# The Archaeology of Death
# in the Ancient Near East

An Assyrian officer receives the severed heads of enemy soldiers. Alabaster wall-relief slab of the reign of the Assyrian king Tiglath-pileser III (745-727 BC). 1.02 x 0.75 m. Archäologische Sammlung der Universität Zürich, inv. no. 1919.

# The Archaeology of Death
# in the Ancient Near East

*Edited by*

*Stuart Campbell*

*&*

*Anthony Green*

Oxbow Monograph 51

*Published by*
Oxbow Books, Park End Place, Oxford OX1 1HN


© Oxbow Books, and the individual authors 1995


ISBN 0 946897 93 X


This book is available direct from
Oxbow Books, Park End Place, Oxford OX1 1HN
*(Phone: 01865-241249; Fax: 01865-794449)*


*and*


The David Brown Book Company
PO Box 511, Oakville, CT 06779
*(Phone: 203-945-9329; Fax: 203-945-9468)*


Printed and bound by Antony Rowe Ltd, Eastbourne

# Contents

# PREFACE AND ACKNOWLEDGEMENTS

By kind invitation of the Victoria University of Manchester, an international residential conference on "The Archaeology of Death in the Ancient Near East" was held at Ashburne Hall, on the Fallowfield Campus, between 16th and 19th December 1992 inclusive. All but three papers, which could not be included for various reasons, appear in this volume. Initiated by aspects of the Editors' research interests and suggested by the lack of any synthetic work on the wide and fascinating topic of funerary practices in the ancient Near East, plans for the conference arose from the overwhelming interest shown at a seminar on the subject at the fourth annual meeting of the British Association for Near Eastern Archaeology, held in Birmingham 9th-11th November 1990.

Many people helped in the organisation of the conference, the preparation of which was enlivened by several unforeseen circumstances. The Editors' particular thanks go to our hosts at Manchester, Mrs Elizabeth Healey, Warden of Ashburne Hall and facilitator of the conference, and Mr Charles Burney, who acted as conference president, both of whom went beyond the call of duty in resolving various crises. The editors would like to take this opportunity of wishing Charles well in his retirement. Without the group of student volunteers who helped out at the conference, total chaos would not have been avoided. Especial thanks should go the unacknowledged 'third administrator' of this conference and publication, Bronwen Campbell, whose assistance was vital at all stages. A debt of gratitude is also due to Rosalie David of the Manchester Museum whose opening lecture set the tone for the rest of the conference.

The conference was sponsored by Manchester University (Small Grants Fund) and the Manchester Egypt and Oriental Society, to whom we are most grateful. The attendance of Sd Abdulaziz Soweileh was made possible by a grant from the British Council in Bahrain, kindly arranged by Dr Robert Killick of the London-Bahrain Archaeological Expedition. Many contributors received financial support from their own institutions, as recorded in their individual acknowledgements, and for this we also give our appreciation. Publication of the book was made possible by a grant towards typesetting and other matters by the Gerald Averay Wainwright Fund for Near Eastern Archaeology, University of Oxford.

Most of all, we thank the scholars who came from various parts of the globe to participate in the conference and to offer their ideas and results for lively debate in a way which made the whole enterprise a pleasurable and, we believe, fruitful event. With their participation, the conference almost ran itself. Their patience in awaiting this publication is appreciated, as are the attempts, notably by St.John Simpson, to avoid too many gross errors in the bibliography.

# Introduction

*When the gods created mankind*
*They appointed death for mankind,*
*Kept eternal life in their own hands.*

Epic of Gilgamesh (Old Babylonian
version) X iii (tr. Dalley 1989, 150)

## Human mortality

Death is the inevitable lot of us all, and fear of death almost universal. When we are young and healthy, we may give it little thought. Then it forces itself upon our attention, as our parents, our friends, partners, sometimes even our children predecease us. Our musings turn to our own mortality. It is an ancient fear. The Epic of Gilgamesh captures the heart of it. In the first half of the poem, Gilgamesh and Enkidu, the dynamic duo, lovers of life, are concerned with heroic exploits and, without a thought of danger or compassion for others, the slaying whoever stands in their way. Then Enkidu himself dies. The second half of the epic, with the desperate, inevitably vain, search of the surviving partner for immortality, is in stark and sorry contrast.

Through myths and cosmologies, ancient people tried to grapple with the reason for death and its mechanics. The protagonist of the Babylonian Legend of Adapa, the first living man, was told by his patron-god Ea not to eat the bread of death nor drink the water of death. When, therefore, on his visit to the heaven of the supreme god Anu, he was offered the bread and the water of life, he refused them, believing them to be the bread and water of death. The implication seems to be that had he consumed them there would have been no human death and all mankind would have enjoyed everlasting life. The biblical equivalent is the story of the Fall, and of the two trees in the Garden of Eden, the Tree of Life and the Tree of Knowledge of Good and Evil, which latter apparently was also known as the Tree of Death. The greatest appeal of Christianity, perhaps, lay in its reversal of the idea of death, with its promise of eternal life.

Despite the physical evidence of post-mortem decomposition, refusal to acknowledge death as the definitive end of human life and personality is strong, and possibly instinctive. The contrasting concept of personal extinction is a comparatively late and philosophically developed idea, unknown, it seems, before Indian Buddhist thinking of the sixth century BC, or in the West until the writings of Epicurus (341-270 BC).

## The value of burial data

*Religion.* It has long been appreciated that mortuary remains provide evidence of ancient religious rites and – apparently – beliefs, while the current interest in "cognitive archaeology" suggests, by the Neo-Assyrian period, at least, the view of the underworld had been transformed. It was now imagined as a complex realm populated by horrifying gods and monsters, a forerunner of the classical underworld and, conceivably, of the medieval vision of hell.

Most strikingly, in the Ur III period, as shown by a funerary poem, there was a belief in differential treatments afforded the deceased dependent on the nature of their burial and the 'gifts' (presumably grave-goods) they were able to present on arrival to the gods of the underworld. Proper burial and provision of funerary offerings, therefore, was of crucial importance to the conditions of the "afterlife" of the deceased.

*Social stratification.* In recent decades, archaeological evaluation of burial data has concentrated less on the light they shed on religious systems and beliefs as on the evidence they provide for the socio-economic ranking. The underlying assumption is that the relative status of an individual in life is maintained, so to speak, in death – in the effort and expense of the burial. Although archaeologists of the ancient Near East have been comparatively slow to adopt procedures for the study of social variability from mortuary analysis, its use in determining aspects of ranked and "egalitarian" societies of the region has begun to receive attention.

*Cultural diversity.* That mortuary data are an effective determinant of cultural groupings, sometimes more reliable than pottery assemblages, has hitherto been little appreciated, and is in this volume put to the test by Elizabeth Carter and Andrea Parker in the first serious study of its kind. Developments in the field of DNA-testing hold out the tantalising possibility of future breakthroughs in the study of population groups and, indeed, family relationships based on burial data.


## Skeletons in the cupboard

No substantial investigation of funerary practices can today entirely ignore the question of ethical attitudes and behaviour in the excavation of human remains. To most archaeologists until the last decade, ethical standards in the excavation of burials, as in archaeological fieldwork in general, was concerned predominantly with questions of archaeological procedure, with 'proper', 'ethically valid' and 'scientific' excavation and recording versus unethical vandalism, tomb-robbing or unacceptably poor standards of archaeological work. Few archaeologists questioned whether their science was, in essence, ethically correct. The matter has been brought to a head, however, by the protests of American Indians against the 'desecration' of the graves of their ancestors, their calls for a halt to such excavations and for the return of the remains of their dead from museum displays and storage rooms for decent reburial. Although it is American Indians who have been most vocal in raising the issue, this question of the root ethics of mortuary archaeology has international implications, and ethical movements against grave-disturbance have gained ground in a number of parts of the world, including the Middle East.

Burials are a particular target for illicit excavation, fuelled by the antiquities market. In many areas of the Middle East a huge depth of archaeological data is threatened with almost total loss by looting. Although the issues involved here go far beyond the narrow concerns of a volume such as this, the conference must express its concern at lack of action on the part of government, in many countries, to control this. The very subject matter of this conference is at risk.

While hardly exhausting a wide and complex field, the papers that follow present some new insights into an interesting and fast developing area of research.

# 1 The Visibility of Prehistoric Burials in the Southern Levant: How Rare are the Upper Palaeolithic/Early Epipalaeolithic Graves?

## Dani Nadel

ABSTRACT— *The paper presents a new look at burial customs from the Middle Palaeolithic - Chalcolithic sequence in the Levant. Although we have data on hundreds from some periods, we know only of a handfull of inhumations from the Upper Palaeolithic - Early Epipalaeolithic period. A quantitative comparison shows that the latter period is very similar to the Middle Palaeolithic period in the number of sites and number of excavated human skeletons. The similarity is not in absolute numbers, but rather in the finds per time unit. However, the period in question does differ from all other periods in the number of burials per site. This could reflect different settlement patterns and unique ways of disposing of the dead.*

## Introduction

The Levant has yielded to the archaeologists one of the richest concentrations of prehistoric graves ever found in one zone; dozens of sites from the Middle Palaeolithic through the Chalcolithic periods have provided hundreds of skeletons and graves. This richness is due to several factors, of which the most important are: a) the long history of archaeological work, b) the density of prehistoric sites, with a continuous sequence from the Lower Palaeolithic to the Chalcolithic period, and, c) the relatively good conditions of preservation of skeletons.

In this paper we will limit ourselves to the southern half of the Levant, where most of the Near Eastern Palaeolithic skeletal material was found. Furthermore, most of the sites with human skeletons/graves were found in a very restricted zone – the centre and north of Israel. However, in order to present the current state of knowledge, the sites surrounding the above-mentioned zone are included. Thus, we actually include Israel, Jordan, Lebanon and south Syria in this paper. Though several isolated and fragmented human skeletal remains have been recovered from Lower Palaeolithic sites (e.g., Ubeidiya,[1]

Gesher Benot-Ya'aqov,[2] Zuttiyeh Cave,[3] Hazorea[4]), they are not thought to represent intentional inhumations. Thus, the earliest examples of mortuary behaviour are found in Middle Palaeolithic sites.

After a century of research in the Levant, there is a plethora of site reports, availability of many anthropological reports, and many publications dealing with the interpretations of prehistoric burial customs. However, a diachronic view of the patterns and changes in mortuary behaviour throughout the long sequence is scarce. A detailed study and interpretation of Natufian and early Neolithic burial customs has been published by Hershkovitz and Gopher.[5] A comparative study of Middle Palaeolithic and Natufian graves has been provided,[6] (Belfer-Cohen and Hovers 1992), and the first general review of the entire southern Levant sequence has recently been published as a catalogue of an exhibition on the subject.[7] Comparisons of Middle and Upper Palaeo-

---

1 Tobias 1966.

2 Gerrads and Tchernov 1983.
3 Gisis & Bar-Yosef 1974.
4 Haas 1973.
5 Hershkovitz & Gopher 1990.
6 Belfer-Cohen & Hovers 1992.
7 Nadel 1992. See also Gilead 1994.

lithic burials in Europe and the Near East have been conducted by Binford and Harrold.[8]

The aim of this paper is to address the issue of the availability of material from Upper Pleistocene and early Holocene sites. The Middle Palaeolithic sample includes tens of skeletons, the samples of Natufian and later periods are in the scale of hundreds. The Upper Palaeolithic/Early Epipalaeolithic sample seems the poorest - only a very few skeletons. A study comparing the periods by presenting the number of finds per time-unit seems to provide a new point of view.

## The Middle Palaeolithic remains

In the excavations of Middle Palaeolithic layers at the Carmel and Galilee caves the skeletal remains of about 80 individuals have been recovered, though most of the individuals are represented by isolated bones/teeth.[9] This number is an explosion in comparison to the scarcity of human skeletal remains from the Lower Palaeolithic. The excavators of Tabun, Skhul, Kebara, Amud and Qafzeh Caves are certain that at least some of the skeletons were intentionally buried. They reached this conclusion from the fact that several skeletons were found in articulation; they were commonly flexed or semi-flexed, usually placed on the back or on the side; and grave goods had been added in at least three cases: Skhul V, with a mandible of a wild bore,[10] Qafzeh 11, with fallow deer antlers[11] and Amud 7 with deer maxilla.[12] This approach has been elaborated by Smirnov, who suggested that Middle Palaeolithic people were burying their dead in a wide variety of ways.[13] A strong argument has been provided for Mousterian burials in the Levant.[14]

## The Upper Palaeolithic/Early Epipalaeolithic remains

The scarcity of human remains from the Upper Palaeolithic/Early Epipalaeolithic period[15] is manifest by the fact that until recently only very few skeletons were amenable for anthropological studies, from both periods. Though in addition to seven articulated burials there were more isolated bones of other individuals, this does seem to be, in absolute numbers, the poorest sample within the Middle Palaeolithic – Chalcolithic sequence in the Levant. What is the meaning of this phenomenon? Is it the result of unfavourable conditions of preservation? Does it

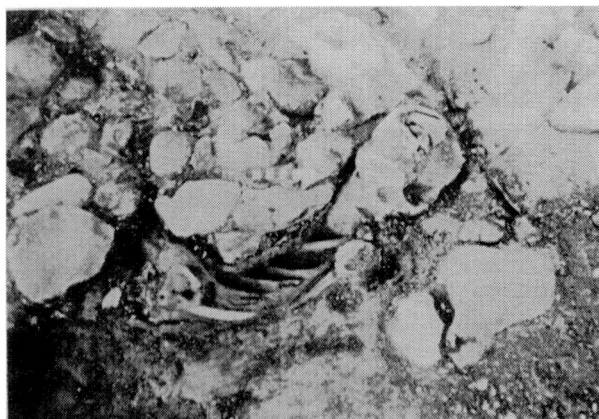

*Fig. 1.1: Discovering the Ohalo II skeleton near the surface.*

reflect a low population density? Does it reflect an unfamiliar burial tradition (e.g., burying away from the habitation site, or disposing of the dead in an above-ground installation)? Are we yet to find many more skeletons which will alter the general trend observed so far, or is the current state of knowledge a true reflection of the past?

Until recently, only six articulated skeletons were known from five sites spanning the Upper Palaeolithic/Early Epipalaeolithic periods: Ksar 'Akil,[16] Nahal Ein Gev I,[17] Ein Gev I,[18] Kharaneh IV (phase B)[19] and Neve David.[20]

Additional isolated human bones and teeth have been recovered, conditions of preservation being too poor to permit any interpretation of burial customs. These were found at Qafzeh Cave,[21] Hayonim Cave,[22] Kebara Cave,[23] El Wad Cave,[24] Ksar 'Akil,[25] Abri Bergy[26] and 'Antelias.[27] These remains represent at least ten and probably more than 15 individuals, in addition to the skeletons mentioned above.

The most complete example of intentional inhumation from this period was found at Ohalo II in 1990. The site was a fisher-hunter-gatherer camp on the shore of the Sea of Galilee, and excellent conditions of preservation have provided a site with unique organic remains.[28] Following recent excavations at the 19,000 years-old site, dated by 26 C-14 determinations,[29] it is now possible to

8 Binford 1968; Harrold 1980. See Gopher and Gophra 1993 for a study of late Neolithic cultures (including burial customs).
9 Cf. Belfer-Cohen & Hovers 1992, Table 2; Bar-Yosef et al. 1992.
10 McCown 1937, 104.
11 Vandermeersch 1970.
12 Rak et al. 1994.
13 Smirnov 1989a; 1989b.
14 Cf. Tillier 1990; Bar-Yosef et al. 1992; Belfer-Cohen & Hovers 1992, Rak et al. 1994.
15 Arensburg 1977, 208; Bar-Yosef & Belfer-Cohen 1988, 29.
16 Ewing 1947; Bergman & Stringer 1989.
17 Bar-Yosef 1973; Arensburg 1977.
18 Arensburg & Bar-Yosef 1973; Bar-Yosef 1978.
19 Muhesein 1988, 358, Pl. 2.
20 Kaufman & Ronen 1987; Kaufman 1989.
21 Vandermeersch 1981.
22 Arensburg et al. 1990.
23 McCown & Keith 1939, 377-378.
24 Ibid., 375-376.
25 Ewing 1947; Bergman & Stringer 1989; Tillier & Tixier 1991.
26 Vallois & Movius 1952.
27 Vallois 1957.
28 Nadel 1990; 1991; Nadel & Hershkovitz 1991; Kislev et al. 1992. Nadel et al. 1994.
29 As n.26; also Carmi & Segal 1992; Hedges et al. 1992; Nadel et al. in press.

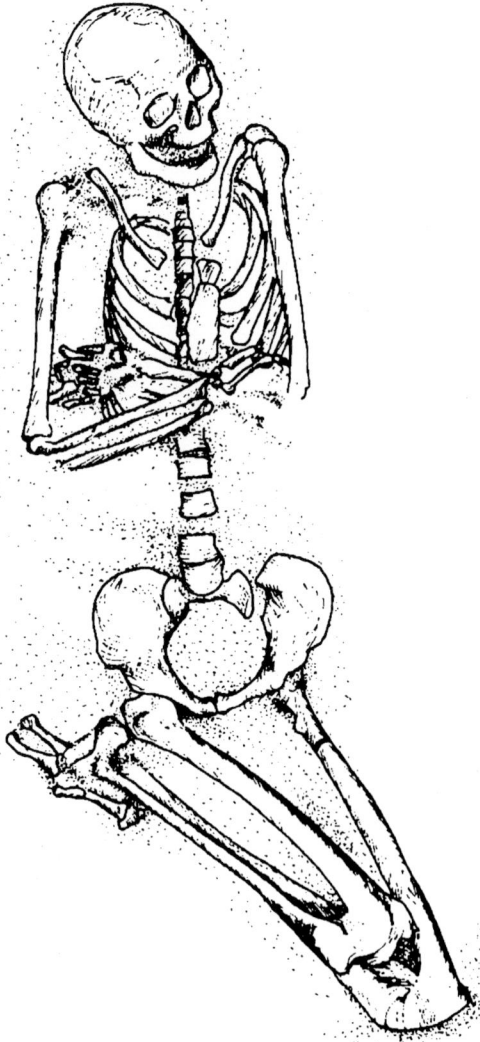

*Fig. 1.2: The Ohalo II skeleton.*

describe in detail a complete and well-dated grave of an adult male.[30]

The Ohalo II skeleton was found in a shallow pit, with the skull and the topmost bones visible above the Lisan Formation bedrock, and covered by recent sand (Figs. 1.2). The grave pit was so shallow, that it seems that the Ohalo II people buried the person without covering the top of the grave with the local muddy clay. They either left some loose sand on top of the grave, or just covered it with perishable materials such as branches or hides, if they covered it at all. The skeleton is of a male who was c. 35-40 years old at death and 1.73 m tall. He was buried on the back, with the hands placed on the chest and knees bent. An incised bone implement was found behind the skull, and was probably placed there intentionally.[31] Other human remains from Ohalo II include a mandible of an adult and isolated bones of an adult and a child. These were found on the surface, and we have no way of

determining whether they derive from a grave, and, if so, where it was located.

## Comparison of periods

In order to perform a quantitative comparison of the Upper Palaeolithic/Early Epipalaeolithic skeletal remains to those from other periods, the relevant data are gathered here in Table 1.1 and the Appendix. It should be noted that the numbers of skeletons (minimum number of individuals) in Table 1.1 are, for some sites, only estimates. Firstly, several publications concerning the skeletal material are not clear as to the exact number of individuals represented by a total count of the remains. Secondly, some of the recently published papers offer revised counts of skeletal material published in the past.[32] In addition, several recent discoveries have not yet been fully published. However, even approximate numbers (from some of the sites) will suffice to demonstrate the general trends. This survey is limited to the southern Levant; Israel, Lebanon, southern Syria and Jordan. The material recovered from the Pre-Pottery Neolithic sites in southern Sinai, as well as the many fourth-third millennia BC Nawamis burial structures in the same area, have not been included here. Also, most of the dolmens in the Jordan Valley have been omitted, as they are commonly ascribed to the Bronze Age.[33]

For the Middle Palaeolithic, we use the data summarised by Belfer-Cohen and Hovers[34] and the detailed counts from Kebara Cave;[35] c. 80 individuals, of which c. 15 are assumed to have been buried. For the Upper Palaeolithic/Early Epipalaeolithic, we estimate from the reports that in addition to the 7 articulated burials, there are bones of at least 15 more individuals. In Natufian and later periods, the number of available skeletons is generally in the hundreds, so we have not made additional counts of isolated bones. It is clear that the earlier two periods are very similar to one another, and very different from the later periods. The number of sites per 1,000 years (an arbitrary unit chosen for comparison) is c. 0.07 - 0.36 for the Middle and Upper Palaeolithic/Early Epipalaeolithic periods, and more than ten times higher for later periods. When the number of skeletons per time-unit is compared, the difference is even more dramatic. The frequencies of skeletons in later periods are over a hundred times higher than in the early ones. Thus, the Upper Palaeolithic/Early Epipalaeolithic period is definitely similar to the Middle Palaeolithic period in the numbers of sites and skeletons, when compared per time-unit. Moreover, even the low percentages of articulated (buried) skeletons out of the total number of individuals (15 out of 80 in the Middle Palaeolithic, and 7 out of 22 for the

---

30  Hershkovitz *et al.* 1993; Nadel 1994.
31  Nadel 1992; 1994.

32  E.g., Belfer-Cohen & Hovers 1992.
33  Cf. Prag, this volume.
34  Belfer-Cohen & Hovers 1992.
35  Bar-Yosef *et al.* 1992.

| Period | no. sites with skeletons | min. no. of individuals | length of period | no. skeletons per 100 years | no. sites per 1,000 years |
|---|---|---|---|---|---|
| Middle Pal. | 8 | 80 | 120,000 | 0.07 | 0.07 |
| Upper Pal. & Early Epipal. | 12 | 22 | 33,000 | 0.067 | 0.36 |
| Late Epipal. | 12 | >420 | 2,200 | >19 | 5 |
| PPNA | 6 | >320 | 700 | >46 | 8.6 |
| PPNB | 19 | >350 | 1,500 | >23 | 12.7 |
| Pottery Neol. 16 | 17 | tens | 2000 | few | 8 |
| Chalcolithic | 34 | thousands | 1,000 | hundreds | 34 |

Numbers of individuals are estimates in some cases. Note the marked difference between the two early periods and the later periods.

*Table 1.1: Prehistoric sites in the southern Levant containing human graves or skeletal remains.*

Upper Palaeolithic/Early Epipalaeolithic) show similar trends, though they are higher in the later period.

It should be pointed out, however, that the period in question differs from the preceding periods in one fundamental aspect. This is the number of burials in one site. Usually we find in excavations only one (or very few) burials in the Upper Palaeolithic/Early Epipalaeolithic sites. Furthermore, even in some of the Middle Palaeolithic caves more than ten burials were found at one site (e.g. Skhul, Qafzeh).

This might be best explainted by the intensity of occupation in those caves and in Natufian and later sites, whereas in the period discussed in this paper the deposits are typically shallow, probably reflecting one or several short occupations. In addition, it seems reasonable to assume that the archaeological visibility of graves belonging to the latter period is rendered difficult due to unique traditions of disposing of the dead. These could have included burial in shallow pits (like at Ohalo II), graves located away from the dwellings (hinted by the location of the grave at Ohalo II)., placing some of the dead in above-ground installations, or a combination of all these possibilities.

There is another aspect to be considered. In some of the Middle Palaeolithic caves (e.g., Skhul, Qafzeh) the skeletons were found in small areas of the sites. In the following period, burials took place at various parts of the sites. At Ein Gev I a skeleton was found under a floor of a cabin, while at Ohalo II the skeleton was not found within any visible structure; it was buried outside the main habitation area (where huts and hearths were located). It would indeed seem that regarding the place of the burial, the relatively homogeneous Middle Palaeolithic tradition, and the more varied Upper Palaeolithic/Early Epipalaeolithic burial customs, did affect our chances of finding the skeletons. Skeletons under thick layers in the caves are relatively well preserved, and so are skeletons from later open-air sites, if they were buried deep enough. Some of the Upper Palaeolithic/Early Epipalaeolithic burials were near the surface or not under a structure in the actual living area of the camp, thus there was less chance of their being found during excavations.

## Discussion

Compared with two well-published and debated groups of skeletons, the Middle Palaeolithic and the Natufian, the Upper Palaeolithic/Early Epipalaeolithic skeletons have not had a strong impact on scholarly discussions. The skeletons are not many and they are not an integral part of any major problem-oriented research.

The claim that there is a particularly poor period has been dealt with here. There are similar low numbers of finds for both Middle Palaeolithic and Upper Palaeolithic/Early Epipalaeolithic periods. Nonetheless, there are more articulated skeletons from the Middle Palaeolithic period. There is a sharp rise in the number of finds from the Late Epipalaeolithic, being more or less constant through several periods thereafter.

A second rise is apparent in the Chalcolithic period. It is self-evident that later sites are better preserved, but this is not the only reason for the observed trends. It should be noted that many of the Chalcolithic skeletons were poorly preserved, but the ossuaries, caves and burial structures in which they were found were easily identified. It is the architecture and furnishings of the Chalcolithic tombs that distinguishes them from earlier ones. This, naturally, is due to the fact that artificial caves, stone built structures (e.g., Shiqmim graveyard,[36] the earliest dolmens, tumuli and Nawamis) and ossuaries (where used) are of non-perishable materials and have good chances of preservation, even if not complete. In addition, some of these burial places, such as the above-ground structures, are conspicuous in the landscape and can be seen from some distance. Thus, Chalcolithic cemeteries composed of caves or stone structures (the Chalcolithic people were the first to bury their dead systematically in cemeteries located away from the habitation sites) are much more visible, in archaeological terms, than earlier graves within the settlements. The graveyard at Eilat is worth mentioning, as it was established towards the end of the Pottery Neolithic period and was also used during the Chalcolithic (according to C-14 dates). It should be noted that some of the more common Chalcolithic practices had already been in use here already during the Pottery

---

36  Levi & Alon 1985; Levi 1987.

4

Neolithic. These include the separation of the burial place from the living site, and the use of above-ground stone installations.[37]

The architecture of the Chalcolithic grave is not manifest in the type of the grave alone. In addition, the bones of the dead were collected into ossuaries (very common along the central coastal plain of Israel), these presenting a wide variety of structures. Furthermore, in some cases small models of ossuaries were found in the bone-containing ossuaries. For Chalcolithic people, it was important to construct an elaborate house for the dead. This was even more important than the complete skeleton, as the custom was to collect certain bones for secondary interment.

Through time, changes in settlement patterns, subsistence strategies and social organisation were closely influencing the spiritual realms of human societies. Mortuary behaviour, as a central aspect of social life,[38] was reflected in these changes. It was only since the establishment of permanent Natufian camps,[39] especially in the open-air, that burial places looked very different from earlier ones. Many tens of articulated skeletons were found at Einan, El Wad, Hayonim and Nahal Oren. Now, more people than ever were buried in one site, reflecting higher population densities (at specific sites and at the regional level) and longer habitation of each site. Several discussions of Natufian burial customs have been offered.[40]

In summary, the data gathered in Table 1.1 and the Appendix clearly show that the Upper Palaeolithic/ Early Epipalaeolithic periods are not outstanding as the poorest time-span with evidence for intentional burial. They are on the same scale (even a little higher) as the Middle Palaeolithic in the number of sites with human skeletal remains and the number of articulated burials, as taken per unit of time.

The well-preserved Ohalo II grave demonstrates the tradition of burying in very shallow pits. This could have been a common tradition, causing many graves to disappear through the ages and to be invisible to archaeologists. Other traditions (unknown to us) practised during this period could have been another factor affecting our capability of reconstructing burial customs. The drastic changes in subsistence and settlement patterns by the end of the Pleistocene are reflected in the types and numbers of graves in Natufian and Neolithic sites. The Chalcolithic graveyards stand out in their numbers and associated architecture, reflecting yet another attitude towards the place of the dead: The construction of separated cemeteries with artificial caves or above-ground stone-built graves.

*Acknowledgements*

This paper is based on research conducted during the preparation of an exhibition entitled 'Bones and Spirits: Prehistoric Burial Customs in Israel' which I curated at the M. Stekelis Museum of Prehistory, Haifa. I would like to thank the staff of the Museum, as well as the Haifa Museum, for assistance during preparation of the exhibition and its catalogue (Nadel 1992). The Haifa Museum generously covered my travel expenses to the Manchester conference. Dr Anna Belfer-Cohen, Professor Baruch Arensburg, and Dr Israel Hershkovitz advised me during my work, giving encouragement and helpful comments. I also wish to thank Ron Hillel for his patience and help, Ofer Bar-Yosef for his help and Irit Zohar for her continuous commitment to the project. Tamar Noy, Yuval Goren, Peter Fabian and Udi Galili have been very kind in providing unpublished data. The Ohalo II project was carried out on behalf of the Israel Antiquities Authority [licence 1679 (1989), 1724 (1990), 93/91 (1991)] and the M. Stekelis Museum of Prehistory. Generous grants were given by the Irene Levi-Sala CARE Archaeological Foundation, the Jerusalem Centre for Anthropological Studies and the L.S.B. Leakey Foundation.

---

37  Avner 1989; 1991.
38  Huntingtion & Metcalf 1987, with many examples.
39  Bar-Yosef & Belfer-Cohen 1989; Tchernov 1991.
40  Wright 1978; Perrot & Ladiray 1980; Belfer-Cohen 1988a; 1988b; Belfer-Cohen & Hovers 1992; Boyd 1992.

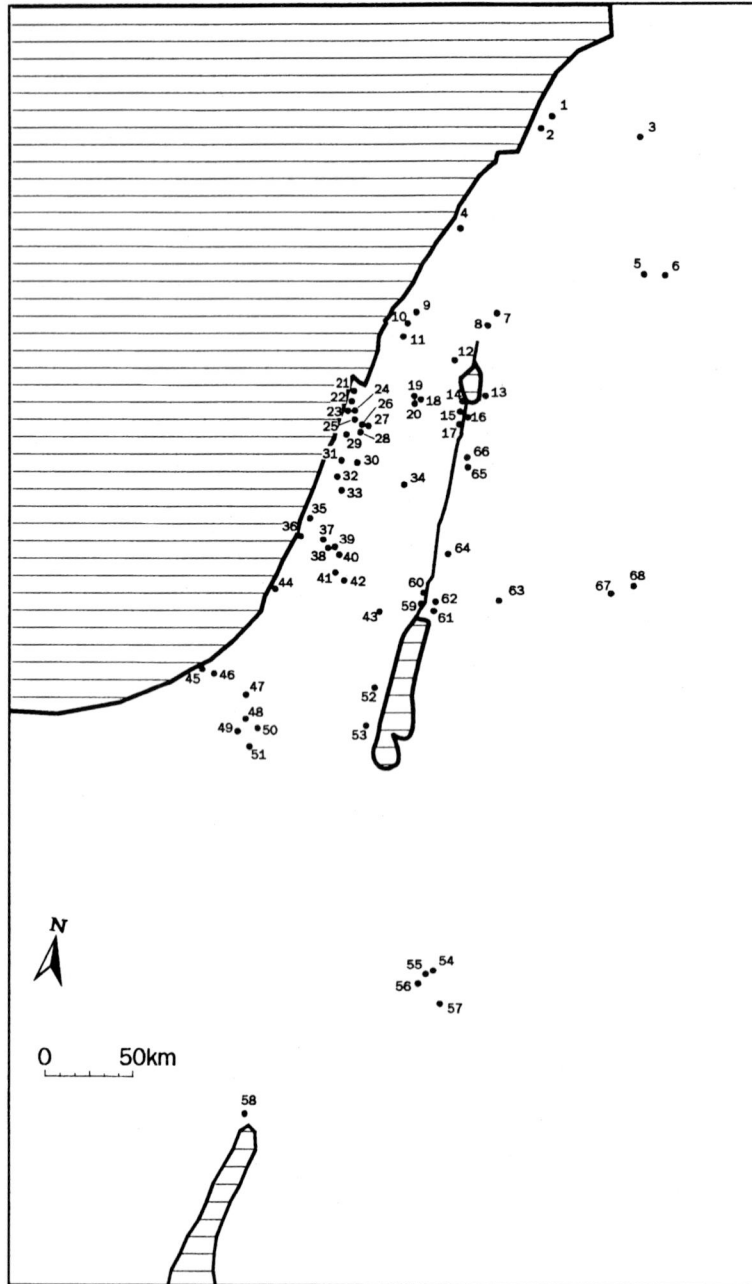

*Fig. 1.3: Location of Middle Palaeolithic - Chalcolithic sites mentioned in text and tables.*

| 1 | Abri Bergi. | 19 | Yiftahel. | 36 | Palmachim. | 54 | Baga 1. |
|---|---|---|---|---|---|---|---|
| 2 | Ksar Akil, Antelias. | 20 | Kfar Hahoresh. | 37 | Azor. | 55 | Beidha. |
| 3 | Saaide II. | 21 | Neve David. | 38 | Ben Shemen, Lod. | 56 | Sabra 1. |
| 4 | Byblos. | 22 | Tel Hreiz. | 39 | Shukbah Cave. | 57 | Basta. |
| 5 | Tel Aswad. | 23 | Atlit Yam, Neve Yam. | 40 | Nahal Qanah. | 58 | Eilat. |
| 6 | Tel Ramad. | 24 | Nahal Oren. | 41 | Hatula. | 59 | Jericho. |
| 7 | Hagoshrim, Kfar Giladi, Tel Dan. | 25 | El Wad, Skhul and Tabun Caves. | 42 | Abu Gosh, Taoz. | 60 | Netiv Hagdud. |
| 8 | Beisamoun, Eynan, Tel Teo. | 26 | Rakefet Cave. | 43 | Erq el-Ahmar, Um Qatafa. | 61 | El Edeimeh. |
| 9 | Horvat Galil, Nahal Bezet. | 27 | Ein el Jerbah. | 44 | Nizanim. | 62 | Teleilat Ghassul. |
| 10 | Kabri. | 28 | Nahal Zehora II. | 45 | Tel Qatif. | 63 | Ain Ghazal. |
| 11 | Hayonim Cave. | 29 | Kebara Cave. | 46 | Nahal Kisufim. | 64 | Wadi Shu'eib. |
| 12 | Amud and Shovakh Caves. | 30 | Mezer. | 47 | Gerar. | 65 | 'raq ed-Dubb. |
| 13 | Ein Gev I, Nahal Ein Gev I. | 31 | Hadera. | 48 | Gilat. | 66 | Wadi Hammeh 27. |
| 14 | Ohalo II. | 32 | Maabarot, Tel Hefer. | 49 | Shiqmim. | 67 | Kharaneh IV. |
| 15 | Sheikh Ali. | 33 | Taibeh. | 50 | Beer-Sheva (Bir Safadi, Horvat Beter, Tel Abu-Matar). | 68 | Azraq 18. |
| 16 | Shaar Hagolan. | 34 | Tel Far'a North (cave). | 51 | Nahal Secher. | | |
| 17 | Munhata. | 35 | Bnei-Braq, Givatayim, Givat Beit Hamitbahayim, Habashan St., Jabotinski St. | 52 | Nahal Mishmar. | | |
| 18 | Kafzeh Cave. | | | 53 | Nahal Hemar. | | |

6

# Appendix

Sites in the southern half of the Levant (Israel, Lebanon, southern Syria and Jordan) containing human burials or human skeletal remains. The reader is referred to the site reports for more details.

*Middle Palaeolithic Period*

| | |
|---|---|
| Amud Cave | Suzuki & Takai 1970 |
| | Rak *et al.* 1994 |
| Hayonim Cave | Arensburg & Nathan 1980; Arensburg *et al.* |
| Kebara Cave | McCown & Keith 1939; Smith & Arensburg 1977; Smith & Tillier 1989; Bar-Yosef *et al.* 1986; 1988; 1992 |
| Qafzeh Cave | Neuville 1934; Vandermeersch 1969; 1970; 1981; Tillier 1989 |
| Shovakh Cave | Binford 1966; Trinkaus 1987 |
| Shukbah Cave | Garrod 1942 |
| Skhul Cave | McCown 1937; McCown & Keith 1939; Ronen 1976 |
| Tabun Cave | McCown & Keith 1939 |

*Upper Palaeolithic and Early Epipalaeolithic Periods*

| | |
|---|---|
| Abri Bergy | Vallois & Movius 1952 |
| 'Antelias | Vallois 1957 |
| Ein Gev I | Arensburg & Bar-Yosef 1973 |
| El Wad Cave | McCown & Keith 1939 |
| Hayonim Cave | Arensburg 1977; Arensburg *et al.* 1990 |
| Kebara Cave | Turville-Petre 1932; McCown & Keith 1939 |
| Kharaneh IV (B) | Muheisen 1988 |
| Ksar 'Akil | Ewing 1947; Bergman & Stringer 1989 |
| Nahal Ein Gev I | Bar-Yosef 1973; Arensburg 1977 |
| Neve David | Kaufman & Ronen 1987; Kaufman 1989 |
| Ohalo II | Nadel & Hershkovitz 1991; Hershkovitz *et al.* 1993; Nadel 1994 |
| Qafzeh Cave | Neuville 1951 |

*Late Epipalaeolithic Period*

| | |
|---|---|
| Azraq 18 | Garrard *et al.* 1987 |
| El Wad Cave & Terrace | |
| | Garrod & Bate 1937; McCown & Keith 1939 |
| Erq el Ahmar | Valloise 1936; Neuville 1951; |
| Eynan | Perrot & Ladiray 1988 |
| Hatula | Lechevallier & Ronen 1985 |
| Hayonim Cave & Terrace | |
| | Belfer-Cohen 1988a; 1988b; Valla *et al.* 1991 |
| Kebara Cave | Unpublished |
| Nahal Oren | Ferembach 1959; Noy, Legge & Higgs 1973; Noy 1989 |
| Rakefet Cave | Higgs & Noy 1971 |

| | |
|---|---|
| Jebel Saaide II | Soliveres 1977; Schroeder 1991 |
| Shukbah Cave | Garrod 1942 |
| Wadi Hammeh 27 | Edwards *et al.* 1988; Edwards 1991 |

*Pre-Pottery Neolithic A Period*

| | |
|---|---|
| Hatula | Lechevallier & Ronen 1985; Le Mort 1989 |
| 'Iraq ed-Dubb | Kuijt *et al.* 1991 |
| Jericho | Cornwell 1981; Kurth & Rohrer-Ertl 1981 |
| Nahal Oren | Noy, personal communication |
| Netiv Hagdud | Belfer-Cohen *et al.* 1990 |
| Tel Aswad IA | Contenson 1972; 1992 |

*Pre-Pottery Neolithic B Period*

| | |
|---|---|
| Abou Gosh | Lechevallier 1978; Arensburg *et al.* 1978 |
| Ain Ghazal | Rollefson 1983; 1986; Rollefson & Simmons 1988 |
| Atlit Yam | Hershkovitz & Galilee 1990; Hershkovitz *et al.* 1991; Galili *et al.* 1993 |
| Baga 1 | Gebel 1988 |
| Basta | Gebel *et al.* 1988; Rohrer-Ertl *et al.* 1988; Nissen *et al.* 1987, 1988. |
| Beidha | Kirkbride 1966; 1967 |
| Beisamoun | Ferembach & Lechevallier 1973; Lechevallier 1978 |
| Hagoshrim (?) | Noy 1980 |
| Horvat Galil | Hershkovitz & Gopher 1988 |
| Jericho | Kurth & Rohrer-Ertl 1981 |
| Kfar Giladi | Unpublished (cf. Arensburg 1977) |
| Kfar Hahoresh | Goring-Morris 1991; and in this volume |
| Nahal Hemar Cave | Bar-Yosef & Alon 1988; Arensburg & Hershkovitz 1988; 1989 |
| Nahal Oren | Noy, Legge & Higgs 1973 |
| Sabra 1 | Rohrer-Ertl *et al.* 1988 |
| Sheikh Ali | Prausnitz 1962; 1970; Haas 1974 |
| Tel Aswad IIB | Contenson 1972; 1992 |
| Tel Ramad | Ferembach 1969; 1970; Contenson 1966; 1967; 1992 |
| Yiftahel | Hershkovitz *et al.* 1986 |

*Pottery Neolithic Period*

| | |
|---|---|
| Byblos | Dunand 1973 |
| Eilat | Avner 1989; 1991 |
| Habashan St, Tel Aviv | |
| | Kaplan 1959, 1970 |
| Jericho | Kurth & Rohrer-Ertl 1981 |
| Lod | Gopher & Orelle, in this volume |
| Munhata | Perrot 1967 |
| Nahal Bezet | Gopher 1989 |
| Nahal Zehorah II | Gopher & Orelle 1991 |
| Neve Yam | Galili, personal communication |
| Nizzanim | Yeivin & Olami 1979 |
| Sha'ar Hagolan | Stekelis 1972 |

| | |
|---|---|
| Sheikh Ali | Prausnitz 1962; Garfinkel, personal communication |
| Tel Dan | Gopher & Greenberg 1987 |
| Tel Hreize | Galili, personal communication |
| Tel Qatif (Y3) | Epstein 1984 |
| Tel Teo | Eisenberg 1986; 1987 |
| Wadi Shu'lib | Simmons *et al.* 1989 |

*Chalcolithic Period*

| | |
|---|---|
| Azor | Perrot 1961; Perrot & Ladiray 1980 |
| El-Adeimeh | Stekelis 1935 |
| Ben-Shemen | Perrot & Ladiray 1980 |
| Bir Safadi | Perrot 1984; Eldar & Baumgarten 1985 |
| Bnei-Braq | Ory 1946; Kaplan 1963 |
| Byblos | Dunand 1973 |
| Eilat | Avner 1989; 1991 |
| Ein el-Jerbah | Kaplan 1969; Arensburg 1970 |
| Gerar | Gilead 1986 |
| Gilat | Levi & Alon 1991 |
| Givat Beit Hamitbahayim | |
| | Kaplan 1959, 1970 |
| Giv'atayim | Sussman & Ben-Arieh 1963 |
| Haderah | Sukenik 1937 |
| Horvat Beter | Dothan 1959b |

| | |
|---|---|
| Jabotinski St, Tel Aviv | |
| | Kaplan 1970 |
| Jericho | Kurth & Rohrer-Ertl 1981 |
| Kabri | Prausnitz 1970 |
| Ma'abarot | Paley & Porath 1979; Porath 1985 |
| Meser | Dothan 1959a |
| Nahal Kisufim | Goren & Fabian 1993 |
| Nahal Mishmar 3 Caves | |
| | Haas & Nathan 1973; Bar-Adon 1980 |
| Nahal Secher | Goren, personal communication |
| Nahal Qanah | Gopher *et al.* 1990 |
| Palmachim | Gophna & Lifshitz 1980 |
| Sheikh Ali | Prausnitz 1962 |
| Shiqmim | Levi & Alon 1982; 1985; Levi 1987 |
| Taibeh | Porath, personal communication |
| Taoz | Perrot & Ladiray 1988; Tadmor 1990 |
| Teleilat Ghassul | Mallon *et al.* 1934; Koeppel *et al.* 1940; Hennessy 1969 |
| Tel Abu Matar | Perrot 1955; 1984 |
| Tel Far'a North (burial cave) | |
| | de Vaux 1970 |
| Tel Hefer | Porath, personal communication |
| Tel Teo | Eisenberg 1987 |
| Um Qatafa | Neuville 1951 |

# 2 Rethinking Social Stratification in the Natufian Culture: The Evidence from Burials

## *Anna Belfer-Cohen*

ABSTRACT—*Social stratification is a tantalising issue. It is tempting to think that it began in the Natufian like many other new customs and traditions. This proposition was offered by Wright, based on differential decoration of the burials from el-Wad. A detailed inspection of the el-Wad graves, as well as the other known burials with personal decoration from the Natufian, presents a very complicated picture. Tempting as it is, the evidence for social stratification inferred from the decorated burials is actually non-existent. Thus we have either to wait for more excavations and new data or look elsewhere for evidence of social ranking.*

## Introduction

The Natufian culture was first described and given an independent status in 1932.[1] Much data had been accumulated since then concerning its geographical and temporal spread, material variety, ways of living, chronological, cultural and spatial sub-divisions, etc.[2] The Natufian is regarded as a transitional phase between two cultural sequences – the Palaeolithic hunter-gatherers on the one hand and the Neolithic agricultural societies on the other. Since its discovery, many C14 dates substantiated this claim chronologically, by placing it between c. 12,800 to 10,300 years ago.[3] The Natufian was subdivided into two or three chronological stages based on techno-typological as well as stratigraphic criteria,[4] a subdivision which has likewise been substantiated by many C14 dates. There is also quite a large body of evidence for continuities of characteristics (material and otherwise) both from the Palaeolithic and into the Neolithic cultures. Indeed, though currently the definition of what may be considered as a Natufian entity is under debate,[5] there is no doubt that the Natufian core-area sites display many attributes that flourish in magnitude and scope in the succeeding Neolithic cultures of the southern Levant.

Prominent among those is the appearance of common burial grounds, with various burial practices such as the removal of the skull, as well as rare decorated burials. In the late 1970s, an attempt was made by Wright to interpret these decorated burials as indicating social stratification in the Natufian society.[6] At that time, all but one of the published decorated burials were recovered from the el-Wad site (Cave and Terrace) in Mount Carmel,[7] dating from the Early Natufian. The only exception was a decorated burial from the Erq el Ahmar rock-shelter in the Judean Desert,[8] but the meagre data available justified its exclusion from Wright's analysis and discussion. There were some preliminary reports of decorated burials from Hayonim Cave and the open-air site of Mallaha (Eynan), but none were published in detail, thus Wright could only make some comments on their presence, while dealing in detail with the data available from el-Wad. He suggested that "the best manner to test the validity of the hypothesized societal partitioning at el-Wad would be through a statistical analysis of the burials from Hayonim Cave and Mallaha, since they are the most recently and presumably the best, excavated sites...".[9]

Wright's interpretation was widely accepted[10] since – though social stratification is considered as a phe-

---

1 By Garrod (1932).
2 Bar-Yosef 1983; Belfer-Cohen 1991a; Bar-Yosef & Valla 1991.
3 E.g., Valla 1987; Weinstein Evron 1991.
4 Valla 1987.
5 Cf. Belfer-Cohen 1991a, with relevant bibliography.

6 Wright 1978.
7 Garrod 1937; Garrod & Bate 1937.
8 Neuville 1951.
9 Wright 1978, 217.
10 Cf., e.g., Henry 1985; 1989.

| Site | Children | Adolescents. | Males* | Females* | Total | Total Population |
|------|----------|--------------|--------|----------|-------|------------------|
| el-Wad | 1 | - | 7 | 1 | 9 | 96 |
| Eynan | 2 | 2 | 3 | 3 | 10 | 105 |
| Hayonim Cave | - | 3 | 1 | - | 4 | 48 |
| Erq el Ahmar | - | - | - | 1 | 1 | 7 |

\* The gender designation is given according to the publications. Preference was given to the designations made while processing the material in the laboratory rather than that made on the site, under field-conditions. In the case of el-Wad, the designation given by McCown (1939) was accepted, even when it is contrary to that given by Garrod in the detailed description of the burials (1937).

*Table 2.1: Decorated burials from the Natufian*

nomenon typical of complex societies – it was felt that its possible existence in the Natufian was just another of those cultural components shared with the Neolithic cultures: Intensification of gathering and/or incipient agriculture, sedentary way of life, a plethora of evidence for communal artistic and symbolic activities, etc.

Since 1978, the decorated burials from both Hayonim Cave and Eynan have been published[11] and new Natufian sites with burials and decorative items have been reported.[12] Besides the accumulation of new data, there is an on-going re-assessment of previous interpretations and various characteristics of Natufian phenomena.[13] It seems that the time has come to follow Wright's advice and examine once more the burial evidence as regards the existence of social stratification in the Natufian.

## The Data-Base

There are at least 12 Natufian sites with human remains, i.e., burials (Fig. 2.1).[14] All of them are located in the Mediterranean climate zone, though not all of them have decorated burials, even sites rich in items of jewellery which elsewhere were recovered from graves.[15] Out of more than 400 burials[16] c. 6% (24 ?) were decorated (Table 2.1). All of them were recovered from only four sites. There is some evidence for possible decorated burials from yet another site, Wadi Hammeh 27, though it is somewhat fragmentary.[17]

Before describing in detail the decorated burials it should be stated that all of them belong to the Early Natufian (c. 12,800 -11,000 BC). It seems that personal adornment of the dead ceased in the Late Natufian, though beads and pendants were recovered from the living areas of many Late Natufian sites. Thus for example, if we check the dentalia recovered from the living areas in Hayonim Cave, in the Early Natufian

there are 416 dentalium beads in all (total volume of 12.6 m$^3$) while from two graves (VIII and XIII) with a volume less than 5 m$^3$ we have 520 dentalia. The numbers of dentalia rise with time – 1,456 beads in the Late Natufian (total volume 26.2 m$^3$) while from the graves of the same time-span (6 graves, 16 burials) there are less than 20 beads. The same applies in general for the bone beads, though most of the complete ones were recovered from the graves. While this is similar to what Garrod observed in el-Wad, where most of the bone pendants were retrieved from the graves[18] in the Early Natufian site of Kebara Cave the situation is reversed. Turville-Petre mentioned 400 bone beads (remarkably similar to those from el-Wad) recovered from the living area and none from the graves in the cave of the same period!![19]

Rare burial offerings were recovered from both Early and Late Natufian adorned and unadorned burials. Thus ochre lumps were recovered from Early Natufian (Wadi Hammeh 27[20]; Erq el Ahmar[21]) as well as from Late Natufian burials (Eynan[22]); a tortoise carapace was recovered from an Early Natufian burial in el-Wad[23] as well as from a Late Natufian burial from Hayonim Terrace.[24] Gazelle horn cores were found in an Early Natufian burial in el-Wad, and in Late Natufian burials from Eynan and Hayonim Terrace. Other, unique, offerings included horse teeth (Erq el Ahmar), a bone dagger (Hayonim Cave) and a Calcite stone human head (el-Wad).

As can be seen from the above, the grave offerings and burial decorations do not encompass the entire range of artistic works known through all the Natufian stages. Thus apart from the bone dagger (Hayonim Cave Grave XIII), there was no intentional representation of the rich and decorative worked-bone assemblages, characteristic of the Natufian culture. Furthermore, only a few ground-stone implements may be associated with the burials. Thus there are some limestone cup-

---

11 Belfer-Cohen 1988a; 1988b; Perrot *et al.* 1988.
12 E.g., by Edwards *et al.* 1988.
13 Belfer-Cohen 1989; Byrd 1989; Olszewski 1991.
14 But cf. Belfer-Cohen & Hovers 1992.
15 Cf., e.g., Turville-Petre 1932 on Kebara Cave.
16 Belfer-Cohen *et al.* 1991; Hershkovitz & Gopher 1990.
17 Edwards *et al.* 1988. Cf. below, p. 14.

18 Garrod & Bate 1937.
19 Turville-Petre 1932.
20 Edwards *et al.* 1988.
21 Neuville 1951.
22 Perrot *et al.* 1988.
23 Garrod & Bate 1937.
24 Valla *et al.* 1991.

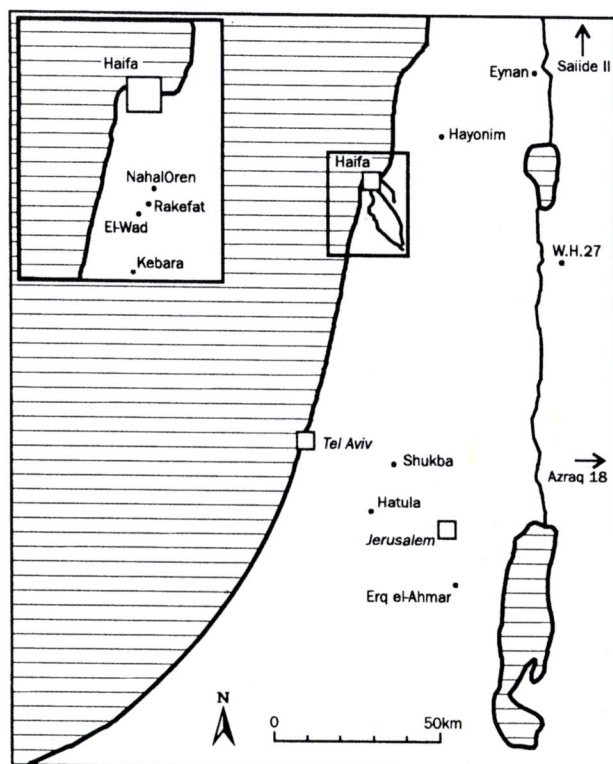

*Fig. 2.1: Natufian sites with burials.*

marks on top of graves in Hayonim Cave[25] as well as breached basalt mortars (i.e., 'stone-pipes') found on top of several burials from Nahal Oren,[26] which could have been used as grave-markers. Possible limestone markers were reported also from graves in Eynan.[27] In el-Wad, some of the specimens in the H. Group 57 burial were arranged in a circle round a broken limestone mortar. No incised pebbles or stone-slabs have been recovered from any Natufian grave, although such items are known from the Natufian layers of Hayonim, el-Wad, Eynan, Wadi Hammeh 27, etc.

The burials are of every possible variety; primary and secondary, interred in pits – sometimes stone-lined or lime-washed – or in constructed graves, occasionally with stone pavements or stone coverings. Some graves had been re-opened to enable the introduction of new burials, while others remained sealed. Burial positions are varied (flexed or extended, on the side, head facing to the north or to the south, etc.), as are the sexes represented and the number of burials per grave. A strict separation was observed between living quarters and burial grounds of the same period.[28]

An outstanding custom observed in the Late Natufian burials is the separation of the skull from the thorax, a practice that continued unto the Neolithic times, culminating in the skull cult of the PPNB.[29]

Indeed, this custom, first reported from the agricultural Neolithic societies, has been considered to be part of an ancestors cult, denoting ownership and emotional ties to a locality and implying the existence of defined and bounded territories. Joint burials of humans and dogs were reported from Eynan (Early Natufian)[30] and Hayonim Terrace (Late Natufian).[31] There were some indications for their existence also in el-Wad.[32] To date, these are the first known instances of domesticated animals in human history.

## The decorated burials from el-Wad

Garrod published 62 burials from the Natufian layers (B1: Upper Natufian; B2: Lower Natufian) in the el-Wad site. From the incomplete descriptions (only 44 were described, as others were considered too fragmentary), it seems that at least some burials, for example H. 23, H. 25, H. Group 57 were actually group burials, thus at least 70 individuals were recorded as recovered from these 62 burials![33] In later investigations, the minimum number of recovered individuals was reassessed at 96.[34] According to Garrod, 10 burials were recovered from inside the cave, 6 near the mouth of the cave and all the rest from the Terrace. The burials from inside the cave, which were a group burial and 3 or 4 burials from the vicinity of the cave entrance were found in an extended position. All the rest were buried in a flexed position (semi-flexed, loosely flexed or tightly flexed). The decorated burials were all recovered from the Terrace. According to Garrod most of the burials belong to the Early Natufian, 5 or 6 were recovered from an area where no clear division could be made between early and late levels, and only about 3 burials were assigned to the Late Natufian stage.[35]

The decorated burials are the following:

1. An adult male (H. 23) with a head-dress of dentalium beads, a necklace of dentalia and twin bone pendants (25 complete and a number of broken ones). One femur had a band or garter of 8 rows of dentalium shells.[36] H. 23 was buried together with H. 23a (fragmentary adult) and H. 23b (a child) – Garrod describes: "The remains of a second, very fragmentary skeleton were found mixed up with H.23, and it appeared that the bodies had been buried side by side, in the same position, and possibly in each other's arms. ... Underneath the adult bodies were the fragmentary remains of a child. All the skeletons were packed into place with large

25  Belfer-Cohen 1988a.
26  Stekelis & Yizraeli 1963.
27  Perrot *et al.* 1988.
28  For a summary, cf. Belfer-Cohen 1991a; Belfer-Cohen *et al.*, in press.
29  Bienert 1991.

30  Perrot *et al.* 1988.
31  Valla *et al.* 1991.
32  Garrod & Bate 1937.
33  Garrod 1937; Garrod & Bate 1937.
34  Belfer-Cohen *et al.* 1991.
35  Garrod & Bate 1937.
36  Garrod & Bate 1937, Pl.VII; Garrod 1937, Pls. 10b, 11a.

fragments of limestone, which had damaged the bones very seriously."[37]

2.  An adult male (H. 25) with a circlet(?) made up of seven rows of dentalia. His was a group grave with four other very fragmentary burials in it (H. 25a-c and H. 26).

3.  The burial (H. Group 28) "contained five fragmentary skeletons packed together in some confusion. On the edge of the group was the incomplete skeleton of a young child, with badly flattened skull. To one side of the head and partly overlying the right parietal lay a group of 32 pendants spaced in such a way as to suggest that they had originally been fastened to a cap or net."[38] The beads were cut from the distal ends of gazelle phalanges; Wright specifies dentalium beads but there are none in Garrod's description.

4.  An adult, perhaps male, H. 41, lavishly decorated. Garrod specifies: "The fourth decorated skeleton (H.41) lay, not in a group, but alongside one other very fragmentary body (H.43)."[39] The decoration consisted of a head-dress made of dentalium shells and bone pendants cut from the tibio-tarsus of partridges; a strip of dentalium shells spread fan-like on the shaft of the right humerus and groups of shells on the shaft of the right femur, which may be a remnant of a cloak or some other garment.

5.  A young adult from a group burial (H. Group 57), sex unspecified due to the fragmentary state of the bones, but Arensburg thinks the skeletal remains are male.[40] Garrod observed that "the head was covered by blocks of limestone, which had crushed the skull very badly, but a mass of bone pendants lying below the mandible was uninjured and when the skull was lifted fairly extensive remains of a shell cap were found on the right side. Part of this was stuck to the bone, and came away with it, while the rest remained in place on the ground."[41] The cap, a narrow fillet made up of three rows of dentalium shells, encircled the head and from this was hung a fringe, four shells deep, which must nearly have reached the shoulders. Mixed with the dentalia were a few tibio-tarsus pendants. There was also a necklace of 31 twin bone pendants as well as dentalium beads. This group burial consisted of seven fragmentary skeletons. The skeletons were placed on their sides with their knees drawn up, and the four which were on top lay in a circle round a broken limestone mortar. The decorated body lay on its right side, at a slightly lower level and partly underneath the other three. Arensburg observed a congenital absence of M3 and a head trauma, a large depression beyond the coronal suture, on the endocranium, with no healing signs. The depression was covered with uncrushed dentalia and twin bone beads.[42]

Other *possible* decorated burials include one observed by Garrod herself.

6.  H. 17: A single flexed burial of a female with one twin bone pendant sticking to the skull. It was designated as Upper (Late) Natufian.

Another is mentioned by Wright.

7.  H. 21: A single flexed burial of a female. According to Wright one bird bone pendant was recovered from this burial. Wright designated the burial as Upper Natufian, but according to Garrod it cannot be assigned definitely to either Early or Upper Natufian.

More decorated skulls were observed by Arensburg in the Peabody collection:

8.  Miss. H. 9: An adult male (dentalium beads adhering to long bones and skull).

9.  Miss. H. 15: A 20-25 year-old male (dentalium beads adhering to long bones and skull).

10. el-Wad B, F, G: An adult, male (fragments of skull and long bones with dentalia).

11. Death Pit: Cranium of an adult male, congenital absence of M3, bone pendant adhering to the skull.

It is of interest to note that out of the 5 mandibles (of the 60 complete mandibles) with congenital absence of M3, two are decorated (H. 57 and Death Pit Cranium). Also Miss. 15 has a congenital missing M3, but in the maxilla.

After long consideration – and being aware that with time and treatment the number of decorated specimens identifiable from those kept in boxes and drawers may increase – it is felt that these specimens should be added to the decorated burials published by Garrod, as obviously she herself did not describe all of the decorated burials but only the most complete ones. It is the same policy she employed in describing the burials in general. Thus she described only 44 in the 'final' report, the additional 18 counted by herself being regarded as "remains of badly preserved burials too fragmentary to describe."[43] Included among the latter were burials H. 38, H. 51 and H. 61, which were described by McCown in his doctoral dissertation. These three crania were intact enough for McCown to record 40 or more measurements on each.[44]

---

37  Garrod 1937, 124.
38  Garrod 1937, 126, and Pl. 12c.
39  Garrod 1937, 126.
40  B. Arensburg, personal communication.
41  Garrod 1937, Pls. 11b, 12a, 125.

42  Belfer-Cohen *et al.* 1991.
43  Garrod & Bate 1937, 19.
44  McCown 1939, cited by Wright 1978, 205.

## The decorated burials from Hayonim Cave

To date, 48 burials and 15 graves have been unearthed at the site of Hayonim Cave.[45] 20 of the burials are considered Early Natufian while 16 belong to the Late Natufian stage. Of the rest, 3 are regarded as intermediate in date, while the remaining 9 cannot be assigned to any particular stage. Though miscellaneous beads and pendants were found in 14 (out of 15) graves, only 4 Early Natufian burials bore definite personal decoration. Extended position was recorded only in burials dating from the Early Natufian (for example, Graves VII and XIII).

The decorated burials are:

1.  A decorated young female found in Grave VII, lying extended side-by-side with a young male (of 20-25 years), apparently pregnant (bones of a foetus were recovered from among the bones of the grave during laboratory examination), together with a child of 7.5-8 years, lying at their feet in a flexed position. The whole setting is reminiscent of the H. 23 group burial from el-Wad. The decoration consisted of a belt and a bracelet (or possibly two), made of bone pendants and dentalium beads, and a dentalium necklace. Two perforated fox teeth were found, one near the woman's head, the other between her legs; perhaps these belonged also to the belt (in total there were 52 bone pendants, 182 dentalia and 2 perforated fox teeth).

Two decorated individuals were recovered from Grave VIII/IX, which contained 10 primary and secondary burials (the tomb had been re-opened and disturbed). Both decorated burials were primary.

2.  H. 17, a male of 20-25 years, in a semi-flexed position. Most of the 155 dentalia recovered from this grave were scattered near his arms, so they were perhaps the remains of a decorated garment?
3.  H. 25, a male of c. 25 years, flexed, on his side, lying on top of H. 27 with his arms folded across his chest. One arm was adorned with a bracelet of 20 partridge tibia-tarsus beads.
4.  H. 33 (Grave XIII), a single extended burial, of a male of less than 25 years. The exact position of the corpse was indeterminable as the legs had been severed by a later wall. Both arms were stretched out along the body and the face was turned to the left, or west. 365 dentalia were found near the neck (a chest dress ?), and there were a belt and an armlet of perforated fox teeth. A unique bone artefact (a dagger or spatula?) was found under the left upper arm.

In most of the undecorated burials only one or a few beads or pendants were recovered, with the exception of (i) Grave III (Intermediate Natufian), which contained one primary and two secondary burials, one of them an infant; the jewellery recovered consisted of two tibio-tarsal beads and 17 dentalia; (ii) Grave VI, which contained both Early and Late Natufian burials (9 primary ones, including a foetus), with 8 bone pendants and 103 dentalia; and (iii) Grave XVI of the Late Natufian, with a single primary burial, 12 dentalia and one bone bead.

## The decorated burials from Eynan (Mallaha)

The open-air site of Eynan provided 105 burials, spanning the whole Natufian time-range. The decorated burials, with one exception, are concentrated in two cemeteries dating to the earliest stages of the Natufian occupation at the site.[46]

There are no final publications concerning the jewellery from either the burials or the living areas.[47] Thus no numbers or detailed descriptions of the various beads are available, but their presence is indicated in all the publications reviewing the Natufian occupations at Eynan, together with many other works of craftsmanship and art.[48]

Cemetery A consists of single, primary and flexed burials – 11 males, females and children – 4 of which were decorated.

1.  H. 6a, an adult male, with a necklace or chest pectoral decoration of dentalia and bone beads made from gazelle distal phalanges.
2.  H. 6b, an adolescent (very fragmentary) – with a bracelet(?) of dentalia.
3.  H. 19, an adult female in a sitting position[49] with either a decorated bonnet or a bandana made of dentalia.
4.  H. 23, a male adolescent (of 15-16 years) with a necklace of pierced shells, dentalia and beads made from gazelle phalanges.

Cemetery B consists of single, primary burials – 12 males, females and children – 5 of which were decorated.

5.  H. 87, an adult male with a necklace and two bracelets of dentalia.
6.  H. 88, a child (of 6 years) with a necklace made of dentalia and other, unspecified beads.[50]
7.  H. 89, an adult male with a necklace of dentalia.
8.  H. 90, an adult female, with a necklace of dentalia.
9.  H. 91, an adult female, with some dentalium beads on the skull, perhaps indicating a head-dress? There were also a necklace, a bracelet, a belt and a garter, all made of dentalium beads.
10. The tenth decorated burial is later in time, though still belonging to the Early Natufian period. It is a

45  Belfer-Cohen 1988a, Table 1.

46  For a detailed description, cf. Perrot *et al.* 1988; Boyd, in this volume.
47  Cf. preliminary publications: Mienis 1987; Marechal 1991.
48  Perrot 1966; Stordeur 1988.
49  Perrot *et al* 1988, Fig. 11.
50  Perrot *et al.* 1988, 25.

foetus burial (H. 43) with a string of dentalia (11 groups of 5 to 7 dentalia in a row) lying across the flexed body.

Thus, out of the 28 Early Natufian burials recovered at Eynan, we have 10 decorated ones, and none from the 8 Intermediate or the 68 Late Natufian burials, save that of a young female (of 19-25 years) (H. 4) with two dentalium beads, most probably originating from the fill material rather than forming part of the burial itself.

The Early Natufian cemeteries were in use for two or three generations, and some of the burials were disturbed while new ones, of the same general time-period, were being dug.[51]

### The decorated burial from Erq el Ahmar

According to Neuville, the Natufian occupation at Erq el Ahmar belongs to the Early Natufian (Natufian I).[52] The decorated burial was part of a group grave. Remains of 7 individuals were placed on a limestone platform, lying haphazardly on a surface area of c. 2 m$^2$. 6 of them – 4 adults and 3 children -were represented by crania alone! The only complete adult, a large female (of 20-30 years), had a necklace composed of bone beads (made from the distal ends of gazelle phalanges) and dentalia. Mixed among the gazelle-phalange beads, were two partridge tibio-tarsus beads. A horse molar tooth was found near each crania.

### The decorated burial from Wadi Hammeh 27

Several burials were recorded from this Early Natufian open-air site.[53] In one of the burial pits (Plot XX J), at least 3 mature individuals (1 male and 2 females) were recovered, associated with grave-goods which included two large chunks of red ochre, and 27 dentalium beads (the remains of a necklace?) bunched under the mandible of one of the adults. It seems that the male burial was primary, tightly flexed and placed in an upright position. One of the females is represented only by fragments of long bones (a secondary burial?).

There were other burials on the site (Plot XX) as well as bone-fragments from children, adolescents and adults found amongst the accumulation of rubbish on the Phase I (uppermost) floors. Most of these are burnt cranial fragments.

## Discussion

In his argument for social stratification on the evidence of the Natufian decorated burials, Wright used only the data from el-Wad, as all the other data presented above (with the exception of the Erq el Ahmar burial) were unavailable at the time. Furthermore, he dealt only with that portion of the el-Wad sample which he considered adequately documented.[54] It consisted of less than half the total sample of 96 individuals, and therefore obscures much of the variation at el-Wad. Wright defined 5 types of burials at the site. The first and second types (I-II) were the group burials (inside the cave and on the terrace). He suggested that the group graves on the Terrace differed in significant ways from those in the Cave. Thus each Terrace group burial contained one primary, dentalium-decorated, flexed burial and one or more secondary burials. In contrast, the Cave group consisted of primary burials in extended position with grave 'furniture' (e.g., grave-goods, hearths or ground-stone fragments). The Cave burial was thought to have been re-opened at least twice, while the Terrace groups were undisturbed. He believed that the two types of group burials were contemporaneous, the earliest on the site and dated early within the Natufian sequence in the Levant. They represented two subgroup affiliations. The dentalium shell symbolised a particular status position that was inherited within one of these affiliations. Thus he considered the dentalium ornaments as having a special significance and limited distribution. The type III burials are represented by the individual burials on the Terrace, which were flexed, and lacked both burial furniture (i.e., limestone or hearths) as well as personal adornment. Type IV burials are the ones located inside of the Cave mouth. These are individual, extended burials with no burial furniture or adornment. Type V is represented by the individual burials outside the Cave mouth. These are flexed and unadorned, but contain burial furniture such as hearths and limestone. Wright thought that while the group burials belonged to the Early Natufian, the individual burials of types II, IV and V all relate to the Late Natufian occupations.

Before debating Wright's arguments for social stratification, it should be pointed out that he was mistaken in his representation of the data, as well as in ignoring the time-trajectory implications by mixing in his typology Early and Late Natufian burials.

He stated that while group burials (his types I and II) represent the customs of the Early Natufian, individual burials are late in the Natufian sequence, thus burials of types III, IV and V are characteristic of the Late Natufian. Yet he included among the type III burials that of H. 56, which he himself, following Garrod's attribution, related elsewhere to the Early Natufian.[55] The same applies to the burial of H. 15, which was related by Wright to the Late Natufian, while Garrod specifically referred to it as Early Natufian. Wright also included in the type III burials that of H. 19, which was specifically listed by Garrod as one of

51 Cf. Perrot *et al.* 1988.
52 Neuville 1951.
53 Edwards *et al.* 1988; Edwards 1991.

54 Wright 1978, 204-205.
55 Wright 1987, 214, as opposed to Table 9.1.

those burials which could not be assigned to any particular Natufian stage, being located in an area where no clear division could be made between the Natufian sublayers B1 and B2. The same is true for burials included by Wright in his type IV. The three burials comprising this type (H. 13, H. 59 and H. 60) were attributed by Garrod to the Early Natufian. As for the type V burials, while Wright considered H. 12, 18, and 62 as Late Natufian, Garrod assigned them to the same group of undetermined date as H. 19.[56]

There are also discrepancies as regards the "burial furniture". Wright considered limestone slabs and fragments as burial furniture and claimed that they were present only in the type I and type V burials.[57] Yet it seems that limestone was found in burials of other types as well. Thus in the burial of H. 21 (type III) Garrod observed a small slab of limestone lying on top of the right humerus, and the right hand rested on this. The same is true for the single burials on the Terrace (Wright's types IV and V). The extended burial of H. 60 is packed with stones and has limestone on the legs and fragments of a broken limestone mortar on the thorax. Though Wright adds a question-mark to his reference to the presence of limestone in burials of type V,[58], the burial of H. 12 is described as having two large blocks of limestone lying immediately on top of the skeleton, which was, in consequence, badly crushed. Likewise for H. 62: On the left side of the skull was a large block of limestone and a smaller one on the right side, while the legs were packed into place by stones of various sizes. Actually there is little difference on this point between the burials of type I and those of type II, though Wright states specifically that the Terrace group "lacked hearths [and] limestone (though four members of Group 6 were arranged around one mortar) and show no evidence of having been re-opened".[59] Conversely, Garrod suggested that there was indeed reopening of these group burials, and even though she equated Natufian burial decoration with high status,[60] she also wrote that the primary decorated burial in the Terrace groups might not be a person of special status, but simply the last individual to be buried.[61] The reopening of the graves damaged the skeletons, and might give the impression of secondary burial.

Furthermore, not every group burial had a decorated individual, and the decorated individual was not always accorded special treatment. For example, in H. Group 57 the skeletons (which were all very fragmentary), were placed on their sides with their knees drawn up, and the four which lay on top were lying in a circle round a broken limestone mortar. As already noted, the decorated body, which was one of the four, lay on its

right side, at a slightly lower level, and partly underneath the other three. This does not sound as if it was a particularly special kind of treatment. It is of interest to note that the skull of the decorated H. 57 burial was covered by blocks of limestone, which had crushed the skull very badly.[62] The same is true for the group burial of H. 23: "All the skeletons [i.e. H.23, H.23a, H.23b] were packed into place with large fragments of limestone, which had damaged the bones very seriously".[63]

Wright's argument for social stratification on the basis of the decorated burials among the group burials on the Terrace (his type II burials) was based on the observations that (i) children and infants were buried with adults; (ii) grave-goods did not differ by the deceased's age or sex; and (iii) there was restricted use of dentalium shell as a decoration.

Yet mixed burials of children and adults are found also among the Mousterian burials in the Levant,[64] and no-one has claimed that they indicate social stratification in the Mousterian culture. Henry notes that the dentalium ornaments have a special significance and limited distribution in the case of Northwest Coast complex hunter-gatherers.[65] Still, dentalium shells were found throughout Natufian sites after decoration of burials ceased.[66] It should be pointed out that the decorated person (a child) of the H. 28 Group burial had no dentalia decoration and had a head-dress made of bone beads.[67] The widespread occurrence of the dentalium beads suggests that they were not of special significance and were not considered to be luxury goods. They are also not as time-consuming to prepare as some of the other ornaments, such as the metapodial bone beads. In fact, Natufian grave-goods include very few decorated bone tools or figurines. The most elaborate decorative goods from the Natufian do not come from graves at all, suggesting that they avoided burying their 'treasures'. If decorated burials are a symbol of social ranking, what happened when they disappeared in the Late Natufian? Decoration could also reflect rituals and customs which underwent changes through time. It could reflect magical protection. Or it could be that the Natufian society did indeed exhibit social stratification, but if so the indications of cultural activities associated with body and skeletal alteration do not provide the evidence for it.[68]

The data from Hayonim Cave and Eynan[69] in part negate the conclusions drawn by Wright from the el-Wad burials. Just as at el-Wad, most of the single burials in Hayonim Cave are Late Natufian. The same is

56  Garrod & Bate 1937, 17.
57  Wright 1978, 211.
58  Ibid., 212.
59  Ibid., 212.
60  Garrod 1937.
61  Cf. the same phenomenon in Hayonim Cave: Belfer-Cohen 1988a.
62  Garrod 1937, 125.
63  Ibid., 124.
64  Belfer-Cohen & Hovers 1992.
65  Henry 1989.
66  Belfer-Cohen 1991b.
67  For description, cf. above, p.3, n. 3.
68  If we use ethnographic data concerning the social structure of present-day incipient agricultural bands (Faris 1983), perhaps we can infer social stratification from the differential responsibilities of males as against females in the provision of food.
69  Cf. above, pp.4-5.

true also for the Late Natufian burials in Nahal Oren. Yet in Eynan the picture is different, with group secondary burials beginning in Late Natufian layers while the Early Natufian burials are all single, primary ones.

The decorated burials are found as both single burials (all the decorated burials from Eynan and H. 33 from Hayonim Cave) or in group burials (as at el-Wad and Graves VII and VIII/IX in Hayonim Cave). Thus there is no basis for the statement that the decorated burials represent the most important individual in a certain group.

At least in Hayonim Cave, the extended burials are the earliest in the sequence. Thus it is quite possible that the Cave group burials at el-Wad, as well as the other extended burials at the site, belong to the earliest phases of the Natufian and not as stipulated by Wright.

As stated above, when Wright presented his hypothesis no data were available for Hayonim Cave and Eynan except very fragmentary and preliminary observations. Following his own suggestion for reconsidering his analysis,[70] it seems that we can now state that the Early Natufian burials are both group and single burials; decorated burials are rare and appear in both group and single burials.

In the Late Natufian, no decorated burials have been reported. While at certain sites most of the graves are group burials with primary but mostly secondary interments (Eynan), at other sites all the burials are single and primary (Nahal Oren). At other sites there are both group and single burials, just as in the Early Natufian (Hayonim Cave). While in both Early and Late Natufian sites, stones were placed over the heads, bodies or limbs (e.g., at el-Wad, Eynan, Nahal Oren, and Kebara), none was observed in Hayonim Cave where stones were placed under bodies or heads (mostly in the Early Natufian burials).

It seems that besides some broad similarities in the treatment of the dead, every site had its very own local set of traditions as regards the burials. Such a pattern of variation has been observed for the jewellery and decorative items of the various Natufian base-sites.[71] Thus it becomes impossible to substantiate general statements like the one made by Wright concerning the existence of social stratification in the Early Natufian. The re-examination of the el-Wad data shows that Wright had made some basic mistakes concerning the differentiation between various types of burials and their relationship, as well as their chronological placement in the Natufian sequence. Apparently there was no basis for such an implication even on the basis of the el-Wad material itself. Tempting as it is, evidence for social stratification in the Natufian, inferred from the decorated burials, is actually non-existent.

---

70  Wright 1978, 217, quoted above.

71  Belfer-Cohen 1991b; Henry 1989.

# 3 Houses and Hearths, Pits and Burials: Natufian Mortuary Practices at Mallaha (Eynan), Upper Jordan Valley

## Brian Boyd

ABSTRACT— *Interpretations of human activity at the Natufian site of Mallaha (Eynan) in the upper Jordan Valley are frustrated by a lack of published detailed descriptions of the stratification and structural sequences. Nevertheless, in one particular area of the site, it is possible to identify a group of human burials underlying a series of superimposed structures, representing successive periods of activity in the same spatial location. François Valla has suggested that as well as the day-to-day "domestic" activities attested in this area, there is also evidence for ritual practices which brought together a number of specific material symbols. This paper aims to go beyond the identification and description of this evidence and attempts to offer some ideas on the nature of the material and how it may have been employed within a very specific type of mortuary practice.*

Every attempt to get at the meaning of life must inevitably face the question of death.

Thielecke 1970.

In attempting to study past mortuary practices, archaeologists often assume that they are seeing a more-or-less direct reflection of those practices, preserved, *recorded,* in the material remains which they dig out of the ground. In this way of thinking it becomes relatively straightforward to set up correlates between, for example, the observed complexity of the burial record and the inferred complexity of the social system responsible for the creation of that record. The sterility of this approach is now widely recognised within recent northwest European mortuary studies, and the view that what we are actually dealing with are the material residues of people's actions which were situated within social practices under specific historical and cultural conditions is becoming relatively uncontentious. It is, therefore, unnecessary to embark upon yet another account of the shortcomings of processual archaeology, despite the fact that the field under investigation here – mortuary practices of the later epipalaeolithic in the southern Levant – remains largely characterised by processual and/or social evolutionary approaches. It would be more profitable to offer a reworking of a specific set of archaeological data in the light of recent theoretical considerations.

## An archaeology of life

As evidence for a particular range of social practices, we can regard mortuary remains as having been employed in strategies carried out by and between certain members of the living community in order to structure, at least partially, their own social relations. Those relations may have involved obligations of kinship, of exchange, of standing within a community, and the mortuary arena was only one of a number of other foci within which such obligations were carried out. It therefore becomes necessary to consider at the heart of our analysis the specific material conditions within which social relations were structured through practices. Material conditions here refer to the ambiguous relationship between the physical (i.e., 'natural') environ-

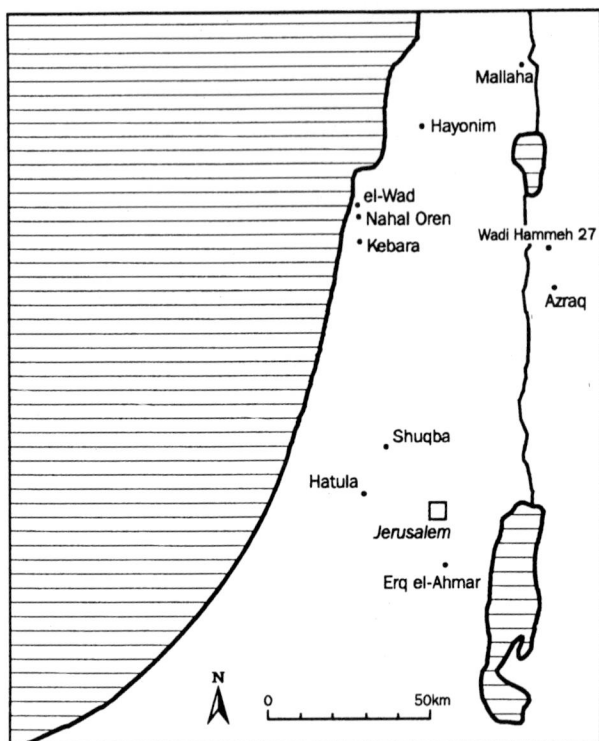

*Fig. 3.1: Map of the southern Levant, showing the location of Mallaha (Eynan) in the upper Jordan Valley, and some toher major Natufian sites.*

ment and the constructed ('lived in' and 'built in'[1]) environment within which people operated and through which they moved on a daily basis. The very nature of archaeology demands that this should be an historical enquiry, and so we must also endeavour to explain something of the historical conditions surrounding our focus of study. In the case of the later epipalaeolithic in the Levant, this requires that we problematise the assumptions which underlie current perceptions of the role of the 'Natufian culture' in the development of sedentism and the earliest stages of food production and animal domestication. Rather than simply accepting that the Natufian represents everywhere in the region some kind of transitory entity, we need to consider the specific details of local cases (where available) and follow the lines of evidence through to a logical and coherent interpretation which is not based on circular inference or analogy from other times and places.

In an effort to demonstrate how we can approach this problem in a way which is both theoretically in-formed and empirically rigorous, I shall now consider how mortuary practices may have intervened in cycles of social reproduction during the early Natufian, so-called, at the site of Mallaha. By social reproduction I simply mean the maintenance or transformation of everyday relationships between people – children, women and men – which, in this case, are likely to be structured

around forms of knowledge relating to concepts of gender, age, kinship, experience, and so on. I am not about to claim that we can infer the specific nature of such relationships through the analysis of the archaeo-logical material, that we can somehow 'read off' the social information from the material 'record'. Rather, the residues of those past practices which constitute our data can allow us partial glimpses of the daily and seasonal activities, those routine practices, which struc-tured and were themselves structured through the social relationships between the people who carried them out. Material culture, as a set of resources, *cultural resources*, is drawn into these relationships, and its significance will depend on the specific nature of the practices in which it is employed and the material conditions fram-ing those practices. We can, therefore, treat mortuary practices as one set of activities which draws upon categories of cultural resources in order to define and negotiate relations between the living, and between the living and the dead.

## Mallaha; the background

Since its discovery in 1954, during the course of a public works project, Mallaha (Hebrew name, Eynan; map reference 204.277), on the western bank of the now-drained Lake Hula in the upper Jordan Valley (Fig. 3.1) has been regarded by many as a, if not *the*, Natufian type-site. This is due, firstly, to the nature of its remains – numerous stone-built structures, rich lithic, bone and groundstone assemblages, abundant faunal remains, and over a hundred human burials – and, secondly, its long stratigraphic sequence which runs from early to (possibly) final Natufian. Surprisingly, only three radiocarbon determinations have been obtained, and these date the earliest known Natufian layers at the site (layers III and IV) to c. 12,000 BP.[2] The later levels have been relatively dated by attributes of the lithic industry, and by cross-site references to what are considered to be securely dated Natufian occurrences such as those at Hayonim Cave B and El Wad B1.[3] Mallaha is notable for another reason: whilst all the other Natufian occur-rences in the modern Mediterranean zone come from cave sites (except one, Wadi Hammeh 27), or on terraces in front of caves, Mallaha is an open site, and one of considerable size (estimated to be at least 2,000 m²).

It should be noted that excavations at the site were, technically-speaking, carried out by three different archaeologists. Jean Perrot (Centre Nationale de Re-cherche Scientifique, Centre de Recherche Français de Jerusalem) directed the initial series of soundings in 1955 and 1956, followed by full excavations from 1959-1961. Successive fieldwork seasons were carried out by Monique Lechevallier (CNRS, CRFJ) in 1971 and 1972,

---

1   Ingold 1992.

2   Davis & Valla 1978.
3   Valla 1987.

and by François R. Valla (CNRS, CRFJ) from 1973 to 1976, although the site was still effectively under the directorship of Perrot himself. This is an important point because if we are to offer a critical evaluation of archaeological evidence, then we must be equally critical of the archaeological practice which structured the ways in which that evidence was excavated, recorded and presented. We have to be able to "expose the social contexts behind the intellectual traditions" which will frame research objectives, excavation strategies and determine the types of questions asked of the empirical data.[4] These are issues pertinent to all archaeological research and, as such, they should be made explicit in excavation notes, preliminary reports and site publications in order to make possible future reworkings, reinterpretations, which can critically accommodate the 'political' motives of the excavators.[5]

In the case of Mallaha, reworking the published material entails consideration of Jean Perrot's initial motives for excavating the site. His early reports[6] state that the soundings carried out in 1955 and 1956 (if one can call a total exposure of 50 m$^2$ a 'sounding') led him to believe that the Mallaha evidence could bridge the gap between the beginnings of intensive food collection by mobile groups and the earliest settled communities with well-established food production. He made some tentative comparisons between Mallaha and the basal levels from the Kenyon-directed excavations at Jericho, and by the close of his first full excavation season in 1959, Perrot felt in a position to claim that Mallaha predated and eclipsed the significance of even that monument: "The discoveries at 'Eynan (Mallaha) throw some light on what led to the first permanent settlement at Jericho"[7] and, "At a time when Natufian hunters roaming the Jordan Valley were visiting the Jericho spring and oasis, 'Eynan, in exceptionally favourable conditions, was already a permanent settlement".[8] More recently, he has written that Mallaha "provides the earliest known example of sedentary life in this country, and perhaps in the entire Near East".[9]

I do not wish to dispute the argument that Mallaha was a permanent site in terms of its structural physicality. However, underlying this is the unquestioned assumption that the site was *occupied* permanently. Perrot never seems to have considered Mallaha as representing anything less, and this premise appears to have strongly influenced his interpretation of the material and structures encountered there. This is not the place to develop this particular argument further, suffice it to say that from the published evidence it is far from clear if occupation was continuous or on a seasonal basis.[10]

Interpretations of the burial data are complicated by differences of opinion between archaeologists as regards certain elements of the site's stratification, particularly in the early phase. For the sake of clarity, I shall briefly outline these differences here. Following the refinement of Natufian chronology in the late 1970s, with sub-divisions into Early, Middle and Late phases, François Valla attempted to correlate the stratigraphic levels at Mallaha with the new sub-divisions.[11] The structural sequence in the early Natufian phase at Mallaha, according to Valla, ran as follows. There existed a structure before the building of shelter 131. As yet, this structure has not been excavated. Following the abandonment of this early structure, shelter 131 was built in the same location. The next major construction, shelter 51, directly overlay 131. Finally, shelter 62 (itself a two-phase structure, with wall 73 representing the earlier of the two phases) was built in the interior of the abandoned 51. For Valla, this whole sequence belongs to the Early Natufian at Mallaha. Perrot, on the other hand, places shelter 62 in a "middle" occupation phase at the site, thereby adding a fourth phase to the chronological/stratigraphic sequence. Also, he fails to discuss the existence of structure (wall) 73.[12]

These differences compel us, again, to examine the possible motives behind the excavation strategy. Perrot and Ladiray's publication on the burial data describes how, during the 1971 season (where Perrot was assisted by Monique Lechevallier), a series of burials was found appertaining to a previously unknown very early level of the site. This occurred during the excavation of a large deep pit (pit 101), which cut through, according to Perrot, the floors of shelters 51 and 62. *Under* this pit, the excavators came across some human bones, and "their excavation immediately became priority".[13] For us, trying to rework this evidence, the shift in excavation strategy during the 1971 season causes severe problems. If we look at Perrot's *"coupe schématique"* of this area,[14] we can see clearly that pit 101, as well as an earlier pit (77), does indeed cut through the floors of shelters 51 and 62. However, it is equally clear that *both pits also cut the floor of shelter 131*, the presence of which the excavators were seemingly unaware. They were, therefore, excavating burials which were stratigraphically under the floor of structure 131, and so the disturbance to this floor (actually found to be two successive floors on their 'discovery' and excavation during the 1975 season) was considerable (Fig. 3.2). In the light of this, it becomes clear why Perrot's own presentation and interpretation of the mortuary data makes little serious attempt to

---

4  After Barrett 1991, 212.
5  Cf. Barrett 1987; and Barrett, Bradley & Green 1991, for effective examples of this approach; Hodder 1989 for further discussion on the topic.
6  E.g., Perrot 1960.
7  Ibid., 22.
8  Ibid.
9  Perrot 1993, 393.

10  E.g., Pichon 1991. The development of recent work on Natufian seasonality (e.g., Lieberman 1993; Valla 1991; 1994) may help to address this problem.
11  Valla 1981; revised 1987.
12  Perrot & Ladiray 1988.
13  Ibid., 23.
14  Ibid., 4.

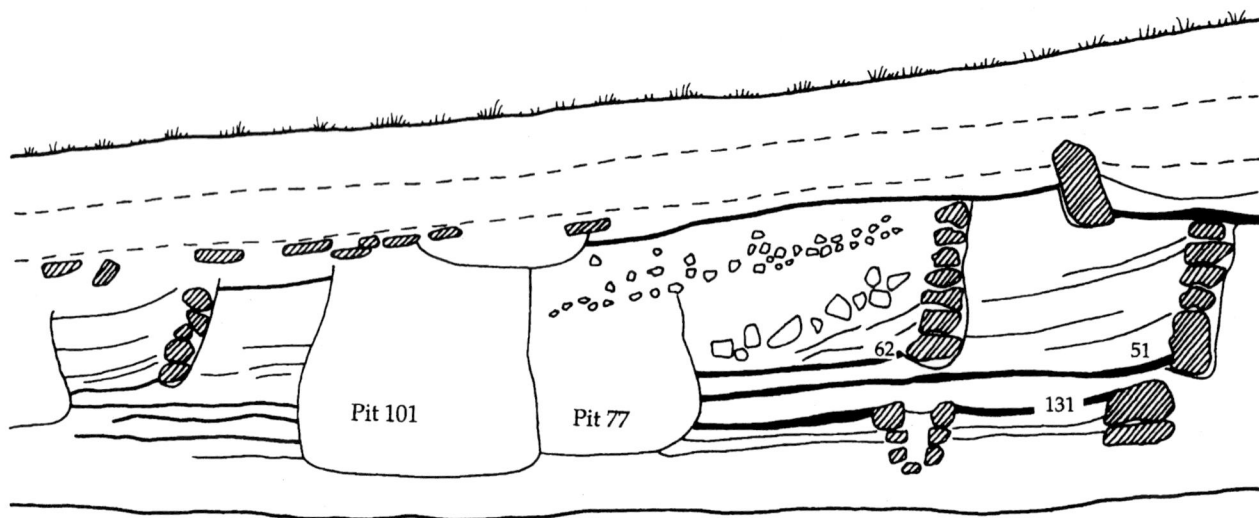

*Fig. 3.2: Mallaha: section showing pits 77 and 101 cutting through floors of shelters 51, 62 and 131
(after Perrot and Ladiray 1988)*

consider the relationship of the burials to the structural remains on the site.

I shall now return to discussion of structure 131 and the area I have chosen within which to examine the relationships between the archaeological remains and the practices which, intentionally or otherwise, produced those remains. I have chosen this particular part of the site for two main reasons. Firstly, it is the only one which has sufficiently detailed published accounts on which to structure a coherent interpretation.[15] Secondly, it was excavated by detailed *décapage horizontale* and the material subjected to, for the first time on the site, wet sieving. We may assume, therefore, that the excavation strategy was executed with rather more integrity than in preceding seasons.

## Structure 131; its material culture

Structure 131 – discovered during the 1975 excavation season – appears to have been a semi-circular structure around 8 m in diameter, covering a surface area of around 25 m². Inside the wall, at about a distance of 1 m, was a series of six roughly circular stone-built features, about 1-1.5 m apart, arranged in a semi-circle respecting the circumference of the wall. A seventh such feature was located towards the interior of the structure. These, it is argued, held posts which together formed a substructure and roof arrangement.[16] Valla identified two occupation floors.[17] The earlier (B) was characterised by a "groupement de 26 objets de pierre", including pestle fragments, a grooved polisher, and objects of

basalt, flint and limestone. The later floor (A) displayed a vast amount of faunal remains and bone and flint artefacts, concentrated towards the area between the wall and the post-holes 143 and 144. *Décapage horizontale* has allowed Valla to identify three clearly-defined groups of material:[18]

1. A collection of 24 small pebbles ("galets") of various colours, some of which were polished or burnt, three grooved basalt stones, flint flakes, and various gazelle, fox, hare and snake remains.
2. A half-buried basalt vase or mortar fragment, along with several stones.
3. Two pestles, a grinding implement, limestone and flint material, a bone point, shells, a tortoise carapace, the cervical vertebrae of a cervid, an ochre-covered stone slab, and various stones.

In addition to these groups of material were pestles, limestone slabs, flint blades, "picks", shells, a gazelle palate, half a canid mandible (probably a domestic dog), and the top of a human infant's cranium (H. 102).

Of particular interest are the hearths. Two hearths, 105 and 147, belong to the upper occupation floor, in association with the material described above. Together, these have been regarded as forming a double or twin hearth.[19] Both are stone-built and occupy an area just inside the semi-circle of post-holes mentioned earlier. Some burnt flint, small fragments of charcoal, shells, and numerous deer and bird bones were recovered from hearth 147, as well as a 23 cm-long polished and incised roe deer antler which showed use-wear traces.[20] Interest-

---

15 Perrot 1966; Perrot & Ladiray 1988; Valla 1981; 1988; 1991.
16 Valla 1988.
17 Valla 1981.

18 Valla 1988; 1991.
19 Valla & Lechevallier 1989.
20 Stordeur 1988, 17-19.

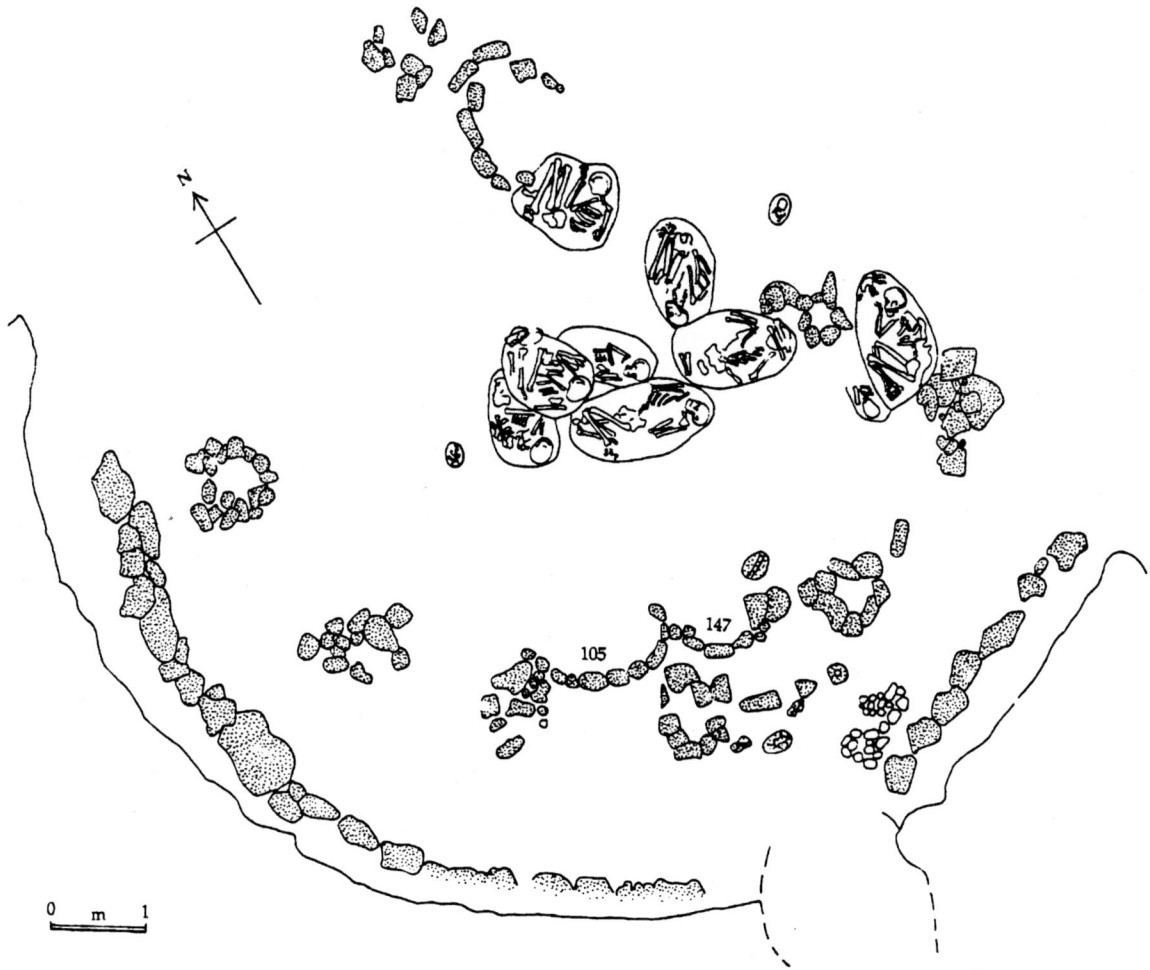

*Fig. 3.3: Mallaha: Composite plan of structure 131, cemetery B. hearths 105 and 147, and groups of cultural material.*

ingly, despite its abundance elsewhere in structure 131, little flint material was found in the zone of the hearth which included this antler. Nearby, between the hearth and two ground stone pestles, two pieces of a small limestone sculpture were found.[21]

## Cemetery B

Underlying the three superimposed houses was "cemetery B", which contained the remains of around 12 skeletons. These (with the exception of H. 92, H. 104 and H. 105) were the skeletons encountered during the excavation of pit 101 in 1971 (see earlier). Five of these were wearing various dentalium shell decorations. The decoration of skeleton H. 91 was particularly elaborate, a possible head-dress, necklace, bracelet, belt and garter. Also in this cemetery lay the well-known "puppy burial" H. 104, which contained an adult female with her left hand resting on a 4-6 month-old canine, in all likelihood

a domestic dog.[22] For the record, there were 3 adult males (H. 87, H. 89, H. 98), 2 of which were decorated (H. 87 and H. 89); 5 adult females (H. 90-H. 93, H. 104), 2 of which were decorated (H. 90, H. 91), 3 newly-born infants (H. 95, H. 97, H. 105); and one decorated child skeleton, unsexed (H. 88).[23] All the burials in this cemetery were individual and primary. Several of them were damaged by the cutting of later pits, or by the placing of their neighbouring burials. All are relatively dated to the early Natufian phase at Mallaha (level IV), although some graves clearly either pre- or post-date others. For example, H. 89 post-dates H. 92, and so on, within the same broad chronological phase.[24]

To reiterate, what we have in the earliest excavated phase at Mallaha, in one particular area of the site, is a large structure with two successive occupation floors, subsequently rebuilt or replaced at least twice in the same spatial location, containing hearths, numerous

---

21  Valla 1988; 1991.

22  Davis & Valla 1978; Perrot & Ladiray 1988, 33-36.
23  Perrot & Ladiray 1988; Soliveres-Massei 1988.
24  Valla 1981.

wild animal bones, pestles and mortars, all in some kind of stratigraphic relationship with a group of human burials. Some of the skeletons are decorated with dentalium shells; there are several possible artefact associations; and one is accompanied by a domestic dog, the only known animal domesticate at the time (Fig. 3.3).

## Structure 131 and cemetery B; domestic space, ritual space

There is certainly no denying the range of everyday activities attested on this part of the site. As Valla has argued, the material remains from the two occupation floors of structure 131 constitute evidence for a wide variety of "domestic" practices; plant processing, lithic and bone artefact production, food discard, and so on.[25] It should be stressed, however, that we have to be able to differentiate between the regular floor debris and the selected, more structured, nature of the discrete groups of material deposited in the area between the structural wall, post-holes 143 and 144, and the double hearth.

If it can be accepted that we are dealing with a semi-circular structure, then let us look again at the positions of the post-holes/supports, the hearths and other cultural material. It seems reasonable to assume that a hearth forms a focus for activity. Here we have a double hearth facing a single hearth, within an arrangement of posts, possibly to support a roof or superstructure.[26] This arrangement would have facilitated and structured the enactment of particular practices (through control of bodily movement, direction of vision, and so on), practices involving deployment of certain material symbols, the cultural resources discussed earlier, and, crucially, making reference to the dead, the remains of the dead, interred in the area of ground between the facing hearths and posts. Perhaps some member(s) of the community would have stood in a particular position, maybe at the hearth, moving around and through the post arrangement, using symbols of authority which would have delineated and legitimised specific forms of understanding, specific forms of knowledge. The cultural resources employed would have been recognisable as 'everyday' or 'mundane' by those participating and/or observing, but also they would have called into existence "meanings and presences which appear to originate beyond the world of everyday experience".[27] And so we see evidence for the use of everyday plant food processing artefacts, wild and domestic animal remains (e.g., daily food discard and/or ceremonial feasting remains), and what may be termed rather uncritically exotics (shells from non-local sources, the coloured pebbles, the limestone sculpture, the incised antler), in a non-mundane con-

text, a ritual context, and calling into existence "meanings and presences" from the past and from the world of the dead, predecessors, maybe even ancestors. I have argued elsewhere that the precise identities of predecessors do not necessarily have to be known to those enacting or observing the rites in order for those rites to be effective.[28] It is enough for symbolic reference to be made to the existence and significance of the remains as a way of legitimising the standing of those involved in the organisation and enactment of the rites.

If we consider that structure 131 was abandoned, its floor covered,[29] and subsequently replaced by structure 51 – also semi-circular – in almost exactly the same location, then what can we say about the timing and significance of these ritual practices? Two issues may be raised:

1. Why abandon and then build something entirely new, rather than simply rebuild the existing structural features?

2. Why was the occupation floor (A) of structure 131 not cleared of its considerable amount of material before it was covered with the floor of structure 51? (and, for that matter, why was floor B not cleared before its replacement by floor A?)

We do not know the length of time which elapsed between the final period of use of 131 and the building of 51. I would venture to suggest that the practices which resulted in the deposition of the groups of material constituted ceremonial activities which either ritually *ended* the occupation and use of structure 131, or ritually began, *founded*, the occupation and use of structure 51. These practices, and the authority of the people who carried them out, would have been legitimised by them making reference to the dead interred under the living area and may have served to, for example, maintain lines of inheritance, land claims and so on. We can now perhaps begin to understand something of the history of this part of the site: the rebuilding of successive structures in the same location, the undoubtedly special nature of the deposits, all overlying a group of ancient human burials.

It is only now, at the end, that we have brought in the dead, and the archaeology of death. The evidence outlined here has rarely been connected with mortuary practices because it appears to have nothing to do with burial, cremation or human remains. It has been traditionally connected with the living, with structures, features and artefacts normally associated with economic subsistence practices and domestic life or, at best, some unspecified type of ritual activity. This highlights a further point: we continue to stress that because they are built out of the same material conditions we should not separate the economic from the symbolic, the mundane from the ritual, the sacred from the profane, and

---

25  Cf. Valla 1988, for a highly detailed description.
26  Valla's (1991) reconstruction of shelter 131 parallels similar structures built and used in recent years by the Bedouin in the northern Negev (personal observation).
27  Parker Pearson 1992, 566.

---

28  Boyd 1992, 27.
29  Valla 1981, 414.

yet we persist in doing just that. We cannot study evidence for specific practices in isolation, whether it is the archaeology of death, of food, of subsistence, of the natural or cultural environments, and so on. To understand something of the significance of such evidence, reference must be made to all the other related "fields of social action".[30] Only in that way can we begin to understand the relationships which existed between different social practices and their contribution to the reproduction of human relations.

## Final comments

The interpretations put forward in this paper are meant to be entirely specific to the practices which may have been carried out in one particular area of one particular site.[31] I have not in any way attempted to draw broader inferences about the applicability or significance of these practices within the Natufian culture and the debatable framework surrounding archaeological explanations of the origins of sedentism and domestication. Suffice it to say it seems likely that the structural setting as well as many of the features and

cultural resources employed in the enactment of the mortuary rites would have been key components in activities connected with the home, plant food acquisition and processing, and the development of human-animal relationships. Similarly, the legitimation of lines of inheritance and land claims do carry certain implications for the development of (semi-)sedentism. However, these connections are more to do with acknowledging the full diversity of the evidence rather than with trying to fit the data into some kind of social or economic totality of our own making.

*Acknowledgements*
This paper began life as a chapter in my 1990 MA dissertation, and so I must thank my supervisor John Barrett for his constant encouragement and inspiration throughout. At the Manchester conference there was a feeling of real optimism and co-operation amongst the participants, which, unfortunately, is not always the case at such academic gatherings. Thanks must also go to Anna Belfer-Cohen, Nigel Goring-Morris, Lesley K. McFadyen, Koji Mizoguchi and François Valla for invaluable discussions and comments during the various stages of the production of the paper. Thanks also to Dr Joshua Pollard for the illustrations. Finally, special thanks to David Gibson and Paul Wheelhouse without whom I would never have made it to Manchester at all.

---

30 Barrett 1988, 40.
31 The practice of building large semi-circular structures, similar to 131 at Mallaha, in some kind of spatial relationship to earlier burials may have been a practice carried out at other Natufian sites, in particular El Wad and Wadi Hammeh 27 (A.N. Goring-Morris, personal communication).

# 4 New Data on Burials from the Pottery Neolithic Period (Sixth–Fifth Millennium BC) in Israel

## Avi Gopher and Estelle Orrelle

ABSTRACT—*The database of Natufian and Pre-Pottery Neolithic period (10,500-6,000 BC) burial customs in the Levant contains details of numerous burials and burial customs. A wealth of data is also available on fourth millennium BC burials. These databases demonstrate significant differences such as the removal of burials from the living site to cemeteries outside. Research on the intervening sixth and fifth millennia BC could contribute towards discussion of this interesting phenomenon but few burials have been previously excavated. Recently excavated burials in three different sites represent different phases of the period. The information gleaned from first examination of these can be summed up in a few points:*

*A.   There appears to have been a continuation of on-site burial during the Pottery Neolithic period.*
*B.   Burials are individual.*
*C.   Burial positions are varied.*
*D.   Skulls are intact in most cases.*
*E.   Skulls are not treated.*
*F.   Burial of young children and foetuses appears to be established behaviour, some of them in jars.*
*G.   Burial offerings are generally absent.*

*A change appears to have occurred in the attitudes of society towards children and foetuses. Adult skulls, on the other hand, are no longer treated. These new trends may indicate change, whose study could enhance our understanding of certain aspects of the society.*

## Introduction

A great deal is known on graves and the buried from the very late Pleistocene and the first half of the Holocene in the southern Levant. The data falls into three main groups: Natufian graves (mainly 10,500-9000 bc); graves of the Pre-Pottery Neolithic A and B period (PPN, mainly 8000-6000 bc); and graves of the Chalcolithic period (mainly 4000-3300 bc). Each of these groups has a sample of tens or hundreds of graves and human skeletons.[1]

An important difference between the earlier two groups of burials (Natufian/PPN) and the later group of burials (Chalcolithic) is the removal of the graves from living sites to separate cemeteries outside the settle-ments. Other differences include aspects such as grave types, accompanying grave goods, treatment of the skeleton, differentiation between the buried, and other elements to be discussed below.

Against this background, the meagre data on burial customs from the Pottery Neolithic period (PN), mainly sixth and fifth millennia BC (5500-4000 bc) is conspicuous. This results from the generally poor state of research of the cultures of these millennia in the southern Levant. The late seventh and the sixth millennia BC were traditionally regarded as a period of crisis to the extent that a settlement gap was suggested for many parts of Israel as a result of a postulated severe climatic deterioration.[2] In the 1970s, however, a number of reassessments were published which suggested that this gap was not a prehistoric reality but a gap in data, the result of inaccurate interpretations stemming from a

---

1   E.g., for the Natufian, Perrot & Ladiray 1988; Belfer-Cohen 1989; for the PPN, Hershkovitz & Gopher 1990; for the Chalcolithic, Perrot & Ladiray 1980; Levy 1986; Gilead 1988.

2   E.g., de Vaux 1966; Perrot 1968; Kenyon 1970.

poor dating capability.[3] In the last decade the research of this period has acquired a new momentum both in Israel and Jordan and the reconstruction of the cultural sequences of the southern Levant has improved especially for the sixth millennium BC.

Today, following Rollefson's suggestion, an extension of the PPN period is proposed – the PPNC, which starts at the very end of the seventh millennium BC and continues deep into the middle of the sixth, thus accounting for nearly half of the settlement gap.[4] Although we have very little data on the cultures of this time-unit, there are a few sites that can be assigned to it where burial evidence has been exposed (such as Ain Ghazal and Atlit Yam, which will be described below).

A recent reconstruction of the sequence of pottery bearing cultures in the southern parts of the Levant has shown that they appear on the scene sometime in the mid-sixth millennium BC. In the region discussed in this paper three major archaeological cultures have been classified – the two early ones are local, small scale cultures – the Yarmukian, which is the earliest and the Lodian (Jericho IX) which is the later, both covering the second half of the sixth millennium BC and early parts of the fifth millennium BC. The third is the Wadi Raba culture, which is a larger-scale culture and is the latest of the three, covering most of the fifth millennium BC.[5] The information on burials and burial customs from these three cultures is very scarce, and publications are even more so. Accordingly, the new burials presented here, from the sixth and fifth millennia BC are significant. A short survey of known burials of the sixth and fifth millennia BC is given, before the new information is presented, followed by a discussion on the contribution which it makes.

## Survey of sixth and fifth millennia BC burials.

### PPNC

*Ain Ghazal* – The PPNC layers of the site of Ain Ghazal are dated mostly to the first half of the sixth millennium BC.[6] All burials are close to or within the houses, in pits, under floors, on floors, in a corner of a house and in a pit by a wall outside a house. In most cases secondary burial is the case, and multiple burials of 2-3 individuals are the rule. One male was found in a semi-flexed position; bodies were "stuffed" into pits and some were "seated semi-flexed".[7] Presence of the skull with the rest of the skeleton is typical for PPNC and skull removal, very common in PPNB, is unattested. One adult male skull, however, was found placed on the floor of a house. Sex-age determinations show a high

rate of infant mortality (over 50% of the sample). No grave-goods are reported, but there is one instance where the bones of a pig were found in the grave of a child. There was no treatment of the skulls.

*Atlit Yam* – This is an underwater single-component site dated radiometrically to between 6100 and 5600 bc.[8] Some 15 skeletons were uncovered in this site in the first season[9] and the sample has grown to over thirty individuals in later seasons.[10] All burials are within or close to the houses. Most graves contain a single skeleton, which is usually in contracted position with skull intact. An exception is a grave containing an adult and a child near one of the structures. Both primary and secondary burials were found,[11] many of them in contracted positions. The sample includes a very low number of children under 14 years of age (2) which must be an under representation when compared to other samples from PPNA-PPNB sites.[12] The conditions of this under-water site must be responsible for causing more damage to the fragile bones of the children. No grave-goods were found in the context of the burials, and no evidence of skull treatment was observed.

### The Yarmukian culture

*Shaar Hagolan* – One grave under a cairn, a hewn stone installation whose base is 2.0 m long and its height 0.60 m, was exposed at this site.[13] The skeleton was in a bad state of preservation, in supine position with slightly contracted legs. The deceased was most probably an adult, and the grave was within a house, in association with a hearth and a pit. No artifacts could be interpreted as grave-goods, but flint tools, animal bones, incised pebbles, bone tools and a stone statuette were found which are most probably related to the floor of the house, but may be connected to the burial as well. Strangely, no pottery sherds were found in this context.

*Habashan Street* – The burial of a young adult in a pit was exposed in the Yarmukian layer of this site in Tel Aviv.[14]

*Munhata* – In the Yarmukian layer of this site, south of Lake Tiberias, a burial was exposed within the living area,[15] but we know very little about it apart from the fact that the deceased was an adult. The skeleton was in contracted position with no skull, and no grave-goods were found.

Additional burials are mentioned in Wadi Shu'eib;[16] it is not clear, however, whether they belong to the Yarmukian or to the later Lodian (Jericho IX) culture. One is a secondary burial of an adult lacking the

---

3   Mellaart 1975, 67-69; Moore 1978; Gopher 1985.
4   Rollefson & Simmons 1986; 1988; Rollefson 1989.
5   Gopher & Gophna 1993.
6   Rollefson 1990.
7   Kafafi *et al.* 1991.
8   Galili 1987; Galili *et al.* 1993.
9   Hershkovitz & Galili 1990.
10  Hershkovitz, personal communication 1992.
11  Hershkowitz & Galili 1988.
12  Cf. Hershkowitz & Gopher 1990.
13  Stekelis 1972.
14  Kaplan 1970.
15  Perrot 1968.
16  Simmons et al. 1989.

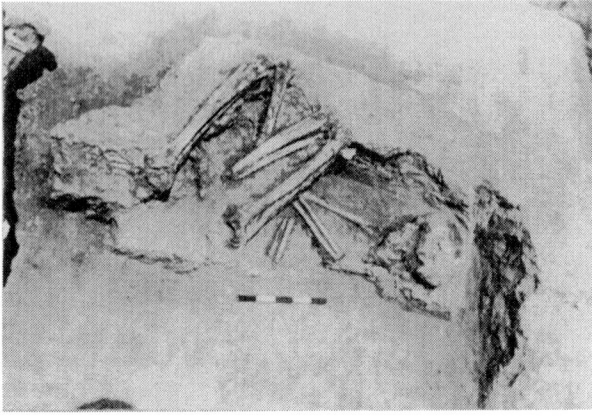

*Fig.4.1: A burial of an adult female from the Lodian layer at Lod. (scale 25cm)*

*Fig.4.2: A burial of an adult from the Pottery Neolithic layer at Nahal Betzet I, upper Galilee. (scale 25cn)*

cranium; and the other is of a child laid in a flexed position within a circle of stones below the floor.

Notably, no definite Yarmukian burials have ever been found at Ain Ghazal. In summary, all the Yarmukian burials known to date in the southern Levant are on-site in the houses, or close to them, and most probably all lacking grave-goods.

To the north, at Byblos, on the Lebanese coast, the 'Néolithique Ancien' layer includes jar burials of babies and infants, juveniles and adults in flexed positions in basin-like installations, and adults in flexed positions lying on their left side, sometimes in a group. All burials are within the settlement area, in and between the houses. Grave-goods appear only within the built basin-like graves and include bone tools and pottery items.[17] The 'Néolithique Ancien' layer at Byblos displays, in a way, a variant to the 'Israeli Yarmukian' and differs from it in some respects, while it has certain resemblances in others. It is relevant in this discussion if only for its chronology. The Byblos 'Néolithique Ancien' data show a diversified set of traditions of burial customs, including a clear differentiation between babies, children and adults, and possibly between different adults as well,[18] which has not been observed in Israel.

## The Lodian (Jericho IX) culture

No burials were exposed in Garstang's layer IX at Jericho, where this culture was first defined, nor in the later seasons of Kenyon (PNA layer). Nor did such finds appear in any other site of the Lodian (Jericho IX) culture. The burials to be presented below, from the 1992 excavations at Lod, are thus primary data. We have mentioned Wadi Shu'eib, whose attribution is not clear, and we should mention too the site of Nizzanim in this context. This site, on the Israeli southern coastal plain, is dated to the early part of the fifth millennium BC and has been assigned to the Lodian (Jericho IX) entity.[19] At

this site, under the floor of a house, two separate graves were found, a secondary burial of an adult, including only shin and foot, and a baby burial, both in small pits. No grave-goods were found.

At Teluliot Batashi, excavated by Kaplan (1958) two skeletons were exposed in level IV that is generally assigned to the Lodian. One was in contracted position on its left side and the other was only partly preserved. The two graves were covered by stones or pebbles. Both burials were most probably of adults; both had their skulls; there were no grave goods.

## The Wadi Raba culture

The Wadi Raba culture includes a range of subcultures spreading over most of the Mediterranean zones of Israel. A burial from the more southerly Qatifian subculture of the late fifth millenium BC is included here, although it is not part of the Wadi Raba culture.[20]

Wadi Raba burials have been only rarely exposed and reported. Three adults were buried under a house floor at Ein el Jarba.[21] They all had their skulls intact and no grave-goods accompanied them. Another adult, to be described below, was found at Nahal Betzet I. A burial of an adult from Kfar Giladi in Upper Galilee cannot be clearly attributed to the Wadi Raba culture, but comes within the same general time-range. All other skeletal remains of the Wadi Raba and related cultures are of babies or foetuses. Those from Nahal Zehora II will be described below. Others include a baby in a jar from Tel Dan,[22] a few jar burials of babies from Tel Teo,[23] and a baby in a jar at the Qatifian site Qatif Y-3.[24] Here too, Byblos must be mentioned for its varied and rich data on burial in the 'Néolithique Moyen' and 'Néolithique Récent' layers covering most probably parts of the time-period we are considering here. The burials there still display most of the characteristics mentioned

---

17  Dunand 1973.
18  de Contenson 1992.
19  Yeivin & Olami 1979.

20  Gilead 1990; Goren 1990.
21  Arensburg 1970.
22  Gopher & Greenberg 1987.
23  Eisenberg 1987.
24  Epstein 1984.

*Fig. 4.3: A fetus burial in a jar from Nahal Zehora II. (scale 25cm)*

*Fig. 4.4: A child burial from Nahal Zehora II. (scale 25cm)*

above for the *Néolithique Ancien* layer. In Teluliot Batashi level III, two burials were exposed (Kaplan 1958) one of an adolescent and one of a baby in a jar; neither had grave goods.

## New data

### Lod

The Lodian layer at the site of Lod was excavated by the authors during a salvage project undertaken in the area by the Antiquities Authority of Israel in spring 1992. The Pottery Neolithic layer was exposed some four meters below the surface and included a series of rounded sunken structures and oval pits filled with dark sediments including faunal remains, lithic artifacts and pottery sherds. Two burials were interred in two such successive pits in the western part of the excavated area.

The lower burial was of an adult in a bad state of preservation, placed in a shallow basin-like pit. The skull was not intact but it was very close to the skeleton (30 cm) and it was facing west. The other bones were for the most part articulated, indicating a primary burial. The position was flexed, but the ribs and spine and one leg were mostly missing. Close to one of the hands a possible bone tool was found, but this still needs to be studied.

The second burial, in a later stage of the same sequence of pits, was that of an adult female in a contracted postion with folded hands. The skull was facing west. The skeleton was fully articulated, testifying to a primary burial. No grave-goods of any kind were found. (Fig. 4.1.)

A third burial, also in a pit, included a few remains, mostly the jaw of an adult, together with animal bones.

All burials are on-site, associated with or are nearby the houses (1-3 m). The better preserved ones are primary single burials, all of adults in contracted position (when observation is possible). It seems that there are no burial gifts.

The finds from Lod are assigned to the Lodian-Jericho IX culture. Radiometric dates of the layer are expected in the coming months. In the meantime, we predict a post-Yarmukian, pre-Wadi Raba chronological position for these finds.[25]

### Nahal Betzet I

A burial of an adult in a shallow pit was exposed in the Pottery Neolithic layer of Nahal Betzet I, in Upper Galilee.[26] The skeleton was in supine position with hands folded on the chest. The skull was not found and no grave-goods were present. (Fig. 4.2.)

The Pottery Neolithic layer of this site was recently assigned to the very end of the sixth or early fifth millennium BC.[27]

### Nahal Zehora II

Three burials were exposed recently in the Wadi Raba layers of Nahal Zehora II, on the southern fringes of the Jezreel Valley.[28] Two foetus burials were found in the north-eastern part of the excavation. One, in a jar, was found close to the wall of a structure (Fig. 4.3), and another in a small 'cist' made of stone slabs. Both skeletons were fully articulated, and await further study.

The third burial was of a child in contracted position, lacking cranial material (Fig. 4.4). The skeleton was surrounded by stones, and a massive stone block took the place of the skull.

All burials of this Wadi Raba site were within-settlement, primary burials. No grave-goods were present, and the buried were all children and foetuses.

## Discussion

A first examination of the new data presented above combined with the known data from past excavations enables some generalisations.

25 Cf. Gopher & Gophna 1993.
26 Gopher 1989.
27 Gopher *et al.* 1992.
28 Gopher & Orrelle 1991.

1. Sixth to Fifth millennia BC burials are on-site, thus continuing the earlier tradition. Therefore, the locating of burial grounds away from the settlement site is probably a later development, belonging to the Chalcolithic.

2. While in the PPNC group burials are common (mostly at Ain Ghazal, but there is also a case at Atlit Yam), the Pottery Neolithic cultures have mostly single burials, both of adults and children/babies/foetuses. (Group burial in the *Néolithique Ancien* is to be noted).

3. While the PPNC burials include secondary burials, as was common for earlier parts of the PPN, the PN adults are in primary burials. Children, babies and foetuses are mostly in primary burials (although some may be in secondary burials).

4. Skulls are intact in most cases both for the PPNC and the PN and are not separated or treated as was the practice during Pre-Pottery Neolithic times.

5. Burial positions are varied, with contracted (and supine ?) positions the more common.

6. Burial offerings are most probably absent altogether for the PPNC and the PN and the possible offerings found in some cases are still in question. (The case of the Byblos *Néolithique Ancien* again is different).

7. In the PN, young children, babies and foetuses are, for the first time in this region, buried in jars. This may reflect changes in PN societies, especially towards the young and probably towards child-bearing, as witnessed by the burial of foetuses. We choose to present a broad speculative reconstruction of social change which will doubtless require further study in the future.

Interpretations have been suggested to account for the phenomenon of separating adult crania and buring them separately in the Pre-Pottery Neolithic period. Although no grave-gifts accompany PPN burials, the treatment of adult skulls is conspicuous and children are not treated equally. It has been suggested that this treatment would only be accorded the initiated. The main argument offered is that family lines are more emphasised in the PPN; and that this finds expression too in customs related to ancestor worship, such as burying adult skulls separately in the PPNA, and plastering and decorating adult skulls separately in the PPNB. This represents a change compared with the non-differentiated Natufian burials.[29] It is interesting to note that a change in Neolithic times to an emphasis on the family unit has been independently suggested by researchers in different parts of the world following discussions on the transition to agriculture.[30] Had orderly conditions after the PPNB continued, we may speculate that the following stages of Neolithic devel-

opment would have brought a higher social complexity and perhaps trends towards a ranked society. But a crisis at the end of the PPNB and the conditions prevailing in the area caused the collapse of the PPNB system and the appearance of a diversified, locally-based set of cultural variants in the PPNC. We no longer see evidence of skull-treatment in burials and in one site (Ain Ghazal) there is a return to group burials. Both these facts may hint at a change resulting from a disturbance in social development that started sometime in the early Neolithic. Only in the mid sixth millennium BC, pottery-using agricultural comunities established themselves with a new social system reflected, amongst other things, in a whole new set of symbolic imagery. The reintegration of local societies and the continued emphasis on family lines in the PN may be the stage at which the trend towards an increase in social complexity begins. Now, as we can speculate from the items of imagery, an investment in the resources of human reproduction is encouraged. Added to this, the slim evidence emerging from this new burial data on children and foetus burial may confirm that children's place in society is becoming established, and perhaps rights in family lines assured.

The PN burials have not, therefore, provided us with evidence for the process of moving burial grounds outside the living site, and we must conclude that this is most probably an innovation of the Chalcolithic period mostly occurring in the fourth millennium BC and related to issues which we cannot explore here. The PN burial customs as presented do, however, reflect changes when compared to the earlier PPN burials. One of these changes may be a new attention to children. Burials of the young (and foetuses) in the recently-introduced ceramic pots may represent the beginning of a tradition of using pottery containers for burial. This gains popularity in the subsequent Chalcolithic period, when vessel and house-like ossuaries appear, belonging to the world of ideas of those communities which connect pottery, women and houses in their symbolic systems. Changing burial customs can contribute to our understanding of socio-economic and cultural change in the PN of the southern Levant, heralding the appearance of more complex entities. We should remember that in the more northerly parts of the Levant and in Mesopotamia, larger scale cultural entities are beginning to appear in the sixth millennium BC, and we suspect that even better evidence for social reconstruction should be available from their burial customs.

*Acknowledgements*
Our grateful thanks to I. Hershkovitz for his valuable help in the field both at Lod and Nahal Zehora II. We also thank I. Zohar and M. Speirs who assisted.

---

29 E.g., Perrot & Ladiray 1988; Gilead 1989; Arensburg *et al.*, in press.

30 Cf., e.g., Gebauer & Price 1992, 9, with papers by Byrde 1992 and Wills 1992.

# 5 Death for the Living in the late Neolithic in north Mesopotamia

## Stuart Campbell

ABSTRACT—*Burials of the late Neolithic in north Mesopotamia (here taken as from about 6,000 uncal BC to 4,500 uncal BC and covering the full range of the Hassuna and the Halaf) exhibit a wide range of types. Although there is a considerable variety in the quantities of grave goods, their interpretation is more problematic. The Binford/Saxe interpretation in terms of the social status of the deceased person does not seem completely convincing on the basis of this data. A particular study is presented based on the large group of published and rich graves from Tell es-Sawwan level I. Using this, together with material from elsewhere, different interpretations are suggested emphasising the role these burial goods may have played for those who deposited them.*

## Introduction

Burials have been studied by archaeologists for many reasons. Indeed, there are potential advantages in examining burials rather than other archaeological remains. Unlike most other deposits, undisturbed burials are deliberate cultural contexts. Items associated with a burial are not discarded or lost but deliberately placed. Whether it is connected with social hierarchy or not, there is an inherent symbolism in the burial and its grave goods. However, in the last twenty years burials have increasingly been studied to obtain information on social structure. The initial theoretical basis that the social position of a person in life will be reflected by their treatment in death was established by Saxe[1] and Binford[2] and this has formed the basis for much subsequent work.[3] It seems clear that, in particular situations, burials can be examined in this way. However, it should not be forgotten that there are cases where any relationship between differentiation in burial and social divisions in life can be very indirect[4] or where burial practices can actually aim to obscure rank in life.[5] Indeed, the Binford/Saxe position can and has been attacked as being an considerable oversimplification.[6] Some more recent work has stressed the fact that the goods associated with a burial represent only the final stage of what may have been a much longer rite of passage. In particular, stress has been laid on the fact that it is the mourners who select the grave goods rather than the deceased and their motives may be very varied.[7]

Graves of the late Neolithic in northern Mesopotamia (the period of the Hassuna and Halaf pottery styles between about 6,000 bc and 4,500 bc at its full extent) are best known in north Iraq and present a varied picture. Although a wide variety of types of burial is present and an equally wide range of burial goods is found in the graves, it is difficult to interpret in terms of social hierarchy.[8] In some cases entirely different burials rituals are used contemporaneously (inhumation, cremation and isolated skull burials all occur in the later Halaf at Yarim Tepe II, for example) without the different circumstances that each denotes being obviously due to the social position of the deceased. In studying the period as a whole, we are usually dealing with small numbers of burials from different sites, which may vary in time, often to an unknown degree. Not only are they usually a small sample, it is certain

1 Saxe 1970.
2 Binford 1971.
3 see Brown 1981 and O'Shea 1984 for a basic endorsement of the Binford/Saxe position.
4 e.g. Ucko 1969.
5 Okley 1979, 86.
6 Hodder 1980; Pader 1982; Metcalf and Huntington 1991.
7 Barrett 1988; Bradley 1990, 94.
8 see Akkermans 1989 and Campbell 1992.

that they only represent a deliberately selected portion of all the burials made by the inhabitants of a settlement. The burials within a settlement may also come from differing social or ritual contexts; there may be many different circumstances surrounding each of the burials which may influence their nature, and when we have only individual examples of burials we cannot be sure what represents a variation within a unified burial rite and an individual occurrence of a completely different rite. Indeed, the small samples warn against making any too subtle interpretations.[9]

Nonetheless, the range of well-defined burial types suggests a rich social organisation and belief system. In view of these difficulties and the inherent potential, rather than embarking on an exhaustive survey of the evidence, a single study will be undertaken in this paper on the largest individual group of burials, those found in the lowest level of Tell es-Sawwan. It is hoped to use this study to point to better ways of interpreting the data from other sites.

## Tell es-Sawwan

Tell es-Sawwan is situated in north-central Iraq on the east bank of the Tigris within the area of the later settlement of Samarra. Although the mounding is quite extensive, it seems likely that only relatively limited areas of the site were inhabited at a single time.[10] Five main levels have been excavated during many seasons of excavation, first by the Iraqi Department of Antiquities and later by a French team. The last three levels have produced large quantities of decorated pottery of the Samarran/Hassuna style dated to around 5,200 bc. The lowest two levels are less easily dated. They produced little painted pottery and what there was may well have been intrusive. I have suggested elsewhere, that the best parallels for the pottery and, in particular, for the large collection of stone bowls lies in the Proto-Hassuna of northern Iraq and the material from Bouqras in Syria.[11] Such a dating would agree with a single C14 date of the middle of the sixth millennium.

Although Tell es-Sawwan has produced a very large number of graves (at least 245, with many more alluded to), the information published about them is very variable indeed. In the first season's preliminary report, 129 graves from level I were published individually.[12] Details of location, approximate age (from the size of the body rather than a full pathological examination) and grave goods are given for each with occasional additional information. The second season's preliminary report contains sketches of at least 44 graves from this

level, although details are often difficult to ascertain and, in the general absence of a scale, it is not even possible to distinguish infant from adult burials.[13] Also, it is unclear whether all the graves excavated are illustrated. It is, however, possible to obtain data on the orientation and position of the burials, their location in some cases, and accompanying grave goods. In the sixth season, 47 more burials were found and some details published.[14] That further burials were found in later seasons is well attested,[15] but few details of these have been published.

There are, therefore, varying details known for a total of 220 burials from level I and their examination, even with incomplete detail, is of considerable interest. The two main sets of data are from the first and second seasons and form the basis of this analysis. The first season, in particular, provides a valuable unselected sample.

It is not entirely clear from the reports whether the burials are all unequivocally associated with the buildings of level I. Al'Adami has argued that they are and that the buildings of level I have a funerary significance.[16] However, Abu es-Soof, writing after a later season, seems to place the burials as a separate cemetery stratigraphically distinct from the level I buildings.[17] With no information other than that already published, no final judgement can be made here although it seems more likely that, given the distribution of the first season's burials beneath the buildings, there is some relationship between at least some of the burials and the buildings of level I.

Some factors are constant in almost all burials. The burials are in shallow, oval graves mainly beneath buildings. The skeletons are in crouched positions where known, except in very rare instances.[18] There are a few cases of the body being wrapped in a mat coated with bitumen.[19] The burials are accompanied by a large variety of material, dealt with in greater detail below, which is notable for the absence of any pottery objects in any of the published graves.

Although there has been a frequent assumption that the graves are part of an infant cemetery, comparable perhaps to that of Tell Abada,[20] this is not strictly true. Amongst the first season's graves there are four types; 13 adult burials, 16 adolescent, 55 infant and 45 burials without bodies. In the report for that season it is suggested[21] that the empty graves may be where the bones have completely decomposed.[22] It is argued below

---

9   see Orton and Hodson 1981, 113-114 for a discussion of the size of samples needed.
10  Breniquet 1991.
11  Campbell 1992 and, for the stone bowls, Bronwen Campbell, personal communication.
12  El-Wailly and Abu es-Soof 1965, 25-28.

13  Al'Adami 1968.
14  Yasin 1970, 7.
15  Abu es-Soof 1971, 5; Salman 1971; Matthews and Wilkinson 1991, 180.
16  Al'Adami 1968, 58-60.
17  Abu es-Soof 1971, 5; also Breniquet 1991, 83.
18  Al'Adami 1968, fig. 4.
19  El-Wailly and Abu es-Soof 1965, numbers 87, 33, 47 and 125; Yasin 1970, 7.
20  Jasim 1985.
21  El-Wailly and Abu es-Soof 1965, 23.
22  El-Wailly and Abu es-Soof 1965; also Al'Adami 1968, 58.

| | Adult | Adolescent | Infant | Empty | Total |
|---|---|---|---|---|---|
| Number | 13 | 16 | 55 | 45 | 129 |
| Number with vessels | 13 | 15 | 54 | 43 | 125 |
| Number of vessels | 35 | 36 | 107 | 54 | 232 |
| Max. Number vessels | 8 | 7 | 4 | 3 | |
| Min. Number vessels | 1 | 0 | 0 | 0 | |
| Number with figurines | 2 | 2 | 8 | 6 | 18 |
| Number of figurines | 7 | 3 | 10 | 6 | 26 |
| Number with beads | 7 | 3 | 21 | 5 | 36 |
| Number with a pendant | 2 | | | | 2 |
| Number with an axe | 1 | 1 | 2 | | 4 |
| Number with lithics | 1 | | 4 | 1 | 6 |
| Number with a phallus | | 1 | 1 | 1 | 3 |
| Number with stone balls | | | 2 | 1 | 3 |
| Number of stone balls | | | 5 | 3 | 8 |
| Number with animal bones | | | 1 | 2 | 3 |
| Graves with single object | | 4 | 13 | 27 | 44 |

*Table 5.1: Summary of Tell es-Sawwan level I burial goods (1st season)*

that the empty burials form a distinct class because of factors other than the absence of bones. It, therefore, seems likely that less than half of the burials from this season, the only one for which we have statistics, are definitely those of children. Nevertheless the proportion of infants is higher than might be expected for a cemetery for a complete population and probably represents

No individual orientations are given for burials in the first season but is noted that most of the skeletons have the heads to the south and more face west than east.[23] There is more information on orientation from 30 of the burials from the second season (Fig. 5.1). There is a single burial with the orientation known from the sixth season with the head to the east, facing south which is not included in this diagram.[24] It is evident from this that, although the orientation to the south is not confirmed, there is a strong concentration (27 out of 31 burials with known orientation) to the arc from north through east to the south – or alternatively an avoidance of burials with the head to the west. Parenthetically, it is worth noting that this avoidance of a westerly orientation is a recurrent theme in prehistoric north Mesopotamian burials. The direction in which the bodies are facing seems too variable to draw any conclusion.

Almost all graves have some burial goods. The variety of objects is considerable, although pottery is notably absent; it does include stone vessels, figurines, beads of a wide range of materials, pendants, stone celts, flint and obsidian blades, stone phalluses, stone balls and animal bones. The quality of much of the stone work is remarkable, both in the artistic sophistication and the investment of labour. Although stone vessels are not uncommon at this period and there are sufficient ex-

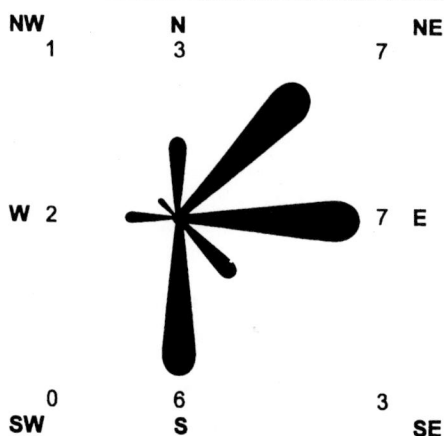

*Fig. 5.1 Frquency of burial orientation in Tell es-Sawwan level I (data from first season).*

amples from the buildings of level I at Tell es-Sawwan to suggest that these are not exclusively funerary objects, these graves goods must represent a considerable degree of 'wealth'.

A very rough index of the 'wealth' of a grave has been made by counting the number of objects in it. Stone vessels and other objects are counted as one object. Beads are counted as a single object no matter the number, in part because the number is never given and in part because many will have come from individual objects such as necklaces. The finds in the graves and the number of objects are summarised in Tables 5.1, 5.2 and 5.3.

---

23  El-Wailly and Abu es-Soof 1965, 23.
24  Yasin 1970, fig. 17.

|  | Number | Mean | Standard Deviation |
|---|---|---|---|
| Adult | 13 | 4.15 | 4.62 |
| Adolescent | 16 | 3.25 | 2.21 |
| Infant | 55 | 2.78 | 1.70 |
| Empty | 45 | 1.71 | 1.01 |

*Table 5.2: Tell es-Sawwan level I burials (1st season). Statistical summary of number of objects per grave*

|  | With Body | Empty | Total |
|---|---|---|---|
| Number | 38 | 6 | 44 |
| Number with vessels | 36 | 6 | 42 |
| Number of vessels | 81 | 9 | 90 |
| Number with figurines | 15 | 3 | 18 |
| Number of figurines | 18 | 3 | 21 |
| Number with beads | 5 |  | 5 |
| Number with phallus |  | 1 | 1 |
| Number Objects | 104 | 13 | 117 |

*Table 5.3: Summary of Tell es-Sawwan levels I/II burial goods (2nd season)*

Several points can be made about these figures. Perhaps the most important single point is the contrast between empty graves and all others. In the first season there were approximately 3.08 objects per grave which had a body in it; there were only 1.71 objects per empty grave. The Mann-Whitney U test is an appropriate statistical test to see whether these frequencies of grave goods could be expected to have come from the same overall population.[25] It makes no assumptions about the distribution of grave goods, which is certainly non-normal, and is unlikely to suggest erroneously that there is a significant difference between the two groups if none exists. A Mann-Whitney U test of the numbers of objects in Table 5.2 for burials with and without bodies indicates that, statistically, the difference is extremely significant (probability greater than 99.9%). This difference is further emphasised as only 20.24% of graves with bodies but 60% of empty graves had a single 'object'. The second season's graves confirm this contrast. There are also several other individual occurrences of stone vessels in the report of the second season which have not been included as it is not certain which ones were actually from burials.[26]

These figures argue convincingly that the empty graves are indeed a distinct category and not simply like other graves but with the body decayed, although a portion of them may be of this type. As far as we know

from the preliminary reports, these empty burials were dug in the same way as the others and they have the same range of objects in them. It could be that, rather than being a genuine empty burial, they represent the burials of the very youngest infants, perhaps including foetuses, which were buried with fewer grave goods and which were systematically badly preserved. Equally, the empty graves may never have had a body in them which would suggest the possibility that they have some ritual significance not primarily connected with disposal of the dead. The other 'graves' might also be such ritual deposits where a body is only a part of a wider ritual – perhaps with the presence of a body giving it greater significance and correlating with richer grave goods of other varieties. Alternatively, there may have been a ritual procedure of burying offerings which could have been used in more than one context. Although the form of the ritual was similar, the graves with and without bodies may have served completely different purposes.

Adult burials have a marginally greater number of objects than adolescents, and adolescents have slightly more than infants (Table 5.2). However, further Mann-Whitney U tests suggest that these differences are not statistically significant; they may be only chance variations. In no instances are adult burials accompanied by only a single item, possibly a more significant trend. The richest adult and adolescent burials also have a larger number of objects than the richest infant burials

---

25  Hamburg 1979, 309-312.
26  Al'Adami 1965, 85-90.

but again the difference is marginal with the exception of Grave 25, which will be discussed below.

It is apparent that there is a considerable range in the quantity of grave goods, many of which were of high quality. This suggests that there may be a significant difference between the richest and poorest burials. It is less certain that this range can be directly related to social hierarchy. Flannery suggested that, at Tell es-Sawwan, the rich grave goods occurring with infants indicate an inherited social status and thereby a ranked society.[27] The direct equation of wealth in child burials with a ranked society seems difficult to prove in any case. In this instance it seems to depend heavily on an impressionistic rather than a quantitative interpretation of the burials. It is true that the statistical evidence suggests that infants were buried in a very similar manner to adults but without a distinct class of poorer burials it cannot be set in context. Redman suggests that small numbers of people controlled religion at Tell es-Sawwan, presumably on the basis of the level I burials.[28] There seems to be no evidence to justify this.

Grave 25, with its 19 objects, is considerably more wealthy than other burials. It may be a clearer instance of social differentiation. However, the report mentions that the grave contains "at least one adult"[29] which leaves the possibility open that the apparent wealth of the burial was due to it being of more than one person. Without a full spectrum of poorer burials it is difficult to interpret the Tell es-Sawwan level I burials as indicating social stratification. Certainly they are the richest set of burials in the late Neolithic of north Mesopotamia. However, this may reflect a regional practice in which the provision of grave goods was of paramount importance or where the richness was associated with a particular site rather than where the wealth was personal or a direct reflection of the deceased person's role in life.

The association of figurines with infant burials has been suggested as significant.[30] This reference is made in the report of the fifth season, for which no information on the level I burials is published, but it is not supported by the available evidence from earlier seasons. The figures for the first season, in Table 5.2, show that the portion of burials with figurines is very much the same for all ages, and indeed for the empty graves as well, and that they only occur in a small percentage of cases. Furthermore, there are considerable variations in the number of figurines per grave, with three in grave 201a,[31] and six in a single grave found in the first season.[32] Similar figures are implied by the limited information available from the 47 burials of the sixth season.[33] It is suggested here that, until there is clear

evidence to the contrary, figurines in these burials should be considered on the same level of significance as any other artefacts. It is also possible that, as the only two occurrences of pendants were in the small number of adults graves, that pendants were only associated with a particular group of adult burials. Likewise stone balls may be associated with infant and empty burials.

## Discussion

As suggested at the start of this paper, it is difficult to see social hierarchy accounting for the range of grave goods at Tell es-Sawwan I. The burials are undoubtedly rich but there is little clear differentiation within them—the only burial with an outstanding number of objects may well be a conflation of more than one. The main contrast is between the empty burials and all the others. Although one should, perhaps, still reserve judgement over whether these empty graves were never associated with human remains, there is some evidence from elsewhere in the late Neolithic in north Mesopotamia for similar crossing between burial and other ritual activity. One can cite the Halaf cremations at Yarim Tepe II in particular (within 200 years either side of 4,800 bc). Here there are deliberate deposits of very fine pottery and other objects, deliberately smashed and associated with burning. In some cases this was associated with cremated human remains[34] and in some cases it was not.[35] Again the suggestion can be made that the inclusion of objects in a burial was only a part of a wider set of ritual activities. At both Yarim Tepe I and Tell Hassuna in the late sixth millennium there are instances of human remains being discovered in structural contexts rather than in graves.[36] The skeletons seem to be dismembered and the rooms are architecturally unusual. Disposal of deceased persons and other areas of ritual seem to be interlocking.

These suggestions that burial was not necessarily a separated activity, isolated from other areas of ritual behaviour and social regulation, suggest other interpretations. Grave goods are deliberately placed with a burial by the living, who may have many motives for this disposal of objects, often valuable. In particular, a funeral may have provided an occasion for this consumption of wealth to have been public and ostentatious. In discussing European hoards, another deliberate consumption of wealth, Bradley has noted that "the distinction between grave goods and hoard finds need not have been as marked as it sometimes seems".[37] The facts that the actual items at Tell es-Sawwan and Yarim Tepe II seem inherently valuable, are found in both the

27  Flannery 1972, 403; see also Brown 1981, 30.
28  Redman 1978, 213.
29  El-Wailly and Abu es-Soof 1965, 25.
30  Abu es-Soof 1971, 5.
31  Al'Adami 1968, 60.
32  El-Wailly and Abu es-Soof 1965, 25.
33  Yasin 1970, 7, figs. 34a-43.

34  e.g. Merpert, Munchaev and Bader 1978, 40-41: Merpert & Munchaev 1993.
35  Munchaev and Merpert 1981, 26.
36  Merpert and Munchaev 1987, 9; Munchaev and Merpert 1981, 84; Lloyd and Safar 1945.
37  Bradley 1990, 94.

funerary and non-funerary deposits and seem unusual in other contexts all tend to support this link.

Bradley has used the ideas of Gregory[38] to interpret the purpose of such deposits. He suggested that in a society in which gift exchange is used as a means of obtaining and maintaining status, it is difficult to avoid repeatedly incurring debt when a gift to a living person is immediately followed by a return gift of greater value. Prestige obtained through giving gifts in this way is always vulnerable to sudden loss. One way of resolving this dilemma may be to give gifts to gods instead. Often this involves the physical destruction of objects or their deposition where they cannot be recovered, often in public and impressive ceremonies. This also has the effect of removing the offerings from circulation permanently, making it more difficult for others to make up comparable prestige.

While we should not automatically adopt this interpretation, it appears to fit the evidence from Tell es-Sawwan closely. The overt purpose of the deposits with and without burials may have been different, but some of their purpose in gaining prestige for certain of the mourners may well have been the same. There is little sign of the competitiveness this suggests in society, either in the Proto-Hassuna or the Halaf, elsewhere in the archaeological record but this is more likely to be a deficiency in other areas of the record. In both the Proto-Hassuna and the Halaf, the accumulation of prestige may have had an important role in society and we may suggest that there were both the means and potential to obtain and maintain power which are not visible elsewhere in the burials of the period.

---

38 Gregory 1982.

# 6

# The Use of Model Objects as Predynastic Egyptian Grave Goods: An Ancient Origin for a Dynastic Tradition

## Sally Swain

ABSTRACT— *The use of models and imitations to act in place of real objects has long been recognised in Egyptian funerary archaeology. The representation could be activated magically, becoming real in the world of the dead tomb owner. This paper seeks to illustrate that the characteristic practice of using models in graves and tombs was already present in the Predynastic period of Egypt. It was carried into the Dynastic period, where its importance was expanded, but this most Egyptian idea had its origins in Egyptian prehistory.*

*Several classes of object are discussed, including model clay vessels, clay vessels which imitate stone ones, tools and weapons, organic items such as garlic cloves, cattle, and cereals, mud used as a substitute for scented fat, beads, and boats. For the most part, models of these things were made of clay or wood and placed in graves, thus releasing more valuable media such as ivory, stone and metal from burial, making them more readily available to the live community, without depriving the dead of those objects necessary to their life in the next world.*

## Introduction

It is well known that the use of model objects as part of the furnishings of Dynastic tombs was widespread in ancient Egypt.[1] In many cases model objects were placed in tombs to stand in for real items. They were believed to become the real items by a series of magical processes, and could be used by the tomb owner after his death to furnish himself with the necessities of life. Such models covered a wide variety of categories including items which were too large to be used in their real state, for example boats. They also included models of cattle, food, servants' houses, and in one famous example from the site of Assuit, a private army of model wooden soldiers.

In short, any item which might have been required in the next world could be represented in the tomb by a model. This served both practical and economic needs, since it is much easier to keep a model cow in a tomb than a real one, it is less expensive to provide and it does not require feeding, cleaning out, or replacing when it

dies. The principal of using models (and, incidentally, painted scenes) is one which is wholly characteristic of ancient Egyptian funerary practices. The aim of this short paper is to illustrate that it had extremely ancient origins within Egypt and to suggest some possible reasons for these origins.

During the Badarian period (c. 5000 to 4000 BC) grave-goods were relatively simple. The graves were shallow round or oval pits, the bodies being placed in contracted positions, with a minimum of possesions, including matting, skins, bead, and pottery.[2] However, during the Naqada I period and, especially, Naqada II period, grave assemblages became increasingly complex and numerous. Status symbols and displays of wealth and power seem to have begun to play an increasingly important role in the burials which are known to us.[3] The following information is taken from findings at several sites of Naqada I and II date including Naqada, El Amrah  Hierakonpolis and Diospolis Parva in Upper Egypt. A number of graves from the site of Naqada con-

---

1  David 1982, 80.

2  Brunton & Caton Thompson 1928, 2-20.
3  Castillos 1983.

tained objects which may be classified as models. It is suggested here that that is exactly what they were; models used in a funerary context to stand for the real thing.

There are four categories of object used as models in Predynastic graves; these are:

1. Models of objects made at the same size as the originals, but in materials which were easier to work and which were readily available.
2. Models of objects made at a smaller scale than the originals.
3. Model servant figures, probably the forerunners of *Ushabti* figurines.
4. Materials intended to substitute for expensive items not readily available for use in graves.

The first of these categories is remarkably similar to model items placed in tombs of the Dynastic period, for example the statues placed in the serdabs of Old Kingdom tombs.[4] These include models of tools, weapons, beads, heads of garlic, and ears of corn made in clay or wood.[5] Each item was life-sized, but clearly intended as a model since the medium selected was both less valuable that flint or copper, and easier to work, and also more durable than the food items.

The second group includes a whole range of items in clay and wood which copy larger paradigms. Notable in this group are clay and wooden boats,[6] a clay model of a house dating to the Naqada II period,[7] and many examples of models of cattle.[8] Also important in this respect is a large number of model pottery vessels. These were made especially to furnish tombs and may be regarded as specific to the funerary cult. The vessels were minute, being so small that they can only have been models. They were certainly too small to have had any practical function. They also had extemely thick walls which reduced the vessel's capacity to a tiny quantity. These minature vessels are known from Naqada, Edfu and Gerzeh,[9] amongst other sites, and date to the Naqada II period. They are surprisingly common. This kind of model came into wide use in Dynastic Egyptian tombs and is, perhaps, best exemplified by wooden models of scenes from daily life found in Middle Kingdom tombs. Stone vessels were also imitated in clay.[10]

The third group of items covers anthropoid figurines. These are most usually of females, but some examples of males are known. They were of considerably more significance in the Badarian and, especially, Naqada I periods than in Naqada II. The figurines which have been found in graves across the whole range of the Predynastic period,[11] have been described as fer-

tility figurines and female goddess figures. It seems likely, however, that many of them were intended to be concubine or servant figures, and may have been the precursor to the idea of placing models of servants in Dynastic graves. They were intended to become real and serve the tomb owner. Some examples may represent something rather different, being goddess figures with upraised arms, similar to the so-called goddess found on painted pottery of the Naqada II period.

The final category cannot strictly be described as model objects, but a notion of substitution is involved in its use, and it has, therefore, been included here. Many Naqada II graves contained wavy-handled jars filled with a scented fatty substance.[12] Over time, however, the proportion of fat was considerably reduced, being replaced by vegetable ashes, a little burnt sand and scraps of animal bone. The fat was increasingly represented only by a thick layer of fatty paste on top of the ashes. It seems likely that the ash was intended to substitute for a proportion of the fat because it was a less valuable substance, but the belief was that if the jar was full, and contained a token proportion of scented fat, the ashes would also become fat in the funerary context, by magical means. Unguents were of great importance in the Dynastic funerary cult. The use of scented fat in Predynastic burials probably had a similar role.

The reasons for the use of models in the Predynastic period may have been very similar to the reasons for their use in Dynastic contexts. Reasons of economy were of paramount importance. In a prehistoric economy items such as tools, weapons, pottery, jewellery and cattle represented considerable wealth, and consumption of materials, skills and time.[13] Models offered an easier way of equiping a grave with many essential but valuable items. They represented a less intensive use of resources but at the same time discharged the responsibility of providing for the dead.

Whether the necessity of using models gave rise to a belief that they would be magically transformed is uncertain, but the presence of female figurines in very early graves suggests that a belief in the efficacy of models was present in early Egyptian prehistory and that this belief continued into the Dynastic period, being elabortated over time. Our knowledge of Predynastic ritual and belief is extremely limited, but it is clear that a sophisticated belief-system existed in which magical practices certainly played an important role. It is by no means impossible that a belief in the power of substitution was in place by the Badarian period.

The second factor which may have influenced the use of models was a constraint on the space available in the grave. It would have been imposible to place a real cow, boat or house in a small pit grave. It would also have been impractical to dig many graves large enough to contain such an assemblage of items. In this case too,

4   David 1982, 78.
5   Petrie 1920, 25, 43-44.
6   Ibid., Pls. VII, XLVII.
7   Aldred 1965, 34.
8   Petrie 1920, 11.
9   Manchester Museum catalogue numbers 3090, 3755, 4549, 5300 and 5926.
10  Petrie 1920, 17.
11  Brunton & Caton Thompson 1928, Pls. II-VI, XXIV.

12  Petrie 1896, 27.
13  Clarke 1979, 350.

models provided an ideal solution to the problem, being small enough to fit into a limited area, whilst also serving the needs of the tomb owner.

In conclusion, it seems from the evidence of the tombs themselves that the use of models and substitution were a significant part of Predynastic Egyptian funerary belief. Hornblower suggests that even painted pottery may have acted in this way, providing painted scenes into which the grave owner could transmute by magical means.[14] In this way, scenes equivalent to those of the painted caves of Palaeolithic Europe were created in an Egyptian environment. This point, however, leads away from the ideas of this paper into a more complex and difficult area which is not for discussion here.

The use of models probably grew up as a result of economic and spatial pressure, becoming an acceptable part of the funerary cult from the Badarian period. By Naqada II their use was entrenched and many of the characteristics of the use of funerary models were in place. These continued to evolve during the Dynastic period, but the essential elements of this utterly Egyptian practice were developed during Egypt's Predynastic phase.

---

14  Hornblower 1930.

# 7 Attitudes to Death with Reference to Cats in Ancient Egypt

## Joyce M. Filer

ABSTRACT— *A variety of sources concerning ancient Egypt indicate the ancient Egyptian attitude towards cats, both in life and in death.*

*The high regard in which cats were held is suggested by the antiquity of a cat cult in Egypt together with the prominence of the cat in Egyptian religion and mythology. Many ancient Egyptian paintings show cats in a close and comfortable association with humans and the many hundreds of cat statues confirm the Egyptian admiration of these animals. Authors from the Classical World commented upon the ancient Egyptian adoration of animals and cats in particular and they suggest cats were never killed.*

*Yet, the biological evidence, ie cat mummies, suggests another facet of the ancient Egyptian attitude towards the cat and its death.*

The extant sources available from ancient Egypt and the Classical world seem to provide conflicting information regarding the ancient Egyptian attitude towards cats and in particular towards the death of a cat. The possible antiquity of a religious cat cult and the depictions of cats in tombs suggest that cats were revered and some written sources even indicate that to harm or kill a cat was a heinous crime. The biological evidence from cat mummies, however, seems to contradict this reverent attitude towards the cat. After a brief examination of some of these sources an attempt will be made to resolve this apparent conflict.

A brief examination of ancient Egyptian religious observances will show that the importance of the cat or certainly felines may be attested from early times. It has been suggested that a stone fragment naming King Den of the First Dynasty (c.2950-2647 BC) and showing a lion (or possibly dog) -like animal[1] may indicate an early feline goddess Mafdet,[2] but it is probable that these animals represent one of the larger cats such as the panther. A deep-rooted reverence for the cat may possibly be seen in the antiquity of the cult of Bastet, a goddess whose earlier representations showed a lion-headed woman. That the cult was originally a local one (spreading through the country at a later period) and that the city of Bubastis (in the eastern Delta) took its name from the established Temple of Bastet does suggest some early regard for the cat.[3] On the other hand, however, the linking of the female cat with the goddess Bastet may not have occurred until the first millennium BC.[4] The city of Bubastis certainly attained a high status when descendants of the Libyan 'great chiefs of the Ma' from Bubastis assumed the throne.[5] Thus the rulers' local animal deity, the cat, also assumed a higher status and became popular throughout Egypt. These descendants, who founded the Twenty-Second Dynasty (945-c.715 BC), established the most important of all Egyptian cat cemeteries, that at Bubastis. It was, however, during the Ptolemaic period (332-330 BC) that the cat reached the apex of its popularity when there was an increase in the popularity of cults associated with animals. It was during this period that the observations were made and the information collected which gave rise to the commentaries of the Classical authors. Thus there is some evidence to suggest a growing regard for felines in a religious context.

---

1 Petrie 1900, 39.
2 Gardiner 1938, 89.
3 Murray 1973, 95.
4 Malek 1993, 73.
5 O'Connor 1986, 235.

In turning to artistic representations of cats in ancient Egypt, those in Egyptian tombs provide a good witness to the developing relationship between the Egyptians and their cats. As all tomb paintings involving cats cannot be discussed here, just a few examples will be described as they are good illustrations of this theme. During the Middle Kingdom period (2025-1606 BC) two attitudes of cats were represented. Firstly, as leading a life apart from humans and often depicted purely as opportunists waiting to misappropriate the fallen prey (usually birds) of Egyptians hunting in the marshland areas.[6] Secondly, they were depicted in association with human activities.[7] This view of the cat as an accepted part of everyday life was a theme that increased in Egyptian art during the New Kingdom period (1539-1070 BC), when cats frequently appear with humans in more sociable settings, notably banqueting (or feasting) scenes and offering scenes. Interestingly, cats only seem to appear under the chairs of women at these banquets, whilst other creatures (notably monkeys and birds) may sit under the chairs of both males and females at these gatherings.[8] There have been attempts to link the occurrence of these animals under chairs with sexual symbolism: the cat with fertility, hence with women, and the monkey with the sexual prowess of the male. Notwithstanding this, such scenes serve to show that cats were regarded as part and parcel of domestic life. In the banqueting scene from the New Kingdom Tomb of the Two Sculptors a cat sits calmly under a female guest's chair whilst a feast is in progress.[9] In another tomb, an offering scene from the Ramesside Tomb of Apy, a mother cat wears a silver ear-ring and seems content that her kitten plays on the tomb owner's lap.[10] That the mother cat is obviously not worried about the safety of her kitten is a good indicator that she is at ease with humans. The fact that the adult cat is wearing an earring and that other New Kingdom tomb scenes show cats wearing collars (and sometimes a lead)[11] would also suggest that the cat had attained the status of a family pet. In addition to depictions of cats in tombs there are many thousands of cat statues and figurines, and whilst the cats are depicted in many attitudes – walking, standing, recumbent, etc. – the popular image of the Egyptian cat is without doubt that of the seated cat with a proudly held body and a self-confident forward gaze. Thus, representations of cats in tomb paintings and statuary serve to underline this idea of respect for the cat and the comfortable familiarity between these felines and humans.

In examining some of the written sources again we are aware of a reverent attitude towards the cat, but here we begin to detect an ambivalent note in attitudes towards the death of a cat. Writing about his visit to Egypt during the 5th century BC, the Greek historian Herodotus reveals what he thought was the Egyptian attitude towards all animals, that "such as there are – both wild and tame – are without exception held to be sacred" (Herodotus II 65), whilst another author notes of the Egyptians that "when any animal dies they mourn for it as deeply as do those who have lost a beloved child ..." (Diodorus Siculus I 84.3-7).[12] This view of the Egyptian's devotion to animals was reiterated by Juvenal (writing about AD 130), who poured vehement scorn upon the practice of animal worship in the words:

Who has not heard, Volusius, of the monstrous deities
Those crazy Egyptians worship? One lot adores crocodiles
Another worships the snake-gorged ibis ...
You'll find whole cities devoted to cats or to river-fish
Or dogs ...

- Juvenal, Satire XV.[13]

Juvenal obviously did not regard cats (or animals in general) with the same devotion as did the ancient Egyptians. Our information about the Egyptian attitude towards cats comes principally from Herodotus who relates what he saw or was told by native Egyptians during his travels in Egypt. He suggests that in a house fire an Egyptian cared more for saving his cat than his home and states that when a cat died the whole household shaved their eyebrows as a sign of mourning. He also tells us that dead cats were embalmed and buried at Bubastis (Herodotus II 66-67). It is important, however, not to let this idea of cat adoration get out of proportion, for the ancient Egyptians venerated most animals. When a dog died, for instance, the inmates of a household shaved their whole body as a sign of mourning and also buried the dog in a sacred place, as they did with all manner of animals including weasels, field mice, ibises and hawks (Herodotus II 66-67). It is possible that certain animals, notably cats and ibises, were held higher in respect, for Diodorus Siculus tells us that to kill one of these animals either intentionally or unintentionally was punishable by death, whereas the death penalty was only incurred for killing other animals intentionally (Herodotus I 83.4-8). He himself witnessed a mob rushing to the house of a Roman to punish him for killing a cat, even though the act had been done accidentally (Herodotus I 83.8) and he reveals that an Egyptian gave a wide berth to a dead cat for fear of being accused of hurting it (Herodotus I 83.4-8).

---

6  Griffith 1900, 2, Pl. 5.
7  For a Middle Kingdom example, cf. 'Tomb No. 15' in Newberry 1893, Pl. VI.
8  Filer 1989, 11.
9  Davies 1925, Pl. VII.
10  Davies 1927, Pl.XXV.
11  Cf., e.g., the Tomb of May (No. 130) in Davies 1936, Pl. XXVII.

---

12  Tr. Oldfield 1933.
13  Tr. Green 1974.

As indicated above, cats (and other animals) were highly regarded and their welfare was of immense importance. It was usually considered a terrible act to kill or harm a cat, but in certain circumstances a cat's deliberate death could benefit a person. A Greek magical papyrus describes how to take revenge on an enemy by drowning a cat. The reciting of a certain formula during the act of drowning ensured that the responsibility for the crime fell upon a designated enemy. The spell is stated to be suitable for every ritual purpose, but it is particularly useful for restraining charioteers in a race and for causing separation and enmity.[14] Thus, written sources from ancient Egypt itself and from the Classical world indicate a high status for the cat, but at the same time when deemed expedient deliberate killing was accepted.

Really it is from the results of the examinations of various cat mummies that this dual attitude towards the death of a cat comes to the fore. X-ray studies on the age at death and cause of death strongly suggest that cats were deliberately killed by having their necks broken and that this occurred within two specific age ranges. The cats were killed either between one and four months, or between nine and twelve months.[15] It is suggested that as these ages at death cannot reflect natural mortality, it was likely they represented the best ages for embalming. It is also possible that by killing and mummifying cats within these age groups, the ancient Egyptians were preserving the animal in the most distinctive phases of its life-cycle: the kitten and the young adult.

Why is this practice of deliberately killing cats as shown by the evidence from cat mummies at odds with the observations and comments of the Classical authors? If, as Diodorus informs us, anyone killing a cat was punished with death, then, with the many thousands of cat mummies that were prepared over the centuries, are we to assume that as many people (i.e., those who prepared the mummies) received the penalty of death? This would seem unlikely else the mummification profession would be severely depleted of practitioners unwilling, literally, 'to risk their own necks'!

From the different types of evidence for the ancient Egyptian attitude towards cats and particularly towards their demise, it seems evident that we are dealing with two categories of cat, the household cat and the temple cat. It was the former that Herodotus and Diodorus witnessed being cherished and which was depicted in the mostly New Kingdom tomb paintings. Those cats which appear to have had their necks broken before being mummified are more likely to have been temple cats, probably specially bred for the purpose of becoming offerings. This would not imply that these temple cats were any less revered or prized than the household pet. The ancient Egyptians were a people who viewed their whole world in terms of opposites: the fertile land versus the desert, Lower Egypt versus Upper Egypt, and so on. They would have no problem with this dichotomy regarding cats. On the other hand, living cats were prized as part of family life, yet on the other hand they were an integral part of an animal-worship cult and, as such, those specially reared in captivity were also honoured by their deaths.

Whilst the extant sources for the ancient Egyptian attitude towards cats – religious contexts, tomb paintings and written information – would seem initially to be at variance with the biological information from cat mummies, the ability of the Egyptians to think in terms of opposites would allow seemingly contrary attitudes to exist side by side. Hence an act of killing, which was unacceptable in everyday society, was more readily accepted when viewed as part of religion.

---

14  Betz 1986, 18-22.
15  Armitage & Clutton-Brock 1980, 185-188.

# 8 Change in Oral Pathology through Time of Nile Valley Populations Predynastic to Roman

## *Francis Thornton*

*ABSTRACT—To compare oral pathology in ancient Nile Valley populations through time, a critical approach was applied to the selection of samples with regard to source, period represented, and number of individuals available. A unified dental recording system was used to ensure reliable comparability. Dentitions from the Predynastic period to Christian era spanning 6000 years were examined. Significant oral pathology trends noted in Egyption populations but less so in Nubia.*

Much has been written since the beginning of this century, concerning the overall severity of dental attrition throughout the whole of the Nile Valley ancient population. Ruffer comments that among the ancient Egyptians, anomalies in position and structure of teeth are rare and that attrition is very marked.[1] Leek reports that teeth from every dynasty examined feature attrition which increases with age, progresses abnormally faster than secondary dentine deposition, exposing the pulp cavity, and is the greatest cause of pathological disturbances.[2]

Although the study reviewed all the oral pathological conditions observed in archaic populations living inside and outside the Nile Valley,[3] in this short paper dental attrition and caries comparisons are the primary concern.

A critical approach to sample selection has been applied to skeletal material of provenanced population groups from the pre-, mid- and post-Dynastic periods, and from specific locations with the ethnographic contexts of Egypt, Nubia, Sudan and the Near East. Reliable samples will ensure that comparisons of pathological features are valid, with age grouping and sex taken into consideration. Fig. 8.1 illustrates the geographical regions from which the samples originated, and the Table 8.1 identifies the samples chronologically.

*Table 8.1 Source and chronology of the samples.*

| Badari | Upper Egypt | Predynastic | 4500-3100 BC |
|---|---|---|---|
| Halfa Degheim | Lower Nubia | A Group | 3300-2800 BC |
| Gizeh | Middle Egypt | Old Kingdom | 2695-2160 BC |
| Sedment | Middle Egypt | 9th Dynasty | 2160-2130 BC |
| Jericho | Palestine | EB-EB/MBA | 2150-1800 BC |
| Kerma | Upper Nubia | 12/13 Dynasty | 1880-1580 BC |
| Gebel Moya | Sudan | Meroitic | 1000-500 BC |
| Hawara | Middle Egypt | Roman | AD 100-200 |
| Kharga Oasis | Upper Egypt | Roman/Coptic | AD 100-600 |
| Biga | Lower Nubia | Christian | AD 550-600 |

---

1  Ruffer 1920.
2  Leek 1966.
3  Thornton 1990.

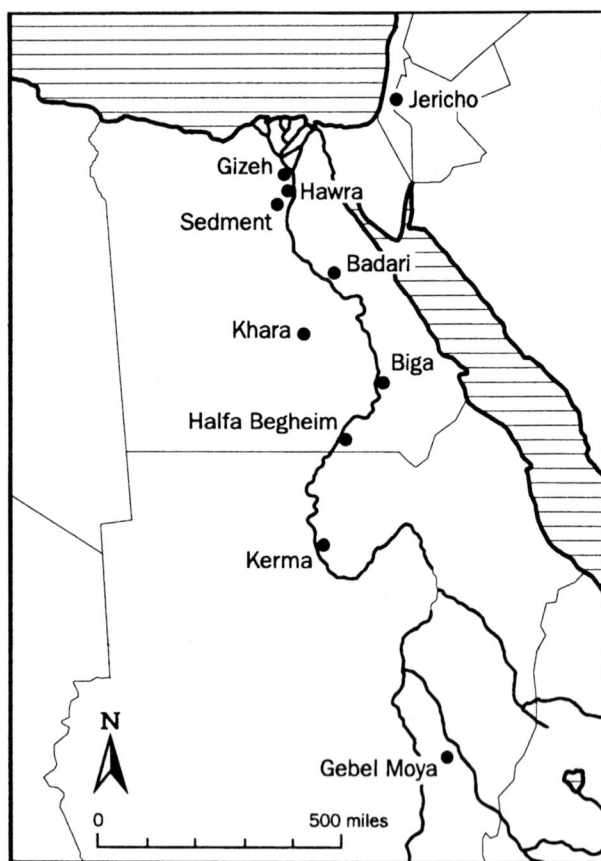

*Fig. 8.1: Location of sites.*

3. Where small differences in the level of attrition were noted between the sexes, males featured the greater wear.
4. Chronologically the Egyptian samples display a decline in attrition through time; this trend is not featured in the Nubian populations. See Fig. 8.2.
5. The concurrent populations outside the Nile valley (Jericho and Gebel Moya) exhibit a lower level of dental attrition.
6. Dental caries, although present in the archaic populations of both Egypt and Nubia has a very low prevalence, i.e., 3% of carious permanent teeth of the total number of permanent teeth with crowns. The increase in prevalence of caries through time is probably a result of dietary changes. See Fig. 8.3.
7. Dental caries is almost non-existent in the Sudanese population of Gebel Moya. This and item 6 to be discussed later.
8. The antemortem tooth loss trend in the Egyption population (Fig. 8.4), declines from the Predynastic to Old Kingdom populations, followed by an increase from 9th Dynasty to Roman/Christian period. when compared with the superimposed trends of attrition and caries, it is evident that in the early period, the antemortem losses can be attributed to gross attrition and the subsequent dental abscesses. In the later populations, severe dental caries is primarily responsible for the apical abscesses, although attrition is still evident. This also supports the dietary and food processing changes.

## Observations and Interpretation

1. Considering the ancient populations in this study, the above results are primarily based on the examination of permanent teeth, as infants and subadults are under-represented in the population samples.
2. The staple diet of coarse bread, made from emmer wheat and barley and with abrasive inclusions, is thought to be the primary cause for the severe level of dental attrition. Samples of bread from tombs analysed by Leek contained inorganic mineral elements. This consisted primarily of rounded desert grains of quartz, which is highly abrasive.[4] The use of saddle querns in milling also contributed to the mineral element. However, the ever-present airborne particles of sand, and the lack of refining techniques which are evident in the later periods, are considered as the main cause of the contamination of the staple diet.
3. The phenomenon of anterior occlusal attrition noted in much later period populations of Hawara and Kharga Oasis may be attributed to the habit of

The detailed analysis of the dentition relies on a comprehensive system of recording and scoring the oral pathologies present. This was achieved by using a common 'dental recording sheet', which also correlated relevant data such as age group, sex and individual serial numbers. The quantification of the various pathologies, subsequent to enhanced visual assessment or measurement, was numerical. This permitted statistical analysis of the visually significant characteristics.

The ability of teeth to survive better than bone permits the study of oral diseases and wear as biological indications of the living individuals health, and age of death within the population sample. This assessment was supported by examination of the skull and postcranial material when present, together with any anthropological data available to assist in age and sex determination and sample reliability from the original excavation reports.

1. The most ancient Egyptian populations did exhibit gross levels of occlusal attrition, and the pathological consequences of the wear in the form of dental abscesses and antemortem losses.
2. As would be expected, generally the chewing zone of the dentition of the 1st molars display the peak level of attrition. The bias to anterior wear on the Kharga Oasis and Hawara samples will be discussed later.

---

4  Leek 1972.

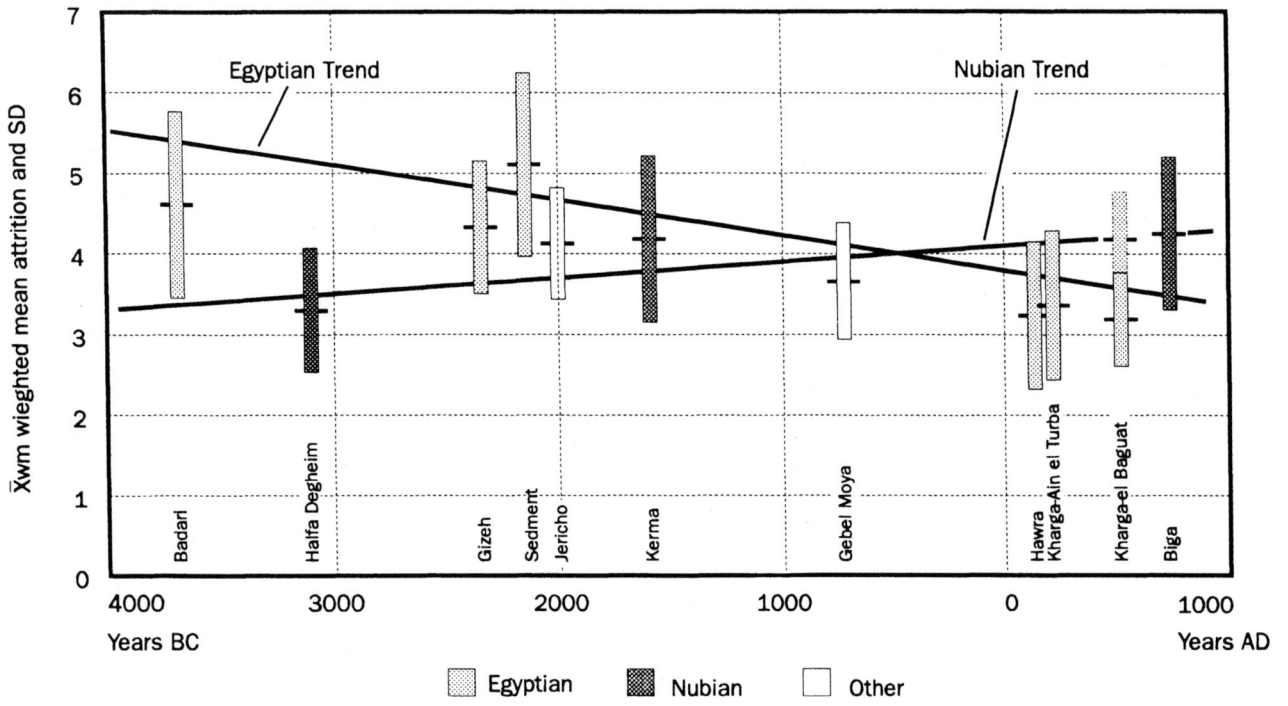

*Fig. 8.2: Chronological attrition analysis: permanent teeth.*

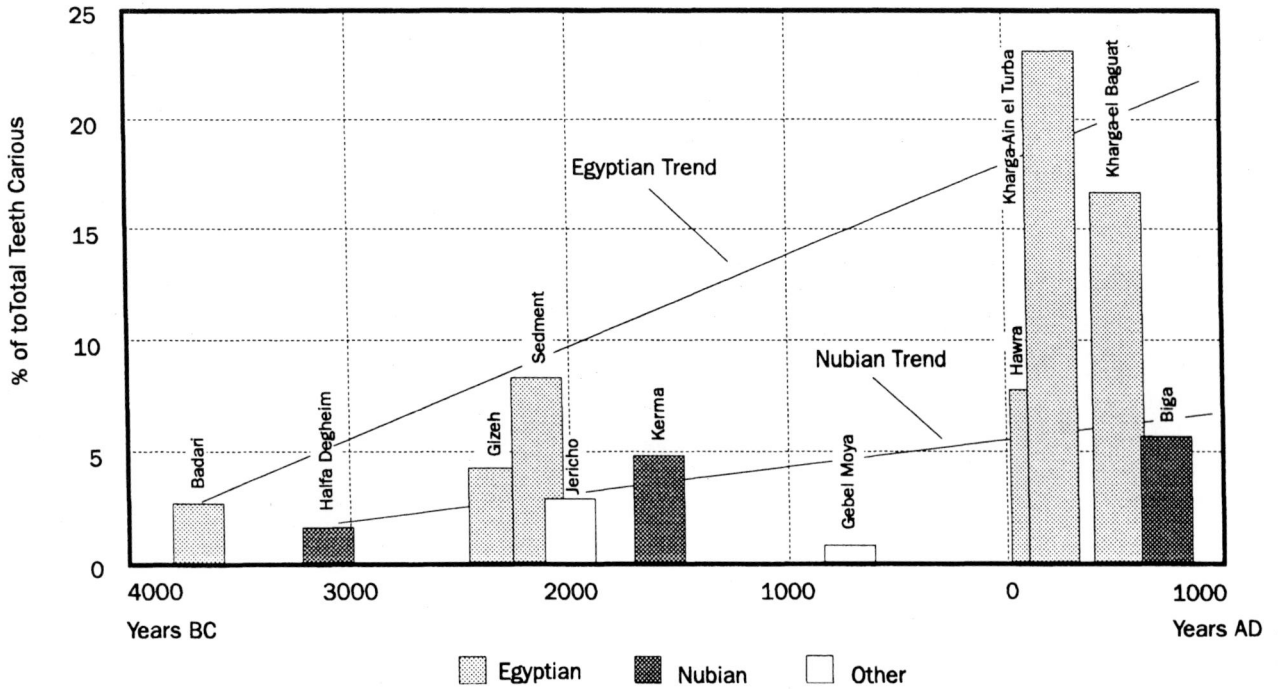

*Fig. 8.3: Chronological caries analysis: permanent teeth.*

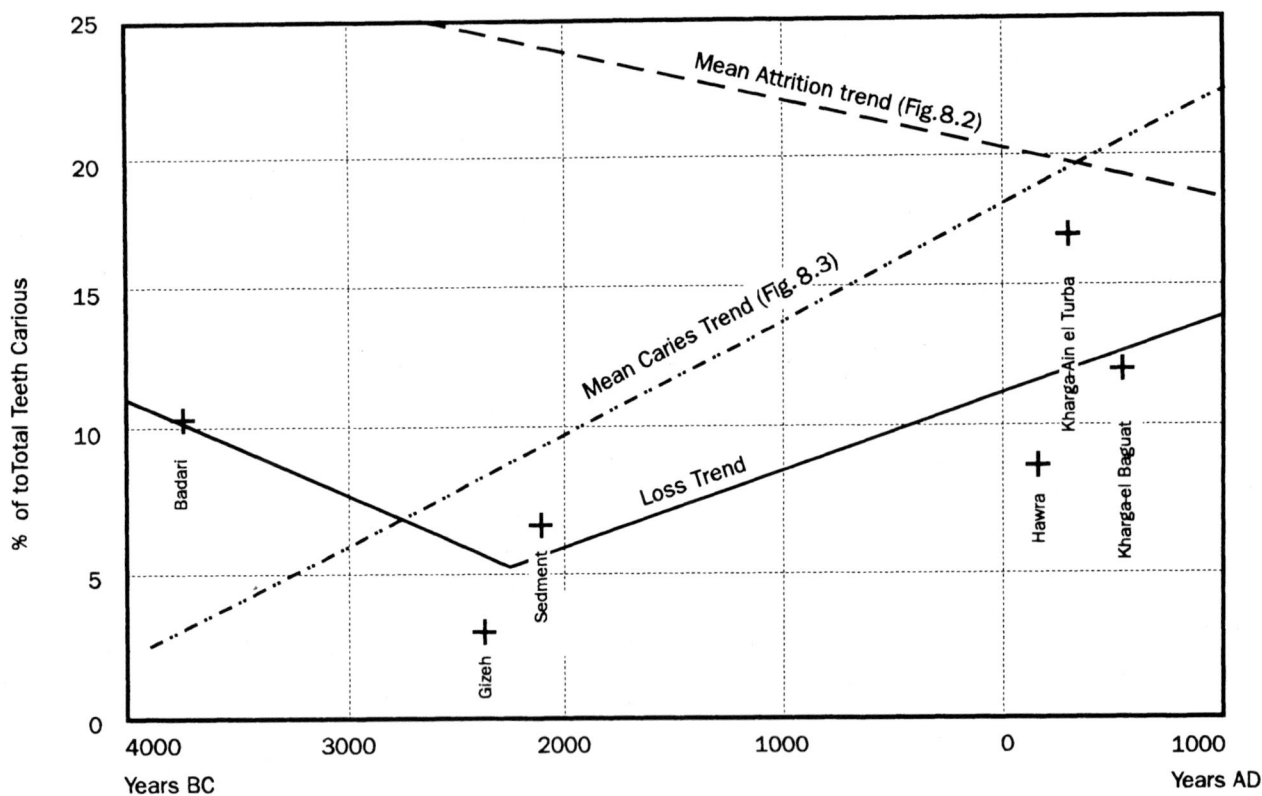

*Fig. 8.4: Antemortem tooth loss trend – Egypt attrition and caries superimposed.*

chewing vegetables masticatories.[5] The habit of chewing papyrus stems uncooked, boiled or roasted, is well attested, and the fibrous structure contains hard amorphous silica particles known as opal rhytoliths. These are naturally abrasive.

4. In humans, sweetening agents are quick energy sources, and the satiation effects and the craving for 'sweets' exists throughout history. Although cane and beet sugar were unknown to ancient Egypt, the date palm, wild fig and honey, all of which provide high sugar levels existed in the Nile valley. The link between sugar and caries is well proven, and the increasing use of sweeteners from the Middle Kingdom would clearly increase the prevalence of dental caries. The lack of any oral hygiene would encourage this morbidity.

5. Considering the decreasing attrition trend and increasing carious trend in the Egyptian population samples through time (Figs 8.2 and 8.3 respectively), there has clearly been a change in oral pathology.

6. The significant reduction in oral pathology noted in the Sudanese population would indicate a different diet. As yet there is no hard evidence of this, but the geographical isolation may have prevented assimilation of Egyptian dietary practices.

7. The Egyptian occupation of Nubia is evident in many cultural aspects, and the chronologically-later oral deterioration of the Nubian dentition is probably a result of Egyptian dietary influences.

5   Dixon 1972.

44

# 9 Deformed Skulls at Tell Arpachiyah: the Social Context

## Theya Molleson and Stuart Campbell

ABSTRACT— *This paper discusses a set of skulls which come from Halaf and Ubaid burials excavated by Max Mallowan in 1933 at Arpachiyah in north Iraq. These date from approximately 4600 bc and 4300 bc respectively. Many of the skulls exhibit a marked degree of deliberate, artificial deformation. This is tentatively related to depictions of heads on pottery and figurines. The possible social context in which this deformation was practised is also discussed. A second point to emerge from the re-examination of the skulls is that there is a strong probability of a direct genetic link between the Halaf skulls and the Ubaid skulls suggesting that there was a considerable measure of continuity in the populations.*

The site of Tell Arpachiyah is some 6 km to the east of Mosul in north Iraq. The relatively small mound was first excavated in 1933 by Max Mallowan using a large number of workmen with little supervision.[1] The levels he excavated were almost exclusively prehistoric, mostly of the Halaf culture (dating to c.5200 bc to 4500 bc) but the top four or five levels at the centre of the site were of a small Ubaid settlement (c. 4400-4200 bc). On the west and northwest slopes of the mound he also excavated an extensive Ubaid cemetery and recovered 45 graves, some with multiple burials, and five more from elsewhere on the site. The material from these graves, together with 9 Halaf burials, was published in a summary form in the publication of the site in 1935. Most of the skeletons were badly damaged but 11 of the better preserved skulls were brought back to Britain, where they were forgotten until 1969 when Mallowan published a report on them in conjunction with Linford.[2] It is the re-examination of these skulls and the interpretation of certain striking features which forms the basis for this paper.

### The Archaeological Context of the Skulls

Although Mallowan's labelling of the skulls is often obscure, most can be identified with specific graves with certainty after an examination of both the published evidence and that contained in the original field notebook (now in the British Museum). In fact, the correlations made here (see Appendix and Fig. 9.1) between skulls and graves may be considered more accurate and reliable than those Mallowan made in 1969. For convenience and to avoid confusion with Mallowan's numbering we have used letters to identify the human remains that are now housed in the Natural History Museum, London.

Three of the remains appear to date from the Halaf occupation of the site. A, the skeleton of a juvenile, can definitely be assigned to published grave 56.[3] Skull C is probably, but not certainly, from Halaf grave 58.[4] The third skull, B, was not published in the original excavation report but there is a reference to it in Mallowan's field notes in the British Museum. This skull seems to have been unassociated with other human or archaeological remains and was found at a depth of 7.5m on the east edge of the tell in what appears to have been an infilled water channel. The depth of the skull suggests that it, too, is almost certainly Halaf. Although both the recording and the excavation technique make it impossible to reconstruct the circumstances of burial further, the obvious parallels for this skull burial are with the skulls found at the same site by Hijara in 1976 at the

---

1  Mallowan & Rose 1935.
2  Mallowan 1969.
3  Mallowan & Rose 1935, 42.
4  ibid., 42.

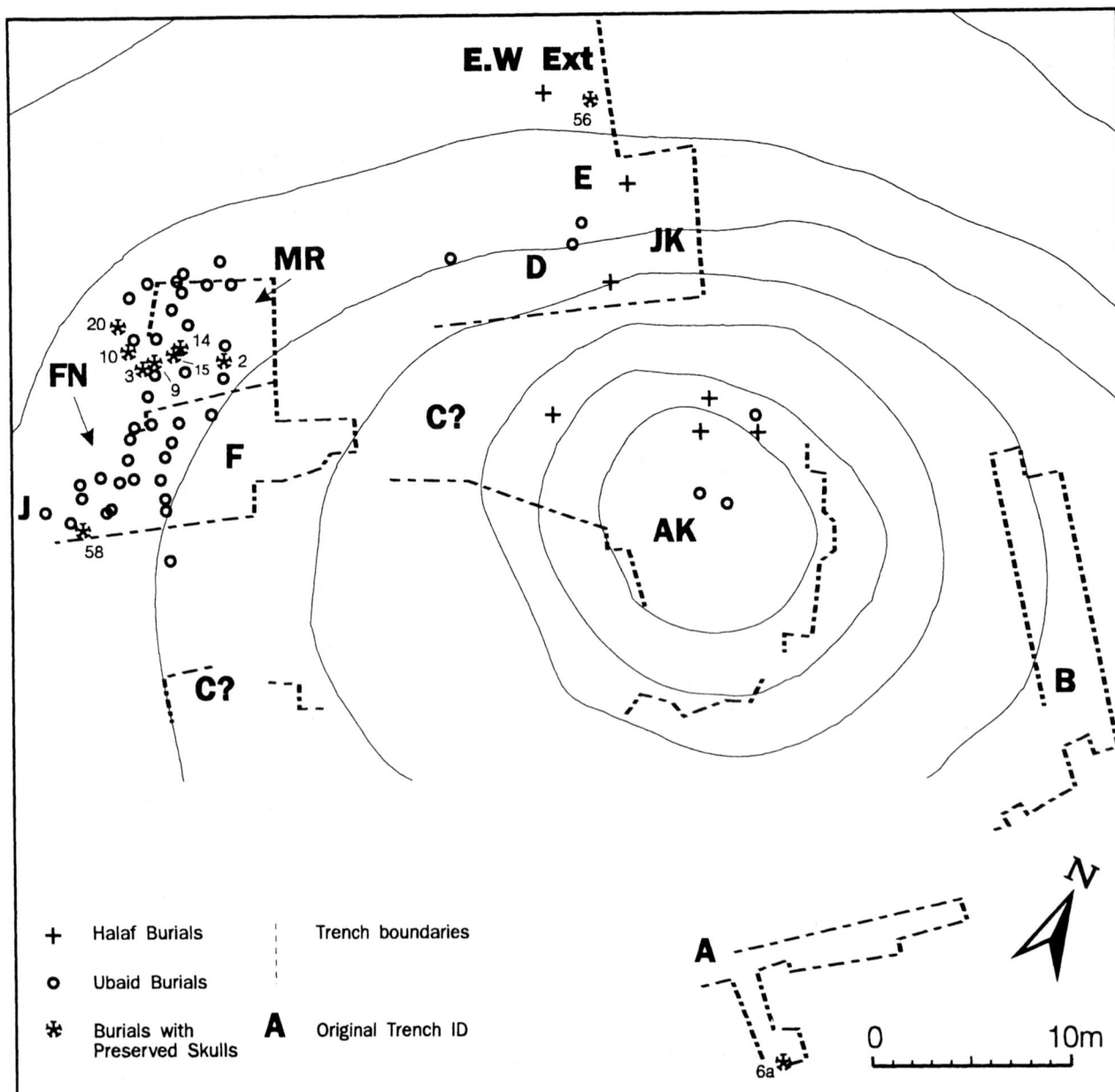

*Fig. 9.1: Plan of Arpachiyah with grave locations and Mallowan's original trench designations.*

centre of the mound[5] and with the single skull interments at the broadly contemporary site of Yarim Tepe II to the south of the Jebel Sinjar.[6] These skull burials differ from what we know otherwise of Halaf burial practices and must have had some special significance but how we should interpret them is unclear. The burials of the Halaf period as a whole are varied, ranging from conventional inhumations with grave goods to cremation burials at Yarim Tepe II.[7]

The definite Halaf occupation at Arpachiyah ends with level TT6. The Ubaid settlement seems to start with level TT4; unfortunately there is too little material available from TT5 to be sure of its status. From the evidence of other sites, there appears to be a phase missing between them – the Halaf-Ubaid transitional.[8] Furthermore, there is tenuous evidence that there was a phase of erosion following TT6.[9] Thus the two groups of burials are separated in time. The Halaf burials certainly belong to the latter part of that period.[10] They should then date from sometime after 4900 bc and before the end of the Halaf c. 4500 bc, probably in the latter part of that range, perhaps around 4600 bc.[11] The Ubaid burials on the other hand must, from the pottery, date to somewhere in the later fifth millennium, perhaps

---

5   Hijara 1978.
6   Merpert, Munchaev & Bader 1978, 40-41; Merpert & Munchaev 1993.
7   see Akkermans 1989 for survey: also Campbell 1992.

8   Davidson 1977; Breniquet 1987, 1990.
9   Campbell 1992, 194.
10  Halaf II A or B according to the terminology proposed in Campbell 1992.
11  for dating see Watkins & Campbell 1987.

around 4300 bc although potentially slightly earlier or later. Thus is there a gap of around three hundred years between the two sets of burials. It may easily have been a slightly greater or smaller period.

The rest of the skulls originate from Ubaid burials within the main area of the cemetery. From the positioning of the graves and from the pottery accompanying the bodies, there seems little reason to suggest that most or all the burials were not made in the same broad time span. This report will therefore consider them as generally of the same date. It is uncertain whether the cemetery represents the burials of the Ubaid settlement at Arpachiyah. That settlement seems to have been small and restricted to the summit of the mound, although the methods of excavation leave this open to a little doubt. No pottery was published from these levels and very little is preserved in museums. However, the very small quantities of unstratified Ubaid sherds amongst the very large quantities of Halaf pottery which has been kept seem to confirm that the settlement was probably very restricted. They provide no useful evidence as to whether it was contemporary with the cemetery. At the end of its Halaf occupation, Arpachiyah seems to have been a site with a specific, high status role in society.[12] There is, however, no indication that this role was continued later. The evidence from the Ubaid settlement certainly does not suggest exceptionally high status and it seems unlikely that we can assume that this was the reason that the Ubaid burials were made on the same mound. They may simply have been placed on a convenient mound close to the settlement from which the deceased came.

The Ubaid graves seem, in general, to have been simple pits of unknown depth, most containing a single body. The main exception is the double burial 14/15 (from which skulls G and H almost certainly come) which comprised a pit reached through a 'passage' and with a cairn of mud brick on top. Although this grave had no associated Ubaid pottery with it, its position in the cemetery makes it all but certain that it, too, was Ubaid.

Mallowan interpreted a third of the burials as fractional, secondary burials.[13] While this remains possible, it seems more likely that they were the result of post-depositional disturbance or poor excavation by very inexperienced workmen (a view ultimately supported by Mallowan himself[14]). The burials were almost always oriented east-west, although Mallowan seems wrong in arguing that the head could be in either direction.[15] Usually the head was placed to the east or south-east. Where body position is mentioned, the skeleton was contracted and in a few cases there was evidence to suggest that they had been wrapped in matting. Hand bones found embedded in the matrix still adhering to

the cranial bones of several of the surviving skulls (D, F, M) give confirmation of the burial position, and suggest that, in these cases, the body was undisturbed, not secondary. Bones of both hands are associated with skull M (from Grave 2), placed palm to palm beneath the right cheek.

Most of the graves either contained no burial goods (15 instances) or contained two pottery vessels (19 instances), suggestive of a more highly structured burial rite than was evident in the Halaf. Only grave 45 contained a large number of vessels and it seems likely to be the conflation of more than one burial.[16] Other, rare grave goods include animal bones, flint and bone tools, beads and two steatite rings.

Generally these burials are in accordance with other Ubaid burials in the north – Tepe Gawra,[17] Telul eth-Thalathat, Yarim Tepe III and Tell Aqab.[18] They contrast markedly with burials from southern Iraq, which at Ur and Eridu are generally extended on their backs and often in mud brick coffins.[19] This suggests that, despite similarities in their pottery, the exact cultural adaptions were different in the two areas.

The surviving skulls which can be assigned to Ubaid burials come from adjacent graves (Fig. 9.2). Although it is conjecture, there must be a high chance that the skulls unassigned to specific burials also came from this area. Presumably, when the skulls were lifted, this was the area under investigation and they may not be representative of the whole cemetery.

## The surviving skulls

The anthropological re-examination of the skulls from Arpachiyah excavated by Mallowan has focused attention on the evidence for artificial cranial deformation displayed by at least six of the surviving thirteen skulls (Fig. 9.2). A high frequency of genetically determined traits raises the possiblity that the material represents the remains of an inbred group.

In summarising his impressions of the cranial material Mallowan observed that "we appear to be confronted with long heads, and there are certain pronounced facial and other characteristics which appear to imply that the possessors of this (Ubaid) pottery had distinctive physical features, which would have made them exceptionally easy to recognise".[20] He asked the questions: Did the distinctive northern Ubaid people differ in facial characteristics from those who used the same pottery in the south? Did the Ubaid peoples differ in their physical characteristics from the Halaf? Did the new Ubaid pottery which displaces the Halaf really imply the presence of intruders from the

---

12  Campbell 1992.
13  Mallowan & Rose 1935, 35.
14  Mallowan 1970, 399.
15  Mallowan & Rose 1935, 35.

16  Mallowan & Rose 1935, 41.
17  Tobler 1950.
18  Davidson & Watkins 1981.
19  Woolley 1954; Forest 1983; Pariselle 1985.
20  Mallowan 1969, 52.

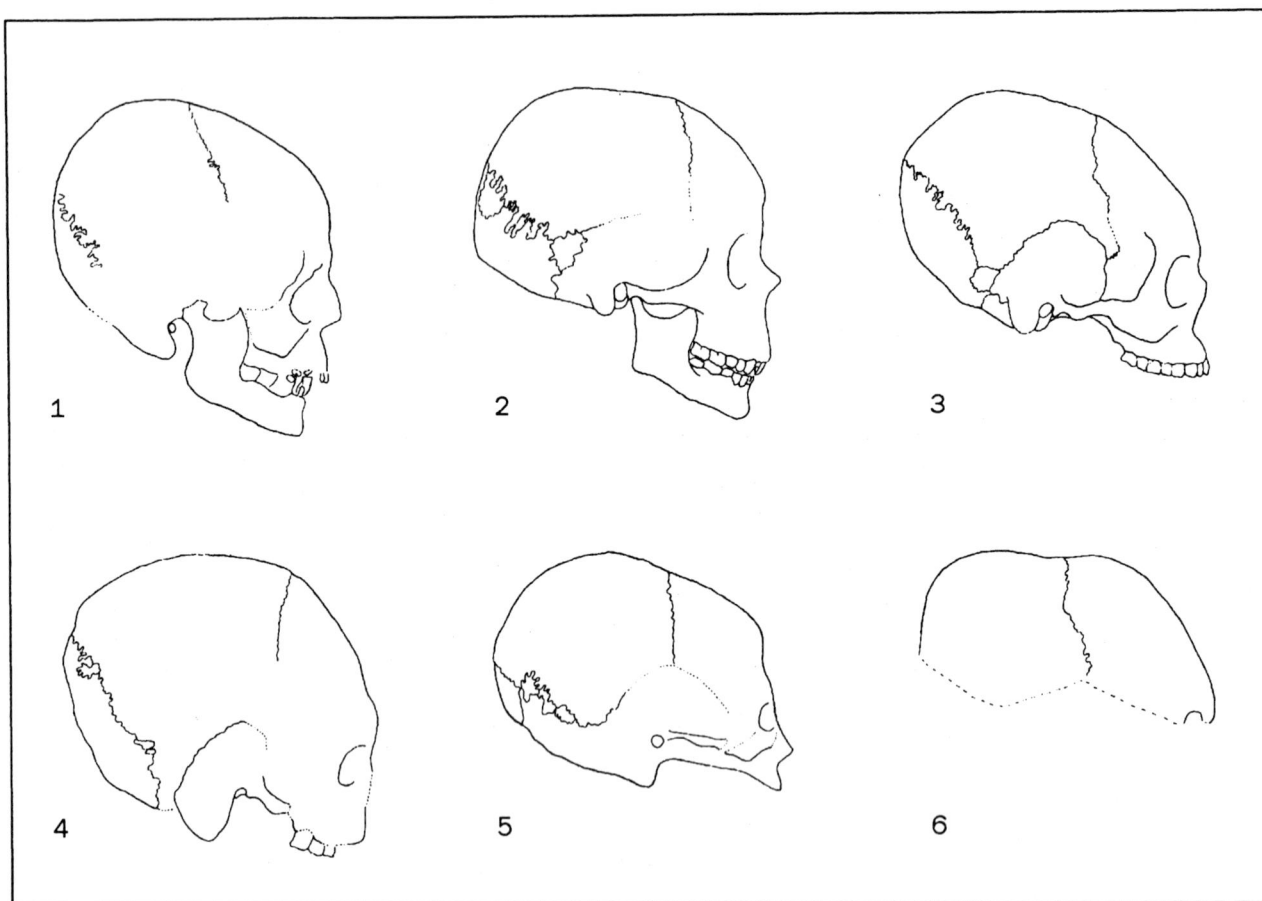

Fig. 9.2: Sagittal outlines of skulls from Arpachiyah showing artificial cranial deformation.
1. Skull H; 2. Skull I; 3. Skull G; 4. Skull C; 5. Skull D; 6. Skull E

southern end of the Tigris Euphrates valley? Only one of the skulls was then noted as showing evidence of artificial deformation.[21]

Melted paraffin wax was poured over the skulls to consolidate the bones for transport. Thus surrounding matrix and the position of neck vertebrae (Fig. 9.5) and hand bones are preserved, but any reconstruction of the skull bones, which are now very friable, would be extremely difficult and has not been attempted. A sandy deposit fills the cavity of several of the skulls. This is layered and apparently water-laid in the case of skull M (Fig. 9.6). Soil compaction and the weight of the overlying burden had caused skull D to be compressed dorso-ventrally and the bones to split apart (Fig. 9.7).

Artificial modification of skull shape can result from the application of pressure to various areas of the skull: a) the occipital region, b) the frontal region c) both frontal and occipital regions, d) along the transverse axis, utilizing circular bands and producing a circular deformity which proportionately lengthens the skull.[22]

Artificial cranial deformation has been widely described in the literature and the criteria by which it can be recognised in archaeological material can be summarised here.

1) The parietal index is greater than 25.[23]
2) The meningeal vessels are dilated and diverted in the direction of compensatory growth as a result of increased intracranial pressure. The posterior-superior area of the parietal bones of the skull are the most markedly affected by the deformation and exhibit a particularly rich provision of arteries. Overall there is reduced vascularisation.[24]
3) The diploe of the cranial bone is underdeveloped in the region where pressure has been applied so that in section or a radiograph of the skull the zone of diploic bone undulates.[25] See Figs 9.5 and 9.8.
4) The coronal suture may be deflected posteriorly.
5) The foramina jugularis is broadened.[26]
6) There is an increase in multiple wurmian bones.[27] This is not a general finding.[28]
7) Sella turcica is flat with a much reduced or largely absent dorsum.[29]

---

21 Mallowan 1969, 54.
22 Stewart 1941, McNeill & Newton 1965, Cheverud et al. 1992.

23 Larnach 1974, Howells 1978.
24 Grupe 1982, 1984.
25 Creutz 1977.
26 Grupe 1982.
27 Ossenberg 1970.
28 Grupe 1982.

| Dentition | Deformed | Skull Shape Not deformed | Indeterminate |
|---|---|---|---|
| Hypodont | C, E?, F | I?, M | L |
| Megadont | H | J | |
| Normal | G | K | |
| Indeterminate | | | A, B |

Frequency of hypodontia = 6/9 or if all the indet. were normal 6/13

*Table 9.1 Association between cranial deformation and reduced dentition (hypodontia or agenesis) in the skulls from Arpachiyah.*

| Ossicles | Deformed | Skull Shape Not deformed | Indeterminate |
|---|---|---|---|
| Present | E,H,C | I? | |
| Absent | G,F,D | M,K | B |
| Indeterminate | | | A,L |

*Table 9.2 Association between cranial deformation and sutural ossicles.*

8) The meningeal vessels are enlarged.[30]

There is great variation in the development and degree of cranial modification even when the same methods to produce the effect are employed. No one change is diagnostic and many cases of artificial deformation must have been overlooked.

In a differential diagnosis post-mortem alteration needs to be excluded; it results primarily in crush fractures of the bones (Fig. 9.7). Remodelling of the bone contour can occur, but in these instances the meningeal vessels and diploic structure, of course, remain normal. Post-mortem distortion is likely to occur where burial is into habitation soils, especially those with a clay component, where the constant passage of people over the area leads to compaction of the soil. Burials under the floors of dwellings will be susceptible, those in the centre of the room would be liable to sustain greater crushing than those at the sides.

Underdevelopment of the diploe of the frontal bone is observed in circular band deformations and where pressure was applied to the frontal. It can be an important indicator of deformation in fragmented material where measurements cannot be taken. The meningeal vessels are not always altered, nor can they be examined in archaeological crania with matrix infill.

At least one of the skulls from Arpachiyah was of the circular type of deformity[31] usually, but not always in the opinion of Stewart,[32] produced by a circular band. Stewart also notes that in two such cases he describes for the United States the deformity is anything but extreme,

which would provide an explanation if the practice has been overlooked.

The deformation at Arpachiyah was probably of two types. A circular bandage encircled the frontal and occipital in infancy to produce an elongated skull, seen clearly in skull G (Fig. 9.9). In other skulls the frontal is flattened as though a board had been placed across it and there is a depression produced by the pressure of the bandages in the parietal bones behind bregma (Fig. 9.10). The inner diploe is constricted in the region of the pressure and expanded away from it, seen in section in skull E (Figs 9.5 and 9.8). It is difficult to determine whether or not an attempt had been made to deform the skull I. The skull is slightly asymmetric and there are large ossicles in the lambdoid suture (Figs 9.11 and 9.12). If it was not artificially deformed it is the only one with extra-sutural ossicles which is not (Table 9.2). These ossicles occur more frequently with artificial deformation[33] but also have a genetic component in their etiology.

The deformation observed at Arpachiyah affects both male and female skulls (3/5 female and 3/7 male). Our sex determinations had to be based on secondary sex characteristics of the skull since no pelvic bones survive; they generally agree with those given by Linford[34] (see Appendix).

It is probable that several of the individuals were related to one another. Hypodontia or congenital absence (agenesis) of third molars (8s), together with the related feature of particularly small teeth, is noted in 6/9 of the dentitions, including individuals both with and without evidence for cranial deformation (Table 9.1).

29  Erdélyi 1930.
30  Grupe 1982.
31  Dingwall 1931, Meiklejohn *et al.* 1992.
32  Stewart 1941.

33  Ossenberg 1970.
34  in Mallowan 1969.

Two, possibly three, of the dentitions have particularly large teeth. There is a strong genetic component in the size, shape, and even presence or absence of teeth.[35] Brook has also shown that megadontia, always rare, is twice as common in first degree relatives as it is in the general population.

The presence of extra-sutural bones in the sutures of the cranium also has a genetic component, although the incidence is increased in artificially deformed skulls.[36] Three of the deformed skulls and one other (4/10) have ossicles at asterion or in the lambdoid suture (Table 9.2).

It is particularly notable that skull C, which is here attributed to the Halaf, has both hypodontia and extra-sutural ossicles in the lambdoid sutures, two characteristics that could link it genetically to the skulls from the Ubaid levels. Mallowan suggested that the Ubaid culture dominated over that of the Halaf in north Iraq through a violent replacement of population. Although this idea has declined considerably in importance[37] the evidence for genetic links between the two populations is striking evidence for continuity. The actual settlement may have moved around during the three hundred years between the abandonment of the Halaf settlement of Arpachiyah and its use as an Ubaid cemetery but there was no complete replacement of the population.

Cranial deformation has been widely practised in the eastern Mediterranean region; it can still be seen today in eastern Turkey and apparently has a very long history.[38] Early examples have been recovered from Jericho, Chalcolithic Byblos, Ganj Dareh, and Ali Kosh.[39] King Midas (738-696 BC) probably had an artificially deformed skull.[40] The practice is of considerable antiquity, extending from the Neolithic in the Near East (Khirokitia, Cyprus) and from 13,000 BP in Australia (eg Kow Swamp) and perhaps 18000-23000 BP in China (Upper Cave, Chou Kou Tien).[41]

Artificially deformed skulls have been recorded from several Ubaid sites, including Tell Madhur,[42] and Eridu.[43] At Telul eth-Thalathat 40km west of Mosul, the Ubaid period contained skeletal remains of a baby whose head was alleged to have been artificially deformed.[44] The 15 crania from Eridu are described by Coon as being "deformed in one fashion or another, presumably after burial, by earth pressure.[45] Some, for example 52B and 181, had been flattened from above. This has made them look superficially like certain Maya Indian crania, deformed intentionally in infancy". Otten commented that the foreheads of the skulls appeared to

be more sloping than those from Ubaid;[46] and Kiszelly noted that there are skulls from Eridu that are artificially deformed.[47] Other skulls were squashed from side to side, as in the case of 2B, while others were bent asymmetrically and look as if they had been "passed through a wringer". This last observation does imply that there had also been some post depositional distortion of the crania, as indeed there has been at Arpachiyah.

The Halaf burial from Kurban Höyük, south east Turkey, has an artificially deformed skull (cranial index: 62.7) and is female.[48] Alpagut compares this skull to the three artificially deformed skulls, which are also female, from Şeyh Höyük (Tell esh-Sheikh), and claimed as the first deformed specimens found among the Chalcolithic and copper age inhabitants of Anatolia.[49] Level 9 of Şeyh Höyük is contemporary with the latter part of the Halaf of northern Iraq and Syria

The majority of deformed skulls appear to be of females (e.g. Byblos), although, as at Arpachiyah, both sexes are involved at Khirokitia and Ganj Dareh.[50] Artificial cranial deformation is too widespread and has too long a history to have a single meaning or cause. At Arpachiyah it involves females and males of an apparently inbred lineage that spans the Halaf-Ubaid.

While the reasons for cranial deformation may be cosmetic, as is usually claimed, the outcome is both distinctive and pragmatic. Pragmatic in the sense that an individual with deformation such as is displayed at Arpachiyah would be unable to carry a load on the head and therefore the deformations would be impractical for anyone destined to labour (from a later date the 'standard' of Ur displays burdens being carried on the head). The distinctive appearance would render the individual identifiable as to class or group even if taken prisoner and stripped of other visible accoutrements of status.[51] The practice has considerable potential for elitism.

The suggestion that artificial deformation at Arpachiyah was practised by a particular group is supported by the evidence, from the dentitions, that they were genetically related. Hypodontia, the congenital absence (agenesis) of third molars, together with the related condition of particularly small (reduced) incisors or premolars is observed in the Arpachiyah skulls at an unusually high frequency, affecting at least two thirds of the sample. Hypodontia affects about 4% of the general population in Britain, rising to 30% among first degree relatives.[52] Extra large or megadont teeth was found in

35 Brook 1984.
36 Bennett 1965, Ossenberg 1970, Gottlieb 1978.
37 see Davidson 1977; Breniquet 1990.
38 Hasluck 1947.
39 Özbek 1974; Hole et al. 1969,.
40 Prag 1988.
41 Angel 1953, Kurth 1958, Brown 1981, Soto-Heim 1986.
42 Downs 1984.
43 Coon 1949, Kiszelly 1991.
44 Egami 1959.
45 Coon 1949.

46 Otten 1948.
47 Kiszelly 1991.
48 Alpagut 1986.
49 Şenyürek & Tunakan 1951.
50 Özbek 1974, Angel 1946, Lambert 1979.
51 Note: Dingwall quotes Ochanine 1925. "The Choresmiens in order to avoid being taken for Turks and sold into slavery to the Persians put heavy packages upon the heads of their children in order to make them broad and short."
52 Brook 1984.

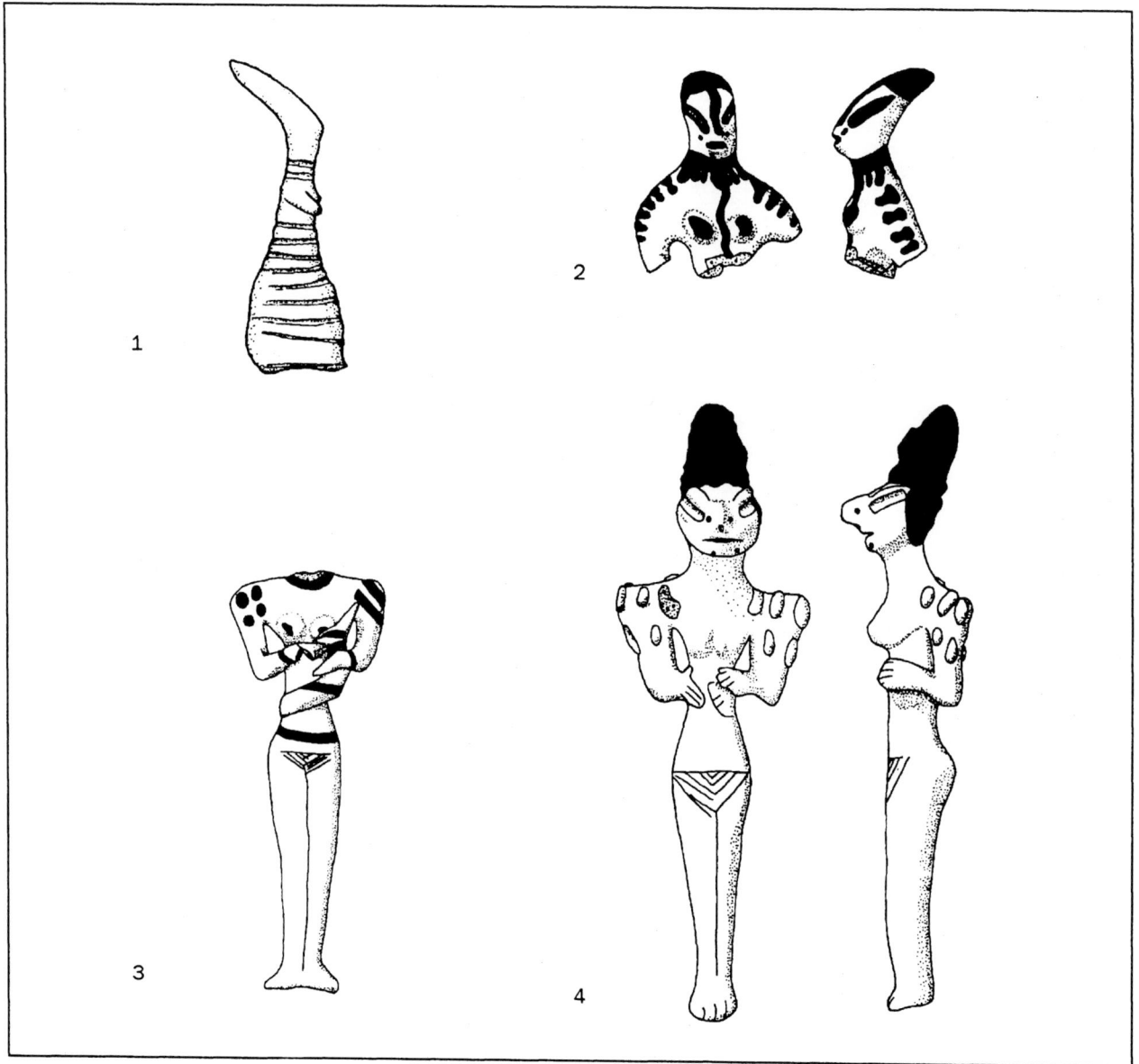

*Fig. 9.3: Figurines with possible skull deformation.*
*1. Yarim Tepe I, c. 5,750 uncal BC; 2-4. Ur, Ubaid period, c.4,200 uncal BC.*
*(2.-4. courtesy Ellen MacAdam).*

1% of Brook's sample (nearly 2% in first degree relatives), so the two cases (2/9) in the small Arpachiyah sample could indicate a genetic relationship between the two. The levels of these genetically determined dental characters at Arpachiyah is higher than would be expected even among parents and siblings and suggests that there was a degree of inbreeding comparable to the prescribed cross-cousin marriages prevalent in the area today. The possibility should perhaps be considered that the Arpachiyah skulls represent members of a hereditary group or class -priests, potters, or princes might be considered.

## Depiction of skull deformation

Realistic depictions of the human form are relatively rare in the Halaf and Ubaid. There are small numbers of humans painted on vessels, more commonly in the Halaf, and a range of figurines. Many of the drawings of humans on pots are either very schematic or have clearly normal heads. A few instances, however, have elongated head, sometimes with hair or feathers shown growing from them. Two particularly clear examples come from the Halaf level of Tell Sabi Abyad in north Syria (Fig. 9.4), although there are also other Halaf parallels. These must represent headdresses, possibly exaggerated hairstyles or, most interestingly in this context, the stylised results of skull deformation. Whichever explanation is correct, they do suggest a

*Fig. 9.4: Possible depictions of skull deformation on pottery. 1.-2. Tell Sabi Adyad, Halaf, c.4900 uncal BC; 3.-4. Tell Madhur, Ubaid, c.4200 uncal BC*

social context in which attempts to emphasise the length of the head may have been of some significance.

The second source of evidence comes from figurines. Again, in many cases, it is clear that the heads are normal in shape or they are schematic, often being little more than pegs. There are certainly many cases where there is a general elongation or flattening of the head. The figures from Ain Gazel are an early instance but they occur very widely. However, the most obviously relevant examples are the lizard headed figures characteristic of the southern Ubaid and with antecendents in the Samarran at Choga Mami and, even earlier, at Yarim Tepe I in north Iraq (Fig. 9.3). These clearly have elongated heads but the faces also protrude in a manner which suggests that something more extensive than a mere deformation of the head is being indicated. The decoration on a pot of the Halaf period from Tell Sabi Abyad shows an elongated head on a human figure but not simply the elongation of the skull but of the face as well with, perhaps, similar intentions to the figurines.

Again, these examples may represent ideals towards which the skull deformation is intended to lead. There are a few examples of Ubaid figurines with heads expanded towards the back and with apparently normal faces. These may be a better parallel to our examples but we must be cautious in picking and choosing parallels from the south of Iraq. The best examples of figurines with clearly elongated heads do seem to occur particularly in the south of Iraq rather than the north.

## Discussion

The instance of skull deformation at Arpachiyah appears, on current knowledge, striking. This is true of the Ubaid and there is evidence of interesting links both in the use of this practice and in population with the preceding late Halaf. Skull deformation seems to occur with regularity at other sites of this general period over a very wide area. The parallels in figurines and on pottery are more ambiguous but still support the idea of a milieu in which shapes of head may have had specific meaning. Although detailed interpretations must await studies on larger samples at more sites, we can advance some hypotheses.

The first is that skull deformation was being used to demarcate a particular elite group, either social or functional. This might have been done visually and, possibly, by restricting the ability to perform certain functions, if carrying objects on the head was prevalent. The close genetic relationship in the sample would suggest that, if this explanation is correct, the group must have been hereditary and closely inbred. The possibility that it may have been maintained from the end of the Halaf into the Ubaid is more speculative but particularly interesting. This hypothesis cannot be disproved on present evidence. In the light of other knowledge of the Ubaid and Halaf, this seems to be a period at which the first moves towards more rigid and institutionalised social divisions may have been beginning and into which the development of institutionalised elites would fit convincingly.

However, the major problem in interpreting the skull deformation as a mark of an elite group is that the trait is so prevalent in the small sample. There seems every reason to believe that Mallowan's criteria for selecting these skulls was either their degree of preservation or because they were being excavated on a particular day, rather than any specific reason to suspect them to be unusual. Therefore it is difficult to argue that this represents the use of a particular exaggerated and artificial physical trait to demarcate a specific social sub-unit within Ubaid society. Rather it may be an attempt to emphasise the exclusivity of an entire social unit in comparison with other units, not dissimilar to the way in which clothing is a frequent, visually immediate, sign of group affiliation. The object of this symbolism may have been the inhabitants of the immediate environs of Arpachiyah. Alternatively, it may have been a unifying and, amongst many other characteristics, a defining feature of the Ubaid of northern Iraq as a whole.

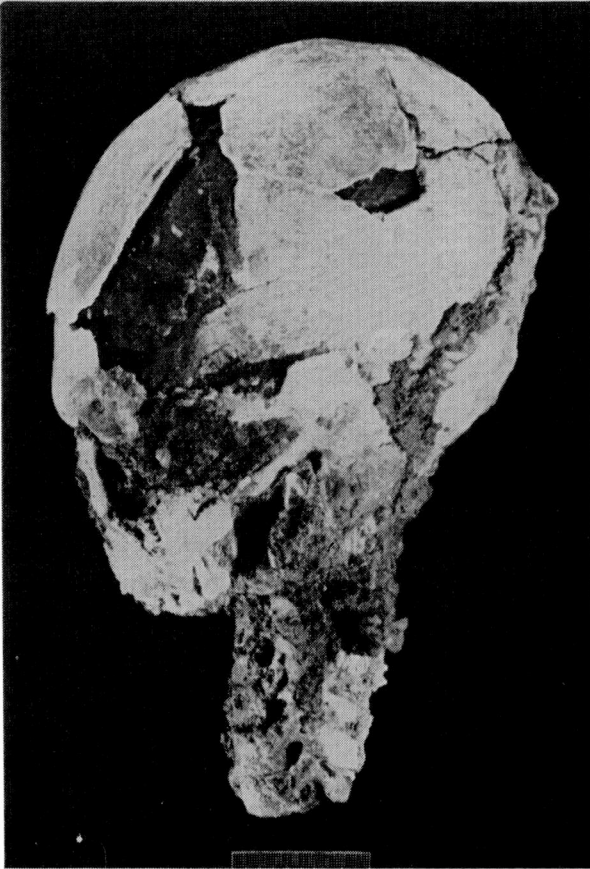

*Fig. 9.5: Posterior lateral view of skull C with neck vertebrae in place. The wedging of the bone through bandage pressure applied to deform the skull can be seen in the section of broken bone (top left). Halaf period.*

## Appendix

For each entry the first line gives three pieces of information. The first letter indicates our new numbering, the second, in brackets, is Mallowan's number,[53] next a transcription of the label associated with the skull or written on the skull itself and, finally, the Arpachiyah grave number with which the skull can be associated. A second paragraph give a commentary on the identification with a grave in the final report. The description of this grave is quoted and a final paragraph summarising the features of the skull.

*Halaf Graves*

A    (11)    E W ext 250/300 (Grave 56)

Two Halaf sherds; 2 pieces of obsidian and 1 piece of flint preserved with this skull are probably just cultural debris.

"At 3m. Skeleton of a child. Body NW by SE. Head SE. Body on left side, face towards the E, in an embryonic position. Body was found in hard red pisé. Objects: in front of the body a fragment of a flint knife, for type cf Fig. 52, no 16. At the same level 1m away from the face a painted bowl of the Tell Halaf period, probably not actually to be associated with the grave but of the same period".[54]

Juvenile (2-3 years) skeleton, deformation and hypodontia indeterminate.

*Fig. 9.6: Layered silty infill of skull M suggests a water-laid deposit.*

B    (10)    A 750 m  (Unpublished)

This Almost certainly refers to trench A, c.35m to the south of the tepe, which was excavated to a depth of 7.5m to ascertain the thickness of deposit and at this depth a skull was found lying in clean sand. Mallowan suggested that this may have been an old river bed that had been used as a rubbish pit/cemetery.[55] The skull is almost certainly Halaf.

Male skull, young adult.

C    (7)    A 7 m (Grave 58?)

(Mallowan adds F170, presumably from a label now lost). If F 170 is correct this must be Grave 58, dating from the Halaf. Otherwise it must be from area A and unpublished like B and, again, Halaf in date given the depth.

"At 1.7m. Body flexed and on right side. Had been disturbed in antiquity. The head was overturned, the lower jaw had fallen away and was lying close to a votive bowl; many of the bones were broken. The soil immediately overlying and surrounding the skull had been stamped down over the bones and was very stiff and compact. Against the head and back of the body were several votive deposits; some of the pottery was smashed and parts were missing. The hard pisé over the head might have been the foundations of a later mud wall, and 0.4m above the body there were traces of ash and sand, probably a house floor, in which case the grave would have been disturbed by later Tell Halaf house builders, but the pottery may have been smashed at the time of the interment, cf. G54, and parallels at Nal etc, where votive deposits often appear to have been smashed at the grave side. Objects: by the head a painted pot, A735, fig.64, no.9. Behind the head three miniature vases unpainted, A493, A494, A495, fig.43, nos.14, 21, 27. Two stone celts, A669, A670. An obsidian knife type, Fig. 52, no.18. White stone amulet with linear markings, A902. A few grains of barley and some human finger bones. The finger bones are a specially interesting form of deposit; they were done in stone in TT6, and may have some ritual significance. Bone implements included awls and scapulae, A720, cf. Plate XIIIa, for awls. There

53  Mallowan 1969,54-55.
54  Mallowan & Rose 1935, 42.

55  Mallowan's excavation records in British Museum, pp.6, 141 and 168.

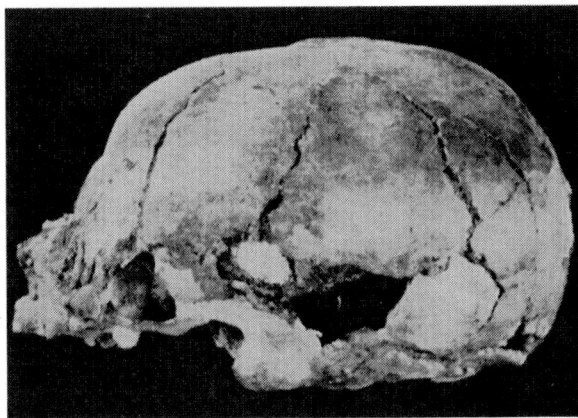

*Fig. 9.7: Post-mortem dorso-ventral crushing of skull D. The skull shape is distorted but the bones are not deformed.*

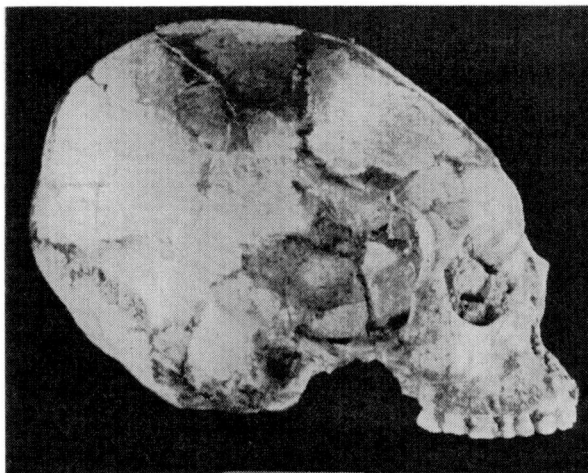

*Fig. 9.9: Lateral view of skull G, showing the elongated head shape, the result of artificial cranial defor-mation, by circular bandaging.*

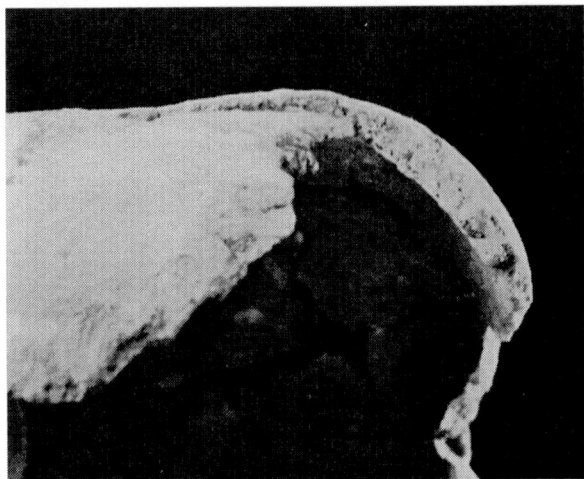

*Fig. 9.8: Wedging of parietal bone of skull E, the result of pressure applied during infancy to deform the natural skull shape.*

*Fig. 9.10: Lateral view of skull E, showing the flattened frontal and sagittal depression, probably the result of pressure from a board and bandage applied to the front of the skull during infancy.*

was also a sherd done with a cable pattern in a lustrous black paint on an apricot ground."[56]

Male cranium, vertebrae, parts of radius, ulna and right hand, young adult, artificially deformed, hypodont (agenesis upper 8s, reduced 2s), lambdoid ossicles (Fig. 9.5). Skull compressed laterally by burial.

*Ubaid Graves*
D    (2)    Archaic 1 F
Exact location unknown but in the main area of the Ubaid cemetery; Mallowan uses Archaic 1 to refer to the Ubaid in his notes and the cemetery is in his area F.

Female skull and hand, mature adult, artificially deformed, ante-mortem loss?. Skull crushed post burial.

E    (1)    F Archaic 1
Exact location unknown but, again, in the main area of the Ubaid cemetery.

Female skull, cervical vertebrae, adolescent (12-16 years), artificially deformed, hypodont (agenesis lower left 8), reduced upper 5s and 7s, ossicle at pterion, metopic.

The only deformed skull recognised by Mallowan and Lindford.[57]

F    (8)    MR G9 (Grave 9)
"At 3.0m. Objects: at head a broken pot unpainted. At feet two painted pots, A169, Fig.27, no.1; A171, Fig.34, no.4. At side of body a fragment of a large unpainted bowl, rim 0.35m, and inside it portion of an infant's skull; complete and fractional burial thus associated."[58]

Male skull and hand bones, young adult, artificially de-formed, hypodont - agenesis upper 8, reduced 5s. Cranium crushed laterally post-mortem.

G    (3)    Pit MR G 14. 'Burnt' room. (Grave 14/15)
Mallowan equates this with Grave 14/15, probably correctly as G14 makes no other sense in the conventions used in his notes. 'Burnt' room is probably very misleading. Usually it refers to the TT6 Burnt House, but this had no skulls within it and was probably not excavated at the time the burials were excavated.

---

56  Mallowan and Rose 1935, 42-43.

57  Mallowan 1969.
58  Mallowan and Rose 1935, 38.

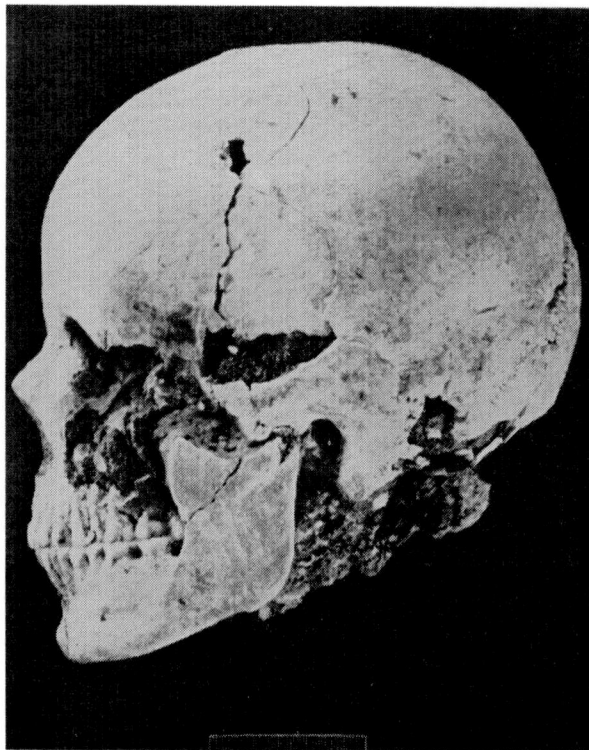

*Fig. 9.11: Lateral view of skull I. An attempt may have been made to deform the skull which is slightly asymmetric and has numerous large ossicles in the lambdoid suture.*

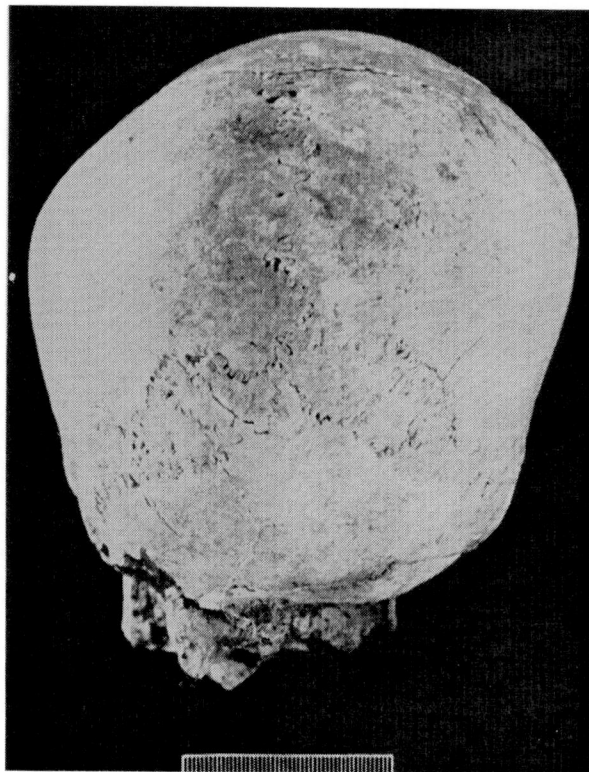

*Fig. 9.12: Posterior view of skull I*

Grave 14/15: "At 3.3m. A circular pit 2.1m deep and 1.6m in diameter. At the bottom of the pit lay two skeletons in the crouched or embryonic position: lack of space would in any case have prevented the bodies from being in a more extended position. The bones were very well preserved and the skulls were entirely free from dirt and in no way crushed. ... One of the bodies had the right hand resting directly on top of the pelvis."[59]

Female skull, mature adult, artificially deformed, agenesis? ante-mortem loss.

H     (3)     Pit MR G 15. 'Burnt' room. (Grave 14/15)
      See Skull G for description.
      Female/Male skull, young adult, artificially deformed, no agenesis, megadont lower 8s, ossicle at asterion. Cranial index: 60.9, 7 cervical vertebrae.

I     (9)     F G20 (Grave 20)
      "At 2.5m. Body, part of which lay in an undug section of the ground, was only partly excavated."[60]
      Female skull, mature adult, not deformed (?) but slightly asymmetric, hypodont (agenesis lower 8s) and megadont. Ossicles at asterion and in lambdoid suture (Figs 9.11 and 9.12).

J     (7)     FN G3 (Grave 3)
      "At 2.5m. Body E by W, Head W. Possibly a reburial, the skull being found 0.9m away from the neck and 0.4m below the level of the body. The head may have been buried first and covered over with earth, the body carefully oriented but placed further

from the skull than was intended. At the feet the skull of a ram or goat. Objects: on the animal's skull an unpainted pot"[61]
Male skull, not deformed, megadont lower 8s.

K     (5)     FN 240 G2
      Grave unknown. Grave 2 is not in the right area or depth. Mallowan appears to have had a provisional grave numbering used in the field which was sometimes different to the published version and to which this may refer. However, in area FN, it is certainly an Ubaid grave from the cemetery area.
      Male skull, not deformed.

L     (6)     FN G10 "teeth from skull" (Grave 10)
      "At 2.6m. Fractional Burial. A few broken bones lying E by W. Objects: three painted pots, A172, Fig.26, no.2; and type on Fig.29, no.5"[62]
      Male mandible, mature adult, hypodont (agenesis lower 8s).

M     (4)     MR G2 -200 (Grave 2)
      This is almost certainly the genuine Grave 2, as in correct area)
      "At 2.2m, probably contemporary with G7, which was close and at the same level. Objects: two painted pots, A164, Fig.33, no.3; A165, Fig.29, no.1. Delicate ware, broken but complete."[63]
      Female skull, clavicle, scapula, and hands placed palm to palm, young adult, not deformed, hypodont (agenesis lower right 8). On the right parietal two healed perforations about 3mm in diameter and 42mm apart. Skull filled with layered and apparently water-laid silt with gypsum crystals (Fig. 9.6).

59  Mallowan and Rose 1935, 38-39.
60  Mallowan and Rose 1935, 39.
61  Mallowan & Rose 1935, 38.
62  Mallowan and Rose 1935, 38.
63  Mallowan & Rose 1935, 38.

# 10 Lemba-Lakkous and Kissonerga-Mosphilia: Evidence from the Dentition in Chalcolithic Cyprus

## Dorothy A. Lunt

ABSTRACT—*The dentition has been examined in two groups of skeletal material from the excavations of the Chalcolithic settlement sites of Lemba Lakkous and Kissonerga Mosphilia, lying to the north of Paphos in western Cyprus. The burials were not in a cemetery, but lay between the houses.*

*A high proportion of the skeletons proved to be those of children or adolescents, and the dentition was of particular value in estimating individual age in this material. Children aged from birth to 12 years formed 65.4% of the material from Lemba Lakkous and 62.5% of that from Kissonerga Mosphilia. Adults over 20 years made up only 26.9% of the Lemba Lakkous groups and 31.2% of the Kissonerga Mosphilia group. An apparent difference in the age distribution of the small numbers of adults in the two groups proved not to be statistically significant.*

*Dental caries was present in both population groups. The prevalence of the disease in adolescents and adults from Lemba Lakkous (6.1% of permanent teeth at risk were affected) was higher than in those from Kissonerga Mosphilia (2.3% permanent teeth affected) and the difference proved to be statistically significant.*

## Material

The skeletal material which forms the basis of this paper derives from two sites in western Cyprus, Lemba-Lakkous and Kissonerga-Mosphilia, both excavated under the auspices of the Lemba Archaeological Project, directed by Dr Edgar Peltenburg.[1] The sites lie in fairly close proximity to one another, some four miles north of Paphos and not far from the coast.

Both sites were village settlements dating mainly from the Chalcolithic period, though at Kissonerga-Mosphilia there was evidence of late Neolithic and early Bronze Age phases. Burials were found between the houses at both sites, and all securely dated burials belong to the Chalcolithic period, 3800-2400 BC. The predominant mode of burial was in a pit, though at Kissonerga-Mosphilia some of the pits had been elaborated by undercutting to form chamber tombs, and two urn burials were also found at Kissonerga-Mosphilia.[2] Many of the graves contained a single burial, though

there were several examples of multiple interments. In some instances a scatter of disturbed material could be identified.

In many cases the skeleton was fragmentary and the dentition was particularly important in providing information concerning the number and ages of persons represented in a grave. Even when bone preservation at first sight seemed moderately good, the skeleton on lifting often fell into small fragments and bone dust, and little could be recovered intact.

Though recovery of the dentition was much more satisfactory than that of the skeleton, the teeth themselves had often suffered *post mortem* damage. As well as fracture and loss of vulnerable parts such as the tips of roots, there was sometimes *post mortem* erosion of the surface of the enamel, which became roughened, dull and chalky in appearance. In some cases there was loss of the enamel surface varying from a slight pitting to gross destruction with blurring of morphological features. The mechanism of this type of erosion is difficult to understand, since the composition of enamel is 96-98% calcium hydroxyapatite, and conditions in the

---

1 Peltenburg 1985.
2 Peltenburg 1991.

graves must have been alkaline as the subsoil is a type of limestone known locally as *'havara'*. This *post mortem* erosion of enamel is quite different from the *post mortem* destruction of the dentine and cementum of the teeth often observed in acid soil conditions. In the latter case it is the fibrous collagenous matrix of the tissues which is attacked, not their mineral content, and since enamel contains no collagen it is unaffected.[3]

The damage caused by *post mortem* erosion of enamel was more extensive in the material from Lemba-Lakkous than in that from Kissonerga-Mosphilia, but the material from both sites contained some specimens which were affected while others were not, and even in the material from a single burial some teeth might be severely eroded while others were completely untouched.

## Methods

The teeth and jaw fragments from each grave were carefully cleaned and the teeth identified. At this stage it was sometimes possible to recognise hitherto unsuspected additional individuals represented in the grave, though such individuals may have derived from earlier disturbed burials rather than from multiple contemporary burials.

The age at death of each person represented by a dentition or part of a dentition was estimated. In juveniles this is done by examining the stage of development of the dentition. A rough approximation of age may be obtained using the eruption status, but a more reliable and detailed estimate is gained from the stage of development of individual teeth, and this technique can also be used when the bone of the jaw has not survived and only a handful of loose teeth is present. When the jaw bone remains intact it is necessary to use radiographs to visualise teeth developing within the alveolus.

Numerous systems have been produced for age estimation in juveniles. Among the best known are the diagrammatic systems of Schour and Massler,[4] Ubelaker,[5] and Hillson.[6] Moorrees, Fanning and Hunt provided detailed charts of the development of most but not quite all teeth, using a system in which development of a tooth is divided into a series of stages.[7] Demirjian, Goldstein and Tanner employed a slightly different series of developmental stages and introduced a method whereby these stages were assigned weighted numerical values for different teeth; the values for different teeth in an individual were combined and the age estimate read off from a table or graph.[8] Of the studies mentioned above, that of Moorrees *et al.* was the only one in which detailed attention was paid to third molars. Johanson made a specific study of third molars and produced a chart of the stages in their development.[9]

There are problems associated with all the above systems, and none is perfect. Of the diagrammatic systems, that of Schour and Massler is by far the best drawn and easiest to use, but is not now considered satisfactory as the nature and quantity of the material on which it was based were not specified. The Ubelaker drawings of tooth development were recommended by Ferembach, Schwidetzky and Stloukal in their attempt to "unify methods in paleodemography".[10] They state that "Only europids were considered", but the Ubelaker chart which they copy is stated in the caption to refer to American Indians. Ubelaker's text indicates that the chart refers to "American Indians and other non-white populations" and gives a series of references from whose data the chart is said to have been compiled. Many of these references contain tooth eruption data only, and give no information concerning the stages of tooth development. While two of the references deal specifically with American Indians, some do not state the racial background of the material, while others indicate that the material was a mixture comprising 70% American White, the remainder being mainly Black with very few American Indian children. The basis of the Ubelaker chart thus seems uncertain. A further difficulty in employing this chart is that the developmental stages of some teeth are inaccurately drawn. The chart published by Hillson is based directly on the Schour and Massler chart.

The charts of tooth development published by Moorrees *et al.* offer the most detailed information concerning tooth development and are based on studies of American White children. In use the charts are difficult to read accurately and it is found that the "most likely age" given by different teeth in the same dentition tends to vary widely, sometimes by as much as three or four years. Age estimates from the Moorrees charts are usually younger, and sometimes considerably younger, than those obtained by other methods.

The method of Demirjian *et al.* was based on a study of French Canadian children. In its original form it depended on the presence of seven permanent teeth, and in the modified form on the presence of four permanent teeth. A method such as this has limitations when applied to skeletal material in which teeth have often been lost *post mortem*. Since both Moorrees' and Demirjian's studies are modern and based on the examination of North American White children, it would be expected that the results they produced would be similar. However, in cases where the Demirjian technique can be used, the resulting age estimate is often closer to the age estimate from the Schour and Massler diagrams.

3 Beeley & Lunt 1980.
4 Schour & Massler 1941.
5 Ubelaker 1989.
6 Hillson 1986.
7 Moorrees, Fanning & Hunt 1963.
8 Demirjian, Goldstein & Tanner 1973; Demirjian & Goldstein 1976.

9 Johanson 1971.
10 Ferembach, Schwidetzky & Stloukal 1980.

|            | Lemba-Lakkous | | Kissonerga-Mosphilia | |
| Age group  | n  | %     | n  | %     |
| ---------- | -- | ----- | -- | ----- |
| 0-5.9      | 25 | 48.1  | 27 | 42.2  |
| 6-12.9     | 9  | 17.3  | 13 | 20.3  |
| 13-19.9    | 4  | 7.7   | 4  | 6.3   |
| 20+        | 14 | 26.9  | 20 | 31.2  |
| Total      | 52 | 100.0 | 64 | 100.0 |

*Table 10.1: Age distribution, Cypriot Chalcolithic sites*

Since no single method seemed entirely satisfactory in use, in the present study age was estimated using as many techniques as possible. The very helpful analysis of tooth formation standards by Smith[11] had not been published at the time that these studies were carried out. The most relevant age diagram was selected from the drawings of Schour and Massler. Ages of individual teeth were assessed from the tables of Moorrees (as sex was unknown, the tables for males were arbitrarily selected), and in the case of third molars the tables and radiographs published by Johanson were used. When the appropriate teeth were present, age was calculated using the method of Demirjian. In most instances it was then possible to establish a median which was then used as the most likely age at death. In making such estimates, it was always necessary to assume that the child was normal and average in the development of its dentition.

The age at death in adults is estimated from the degree of attrition of the permanent molars, which erupt at something approaching six year intervals and therefore show a gradient in attrition which is maintained throughout adult life. A scale in which age is plotted against the degree of attrition of all three molars was published by Miles based on a population of Anglo-Saxon skeletons.[12] The baseline was achieved by a study of the developmental age in the juveniles. The degree of attrition in the juveniles was then related to the developmental age and the correlation extrapolated forward to provide estimates of age in the adults. In applying this technique to other population groups, a similar method should be used, i.e., extrapolation forward of data gained by a study of juveniles. Unfortunately there are seldom enough juveniles of the appropriate age group, c.12-19 (the younger juveniles do not give the required information), to make this procedure feasible, and recourse must be had to published tables. It was felt that the very precise table of Miles would probably be inappropriate for use on Chalcolithic dentitions from Cyprus, and a more generalised table, based on the Miles method and published by Brothwell, was employed.[13] The adults were divided on this basis into categories 20-25, 25-35, 35-45 and 45+, but these were regarded as indicating successive stages in adult life rather than precise age limits.

In addition to recording all the data on tooth development and attrition which were necessary for age estimation, detailed records were also made of developmental abnormalities, morphological features and anomalies, and dental pathological conditions.

## Results

### Age distribution

An important aspect of the study of this material was the assessment of individual age at death, and subsequently an analysis of the age distribution within the two population groups. With respect to the juveniles from both sites, age could be assessed with a moderate degree of confidence in most instances. In some dentitions, the teeth were all at a stage of development appropriate to a particular age in the chronological tables. In others there were some slight discrepancies in the stages of development of different teeth, and in a few these discrepancies were quite large, with a gap of two or three years between the most probable age derived from some teeth and the figure obtained from others. In such cases there is no means of knowing whether some teeth are retarded or others advanced with reference to the true age of the individual. Some teeth are considered to be less variable in their development than others, e.g., the first permanent molars are considered to be relatively stable teeth which show less variation in development than the second or third permanent molars. In difficult cases, more weight would be placed on the 'stable' teeth in age assessment.

Assessment of adult age, based on the degree of attrition of the permanent molars, could be attempted in most specimens from Kissonerga-Mosphilia. The severity of *post mortem* erosion and the presence of extensive dental disease made age estimation much more difficult in the adults from Lemba-Lakkous. In some cases no closer estimate could be made than mature adult. This vague category also had to be used when insufficient teeth were present on which to base a closer estimate.

---

11  Smith 1991.
12  Miles 1963.
13  Brothwell 1972.

**Lemba-Lakkous**  **Kissonerga-Mosphelia**

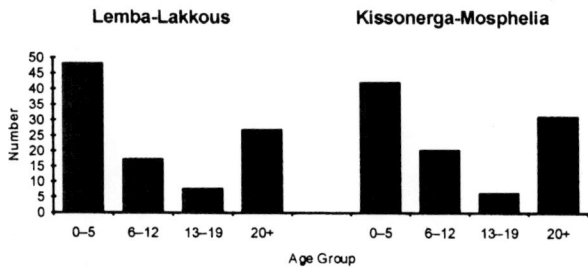

Fig. 10.1 Histogram showing age distribution in the
skeletal material from the sites at Lemba-Lakkous and
Kissonerga-Mosphelia

For the analysis of age distribution at the two sites,
the material was first grouped into the following categories: birth to 5.9 years, 6 to 12.9 years, 13 to 19.9 years, and
all those over 20 years. The resulting age distribution is
shown in Table 10.1 and Fig. 10.1.

The age distribution pattern is virtually identical in
the material from the two sites. In both groups there is a
marked preponderance of juveniles. Only 27% of individuals recovered from Lemba-Lakkous and 31% of those
from Kissonerga-Mosphilia were aged over 20 years at the
time of death.

An attempt has been made to examine the age distribution among the adults, though the numbers are small,
and the difficulties of assessing age in the Lemba-
Lakkous adults have been mentioned. The results are
shown in Table 10.2.

The age distribution of the Lemba-Lakkous adults is
undoubtedly skewed as a result of the high proportion
classified simply as mature adult. In fact, many of these
were thought to be relatively elderly and none could have
been in the category 20-25. The figures for the Kissonerga-
Mosphilia group reflect a truer picture of the age distribution in that group. In spite of the difficulties inherent
in attempting to compare the two groups of adults, it
appears that there is a somewhat higher proportion of the
youngest adults in the Kissonerga-Mosphilia group and a
higher proportion of the older adults at Lemba-Lakkous.
However, when the number of adults in the 20-25 category
in each group was compared with the number at all other
ages, a $\chi^2$ test showed that there was no statistically
significant difference between the groups.

The overall picture for both sites is that of skeletal
material consisting largely of juveniles with a small
proportion of adults.

## Dental pathology

There was evidence of dental disease among the
Chalcolithic people of western Cyprus. In prehistoric and
mediaeval populations, dental disease is found mainly
among the adults, and this proved to be the case in the
Cypriot Chalcolithic material.

The lesions of dental caries were plain to see, a few
located on the occlusal aspects of the crowns of the teeth,
but the majority situated at the necks of the teeth either
on an approximal surface or on the buccal surface. Some
of the larger lesions were sufficiently deep to have caused
exposure of the pulp of the tooth. This situation resulted
in pulp infection, which then tracked through the root
canal to the apex of the root, and if the tooth was still in
situ in the alveolar bone, an abscess cavity could usually
be observed around the root apex. In multi-rooted teeth
such as molars more than one root might be affected. In
some instances, carious destruction of the tooth had
progressed so far that the crown had been lost and only a
root stump remained.

Sufficient material was present to allow figures for
the prevalence of dental caries in the two Cypriot population groups to be calculated. In skeletal material such as
this, few dentitions are complete and it is therefore
impossible to assess the presence of caries on an individual basis, or to express caries prevalence in terms of the
'DMFS index' (decayed, missing and filled surfaces)
which is employed in the study of dental caries in living
populations. Instead, a simpler procedure must be followed, that of calculating the number of teeth which show
carious lesions as a percentage of all teeth erupted and
therefore at risk of caries.

The percentage prevalence of dental caries in adolescents and adults of the two Cypriot groups is shown in
Table 10.3.

In the Lemba-Lakkous group, adolescents, young
adults and mature adults had been equally affected by
dental caries, with some 6% of permanent teeth erupted
and at risk showing evidence of the disease. The Kisson-

Table 10.2: Age distribution, Cypriot Chalcolithic sites

| Age group | Lemba-Lakkous | | Kissonerga-Mosphilia | |
|---|---|---|---|---|
| | n | % | n | % |
| 20-25 | 3 | 21.4 | 9 | 45.0 |
| 25-35 | 1 | 7.2 | 5 | 25.0 |
| 35-45 | 2 | 14.3 | 3 | 15.0 |
| 45+ | 0 | 0 | 0 | 0 |
| mature adult | 8 | 57.1 | 3 | 15.0 |
| *Total* | 14 | 100.0 | 20 | 100.0 |

| | Lemba-Lakkous | | | Kissonerga-Mosphilia | | |
|---|---|---|---|---|---|---|
| Age group | No. Teeth erupted | No. Teeth carious | % teeth carious | No. Teeth erupted | No. Teeth carious | % teeth carious |
| 13-19.9 | 99 | 6 | 6.1 | 101 | 0 | 0 |
| 20-25 | 68 | 4 | 5.9 | 161 | 1 | 0.6 |
| mature | 161 | 10 | 6.2 | 177 | 9 | 5.1 |
| *Total* | 328 | 20 | 6.1 | 439 | 10 | 2.3 |

*Table 10.3 Caries prevalence, Cypriot Chalcolithic Sites*

erga-Mosphilia group showed a different pattern; there was no evidence of dental caries in the adolescents, while young adults were only slightly affected, and dental caries appeared mainly in the mature adults. Even in the latter group, the prevalence of dental caries was lower than that observed in the Lemba-Lakkous group. There is a noticeable difference in overall caries prevalence between the sites: 6.1% at Lemba-Lakkous and 2.3% at Kissonerga-Mosphilia. A $\chi^2$ test applied to the overall caries prevalence figures showed that the difference between the sites was statistically significant at the 1% level of significance.

There was less evidence of dental caries in juveniles below the age of 12.9 years, but even here caries appeared at a lower rate in the Kissonerga-Mosphilia group than at Lemba-Lakkous. In those aged 6-12.9, none of 78 erupted permanent teeth showed caries in the Kissonerga-Mosphilia children, while 2 of 85 erupted permanent teeth showed carious lesions in the Lemba-Lakkous group (2.4%). With respect to the deciduous dentition, 2 of 256 deciduous teeth at Kissonerga-Mosphilia were carious (0.78%), but 2 of 194 deciduous teeth at Lemba-Lakkous (1.03%).

Other dental pathological conditions were observed in both Lemba-Lakkous and Kissonerga-Mosphilia dentitions. These included dental abscesses or cysts, due either to extensive dental caries or to severe attrition exposing the pulps of the teeth; periodontal disease; and *in vivo* loss of teeth. Good preservation of alveolar bone is necessary in order to make a satisfactory study of these conditions, and unfortunately *post mortem* damage to bone in the Cypriot Chalcolithic skeletons precluded a full investigation in this material.

## Anomalies of dental development

Congenital absence of teeth, which indicates failure of the tooth germ to develop, was observed in a few instances. One or more of the third molars were congenitally absent in two individuals from Lemba-Lakkous and in five from Kissonerga-Mosphilia. One of the Lemba-Lakkous individuals lacking third molars also showed congenital absence of both mandibular second premolars. A maxillary permanent lateral incisor may have been congenitally absent in another child from Lemba-Lakkous. In one of the Kissonerga-Mosphilia individuals lacking third molars, one mandibular second premolar

was congenitally absent and its counterpart was embedded, i.e., had developed but failed to erupt.

An embedded canine was observed in one maxilla from Lemba-Lakkous, and the same condition was seen in two maxillae from Kissonerga-Mosphilia. An embedded mandibular second premolar from Kissonerga-Mosphilia has been mentioned above.

One specimen from Lemba-Lakkous showed a supernumerary tooth, in the form of a peg-shaped incisor, and a midline supernumerary incisor, known as a mesiodens, was observed in one dentition from Kissonerga-Mosphilia.

A very rare anomaly of tooth development known as a dilated composite odontome, in which the dental tissues are arranged in a bizarre form not resembling a normal tooth, was observed in an individual from Kissonerga-Mosphilia.

The presence of *post mortem* erosion of enamel, particularly in the Lemba-Lakkous material, made difficult the assessment of the developmental defect of enamel known as enamel hypoplasia. Some degree of hypoplasia was observed in two of the Lemba-Lakkous children and in six individuals from Kissonerga-Mosphilia. The condition affected only a few teeth in each individual, and other teeth which must have been developing at the same time were unaffected. Gross hypoplasia with pitted defects of many teeth was not observed at either site.

A nasopalatine cyst (a developmental bone cyst of the maxilla) was observed in one individual from Kissonerga-Mosphilia, and a bone cyst of unknown aetiology was seen in the mandible of another individual from the same site.

## Discussion

The preponderance of juveniles in both the Lemba-Lakkous and Kissonerga-Mosphilia groups is remarkable. Even taking into account the high mortality rate expected among young children in prehistoric populations, it seems unlikely that the age distribution of the skeletal material found can accurately represent the pattern of mortality of these village groups. Taking into consideration the length of occupation proposed for the sites, a far greater number of adult burials would be expected. It seems probable that most of the adults were buried elsewhere. Whether all the children were buried around the houses, or whether those so treated formed a special group within the community, must be a matter for speculation.

The statistically significant difference in caries prevalence between Lemba-Lakkous and Kissonerga-Mosphilia was unexpected. Factors involved in controlling dental caries may be genetic, dietary or bacteriological, and it is impossible to say which may have been at work here.

The published skeletal material which is geographically closest to Lemba-Lakkous and Kissonerga-Mosphilia comes from the Neolithic site at Khirokitia.[14] Caries prevalence in this report appears to have been calculated in a slightly different way to that employed in the present work, but a little reworking of the figures suggests that the caries prevalence at Khirokitia may have been 2.3% of the teeth at risk, which is exactly the prevalence observed at Kissonerga-Mosphilia. Dascoulis recorded a caries prevalence of 2.3% in Greek skeletal material from c.2000 BC.[15] For Predynastic Egyptian material, a caries prevalence of 2.3% has also been recorded,[16] though Grilletto recorded caries prevalence of 5.72 % for Predynastic Egyptian and 4.65% for Dynastic Egyptian material.[17]

The caries prevalence at Kissonerga-Mosphilia is also fairly close to figures produced for some western European prehistoric populations. For example, the percentages of carious teeth in the Scottish Neolithic and Bronze Age groups were 1.7% and 1.8% respectively.[18] Similar figures of between 1.5% and 3.0% have been recorded for several other Neolithic populations in Europe (England, Germany, Sweden and Denmark).[19] Several groups of French Neolithic skeletons have produced caries prevalence figures varying from 3.2%[20] to 4.2%.[21]

By contrast with these figures, the caries prevalence of 6.1% at Lemba-Lakkous seems relatively high (a level as high as this was not reached in Scotland until the high mediaeval period). However, even higher prevalence figures have been recorded in the eastern Mediterranean: 12.1% for Greece in the Neolithic-Early Helladic period[22] and 9.0% for second millennium BC Crete.[23] Some higher caries prevalence figures have also been published for western European Neolithic groups, e.g., 7.2% in Provence[24] and 8.3% in Switzerland.[25]

In order to find an explanation for the relatively high caries prevalence at Lemba-Lakkous, it was suggested in an earlier publication that the Lemba diet may have been softer, stickier and richer in carbohydrates than some other prehistoric diets.[26] This may still be correct. But is it reasonable to suppose that the diet at Kissonerga-Mosphilia, only a mile away, was markedly different - or is some other explanation to be sought for the difference in caries prevalence? In view of the considerable variability in caries prevalence recorded for Neolithic material in Europe and the Near East, it may be wiser merely to indicate the difference in caries prevalence between the two Cypriot Chalcolithic groups without attempting an explanation. It should of course be pointed out that the figures for caries prevalence which have been quoted above have been obtained by many different observers whose criteria for the diagnosis of dental caries may not be comparable.

The increase in caries prevalence with age in the Kissonerga-Mosphilia group is in accordance with observations of caries prevalence in Scottish mediaeval skeletal material.[27] The Lemba-Lakkous group is unusual in having a similar caries rate in adolescents and adults.

*Acknowledgements*

I am indebted to Professor Edgar Peltenburg, Department of Archaeology, University of Edinburgh for allowing me to study the human dentitions from Lemba-Lakkous and Kissonerga-Mosphilia. I am also grateful to Dr M.E.Watt, Department of Oral Sciences, University of Glasgow Dental School for assistance with the computer processing of data.

14 Angel 1953.
15 Dascoulis 1956.
16 Brothwell 1963b.
17 Grilletto 1973.
18 Lunt 1974.
19 Quoted by Brothwell 1963b.
20 Hartweg 1945.
21 Brabant 1969; Maytie 1972.
22 Angel 1944.
23 Carr 1960.
24 Puech 1977.
25 Brabant 1971.
26 Lunt 1985.
27 Lunt 1986.

# 11 Approaches to the Archaeological Study of Death with Particular Reference to Ancient Cyprus

## Lynn Bright

ABSTRACT— *There has been a lack of interest in 'Q anatss' in Bronze and Iron Age Cyprus. Death, is one area of research which, despite the overwhelming material evidence available has until recently, remained conspicuously absent. This paper, is a survey of one important aspect of the archaeology of death, the anthropology of ancient Cyprus, with some suggestions for future directions in research.*

## Early Interest in Cypriot Burial Sites

Cyprus attracted travellers and treasure hunters to her shores long before the advent of official archaeology. The island's position in the Eastern Mediterranean resulted in it being used, especially in the Middle Ages, by pilgrims on their way to the Holy Land. Some of these travellers were no doubt content to roam around, exploring and enjoying the beauty of the countryside but it seems that many were interested in the ancient monuments, particularly locating lost sites.[1] It was not long, however, before the attention of some men turned to the financial gains to be made from the age old business of tomb robbing.

Luigi Palma di Cesnola and Hamilton Lang were but two of the many men who were interested in Cypriot tombs, prior to the instigation of the rule allowing only official excavations on the island. Those who engaged in excavation were unscrupulous in their quest for gold, jewellery and other precious objects which were usually sold for personal financial gain or for expanding their own private collections of artefacts. Even the local Cypriots themselves, were not above robbing their ancestors for valuable pieces.[2] There is a description of local tomb

looting as early as 1573.[3] Indeed there are many tombs which may have been robbed in antiquity and most ancient sites boast some examples of looting. Bamboula at Kourion, for example, was found to have more than a quarter of the total number of Late Cypriot tombs plundered.[4]

I shall not attempt to produce a comprehensive history of illicit Cypriot excavations here, as it has been adequately covered by others. Nor do I intend to chart the early history of official excavation on the island. I refer the reader instead to Elizabeth Goring's excellent guide to the Royal Museum of Scotland's exhibition 'Aphrodite's Island: art and archaeology of ancient Cyprus'.[5]

## Interest in Cypriot Burial Practices

Both the Bronze and Iron Ages have been known and available for study to both archaeologists and anthropologists since the first excavations in the nineteenth century and much research has already been devoted to them. Studies have been made of various aspects of tombs notably tomb architecture and grave goods, especially ceramics and jewellery. Death itself, however, has largely been ignored. This is particularly surprising when one considers the nature of a great many of the published excavation reports, particularly the great tomes of the Swedish Cyprus Expedition. For despite the fact that

---

1    Two such Medieval cleric pilgrims were Bishop Wilbrand von Oldenburg [1211] and the Westphalian priest Ludolf von Suchen [1336]. (Cf. Cobham 1908, 14, 19 and Maier & Karageorghis 1984, 16) whilst two later pilgrims, Ludwig Tschudi (1519) and Francesco Attar (c. 1540) correctly identified the ruins at Kouklia. (Cf.Maier & Karageorghis 1984, 16 and nt.3). Scholars, like R. Pococke and the Oriental scholar Joseph Hammer von Purgstall, began to follow in the footsteps of the pilgrims (Cf. Maier & Karageorghis 1984, 16 and nt.5.).

2    Goring 1988, 1.

3    Maier & Karageorghis 1984, 16.
4    Benson 1972, 10ff.
5 .   The exhibition which was held in Edinburgh ran from 14th April to 4th September 1988. Elizabeth Goring also explored the early history of Cypriot excavation (Goring 1983).

thousands of pages have been devoted to the description of tombs and their contents and that the vast majority of the artefacts adorning the museums have come from tombs, with the notable exception of H. Cassimatis (who produced a lengthy article on the burial customs on the island from the Early Bronze Age through to and including the Cypro-Archaic period),[6] no one has yet seen fit to draw together the mass of scattered information relating to death in the Cypriot Bronze and Iron Ages. It is paradoxical that the archaeology that has for so many years concentrated on tombs in Cyprus has, by the same token, ignored the study of death. It is a situation which is mirrored in the ancient Near East.[7]

Several scholars over the years have, of course, referred to the burial practices. They are numerous, not least because almost all of our knowledge of the Early and Middle Cypriot period, for example, comes from tombs and any writer incorporating these periods into a study is therefore almost certain to refer, however briefly, to some aspect of the burial customs. The approach that these writers have assumed takes two forms. Firstly, there are those like E. Gjerstad[8] who list the salient features of the practices, noting in particular the rite of inhumation, the form of the tomb (architecture), the occurrence of multiple burial, the type of grave goods accompanying the dead and so on. Examples of sites displaying each trait are included for illustration. The second approach concentrates on a particular site or tomb as the case may be and develops a more general account of the burial customs. The practices are then charted and parallels are drawn from elsewhere both in and outside the island. An example of this type of approach can be seen in the publication of Tomb 23 (LCIII) at Hala Sultan Tekké by Karin Niklasson.[9] In this particular study, Niklasson attempted not only to publish the finds from the tomb in question but also to give an outline of the burial customs to be found in Cyprus during that period. More recently, some scholars have turned towards a social anthropological approach. Rupp[10] and Keswani[11] in particular, have used mortuary data to discuss social status and hierarchy in Late Bronze and Iron Age Cyprus.

## Early Interest in Human Skeletal Remains

Although people have been interested in the human body for many years, it has tended to be either from a medical standpoint or an artistic one. From the Renaissance onwards Western societies have focused their attention on human origins, although at first it seems the only evidence about early man came from ancient writings or from encounters between Western people and so called 'primitive' societies. Interestingly, as early as 1668, the English mathematician Robert Hooke suggested that fossils could be used to define a geological timetable but the dearth of fossil evidence, particularly relating to humans, and the lack of sophisticated archaeological techniques together prevented any progress in the development of what is now termed physical or palaeoanthropology.[12] At the same time other evidence was slowly being discovered which would later help to document the evolution of man's achievements. A flint tool found in Grays Inn Road in 1690 by Conyers was associated with the bones of an elephant and later antiquarians dated it to the Roman period. Further flint implements were found by Frere in 1797 at Hoxne in Suffolk. He declared that they belonged 'to a very ancient period indeed, even before that of the present world'.[13] It was not until much later that their true origin and date was discovered.

The social and physical development of man were controversial subjects to discuss, involving moral questions and dispute over biblical teaching. Archbishop Ussher had worked out that the creation of man occurred on the 23rd March 4004 BC and this view was still widely held. One wonders of course, what the reaction would have been to recent genetic evidence which has led some to suggest that apes should be classed as a separate species of man! Palaeontology and general vertebrate taxonomy had begun to develop in the 18th century but there was virtually no fossil evidence. Fossils found in 1820 by von Schlottheim in Upper Saxony attracted little public attention, and the find was not described in the 'Anthropological Review' until over 40 years later. Robert Chambers' book of 1843, 'Vestiges of the natural history of Creation', though inaccurate and somewhat unscientific brought the idea of the creation as a form of development over time to the general public. When Darwin's 'Origin of Species' appeared in 1859 some criticism of this work seems to have derived from confusion between Chambers' ideas and Darwin's more cautiously scientific discussion. In Britain, it was Richard Owen, a distinguished anatomist and palaeontologist, who led the opposition to the evolutionary theory at this time. The London Ethnological Society was formed in 1843 and the London Anthropological Society in 1863. Both societies published journals covering aspects of physical and palaeoanthropogy. The Anthropological Institute of Great Britain and Ireland (now the Royal Anthropological Institute) was formed in

---

6  Cassimatis 1973, 118ff.
7  As the organisers of this conference noted in their first circular, 'Despite the number of excavated burials mentioned or detailed in archaeological reports burial practices in the ancient Near East have received little attention'.
8  Gjerstad 1926, 52ff.
9  Niklasson 1983.
10  Rupp 1985 and 1989.
11  Keswani 1988.

12  The literature seems to make a distinction in the between the idea of 'palaeoanthropology', the history of which can be clearly documented as the search for the evolutionary development of humans, and that of physical anthropology (or just anthropology) which was concerned with the different characteristics of 'homo sapiens', work on which is bound to shade into archaeology or even cultural or social anthropology. As will be seen below, the scientific emphasis of anthropologists, anatomists, palaeontologists etc working around 1850 to mid 20th century centred around probably the most important *anthropological* question of the time, the search for man's origins.
13  Oakley 1972, 3f.

1871 from the union of these two societies. At the time of the early (official and unofficial) excavations on Cyprus, therefore, there was little academic interest in human skeletal material, which did not help to answer the question of the origin of man. This probably explains why there is little or nothing written on that subject dating from that period.

By 1908 when J.G. Frazer took up the first professorship of social anthropology in Britain at Liverpool University, further fossil finds had confirmed the existence of a neanderthal race but apart from this and Dubois' finds in Java there was still very little evidence for early man. During the first part of this century the main British evidence was that of Piltdown Man, which had not yet been exposed as a hoax. In Britain, paleoanthropology was mainly developed by leading figures either in anatomy or geology, men like Grafton Elliot Smith an anatomist specialising in the study of the brain (who worked on Egyptian material); Arthur Smith Woodward, Keeper of Geology at the Natural History Museum and palaeontologist; and Arthur Keith the anatomist.

Unlike archaeologists, physical anthropologists or palaeontologists are not concerned with the accoutrements of death but tend to focus solely on the tangible evidence of the corpse. The history of interest in human skeletons, like interest in grave goods, did not begin with the birth of archaeology. During some periods in the past, a certain class of human remains has had an intrinsic value. The bones of those thought to be saints were often used as holy relics, a word taken from the Latin reliquiae meaning 'remains'.[14]

The men who were digging up human remains in Cyprus, both as a by-product of tomb robbing and in the early days of excavation, however, were not interested in them because they did not represent examples of venerated ancestors, saints or heroes. The skeletons were in the majority of cases treated with utter disrespect, even by some of the so-called scientists (archaeologists). Having said that, it is only fair to point out, however, that the literature also highlights a few examples of men who were somewhat concerned about the plundering of the tombs of the dead. In his book, 'Cyprus As I Saw it in 1879', Sir Samuel Baker wrote, 'It is a curious contradiction in our

ideas of propriety.... that we regard as felonious a man who disinters a body and steals a ring from the fingers of the corpse a few days after burial in an English churchyard, but we honour and admire an individual who upon a wholesale scale digs up old cemeteries and scatters the bones ... and having collected the jewellery, arms and objects of vanity that were buried with them, neglects the once honoured bones but sells the gold and pottery to the highest bidder.'[15] Several years later in 1888 and 1890 respectively, two archaeologists wrote about the bodies which they had encountered during the course of their excavations. Hogarth wrote, 'May I remark that the bones of the Paphians were restored to their resting-place after their graves had been plundered.'[16] Munro wrote, 'In conclusion it may be remarked that, although we have spoken throughout of our unhallowed depredations with the professional callousness of the hardened digger, yet the sacred peace of the dead was as little disturbed as the nature of our task permitted. They were robbed of their vessels and their trinkets, but their bones were respected and their resting-places closed again for their tranquil possession. Requiescent in pace.'[17] It is not the general practice in archaeology today to re-bury the bones of the dead discovered during excavation although there are of course incidences where this does occur such as the fairly recent excavation at Spitalfields in London.

In 1878, the year of the signing of the Convention of Defensive Alliance between Great Britain and Turkey, unauthorised excavations in Cyprus were banned. Amongst those terminated was that of A.P. di Cesnola at Salamis. Despite hints that perhaps a few illicit excavations persisted, a period of 'official' excavating took place. Ohnefalsch Richter was amongst the most active of the early excavators, digging at sites such as Tamassos and Idalion (the title of his famous unpublished manuscript. Despite Myres desire for archaeology to be used as a 'weapon of historical science', the improvements cannot always be detected and the information collected was often unreliable. As Goring comments, 'Archaeology in Cyprus continued to be dogged by poor standards, despite Myres' refreshing professionalism, and the British Museum's subsequent excavations at Kourion and Enkomi can hardly be called scientific.... The damage was such that the material from these excavations is scarcely more valuable in terms of archaeological evidence than the finds made by Lang or Cesnola.'[18] The position regarding the skeletons unfortunately remained the same and excavators continued to find them of little academic interest. An example of such a reference to the human remains around the turn of the century is the publication of Tomb 47 at Enkomi. A simple, single sentence describes them: 'This tomb contained about 4ft of human bones.'[19]

---

14 Many Greek cities had temples which housed the remains of their legendary heroes which were purported to protect the city. Plutarch, for example, relates how Cimon brought the bones of Theseus back to Athens from Scyros and reburied them there. (Cf. Plutarch, The Rise and Fall of Athens, 1:36) Other similar Greek examples are the cities of Epidaurus (Asclepios), Elis (Pelops) and Argos (Tantalus). Geoffrey Ashe quotes the earliest reliable (Christian) relics story as that originating in a letter from Smyrna in A.D. 156 which describes how the bones of St. Polycarp, who was burnt at the stake, were gathered up by his followers: 'We took up his bones, more precious than jewels and finer than refined gold, and laid them in a suitable place where the Lord will permit us to gather ourselves together, and celebrate the anniversary of his martyrdom.' (Cf. Ashe 1971, 2353). Relics of this kind assumed great importance during the Middle Ages and resting place of the more prominent saints added to the status of the church where they were housed and inspiring devout Christians to go on pilgrimages.

---

15 Baker, 1879, 53.
16 Gardner *et al.* 1888, 271.
17 Munro & Tubbs, 1890, 31.
18 Goring 1988, 29.
19 Murray *et al.* 1900, 50.

Modern writers and excavators are happily more en-
lightened, although not many can be said to be actually
excited by human remains. As Brothwell noted in 1963
and again in 1981, 'Bones are commonly an embarrass-
ment to archaeologists, even though the skeleton offers a
no less fruitful subject of enquiry than ceramics, metals,
architecture or any other field of historical or prehistorical
study.' The situation is not, therefore, confined to Cyprus
alone but it seems is common almost everywhere.[20]

The Swedes have emerged in the forefront of early
palaeoanthropological work on Cypriot human material.
Perhaps the reason for this lies in the fact that Sweden
already had a series of flourishing Palaeontological
Institutes such as that at Upsaala which had handled
material of international importance. For a time, fossil
finds from China overshadowed Raymond Dart's find
from Taung.[21] The National Geological Survey of China
liaised with various Swedish institutions (aided by
J.G. Andersson, a Swedish mining adviser to the Chinese
and a committee chaired by the Crown Prince of Sweden).
From 1921 onwards many fossils of both humans and
animals were recovered and sent to Professor Wiman's
Palaeontological Institute at Uppsala. When the Swedish
Cyprus Expedition excavated on the island much of the
human material, which consisted mainly of crania, was
also sent to Sweden. It was, however, not studied immediately even though the institutions were well equipped to
deal with it, perhaps because it was not deemed to be as
important as the Chinese material for example.

The other question with which anthropologists were
concerned, was race. I think that might go some way
towards explaining why only the (perfect) skulls were kept
from some of the early excavations, such as those noted
above because it was cranial measurements which formed
the bases of the studies of racial distinction. The first
study on the anthropology of Cyprus was published by
Buxton in 1920.[22] This was concerned with a living
sample of males and a small group of ancient crania. The
first specific report on the anthropology of the prehistoric
population of Cyprus did not emerge until Fürst's work of
1933,[23] although as will be seen below, only a general
description undertaken by the archaeologist, rather than
an anthropologist, usually appears.

The physical anthropologist is primarily interested
in the physical attributes of a specimen. The first task is to
establish its age and sex and subsequently examines it in

the light of stature, health, ethnic affinity and so on. In its
simplest form, the evidence for sex and age in modern
burials might take the form of information obtained from
a study of tombstones. In older cemeteries, however, more
complex methods are often necessary to determine even
this most basic information. On rare occasions an
excavation takes place where the traditional anthropological techniques are used to examine the osteological
material but where tombstones or other inscriptions are
available at the same time which act as both an independent check and as an additional source of information.
One such extraordinary excavation was that of the crypt of
Christ Church at Spitalfields, in the City of London,
referred to above.

We have no demographic information from ancient
tombstones or the like. Even in the latter part of the
period when Cypriots were able to write, The earliest
Cypriot tomb inscription is written in Phoenician and has
been dated to the 9thC BC but this is without provenance.
Although tomb inscriptions become common at sites such
as Kition from c.800 BC no age or sex is recorded for an
examinable skeleton. When dealing with the Cypriot
Bronze and Iron Age material, the sole source of information is, in the majority of cases, that of the often meagre
osteological descriptions in the site publications. I hesitate
to use the term 'report' as full reports for earlier excavations are relatively rare. An example of this is the description of the material from Tomb 301 Chamber B of the
Swedish excavations in 1927 at Lapithos Vrysi tou
Barba.[24] 'In the centre of the chamber were found the
remains of a corpse, which had originally been placed,
sitting with the arms clasped around the knees and facing
south. The pelvis and some of the vertebrae had fallen
backwards and were found in a dorsal position, but the
position of the femur and fragments of the humerus gave
conclusive evidence as regards the original position'.
These remarks are very interesting as regards burial
customs but it is unfortunately the only information in the
publication about this particular skeleton. In addition
to this there is no other reference to an anthropological
study for this or any other tomb from the necropolis at
Lapithos Vrysi tou Barba. Again writing about Tomb 301
from this cemetery Gjerstad states, 'It is worth mentioning
that Chamber A and Chamber B seemed to contain only
female skeletons, and that of the only male skeleton was
found in Chamber C.' The sex of these skeletons appears
not to have been determined by any anthropological
examination or if it was this remained unmentioned. The
evidence seems to have hinged instead on the associated
grave offerings. In addition to two Red Polished II
cooking pots (Nos. 7 and 9), Chamber A contained a Red
Polished spindle-whorl (No. 8). No bronze objects were
found in Chambers A or B. The skeleton in Chamber C
on the other hand, which was identified as being that of a
male was furnished with two bronze swords (Nos. 3 and
13), three knives (Nos. 6, 7 and 15), a scraper (No.5) and

20  Brothwell 1963 and 1981, Introduction. In the 1981 (third)
    edition the word 'embarrassment' has been replaced by
    'problem'.
21  Raymond Dart was a junior colleague of Elliott Smith at UCL
    and it was he (as Professor of Anatomy at the Witwatersrand
    University) who discovered the first remains of Australo pith-
    ecus africanus at Taung, South Africa in 1922. However, it was
    not until the mid 1930s onwards in the light of subsequent finds
    by Robert Broom at Taung, Sterkfontein and Kromdraai, that
    their true significance was realised by British anthropologists.
    These later finds were classified as two types of australopith-
    ecus- 'africanus' and the heavier 'robustus'.
22  Buxton 1920.
23  Fürst 1933.

24  Gjerstad et al. 1934, 37.

two bronze tweezers (Nos. 4 and 14).[25] Bronze and 'weapons' appear to be seen here as exclusively male accoutrements. This is an improvement on the burial description of Enkomi Tomb 47 but in 1927 it appears that despite the advancement in excavation technique there was a long way to go with regard to anthropology.

As has been seen above, relatively little anthropological work was carried out on the early excavated material from Cyprus, indeed much of it seems to have been simply thrown away. Modern researchers interested in examining or re-examining the material are lucky to be able to find the skulls, as these often seem to be the only part of the skeleton kept. In Percy Christian's letter to Murray dated May 25th 1896 (quoted by Goring, 1988) he writes 'We had a very interesting tomb with about 4ft of human bones ... I will send you as many skulls as I can get perfect.'[26] An example of such a collection of Cypriot skulls is that stored in the Department of Anatomy in the University of Lünd, Sweden. There is a certain amount of other skeletal material in this collection but it apparently consists mainly of skulls from a variety of sites. Enkomi and Ayios Iakovos, Melia are well represented in this collection whilst there are, for example, only four skulls originating from Bellapais Vounous. The exact excavation and tomb to which each belonged is not always clear, for example Skull No. III and Skull No. IV from Vounous could have been from a French or a Cypriot excavation as the tomb numbers are unknown.[27] To be fair to the excavators, on the other hand, it was the skulls that were one of the most likely parts of the body to be preserved in the majority of cases and they presumably thought misguidedly that the skull contained all the information that it was necessary to know.

When work was carried out on the material, it appears to have sometimes been ignored in the site publication and subsequent discussions. Gjerstad for example, does not refer to anthropological work carried out by Fürst, in the excavation reports even though some age and sex estimates had already been attempted. In other instances the work is mentioned but perhaps because the work was never published or a reference was not quoted, the original source of the information can never be examined. A good example of this is the article by George McFadden on Tomb 40 at Kaloriziki. He wrote that the cremated remains from this tomb were examined by Gejvall and proceeded to summarise the findings. 'Professor N.G. Gejvall of the Royal Academy of Antiquities and History at Stockholm, who was kind enough to examine them, identified ten pieces of a human skull belonging to a person between 50 and 70 years of age whom he believed to be almost certainly a woman....'[28] He failed, however, to quote the reference, if indeed there was one, for this very important work. The information is in effect very much second-hand information and as such

may be confusing. On the previous page McFadden says, 'It is the opinion of Professor N.G. Gejvall, the Swedish anthropologist who was kind enough to examine the cremated remains, that they belonged almost beyond question to a woman in middle life.'[29] As the quote from McFadden's following page illustrates, there are now two statements regarding the age of this cremated individual. Firstly, 'she' was middle-aged and secondly, 'she' was between 50 and 70 years old. A question must be raised here as to whether the statements are indeed compatible as most anthropologists regard archaeological specimens with an age of 50+ as 'mature' or even 'old' rather than middle-aged for statistical purposes. It would, therefore, be desirable to have access to the source, in this case Gejvall's report in order to check these points.

## Patterns of Past Research on Cypriot Skeletal Remains

Past research on the Cypriot osteological material can be divided into five main categories.[30] Firstly, there was Buxton who produced his 'Anthropology of Cyprus' in 1920.[31] He was essentially interested in the living population. He took a sample of modern males (he did not bother to sample women) and noted their age and key measurements. He included a few specimens from ancient Cyprus but his sample was relatively small. Secondly, there are those who produced a purely anthropological examination aimed at a general anthropological description of the ancient Cypriot population rather than confining an investigation into one particular site. The Swedes, Fürst[32] and Hortsjö,[33] in particular favoured this approach. It is probably true to say that Fürst and Hortsjö displayed a bias towards identifying racial affinity.

The third category of specialists which include Angel,[34] Charles[35] and Schwartz[36] are for the most part concerned in the literature with what could perhaps be called osteological site reports, as they deal mainly with material extracted from a particular site and the findings are included in the final publication. Although the members of this group are all appended to a site report it does not follow that their approach is universal as the following brief survey shows.

'Excavations in the Necropolis of Salamis I (Text and Plates)' was published by V. Karageorghis in 1967. Appendix VI by R.P. Charles was devoted to the human remains. He examined ten individuals from the site and as the title of the Appendix (Études des Restes Humains

---

25  Ibid.
26  Goring 1988, n.63.
27  Fischer 1986, 28.
28  McFadden 1954, 131ff.

29  op. cit., 133.
30  The following are examples of the kind of work carried out on the Cypriot material and are not intended to represent an exhaustive list.
31  Buxton 1920.
32  Cf. Fürst 1933.
33  Cf. Hjortsjö 1947.
34  Angel 1972, 148ff.
35  Charles 1967, 147ff.
36  Schwartz 1974, 151ff.

de la Tombe 31) demonstrates, all of the subjects came from the same tomb. It contains a purely anthropological examination of the material with no discussions included, either general or specific. It therefore required no bibliography. Charles was naturally concerned in the first instance with ageing and sexing his ten subjects and went on to make certain observations of the skull. He was particularly concerned with typology. Only three skulls (A, C and G) seem to have been well enough preserved for this observation and he classed all three of them as néo-méditerranéen.[37] He also supplied cranial measurements and indices for the afore mentioned skulls. Subject A was well enough preserved to afford Charles the opportunity of taking post-cranial measurements. The ones he included are for the mandible, right humerus, right radius, femurs and tibias. In addition to these tables, three diagrams are incorporated into the text (Figs 11.1–3). They are all similar and represent and I quote 'Diagramme sagittal du crâne 31(A/B/C) de Salamine (GN:2).'

In 1972 the results of Lawrence Angel's examinations of the skeletal remains of 81 individuals from the Late Cypriot site of Bamboula at Kourion were published as an Appendix (Appendix B) of the site publication by J.L. Benson.[38] He had studied the remains of sixty-one individuals from Bamboula as early as 1949 and a further twenty individuals from J.L. Benson's 1956 excavations both in that year and in 1958. The 1972 report was concerned with the Late Cypriot evidence, Late Cypriot III in particular, as that was the period dealt with in the main site publication. He, therefore, omitted the eleven individuals that he had studied from the Hellenistic tombs at Ayios Ermoyenis near Episkopi[39] and the twenty-five year old woman from Bamboula Tomb 34 as this was of uncertain date.[40] Some of the material described by Angel had previously been published by Hjortsjö and Axmacher in 1959.[41] Angel commments on some of the mistakes that they made in this publication, such as wrongly naming the excavator of the site.[42] In addition to ageing and sexing the material, which consisted for the most part of skulls, he considers each individual in a highly informative manner, providing measurements where appropriate. An overview of topics such as artificial cranial deformation, metopic sutures, browridge sizes, supra-mastoid crests and morphological types is given. The main discussion, however, centres on three main issues (a) a comparison of the population of Late Cypriot Bamboula with both other Cypriots and people from contemporary Mainland Greece (b) the incidence of artificial cranial deformation and (c) the occurrence of thalassaemia and malaria in Cyprus. A summary of the main findings is provided together with a fairly extensive bibliography. Four Tables accompany the text containing: the individual bones with information such as age, sex and so on listed in tabular form; individual measurements and indices; comparative information ('Mean measurements of undeformed male skulls from prehistoric sites in Cyprus and from Mycenaean Greece') and the mean percentage occurrence of morphological types in total adult samples (including deformed skulls) in prehistoric Cyprus and Mycenaean Greece. In short, Angel provides a highly informative report on the Late Cypriot skeletal remains from Bamboula at Kourion and combines anthropological examination with a feasible interpretation.

'The Human Remains from Kition and Hala Sultan Tekké: A Cultural Interpretation by Jeffrey, H. Schwartz appeared as Appendix IV in 'Excavations at Kition I: 1. The tombs (text)' by V. Karageorghis in 1974.[43] He examined eleven individuals (skulls) from Kition and a further eleven from Hala Sultan Tekké (also skulls) as well as samples from Akhera and Pendaiya. A bibliography is supplied at the end of his discussions on this material. It is evident from the outset that Schwartz's interest lies with artificial cranial deformation. He makes no apology for this bias. Three figures and three tables accompany the text. Fig. 1 shows the various types of cranial deformation which could be practised using a cradle-board. Figs 2 and 3 are in fact photographic plates of skulls from Hala Sultan Tekké and Pendaiya/Akhera respectively. His tables include an age and sex distribution chart; non-metric analysis of Late Bronze Age cranial material and the percentage of non-metric traits in individual and total number of sites. Schwartz explains that his approach is 'more qualitative than quantative'[44] and goes on to explain his reasons for not including metric variables.'[45]

The fourth class of study is that where Cypriot material is looked at for more specific traits and where the Cypriot samples form part of a larger international group. An example of this is the study carried out by Jonathan Musgrave and Suzanne Evans of the Department of Anatomy and Computer Centre, University of Bristol. They dealt with ancient crania from Crete, Mainland Greece, Cyprus, Israel and Egypt. They applied the technique of Principal Coordinate Analysis to these skulls in an attempt to ascertain the 'degree of affinity between groups of ancient human populations'[46] Sixteen groups of

37 Charles 1967, 147ff.
38 Angel 1972, 148ff.
39 Angel 1955, 70.
40 Angel 1972, 148.
41 Axmacher and Hjortsjö 1959.
42 Angel 1972, 148.

43 Schwartz 1974, 151ff.
44 Schwartz 1974, 151.
45 'The omission of discussions of metric variables is based on inconsistencies which arose when various approaches... to statistics-for-small-samples were applied to the data: that is to say, for example, when applying the Student's t-test where one equation would give a significant difference in head length between males and females, another would not. Rather than misuse the data and the statistics, this analysis will be reserved for a later date when larger sample sizes are available for study.
46 The papers referred to were two given in 1978 by Musgrave and Evans, the first at a meeting of the Society for the Study of Human Biology in Cambridge in April and the second at the XI International Congress of Classical Archaeology held at University College, London in September 1978.

crania were used: Ancient Cretans (Groups 1 to 3), Modern Cretans (Group 4), Bronze Age Mainland Greeks (Groups 5, 6 and 7), Classical Greeks (Group 8), Neolithic Cypriots (Group 9) and Ancient Egyptians (Groups 11 to 16). It is hoped that future multivariate analyses will be carried out on both Neolithic and later material.[47]

The fifth and final category displays a very much more modern approach and incorporates as far as is possible interdisciplinary studies but in particular combines the disciplines of anthropology and archaeology. Two examples of this, taken from 'both sides of the fence' are A. Le Brun and Peter Fischer. In the first example Le Brun writes mainly from an archaeological standpoint but incorporates a degree of anthropological data to describe 'Le traitement des morts et les représentations des vivants a Khirokitia'.[48] Peter Fischer, on the other hand writes as an anthropologist who examined a large collection of crania expanded his field of study to include physiological and pathological information.[49] Part 1 of his work 'Prehistoric Cypriot Skulls' attempts a medico-anthropological investigation. In Part II: The find context. Datings, references, burials and finds, Fischer attempts to correct some of the omissions of the excavators and tomb plan illustrators and tries as far as is possible to match up the existing remains with the archaeological context and associated finds. Part III: Trace element studies by Secondary-Ion-Mass Spectrometry (SIMS) of teeth from archaeological sites on Cyprus is a pilot study attempting to deal with a series of questions relating to the extent to which trace elements can be traced in teeth and used for dating archaeological specimens.

Interestingly, anthropologists such as Domurad are still chasing the elusive question, 'whence the first Cypriots?'[50] Happily, the new search incorporates not only new methods of computer assisted multivariate analyses but more importantly combines the disciplines of anthropology and archaeology. Optimistically, she notes 'Fortunately, the prospects for further study are improving steadily. The importance of human bones as archaeological material has been recognised, and archaeologists have begun to consolidate bones before excavating them, resulting in more representative samples in a better state of preservation. New skeletons are being found at current excavations in the Kalavassos Valley, Khirokitia and Lemba which add to the sample available for comparison.'[51]

## The Cypriot Archaeology of Death - Future Directions

Cypriot archaeology relies heavily on traditional methods and tends not to be interdisciplinary. When death is discussed, its scope is often limited. Traditionally, the archaeological study of death has been synonymous with Burial Customs. Perhaps if the restrictive boundaries of the phrase 'Burial Customs' were to be lifted then perhaps new life would be breathed into the subject of death. A new title might lead to a new approach. This is precisely what seems to have taken place elsewhere. The whole subject of death is no longer simply dubbed Burial Customs but The Archaeology of Death!

An analysis of funerary rites forms an integral part of the study of death and yet the aim of such a study should not be merely to produce a discussion of the material but to identify, as far as is possible, and to discuss, the relationship between both the objects themselves and the living and the dead. It should be as much concerned with what the customs reveal about the person who was buried there, the people who performed particular rites for their dead and the society in which they all once lived. Elizabeth Goring was no doubt aware of this when at a conference in Edinburgh in 1988 she called her portrait of a LCIIA tomb from Kalavasos Ayios Demetrios, *Death in Everyday Life*.[52]

Burial custom studies deal primarily with cemetery evidence. Tomb data is first collected and then subsequently classified. It has been the brief of the excavation report to produce a series of facts and figures relating to a site sometimes with little else by way of discussion. A site report is a primary report and is by its very nature for the most part meant to avoid interpretation. It is left to others to interpret. Many of the interpreters who purport to be interested in death, however, often appear to be only interested in the accoutrements of death displaying no apparent interest in the deceased at all. As I have shown early excavators in Cyprus found skeletons of little academic interest. Their attitude has meant that such material was not kept and is consequently now unavailable to modern scholars. To be fair to the excavators, bearing in mind the often rudimentary methods of excavation, it was the skulls that were one of the most likely parts of the body to be preserved in the majority of cases and they presumably thought misguidedly that the skull contained all the information that it was necessary to know. When Cypriot skeletal material has been examined the results have more often than not been appended to the site report. The anthropologist tends not to refer to the other archaeological evidence and vice versa. Each discipline is treated as a separate entity thus losing much potentially useful discussion.

In some areas the two branches of archaeology are beginning to come closer together. Whilst the traditional

---

47  The extent of the Cypriot groups for later inclusion in these studies are as follows: 1. Bamboula (Late Bronze Age), 2. Enkomi (Late Bronze Age, 3. Iskender (Geometric-Hellenistic), 4. Karavas (Neolithic), 5. Lapethos (Bronze Age), 6. Lapithos (Iron Age), 7. Melia, Enkomi (Bronze Age) and 8. Vounous (Early Bronze Age).
48  Le Brun 1989, 71ff.
49  Fischer 1986.
50  Domurad 1989, 66-70.
51  Domurad 1989, 69.

52  Goring 1989, 95ff.

branch is now ready and willing to take at least some new ideas on board, the new archaeology is at the same time working towards a more cognitive approach. An example of how archaeologists and anthropologists of the 1990s are trying to work towards a greater understanding of each others contributions was the recent informal seminar held by the Royal Anthropological Institute entitled 'Death, Exchange and Deposition'.[53] Although a valiant attempt was made to get the archaeologists and anthropologists to talk to each other, the problem of language and terminology still intervened. The archaeologists tried not to get bogged down in ceramic typology and the anthropologists found it hard not to mention the mother's mother's brother and other kinship terms but with a great deal of effort it was possible to find underlying similarities in the societies about which each side was talking. Collections of articles from writers with different specialist knowledge are also being published. One example of just such an interesting collection, is the book 'Death, Decay and Reconstruction', edited by Boddington, Garland and Janaway. Contributors include archaeologists, anthropologists and forensic scientists. However, Sally Humphreys' observation of 1978 is still largely true today in Cyprus, Greece, Egypt and the Near East, '... archaeology in Greece has still scarcely been touched by the new ideas developing in other fields. It is still oriented towards the study of artifacts and excavation sites rather than the study of communities and their culture.'[54] 'It is true that studies such as that of Maureen J. Alden[55] have now penetrated the ancient Greek world. (Alden concentrated her efforts on plotting Bronze Age population fluctuations in the Argolid using the evidence of the Mycenaean tombs.) but there is a long way to go. As for Cyprus, the main publication for articles on Cypriot archaeology is 'Report of the Department of Antiquities on Cyprus' (RDAC). A glance through backcopies for recent years shows that the emphasis is overwhelmingly that described by Sally Humphreys for Greece in 1978 'the study of artifacts and excavation sites'. The other main publication series is Åström's 'Studies in Mediterranean Archaeology' (SIMA). This list is equally revealing as the bias is similar but with some notable exceptions. Although I have raised this criticism of Cypriot archaeology it must be borne in mind that as Karageorghis said in the Thirteenth J.L. Myres Memorial Lecture of 1985 'A small island has managed to raise the study of its past into a special branch of archaeology which far surpasses its size. We know more perhaps about the archaeology of Cyprus than of any other island of similar size, including Crete.'[56] I firmly believe that 'The Cypriot archaeology of death' has, in the 1990s, a wider scope than pure archaeology alone. Indeed, like the Egyptian udjat, eye of Horus, the phrase itself now seems to encompass something far greater than the sum of the individual parts. This is probably due to two major

influences, the advent of 'new archaeology' in the 1960s and the 'social archaeology' of the 1980s. In order to examine the archaeology of death in its new totality, it is necessary, therefore, to look at the Cypriot evidence in the light of the related disciplines and the methods and techniques they employ rather than in terms of archaeology per se. The work of Rupp has already been mentioned and it is refreshing to look through his bibliography which is peppered with social anthropological references.

New and exciting techniques are also becoming available, such as those borrowed from forensic science. Boddington, Garland and Janaway summed these up in the following paragraph taken from 'Flesh, bones, dust and society'.[57] 'For any cemetery, whether the dead are provided with artefacts or not, the variety of potential analytical techniques is broad. The archaeological investigations of survival, position and association may be complemented with macroscopic and microscopic studies of bone. Observations of morphology, pathology and osteometry may be integrated with techniques such as radiology, histology, chemical analysis, serology, and more recent developments such as DNA extraction, to substantially increase the information recovered from human remains. Such techniques can improve our ability to make statements on age at death, the biological relationships between communities, reconstruction of diets, the diagnosis of palaeo-pathological specimens and the rate of growth during childhood.... Such statements are not, however, achieved by the use of techniques in isolation, as is common practice, but by their use together in an integrated programme of analysis.' As this paragraph reveals, the potential for further results given these techniques is enormous and is steadily growing. Unfortunately few of these sophisticated techniques have yet been applied to the Cypriot material although the work of Fischer for example, is a great step in the right direction.[58]

## A Suggested Research Programme for the Study of the Archaeology of Death

There is always a need for a structured research programme. There is no point in the indiscriminate gathering of facts without any preconception of what they are going to be used for or what they might mean. Adequate research designs are crucial for productive excavations but it is also true that they are invaluable for effective data analysis and problem solving. In order to set up a research programme a set of assumptions must first be made. Taking the example of the relationship between the living and the dead as an example, a series of core assumptions for exploring this relationship might be: firstly, that there was a relationship between the living and the dead during all the archaeological periods under review, irrespective of

53   6th October 1990.
54   Humphreys 1981, 6.
55   Alden 1981.
56   Karageorghis 1987, 15.

57   Boddington et al 1987, 3ff.
58   Fischer 1986.

1. = deceased
2. + living
3. * ritual
4. G grave offerings
5. D domestic/other items
6. T tomb
7. R residence unit

8. B burial place/cemetery
9. S settlement
10. A other activity area
11. ^^environment
12. [] within the island
13. ][ abroad
14. E enquirer

*Fig. 11.1: Burial Custom Variables*

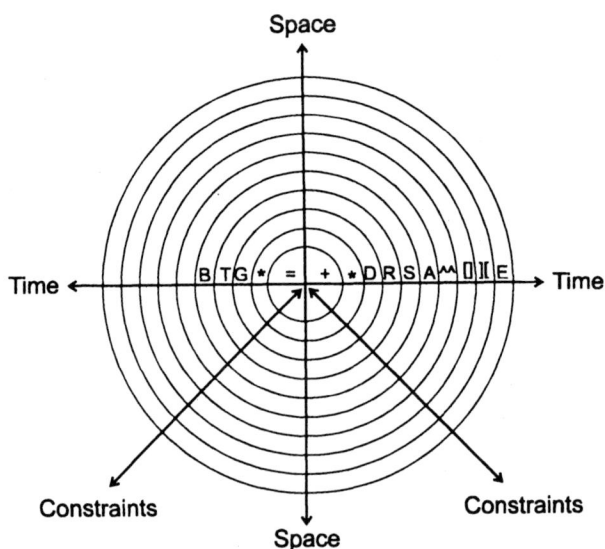

*Fig. 11.2: Research Design*

the number or nature of the archaeological evidence. Secondly, that this relationship was not a static one and thirdly, that the relationship took different forms each of which were bound by a series of constraining factors.

In order to recognise and to explore a series of potential comparisons it is necessary to identify the variables with which one is proposing to work. In the following example I have identified fourteen variables and have assigned each a symbol as can be seen in Fig. 11.1. I chose the fourteen 'variables' on the following basis. Firstly, I assumed that I needed to identify the basic elements which were crucial to any discussion of the dead and the burial customs practised by the living. My initial list therefore included: the skeletal evidence, the accompanying grave offerings, the burial ritual, the tomb, the cemetery or 'burial place' and the local area or 'environment' as I have called it. These six elements are crucial to burial custom description. I deliberately excluded aspects such as the preparation of the body and orientation (of corpse and tomb) as these would be adequately discussed under one of the above headings. I then added an element which I called 'within the island', this being related to the site's position. I avoided the use of the term 'region' because I decided it did not embrace the feeling of its relationship with the entire island in the same way that 'environment' did not. I also included a further element which I called 'abroad', which in burial custom description is covered by terms such as 'parallels elsewhere' and 'foreign influences'.

Although the majority of the evidence is funerary, the relationship between the living and the dead is not concerned solely with the dead. I therefore widened my initial parameters to embrace the sphere of the living population. The first of these new elements I termed quite simply 'the living'. I then included the items used during the course of day to day living, that is to say, 'domestic and other items'. The homes in which these people lived (residence units) and their settlements joined the growing list. The living population differs from the dead in that they engage in a variety of activities. The tools and paraphernalia of these activities were already included under the blanket term 'domestic and other items' but it was necessary to add a further element which I called 'other activity area' because these areas do not always coincide with the place of settlement. Examples of other such activity areas might include sanctuaries and industrial zones. Some of these variables apply primarily to the dead, some to the living and others such as 'environment'

are very obviously, shared by both. Finally, I added the 'enquirer' as I felt that if my historical and anthropological training had taught me anything it was that the information used in research can be profoundly affected by its source.

Rather than allocate a separate circle to each component (Fig. 11.2), I have grouped the similar ones together where possible. The living and the dead share one area as do tombs and residence units and burial places (cemeteries) and settlements. The elements relating to the dead (tomb and burial place) appear on the left side of the diagram and those pertaining to the living (residence unit and settlement) appear on the right. Some circles depict the same symbol on both the left and right hand side, for example ^^ (environment) as this is an element shared by both the living and the dead.

It may be argued that the order of the fourteen variables is immaterial but if research is to be problem oriented it is essential to begin with the central issue. I have, therefore, begun with the central characters, i.e. the deceased and the living and in effect worked outwards in a series of concentric circles, threading the various components together to form a coherent whole. This can be seen in Fig. 11.2 which illustrates my Research Design. It is the opposite approach to a site report or general description which usually begins with the background to the enquiry (variable no.14), moving on to where the site is located (variables 13, 12, 11) and working through the list in roughly the reverse order.

As can be seen in Fig. 11.3 the number of possible combinations jumps from fourteen to a staggering one-hundred-and-five and even this number is not necessarily definitive. Not all of these will be relevant of course and many will not produce fruitful lines of enquiry, perhaps because vital evidence is missing. The aim of identifying them is primarily to raise the awareness of their existence because different combinations of the same basic 'components' could lead to an entirely

| | | | | |
|---|---|---|---|---|
| 1. | = <—> = | 54. | D <—> B | |
| 2. | = <—> + | 55. | D <—> S | |
| 3. | = <—> * | 56. | D <—> A | |
| 4. | = <—> G | 57. | D <—> ^^ | |
| 5. | = <—> D | 58. | D <—> [] | |
| 6. | = <—> T | 59. | D <—> ][ | |
| 7. | = <—> R | 60. | D <—> E | |
| 8. | = <—> B | 61. | T <—> T | |
| 9. | = <—> S | 62. | T <—> R | |
| 10. | = <—> A | 63. | T <—> B | |
| 11. | = <—> ^^ | 64. | T <—> S | |
| 12. | = <—> [] | 65. | T <—> A | |
| 13. | = <—> ][ | 66. | T <—> ^^ | |
| 14. | = <—> E | 67. | T <—> [] | |
| 15. | + <—> + | 68. | T <—> ][ | |
| 16. | + <—> * | 69. | T <—> E | |
| 17. | + <—> G | 70. | R <—> R | |
| 18. | + <—> D | 71. | R <—> B | |
| 19. | + <—> T | 72. | R <—> S | |
| 20. | + <—> R | 73. | R <—> A | |
| 21. | + <—> B | 74. | R <—> ^^ | |
| 22. | + <—> S | 75. | R <—> [] | |
| 23. | + <—> A | 76. | R <—> ][ | |
| 24. | + <—> ^^ | 77. | R <—> E | |
| 25. | + <—> [] | 78. | B <—> B | |
| 26. | + <—> ][ | 79. | B <—> S | |
| 27. | + <—> E | 80. | B <—> A | |
| 28. | * <—> * | 81. | B <—> ^^ | |
| 29. | * <—> G | 82. | B <—> [] | |
| 30. | * <—> D | 83. | B <—> ][ | |
| 31. | * <—> T | 84. | B <—> E | |
| 32. | * <—> R | 85. | S <—> S | |
| 33. | * <—> B | 86. | S <—> A | |
| 34. | * <—> S | 87. | S <—> ^^ | |
| 35. | * <—> A | 88. | S <—> [] | |
| 36. | * <—> ^^ | 89. | S <—> ][ | |
| 37. | * <—> [] | 90. | S <—> E | |
| 38. | * <—> ][ | 91. | A <—> A | |
| 39. | * <—> E | 92. | A <—> ^^ | |
| 40. | G <—> G | 93. | A <—> [] | |
| 41. | G <—> D | 94. | A <—> ][ | |
| 42. | G <—> T | 95. | A <—> E | |
| 43. | G <—> R | 96. | ^^ <—> ^^ | |
| 44. | G <—> B | 97. | ^^ <—> [] | |
| 45. | G <—> S | 98. | ^^ <—> ][ | |
| 46. | G <—> A | 99. | ^^ <—> E | |
| 47. | G <—> ^^ | 100. | [] <—> [] | |
| 48. | G <—> [] | 101. | [] <—> ][ | |
| 49. | G <—> ][ | 102. | [] <—> E | |
| 50. | G <—> E | 103. | ][ <—> ][ | |
| 51. | D <—> D | 104. | ][ <—> E | |
| 52. | D <—> T | 105. | E <—> E | |
| 53. | D <—> R | | | |

*Fig. 11.3: Table of Burial Custom Relationship Possibilities*

different set of conclusions. It can be likened to the popular game of Cluedo with the board representing the island and the rooms the archaeological sites. 'Colonel Mustard in the Library with the Candlestick' will produce a totally different scenario and solution for the detective/player to 'Professor Plum in the Kitchen with the Dagger'!

Furthermore, the number of variables does not end there. Although each symbol represents a variable it does not necessarily represent a single unit. The equals symbol =, for example, stands for the deceased without indicating the age, sex, social status and so on of that individual in life or the treatment the body received after death. This is information which may prove crucial to a community where there is a practice of for example, sexual differentiation. In this instance, a different relationship may exist between a deceased female and her grave offerings and a deceased male and his offerings. In the past some Cypriot archaeologists have attributed weapons to male incumbents and jewellery to women although later anthropological research has shown this differentiation to be incorrect. Tomb gifts of Skull FCL3 from a tomb at Lapithos dated to the transition from Early to Middle Cypriot included a sword, a dagger, two knives, fourteen spindlewhorls, a necklace of paste beads and the skeleton of a horse. The sex determination based on anatomical sexual characteristics, however, revealed an 18-24 year old female.[59] In Cyprus, necklaces and diadems accompanied both males and females and Skull FCM 37 from LCIIB Lapithos was found to have spiral hair-rings despite being a forty-eight year old male.[60] Similarly, E stands for the 'enquirer' meaning someone who is seeking the evidence but without any indication of whether a particular enquirer is or was, a looter or an archaeologist!

Fig. 11.4 illustrates in tabular form, examples of the many additional variations which are possible in each group. The relationship sets can also be re-grouped under umbrella headings because the term 'relationship' itself is multi-faceted. Examples of such re-groupings might include: physiological, physical, geographical, environmental, spatial, political, ideological, economic, social and ritual relationships.

To take an example from my own work, when looking at the relationship between the deceased and the deceased (=<—>=) from a physical aspect I identified four possible lines of enquiry: skeletal assemblages, palaeodemography, consanguinity and ethnic affinity. The amount of Cypriot skeletal material available for study is limited due to the constraints of poor preservation and subsequent lack of conservation. The question remains, however, can the men and women buried in Ancient Cypriot tombs tell us anything? Late Cypriot skeletal assemblages for example are solely concerned with the physical remains and their number but once

59  Fischer 1986, 29.
60  Fischer 1986, 33.

again there is more than one avenue to be explored. I initially asked the traditional questions about whether the incumbents were buried singly, multiply or en masse before turning my attention to the point of view of age and sex.

The Swedish anthropologist, Peter Fischer examined some material from Late Cypriot Ayios Iakovos *Melia* and Enkomi and some Cypro-Geometric skulls from Lapithos *Plakes*, which were stored in the University of Lund in Sweden. He discovered to his apparent astonishment that there appeared to be more male specimens than female. He suggested that perhaps males and females were buried separately at these sites or that male skulls survived better post-mortem than their female counterparts. He found no evidence to support either suggestion and decided that the question would remain unanswered. The question Fischer concentrated on was where were the missing female adults?

I have argued above that relationships are rarely simple and that as many combinations as possible should be related to each other. Although Fischer also drew attention to a second problem with the data, the below average incidence of child burial from these sites, he did not connect the two once he had established that women and children did not receive separate burial. I have recently suggested that the answer may lie elsewhere and that perhaps what we are seeing in this negative evidence is the practice of female abandonment.[61] There are further lines of enquiry which I am currently pursuing which may also prove to be interconnected. Enkomi was a site where intramural burial was practised for the first time in Late Bronze Age Cyprus. Lapithos *Plakes* is also a little unusual in that it apparently used two separate cemeteries for different ethnic groups, one Greek and one Eteo-Cypriot. Furthermore, all three sites were important, relatively wealthy, urban rather than rural sites. Do these facts perhaps hold clues to differential customs?

An analysis of the relationship between the living and the dead also relies on comparisons between different sets of variables at different periods in time. The examination of the changing relationship is concerned with cataloguing and classifying the evidence, recognising any changes that have taken place and identifying (where possible) the processes involved in these changes. Although the outward significators of social change should be sought it is necessary to steer clear of simplistic cause-and-effect solutions based purely on data viewed chronologically. It is all very well identifying and describing the variables and the relationships which may exist between them but the real difficulty lies in attributing a social meaning to them as was seen in the example of the missing women and children. The two questions which must remain uppermost are firstly, from whose point of view does a relationship between variables exist and secondly, from whose perspective is a perceived change significant? In each case there are at least three possible

---

61   Bright 1994.

| = | deceased | quantity, age, sex, health, wealth, rank, social status, clothing, possessions (group and individual) |
|---|---|---|
| + | living | as above (=) |
| * | ritual | rites, place, paraphernalia, ideology religion |
| G | grave offering | quantity, types: jewellery (various), pottery (fabric,shape,decoration,quality), weapons and tools (various), furniture, models, toys, food and drink, miscellaneous |
| D | domestic/other | as above (G) |
| T | tomb | quantity, size, shape, niches, ledges, entrance, decoration, orientation |
| R | residence unit | as above (T) |
| B | burial place/cemetery | location, size, shape, layout |
| S | settlement | as above (B) |
| A | activity areas | cult places, agricultural areas, industrial areas, mines, trading areas |
| ^^ | topography | micro: geology, geography, soil, contour, flora, fauna |
| [] | island | macro: as above (^^) |
| ][ | abroad | combination of all variables listed above parallels, influences |
| E | | enquirer, traveller, collector, scholar, archaeologist, looter etc. |

*Fig.11.4: Variation Possibilities for Individual Symbols*

---

standpoints (a) those of the characters involved that is to say, the living and the dead (b) those of the enquirer and (c) those of the subsequent reader of the completed research text. The irrevocable situation in most studies is that even though the method of enquiry is made as 'scientific' or objective as possible, the final conclusions may remain forever personal. To add to this, new evidence may provide new information which may lead to new conclusions. One of the best Cypriot examples of this was the Swedish discovery of Bronze Age tombs at Enkomi. With the knowledge available to Gjerstad in 1926 he wrote 'wherever settlements have been found, the necropolies always are in their close vicinity, but in no locality from the earliest to the latest period of the Bronze Age been found within the settlements. A distinct limit between the living and the dead is maintained.' What he was unaware of was that the Enkomi tombs were in fact intramural and occurred within the courtyards of the houses.

The constraints which were in operation at the time of burial and the constraints which have been and continue to be in operation ever since, play a vital role in any reconstruction of past social reality. An historical problem shared by both field anthropologists and archaeologists alike is the dual sense of import and data ownership. Each living tribe or culture is seen to be unique and the kinship patterns and cognitive systems unravelled by it's ethnographer seem to assume a personal importance which is seldom truly shared. In the past many field archaeologists have fallen foul of the same trap. Certain sites, whatever their geographical location, have an intrinsic prestige value and their discoverers tend to expend a great deal of time asserting that their finds are far more important than other contemporary ones. When looking at the contents of Tutankhamun's tomb it is easy to forget that his tomb was one of the smaller ones in the Valley of the Kings and that he was but a minor pharaoh. Cypriot archaeologists who found richly endowed tombs in northern Cyprus at sites such as Vounous *Bellapais*[62] attributed great importance to them. The ceramic sequences found in the north formed the type for the whole island. Their unwitting propaganda was so successful that for years the areas in the south of the island were looked on as extremely backward simply because they failed to produce the White Painted II Ware that was thought to have heralded the onset of the Middle Cypriot Period. In reality the island was not homogeneous but as Ellen Herscher[63] and Stuart Swiny[64] later pointed out, was merely regional and northern ceramic fashions were just not greatly appreciated in the south. Despite the new information that the Late Cypriot population of Enkomi favoured intramural burial, we still cannot afford to be complacent about the state of our knowledge. Two key assumptions have been made about these intramural tombs. Due to the importance which has been attributed to Enkomi it has been assumed that it was representative of the entire island and that intramural burial was the norm. It has also been assumed that the rich intramural burials were contemporary with the buildings in whose courtyards they stood. Surprisingly, however, neither of these core assumptions has ever been seriously questioned.

Some archaeologists also appear to feel that because he or she discovered or excavated a site that it in some way the data belongs to them. There is, therefore, no compulsion to share the findings and no obligation to publish. Students of Cypriot archaeology have been extremely fortunate in this respect due mainly to the influence of Dr Vassos Karageorghis. He has been a prolific writer himself and has actively encouraged others to produce interim reports and early publication. A trend I hope will be continued.

My Research Design diagram, Fig. 11.2 illustrates the boundaries which exist between the individual variables by means of ink circles and lines. It also depicts in abstract form, the constraints which put pressure on the concentric circles representing the fourteen variables. They begin from outside the circles and exert a force towards the centre. I have shown them in this way because the relationships between both the central characters and the other elements may be affected by each circle in turn.

For example the outer circle 'E' (the enquirer) may alter our perception of the situation occurring in all the spheres of the diagram purely by the manner in which the evidence was recorded. Similarly, the shape of a tomb (T) may have been affected by (R) the shape of the residence unit and/or the environment ($^\frown$) in which it was built. The environment itself, moreover, may add a further constraint in the form of the degree of preservation it would allow through time. The constraints may of course operate in the reverse direction too, that is to say beginning at a point somewhere inside of the diagram and exerting pressure on the elements towards the outer edge. The present world concern about the disappearing rainforest is testament to the effect that Man can have on his environment. At times it seems that the pressure may even be greatest at the boundary between the individual circles.

In addition to the constraints, Fig. 11.2 also depicts two intersecting arrows, labelled time and space respectively. In reality their compass directions are not important because they travel both into and out of the circles in all directions. In some cases, moreover, space and time may even be coextensive. Space as used here has several meanings and is not restricted to a measurable distance on the ground, although this aspect is of course of considerable importance. It may for instance refer to a distance between two points (in more than one dimension), an occupied area, an interval of time or even a kinship relationship. The dimension of time plays a vital role, not least because of the changes which occurred over a series of archaeological periods. Each set of variables (Fig. 11.3) should be understood as having two arrows attached to it rather than the broken one I have shown running horizontally (<—>). It must always be borne in mind, therefore, that there is also an imaginary vertical line with arrow 'heads' pointing in two directions thus indicating both forwards and backwards in time. Time in this context, moreover, is not simply coterminous with chronology. For instance, two grave offerings may be deposited in a single instant in time or at an interval of a few weeks or months within the same archaeological and yet the nature of our subsequent reading of the evidence might lead an excavator to date it to within plus or minus fifty years! A distinction must also be made for example between seasonal time and ritual time.

The one-hundred-and-five relationships operate on six distinct levels which serve to illustrate the major areas in which space and time are seen to operate. Comparisons are necessary between: (i) contemporary material from the same tomb (ii) contemporary material from other tombs at the same site (iii) contemporary material from other sites (iv) material of other periods from the same tomb (v) material of other periods from the same site (vi) material of other periods from different sites.

Both the individual burial components and their relationships also display a series of underlying dichotomies, some of which are of considerable importance. The symbols themselves fall into categories such as 'within'

62 Dikaios 1938.
63 Herscher 1981.
64 Swiny 1981.

and 'without', the tomb and the cemetery and the island and abroad. Other similar social and economic dualities may also exist. A dichotomy may exist, for example, between coastal and inland areas or between the practices of foreigners and those of the indigenous population, in this case the Eteo-Cypriots. Other possibilities are the rich and poor, farmers and traders, male and female, child and adult and so on. Although the various elements are often seen as being in opposition, in reality one can rarely exist without the other. The dead are recognised as differing from the living but there can be no death without life. Similarly, a male and female may appear to be opposites but without this duality there would be no people. Duality in this context should be understood as 'heads and tails', the two opposing sides of the same coin. Duality is also linked with the existence, real or imaginary, of boundaries.

I have shown that the term 'relationship' in this context has a far wider meaning and many more connotations than is at first apparent and that there are numerous possible lines of enquiry. A comprehensive appraisal of each of these, making full use of interdisciplinary methods, would be a truly gargantuan task for dealing with Cypriot or indeed any other burials but I make no apology for my suggestions. I have chosen avenues which appear to me to be the most significant but that does not make them definitive. I merely hope that by drawing attention to them they will serve to highlight problem areas which deserve further research. Each enquirer has a role to play in both the description and the evaluation of the archaeological material. In effect I myself, form part of my own Research Design diagram, appearing as 'E' in the outer circle. Some of my conclusions about the relationship between the living and the dead will, therefore, remain forever subjective as it is I, the enquirer who has inevitably contributed to their significance. Likewise, it is the predisposition of the archaeologists, anthropologists and other specialists involved which governs the future of the archaeology of death.

# 12 The Dead Sea Dolmens: Death and the Landscape

## Kay Prag

ABSTRACT—*Dolmen fields are found in the area north-east of the Dead Sea in Jordan. They have been the focus of various studies since the nineteenth century. These studies suggest that the construction of some dolmens dates to the late fourth millennium BC (the Early Bronze I period). The dolmens are usually perceived and studied in isolation. This paper approaches them in the context of regional survey and excavations at Tell Iktanu and Tell al-Hammam. Three factors may give alternative perceptions: the relationship between dolmens and the environment, with its potential for transhumant grazing; evidence for a flexible settlement pattern in the Early Bronze I period, with sites ranging from incipient towns to animal pens; and the study of recent burial practices among transhumant pastoralists in the area, who constructed monumental tombs in the same landscape. Finally the evidence is compared to existing theoretical frameworks.*

## Introduction

The definition of a dolmen adopted here is that of Conder,[1] one of the first to give a detailed description of many of the monuments forming the substance of this paper. In his 1881 survey on behalf of the Palestine Exploration Fund in the area north-east of the Dead Sea he listed cairns, stone circles, menhirs (single standing stones), dolmens (usually single chamber structures with a capstone supported on upright stones) and demi-dolmens (dolmens built on a hillside with one end of the capstone resting on the ground). Many of the dolmens have capstones from two to three metres in length. Irby and Mangles were the first to refer to such monuments in this area,[2] but Conder's detailed publication is still a primary source for many megalithic structures which have since been destroyed or damaged. The Transjordan dolmens do not conform to the "most widely accepted definition" of Arnal: "The dolmen is an open sepulchral chamber, usually megalithic, covered by a mound and intended to house several burials".[3] Evidence for mounds, tumuli or cairns over the dolmens in central Jordan is uncommon. After commenting on the density of the distribution,

Conder concluded that the dolmens in this area were not tombs, as they frequently rested directly on the rock, and had never been covered by earthen mounds or tumuli, but were more likely to be habitations, altars or offering places.[4] The latter suggestion was due to the fact that many of the capstones appeared to have cup-holes, hollows or channels carved in the surface which he thought were contemporary with their construction. Conder and Mantell described, photographed and drew many of the megalithic remains. These dolmen fields form only a part of the very extensive dolmen distribution in north and central Palestine and north and central Transjordan.

## Distribution of dolmen fields (Fig. 12.1)

On the western fringes of the Transjordanian plateau area, c. 800 m above sea level, the dolmens are usually located on the slopes and ridges overlooking the steep wadis which characterise this area, where pastoralism but little cultivation is possible except in the narrow valley bottoms or on the less steep slopes. Here Conder noted ten dolmens on the upper Wadi Zirqa in the area that is now

---

1 Conder 1889, 302.
2 Irby & Mangles 1823, 321-324, 466.
3 Quoted by Joussaume 1985/1988, 18.

4 Conder 1889, 302-304.

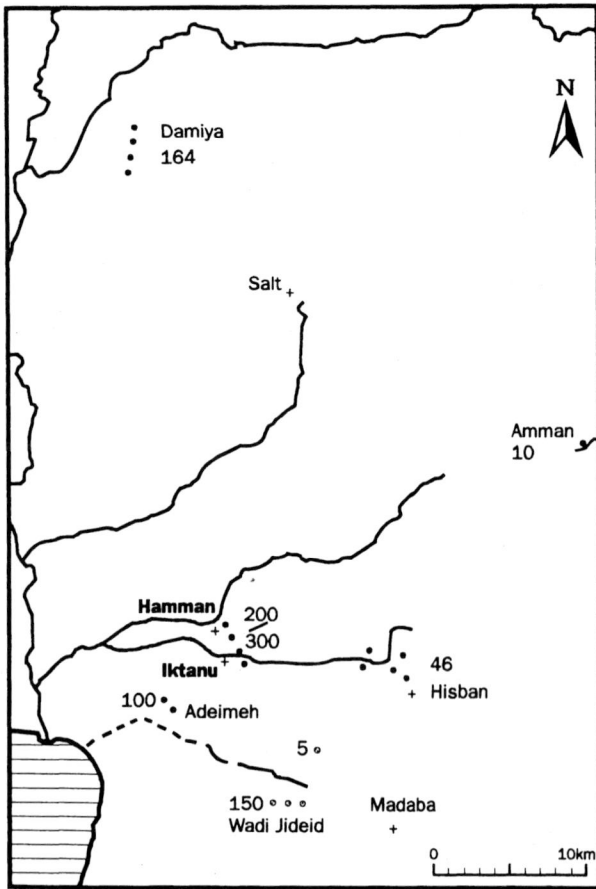

*Fig. 12.1: Distribution of dolmens in the area north-east of the Dead Sea.*

The Adeimeh dolmens were first recorded by de Saulcy;[10] Mallon and Neuville excavated six dolmens there in 1930;[11] Stekelis undertook the detailed study and excavation of part of the Adeimeh cemetery in 1933.[12]

At Adeimeh Stekelis excavated 11 tumuli and 168 cist burials. From the cist graves he took several groups of Chalcolithic pottery, similar to material from the Chalcolithic type site at Teleilat Ghassul less than 2 km to the north-west.[13] All the cists had nearby hearths; 130 cists contained badly preserved bones but the mode of burial was only discernable in one instance, where the body appears to have been placed in an upright position, squatting on the heels, head facing east.[14] The cists were generally too small for extended burial, their length ranging from 0.50-1.52 m. Hanbury-Tenison suggests the lack of bones indicates that the body was an inessential part of the funeral process, and many of the cists may have been token graves;[15] given the numbers of cists which did have some bone, it seems more likely that the sparse skeletal evidence is due in part to ancient or modern disturbance. There are numerous parallels between the Adeimeh cists and the large Chalcolithic cemetery at Shiqmim in the north Negev.[16]

At least six similar cemeteries of cist graves occur round the edge of the foothills from Adeimeh eastwards towards Tell Iktanu.[17] Some cists south of Iktanu were excavated in 1966;[18] no primary deposits associated with them were found but the single sherd discovered in the fill is also Chalcolithic. J.B. Hennessy also notes the resemblance of these cists to silos he excavated in Chalcolithic domestic contexts at Teleilat Ghassul.[19]

There were no dolmens in the area excavated by Stekelis at Adeimeh, but one stood just 35 m to the south on the edge of the Wadi al-Siyala.[20] Stekelis mentions more than 100 dolmens in the Adeimeh area.[21] Webley noted that these dolmens were located directly on a boulder-strewn, water-eroded surface on barren land adjacent to the alluvial soils.[22] Mallon and Neuville excavated six of the dolmens, but found nothing that could be used to date them, despite lifting the floor slabs, which were set directly on small stones, natural soil or rock.[23] Some of the capstones had cup marks and channels cut into the upper surfaces. Stekelis noted similarities in building technique between the cists and the dolmens, and suggested that they were contemporary, with dolmens

covered by central Amman;[5] about 46 dolmens on the upper Wadi Hisban at al-Kurmiyeh, Wadi Umm Shuamir, Sumia and al-Kalua;[6] about five in the vicinity of Mt Nebo;[7] about 150 dolmens on the upper Wadi Jideid, especially at Hadanieh and al-Kuejiyeh;[8] another group with more than 150 dolmens lies a little further south, at al-Mareighat on the north slopes of the upper Wadi Zirqa Ma'in (south of the area shown in Fig. 12.1).[9] Almost no work has since been done on these dolmens, and many have been destroyed during the twentieth century by expanding populations and agriculture.

Below the plateau, on the edges of the Jordan Valley, other groups are located on the lower western courses of these same wadis, between the -300 and +200 metre contours. They are sited on stoney ground adjacent to the cultivated alluvial soils. A large dolmen field at Adeimeh (c. 5 km north-east of the Dead Sea) was not explored by Conder, although it lay within his survey area. There has been much confusion over the courses and names of the many seasonal wadis in this area, but the Wadi Adeimeh appears to be the lower course of Conder's Wadi Jideid.

---

5   Ibid., 20-26.
6   Ibid., 159-171, 222, 277.
7   Ibid., 201-202.
8   Ibid., 254-274.
9   Ibid., 184-189.
10  de Saulcy 1865, 312.
11  Neuville 1930.
12  Stekelis 1935.
13  Note cists 54, 55, [126, 134, 146, 147, 150, 151], and 164 in particular; ibid., 71-76, Figs. 19, 20; Pls. IV, V.
14  See cist 32; ibid., 54, 65-66, Pl. I:2.
15  Hanbury-Tenison 1986, 224, 230.
16  Levy 1991, 409.
17  Prag 1990, 126, Fig. 7, Pl. II:1-2.
18  Prag 1971, 279, Fig. 60.
19  J.B. Hennessy, personal communication.
20  Stekelis 1935, 67.
21  Stekelis 1935, 38; Pl. II:1-2. This is currently a military area and I have not seen the present state of the dolmens.
22  Webley 1969a, 42-43.
23  Neuville 1930, 249-265.

occurring instead of cists where suitable local stone was available. The close proximity of dolmens and cists at Adeimeh to some extent contradicts this view. In the Adeimeh area there was evidence for later use of the cemetery, particularly connected with the tumuli.

In 1942-43 Stekelis moved north to the Damiya/Ala-Safat dolmen field, which lies just to the south of the lower course of the Wadi Zirqa. At Damiya/Ala-Safat (c. 35 km north of Adeimeh) Stekelis recorded 164 built dolmens, 3 rock-carved dolmens, 14 cists, and some tumuli and stone circles. They are located on a rocky ridge some 4 km in length, overlooking the alluvium from the east. In the summer the ridge is barren, but is a paradise of grass and flowers in the spring, and almost all the dolmens are still in an excellent state of preservation. Here the dolmens are large and regular, built of the available natural rock slabs. These dolmens usually have a capstone, four side slabs, floor slabs and a stone circle/terrace platform around the base with an average diameter of c. 6 m. The capstone is regularly over 2 m long, and several were over 3 m; the supporting uprights were also very large single slabs, in the case of Dolmen no. 114 the supporting slabs were 4 m long, and 2 m high; one supporting slab for Dolmen no. 180 was 4.60 m long. Many at the north end of the cemetery had a carved porthole entry in the narrow north end. Most were oriented north-south, eight were oriented east-west. The field was mapped by Swauger in 1962.[24] Human bones indicated both primary contracted burial, and cremation rites.[25] Cremation is rare in ancient Palestine, but is occasionally attested in the EB I period, at, e.g., Jericho, and sporadically at other times including possibly the Chalcolithic at Byblos,[26] as well as in the Roman period. Other possible evidence for a cremation rite connected with dolmens came from Turville Petre's work at Khirbet Keraziye just north-west of the Sea of Galilee, and from Schumacher's exploration in Ajlun,[27] but it is impossible to date these remains, which could be Roman or earlier.

The pottery associated with the primary use of the Damiya dolmens was clearly dated to the EB I period (c. 3200-2800 BC).[28] This EB I chronology was further indicated by K. Yassine who found quite complete deposits in the lower storey and beneath floor slabs of dolmens at Damiya.[29] Stekelis concluded that it was absurd to attribute the large monuments at Damiya to nomadic tribesmen; he supposed they were the work of a well-organized, agricultural, sedentary society cultivating the nearby rich soils of the Jordan Valley. He noted that similar pottery had been found on contemporary

settlement sites. Though noting that a possible reason for the generally rather isolated situation of dolmen fields accorded with newcomers arriving in Palestine, Yassine also notes that the Jordan Valley dolmens do not stand isolated from settlements. The latter point is also made in relation to the more recent discovery of several large dolmen fields further to the north, on the Wadi al-Yabis.[30]

Stekelis recorded that many of the tombs at Damiya had been re-used in the Middle or Late Bronze Age,[31] when the earlier interments were cleared out, but enough fragments of earlier pottery remained to indicate secondary use. He concluded that dolmens with some typological variations continued to be constructed at later dates also.[32] Swauger found only Iron Age, Roman, Byzantine and modern pottery on the surface at the Damiya site, but did not publish any of it.

Returning south towards the Dead Sea area, the al-Mataba/Hisban field comprises several groups. The main work has been that of Conder and Mantell,[33] Swauger[34] and Rafik W. Dajani.[35] This, the largest dolmen field Conder explored, stretches along the edge of the foothills from al-Mataba, just south of the lower Wadi Hisban near Iktanu, to just south of the lower Wadi Kafrain near Hammam, and contained from 200 to 300 dolmens.[36] He comments that the Wadi Hisban seemed particularly rich in these remains. The dolmens were not found north of the Wadi Kafrain, nor on the Wadi Shu'aib, although Conder's survey did not cover the central and upper sections of the Wadi Shu'aib.

The al-Mataba group, on the south bank of the Wadi Hisban just east of Iktanu, comprises 16 dolmens built of rather poor quality stone, which have generally collapsed and survive in rather poor condition today. They are (relative to those at Damiya) rather unimpressive, but average 2.04 m in length and 0.63 m in width. They also have floor slabs and are set on circular terraces. Only three capstones were still measurable in 1962, one being 2.90 m in length. The majority was again oriented north-south; some were said to resemble cist graves built partially above ground. They resembled the dolmens at Damiya more closely than those in the group immediately to the north of al-Mataba, on the north bank of the Wadi Hisban at Umm al-Quttain.[37] At Umm al-Quttain the five dolmens are larger, with side walls averaging 4.68 m in length, with one side wall being 7.25 m in length, but made up of more than one slab; they are unusual in plan, being back-to-back, 'semi-detached' or double dolmens, one containing a type of 'port hole' in the intermediate partition. They have terraces variously 7, 10 and 15 x 12 m in diameter. Dajani found evidence that the dolmens he

24 Swauger 1965, 3-36.
25 Stekelis 1961, 56-57.
26 Bienkowski 1982, 89; Eldar & Baumgarten 1985, 138; Prag 1986, 65.
27 Both summarised by Broome 1940, 479-497, esp. 484.
28 E.g., dolmens 49, 82, 83, 84; Stekelis 1961, 63; Figs. 14, 15, 18, 19, 20. Though note Hanbury-Tenison 1986, 245, who does not regard the EB I date at Ala-Safat as proven; but he is inclined to think the 1000 dolmens at Jebel Mutawwaq, east of Jerash, might also date to the EB I period.
29 Yassine 1988, 51.

30 Palumbo, Mabry & Kuijt 1990, 480.
31 E.g., Stekelis 1961, Fig. 16:37-41, from Dolmen 19.
32 Ibid., 94-95.
33 Conder 1889, 232.
34 Swauger 1965, 2-36.
35 Dajani 1968, 56-64.
36 Conder 1889, 230-236.
37 Conder 1889, 16. Apparently the same group is described under the heading Akwek by Mallon 1929, 225.

excavated in this group at Umm al-Quttain had been built in EB I, then reused in the Iron Age. Many more dolmens cover the slopes further north, immediately east of Rawda, and south-east of Hammam; occasionally there are isolated examples. They also utilise local stone, and are set on round terraces. There are many stone circles in this area as well.

In conclusion, one should note that the wadis in this region all demonstrated a similar pattern. In the north, the Wadi Zirqa had 10 dolmens near the headwaters on the plateau, and 164 in the Jordan Valley near its lower western course. The Wadi Hisban had about 50 dolmens in the region of its headwaters, and 200-300 in the lower foothills on its lower western course. The Wadi Jideid/Adeimeh has 150 near its headwaters, and around 100 at its foot. These areas accord well with the summer and winter grazing zones of nineteenth- and twentieth-century transhumant pastoralists. The upper areas provide temperate climates, water and grazing in the summer (May to October) and are cold in winter; the lower areas are hot and lack grazing in summer, but have a temperate winter climate and good grazing after early and late winter rain (November to April). There appear to be no dolmens associated with the Wadi Shu'aib and the Wadi Kafrain. The exact numbers rely heavily on the records of nineteenth-century explorers.

## Date of the dolmens

There is insufficient evidence to be dogmatic about the date and use of the dolmens in this area, but evidence thus far obtained seems at least consistent. It seems likely that cist burials were extensively employed in the Chalcolithic period,[38] and to some extent were succeeded in the EB I period by more megalithic dolmen building which occurs in hilly/stoney areas where large slabs of stone can be obtained locally, and slid downhill into position.

That there was later building and re-use of both types is not excluded by this evidence. Epstein excavated 36 dolmens from 12 different sites in the extensive dolmen fields in the Golan north-east of the Sea of Galilee, where hundreds more dolmens exist.[39] She divided them into six more or less overlapping types, of which types 1a, 1b and 2a seem to be typologically closer to those we have mentioned further south.[40] The earliest pottery found on their floors dated to the EB.MB (EB IV) period. Epstein noted that earlier burials might have been cleared out, but if so the process was tidier and more complete than at Damiya. These dolmens had also been reused in the Middle and Late Bronze and Iron Ages. Epstein also corroborated (on stratigraphic evidence) that the dolmens post-dated one of her Chalcolithic houses. She thought it likely that the various dolmen cemeteries

were tribal, "with an occasional isolated dolmen indicating the tomb of a person who was not brought to rest at the main burial place".[41] Vinitzky in reassessing the evidence for dolmens in the Golan and Galilee, dates them to the EB II and III periods.[42]

## Dolmens in context

Nearly all those who have worked on these dolmens have studied them in isolation; a few have perceived them in varied relationships to contemporary sites, and to the landscape. Several have seen them and other megalithic structures as tribal cemeteries or gathering places, generally connected with pastoralist societies. For the wider distribution of 'megalithic monuments' in Palestine, note Stekelis' map and extensive summary, more recently up-dated by Zohar.[43] Such views have been reinforced by the recent discoveries in the hill country west of the Jordan, at Ain Samiya/Dhahr Mirzbaneh[44] and Jebel Qa'aqir,[45] where large shaft grave cemeteries and small settlements of the late third millennium BC [EB.MB=IB=EB IV] are interpreted as centres for dispersed populations or winter centres for transhumant groups. Finkelstein has developed this in a more complex way to account for both sedentary and pastoralist use of the landscape, with exploitation of varied eco-zones and a multi-variant population.[46] The more complex explanations are more in keeping with the evidence emerging particularly east of the Jordan during the last thirty years.

The region immediately north-east of the Dead Sea is geographically varied. The floor of the Rift Valley is occupied by lacustrine marls capped by alluvial deposits, through which the Jordan River flows to the Dead Sea. The alluvial soils, and the mainly limestone foothills of the plateau to the east, are deeply dissected by a series of perennial and seasonal streams. Most of the foothill land is semi-arid, steep marginal land suitable for seasonal grazing rather than agriculture. Although the distribution of sites of the Chalcolithic and Early Bronze Age periods at first sight seems general, 13 of the possible 16 Chalcolithic sites noted in surveys lie in the flat alluvial soils, in the west of the area, around the present -300 m contour; 8 of the 15 EBA sites noted lie to the east at the edge of the foothills; the 3 certain Chalcolithic sites all lie near the -300 m contour, 7 of the 8 'certain' EB I sites lie further east between the -200/-100 m contours. In both periods sites are regularly located along wadis which are today perennial, especially the Wadi Shu'aib, but in the EBA sites seem to be restricted to this location, perhaps reflecting the onset of drier conditions than had

---

38 Hanbury-Tenison 1986, 218.
39 Epstein 1985, 22, see esp. Map 1.
40 Ibid., Fig. 1.

41 Ibid., 21.
42 Vinitzky 1992.
43 Stekelis 1935, 25; Zohar 1989, 26 n. 16.
44 Finkelstein 1991, 19-45.
45 Dever 1980, 57.
46 Finkelstein 1991, 34; cf. Helms 1987, 52, "plural societies".

previously existed in the vicinity of Ghassul in the Chalcolithic period.[47] Teleilat Ghassul, the type site for the Chalcolithic period, which is so far the largest village settlement of the period to be excavated, lies in the flat alluvial soils, 2 km from the concentrations of cist burials at Adeimeh. This site, with its temple complex and wall paintings, may have been a social, economic and religious centre for smaller settlements in the vicinity and for people occupying a wider area. Adeimeh has often been interpreted as its cemetery.[48]

Despite the weight of evidence for cultural continuity, following the abandonment of the large Chalcolithic settlement in the plain at Ghassul – and perhaps that of a number of smaller satellite sites – there appears to be a shift of settlement emphasis eastwards at the beginning of the EB I period, towards the foothills. Sites such as Iktanu and Hammam are then newly occupied, whether for environmental or strategic/political/demographic reasons is as yet unclear.[49] In the following period (EB II) there seem to be fewer sites in the region, and by the EB III period the population may have been concentrated in just two large, defended sites, the most important of which was at Hammam on the Wadi Kafrain, the other at Tell Mustah on the Wadi Shu'aib. The excavation evidence from Iktanu and Hammam thus far would support this hypothesis, but more detailed survey material is required.

The distribution of EB I sites in the area correlates quite well with the location of the dolmen fields at Adeimeh and al-Mataba. EB I sites have been noted at Mweis and Azeimeh/Adeimeh on the Wadi Azeimeh/Adeimeh[50] not far from the Adeimeh dolmens. Some of the largest dolmen fields are located in the foothills between the Wadi Kafrain and the Wadi Hisban, immediately east of the EB I settlement sites of Hammam on the Wadi Kafrain and Iktanu on the Wadi Hisban. The evidence from excavation at Iktanu suggests the EB I settlement was unfortified; the Early Bronze Age fortification walls at Hammam have not yet been dated. At Hammam two structures which must have been dolmens occur on the western edge of the site. Both have lost their capstones, but otherwise exhibit classic local dolmen structure. One is just inside the line of Early Bronze Age walls, the other on the slope just outside. Local people say that 'Roman' glass and pottery were found inside the former some years ago. If they were built in the EB I period, then it would seem likely that they were built before settlement or fortifications had spread to this part of the site.

There are, as many travellers have noted, many undated megalithic remains in the vicinity, especially south of Hammam and in the hills to the east. They consist of enclosures and circles, as well as dolmens. Rawda Site 3 lies c. 500 m south-east of Hammam,

directly east of the town of Rawda, built against the rock face which here forms the dramatic east wall of the Jordan Valley Rift. The slopes at Rawda Site 3 form two knolls; that on the north has a ruined dolmen. The southern knoll has one well-preserved dolmen and two rather collapsed specimens. These are constructed in the very characteristic limestone of the area which weathers to a deep shade of purple. The same stone has been used to construct straggling megalithic enclosures, which could be interpreted as animal pens. The pottery found at Rawda Site 3 is EBA (certainly no EB.MB pottery), possibly EB I, but no excavation has been made at this site.

At Iktanu the EB I settlement was abandoned either towards the end of EB I or early in EB II, and extensively reoccupied in the EB.MB (EB IV) period. It seems likely that the al-Mataba dolmen field a few hundred metres to the east of Iktanu should date from the EB I period[51] but when Mallon explored it in 1929, he found that the one dolmen which then still had its cover slab had recently been vandalized, and he thought that an EB.MB cup came from this dolmen. However he clearly did not see this excavation and he might have been misled about the provenance of the cup.[52] Its provenance therefore is not assured. The primary evidence suggests that the al-Mataba dolmens were built in the EB I period, and though it is possible they were built in the EB.MB period, it is more likely they were re-used in the EB.MB period. No other cemetery for the EB.MB period at Iktanu has yet been discovered. There are megalithic enclosures at the west end of the south hill at Iktanu, and an isolated rectangular structure just beyond. The former must date to the EB.MB period, and the latter probably so.[53]

Hanbury-Tenison concludes that the most likely date for the Transjordan dolmens is EB I or EB IV.[54] Both periods reveal less nucleated, more dispersed settlement patterns than during the rest of the Bronze Age, and many of the megalithic monuments have from time to time been dated to the EB.MB (EB IV) period, usually on rather slight evidence. Further possible evidence comes from the Ajlun district.[55] It is quite possible therefore to conclude that dolmens were built and used in both EB I and EB.MB periods.

## Ethnographic evidence

Ethnographic material from the survey area was collected with equal care by Conder. He noted not just the traditions and folklore about the dolmens and other remains circulating among the Arab tribes in 1881, but the contemporary burial and building practices of these pastoralist tribes who practised transhumance within a

47  Webley 1969b, 21-23.
48  see Hanbury-Tenison 1986, 218.
49  Prag 1992, 155.
50  Yassine 1988.
51  Dajani 1968.
52  Mallon 1929, 226, Pl. III:2, "c'est assurément de là que provient le beau vase caliciform".
53  Prag 1990, 123.
54  Hanbury-Tenison 1986, 245.
55  Steuernagel 1925, 51-58, especially the Dalma dolmen, p. 56, Fig.13.

*Fig. 12.2: Modern grave circle at 'Ain Hisban (after Conder 1889, 8); c. 6.8 m in diameter.*

limited geographical zone.[56] The building practices of tent-dwelling pastoralists, which included construction of monumental tombs, barns, mills and forts in stone, were certainly initiated by the pastoralists, though it is not clear who was employed in the construction work; some trained labour must have been employed for the construction of the Adwan forts, possibly the same employed by the Ottoman government in the area.[57]

Conder distinguished both modern and ancient megalithic circles in the area. The ancient ones are numerous but undated, and at the top of the range include the great oval (c. 76 m in major diameter) on the ridge at Hadanieh/Wadi Jideid.[58] Modern (nineteenth-century AD) burials were often placed near the ancient circles, in pits and under cairns, and clearly the ancient circles were accorded a special status in the nineteenth century which made them attractive as burial sites. Revered tribesmen were interred inside modern stone circles. Members of the pastoralist Adwan tribe said these circles were built to mark the graves of sacred persons.[59] Conder described a typical modern circle at 'Ain Hisban in the upper Wadi Hisban (Fig. 12.2). It was nine paces in diameter (three paces = 7½ feet, nine paces = c. 6.86 m),[60] built of some very large, uncut blocks, some over a metre in length. On the west side of the circle was a gate or altar, a trilithon of squared ashlar (jambs 2 feet = 0.609 m high, lintel 3 feet

= 0.914 m long), on which were placed small offerings of glass beads and pottery chips (elsewhere a few coins were noted). The tribal mark of the Ajarma tribe (local pastoralists) was cut on the stones.[61] These were regular features of other circles also; equally regular was the use of the circles for the safe-keeping of objects such as ploughs, gun-locks and axe-heads. The modern circles possessed a sanctity, perhaps derived from the person buried there, which protected objects left in them from theft or damage (Fig. 12.3). A wooden coffee mortar was also placed there, but whether as votive or for its safe-keeping, or as indicating the generous hospitality of the dead person is not clear. Sixteen very similar circles were noted at Abu al-Kauwukah,[62] Abu Lozeh,[63] Ain al-Minyeh,[64] al-'Al,[65] 'Ain Amman,[66] Butmet al-Terki,[67] Hadanieh,[68] Hisban, south of the tell,[69] al-Jereineh,[70] Kabr Abdullah between Hisban and Nebo,[71] Kefeir Abu Bedd,[72] Khirbet

56  Conder 1889; Prag 1992.
57  Prag 1991, 50-52; Petersen 1989.
58  Conder 1889, 98-100 and Fig. facing page 100.
59  Conder 1889, 134.
60  Ibid., 27.

61  Ibid., 8.
62  Ibid., 2.
63  Ibid.
64  Ibid., 10.
65  Ibid., 16.
66  Ibid., 52-53.
67  Ibid., 93.
68  Ibid., 99, and Fig. facing p. 104.
69  Ibid., 105.
70  Ibid., 110.
71  Ibid., 113.
72  Ibid., 134.

*Fig. 12.3: Modern grave circle at Hadanieh (from Conder 1889, facing p. 104); c. 5.85 m external diameter. Small offerings on the entrance stone include a shaykh's crutch-headed stick and two knife-blades; within the circle were stored two swords, two wooden ploughs, coffee mortars and a metal coffee-jug.*

al-Dubbeh,[73] al-Kuejiyeh,[74] Rujm Saaur,[75] Sheikh Subeih[76] and Umm al-Hanafish.[77]

As well as the grave circles Conder noted at least 45 Arab cemeteries or isolated burials in pits/rough cairns in the survey area which testified to considerable diversity of burial practices. None of the cemeteries or burials belonged to contemporary villages/settlements. They were either the burials of tent-dwelling pastoralists (the Ajarma seem to have temporarily occupied caves and ruins on occasion also), or of fellaheen/cultivators working for the Adwan shaykhs, who mainly inhabited isolated huts, caves or occasionally small modern cottages. Cemeteries appeared to be mainly tribal and grouped around an important burial, as that of the Ajarma at 'Ain Hisban mentioned above. But it is clear that almost any ruin or prominent spot could attract a burial to it, and not necessarily that of a person of elite status.

As remarkable as the circles built for venerated persons, are the monumental tombs built to house high-status people, especially important shaykhs, such as the tomb of Shaykh Findi al-Faiz of the Bani Sakhr tribe, one

of the most powerful chiefs of his day, who died not earlier than 1877.[78] Thanks to Conder, this is a particularly well-documented example.[79] The shaykh died when returning to his home territory near Madaba probably from a visit to Nazareth and Nablus; he was buried in Adwan territory (NB, at place of death, not in home territory or tribal cemetery) at the junction of the Wadi Kafrain and Wadi Rama. His tomb, built of masonry, cemented and white-washed, was a very prominent monument located on flat land. It was probably a solid monument, with the burial in the ground beneath. It appears to be a rough copy of a Roman sarcophagus, 10 feet = 3.05 m long, 6½ feet = 1.98 m wide, 10 feet = 3.05 m high at the ridge (Fig. 12.4). It had a crude denticulated string course, and relief-carved decoration consisting of a tribal mark, crutch-headed sticks ("Osirian" symbols of power), sword (warrior), coffee cups, coffee pot, coffee mill, coffee jug, tongs and spoon (liberal hospitality). There were niches in the side and ends for offerings. The monument was surrounded by a low wall, quadrangular, with rounded corners, 17 feet x 15 feet (= 5.18 x 4.57 m), with on the west a kind of trilithon about 2 feet (= 0.609 m) high, not unlike those of the circles. Though it was in good repair when Conder

---

73  Ibid., 148.
74  Ibid., 158.
75  Ibid., 207-208.
76  Ibid., 216.
77  Ibid., 247-248.

78  Prag 1991, 59; 1992, 157.
79  Conder 1889, 113-115.

visited it in 1881, and was photographed by Vita-Finzi in 1962-63,[80] it had been torn apart when I visited it first in 1989, but the masonry lying round clearly derived from the monument described by Conder. One is reminded of Epstein's explanation of isolated dolmens constructed for members of the tribe who died away from home.[81] Today it is surrounded by modern graves. At least five other such monuments existed, which marked territorial as well as tribal status. Those of the Adwan shaykhs (transhumant pastoralists) were located on prominent tells at the winter centres at Tell Nimrin,[82] Kafrain,[83] and at Tell al-Rama;[84] that of Shaykh Shehab al-Fuliyeh of the Ajarma at 'Ain Hisban had relief carving of the tribal mark, a bow, a coffee mortar and pestle, and a man on horseback with a sword and a bow above him;[85] other relief-carved tombs of the chiefs of the Ghaneimat tribe were noted at Kabr Abdullah.[86]

Although these monuments are not megalithic, they have a number of points in common with the ancient dolmens and circles. It is reasonable to assume that Stekelis was not correct in assuming that unsedentarised tribal groups were incapable of building the dolmens at Damiya. The Adwan, though living in tents and practising a regular pattern of transhumance from Jordan Valley to plateau, built or maintained not just large tombs, but forts/stores, water-mills and possibly shrines in masonry. But neither should these monuments be viewed in isolation from settlement sites: the Adwan relied on poor fellaheen and subsidiary tribes working for them to produce cereal and other crops within their territory; the Adwan (and the Bani Sakhr) had close relations with townspeople at Salt, visited the towns (Jerusalem, Nablus, Nazareth, etc.) west of the Jordan, and had dealings with the markets and merchants of Damascus, all under very nominal Ottoman rule. They formed segments of a highly stratified society. The Ottoman administration, apart from the forts which guarded the pilgrim route to Mecca (one in the eastern Balqa, at Dab'a, restored in the sixteenth and eighteenth centuries),[87] by 1867 was also building forts or block houses at Salt, Hisban and Nimrin. According to an inscription collected by Conder, the Adwan had built at least one (possibly three) sizeable stone fort in 1777 which was used to store weapons and food.[88]

The distribution of these nineteenth-century burials (in large and small clusters, as well as isolated occurences), located along routes of pastoral transhumance and particularly close to summer and

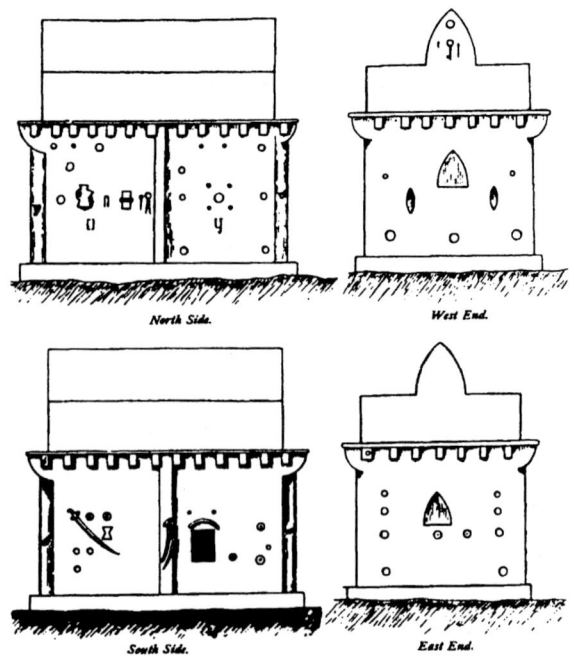

*Fig. 12.4: The grave monument of Shaykh Findi al-Faiz of the Bani Sakhr, south Jordan Valley, c. AD 1877.*

winter quarters, bears considerable resemblance to the distribution of the dolmen fields, scattered in large and small clusters over a wide area, but particularly concentrated on the lower and upper courses of wadis in a way which can be seen to parallel the summer and winter patterns of transhumance in the region. It is interesting to note the views of Zohar, who suggests that interplay between the pastoralist and the sedentary peasants led to construction of megalithic monuments, and who stresses the importance of main roads in this process.[89] There were few towns or settlements in the survey area in 1881. Salt was the only existing one, though the redevelopment of Hisban and Madaba was beginning c.1880. The main route from the plateau via Salt to the Jordan ford from Neolithic times onwards should have been the Wadi Shu'aib, which notably lacks dolmens. Although there was a road from Hisban to Rama in Roman times and probably earlier, it followed the south ridge above the Wadi Hisban. The dolmens and the nineteenth-century cemeteries in the Hisban are located much closer to the places which were the favoured seasonal camping centres for the nineteenth-century AD pastoralists.[90] There is probably a copy-cat element in the nineteenth-century patterns, when the circles and trilithons with offering hollows seem in part to copy the older monuments, but the nineteenth- century evidence may parallel the patterns and practices of ancient pastoralists in a marginal zone, notably in both the upper and lower Wadi Hisban. The

---

80  Vita-Finzi 1964, Pl. XII.A, opposite p. 27.
81  Cf. above, note 41.
82  Conder 1889, 238. Warren visited it in 1870, and noted a relief carving of a horseman with a sword, which Conder did not see. warren 1870, 285.
83  Ibid., 116, 140, grave of Shaykh al-Mujahad, said to have been very similar to that of Findi al-Faiz.
84  Ibid., 113.
85  Ibid., 8-9.
86  Ibid., 113.
87  Petersen 1989, 100.
88  Conder 1889, 216-217; Prag 1991, 50-53.

89  Zohar 1989, 18-31, esp. p. 27.
90  Prag 1991.

locations of dolmen fields can therefore be paralleled very closely by pastoralist patterns rather than influenced by the proximity of major routes.

In earlier times, the juxtaposition of extensive dolmen fields and settlements as at Iktanu and al-Mataba, particularly in periods of rather flexible settlement such as during the EB I and EB.MB periods, may suggest an interplay of tribal pastoralists and more sedentary cultivator-pastoralists in the normal environment of a site and its hinterland. Such a combination may exist at any time – the suggested re-use of dolmens in the Middle and Late Bronze and in the Iron Age may be indicators of just such mobile elements in the population.

## Theoretical implications

Joussaume accords little space to the dolmens in Palestine and Transjordan, and none to recent work there.[91] He is primarily concerned with the chronology, to make clear the independent origin of the European dolmens from those of the Near East; "the dragon of hyper-diffusionism is dead".[92] The emphasis now is on independent models of explanation, impirical or more regional.

Theoretical archaeology has attempted alternative models of explanation for the widespread appearance of dolmens. Renfrew proposed a unitary explanation rather than a diffusionist model for the appearance of the megalithic tombs on the North Sea/Atlantic seabord. He proposed that they were "an expression of territorial behaviour in small-scale segmentary societies ... especially in circumstances of population stress". Such segmentary societies lack the centralised hierarchical structure of a chiefdom or state, consisting of cellular and modular autonomous units.[93] These segmentary societies are definable in early Neolithic farming communities in Europe, and the theoretical demographic stresses relate to population growth within them; in circumstances where the farming community is joined by pre-existing fisher/gatherers/hunters there is even more rapid population increase; in addition some fisher/gatherers might adopt farming while not giving up existing food resources; all of which intensifies land competition.[94]

Can this theoretical base be applied if we accept an EB I date for the construction of the dolmens in our area? The existing Chalcolithic farming/pastoral community was quite large (the site of Teleilat Ghassul occupied 20 ha). Although much of the evidence from the economy and burials indicates simple egalitarian commmunities, the wall paintings, the metalworking and the temples suggest a degree of social complexity in the Chalcolithic. These communities may nevertheless be regarded as segmentary societies, lacking a centralised chief or state

authority. Taking into account the size of the Chalcolithic settlements in the western alluvial soils, and the proposed increasing dessication of the western alluvial zone, which may have led late in the Chaalcolithic period to a shift eastwards towards the higher rainfall zones in the foothills in the EB I period, the combination of such change and the pre-existence of other farming/pastoralist communities in the foothills may be assumed to have given rise to considerable population stress and competition for land between people exploiting both economic systems. It is still debateable whether the new factors appearing in the EB I period are also in part the result of immigration from a wider area, and if observed changes in agricultural processes can be seen as cause or effect in these processes.[95]

Chippindale notes that a strong concern of recent British archaeology "has been the making of social inferences, seeing ... if megalithic monuments, and the remains found in them, can indicate whether they were built by stratified societies under the command of chiefs and nobles or by egalitarian societies".[96] The contents are so rarely known in the Jordan dolmens that such inferences remain inferences. As to whether they are egalitarian or élitist monuments, the dolmens in Jordan are so widely distributed, in such numbers, that it would seem these are the normal form for disposal of the dead of a large part of the population over a long period; the varying sizes may simply relate to the availability of good slabs of stone. There seems to be no distinction between élite and non-élite as is seen in the nineteenth century AD, between the monuments constructed for venerated persons and tribal chiefs and the simple pit or cairn burials of lesser men. The inference is that we are looking at the product of an egalitarian society.

If the EB I peoples are the indigenous descendants of the Chalcolithic farming community and are viewed as the dolmen builders, the dolmens could be interpreted as above-ground territorial markers, as described by Chapman. Discussing the European dolmens, Chapman suggests that the appearance of the megaliths must be linked to contemporary agricultural societies, and concepts of descent, marriage and ancestor cults through which a permanent claim to the use of the land and critical resources is established; and in particular that the appearance of megaliths (e.g., dolmens) in succession to a flat cemetery (e.g., cists) might argue "that the reasons for the change were the greater pressure upon the critical resources and greater strains within the social system, necessitating ... symbolized control of these resources in a more impressive, visible manner".[97] In the nineteenth century AD in Transjordan many of these factors applied to pastoralists to whom concepts of descent, marriage and territory were equally important in terms of grazing rights as a critical resource, and who were subject to continuous inter-tribal stress and competition for land.

91  Joussaume 1988, 251-258.
92  Sherrat 1989, 59.
93  Renfrew 1976, 200, 206.
94  Ibid., 218.

95  Hanbury-Tenison 1986.
96  In Joussaume 1988, 13.
97  Chapman, Kinnes & Randsborg 1981, 73, 80.

Generally there seems to be increasing agreement that the dolmen cemeteries are those of tribal pastoralists (isolated cemeteries on hill slopes at a distance from settlements and arable land), who are in contact with sedentary groups, possibly closely linked in social and economic patterns, or who are themselves sometimes semi-sedentary or sedentarising (cemeteries close to arable land and settlements).[98] The former conditions exist in the upper Wadi Hisban where the distribution of the dolmens relates quite closely to that of nineteenth century transhumant pastoralists, their campsites and their tribal cemeteries, rather than to main routes and agricultural land. The latter conditions exist in the Adeimeh, al-Mataba and Damiya fields adjacent to alluvial soils and contemporary sites.

A more complex solution is to see the dolmens as the result of pressures between closely inter-related communities, with the competition between the users of agricultural land who undoubtedly have flocks, and pastoralists using more marginal zones who may also cultivate, being brought into a situation of greater stress by increased population (by birth and migration),

increasing dessication of the western alluvial soils in the south Jordan Valley in the late fourth millennium, and new settlement patterns which increasingly demanded defensive locations and defensive walls in foothill zones of slightly higher rainfall. With these changing balances, much of the population may well have adopted dolmen burial (cist burials above ground?), primarily as a territorial marker, and secondarily as tribal/religious status symbols. The building of dolmens may reflect particular periods of territorial stress and change in EB I and EB.MB (EB IV) when more dispersed settlement patterns are evident. The establishment of permanent, fortified settlements in EB II/III and MB I/II, when the fortifications themselves marked and defended territorial rights, permitted and necessitated the urban inhabitants to revert to a norm of below-ground burial, in caves, shaft graves and charnel houses. The evidence that the building and use of dolmens may continue throughout the Bronze Age and later alongside the more common below-ground interments may simply reflect conservative traditions and pragmatic choices among the more pastoralist sections of society. If there is an available charnel house, use it.

---

98  Cf. Zohar 1989; Carter & Parker, in this volume.

# 13 The Complex Nomads: Death and Social Stratification in EB IV Southern Levant

## *Evi Baxevani*

ABSTRACT— *The present paper comprises an effort to monitor mortuary variability and social differentiation in two well known EB IV Levantine cemeteries, Jericho and Tell Ajjul. The results of this work are discussed with reference to existing models regarding the social structure of EB IV communities in the southern Levant and with special emphasis on the limitations of the archaeological record. In the conclusive part, a discussion pertaining to the trajectory of complexity in EBA southern Levant is offered in order to provide a context for the results of this research.*

## Introduction

The end of the Early Bronze Age (EBA) in the southern Levant has been characterised by archaeologists as a period of major disruption marked by the collapse and fragmentation of the urban centres and accompanied by a series of changes in the settlement and mortuary record. This apparent discontinuity in the archaeological record has been widely discussed by scholars like Kenyon,[1] Prag,[2] Shay,[3] Palumbo,[4] Bentley[5] – to cite but a few – and more recently by Dever.[6]

Changes in the settlement pattern include the breakdown of urban settlements and subsequent small scale occupation. Continuation of *tell* occupation has been documented for several sites,[7] but is usually described as of non permanent character. This distinct modification of the settlement pattern has led to a series of interpretations suggesting a mobile character for some of the EB IV Levantine communities.

Environmental reasons, such as deterioration of the climate,[8] population influx,[9] and/or geopolitical explanations[10] have been provided. Recent fieldwork undertaken on sites with well documented EBA sequences in Transjordan, like Bab edh Dhrah',[11] has highlighted our knowledge of the EB IV phase and its variations. Most scholars now agree that the apparent discontinuity in the record is not a "gap", as previously thought. It seems that a widely accepted explanatory model is only emerging through the amalgamation of former theories. Population immigration models like the one forwarded by Kenyon[12] have not yet been totally dismissed, despite the appearance of more recent alternative explanations.

Recent research in the Jordan Valley, Transjordan and Israel by a number of expeditions[13] now shows that the number of EB IV sites in the southern Levant may exceed 1500, or more. Contrary to the views that regarded the EB IV southern Levant as a depopulated area, it is now shown that although settlement patterns and subsistence strategies had changed, sedentary occupation in agricultural village agglomerations was still the norm to a very large extent; in addition, recent excavations in these areas indicate that some of the EB IV sites were of 'urban' character.

The main corpus of published evidence, however, still comes from EB IV funerary contexts. The bulk of studies discussing the social horizon of the EB IV predominantly consists of mortuary analyses conducted on formal burial sites such as Jericho.[14] The relationship

1   Kenyon 1960
2   Prag 1974
3   Shay 1983
4   Palumbo 1987
5   Bently 1987
6   Dever 1992
7   e.g. Prag 1974; Davies 1986
8   e.g. Richard 1980
9   e.g. Kenyon 1960; 1979
10  e.g. Rast 1980

11  Schaub and Rast 1989
12  Kenyon 1979: 186-210
13  see Dever 1992
14  e.g. Shay 1983; Palumbo 1987

between mortuary differentiation and complexity established by the anthropological theory of the seventies[15] still dominates archaeological studies of death. The principles of mortuary variability first set by O'Shea[16] have determined the methodology of archaeologists working on cemetery material in other parts of the East Mediterranean, too,[17] including the present author.[18]

In this paper, the results of an analysis of mortuary variability in two major EB IV sites, Jericho and Tell Ajjul are presented in an attempt to establish the archaeological correlates of complexity in the EB IV southern Levant. The results of this analysis are then discussed in relation to existing theories regarding the collapse, or regression of complexity during the EB IV. The view promoted here is that the discontinuity in the archaeological record of EB IV southern Levant reflects a *fluctuation* in the process of complexity of Bronze Age communities, and not a state of *regression* as often assumed due to the demise of the urban idiom.

## Nomadic Theory and Social Complexity

The model of Pastoral Nomadism has been long held to best describe the character of EB IV southern Levantine society.[19] Even in the traditional invasion theories[20] the 'newcomers' were characterised as 'nomads'. Further study of the archaeological evidence available led to considerable modification of this hypothesis and moreover questioned the equation between nomadism and egalitarianism.[21] This question is closely related to the characterisation of EB IV society as complex, since social stratification is regarded as a prime correlate of complexity.

A relatively recent review of the nomadic theories by Bentley[22] has established an alternative view of the nomadic hypothesis, namely that the degree of complexity and variation of expression in nomadic pastoralist economies is much higher than often assumed, a view also expressed by Tubb[23] earlier on. At present, it is more or less widely acknowledged that EB IV southern Levantine communities exercised a mixed economy where sedentism and agriculture comprised a major part in the subsistence strategies involved. Moreover, it has been argued that the nature of the settlement record tends to over-emphasise the *nomadic* character of the society.[24]

An examination of the mortuary record of the southern Levant indicates that patterns of social differentiation – widely considered as clear correlates of complexity – are displayed in EB IV funerary domains. Evidently, the equation between *nomadism* and *egalitarianism* is a false one since it does not account for the variability apparent in the record. Similarly, urbanism is not always positively correlated to complexity, i.e a decline in the urbanisation process of an area does not necessarily imply a regression in complexity. Bearing in mind the theories proposed for the demise of EB III settlements in the southern Levant,[25] it is necessary to understand the parameters of economic and political adaptation dictating structural changes in the sociopolitical format of human communities without introducing simplistic arguments in favour of "egalitarian", non-complex social structures.[26] Such views cannot satisfactorily explain the emergence of a *fully* developed urbanism in the MBA. Yet, the 're-urbanisation' process could not have taken place in a sociopolitical vacuum.

An interesting point maintained by modern scholars[27] has been that attention should be drawn to the distinctive character of EBA urbanism in the southern Levant marked by the absence of any written archives to offer detailed insights as to the urbanisation process in the area. Indeed, several aspects of EBA urbanism in southern Levant point to the *less* urban idiom of the area when compared with the fully urban character of Syria, Mesopotamia, and the southern Levant itself in the MBA. More recently, the notion of scale in complexity has been introduced[28] to help realise that the archaeological correlates of complexity may vary a great deal among different societies, or even different human communities within the same area. Both the nomadic and urbanisation theories may need to be reconsidered with reference to this particular point so that the peculiarities of the Levantine record may be accommodated within their theoretical frameworks.

## The archaeological evidence: Jericho and Tell Ajjul

A study of mortuary variability on the major EB IV cemetery of Jericho[29] indicates that the skeletal population was differentiated in several aspects of the burial program involved the most prominent of which were methods of disposal and grave inclusions. Unfortunately, sex and age data are biased to such an extent that it is impossible to treat the skeletal sample in quantitative terms.[30] However, the distinct pattern of burial

15 Saxe 1970; Binford 1971
16 O'Shea 1984
17 e.g. Keswani 1989a for Cyprus, Bard 1989 for Egypt
18 Baxevani 1994 for Cyprus, Crete, and the southern Levant
19 Dever 1980, 1992; Palumbo 1987
20 Kenyon 1960
21 Palumbo 1987
22 Bently 1987
23 Tubb 1983
24 Prag 1985

25 see Bentley 1987
26 *contra* Shay 1983
27 e.g. Bentley 1987; Philip 1989
28 Joffe 1991
29 Palumbo 1987
30 *contra* Shay 1983

treatment that the mortuary population received and the variations in funerary equipment led Palumbo[31] to conclude that social stratification was manifested in the burial record of the site. Apart from the quantity of grave goods it can also be argued that the quality of furnishings further differentiates the burials. For instance, only pottery and/or beads accompany the disarticulated inhumations, whereas metal comprises the consistent grave good of single and intact interments. Moreover, in terms of energy expenditure, the most elaborate chambers on the site – Kenyon's Outsize and Square shaft types – are associated with *both* metalwork and pottery.

Similarly, at the site of Tell Ajjul patterns of sharp social differentiation are displayed in the tombs. The site was re-examined by Kenyon[32] and it is from her publication that the data used in this paper are drawn.

The present analysis examines five variables with regard to mortuary differentiation: a) biological and demographic data, b) treatment of the deceased and methods of disposal, c) grave equipment, d) spatial arrangement of tombs and skeletons, and e) energy/labour expenditure towards the construction of tomb facilities. These variables have been used for the cemetery analysis on both sites.

Reference should be made to the limitations of the archaeological record itself in this area and the poor publication standards which determined to a very large extent the methodology of this research. In order to avoid introducing any further bias in the study of this corpus of data, a set of Data Quality Control Factors were established to help cope with the difficulties of handling such a fragmentary and often unreliable material. These factors are discussed in detail elsewhere,[33] but a brief outline for each cemetery follows.

*Jericho Data Quality Control Factors*
a)  Fragmentary pottery vessels or sherdage are not used in this analysis
b)  Pottery, or other finds, which come from unstratified parts of the tombs, have been excluded from this research since their context is unknown
c)  Finds deriving from sieving have also been excluded
d)  Tombs which only survive as deep pits, or fissures, or have been partially excavated have not been included in the present sample
e)  Pottery vessels mended from sherdage are not included since their description is not provided in the publication
f)  With particular reference to the EB IV tombs of Jericho published by Kenyon,[34] 'facing' refers to the *position of the skull* (head to), and not to the actual

direction to which the face is pointed. This piece of information is not published.

*Tell Ajjul Data Quality Control Factors*
a)  Tombs which do not contain human remains are excluded from the present sample
b)  Pottery which is not illustrated in the original publication of Petrie,[35] or described in the republication of Kenyon[36] is not included
c)  Individual discrepancies between the two publications have been noted. In these cases, the relevant tombs or artefacts have been excluded from this analysis.

# Jericho

## a) Biological and Demograhic Data

Anthropological evidence is available for a number of EB IV tombs. Kenyon[37] makes an estimate of ca. 356 individuals in the EB IV burial facilities. The demographic structure of the population cannot be reconstructed with certainty due to the fragmentary nature of the anthropological evidence.[38] The sample is biased for several reasons, the most important of which are the number of disarticulated burials and the distinct lack of female skeletons.

Disarticulation processes render the mortuary population sample unverifiable. The gender representation ratios also indicate the bias. Since the identification of age and gender depends on the state of preservation of each skeleton it becomes evident that only assumptions can be made with regard to the disarticulated segment of the population.

## b) Treatment of the Deceased and Methods of Disposal

The majority of the EB IV skeletal population comprised disarticulated burials (n=47), and less than half were single intact inhumations in flexed (n=4) and crouched (n=25) positions (Fig. 13.1). Of the aligned burials (n=14) most had a general E-W orientation (n=13), and were facing W. Although the population was mainly adult (n=30) there were at least some children (n=4) and infants (n=4) interred (Fig. 13.2).

There are two distinct patterns of post-mortem treatment, that of articulated, primary inhumation and that of disarticulated, secondary burial. For the moment, no discussion is made concerning the significance of these patterns in relation to mortuary differentiation; however, this aspect of mortuary variability focuses our attention on age/sex as opposed to status distinctions.

31  Palumbo 1987
32  Kenyon 1956
33  Baxevani 1994
34  Kenyon 1960

35  Petrie 1931
36  Kenyon 1956
37  Kenyon *Jericho II*: 1
38  *contra* Shay 1983

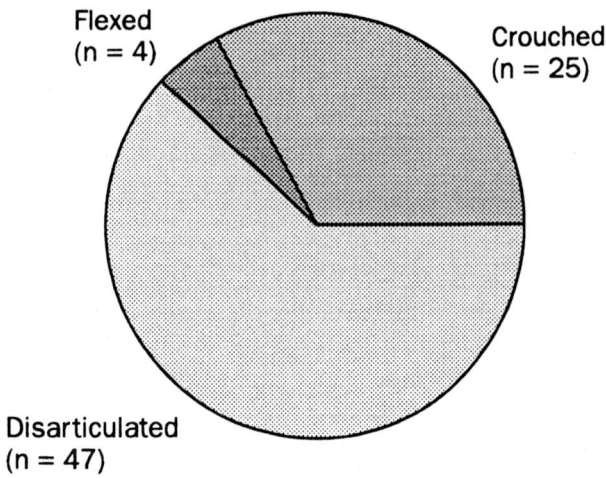

*Fig. 13.1: Jericho EB IV burial positions*

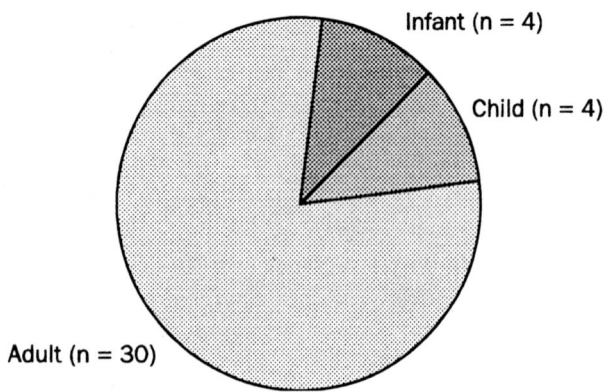

*Fig. 13.2: Jericho EB IV age of individuals*

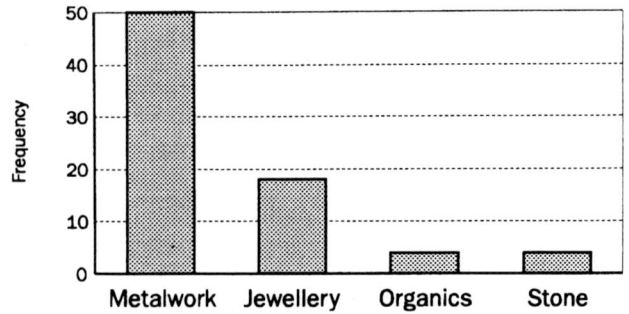

*Fig. 13.3: Jericho EB IV frequencies of grave equipment*

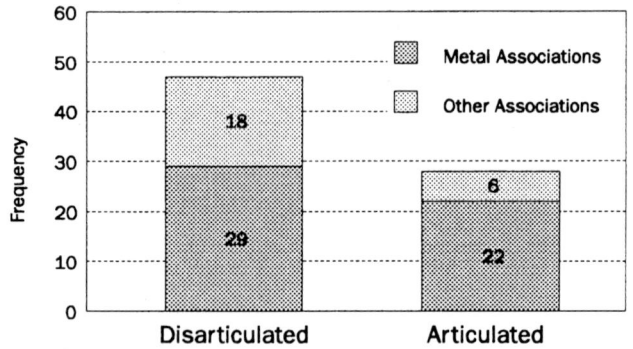

*Fig. 13.4: Jericho EB IV number of associations with metalwork*

possibility that at least three burials (Tombs J 3, J 37, J 105 in Area A) may have been those of women on the basis of their associations (a pin and a bead for each interment); these are all single, articulated inhumations. However, sex cannot be safely postulated on the basis of artefactual associations only, therefore, this piece of data is unreliable.

### c) Grave Equipment

A different situation appears in the EB IV tombs at Jericho. Metalwork (n=50) is predominant in these contexts (Fig. 13.3); most items are daggers (n=14) and pins (n=12). All the other categories have lower frequencies. A correlation between post-mortem treatment and metal deposition shows that almost all of the articulated individuals (n=29) were accompanied by metal items (n=22). Of the disarticulated individuals (n=47), the majority (n=28) were buried with metal artefacts and pottery.

The ceramic industry is very standardised during this period and the range of shapes is rather poor. There are selective patterns of ceramic deposition evident in the association between specific tomb types and pottery[46]. The sample indicates that pottery comprises the major correlate of disarticulated inhumations as opposed to articulated skeletons which are foremost associated with metal weapons (Figs 13.4 and 13.5). Only a few articulated inhumations (n=5) were associated with ceramics only, whereas most of the disarticu-

With reference to EB IV Jericho, research is divided; some scholars maintain that post-mortem treatment here is associated with age/sex distinctions, or even ethnic ones.[39] Others – including the author – argue in favour of social stratification manifested in these contexts.[40]

Statistical methods were employed to examine the skeletal population in demographic terms and even extract biological and social information from the EB IV burials.[41] Shay[42] infers that the distinct absence of female skeletons is due to pre-interment disarticulation treatment of the female segment of the population and that non-disarticulation was reserved solely for males. Her observations are based on the sexing of EB IV skeletons from the 1955-58 season[43] which showed that all female skeletons were completely disarticulated.

Unfortunately, anthropological information is not available for the EB IV tombs which were excavated during 1954-55[44]. According to Kenyon[45], there is a

39   Kenyon 1969; Prag 1974; Shay 1983
40   Philip 1989; Palumbo 1987; Baxevani 1994
41   Shay 1983
42   Ibid., 31
43   Kenyon 1965, Appendix H: 665
44   Kenyon 1960.
45   Ibid., 187

46   Kenyon 1960, 199-205.

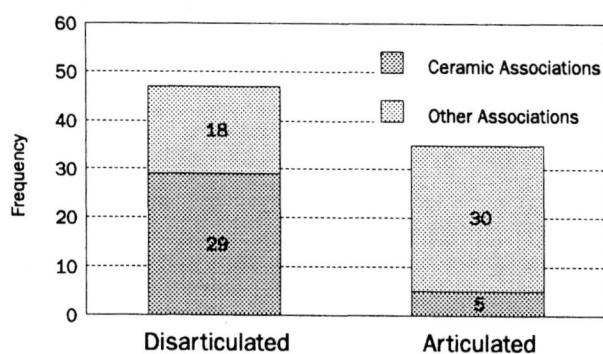

*Fig. 13.5: Jericho EB IV number of associations
with ceramics*

lated burials (n=28) were accompanied by pottery and occasionally metal.

The examination of post-mortem treatment and grave equipment in the EB IV tombs at the site indicates that at least two variables point to a pattern of mortuary differentiation. Two more variables are examined in the following pages in order to verify this pattern.

*d) Spatial arrangement*

The spatial arrangement of tomb types during the EB IV, when correlated to all aspects of mortuary variability, points to a lucid expression of differentiation in the Jericho burial domains. Kenyon's discussion on the EB IV tomb groups[47] reveals the highly structured nature of EB IV burials. Each tomb type has its own characteristics in terms of location, post-mortem treatment, grave equipment and funerary architecture. Evidently, the differences observed among these distinct tomb groups require explanation. Since the chronological argument is dropped by the excavator herself[48] and the mingling of characteristics in some of these domains[49] weakens the ethnic argument, it is only possible to look for social interpretation. This interpretation is sought at the end of the analysis of this cemetery, after tomb typology and energy flow have also been examined.

*e) Energy/labour expenditure*

Measures of energy flow in the EB IV are related to the tomb typology proposed by Kenyon.[50] Accordingly, the most "expensive" tombs were the Outsize, Square Shaft and Pottery type tombs; the Dagger and Bead type tombs were of smaller size and thus required less labour for their construction.

Despite the fact that measures of energy expenditure have been disputed as measures of social status,[51] energy flow when correlated with other aspects of mortuary variability in the present sample shows that

differentiation was also made in terms of labour expenditure.

## Patterns of Mortuary Differentiation at EBA Jericho

In order to better visualise the changes in mortuary symbolism and ritual that took place in the EB IV of the southern Levant, it is necessary to view briefly the main characteristics of mortuary ritual at Jericho throughout the EBA, and also to recall the evidence from other contemporary sites in the southern Levant. In this case, the recently published site of Bab edh Dhrah' in Transjordan[52] offers a parallel for comparison.

The number of EB I-III tombs at the site is very small to allow for any distinct patterns to emerge. Multiple burial also renders meaningful contextual analysis impossible. Apart from evidence for cremation in EB I Tomb A 94[53], the inhumation of a vast number of individuals in this tomb distinguishes this context from its counterparts at other sites, like Bab edh Dhrah' in Transjordan. It is important to note that the EB I tombs on both Jericho and Bab edh Dhrah' contain a smaller number of skeletons in comparison to the EB II-III tombs which accommodate a vast number of individuals. This piece of data indicates that the mode of interment changes through the early EBA from *communal* to *collective*. This change also marks the beginnings of urban life in the associated settlements on both sites.[54]

However, some EB I tombs at Jericho (e.g. A 94[55]) have yielded an enormous number of burials and finds. Some 113 individuals are estimated for A 94, a total that by far surpasses the contemporary Bab edh Dhrah' contexts; other EB I Jericho tombs (e.g. A 13[56]) are of comparable size in mortuary population and finds.

Another similarity between the EB I tombs on both sites is in the post-mortem treatment of the deceased individuals. They all comprise disarticulated inhumations deliberately arranged within the burial chamber; the long bones are usually piled up in the centre of the chamber while the skulls are situated in a separate row. Unfortunately, this pattern of internal arrangement was not as clear in Jericho due to the more cumulative nature of its deposits.

The evidence shows that on both sites, the EB II-III tombs contain a huge number of skeletons. In Bab edh Dhrah' this change is marked by the introduction of different mortuary facilities to accommodate the dead (charnell houses). In Jericho the same rock-cut tombs are used and some of the EB I-III chambers re-used.

47  Kenyon 1960, 180-185.
48  Ibid., 182.
49  Ibid., 182
50  Ibid., 180-185.
51  Tainter 1978; Bentley 1987

52  Shaub and Rast 1989.
53  Kenyon 1960, 8.
54  Kenyon 1979, 167-185; Schaub and Rast 1989, 547.
55  Kenyon 1960, 16-25.
56  Ibid., 47-48.

| Type | Main Location | Burial | Grave Goods |
|---|---|---|---|
| Square Shaft | Area J | Single Intact | Metal Weapon-Pottery |
| Dagger | Area A | Single Intact | Metal Weapon |
| Outsize | Areas O, P | Disarticulated-Intact | Pottery-Metal Weapon |
| Pottery | Areas H, G | Disarticulated | Pottery |
| Bead | Areas K, D | Disarticulated | Beads, occasional metal |

*Table 13.1: General features of Jericho tombs.*

Thus the continuity in burial architecture is not disrupted in Jericho as it is in Bab edh Dhrah'.

The quality of grave goods also changes on both sites between the EB I and EB II-III, with the introduction of an enhanced artefactual repertoire present in both the settlement and burial contexts. Carinated vessels appear in the EB II-III contexts at both Jericho and Bab edh Dhra and new metal weapon types are introduced (e.g the fenestrated axe). Moreover, the quantity of grave furnishings increases, though in accordance with the number of inhumations in these tombs.

The evidence from Tomb A 94 in Jericho is indicative of a collective mode of interment as early as the EB I. This may be of significance in terms of social inferences since it may suggest there was not a gradual development from *communal* to *collective* interment. The latter was already practised in EB I Jericho.

The major point to be made with regard to the EB I and II-III tombs is that they manifest a reluctance on behalf of the burying group to exhibit differentiation among the deceased members of the society. The communal/collective mode of interment points to intentionally minimal differentiation during a period that has been associated with more complex sociopolitical organisation in the Levant. Social distinctions that may have existed are not detected in the record; inequalities in access to resources, post-mortem treatment and energy expenditure are not visible either.

The EB II-III burial mode is in marked contrast with the situation in the EB IV contexts. In the previous paragraphs it was shown that there seems to be a correlation between the rise of urbanism in the southern Levant and change in the format and execution of burial programmes. Change in the social structure of EB II-III southern Levantine communities is sustained by the burial record, while the settlement record yields evidence for organisational change too.

In this respect, the EB IV situation stands in marked contrast to what went on before. At Jericho, in particular, mortuary variability is enhanced by the highly formal nature of burial programmes during this period.

Methods of disposal indicate radical change, from multiple disarticulated/articulated inhumations to single, intact interments for a certain segment of the population. This differentiation by post-mortem treatment is further emphasised by the presence of different grave good packages for each mode of inter-ment. In relation to the above mentioned, labour expenditure varies for each mode of interment with its associated grave kit, and spatial location is used to discern among the different tomb groups.

All variables used in this sample to detect mortuary differentiation indicate that different statuses are undoubtedly displayed in the EB IV domains. The point is that the substantial changes in the execution of burial programmes during the EB IV, and the vivid manifestation of mortuary differentiation in these domains, has to be interpreted.

A general discussion on the EBA is found in the concluding part of this paper. It is necessary at this point, however, to discuss the Jericho evidence in more detail, since it comprises the best preserved evidence for the period. First, it is important to isolate the characteristics of the EB IV tomb groups in relation to both Kenyon's typology and observations[57], and the results of this analysis. The table 13.1 gives a description of the main features of these tombs:

Measures of energy flow indicate that the Outsize, Square Shaft and Pottery type tombs were the largest facilities on the site. When all variables are pulled together it becomes evident that the most "elaborate" type is the Square Shaft tomb followed by the rest of tomb types in the sequence presented in the above summary.

This clear-cut pattern of burial programmes points to different statuses held by the deceased in these domains. It does not necessarily follow that the higher status individuals were the ones buried in Square Shaft tombs, however, since the manifestation of differentiation is so distinct, it must be acknowledged that social distinctions were sharp and inequalities had to be apparent. The reasons dictating this behaviour on behalf of the burying group must be sought in the social structure of the EB IV Jericho community that required the maximisation of differentiation in burial domains.

Although this may involve different ethnic groups and horizontal distinctions not discernible in the archaeological record, vertical distinctions are far more evident.[58] The fact that only a segment of the population had access to metal resources for instance, or the differentiation between intact and disarticulated skeletons is indicative of a high degree of inequality in the Jericho community. Again, it is not clear which post-

---

57 Kenyon 1960, 180-185.
58 Palumbo 1987; *contra* Shay 1983.

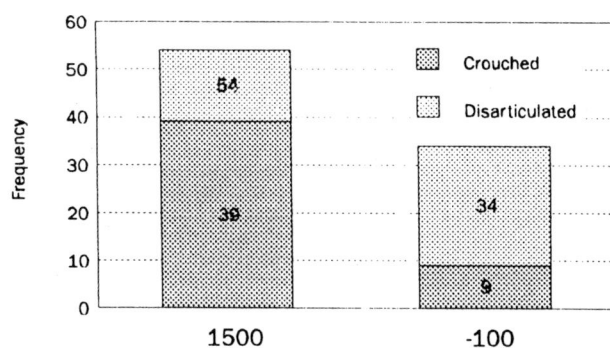

Fig. 6: Tell Ajjul EB IV post-mortem treatment

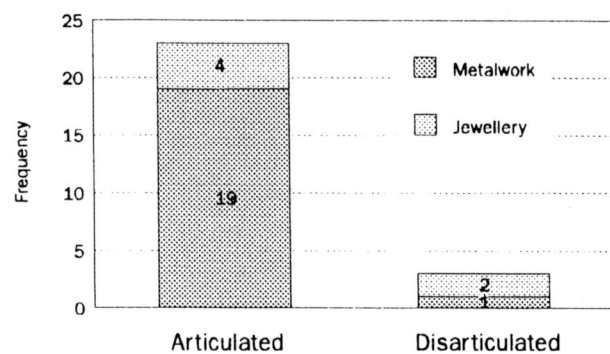

Fig. 13.8: Tell Ajjul EB IV burials with
ceramic associations

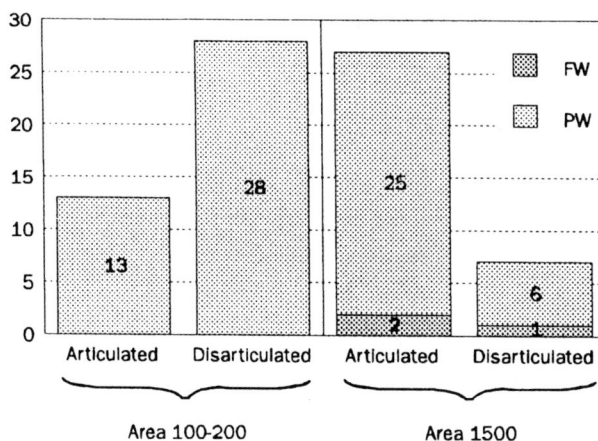

Fig. 13.7: Tell Ajjul EB IV burials with metalwork
and jewellery associations

post-mortem treatment is a correlate of high status, but the distinction is so sharp that inequality is deliberately displayed; similarly, the differences between grave goods (metal vs pottery or beads) are compelling indicators of vertical social distinctions. Clear-cut levels of social stratification are difficult to establish, however, stratification is obvious in these contexts.

The analysis of the Tell Ajjul cemetery corroborates the Jericho evidence with regard to the manifestation of mortuary differentiation and social inequalities. Evidently, major structural change took place in EB IV southern Levant evident in both the disruption of the settlement record and the implementation of different burial programmes in which mortuary differentiation was clearly manifested.

## Tell Ajjul

### a) Biological and Demographic Data

Due to the complete lack of anthropological data biological and demographic evidence is missing. The only relevant piece of information derives from the association between the extent of the cemetery and its mortuary population, and the *tell* evidence, which is virtually non-existent. This corroborates the argument that during the EB IV settlement occupation was sparse or absent at the Tell Ajjul excavated area.

### b) Treatment of the Deceased and Methods of Disposal

Information related to post-mortem treatment and pre-interment practices is indicated in the disarticulation of several burials on the site. On the basis of the data there are some marked differences in patterns of post-mortem treatment between the two areas of the cemetery.

There is a total of 105 (n=105) inhumations from Tell Ajjul (Fig. 13.6). Area 1500 contains 48 burials (n=48), whereas area 100-200 contains 57 inhumations (n=57). The majority of skeletons (n=39) in area 1500 are intact, in crouched position, aligned E-W (n=28) with head to north. They are all single burials. The majority of burials in area 100-200 are disarticulated skeletons (n=25). Some of the articulated, crouched burials (n=15) are aligned E-W (n=5) with head to north. They comprise single burials like in area 1500.

There is a distinct pattern of post-mortem treatment discerning between the two areas of the cemetery . As in the case of EB IV Jericho where different treatment was associated with different burial and spatial domains, post-mortem treatment at Tell Ajjul has a definite spatial correlate. The validity of this information is demonstrated when all other aspects of mortuary variability are examined.

### c) Grave Equipment

The standard grave good furnishings consist of Plain Ware (PW) pottery, jewellery (mainly beads) and metalwork (copper daggers). An interesting pattern emerges when the information on grave goods is examined spatially. The vast majority of finds from area 1500 are copper daggers (n=19) associated with single intact skeletons in crouched position (Fig. 13.7). Two bead groups (n=2) of unknown material and two (n=2) stone rings were also found. In area 100-200 the majority of skeletons are accompanied by PW pottery (n=28). Only one inhumation (n=1) was found with a

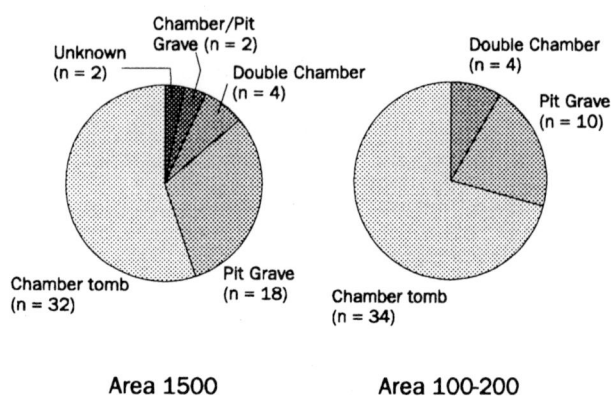

*Fig. 13.9: Tell Ajjul EB IV spatial distribution
of tomb types*

dagger, and another two (n=2) with a stone ring and some beads.

In terms of pottery equipment, area 1500 shows that usually only the articulated skeletons were accompanied by ceramic vessels, mostly PW (n=25), whereas the disarticulated ones were only occasionally found associated with ceramics (n=6) (Fig. 13.8). Area 100-200 demonstrates that the disarticulated burials (the majority) were mostly accompanied by pottery vessels (n=28) (Fig. 13.8).

### d) Spatial Arrangement

The spatial aspect of mortuary differentiation is best exemplified in this cemetery. Areas 1500 and 100-200 display distinct differences in all dimensions of funerary variability, including the last variable, energy flow, which is examined in the next section.

This pattern of spatial differentiation, though an evident one, is not as clear-cut, since both types of post-mortem treatment are represented in both cemeteries and there are, even sporadic, occurrences of grave goods that are clearly associated with each of them. Differences seem to cross-cut the two areas and this renders its interpretation more complicated.

What is noteworthy is the fact that the spatial element is employed on top of all other variables to emphasise differentiation in the specific contexts. Whether this differentiation was based on age/sex or status distinctions is almost impossible to assess because the anthropological data is lacking; nevertheless, the distribution of metal between the two areas is a compelling indicator of sharp inequality among the deceased. As in the case of EB IV Jericho spatial distributions of post-mortem treatment and grave equipment points to distinct burial programmes that serve to emphasise differentiation in these domains.

### e) Energy/labour Expenditure

There are three different tomb types excavated in area 1500 of the Tell Ajjul cemetery. These are, simple

pit graves (type 2), built tombs (type 5) and chamber tombs (type 4). In area 100-200, only pit graves and chamber tombs were excavated (Fig. 13.9).

In terms of relative energy flow area 1500 type 5 tombs are the smaller facilities used. Types 2 and 4 have dimensions that exceed 1.50m. An interesting contrast appears when area 100-200 tombs are examined; both tomb types in this area have considerable dimensions and when the two areas are compared it is shown that area 100-200 tombs were more "expensive" in terms of labour spent over their construction. Energy expenditure measures, therefore, do not point to the same kind of differentiation established by the other variables.

The dagger burials occur solely in chamber tombs, thus pointing to a possible association between this type of interment and specific mortuary architecture. In view of the quantity and quality of grave equipment area 100-200 may be characterised as a "poorer" cemetery despite the fact that measures of energy flow do not support this view.

### 5) Patterns of Mortuary Differentiation at EB IV Tell Ajjul

The examination of mortuary variability on the site, shows a predominant pattern of differentiation expressed in spatial terms. There are several parameters to be considered before any clear-cut distinction between a "rich" and a "poor" disposal area are made.

First, it is important to remember that sex and age data is lacking for both areas. Second, the two patterns of post-mortem treatment observed in both areas have to be interpreted using the evidence from other EB IV cemeteries in the southern Levant. Third, the variety of mortuary architecture employed for these burials is noteworthy, particularly since most EB IV burial sites contain only chamber tombs.

Other points worth considering are the contrasting evidence derived from energy flow measures and the cross-cutting of post-mortem treatment, grave equipment and tomb types in both areas of the cemetery. These features are present to a greater or lesser degree in both areas. The interpretation of the particular cemetery, therefore, involves several aspects which merit consideration. Tell Ajjul, like most EB IV cemeteries in the region displays the new elements of the era, namely the metalwork tombs containing single inhumations. It is a far reaching conclusion to maintain an association between males and metal weapons since no sex data exists.

Patterns of mortuary differentiation point to the formality of EB IV burial programmes at Tell Ajjul and the intentional expression of differentiation in mortuary domains. Like EB IV Jericho, Tell Ajjul bears evidence for sharp distinctions which call for an interpretation that goes beyond the dichotomies of rich/poor burials and seeks to explain the reasons behind such a distinct expression in mortuary symbolism and ritual.

# Conclusion: A discussion on the trajectory of complexity in EBA southern Levant

In this section of the paper an effort is made to monitor the rise of complex society in the southern Levant through the manifestation of this process in the mortuary record. The theoretical context of this discussion includes several parameters related to the interpretation of exclusively burial data to detect sociopolitical development and change. The most crucial constraint imposed upon the manipulation of such data is the highly symbolic nature of the funerary remains.

The evidence for mortuary differentiation has been long considered to comprise an important archaeological correlate of social complexity, however, this correlation is not a direct one; it is related to changing rules of mortuary ritual and symbolic expression that reflect the ideal social order, rather than daily sociopolitical organisation and interaction.[59]

Patterns of mortuary differentiation, therefore, are filtered through this ideal social order and their meaningful intepretation depends upon the flexibility of the research design to provide alternative sets of correlates for complexity. As such, the manifestation of differentiation in burial domains is subject to rules and regulations determined by the burying group, i.e the living community. The display of equal/unequal treatment in all aspects of mortuary variability comprises a conspicuous expression on behalf of the society to portray the social personae of its deceased population. Mortuary variability is, foremost, a highly artificial expression of the social order. The funerary evidence from EBA southern Levant is tested against this theoretical perspective in order to provide insights into the evolution of socioeconomic and political organisation and rising complexity.

There are several issues to consider with regard to the trajectory of social evolution in the southern Levant. One is the rise of urban culture and increased complexity as a result of foreign, versus indigenous development.[60] Second is the notion of fluctuations in social complexity attested for the southern Levant during the third millenium BC.[61] The archaeological record of the area exhibits discontinuities which point to cycles of collapsing and rising complexity that need to be explained. With particular regard to the burial record, a fluctuating pattern of complexity is evident in the changing patterns of mortuary ritual. The final issue is related to the re-emergence of urban societies in MBA southern Levant and the beginnings of international economic and political interconnections in the East Mediterranean region.

With regard to the first point, there is a wide literature dealing with the discontinuities between the Chalcolithic and the EBA and the trajectories of

transition from a village-level, small-scale society to one of increasing integration and complexity.[62] Some scholars maintain that the evolutionary trajectory of southern Levant was determined by the qualitative reorganisation of the society as early as the EB I, which is considered as the key to understanding later developments.[63]

The archaeological evidence points to a variety of settlement agglomerations in different parts of the southern Levant; in the south for instance, evidence for settlement occupation includes Chalcolithic elements[64] and indicates Egyptian influence. At Bab edh Dhrah', the EB IA phase comprises ephemeral occupation.[65] In the north, reduction in settlement size and number of settlements is noted.[66]

The mortuary record consists of chamber tombs used for the inhumation of several individuals accompanied by a highly standardised equipment. The examination of mortuary variability on EB IA Bab edh Dhrah' indicates differentiation on the basis of post-mortem treatment. However, in terms of other variables, no significant differentiation can be postulated. Burial data from this particular site point to kin, or lineage-based social units[67] which were clearly resistant to social distinctions; patterns of grave equipment deposition present a high degree of similarity and formality, thus indicating a conscious effort to eliminate differentiation.

The later part of the EB I (EB IB), is characterised by higher levels of societal organisation evident in the expanded settlement pattern of the southern Levant.[68] Mortuary evidence from this phase at Bab edh Dhrah' points to continuity in patterns of post-mortem treatment, however, both grave equipment and mortuary architecture demonstrate changes in death ritual; the most prominent is the evolution of the charnel house as a distinct type of burial architecture and the appearance of metal weaponry in this context. Clearly, the changing pattern of burial practice is indicative of changes in the societal format of late EB I communities. The introduction of larger mortuary facilities like the charnel houses in the EB II-III points to the emergence of larger social units, and the deposition of metalwork, "a slender currency",[69] raises questions related to resource access and control.

The process of development towards increasing complexity and change during early EBA has been often linked to contemporary sociopolitical developments in neighbouring areas, mainly Egypt.[70] The crucial question here is to what extent social evolution in the

---

59 e.g. Pader 1982; Morris 1987; Keswani 1989a.
60 Joffe 1991, 3.
61 Joffe 1991, 5.
62 e.g. Esse 1991; Joffe 1991.
63 Joffe 1991.
64 see Lachish Area 15600, Tell el Hesi, Azor Installation C, in Joffe 1991, 13.
65 Schaub and Rast 1989, 554.
66 Joffe 1991, 13-15.
67 Bentley 1987; Joffe 1991.
68 Joffe 1991.
69 Joffe 1991, 29.
70 Rast 1980; Joffe 1991.

southern Levant was affected by the Egyptian presence in the area; although the impetus for a re-organisation of southern Levantine society may have been provided by the interaction with the highly complex, state society of Egypt, the archaeological record of the southern Levant displays a high degree of individualism in this process of increasing complexity.

Interaction with Egypt never produced a Levantine society which borrowed, or emulated the Egyptian model. Selective mechanisms developed by the Levantine communities must be inferred in order to explain such a pattern of contact and exchange. Environmental constraints have certainly played a significant role in the creation of a "pre-adapted" society that would certainly follow a different path towards complexity.[71] However, the environmental argument does not suffice to explain intensive levels of interaction but much lower levels of emulation. On the basis of this less composite (i.e small-scale) nature of complexity, southern Levantine society has often been considered as underdeveloped in comparison to its neighbours. This notion has been sufficiently argued against by Joffe who introduced the concept of scale in the examination of Levantine complexity.

The EB II-III period in the southern Levant is marked by changes in the settlement pattern which now becomes expanded with more sites demonstrating urban features and providing more identifiable forms of complexity.[72] The mortuary record of this period bears evidence for further social re-organisation, featuring predominantly collective inhumations in large chambered or built tombs and an abundance of grave equipment. Patterns of mortuary differentiation are difficult to assess in these contexts. The number and range of burial goods point to intensified contact with both Egypt and Syro-Mesopotamia.[73] The establishment of the charnel house at Bab edh Dhra as the main burial facility for EB II-III inhumations is indicative of an increase in the scale of societal organisation and of a much greater degree of sedentism, associated with the main urban phase on the settlement.

The new configuration of fortified, urban, settlements actively involved in exchange networks and centralised economic and political activity, consolidated socioeconomic relations that were based upon efficient resource control and exploitation. Whether the economic power was in the hands of small-scale elites which became crystallised in the urban environment is difficult to assess on the basis of the mortuary evidence, due to the collective nature of the EB II-III deposits and the limited size of the sample of early EBA tombs.

The evidence for social differentiation in mortuary domains continues to be minimal. The accumulation of hundreds of burials in each tomb eliminates individualism and underlines a collective sense in the manifesta-

tion of the social order. The transformation of the communal idiom of the EB I into a collective one in the EB II-III points to a concomitant change in sociopolitical organisation. Collective interment becomes a correlate of urban society in this respect.

It is beyond the scope of this thesis to examine Levantine urbanism and its manifestations in the EBA archaeological record in detail; however, the results of the analysis indicate that the trajectory of urbanism in the EBA southern Levant is highly individualistic and its correlates vastly differentiated from its counterparts in other urban societies of the Near East, like Syria and Mesopotamia, where elite burials provide a correlate of urbanism. The nature of EBA urbanism in the southern Levant has been questioned;[74] the settlement record provides evidence for defended urban centres and relevant population aggregates, but the burial record does not provide the necessary evidence for social inequality and stratification.[75]

It has been suggested that the communal element present in the social structure of southern Levantine communities may have determined the trajectory of urbanism and complexity in the area.[76] However, this element is transformed in the EB II-III period into a collective idiom; it may be that this is an expression of small-scale urbanism, or that urbanism itself is not yet fully developed. A comparison between the EBA and the MBA in southern Levant itself shows that evidence for social stratification is present in the MBA burial record.[77] It is suggested, therefore, that the archaeological correlates of EBA urban society in the southern Levant may be radically different from relevant sets of correlates in other areas of the Near East. In the EBA context, collective interment is one such correlate. Attention must be drawn to the fact that "collective" does not necessarily imply "egalitarian".[78] Rather, a collective mode of interment serves to mask actual inequalities and distinctions that probably existed in the living society.

The final phase of the EBA bears evidence for a fluctuation in the trajectory of complexity in the southern Levantine communities. The abandonment of tell occupation to a large extent and the "replacement" of the "domestic mode of production"[79] by multi-resource subsistence patterns marks a distinct change in sociopolitical organisation and socioeconomic relations, emphasized by considerable amounts of metal goods of localised production and their conspicuous consumption in tomb contexts.[80]

The examination of mortuary variability from EB IV disposal areas displays several levels of differentiation with regard to the variables employed. The

---

71  Joffe 1991: 7.
72  Kenyon 1960; Prag 1974; Rast 1980; Joffe 1991.
73  Rast 1980.

74  e.g. Philip 1989, 195.
75  also Philip 1989, 195.
76  Philip 1989: 195.
77  e.g. Philip 1989, 207-216.
78  also Soles 1988.
79  Joffe 1991, 36.
80  Philip 1989.

crucial parameters of that differentiation are epitomised by the highly structured implementation of burial programmes.

Evidence for social and economic inequalities is found in these contexts and although a clear-cut pattern of social stratification has not emerged, these deposits emphasize differentiation to such an extent that, if mortuary differentiation is accepted as a correlate of complexity, it is difficult to maintain a significant regression in complexity during the EB IV period. It is, therefore, suggested that the EB IV comprises a period of qualitative re-organisation of southern Levantine communities. The distinct artefactual repertoire of the tombs in relation to the contemporary settlement evidence points to a change in the societal configurations that may be related to environmental or geopolitical change.

Lower levels of complexity may be assessed for the EB IV since it is during that period that an emergence of elite groups can be sustained on the basis of burial data. The evidence from Jericho and Tell Ajjul points to the existence of small groups who had differential access to resources. This argument shows that a correlation between elite mechanisms and rising complexity is problematic, particularly since highly restricted resource control does not trigger highly complex forms of sociopolitical organisation.[81]

To conclude, the trajectory of social complexity in the southern Levant was determined by several factors which were not always in the form of constraints, but often a product of socially selected procedures related to the small-scale nature of the society. The fluctuations of organisational complexity well attested in the mortuary record of the area point to the EBA southern Levant being a "middle-range"[82] society where the evolution of sociopolitical complexity was markedly different from other complex societies in the Near East, both in terms of quality and scale.

---

81   Tainter 1988.
82   Upham 1990.

# 14 Pots, People and The Archaeology of Death in Northern Syria and Southern Anatolia in the latter half of the Third Millennium BC

## *Elizabeth Carter and Andrea Parker*

ABSTRACT—*The paper presents an overview of burial practices in sites dated to the later third millennium in North Syria and Southern Analtolia. The discussion focuses on Hadidi, Tawi and Halawa on the middle Euphrates; Ansari-Aleppo, Barsip and Ebla in northern Syria, Lidar, Titris and Kurban Höyük in the Atatürk dam region of southern Turkey; and Oylum, Gedikli and Tilmen Höyük in the Taurus foothills of southern Turkey. The distribution of the ceramic horizons of the period, often equated to distinct cultural zones by other researchers, are compared and contrasted with the contemporary burial types (inhumations, pithos, cooking pot, cist, stone-built tombs etc.) in the region. It is argued that if the presumed equation of ceramic distributions with cultural groups is correct, then some significant overlap between the ceramic horizons and the distribution of funerary customs should occur.*

*Shared ceramic traditions appear to be misleading indicators of cultural zones, best illustrated in the case of the nothern caliciform horizon which is supposedly centered around Ebla. In this instance ceramic homogeneity appears to mirror patterns of inter- or intra-regional interaction independent of regional identity or socio-economic complexity. The study of the burial types and their ceramic, metal and other offerings suggests that their variability may reflect the multi-ethnic composition of the urban settlements of the late third millennium BC. The paper concludes, however, with some alternative explanations for the observed differences in mortuary customs (i.e., chronological, regional, socio-economic, cultural identity, gender) first within each site and then across the sites.*

## Background and methodology

Excavations in the Middle Euphrates, in northern Syria and in southern Anatolia document an increase in urbanism and the rapid spread of a particular style of mass-produced, fast-wheel-made ceramics during the latter half of the third millennium BC.[1] The time-frame when these two phenomena are observed in the region extends roughly c. 2600-2000 BC. In cultural terms, this time period in northern Syria and southern Anatolia is usually referred to as the EB III and/or IV period.[2] The mass-produced ceramics that are deemed characteristic

---

1   E.g., Mazzoni 1985a; 1985b; Dornemann 1990.

2   Thissen (1989, 207 n.1) dates EB III to c. 2500-2300 BC and EBIV 2300-2200 BC, "the mature Akkad period". The C-14 dates he cites for EB III (first burned level) range from c. 2600-2300 BC; and for EB IV (second burned level) range from c. 2650-2450 BC. These do not inspire confidence in the Hammam chronology. Mazzoni regards Mardikh IIB1 as EB IVA (pre-Palace G destruction) and EBIVB as the post-destruction phase of the caliciform horizon. Schwartz (personal communication) dates EB IVA = Mardikh IIB1/Amuq I = Phases I-II of Selenkahiye (2600-2350 BC = early in reign of Sargon for Palace G destruction) and EB IVB = Mardikh IIB2 and Amuq J (2350-2000 BC) = Phases III-IV at Selenkahiye.

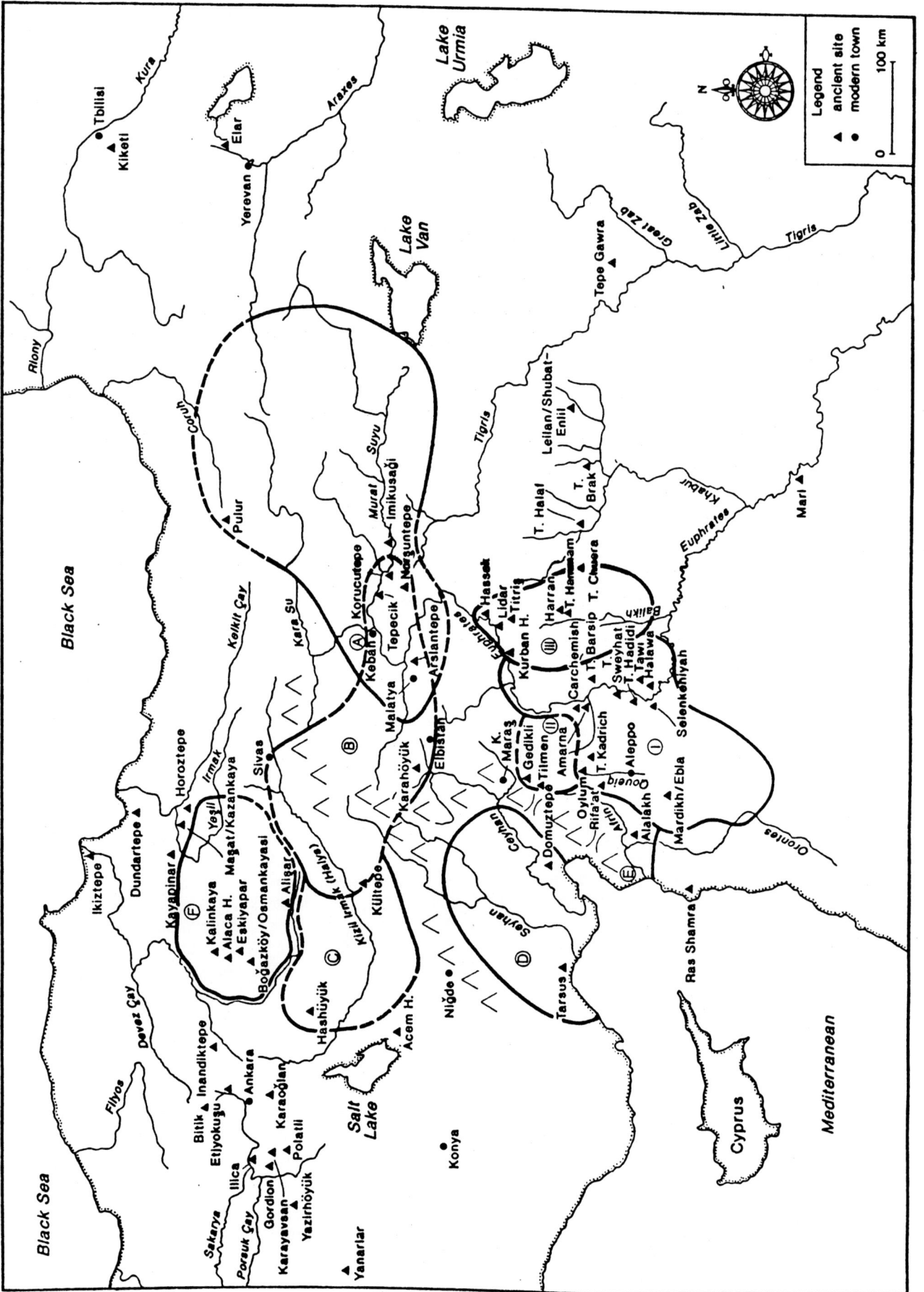

*Fig. 14.1: Ceramic regions in northern Syria and southern Turkey in the late third millennium BC.*

of the EB III/IV period in this region are widely known as 'caliciform ware'.

The interpretation that is to be assigned to the diffusion of the caliciform ceramic style across the region and up the Euphrates in the course of the latter half of the third millennium BC is unclear. The fact that the spread of these mass-produced ceramic types generally coincides with a rise in urbanism in Ebla and the Middle Euphrates has led some researchers to regard both phenomena as interdependent and to relate the caliciform ceramic horizon in northern Syria and southern Anatolia c. 2600-2000 BC to a distinct cultural group. Mazzoni, for example, links the appearance of the 'caliciform ceramic horizon' during the latter half of the third millennium BC to the expansion of a specific culture and urban lifestyle centered at Ebla in northwestern Syria: "It is not unlikely that in this case the geographic and environmental limits correspond with the cultural borders. The area of the 'caliciform' culture lies to the north (of the Palestinian steppe zone, suited to pastoral nomadism), where the fertile area begins, permitting efficient water exploitation, increased economic prosperity, and finally a high level of urbanization."[3] Dornemann, viewing the scene from the Middle Euphrates, agrees with her perception of the caliciform ceramic horizon as a relatively homogeneous culture group. He refers to the EB III/IV time period in which caliciform ware is predominant in northwestern Syria and southern Anatolia as "the EB III/IV culture" and even "the EB III/IV civilization".[4] Bonechi has gone a step further and attempted to match the distribution of personal names in the Ebla texts to the pottery regions outlined by Mazzoni.[5]

Other archaeologists working in neighbouring geographical areas have taken up Dornemann's and Mazzoni's trail and have also proposed that their ceramic provinces represent distinct cultures in the socio-political sense. Thissen, for example, has identified a mid-to-late third millennium BC 'Balikh-Chuera' pottery region[6] which he equates to the patchwork of EB III (c. 2500-2300 BC) political entities in the Balikh region of northern Syria during that period,[7] followed by an EB IV political entity, represented by Hammam et-Turkman VI west (c. 2300-2000 BC). In Cilicia, Mellink interprets the appearance of a new EB III pottery style at Tarsus c. 2400 BC as a change in eating and drinking customs.[8] Due to the new pottery's close parallels with Troy II, and the widespread conflagration at Tarsus that preceded its appearance, she suggests that the new EB III ceramic style at Tarsus appears "suddenly and en masse".[9] A more subtle reference to the arrival of uninvited immigrants into Cilicia from western Anatolia c. 2400 BC can scarcely be made.

The tendency to equate pots with people in third-millennium BC Anatolia and northern Mesopotamia is not new. Alkim already suggested that the 'Brittle Orange Ware', at home in the Tilmen-Gedikli region (EB II-III),[10] should be linked to the political entity that built the EB II/III palaces and cist tombs in the region.[11] Sagona and many others see the diffusion of the EB II-III 'Kura-Araks/Early Transcaucasian' (ETC) ceramic tradition in south central Anatolia and the Levant as reflections of the migration of eastern Anatolian 'folk'.[12]

What is new is the tone of confidence with which pottery zones are now resuscitated as evidence for cultural zones. This tendency persists despite growing evidence of overlap between the boundaries of the various ceramic zones that have been identified during the latter half of the third millennium BC in northern Syria and southern Anatolia. Some of this overlap may be dismissed as stemming from the rather broad and/or vague time-frames that have been ascribed to the different ceramic 'cultures' in question. Long or ambiguous chronological labels such as '2700-2000 BC', or 'EB III/IV' blur distinctions and the ceramic zones appear to merge. Yet, as more and more radiocarbon dates become available from various sites in the region, what used to be dismissible as merely 'apparent' chronological and geographical overlap between some ceramic horizons becomes increasingly difficult to ignore and begs a more thorough explanation than the one presently provided by the pots-equal-people hypothesis. The encroachment of one ceramic zone on another is now apparent, in our opinion, in the case of the caliciform and Balikh ceramic zones around Titriş in the area of the Atatürk Dam (Fig. 14.1: I-III) and further south on the east bank of the Euphrates around Halawa. Infringement is also beginning to be apparent between the Gedikli area (Fig. 14.1: I-II) and caliciform zones in the area of Oylum.[13]

The goal of this paper is to re-examine the proposition that the ceramic zones that have been identified in the second half of the third millennium BC in northern Syria and southern Anatolia coincide or overlap in any consistent way with any particular cultural (e.g., Eblaite) or socio-political forms (i.e., city state, urbanism, etc.). To this end, the ceramic horizons in question (Fig. 14.1) are compared to a map of the region (Fig. 14.2) that is based on mortuary customs, another category of archaeological data that are also widely considered to represent cultural 'fingerprints'.

Despite debate on the subject, it is widely agreed that mortuary traditions do often reflect the prevailing

3    Mazzoni 1985a, 15.
4    Dornemann 1990, 86.
5    Bonechi 1991.
6    Thissen 1989, 195.
7    Ibid., 207.
8    Mellink 1989, 325.
9    Mellink 1992, 216.

10   Alkim 1968, 95; Mellink 1989, 322.
11   Alkim 1968, 93-97.
12   Sagona 1984, and Map C p.15. Cf. Marro 1993 for a recent summary of opinions.
13   Özgen & Carter 1991; Özgen 1989-1990.

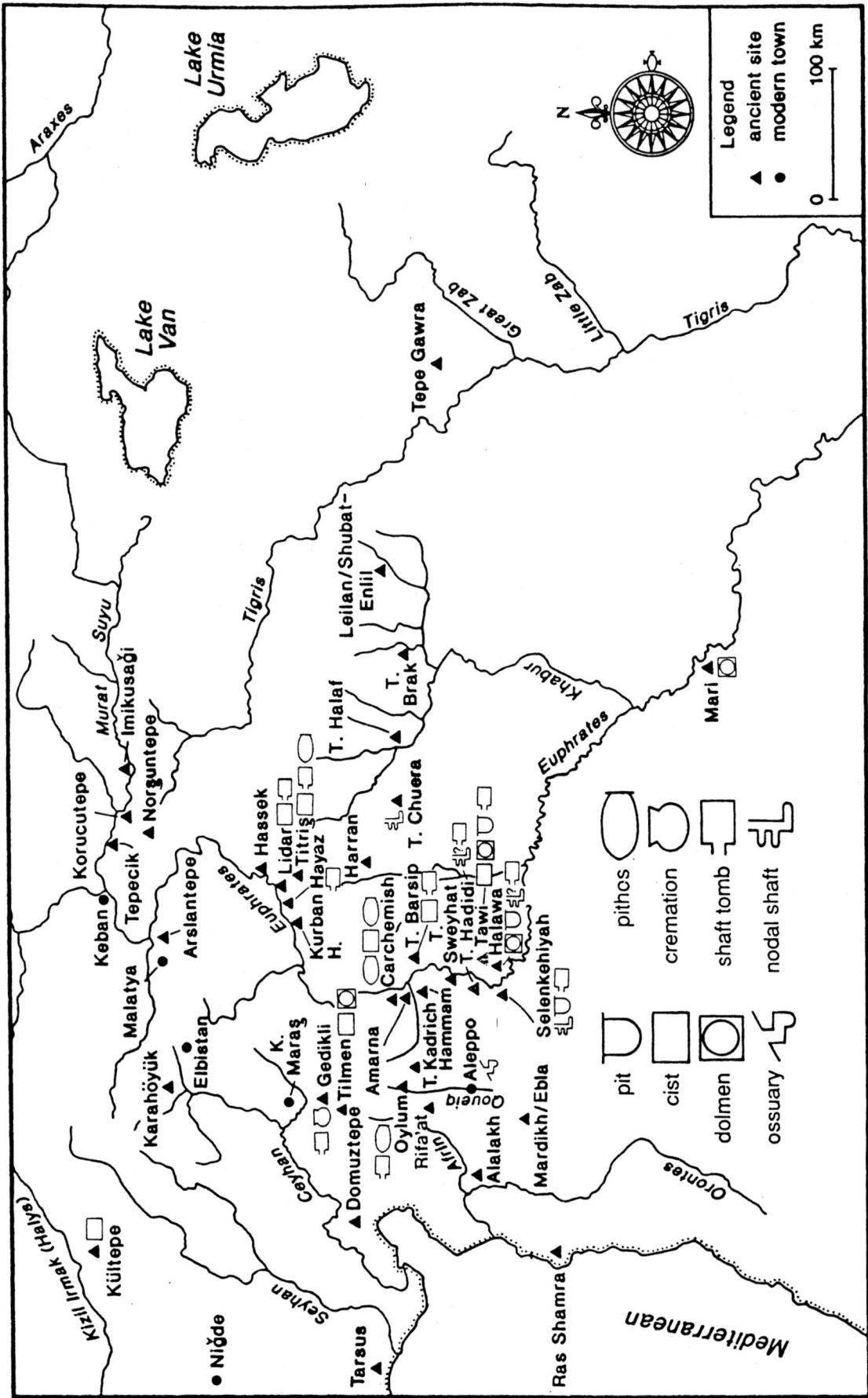

Fig. 14.2: Distribution map of burial types in northern Syria and southern Turkey in the late third millennium BC.

ideology of any particular social group,[14] something that ceramics cannot claim as readily. Because burials are linked to ideology, efficiency should play a less significant role in the changes in burial form over time than ritual requirements.[15] Therefore, this paper proceeds under the assumption that mortuary traditions are at least as accurate indicators of cultural groups as ceramic traditions, and that consequently some significant geographical and chronological overlap between mortuary traditions and ceramic horizons will be seen, if the diffusion of the EB III/IV ceramic assemblage is, for example, related to the spread of an EB III/IV 'culture' or 'civilisation' across northern Syria and southern Anatolia.[16]

At present, a major impediment to a synthetic understanding of the relationship between ceramic zones, urbanism and socio-political entities in northern Syria and southern Anatolia during the latter half of the third millennium BC is the lack of a common chronological framework within which to compare these three phenomena. Different names for the same time period across different regions, or even within the same region, have led to confusion over how to synchronise events at sites both inter- and intra-regionally.[17] In this paper, the comparison of ceramic and mortuary data among sites and across regions is performed within a fairly absolute chronological framework, based on the recalibration of radiocarbon dates from numerous sites in the region using one standard calibration method. Although this approach will not sort out the terminological confusions that persist, or fill in the many gaps that remain, it should permit a more accurate evaluation than those currently available of both the boundaries of the various pottery traditions over the time-frame examined (c. 2600-2000 BC) and the relationship of the pottery zones to the varying funerary practices.[18]

The period covered equates to the ED III through Ur III periods in Mesopotamian chronologies and to the EB II-III period in south-central Anatolia and Cilician chronologies (Tarsus, Gedikli), and to the EB IV A and B or EB III-IV period in northern Syria and Middle Euphrates chronologies (Hadidi, Selenkahiye, and Atatürk Dam).[19]

## The ceramic zones of northern Syria and southern Anatolia c. 2600-2000 BC (Fig. 14.1)

Our discussion focuses on the area delimited and defined by the Atatürk Dam sites, the Middle Euphrates sites, Ansari-Aleppo, and the Gaziantep/Gedikli region (Oylum, Tilmen, Gedikli), but the geographical area covered is extended for comparative purposes to include the contemporary ceramic regions of the Anatolian plateau, the Keban region in east and the Cilician and Amuq regions in the west in order to draw attention to the role these areas had in the cultural development of the transitional zone between the Anatolian highlands, the Syrian steppe and the Mediterranean. The main focus of this paper is on three ceramic horizons: I. the so-called 'caliciform'; II. the Balikh; and III. the Brittle Orange Ware (Fig. 14.1:I, II, III). Other contemporary ceramic regions have been identified more or less explicitly by various authors and are listed below and shown graphically on Fig. 14.1. The purpose of this overview is to provide a general guide to the ceramic distribution patterns so that they may be compared in the following section to the map of the burial types. The ceramic provinces shown on this map are reconstructed from published information, are approximate, and are heavily dependent on the locations of excavated sites and surveys.

### I. 'Caliciform Ware' horizon c. 2600-2000 BC

Description: Light coloured, fast wheel-made pottery; including goblets, cups and bowls. The goblets have either plain or corrugated exterior walls and are known in plain or painted varieties; the plain-ware bowls have upright plain or indented band rims that show some relationship with Mesopotamian types of the Akkadian and Ur III periods.[20] Mazzoni notes the regional variations in her articles, but the basic mass-produced goblet and bowl types form the bulk of the assemblage in her southern and northern regions.

Distribution: Middle Euphrates (Hadidi, Tawi, Halawa, Selenkahiye) and Upper Middle Euphrates/Atatürk Dam area (Lidar, Hayaz, Kurban III; Barsip, Carchemish); northern Syria (Qoueiq, Ansari-Aleppo, Ebla), southern Anatolia (Oylum, Gedikli).

---

14   Vernant, J-P. 1982, 6.
15   Cf. Metcalf & Huntington 1991.
16   This is somewhat similar to the method taken by Akkermans (1989, 75) in his comparison of Halaf mortuary practices and the theory of a 'Halaf' cultural horizon.
17   Cf. above, n. 2.
18   There are no C-14 dates available from Ebla since the date of the destruction of Palace G is still disputed (cf. Pettinato 1991, 58-64, for a recent summary of the evidence). Here we have adopted Matthiae's (1988) position and placed the destruction early in the reign of Sargon c. 2330BC, but are aware of the historical and paleographical problems of this dating which may have to be pushed even earlier. The beginning date of the caliciform horizon remains difficult to establish (cf. Curvers 1989, 175-6 for a discussion). The equation of what was a relatively short occupation level in Palace G with an apparently longer-lived ceramic period has also led to some terminological confusion.

19   Cf. Table 14.1 for a chronological overview, and Appendix for [14]C dates.
20   Mazzoni 1985a: Fig. 6-7, 9-17, 22; 1985b, 572-573; Yakar 1985, 353, Fig. XXVI, 350; Algaze 1990, 311-389; Dornemann 1990, Pls. 18-19.

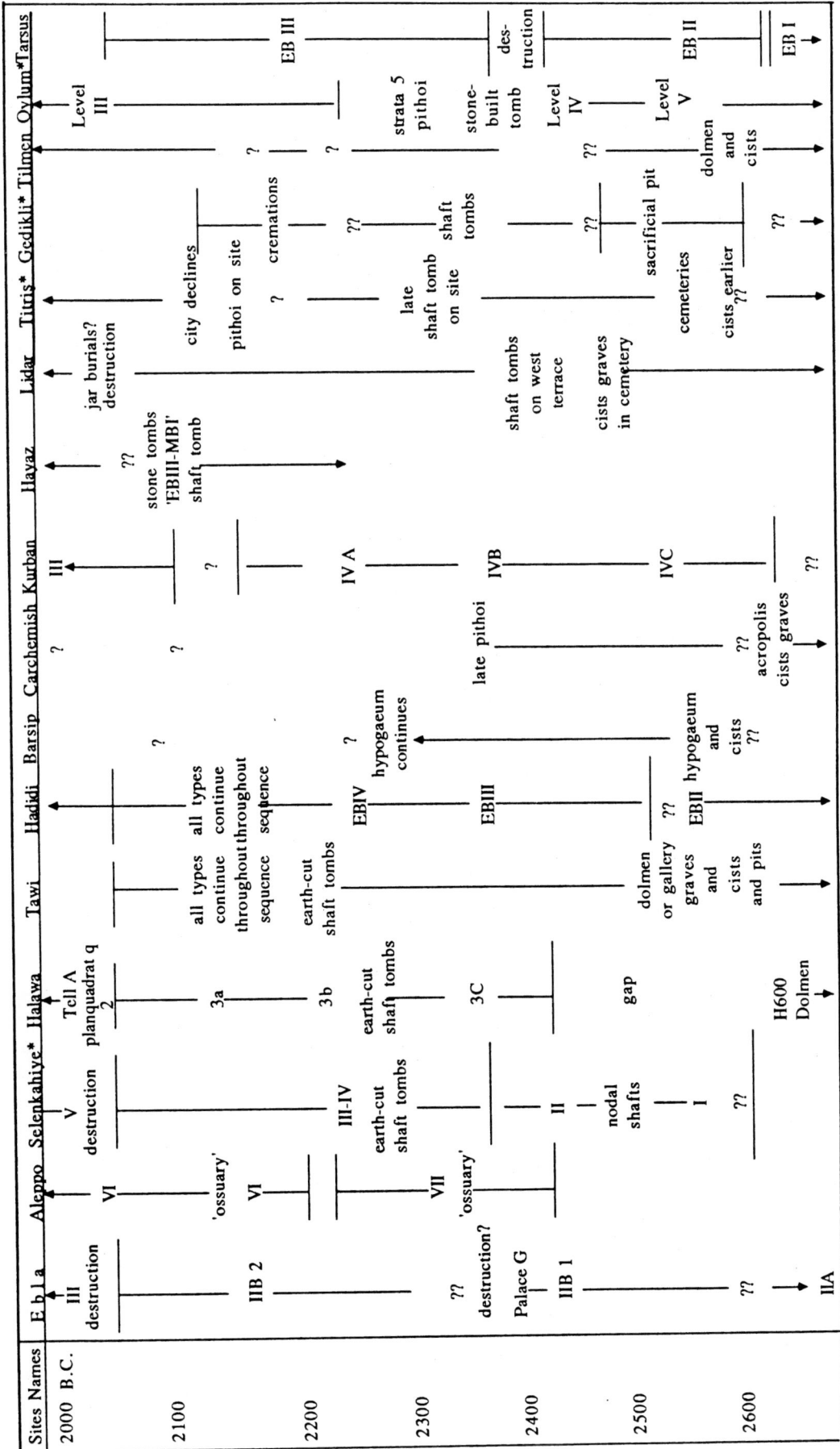

Table 14.1: Relative chronology of burials found in northern Syria and southern Turkey, c.2600–2000BC.

| Sites Names / B.C. | Ebla | Aleppo | Selenkahiye* | Halawa | Tawi | Hadidi Barsip | Carchemish | Kurban | Ilavaz | Lidar | Titris* | Gedikli* | Tilmen Oylum* | Tarsus |
|---|---|---|---|---|---|---|---|---|---|---|---|---|---|---|
| 2000 | III destruction | | destruction | Tell A planquadrat q 2 | | | ? | III | | | | | Level III | |
| 2100 | IIB 2 | VI | V | 3a | all types continue throughout sequence | 'ossuary' VI ? | ? | ? | ?? stone tombs 'EBIII-MBI' shaft tomb | jar burials? destruction | city declines pithoi on site | cremations | | EB III |
| 2200 | | VII | III-IV earth-cut shaft tombs | 3b earth-cut shaft tombs | earth-cut shaft tombs | 'ossuary' EBIV hypogaeum continues ? | | IVA | | | ? | ?? shaft tombs | strata 5 pithoi | |
| 2300 | | | II nodal shafts | 3C | | EBIII | late pithoi | IVB | | shaft tombs on west terrace | late shaft tomb on site | | stone-built tomb destruction | EB II |
| 2400 | destruction? Palace G | | I | gap | dolmen or gallery graves and cists and pits | ?? EBII hypogaeum and cists ?? | ?? acropolis cists graves | IVC | | | sacrificial pit cemeteries | sacrificial pit cemeteries | Level IV | |
| 2500 | IIB 1 | | ?? | H600 Dolmen | | | | ?? | | cist graves in cemetery | cists earlier ?? | cists earlier | Level V dolmen and cists | EB I |
| 2600 | ?? IIA | | | | | | | | | | ?? | ?? | | |

*=Sites with C-14 dates

101

## II. Balikh Ware horizon

Description: Plain simple ware, a shared preference for more specialized wares such as metallic (also known as stone-ware) and calcite-tempered cooking ware with triangular lug handles in the EB III (EB IVA).[21] In the later phase (Hamman VI west = EB IVB) collared-rim goblets and vertical rim bowls are present. No corrugated goblets were found in Hamman VI, although plain ware 'calciform' goblets were numerous.[22]

Distribution: Hammam et-Turkman, Chuera, Harran and in the Atatürk Dam region. In the Kurban IV period ther are close links with the Balikh assemblages.[23] The later phase known as Hamman is less like the western Syrian caliciform assemblage than the Kurban III assemblage in the Atatürk Dam region; this discontinuity, however, may be due as much to the lack of a continuous sequence spanning the period as to regional difference.

## II. Orange Brittle Ware horizon
## c. 2700-2000 BC

Description: "Reddish-orange ware with or without decoration; bell-shaped pedestal bases, rather squat fruit-stands with bell-shaped bases, fruit stands of the normal type, bowls, small vessels with basket handles, small jugs and beige cups with parallel horizontal grooves on the outside."[24] The latter are closely linked to the caliciform types described above, the other material is distinctive in ware, shape and decoration.

Distribution: Gedikli, Tilmen, Zinçirli, general Gaziantep region (e.g., Leylit H, near Oylum), imported examples in the Amuq, Khabur (Tell Brak) and Cilicia (Tarsus).[25]

## A. ETC (Early Transcacuçasian II-III) Ware zone c. 3300-2000 (?) BC[26]

Description: ETC Ware is characterized by open forms with soft and sinuous profiles and bases which are very small in proportion to the rim diameter, explaining the widespread use of pot stands with these vessels. The pots are never wheel-turned. All are covered with a thick slip and fired to red, black or both, and highly burnished. The vessels are also often decorated in relief, some with ribbing, others with nipple-like protuberances and circles. Lids and pot stands bear incised decoration'.[27]

Distribution: Widespread, stretching from western Iran to northern Israel. In the Caucasus, the pottery is referred to as Kura-Araks Ware;[28] in the Amuq and the

Malatya region, RBBW= Red-Black Burnished Ware;[29] in eastern Anatolia, 'Karaz' Ware.[30] The generic term for the ceramic type in Anatolia is commonly ETC = Early Transcaucasian Ware.[31] In Israel and the Levant, the same pottery is known as Khirbet Kerak Ware or Beth Yerah Ware.[32]

Generally speaking, the amount of ETC Ware found at Upper Euphrates sites increases from c. 2900 to 2400 BC, then diminishes from 2400-2000 BC.[33] It is considered intrusive in the Upper Euphrates valley during the third millennium BC and its appearance coincides with a break in the flow of Syrian culture into the Upper Euphrates region.[34] Indeed the percentage of ETC vs PSW ('Plain Simple Ware' of Syrian style) at any particular site in the Upper Euphrates valley is commonly used as an indicator of the degree of eastern Anatolian or Syrian influence at the site.[35]

## B. 'Old' Red-Violet Painted Ware or South Central Anatolian Ware c. 2900-2400 BC

Description: ETC Ware overwhelmingly characterises the non-Syrian ceramic component of the assemblages found at Upper Euphrates sites during the entire third millennium BC. Another type of ceramics, however, called Painted Ware, is also found around 2600 BC.

Distribution: Marro, among others, considers Painted Ware ceramics in the Upper Euphrates to represent an isolated development disconnected from both the ETC and Syrian traditions, as well as from any neighbouring Anatolian traditions.[36] We prefer to group the Painted Ware that is found at Upper Euphrates sites during the third millennium BC under the category of 'South Central Anatolian Ware'. This ceramic ware is also known as Malatya-Elazig Painted Pottery, Simple and Finer styles.[37] It is contemporary with the ETC ceramic horizon, with which it is associated, and found at Arslantepe, Değirmentepe, Gelinciktepe, Han I bramin Sah, İmamoğlu, Köşkerbaba, Korucutepe, Norş untepe, Pulur, Şemsiyetepe, and Tepecik.[38] Contrary to Marro's perception of the Painted Wares as an isolated ceramic tradition not connected to styles east or west of the Upper Euphrates, a recent study by Andrea Parker suggests that Painted Ware is characterised by a certain number of design motifs which are found on ceramics of both central and eastern Anatolia.[39] These motifs, such as whirling disks, stags, and the 'column of lozenges',

21  Thissen 1989; above, n. 2.
22  Curvers 1988, 382.
23  Cf. Algaze 1990, 343-350, for a discussion of the early phase.
24  Alkim 1968, 93-95.
25  Alkim 1968, Fig. 48; Mellink 1989, 322; Yakar 1985, 361.
26  Sagona 1984, Table 2, phases II-III.
27  Ben-Tor 1992b, 109; Marro 1993.
28  Sagona 1984.
29  Braidwood & Braidwood 1960, 361-368; Frangipane & Palmieri 1983c, 536-542.
30  Marro 1993, 58-61.
31  Burney 1971, 43-85; Kelly-Buccellati 1978; Yakar 1985.
32  Ben-Tor 1992b, 109-112.
33  Sagona 1984, 126-127, Table 2.
34  Frangipane & Palmieri 1983c, 572.
35  Marro 1993,62-63.
36  Ibid., 61-62.
37  Sagona 1984, 68-69 and Figs. 111-114.
38  Marro 1993, Table 1, p. 59..
39  Parker, in preparation.

appear c. 2900-2300 BC in Transcaucasia, within the ETC ceramic horizon, and in Cappadocia, outside the ETC horizon. Parker proposes that they represent an iconographic repertoire that is neither ETC nor Cappadocian, but probably Hattic or proto-Hittite, based on the frequent association of the same motifs on Hittite cult vessels.[40]

## C. Cappadocian Ware

Description: Orthmann describes a black on cream painted ceramic tradition that appears in EB II (c. 2700 BC ?) at Kültepe.[41]

Distribution: Roughly from Kültepe to Alishar, and from Acem Höyük to Hashüyük. The ceramic region that lies to the west is characterised by a subgroup of the handmade 'metallic' ware found at sites in the Konya and Aksaray-Niğde plains. Goldman describes it as "buff-yellowish slipped and painted in a purplish, sometimes shining, paint."[42]

## D. Cilician Ware

Description: The type fossil of the EB II (c. 2600-2400 BC) period at Tarsus is the light clay bowl made on the tournette. Found with the bowls are pitchers and jars made in similar ware. These vessels are cross dated by an example discovered in the cemetery at Giza dated to Early Dynasty IV c. 2566 BC. Hand-made "red-gritty Anatolian wares", best represented by pitchers and pithoi of "sturdy red-brick ware" complete the assemblage. Imported items, useful for cross-dating and indicative of contacts with Syria and across the Amanus include 'Brittle Orange Ware', caliciform goblets, and Early Khabur Ware. Connections with Anatolia are attested by the presence of 'Old Red-violet painted ware'.[43]

In EB IIIA and B (c. 2400-2000 BC) the nature of the assemblage changes and a sudden influx of west Anatolian pottery types, best known from Troy II, appears at Tarsus.[44] Bowls, plates, platters, tankards, depa, lentoids, and jars in polished red ware and 'Copper Age Wares' represent a change in eating and drinking customs.[45] In addition to various local types, corrugated goblets both plain and painted of Syrian type,[46] metallic ware and the obviously long-lived Syrian bottle are found in these layers at Tarsus.

Distribution: Little outside the immediate region of Tarsus is known. Isolated examples of depa occur in the Amuq, and at Selenkahiye and Titriş.[47]

## E. Amuq Wares horizon

Description: Amuq I is defined ceramically and the assemblage includes three wares which continue from phase H: Red-Black Burnished Wares (= ETC or Karaz Wares), Brittle Orange Ware and Reserved-slip wares; and three new wares: Simple ware with 'caliciform' shapes, Painted Simple Ware and Smeared Wash Ware.[48] Mazzoni notes that the Ebla Palace G assemblage is distinguished from the Amuq by its lack of Red-Black Burnished Ware.[49] Amuq J like Ebla IIB2 is characterised by the common use of Painted Simple Ware goblets with designs incised through dark paint to the light clay beneath. Red-black Burnished Wares are now limited to 'cooking-pot' wares but Smeared Wash Ware increased in popularity in this phase and Brittle Orange Ware dies out completely. Imports include a Syrian bottle and a depas which tie this phase to the north (the Gaziantep region) and the west (Cilicia).[50]

Distribution: The Orontes valley as far south as Hama, in the early phase includes Ugarit.

## F. Anatolian Central Plateau Wares

Description: This ceramic zone lies somewhat outside our survey and is not discussed excepting to note that it is quite different from the two Painted Ware ceramic zones that lie to its south (B and C). Central plateau ceramics during the third millennium BC are characterised by monochrome polished pottery and the general absence of paint (except at Alaca).[51]

## Mortuary traditions in northern Syria and southern Anatolia c. 2600-2000 BC (Fig. 14.2)

Mortuary traditions in isolation are not the ideal, or only gauge, of the geographical extent of any particular cultural zone, but they are an important component of any archaeological culture. If ceramics distribution patterns are representative of a common EB III/IV culture, then these groupings should coincide with the distribution patterns of contemporary mortuary evidence.

Morris has identified five aspects of burial data that permit them to be interpreted as cultural evidence. These are burial typology, chronology, grave-goods/context of burial, spatial arrangement of burial

---

40  E.g., the jar from Kültepe, 1b, described by Özgüç (1978, Fig. 110); . Özgüç 1988, 120-121.
41  Orthmann 1963, 98-99, Table 9.
42  Mellink 1992, 215; citing Goldman 1956, Fig. 247.
43  Mellink 1989, 321.
44  Mellink 1989, 325; 1992, 214-216.
45  Mellink 1989, 325.
46  Mazzoni 1985a, 11.

47  Mellink 1989, 327; Algaze 1992, Fig. 16.
48  Braidwood & Braidwood 1960, 396-398.
49  Mazzoni 1985a, 10; 1985b.
50  Braidwood & Braidwood 1960, 429-451.
51  Huot 1982, 765 and Map 73.

INHUMATIONS (NOT BUILT) — TOP ENTRY — PITS — with stone cover / without stone cover

EXCAVATED (NOT BUILT) — SIDE ENTRY — 'OSSUARIES'

CERAMIC CONTAINER — TOP ENTRY — PITHOI / CREMATION URNS / COOKING POTS

CONSTRUCTED TOMBS
— TOP ENTRY — CISTS / DOLMEN OR GALLERY GRAVES — with stone sides / with earth sides
— SIDE ENTRY — DROMOS + ROOM / SHAFT + NODE(S) / SHAFT + ROOM(S) — earth or bedrock walls / stone built walls

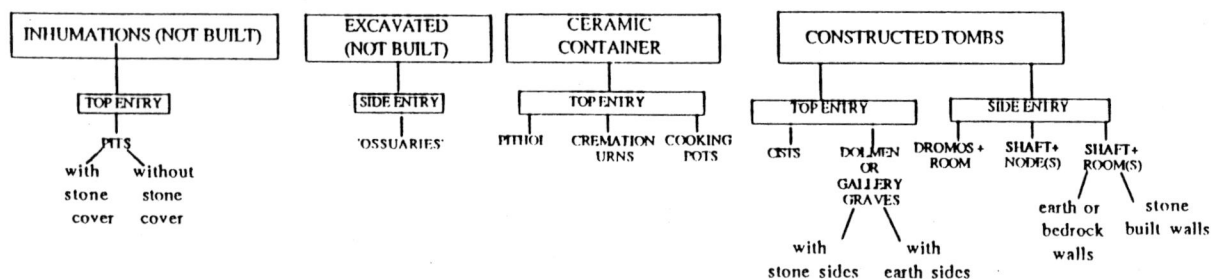

*Table 14.2: Typological analysis of burial types in Syro-Anatolia c.2600-2000BC.*

vis à vis settlement, and demographics.[52] We have relatively good data for only two of these categories, typology and chronology. A third, grave-goods, is partly complete. The data on demographics and internal spatial relationships are very spotty. The distribution map based on burial data of such limited quality will, necessarily, be somewhat sketchy, but by the end of this section we should be in a position at least preliminarily to assess the accuracy of the cultural map based on ceramics. Our overall conclusions must therefore be deemed tentative, but "finding a suitable typology is often the last stage as well as the first stage of a study".[53]

Three topics will be covered in the following section: (A) typology, (B) grave- goods and internal spatial relationships, and (C) chronology.

## Burial typology (Tables 14.2 and 14.3)

We have identified seven distinct burial types, most with subtypes, in regions I, II, III, A and C (Fig. 14.2) between c. 2600-2000 BC. The bulk of the evidence from which our typology is derived comes from ceramic horizons I, II and III. Zones B, D and E, are represented ceramically by excavations in the Malatya region and a surface survey.[54] Tarsus and the Amuq respectively, provide no burial data. Ceramic zone A (Upper Euphrates) provides only burial data that precedes our period (notably Korucutepe timber-roofed brick cist tombs, similar to Alaca, but dated c. 3000 BC). Ceramic horizons C (Kültepe, Alishar, etc.) and F (Alaca, Kalinkaya, etc.) provide the Anatolian burial data that corresponds to our time-frame of 2600-2000 BC.

The typological scheme, illustrated in Tables 14.2 and 14.3, is based primarily on whether the burials are simple inhumations or constructions; and on their mode of entry, either from the top or the side. Pits, cists, and gallery graves are typically entered from the top, while 'ossuaries', nodal shafts and chamber tombs (shaft or dromos subtypes) are normally entered from the side. Pottery containers are obviously entered from the top, but their placement vertically or horizontally in the

earth may be of some significance. In general, pits and pithoi, and cremations, were one-time, individual burial structures, whereas 'ossuaries', cists, nodal shafts, gallery graves and shaft/dromos chamber tombs appear to have been frequently re-used, sometimes for centuries (Barsip), for the interment of one or two individuals at a time. There is no surviving skeletal evidence from any of the tombs that suggests that any were constructed for mass burials.

Since words such as 'cist', 'gallery grave' and 'shaft tomb' appear frequently in the archaeological literature of the ancient Near East, often with different meaning according to different authors, we offer explanations and examples of each of our burial types below, in order to prevent misunderstandings. Many of the examples that we list are from Tawi and Halawa.[55] These sites, although looted, yielded a wide variety of the grave types in question and were well excavated and published.

### 1. Pit burials

In the areas under consideration here, the key characteristic of the pit burial type is that it is relatively small and not lined with stone walls (we are not referring to the accidental or casual pit burial here). Two subtypes can be identified in the Middle Euphrates; (a) plain earth covers; and (b) stone covers.

a. Earth-covered pit graves are small (1 x 1 m) and rarely more than 0.50 m deep.[56]

b. Stone-covered pit burials are covered with stone slabs and dirt, and usually ringed with small stones. Pit graves of this type are larger, deeper (1.50 m) and are often more sub-rectangular than the oval shape of the earth-covered pit burials (1a).[57] At Tawi and Halawa, the only sites where simple pit graves have

---

52 Morris 1992, 24-29.

53 Morris 1992, 25.

54 Marro 1993; Yakar & Gürsan-Salzmann 1979.

55 Kampschulte & Orthmann 1984; Orthmann 1980; 1981; 1987; 1989.

56 E.g., Orthmann 1981, H103; ?H104; H106-8; H110-2; H116-7, Plates 36-38; Kampschulte & Orthmann 1984, Abb. 12, T23-T27. Five pit burials that contained caliciform pottery are briefly described from Tell Rifa'at, just north of Aleppo, but without adequate illustration. One of these (burial 4) may have been a mud-brick cist similar to the one found at Barsip (Matthers 1981, 328-329, 332-333).

57 Orthmann 1980, 100, Fig. 4; Kampschulte & Orthmann 1984, fig. 18.

| BURIAL TYPE / SITE NAMES | INHUMATIONS (NON-BUILT TOMBS) TOP ENTRY — Pits (dirt cover) | Pits (stone cover) | SIDE ENTRY 'Ossuaries' Non-built, excavated in hillside | CERAMIC CONTAINERS TOP ENTRY — Pithoi & Cremation Urns | CONSTRUCTED TOMBS TOP ENTRY — Cists (plain earth) | Cists (stone built or lined) | Gallery Graves; and "Dolmens" (nodal shafts) | SIDE ENTRY Shaft and Chamber (Dug into earth or bedrock; single or multiple niched chambers + vaulted roof) | Stone built | References |
|---|---|---|---|---|---|---|---|---|---|---|
| Halawa | H103-4 H106-8 H110-2 H116-7 | | | | | H600 | | H2, H31,32, H34,35 37, H64,70,119 | | Orthmann 1977, 97-105; Orthmann 1981, 1989 |
| Tawi | T23-7 | T32-4, T37-8, T44, T51, 53 T62-7 | | | T29-31, T46 | T70,71, T16,19, T20, 21 | T5 | T6, T9, T22 | | Orthmann 1977; 97-106; Kampschulte and Orthmann 1984 |
| Hadidi | | | | | | | ? probably present | Areas K and K | Area L1; Area D= two chambers | Dornemann 1979, 117-132 |
| Barsip | | | | | Tombs 1-5 (intramural) | | | | Hypogacum (two persons) | Thureau-Dangin 1936, 97,108-9 |
| Carchemish | | | | KPB4 | KCG1-2, KCG6-9 (intramural) | | | | Possibly tomb at Kara Hasan | Woolley 1952, 215-222; Woolley 1914, 89-90 |
| Lidar | | | | | Cemetery east of Lidar village on the edge of the ancient site | | | | F/G 33/34 | Hauptmann 1982-3, 96-97, 104-109; 1987, 8-10 |
| Titriş | x? | x? | | Cemetery 2 & on site 69/54 & 35/18 | Cemetery 2 off site and on site in 81/81 | | | | Cemeteries 1 & 2, on site in 69/54 | Algaze et al.1992, 38-9; Algaze n.d.; Helwing 1991, 25-26 |
| Hayaz | | | | | | | | | 12 persons sheep & goat | Roodenberg 1979-1980, 8-10 |
| Selenk-ahiye | U22 W12 R21 W43 | | | | | | W13 OCC III, VII Q26 | W12 Q26 | | Van Loon 1967, 1973, 1979, Meijer 1977 |
| Aleppo Ansari | | | Ossuary-dromos +chamber | | | | | | | Suleimann 1984, 1-16 |
| Oylum | | | | Strata 5 cemetery, 16 pithoi | | | | | N170E75.1 | Özgen and Carter 1990; Özgen et al. nd. |
| Tilmen | | | | | M1, M2 | M3 | | | | Alkım 1962,455-6, 1964, 174, 1968, 93-94; Alkım 1970, Pls.29, 30 |
| Gedikli | | | | Cremation cemetery | | | | | M1, 2 (?); M4-(dromos entry), M5-6 | Alkım and Alkım 1966, 40ff; Alkım 1970, 95-7, Pls. 35-37;. |

Table 14.3: Burial types in Syro-Anatolia, c.2600-2000BC.

been published, there is little evidence of successive interments in this type of burial. The small pit graves (unrobbed) contained only one individual, in a flexed position.

## 2. Ossuaries

At Ansari-Aleppo a burial of similar shape and size to the Middle Euphrates hollowed-out shaft tombs is illustrated, but it is called an ossuary by the excavator. The tomb chamber was dug into a limestone rocky hill. It is accessed via a short, diagonal shaft different from the vertical shafts that characterise Middle Euphrates shaft tombs. The side walls are reported to have been covered with plaster.[58] A jumble of ceramics and animal bones, but at least five intact skeletons, were found in the tomb. What can be attributed to looting and what to long-term use is unclear. Stratigraphic considerations and comparative materials suggest that the tomb was in use from the EB IV through the Middle Bronze Age. Burials of this type appear to be closely related to the later MBA tombs at Ebla (the tombs of the Princess and the Lord of the Goats).[59] A portion of such an 'ossuary' may have been discovered at Oylum where a number of pithos burials were found jumbled in a plaster lined pit.[60]

## 3. Cists

Cist graves are characterised by walls built with stone slabs (with two brick-wall exceptions[61]), and the absence of a shaft or dromos. The walls of the cists tombs in our survey are built by setting the stone slabs on edge, as at Lidar Höyük.[62] There are no published examples of cist walls built by laying the stones on their flat sides. The one in-place cist cover from Titriş indicates that a single smoothed flat slab was used to cover these graves.[63]

Both small (1m²) and large (c. 1.5 x 1 m) cists were used for single burials. The small cists found at Tilmen Höyük[64] and Carchemish[65] contained infants. A small mud-brick "cist" at Til Barsip also contained a child.[66] Curiously, its brick walls were constructed similarly to those of its three neighbouring stone cists; by setting the bricks on edge.[67] Larger cists known from Lidar,[68] Titriş

Höyük,[69] Carchemish,[70] Til Barsip[71] and Tawi[72] may have been destined for adults, but sufficient skeletal remains are not available to support this suspicion. At Lidar, these cists were frequently cleared out and reused.[73]

## 4. Burials in ceramic containers, including burials in (a) cooking pots, (b) pithoi, and (c) cremation urns

a. Cooking-pot burials
These burials contain the remains of infants or young children and are located under house-floors. They have been excluded from the present study because not enough data is published on this apparently widespread and long-lived custom.

b. Pithos burials
We distinguish two groups, pithoi laid horizontally, and those set vertically in the soil. The horizontal pithos burials in our survey are similar in concept to the ones that characterise the EB II-III cemetery at Karataş[74] and the EB I cemetery at Hassek.[75]

1. Typical horizontal pithos burials are found at Oylum, where 16 pithoi, probably part of a cemetery, were excavated in 1989 and 1990. The burial jars from the Oylum cemetery are ovoid in shape, about 1 m in height and often have a knobbed base and slightly thickened or folded rim. Four were found with stones blocking the rim.[76] The difficulty of getting a body through the mouth of the jars suggests the possibility of a multi-staged funerary rite where the body was placed in the pithos after some period of exposure.

2. The only vertical pithos burials in our survey are found at Titriş, Oylum and Carchemish. The Titriş burial pithoi themselves were of the long-lived grooved-rim jar type that was used throughout the second half of the third millennium BC.[77] These vessels were set vertically into a level of mid-late third-millennium BC date and unassociated with any living floor. The pithos sherds found in the cemeteries at Titriş may date as late as the EB-MB (Kurban III period) or the early MBA.[78] At Oylum three vertical pithoi clearly postdate the horizontal pithoi and are

58  Suleimann 1984, 2-3, Pl. 1.
59  Matthiae 1980.
60  Özgen, Carter, Parker, Ziadeh n.d..
61  In addition to the Barsip and Rifa'at cists; a mud-brick cist was also found at Gritille of EBI date (R. Ellis, personal communication).
62  Hauptmann 1982b, 97, 108, Fig.11. Some of the Lidar Höyük cist slabs appear to have been quite finely worked; the same is not true for those from Titriş Carchemish, Tawi or Tilmen, but until detailed descriptions have been published we must group all the cist burials together.
63  Algaze, 1992, 39, Fig. 8.
64  Alkim 1962, 455-456, Figs. 29-30.
65  Woolley 1952, 219.
66  Thureau-Dangin & Dunand 1936, 109, Tomb 3.
67  Ibid, 108-109, Tombs 1-2, 4.

68  Hauptmann 1982b, 97.
69  Helwing 1991, 22-26.
70  Woolley 1952, 220-22
71  Thureau-Dangin & Dunand 1936, 109-110, Tomb 5.
72  Kampschulte & Orthmann 1984, T 31-39, 46, 48, 55, 58, 60.
73  Hauptmann 1982b, 97.
74  Mellink 1967, 251-257, 267.
75  Behm-Blancke 1984, 52-58.
76  Özgen 1989-1990; Özgen 1993, 469.
77  Cf. Algaze 1990, 376, jar type 21; Algaze pers. comm.
78  Cf. Helwing 1991, 23; Algaze pers. comm.

dated to the Middle-Bronze Age layers by their context and contents.[79]

Similar pithos burials are recorded from the "Chalcolithic" at Carchemish, but at least in one instance, the knobbed pithoi and the vessel and jewellery found in the burial suggest a late third millennium BC date.[80]

c.  Cremation urns

Urns of several different types were found only at the site of Gedikli. These jars include nearly spherical pots with outward flaring rims made of a "brittle baked clay" often called 'cooking pot ware' and coarser specimens of the ceramic types found in the contemporary stone-built cist or chamber tombs: Reddish-orange deep bowls, squat "fruitstands", variously shaped pots and caliciform goblets.[81] They are dated to the very late third millennium BC.

## 5. *Gallery graves ('ditch' graves and 'dolmens')*

These tombs are long (>3m),[82] relatively narrow pits covered with large stone slabs without an entry shaft or side door. Two subtypes are known, based on wall-construction material; (a) plain earth walls covered with stone slabs (gallery or 'ditch graves'); and (b) stone walls covered with stone slabs ('dolmens').

a.  Gallery or ditch graves

The only site with graves of this type is Tawi. The large sub-rectangular pits with stone slab covers[83] are deep (> 1m), long (4-8 m), relatively narrow (1-1.50 m) ditches cut into sterile soil and covered with large stone slabs. There is some evidence that these graves were reused, but no evidence that they were meant to be communal graves.[84] At Tawi in 13/L five of these large ditch (earth-gallery) graves were surrounded by smaller, poorer pit graves. These gallery graves were constructed following a somewhat illogical, but very distinctive, sequence of construction stages, unparalleled elsewhere: (1) the upper surface level was cleared out to the level of virgin soil over the planned total size of the grave; (2) in the clearing a flat pit was dug, which was scarcely larger than the planned cover; (3) in this shallow ditch the cover stones were installed and remaining small empty spaces both in the stone cracks as well as between the stones and the virgin soil were coated with mud, larger gaps were

filled with small stony material; (4) finally the real grave pit was excavated under the stones.[85]

The large ditch graves can incorporate a small window, or port-hole, at surface level at one end of the grave.[86] The opening is large enough to permit viewing of the bones inside, or the addition of occasional pots and food offering to the dead from outside the tomb, but is too small to permit a live individual from actually entering the tomb, and probably also of successive interments to the tomb in any but a jumbled fashion, unless this was done through the roof. One 'ditch grave' at Tawi (T22) seems to have elaborated on the port-hole concept and had crude steps that led into the earthen-walled chamber. In our typology, this apparent innovation or deviation from the 'ditch grave' type makes the T22 grave at Tawi technically a shaft and chamber tomb.

b.  'Dolmens' or gallery graves

Three dolmens are known, one each at Tawi,[87] Halawa[88] and Tilmen.[89] Although all three consist of piled up stone walls covered by monolithic stone slabs, perhaps some further sub-divisions might be made on the basis of the angularity of the wall corners; the Tilmen M3 and Tawi T5 dolmens have squared internal corners, while the Halawa dolmen has rounded internal corners.

These burials consist of pits that are not quite as long and narrow as ditch graves, but much longer than the proportions found among cists. The walls are of roughly quarried stones. The Tawi dolmen (4.50 x 1.25 m) was corbelled inwards at the top and covered with huge stone slabs; the dolmen at Halawa (5 x 1.30 m) was nearly straight-sided and the stone-built walls were coated with mud-plaster, the cover was not preserved. The corners were rounded through use of mud plaster. Mud and plaster filled the gap between the stones and the ditch for the grave. No construction details are available on the Tilmen dolmen other than its size (l = 4m, w = 1.5-1.9m, h = 2.2m).

The mid-third millennium BC burnt brick tomb excavated at Habuba Kabira is likely a variant of the top-entry dolmen or gallery grave type. The indentation on the side of the long wall is interpreted as the location of the top entry way.[90]

## 6. *Nodal shaft graves*

This is a burial type that in our survey is described only inside the city walls at Selenkahiye during the

---

79  Özgen, Carter, Parker, Ziadeh n.d.
80  Cf. Woolley 1952, 215-216, KPG 15.
81  Alkim and Alkim 1966, 43-44, Figs. 28-30.
82  Kampschulte & Orthmann 1984, 109, draw the line between pit and gallery graves at l = 4+ m; we have included graves T70-71 in the l = 3 m range here because of their cover type and ditch-like substructure.
83  Kampschulte & Orthmann 1984, T70-71 (l = 3-3.10 m), T16, 19-21 (l = 4+ m).
84  Ibid., 93-102.
85  Ibid., 31.
86  Ibid., T21, T22, T70.
87  Orthmann 1977, 101-102; Kampschulte & Orthmann 1984, T5.
88  Meyer in Orthmann 1989, 50-54, H600.
89  Alkim 1968, 93.
90  Sürenhagen 1973, 33-38.

latter half of the third millennium BC. Judging by the descriptions, nodal shafts are also present at Hadidi. One example is published from Tell Chuera, outside our region.[91] The burials, as described at Selenkahiye, consist of a deep vertical shaft which leads to one (early period) or many (later period) chambers approximately 1 m in diameter located laterally off the shaft.[92] These chambers which resemble nodes (hence the name of the type) were hollowed out of the subsoil or the earlier occupation levels, and contained the dead. None of these are illustrated, but each node was clearly intended to be for a single individual. In later periods, the shafts that accessed each chamber were re-used to carve out new chambers, but the chambers themselves were rarely cleared out and re-used. Additional small burial chambers were carved out higher up in the side of the shaft, taking care not to disturb earlier burials. In one instance a mud-brick partition had been built to separate the grave goods of two neighbouring chambers.[93]

## 7. Shaft tombs

Shaft tombs, like the gallery or ditch graves, may be either dug into bedrock, hard sterile soil or stone-built. Unlike pits, cists, ditch graves or dolmens, they are accessed from a side door. The shaft (generally 1 m² and often 3 m deep) may not always be as deep as the actual tomb but it is not a mere window at surface level, as in the ditch or earth-gallery graves. The shaft usually connects to the tomb via a door that is covered with a vertical, removable stone.[94] The opening in the large tombs is usually large enough to allow the passage of an adult into the tomb, suggesting that the shaft tombs were intended for multiple burials involving the intervention inside the tomb (to arrange the bones or corpses) of living individuals. Shaft tombs may have single or multiple burial chambers. We distinguish two major subtypes, (a) stone-built; and (b) cut into earth or bed-rock.

a. The single-chambered stone-built shaft tombs are widespread in north Syria and southern Anatolia. Side-entry stone-built tombs can be further subdivided according to the kind of access that is actually recovered, either horizontally via a dromos (only one example of this type is reported[95]) or vertically via a vertical shaft to the surface.

The most usual forms are stone-built and consist of straight-, or slightly corbelled-walled rectangular or nearly rectangular chambers with a vertical entry slab in the short end, roughly at the level of the tomb floor; examples include Titriş,

Lidar, Hayaz, Oylum, Gedikli, and Hadidi (cf. Table 14.2).

The 'hypogaeum' at Til Barsip is the classic example of a large (5.4 x 3 m) single-room stone-built shaft tomb. It is entered by a side door connecting to a shaft ending above ground level. The 'clay cones' placed in the side walls are unparalleled.[96] The date range of the finds suggest that the 'hypogaeum' was reused, or at least ceramics were added to the burial offerings, between c. 2600 and 2100 BC.[97] The only example of a multiple-roomed stone-built shaft tomb is at Hadidi. A shaft with stairs leads to a small rectangular chamber which has burial chambers to the north and south.[98] The tomb chamber walls are corbelled inward and doorways are built with shaped sills, jambs and lintels. This tomb was reused in the Late Bronze Age and subsequently robbed.

b. The earth or rock-cut shaft tombs are common in the Middle Euphrates[99] and are known in both single- and multi-room varieties. The elaborate shaft tombs of Halawa consist of a deep (3 m) shaft that opens into one or more irregularly shaped rooms. These underground structures are most closely paralleled by the ones at Selenkahiye, which are unpublished. Unlike the nodal shafts of Selenkahiye, the chambers are all on more or less the same level. All the reported tombs of this type have vaulted roofs, most have benches and niches; some have built-in 'pillows' and 'windows', giving the burial chamber or chambers the appearance of underground bedrooms or houses.[100] In one of the Halawa burials the women were placed on these benches, while the men and a single child were on the floor.[101] There is some suggestion that the practice of burying more than one body in each shaft grave only dates to the later phases of Selenkahiye's occupation, but the full publication of this information is not yet available.[102]

## Burial gifts and internal spatial relationships as measures of social groups

In spite of the incomplete record of grave-goods at many of the sites covered in this survey, certain observations can be made regarding: (1) the diversity of grave-goods at and between the sites; and (2) the spatial relationships of grave types within and among the various sites. These observations, in turn, can lead to

91  Orthmann, Klein, Lüth 1986, 48-50.
92  van Loon 1973, 146-147; 1979.
93  van Loon 1968, 26.
94  E.g., Kampschulte & Orthmann 1984, T 22.
95  Alkim 1968, 95, M4, Pl. 37.

96  Thureau-Dangin & Dunand 1936, 96-108.
97  Cf. Helwing 1991, 110-111 for a discussion of the ceramics.
98  Dornemann 1979, 120, Figs. 7-8.
99  Orthmann 1980, 97-98.
100  Ibid., 101-104.
101  Orthmann 1981, 70, H37; pl. 35.
102  Meijer 1980, 125.

speculations about the existence of social, commercial and ritual ties at the site or sites in question.

## 1. Grave-goods

The richest and most diversely furnished burials in the ceramic regions I-III (Fig. 14.1) were found in the shaft tombs of Selenkahiye and nearby Wreyde. The personal ornaments in the shaft graves consisted of silver frontal diadems, metal torques, earrings and bronze axes, adzes, daggers and pins.[103] The contemporary pit graves in Selenkahiye, to judge by preliminary reports, were poorer, having only a few pots and a pin or two. From this it might be inferred that at least two social classes co-existed at Selenkahiye between c. 2400-2000 BC.

The Oylum pithos burials have the same types of personal ornaments (earrings, bracelets, torques, pins, and one grave with a gold frontlet and cylinder seals) and ceramics (upright-rim bowls, corrugated caliciform goblets) as the burial gifts found in the Selenkahiye shaft tombs, although the Oylum pithoi lack the weapons of the Selenkahiye shaft graves.[104] A haematite workshop found in Selenkahiye[105] may offer a clue to the nature of the ties between the two sites, since haematite is known to have existed in the third-millennium BC mining regions of the Taurus mountains northwest of Gedikli,[106] accessible via Oylum. A commercial link, perhaps based in part on a trade in haematite, between the élites of Oylum and Selenkahiye c. 2400-2200 BC might explain the close parallels in burial gifts and the completely different funerary rituals.

To date, no such similarity in grave-goods is found between Oylum and any other site in the caliciform-ceramic horizon, although admittedly most of the other sites have been robbed. The burial rituals identified in Selenkahiye and Halawa, however, appear to be linked. In a shaft of a tomb under court Q26 at Selenkahiye, the skeleton of a slaughtered ox and a dog buried intact were found.[107] A similar custom is attested in a partially destroyed but unrobbed Halawa shaft tomb, Halawa tomb 70, where the remains of an equid were identified in the fill above the skeletons.[108] Another parallel in the burial rituals at Halawa and Selenkahiye may be the inclusion of crude limestone 'reserve bodies'.[109] These resemblances in ritual as well as the similarities in the tomb architecture suggest a common burial tradition of the upper classes at the two sites.

The 'hypogaeum' at Til Barsip, a stone-built shaft tomb, contained an almost incredible number of pots (1,045 complete vessels) along with a smaller number of elaborate metal objects.[110] There seems no question that

the tomb was used over a number of generations, but only two articulated skeletons were found in it. Roof-fall had damaged the skeletal remains; however, the bodies do not seem to have worn the bracelets, frontlets, or other jewellery of precious metals known at Selenkahiye or Oylum . The smaller cist graves adjacent to the large grave at Barsip show a similar lack of diversity in their burial offerings, the basic assemblage consisting of pots and a few beads. Shaft tombs that were used repeatedly are found at all three sites, but the Barsip tomb was stone-built not earth-cut, and the number, rather than the diversity, of the grave-offerings appears to have conferred status on the deceased.

The incomplete data from Tawi and Halawa also indicate that grave size and the number (not the diversity) of objects relate to the wealth or social standing of the deceased in these sites. This conclusion is based on the disproportionate increase in the number of pots between pit graves with single individuals[111] and large shaft graves, such as H70, which contained 2 individuals, 37 pots, 9 toggle pins, 2 dagger blades and an equid skeleton. The diversity of the grave-goods remains relatively constant between small pit graves and larger gallery graves from Tawi.[112] T70 is a gallery or ditch grave that contained a male and a female skeleton, accompanied by 15 pots. The only other find was a small piece of incised bone associated with the male skeleton. Since T70 was undisturbed, but used more than once, it seems possible, but not certain, that the more valuable metal objects were removed and/or recycled by the time of the excavations. The male skeleton in T70 was accompanied by a more numerous (10, as against 5, pots) and somewhat finer collection of ceramics (well-made 'Painted Euphrates Ware') than the female.[113] If an increase in the number of pots corresponded to higher status, then more burials with similar differential associations of goods between male and female might offer some insights into the status distinctions between the sexes.

The northern part of the Lidar necropolis contained approximately 200 large and small cists. Overall the cist graves found at Lidar are poorer in the quality and diversity of their finds than the shaft tombs from the same site.[114] Some of the cist graves are dated to early in the third millennium BC, but others are clearly later and were in use at the same time as the two stone-built shaft tombs in F/G 33/4 on the west terrace of the site which date to the mid to late third millennium BC.[115] Hauptmann posits that the Lidar shaft tombs, like those excavated in the cemetery at Titriş Höyük, 9 km away, originally contained much more diverse metal finds, such as pins, dagger blades, rings and pendants,

---

103  van Loon 1968, 27.
104  Özgen, Carter, Parker, Ziadeh n.d.; Özgen 1993.
105  van Loon 1968, 31.
106  Yener, H. Özbal, E. Kaptan, A. Necip 1989,  201.
107  van Loon 1979, 105-106.
108  Orthmann 1981, 54, 101.
109  van Loon 1979, 106; Orthmann 1989, 79, 82.
110  Thureau-Dangin & Dunand 1936, 97-110.

111  E.g., Kunter in Orthmann 1981, 81-82, H103, H108, H111; Kampschulte & Orthmann 1984, T62-65, T67-68.
112  E.g., cf. ibid., T63-64, T70-71.
113  Ibid., 97.
114  Cf. Hauptmann 1993, 12.
115  Hauptmann 1982b, 96-97, 109, Fig. 12; 1982c, 18; 1993.

and suggests that the shaft tombs are to be regarded as the high status tombs of third-millennium BC Lidar.[116] Since some of the cist burials are contemporary with the shaft tombs and both show evidence of frequent reuse, we might also reconstruct a multi-stage funerary ritual in which the remains of the deceased were moved from one place to another at various stages in the funerary rites. The full publication of the Lidar tombs and cemetery should shed considerable light on both class differences and funerary rituals in the Atatürk region.

## 2. Spatial relationships

At Titriş Höyük two cemetery areas off the edge of the site have been briefly excavated by Adnan Misir and H. Hauptmann.[117] Recent excavations in the site have shown that intramural burial was also commonly practiced as well in the late EBA.[118] Contemporary intramural burials and large extramural cemeteries have also been identified at Hadidi[119] and Selenkahiye.[120] Extensive cemetery areas lay in groups around most of the Middle Euphrates sites, but at Selenkahiye a number of shaft tombs were placed beneath the house and courtyard floors. These burials appear to be contemporary with the numerous burials found outside the settlement.[121] Around Tell A at Halawa several groups of shaft graves were investigated just outside the fortification wall. Orthmann has suggested that the elaborate earth-cut or rock-cut shaft tombs at Halawa were the cemeteries of the urban élite whose prerogative was burial next to the city wall.[122]

Who then was buried under the house and courtyard floors and who outside the settlement? In southern Mesopotamia, in the roughly contemporary ED III period, cemeteries were possibly the preferred resting places for members of state institutions, but members of private and occasionally administrative (public) households were more likely than not to be placed beneath their house floors.[123] It therefore seems possible that there were similar practices in the Middle Euphrates. Another plausible interpretation is that rural or mobile population groups buried their dead in the cemeteries outside the city, and residents buried them under the house floors next to the city wall. More difficult to explain is why pit graves with stone covers were located in the flatlands and shaft graves were dug into the slopes of the mounds and hillsides at Tawi and Halawa.[124]

At Oylum the cemetery was situated on the eastern edge of the main mound. A stone-built shaft tomb

within the cemetery appears to have predated, if only slightly, the pithoi. One of the richest burial pithoi (N160E65, burial 13) was placed at a right angle against the south wall of the tomb. Some of the pithoi were placed in a group in a plaster-lined pit[125] less than 5 m south-southwest of the stone tomb; other pithoi were simply placed at the bottom of a relatively shallow pit dug for the jar.[126] At present the pithoi all appear to have been located near the stone-built shaft tomb.

At Gedikli, as at Oylum, there was a cemetery area on the main mound. The cremation cemetery and stone-built tombs (M1-5) are next to each other and both burial types contained Brittle Orange Wares as gifts, thus the interval between the two burial customs is considered short.[127] The relationship of the stone tombs and the cremation burials at Gedikli might well be similar to that observed at Oylum between the stone-built tomb and adjacent pithoi, suggesting that individuals wished to be buried around a person or persons who were interred in the large stone-built tombs.

## Chronology

Burials, especially those that have been recycled or robbed, are notoriously difficult to date based on their contents. As an example we cite two earth-gallery or ditch graves at Tawi (T19-20). The pottery includes "early-Khabur types",[128] corrugated caliciform types[129] and Balikh EB III types.[130] The mixture of ceramic types is probably indicative of the re-use of the tombs over several generations during which time Balikh ceramics were replaced by caliciform style pottery. This hypothesis is supported to a certain extent by the stratigraphic distinction between Kurban IV and III[131] where the caliciform goblets with convex walls only appear in Kurban III. But it is also within the realm of possibility that the different ceramic types are more-or-less contemporary and were meant to accompany individuals from different tribes or social groups.

Ideally, the question of contemporaneity of ceramic types could be resolved by using absolute dates. Therefore we have recalibrated the available C-14 dates and have utilised them as a framework for our analysis (Table 14.1). The following sequence of burial types in Syro-Anatolia can be suggested, then, based both on the ceramic and the internal criteria outlined in the preceding sections and the C-14 evidence presented in the Appendix.

116 Hauptmann 1993, 12.
117 Helwing 1991, 2-3.
118 Algaze 1992, 38-39; Algaze, in press.
119 Dornemann, Algaze, Misir and Wilkinson 1979, 117-118.
120 Schwartz, G. pers. comm.
121 Ibid.
122 Orthmann 1980, 103-104.
123 Steele 1990, 207-217.
124 Orthmann 1980, 99-100; 1981, 3-4, 6, Pl. 21.

125 Özgen, Carter, Parker & Ziadeh, Figs. 8, 13: N165E70, burials 26-30; N165E65, burials 3, 8, 11, 19, 25.
126 E.g., Ibid., Fig. 15: N160E75, burial 14.
127 Alkim & Alkim 1966, 44-47.
128 Kampschulte & Orthmann 1984, Pl. 26: 211-220.
129 Ibid., Pls. 21: 80, 87.
130 E.g., ibid., Pls.16:8, 20:68.
131 Verhaaren 1989, 172-176, Table 80; Algaze 1990, 369-387.

1. An early phase (c. 2800/2600-2450 BC) in which cists, and dolmen or gallery graves are more frequent than the shaft and chamber burials. The early phase nodal shafts from Selenkahiye should probably be assigned to this phase as well. The beginning date is very uncertain but by 2600 BC the pattern is clear.

2. A middle phase (c. 2450-2350 BC) in which stone-built shaft tombs spread across southern Anatolia (Oylum, Gedikli) and continue in use in the Middle Euphrates and Atatürk Dam areas (Hadidi, Barsip, Titriş). Nodal shafts become more complex and elaborate earth-cut shaft tombs make their appearance (Selenkahiye, Halawa).

3. A late phase (c. 2350-2000 BC) in which pithoi, after their use in the late fourth millennium BC, reappear in Oylum, Titriş, and Carchemish; and, finally, at Gedikli the practice of cremation is introduced. Stone-built shaft tombs continue in use (e.g., at Hayaz, Hadidi); cists and dolmens or gallery graves die out and rock or earth-cut shafts and chamber tombs predominate in the Middle Euphrates.

Kampschulte and Orthmann writing about Tawi could detect no meaningful change in burial customs in the period between c. 2800-2000 BC.[132] By 1989, however, it became clear that the dolmen found in the nearby site of Halawa (H600)[133] was earlier than the first occupation level, on virgin soil, of Tell A, 3c *Planquadrat* q, and that H600's construction date was probably contemporary with the last phase of Tell B, or ED I-II, c. 2800-2600 BC.[134] A late ED 1 date is suggested for the dolmens beneath the temple of Ishtar at Mari.[135]

No one site provides a completely satisfactory sequence. The best available sequences come from Selenkahiye and Titriş. Oylum and Gedikli provide shorter segments of the sequence, but have some reliable C-14 dates. Most of the 'early group' of burial types has even earlier antecedents, with the important exception of the stone-built shaft tombs. Pithos burials also have earlier antecedents in the region at Carchemish, where some date to the Uruk period.[136] Some of the later pithos burials were found beneath the floor of the same room as the cists and were considered by Woolley to be contemporary with the cist graves.[137]

Some of the stone-built shaft tombs found in cemetery 2 at Titriş cut into the cist graves.[138] A study of the ceramics from this cemetery further demonstrates that the cists, especially those constructed of smoothed limestone slabs, belong to the early to mid third

millennium BC.[139] The stone-built shaft tombs from Titriş (and presumably Lidar) appear to begin slightly later (c. 2600-2500 BC)[140] but continue in use until about 2200-2100 BC (the end of Kurban IVA) at Titriş and until the MBA in the region (e.g., at Hayaz). Pithoi are reintroduced in the late phase at Titriş, Lidar (?) and Carchemish.

The recent excavations at Titriş support the dating outlined in the preceding section. Two cist graves excavated in 81/81, one large and one small, were cut into virgin soil. The ceramics associated with the larger of the two included a "champagne cup", a Karababa painted ware footed-pot, and several Simple Ware cups and bowls. The latter have close parallels with the Balikh EB III or early Kurban IVB-C pottery (c. 2600-2300 BC).[141] A stone-built shaft tomb found in square 69/54 (locus 016) was cut into an eroded level of late third-millennium date; it had a vertical stone slab in the short end providing an entry from the shaft which is not preserved.[142] This burial, although disturbed, contained among other things two Syrian bottles, an early Khabur Ware jar and three vertical-lugged jars. In short, an assemblage that dates to the end of Kurban IVA (c. 2300-2100 BC).

At Oylum the stone-built shaft tomb appears to predate the pithoi. The absolute dates from Oylum suggest a date of c. 2300-2200 BC for the pithoi, which would put the stone shaft tomb at c. 2400-2300 BC. At Gedikli the radiocarbon dates indicate that the stone-built shaft tombs (c. 2400-2200 BC) are followed by cremations (c. 2200-2100 BC).

In summary, there is no single site with all the burial types in proper sequential order. Nevertheless the variability in funerary practices is not due simply to changes in form, over time, from simple to more complex; from pits, cists and dolmens to shaft tombs. There were a number of different but contemporaneous burial practices in the regions under discussion.

## Comparison of ceramic distributions and funerary practices

A comparison of the map of ceramic distributions (Fig. 14.1) with the map based on burial types (Fig. 14.2) shows that to attribute the distribution of any particular burial type or types to an expansion of any particular group out of the caliciform heartland around Ebla would be erroneous. Caliciform ceramics of the

132 Kampschulte & Orthmann 1984, 110.
133 Meyer, in Orthmann 1989, 50-54.
134 Lüth 1989, 109.
135 Jean-Marie 1990. For the ceramics, cf. Lebeau 1990, 349-74; of particular significance for this study are the ceramic parallels with Halawa Tell B.
136 Woolley 1952, 215-218.
137 Woolley 1952, 217-218, graves 16-17.
138 Helwing 1991, 25-26.

139 Ibid., 85-87, 113.
140 Hauptmann 1993, 13, illustrates one of the ED II-IIIa (Fara style) seals from a Titriş shaft tomb which is rendered in the hatched manner common in Syria during the late third millennium BC (cf. Collon 1987, 24, and Figs. 71, 74). More seals and marble figurines of western Anatolian type on display in the Urfa Museum further support this dating for the shaft tombs.
141 Algaze, nd.
142 Algaze, Misir and Wilkinson 1992, Figs. 10-11.

convex-walled Ebla type were found in the large stone-built shaft tombs at Hadidi, Barsip, and Oylum; but in the area around Ebla where the caliciform ceramics are believed to be most indigenous, indeed manufactured, no shaft tombs (or pithoi) have yet been found. From current evidence, the burial type instead seems to be the simple pits at Tell Rifa'at[143] and the ossuary at Ansari-Aleppo. Farther up the Qoueiq, caliciform pottery appears at Oylum[144] both in a stone-built shaft tomb and the associated pithoi.

Therefore EB III-IV ceramic assemblage should not be seen as a single 'culture' which was the direct expression of a highly urbanised situation.[145] It is rather a ceramic assemblage whose mass-produced types give the impression of a 'standardised', 'factory-made product', since they were thrown from the 'hump.' This standardisation of forms is primarily due to the technology and cannot on present evidence be tied either to urbanisation or to a single cultural group. The currently available data points to local production in workshops. A study of the kiln site of Tell Kadrich, 100 km northeast of Ebla, and an analysis of the sherds found there and in the region concludes that there were a number of local ceramic workshops.[146] The kilns found in the town site of Lidar and some evidence for ceramic production at the nearby village site of Kurban also suggest the presence of local workshops in the Atatürk Dam region. Finally, evidence from the Ebla texts indicates that the urban élite of the city were not directly involved in ceramic production or distribution.[147]

The popularity of the particular Ebla types of goblets and bowls originally might have been linked in part to their use by powerful urban élites, as attested by their discovery in a palatial context at Ebla. The widespread distribution of these ceramics was probably the result of a demand for specialist-produced goods among the non-élite, where efficiency of production was of greater importance than the centralised control of the industry.[148] Production of pottery at scattered sites where the cost of the raw material was minimal would have reduced transportation and fuel costs.

# Conclusions

Explaining the existence of differing contemporary burial practices within the ceramic horizons of Syro-Anatolia depends upon several factors, which change according to the nature of the data and the time-frame in question. The various contemporary burial patterns

identified in the regions discussed may mirror the heterogeneous composition of the states of the late third millennium BC, local customs and preferences, external contacts (including migrants from other areas) as well as internal social structures. The extensive distribution of the shaft tombs, as opposed to the more restricted areas in which the more numerous grave types (e.g., pithoi, cists, pits, cremations, gallery graves) occur (Fig. 14.2) suggests that a study of the variability of the common burials at the shaft-grave sites might be an effective way to trace indigenous preferences and gauge socio-cultural differences in each region. Some inferences can be drawn from the regional distribution patterns regarding the cultural antecedents and/or links of the different burial types identified in the region. The lack of published data prevents us from drawing any firm conclusions; nevertheless, we hope that the speculations that follow may serve as a guide for future research.

## 1. Pits

A cemetery in Tawi (*Planquadrat* 2W) showed that earthen pits and stone cists could occur together in the same cemetery. A combination of careful observation and limited excavations showed that the graves were arranged in regular rows. The seven unplundered excavated graves showed little variation in their size or in the types or quantities of burial gifts.[149] Some similarities in the placement of the skeletons in the pit graves of Tawi and Halawa have been identified and suggest a shared funerary ritual.[150]

## 2. Pithoi

The pithos burial tradition appears to be well-entrenched in central and southern Anatolia from Karataş to the Euphrates by c. 2400 BC Cists and pithoi are found together in the EB I (c. 3000 BC) cemetery of Demecihüyük-Sariket in central Anatolia, although the dates of the different burials in this cemetery are not clear.[151] Kalinkaya, just north of Alaca, in ceramic zone F, provides a well-dated example of an EBA Anatolian pit and pithos cemetery. The burials found there date from c. 3100-2300 BC.[152] Thirteen burials were in pithoi with flat stone lids under house floors. Many of the grave-gifts have parallels with objects found in the "royal" tombs at Alaca, suggesting a date for these pithoi at c. 2500-2400 BC. However, the gifts in the Kalinkaya pithoi (small simple sun disks, animal figurines, shaft-hole axes, miniature votive items and lead cups) are more modest in material than those at Alaca, suggesting that the interred represent a farming/craftsman class of

---

143  Matthers 1981b, 328-329.
144  Although this tomb was thoroughly robbed, large numbers of sherds of both upright-rimmed bowls and caliciform cups left behind in the tomb indicate that these vessels were part of the original tomb inventory (Özgen 1989-90).
145  Mazzoni 1985a; 1985b.
146  Matthers 1981b, 327-348; Riley 1981, 349-360.
147  Wattenmaker 1990, 273-275; Archi 1982, 208-212.
148  Wattenmaker 1990, 279.

149  Orthmann 1980, 100-101; Kampschulte & Orthmann 1984, 75-91.
150  Kunter, in Orthmann 1981, 82.
151  Seeher 1993, 5.
152  Angel & Bisel 1986, 12.

the same or similar population group as that of Alaca.[153] At Hassek Hüyük in the Atatürk Dam region a pithos cemetery dates from c. 2800-2600 BC.[154] Pithos burials are also known from Titriş, Lidar (?) and Oylum where they are dated to the last centuries of the third millennium BC.

In Syria the pithos burials are episodic. Could the pithos burials be seen as coinciding with a periodic resurgence of an Anatolian-oriented population that inhabited the region north of Ebla during the course of the third millennium BC, possibly centered at Carchemish? Parker has proposed – on the basis of strong iconographic similarities between the decorative motifs on late third millennium BC Upper-Euphrates Old Painted Ware and Cappadocian Ware with Hittite iconography – that Hattic/Hittite populations inhabited the Upper Euphrates by c. 2400 BC. She presumes that they participated in the ebb-and-flow of north Syrian interaction with the Upper Euphrates and proposes that the late third-millennium BC pithos burial tradition is related to their culture.[155]

## 3. Cists

The cemetery in our area with the largest known number of cist graves is at Lidar, where approximately 200 cists, dated from EB I-EB III, were excavated. Cists and pithoi found together in Carchemish were dated roughly to the same time-range. To the south, cist graves from Apamea in the Orontes valley[156] contain material of Kurban V date[157] and thus should probably be dated slightly earlier than the c. 2500-2300 BC date-range given by the excavators. The relationship between cists and pithoi remains unclear in the areas considered here, but at Demirchüyük-Sariket, near Eskişehir, cist and pithos burials were found alongside each other in the EBA cemeteries, and the combination appears to be an innovation of the Anatolian EBA in general.[158] The publication of the finds from the Lidar cist grave cemetery will be of the greatest importance for clarifying whether the cist and pithos burial traditions are part of the same or different mortuary rituals.

The archaeological record has led some to postulate Hurrians or proto-Hurrians migrating into the area from eastern Anatolia, whose traces might be expected to be visible in the burial patterns and/or archaeological record of Syro-Anatolia. Written records also point to the existence of small Hurrian states to the north and northeast of Akkad in the late third millennium BC, and to the presence of Hurrians in the Khabur.[159] Hauptmann sees Lidar as a Hurrian city in the early second millennium BC that was possibly destroyed by

Hattusili I c. 1650 BC.[160] Given the widespread popularity of cist burials in Anatolia it seems possible that the cist burial tradition is to be linked to Anatolian/Hurrian populations.

## 4. Gallery graves or dolmens

The main cemetery at Tawi (*Planquadrat* 13/L) had 5 long (>4m) earth-ditch graves at its core and was surrounded by small burials.[161] The location of these graves in the flatlands and their distinctive construction separates them from the other cemeteries at Tawi and in the region. But who was buried in these tombs – a mobile population, perhaps, with loose ties to the town?[162]

## 5. Shaft tombs

In our opinion, the most likely burial type linked to funerary customs farther south are the stone-built side-entry (shaft or dromos) tombs.[163] Moreover, our burial type distribution map indicates that the stone-built shaft tomb represents a mortuary tradition that is distinct from the various other local burial practices, e.g., stone shaft tomb with pithoi at Oylum, with cists at Barsip, Lidar and Titriş, and with cremations at Gedikli. The burial evidence points to shaft tombs as non-local and associated with an élite; we suggest that the shaft tomb, as a type, may reflect ED III/Akkadian commercial expansion towards the Amanus and the Upper Euphrates which was accompanied by certain cultural traditions, namely administrative practice, and palace and burial construction.[164]

The northern cities of the Syro-Anatolian plains may have been loosely integrated into the Mesopotamian imperial systems of the late third millennium BC, but most appear to be separate entities each commanding a small surrounding region whose own interactions with each other were at least as significant as their relationships with southern Mesopotamia.[165] The Ebla texts further demonstrate that third-millennium polities in the Syro-Anatolian region were linked together in commercial and diplomatic relationships that stretched in an arc across northern Mesopotamia.[166] The size, locations and excavations at the major cities of the Syro-Anatolian plains[167] demonstrate that these sites were

---

153  Mellink 1972, 169-170.
154  Behm-Blancke 1984, 53-58.
155  Parker, in preparation.
156  Collon & Otte 1975, 107-158.
157  Cf. Algaze 1990, Pls. 43, 44, 45:E-F, 49:C.
158  Cf. Seeher 1993, 5-6.
159  Wilhelm 1989, 1-10; Milano 1991.

160  Hauptmann 1993, 12.
161  Kampschulte & Orthmann 1984, 31.
162  Cf. Prag, in this volume.
163  Although we can point to no exact Mesopotamian parallels, we note that the 16 Royal Tombs of the Ur cemetery are distinguished from ordinary burials in part on the basis of their construction in either stone, stone and baked-brick, or mud-brick, and consisted of one or more rooms. The rituals are known to involve human sacrifice and the complex refilling of the shaft entry to the tombs (Moorey 1982b, 60).
164  Cf. Alkim 1969, 280-289.
165  E.g., Michalowski 1985; Thissen 1989.
166  Michalowski 1985; Pettinato 1991.
167  Weiss 1983; 1990.

multi-ethnic, urban centres in touch with each other, as well as the more distant mountain areas the southern alluvium.

All of these cities, and even some of the towns, regardless of their diverse local ethnic backgrounds,[168] show signs of Mesopotamian cultural influence during the second half of the third millennium BC; e.g., the adoption of the Sumero-Akkadian writing and administrative systems (Ebla, Brak, Mozan, Hammam et-Turkman); the emulation of Mesopotamian artistic styles and religious symbolism (statuary at Tell Chuera, Selenkahiye; seals and sealings from all sites). The late Early Dynastic cultural impact in the Euphrates valley and the areas to the west appears to have had a stronger and possibly longer-lasting effect than did Akkadian traditions.[169] Local authorities or élites may have sought legitimation through copying southern styles, or, in fact, were consciously attempting to associate themselves with the southern city-states to underscore their access to, or good relations with, the major urban powers of Sumer, for commercial, political or religious reasons. Given the southern features in other cultural traits associated with social or religious élites of Syro-Anatolia, it seems reasonable to expect that some relationship to Mesopotamian burial practices of the late third millennium BC might be found.

The earth or rock-cut shaft tombs on the other hand may possibly be the best example of a local north Syrian development. Simple versions of nodal shafts are known from Selenkahiye and Chuera that predate the more wide-spread elaborate versions of this tomb type. It is conceivable that the elaboration of the type into a shaft tomb was encouraged by contacts with Mesopotamia. The multi-nodal shaft and multi-roomed tombs, however, appear to represent successive generations of use and suggest the serious investment of labour and attachment to a place. They are associated with urban populations and possibly with established lineages. In Selenkahiye, on a rock forming the corner of two doorways linking the shaft and tomb chambers six strokes had been scratched as if to indicate the number of times the shaft had been opened/closed.[170] The ossuary of Ansari-Aleppo may also be a variant form of this burial practice. Burials of this type appear to have their origins in the mid third millennium BC and in their more elaborate forms appear to be closely related to the EB-MB tombs of the Levant[171] and the later MBA

tombs at Ebla (the tombs of the Princess and the Lord of the Goats).[172]

## 6. Cremations

The Indoeuropean Luwians are thought to have moved primarily into Cilicia and, less certainly, into south central Anatolia and northern Syria beginning c. 2500 BC (EB III at Tarsus) – on the basis of ceramic forms deemed representative of western Anatolia.[173] These peoples did not leave any recovered burial traditions, although one pot burial is recorded from Acem Höyük on the Salt Plain (with a two-handled tankard and a one-handled cup, dated to c. 2400 BC).[174]

Cremation burials are usually associated with later west Anatolian culture, and the oldest cremation burials in Anatolia were found in Gedikli. This mode of interment spread widely in Anatolia during the second millennium BC.[175] The debate concerning the cultural affiliations of cremation as a mortuary tradition are too extensive to include in this discussion, but the absence, at this time, of cremations further east than Gedikli, and their association with the imported (?) west Anatolian depas perhaps supports the theory that they are related to western Anatolian, and probably Indoeuorpean, customs arriving in the Gedikli area from Tarsus towards the end of the third millennium BC. Nevertheless the localised nature of the phenomenon could be as easily interpreted as regional or family preference.

## Summary

The EB III/IV ceramic horizon represents one of the most continuous and best known ceramic complexes from Syria and southern Anatolia during the latter half of the third millennium BC.[176] The interpretation, however, of the ceramic data with regard to other developments in the region, such as growing urbanism and changing ethnic groups, remains uncertain. One widely held hypothesis proposes that the EB III/IV ceramic horizon, as well as some of its contemporary, neighbouring ceramic horizons, should be directly correlated to spheres of influence of particular political entities in the region, in turn represented by specific cities. According to this view, the boundaries of the various ceramic horizons at different points in time during the second half of the third millennium BC should be equated to the political spheres of influence of various city-states. We have investigated the validity of the 'pots equals people' interpretation of the ceramic data, by comparing some of the the ceramic zones (or

---

168 Cf., e.g., Weiss 1990, 213-218.
169 Obviously this is not something easily measured; nevertheless, the contrast between the strong influence of Akkadian culture in Elam and the areas of the Trans-Tigridian corridor stands in contrast to the regions in the west where ties to the late Early Dynastic culture of Mesopotamia are far more visible in the archaeological record than those of the Akkad period.
170 van Loon 1979, 102.
171 Cf. Gophna 1992, 139.

---

172 Matthiae 1980.
173 Gimbutas 1985; Mellink 1989, 325-326; Cate 1990, 902.
174 Özgüç 1986, 41, Figs. 3:34-35.
175 Seeher 1993, 7-8.
176 Dornemann 1990, 85-86; Mazzoni 1985a; 1985b; Thissen 1989.

'horizons') in question (Fig. 14.1) with another map of the same region based on a different set of archaeological data that are at least equally indicative of cultural groups, namely burial customs (Fig. 14.2, Tables 14.2 and 14.3). After inserting both types of evidence within a common chronological framework (Table 14.1; Appendix), we have tried to show that pottery distributions correlate better with economic and technological activities than with the socio-political or ethnic developments in the region during the latter half of the third millennium BC. The lack of coincidence between the pottery regions as defined by Mazzoni and Thissen[177] and the various burial patterns identified in the Syro-Anatolian area in the late third millennium BC

demonstrate that the mass-produced caliciform pottery should not be referred to as a 'culture' or 'civilisation'. We hope that this review will encourage the publication of relevant data, stimulate further research and discussion, and provide a framework for future studies on the archaeology of death in Syro-Anatolia.

*Acknowledgements*
We would like to thank the participants at the conference for their comments, and G. Algaze, R. Berger, R. Ellis, H. Hauptmann, B. Helwing, E. Özgen, and G. Schwartz for their help in providing us with unpublished information. We, of course, are responsible for any errors or omissions. W. Patrick Finnerty and Jean E. Selles drafted the maps and tables.

---

177 Mazzoni 1985a; Thissen 1989.

## *Appendix: Radiocarbon dates from relevant sites*

| Lab. Number | Site | Context | uncal. BP | Cal. BC | Reference |
|---|---|---|---|---|---|
| **Ur III** | | | | | |
| BM-2555 | Brak | FS 1093 floor with post-Akkad seal | 3730±50 BP | 2199-1980 | Bowman & Ambers 1989 |
| BM-2556 | Brak | FS 1383 | 3960±50 BP | 2553-2350 | Bowman & Ambers 1989 |
| P-1464 | Gedikli | Amuq J cremation | 3767±50 BP | 2273-2041 | Hassan & Robinson 1987, 35 |
| P-1794 | Selenkahiye | IV, Ur III | 3730±57 BP | 2200-1979 | van Loon 1973, 147 |
| P-2324 | Sweyhat | Ur III | 3640±70 BP | 2128-1834 | Holland 1977, 62 |
| P-2338 | Sweyhat | Ur III | 3730±70 BP | 2265-1976 | Holland 1977, 62 |
| UCLA-2850B | Oylum | Level III | 3700±75 BP | 2198-1942 | Parker & Berger n.d. |
| **Akkad** | | | | | |
| GrN-5581 | Gedikli | Amuq J tomb | 3820±40 BP | 2398-2144 | Ehrich 1992, 178 |
| P-1461 | Gedikli | Amuj I-J | 3877±57 BP | 2465-2205 | Hassan & Robinson 1987, 135 |
| R-1008α | Arslantepe | VID: post ETC rebuild | 3800±50 BP | 2397-2072 | Ehrich 1992, 178 |
| R-1012α | Arslantepe | VID: post ETC | 3840±110 BP | 2467-2051 | Ehrich 1992, 178 |
| UCLA-2850A | Oylum (East Cut) | Level IVC/V | 3885±65 BP | 2467-2205 | Parker & Berger n.d. |
| **ED IIIb/Akkad** | | | | | |
| BM-2511 | Brak | CH 450 late EDIII prior to Naram-Sin | 3960±90 BP | 2569-2294 | Bowman & Ambers 1989 |
| BM-2554 | Brak | FS 504 building dated to Naram-Sin | 3990±50 BP | 2567-2460 | Bowman & Ambers 1989 |
| GrN-5580 | Gedikli | EBIII-MB sacrificial pit | 3990±40 BP | 2564-2465 | Ehrich 1992, 178 |
| P-1788 | Selenkahiye | Phase I habitation layer | 4015±63 BP | 2619-2466 | van Loon 1973, 146 |
| P-1789 | Selenkahiye | Phase I habitation layer | 3975±73 BP | 2569-2346 | van Loon 1973, 146 |

*Note:* Calibrated dates in the last column are rounded to the nearest five years and are based on calibration tables of Stuiver, M. and Reiner, P.J. 1993, *Radiocarbon* 35, 215-230 and Stuiver, M. and Becker, B. 1993, *Radiocarbon* 35, 35-65.

# 15 Mortuary Practices at Tel Dan in the Middle Bronze Age: a Reflection of Canaanite Society and Ideology

## David Ilan

ABSTRACT—*Tel Dan (Tel el-Qadi) is a 20 ha, multi-period site located at the major source of the Jordan River. Twenty-eight years of excavation have revealed four major strata of Middle Bronze Age occupation with tombs of different types underlying the living surfaces of each stratum. No contemporaneous extramural necropolis has been identified in the surrounding countryside. The stratified context of the MB tombs provides a rare opportunity to identify diachronic patterns and processes over approximately 400 years.*

*Four tomb types have been distinguished. Jar burials are reserved for infants under the age of 2 years (with one interesting exception), cist tombs for older, generally sub-puberty children (and possibly only males), chamber tombs for post-puberty individuals of both sexes, and the single shaft burial contains adult interments in association with a chamber tomb. Hence, tomb type is associated with demographic status. Consanguinity is indicated since most, if not all, the tombs underlay domestic architecture (as they do at several other MB and LB sites in the Levant). Textual evidence points in this direction as well). Contrary to other archaeological evidence for such differential wealth or ascribed ranking is not discerned in the mortuary remains.*

*The motifs of rebirth and the interconnexion of death and fertility are inherent to many of the archaeologically observable burial practices. All tomb types suggest a simulation of the womb; the cadaver is almost always placed in a flexed ('fetal') position with the head toward the tomb opening. Offerings (kispum in the western Semitic texts) reflect sustenance and paraphernalia consistent with social persona in another, or continued, existence. The general picture correlates quite well with cosmology and ideas of death and fertility represented in the Ugaritic Baal Epic and the Tale of Aqhat, as well as the Bible (Genesis 3:17-19). These ideas were still with the ancient Israelites to the prophets' chagrin (Isaiah 57:5-6).*

## Introduction; research strategy

The archaeological remains of funerary practices can be approached from a number of perspectives, a point amply demonstrated by the variety of papers in this volume. In what is still the best concise summary of the analytical traditions that dominate the field, Chapman and Randsborg have identified three general research orientations: the chronology-typology (or "normative") approach, the social organisation approach, and that concerned with religious interpretation (or the "rationalist-idealist" approach).[1]

Most work carried out in the rich and varied cemetery remains of the Levant in this century utilised them to define cultures, their native regions and their diffusion, or the diffusion of their parts and ideas, following the Childean paradigm.[2] Kathleen Kenyon, relying largely on tomb assemblages from Jericho and Megiddo, was perhaps the doyenne of this approach, rigidly attributing culture change to the movement of human groups, mainly from Syria and Mesopotamia, into the southern Levant.[3] Her influence was crucial in determining the methods and fields of inquiry adopted

---

1 Chapman & Randsborg 1981, 1-24.

2 E.g., Childe 1956; 1957.
3 E.g., Kenyon 1966; 1979.

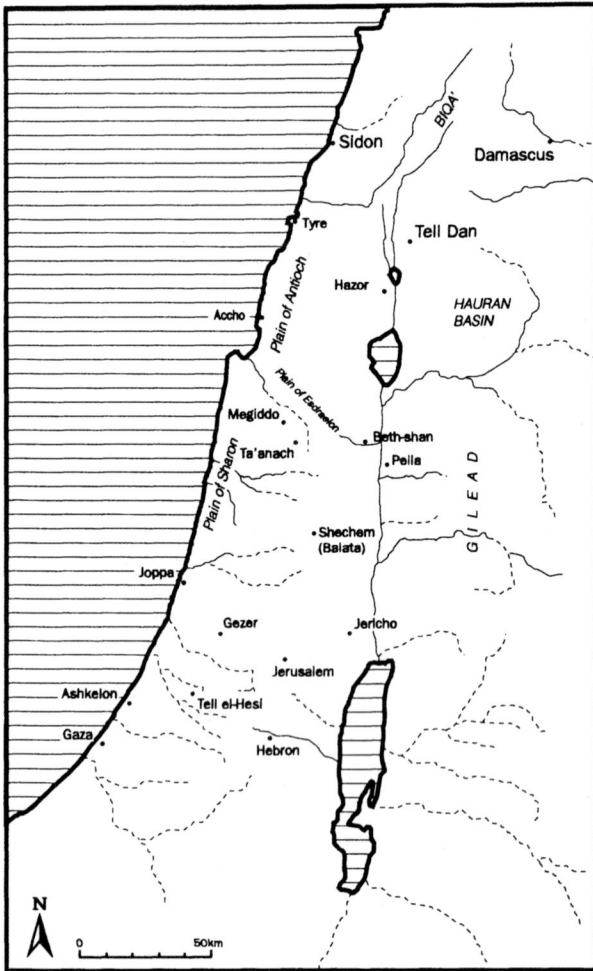

*Fig. 15.1. Location map after CAH II/2 (1975), Map 2.*

by archaeological research from the sixties through the eighties of this century.

Re-examination of past methods has shown that the use of funerary remains to forward strictly chronological or typological studies results in interpretations that are likely to be skewed and non-representational.[4] Of course, the proper culture history approach to mortuary contexts requires that temporal and geographical ranges be defined for individual components of material culture, to be followed by investigation into the meaning of patterns present.

Reliance on burial contexts also gave rise to some mistaken conceptions concerning the extent of cultural homogeneity. With more excavation of settlement sites and the rise of contemporary ethnographic studies it became clear that certain burial characteristics, and particularly the degree of variability in burial methods, were common to many, unrelated cultures.[5] This

realisation led to the resurgence of the social approach which sought to understand funerary practices as indicators of social phenomena such as rank and *social persona*. Binford was perhaps the first to expound this view on a theoretical level and to test (and to some degree validate) hypotheses using a more positivist approach.[6] Upon this foundation, the social approach has since become the predominant one, adopted by scholars who have refined, broadened and corrected Binford's early work.[7]

It would be convenient to confine our study to a single line of inquiry, either one of typology and culture history, one of beliefs and ideas (the 'trationalist-idealist' approach), or one of social meanings. It seems to me, however, that no one of these can, by itself, explain both the patterns and the variability manifest in mortuary remains, whether these be inter- or intra-cultural. Therefore, the approach adopted here combines all three lines of inquiry, accepting the risk of watering down the theoretical validity of each.

On a more primary level, it seems expedient to adopt, at least initially, a more inductive and more empirical programme, as opposed to the deductive method favoured by most social archaeologists. If research strategies (paradigms) and underlying assumptions are made explicit, data can more honestly speak for themselves, and suggest hypotheses for testing in other contexts. In real life, deduction is always founded on pre-existing, inductively derived information. The present writer has not yet encountered any theory of mortuary behaviour to account for all aspects of cross-cultural variability; Ucko's warning about the complex nature of burial practices stands as much a beacon today as when it was first written.[8]

Four basic, perhaps self-evident, assumptions underlie this study and its research goals:

1. Death is a central event in human experience.
2. A human being's reaction to death reflects his or her cultural values and life experience.
3. Patterns detected in the mortuary remains of the past will reflect cultural values, held by a community and not just by an individual.
4. Tomb offerings are socially selected and do not represent a random sample.[9]

These assumptions, whether stated or not, are universal in anthropological and archaeological research concerned with death and mortuary practices, and are common to the normative, social and idealist approaches.[10] The last two assumptions – those dealing with patterns in the archaeological remains of funerary

4   E.g., Kendall 1963, on some pitfalls in Petrie's sequence dating of Predynastic tombs in Egypt; Bienkowski 1989, on types present on the tel of Jericho but not in contemporary tombs; Hanbury-Tenison 1986, on the differences between tomb and settlement assemblages and their interpretative ramifications.
5   Chapman & Randsborg 1981, 4-6.

6   E.g., Binford 1971.
7   Some of the more important are Brown 1971; Morris 1987; O'Shea 1984; Saxe 1970, etc.; and Tainter 1975, 1978, etc.
8   Ucko 1969.
9   Piggot 1969, 558.
10  E.g., Huntington & Metcalf 1979, 1-2; Chapman & Randsborg 1981, 1-2; Humphreys & King 1981; Bloch & Parry 1982, 1-44.

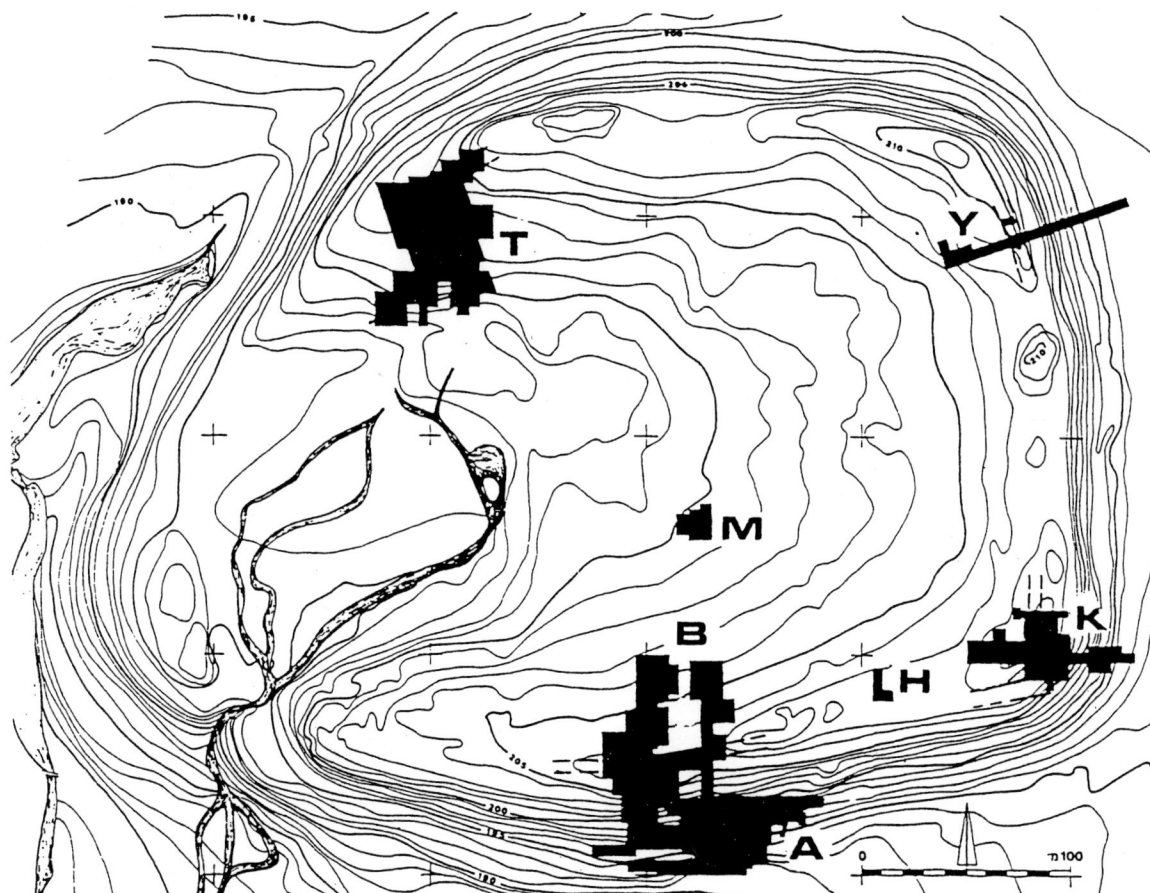

*Fig. 15.2. Tel Dan, topographic plan and location of excavation fields.*

practices – provide the most fertile ground for archaeological investigation.

In this study we have sought answers to four major types of question concerning the Middle Bronze Age burial assemblages found at Tel Dan:

1. What patterns exist in the burial practices at Tel Dan? For example, the orientation and position of the interred; the number of interments per tomb and per burial type; the age/sex distribution of interments per burial or tomb type; burial goods: How are they positioned relative to the cadaver and what are the frequencies of different types?

2. What do patterns in burial practice indicate on the social and ideological plane? Do particular burial or tomb types, burial goods, interment methods, etc., indicate ecological circumstances, social status, wealth, or a belief system? What do deviations from recognised patterns mean?

3. Which patterns present at Tel Dan occur elsewhere and which do not, and why?

4. Where do burial practices originate? How much cultural homogeneity and continuity exists in the Near East in the Middle Bronze Age and what does this homogeneity and continuity, or lack of it, re-veal about the diffusion of ideas and/or movement of peoples?

This is a potentially massive undertaking, which, to approach completeness must take into account all contemporary burial assemblages in the Levant and much data from beyond. It should involve statistical analysis and associated interpretative tools. For the present however, social and ideological aspects are dealt with on a more impressionistic level and with an interpretive scope limited largely to the material from Tel Dan. Confined though it be, this approach can be used as a means of laying down hypotheses for further study.

The present paper proceeds in the following manner: a brief description of Middle Bronze Age Tel Dan in its natural and human environment is followed by a synopsis of the basic mortuary data. A temporal and cultural framework is then offered based on material-culture analogies.[11] This includes a discussion of the typological development, chronological range and geographical distribution of tomb types and burial techniques. The concluding section will deliberate on

---

11  Not discussed here in detail, but cf. Ilan, in press.

| Stratum | Period | Area A | Tombs | Area B | Tombs | Area M | Tombs | Area Y | Tombs |
|---|---|---|---|---|---|---|---|---|---|
| XII | MB I | 1 | 23 | 1 | | | | 1 | 902b-d |
| | | 2 | | 2 | 4244 | | | 2 | 1025, 3050 |
| | | 3 | | 3 | | a | | 3 | 3126 |
| | | | | 4 | 4242 4356 | | | 4 | |
| XI | MB II | 4 | | 5 | | | | 5 | 1062 |
| | | | | 6 | | b | 8096a | | |
| | | | | | | b | 8185? | | |
| | | | | 7 | | | | | |
| X | MB II | | | 8 | 4663 | c | | 6 | 3004 |
| IX | MB III | | | 9 | 349, 187, 328, 367, | d | 8096b 8186c | | |
| | | | | 10 | 368, 371, 393, 4648, 4652, 7161 | e | | | |

*Table 15.1. The Middle Bronze Age stratigraphy of Tel Dan: A correlation of area phases and tomb assemblages (approximate)*

the social and ideological implications inherent in the mortuary remains.

## The stratigraphy and nature of the Middle Bronze Age remains at Tel Dan

Tel Dan (Tel el-Qadi) is located in the north of Israel, in the northern reaches of the Hula valley, at the foot of the Mt Hermon massif, which provides the snow melt that percolates downward to form the major source of the Jordan River, the Dan (Fig. 15.1). The tel is situated at the headwaters of the Dan, on a low travertine outcropping, and today rises up to 18 m (c. 200m above sea level) above the surrounding alluvial plain, itself littered profusely with rounded, often slab-shaped, basalt boulders (when these have not been removed as a result of cultivation). Over some twenty-seven seasons of excavation at this large (20 ha) site, six major fields have been opened (Areas A+B, K, M, T, and Y, see Fig. 15.2) and four general strata of Middle Bronze Age occupation discerned.[12] These strata comprise the cumulation of finds from all areas, but their determination is founded chiefly on the two areas with the most complete stratigraphic sequences, Areas A-B and Y.

The earliest MB (MB I, Stratum XII) remains uncovered at Tel Dan consist of domestic structures and courtyards in a settlement established inside the existing Early Bronze Age fortifications. Several phases of occupation were recognised in the area around the perimeter of the site, testifying to continuity and dynamism in settlement over some length of time in the early MB I. Later in the MB I (late Stratum XII), the existing EB fortifications (which included a massive stone wall with offsets and a brick superstructure abutted by a terre pisée glacis) were supplemented by the addition of a massive earthen embankment[13] crowned by another wall, a hallmark of the MB in Canaan and an important indicator of social organisation and complexity.[14]

Following the construction of the embankment, settlement apparently concentrated in the more level interior. Only by the MB III was the interior embankment slope utilised – thus far most strikingly apparent in Area B – including the practice of intramural burial. Several explanations alone or in combination might be offered for occupation of the interior embankment slope:

a. With population pressure mounting and house-holds extending, there was no longer enough space on level ground.
b. The level, cultivable land inside the rampart was needed for crops, possibly due to population pressure and possibly due to the need to assure culti-vable land in time of siege. This area could be irri-gated from the site's protected inner spring.[15]
c. Slopes were utilised to avoid the winter flooding that struck the basin.

Approximately five post-embankment occupational phases have been recognised in Area B (local Phases 6-10), and at least two in Area Y (local Phases 5 and 6) (see Table 15.1). These levels also appear domestic in character. Unlike the MB remains excavated at Hazor, Megiddo, Kabri, Tel Ifshar, Tell el-Hayyat and Aphek, the small areas uncovered at Tel Dan have not yet revealed obviously palatial or cultic architecture, although there is some evidence to suggest a more

---

12  Biran 1994.

13  Ibid.
14  E.g., Bunimovitz 1992; Finkelstein 1992.
15  cf. Kempinski 1992.

monumental edifice under the Iron Age cultic platform of Area T.

Since most of the MB remains were exposed along, or just inside the perimeter of the tel, most of the burials have some discernible stratigraphic relationship with the fortifications. MB I burials are generally under the MB earthen embankments, MB III burials surmount and penetrate the earthen embankments, and the few MB II burials are located at the base of the interior embankments' slope (e.g., T. 4663). This array demonstrates the effect of excavation strategy on sample recovery. Had excavation concentrated further towards the tel's interior, a larger MB II burial sample would have been provided. In the key area for testing this hypothesis, Area M (located near the centre of the site), only a few square metres of the MB levels were exposed. Much of this small exposure was disturbed by Iron I silos, and Tombs 8096 and T. 8185, which though perhaps constructed in the late MB I or early MB II, were mostly utilised in the MB III. These factors created a degree of disturbance which hinders determining whether an MB settlement existed here.

## Tombs in stratigraphy; an explanation of method

In reworking the sequence of the Middle Bronze Age tombs at Megiddo, Kenyon was the first to illustrate the means by which subterranean tomb assemblages must be associated (or disassociated) with material from occupational strata.[16] While her scheme inevitably required some reworking,[17] Kenyon succeeded in establishing both a stratigraphic and typological framework for analysing Megiddo's occupational strata that is now implemented, with some alteration, in most ceramic studies of the Middle Bronze Age,[18] including that carried out on the Tel Dan material.

Stratigraphic aids such as baulk-sections and the frequent assigning of find baskets are crucial for isolating the levels from which tombs were dug and/or built and for detecting associated deposits outside such tombs. At the risk of stating the obvious, it should be emphasised that the more extensive the sounding, the clearer the tomb's surrounding context. The larger and deeper the area excavated, the greater the number of tombs and burials exposed.

The foregoing brief account reveals two distinct advantages that invite a diachronic analysis of the Middle Bronze Age mortuary practices at Tel Dan. For one thing, the site contains a largely, if not completely, continuous sequence of occupation and burial from early to late MB, allowing one to follow the development of mortuary behaviour over an extended period of time.

| type of burial[*] | no. of tombs | no. of interred individuals | MB date-range |
|---|---|---|---|
| chamber tombs | 4/5 | 10/17+ | MB I-III |
| cist tombs | 5/6 | 7/14 | MB I-III |
| jar burials[**] | 22 | 21 | MB I-III |
| shaft burials | 1 | 4+ | MB I |
| *Totals* | 33 | 49+ | |

[*] The number of chamber and cist tombs and number of burials they contain depend on whether T.187b is called a cist or chamber tomb. The larger total for each category indicates its inclusion.

[**] Jar burial totals include two (T.902c-d) for which no skeletal material was reported.

*Table 15.2. The MB burials at Tel Dan: Burial types, their frequency, total number of interments by type, and MB date-range*

Secondly, the burial assemblages are relatively small and undisturbed, never containing more than eight individuals. It is usually possible to determine the last interment and its accompanying furniture. On the minus side, it must be stated that most MB burials, and constructed chamber tombs in particular, were encountered in deep probes lacking the areal exposure necessary to assess living floor context. Their stratigraphic assignation is often problematic as well. Built cist tombs and jar burials however, are usually easier to assign. A further disadvantage exists in the relatively small size of the overall sample, obviating the utility of more powerful quantitative methods such as cluster analysis.

## Tomb typology and burial techniques[19]

Burials were encountered wherever excavation reached Middle Bronze Age levels, except in Area K, where the Middle Bronze Age mud brick arched gate was found.[20] Interment was largely, and perhaps solely, subterranean and intramural, i.e., located under the floors of dwellings and courtyards. Despite extensive survey in the immediate area, no adjacent extramural cemetery has been found, though the finds from contemporary sites such as Jericho,[21] Gibeon[22] and Megiddo[23] indicate that the possibility should not be discounted. The nearest known MB necropoli are found at Hagosherim (4 km west, early MB I)[24] and Kfar Szold (4 km south, mid to late MB I).[25]

Four basic burial types have been recognised in the Middle Bronze Age layers at Tel Dan, (1) jar burials, (2) built cist tombs, (3) built chamber tombs and (4) a

---

16  Kenyon 1969.
17  E.g., Müller 1970.
18  E.g., Cole 1984; Kempinski 1983.
19  In the attribute tables that accompany this section all tombs are listed from earliest to latest.
20  E.g., Biran 1981; 1993.
21  Kenyon 1960; 1965.
22  Pritchard 1963.
23  Guy 1938.
24  Covello-Paran, in press.
25  Epstein 1974.

| Tomb | length (m) | width (m) | height (m) | orientation and entry | burial mode |
|---|---|---|---|---|---|
| 1025 | 2.70 | 1.50 | 1.20 | E-W – entry west via shaft | primary, multiple, successive |
| 4663 | 4.60 | 2.20 | 2.20 | NE-SW – SW entry via shaft | no burials |
| 8096 | 2.40 | 2.40 | 1.40 | N-S – entry south via shaft or dromos | primary, multiple, successive |
| 8185a | 2.20 | 1.70 | 1.45 | E-W – west? no further data | no burials |
| 187 | 2.25 | 1.40 | 1.04 | N-S – entry via roof | primary, multiple, successive |
| *average* | 2.83 | 1.84 | 1.46 | | |

*Table 15.3. Attributes of built chamber tombs.*

single shaft burial.[26] The criteria for the distinction of different types are discussed below. Table 15.2 comprises a breakdown of the different burial types and their respective number of interred individuals. Table 15.6 is a more detailed summary of the data from all tombs.

*Built chamber tombs* (Figs 15.3-15.8)

At most Middle Bronze Age sites rock hewn caves are the rule for multiple, successive burial of mature individuals;[27] but Tel Dan is located on an alluvial plain with no nearby bedrock suitable for the hewing of tombs. Indeed, the availability of solid but easily worked bedrock is the most obvious factor accounting for the relative rarity of built tombs, as opposed to rock-cut tombs in Canaan. Middle Bronze Age towns like Hazor, Tell-el-Farah (N), Aphek, Jericho and Pella have revealed no large built tombs, the dominant mode being the rock-cut and pit or cist tombs. On the other hand, large built chamber tombs have been found at Megiddo and Kabri, both of which have good bedrock, which at Megiddo at least, was also utilised for burial. This suggests that another explanation, beyond the mere availability of bedrock, must be sought for the presence of built tombs, one that may be related to cultural factors.

These are the largest tombs and required the most effort to construct. Table 15.3 summarises their attributes.

The following is a typological feature summary of the built chamber tombs:

1.  *Size*: The large built tombs average 2.83 m long, 1.84 m wide, and 1.46 m high. Too much weight should not be given these averages since, (a) T. 4663 is substantially longer and higher than the others and skews the averages, and (b) T.8096 has a sort of curvilinear trapezoid plan as opposed to the more usual rectangular plan.

2.  *Access*: The shaft entrance appears to have been the predominant if not exclusive means of access into the chamber tombs at Dan. The shaft entrance into T.4663 was surprisingly insubstantial and may have been constructed at a later stage. The entry side of T.8096 was in the baulk, but the other tombs at Dan and tomb parallels at Megiddo[28] suggest that a shaft entry can be assumed. The south side of T.187 was also in the baulk, although its interior was exposed, showing the chamber to be built around its entire circumference, indicating access from the roof, making T.187 a cist tomb in this respect. T.8185 was re-used and its construction altered; no clear entry was discerned. T.1025 was excavated beyond its entryway and the baulk was conveniently placed in a position that allowed the shaft to be seen quite clearly in the section. The finely constructed entry passage of T.8096 is thus far unique at Tel Dan but is found elsewhere.[29]

3.  *Roofing*: Roofing consisted of large stone slabs placed above walls corbelled moderately inward. T.8096 is unique so far at Dan in being constructed of a curvilinear 'beehive' type corbelling and a radial pattern roof (see Fig. 15.6). The true vault was not used in tomb roofing at Tel Dan – one might assume that the abundance of large stone slabs occurring naturally obviated the need for the arduous process of vaulting in the construction of more diminutive structures. Vaulting was utilised extensively in the MB tombs at, for example, Tel el-Dab'a[30] and Ur[31] – places where stone was less readily

---

26  Technically, jar burials, chamber tombs and shaft burials are also cist tombs; the term 'cist' refers simply to a subsurface cavity.
27  E.g., Wright 1985, 329.
28  E.g., T.3095: Loud 1948, Figs. 203-204.
29  Cf. parallels in Appendix.
30  van den Brink 1982.
31  Woolley 1934; 1954; 1976.

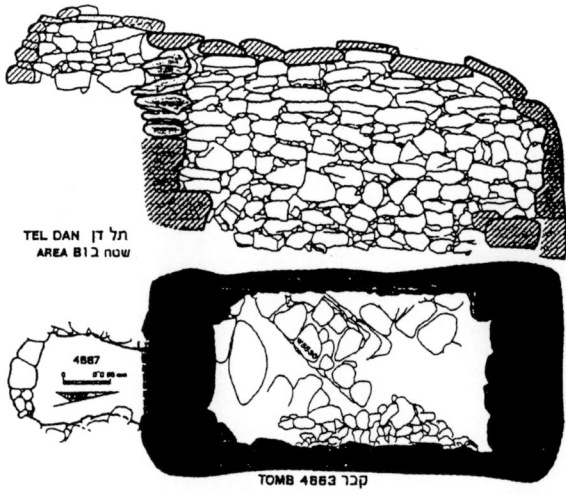

*Fig. 15.3: Chamber Tomb 4663, top plan and section.*

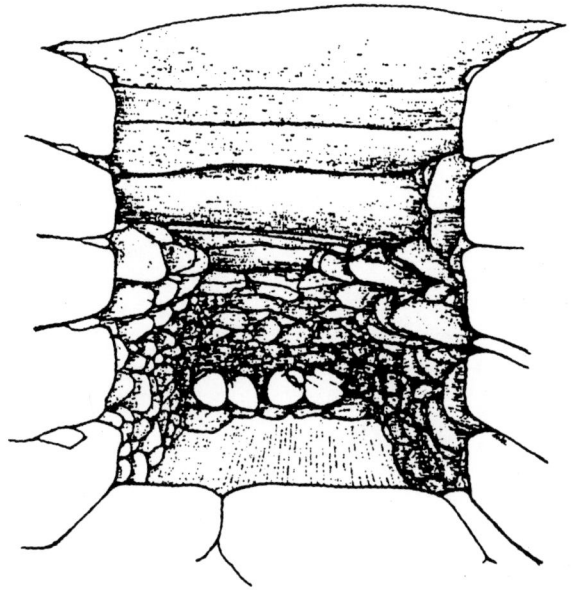

*Fig. 15.4: Chamber Tomb 4663, artists portrayal looking through the tomb opening toward the back (G. Cook). Note the bench bearing the four vessels..*

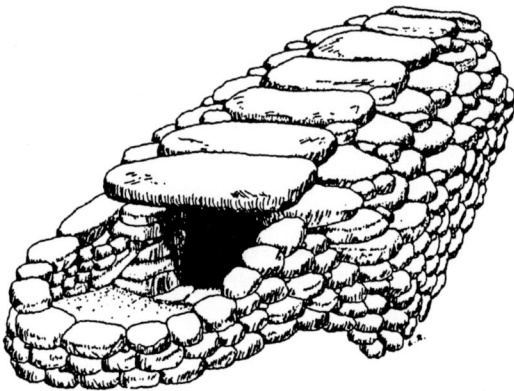

*Fig. 15.5: Chamber Tomb 4663, drawing (L.Ritmeyer).*

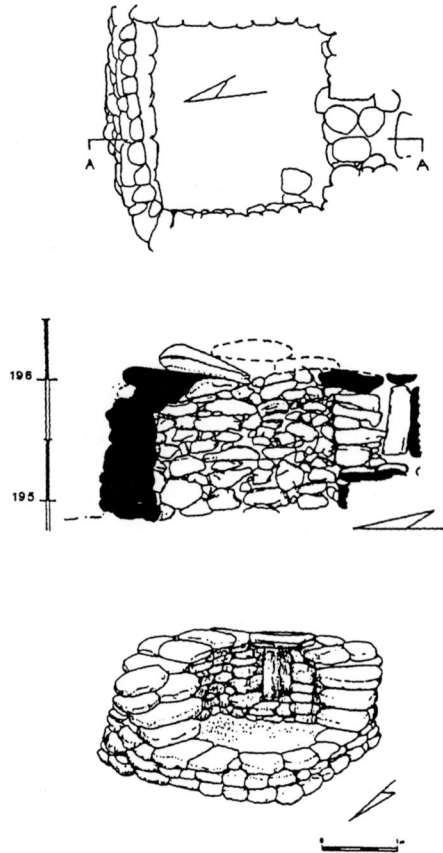

*Fig. 15.6: Chamber Tomb 8096, top plan, section and artists drawing (G.Cook).*

123

| Tomb | length (m) | width (m) | height (m) | orientation /direction of head | burial mode |
|------|-----------|-----------|-----------|--------------------------------|-------------|
| 23 | 1.75 | 1.05 | 0.45 | N-S /N | primary, single, flexed, left side |
| 4244 | 1.60 | 1.24 | 0.50 | E-W /E | primary, single, flexed, right side |
| 3004 | ? | ? | ? | ? | single (?), no other data available |
| 371c | 1.02 | 0.92 | 0.39 | N-S /? | multiple, successive, no other data available |
| 187a | ? | ? | ? | ? | single, disturbed |
| *average* | 1.46 | 1.07 | 0.67 | | |

*Table 15.4. Attributes of built cist tombs*

available. Gonen has also posited that corbelling is a stronger construction method.[32]

4. *Entry passages*: Where discerned, the entry passages take the form of a linteled and posted square opening located in one of the short walls at its midpoint, or in the case of T.8096, somewhat off-centre. A step leads from the original tomb floor to the opening. As noted above, T.187b did not have a side opening and was accessed from the roof.

5. The only other constructional feature worthy of note is the *stone bench or shelf* found in T.4663 built against the wall opposite the opening.

6. *Number of interments*: Of the four burial types, the built chamber tombs contain the largest number of interments (with the exception of T.4663 and T.8185b). They range from 4 to 8 individuals, and generally contain the greatest number of burial goods (see Tables 15.6 and 15.7).

7. *Demographic characteristics of interred*: Our data are not sufficient to allow conclusions with wider applications. Tombs 4663 and 8186b contained few or no human remains. Only a preliminary study was made of the bones from T.1025, which were fragmentary in any case. T.187 contained only males and T.8096 held individuals of various ages and both sexes. These insubstantial data will be considered later.

*Built cist tombs* (Figs 15.9-15.10)

The cist tombs are smaller versions of the larger chamber tombs. In both cases a pit was first excavated under the living surface, followed by the construction of a roofed stone tomb. However, the cist tomb was entered via the roof, while the chamber tomb included a side entry. As noted above, T.187b is, from the standpoint of entry, a cist tomb. Table 15.4 summarises the main attributes of cist tombs.

Several patterns are apparent with reference to cist tombs:

1. Cist tombs tend to be more square in plan and to be smaller than chamber tombs. It is worth noting that a similar tendency exists in rock-cut tombs (of all periods) where curvilinear tombs tend to be smaller than rectangular ones.[33] Being less solid, the construction of cist tombs also tends to be more easily disturbed.

2. By definition, access to the cist burial is via the roof; no dromos or shaft is present (T.187 is referred to as a chamber tomb because of its size). However, in most cases (T.4244 is the exception), at least one of the short sides is open, i.e., lacking a stone lining. This may be the outcome of expedience or have some ideological importance.

3. One interment is the usual number, the exception being T.371, which contained four burials in the cist (two successive jar burials were placed over the roof of the tomb).

4. Correlating to the smaller number of interments, cist tombs tend to contain fewer burial goods (see Table 15.7).

5. Cist tombs are generally reserved for juveniles from 3-12 years of age.

*Shaft burial* (Fig. 15.8)

Shaft burial T.3126 is clearly associated with chamber tomb T.1025 (Fig. 15.8), the shaft probably comprising the original access to the chamber tomb from a surface about 0.5 m above. When the massive earthen embankment was deposited over the remains of the previous occupation and tomb shaft, a new shaft (Shaft 3090), approximately 2.30 m deep, was dug out. The question is whether the 3126 burials date to the shallow, pre-embankment shaft or the deeper post-embankment shaft. At least four individuals with burial goods were interred here; the uppermost was flexed and relatively intact. The configuration of flexed position and burial goods rules out the simple disposal of refuse.

---

32  Gonen 1992c, 159-160.

33  Wright 1985, 325.

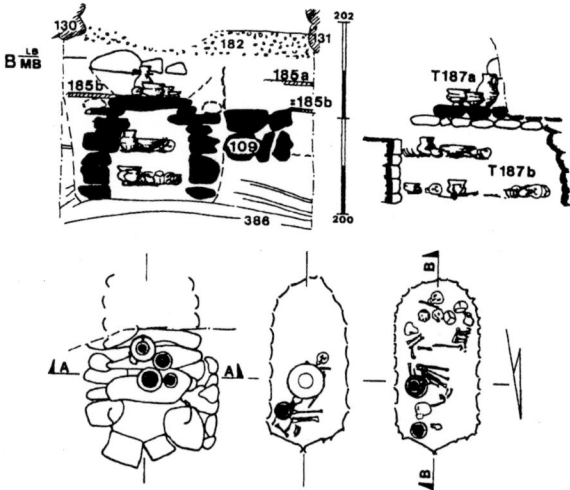

Fig. 15.7: Chamber/cist Tomb 187a and 187b,
sections and top plans of diferent phases.

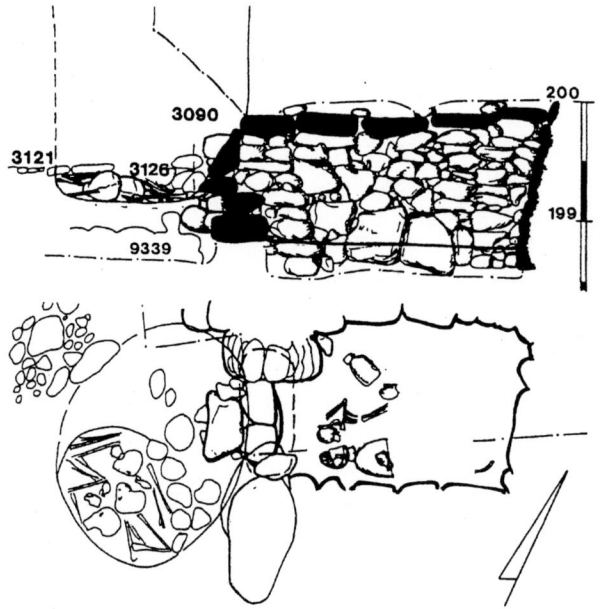

Fig. 15.8: Chamber Tomb 1025, Shaft 3090 and
shaft Tomb 3126, section, top plan
and artists drawing (G. Solar & G. Cook).

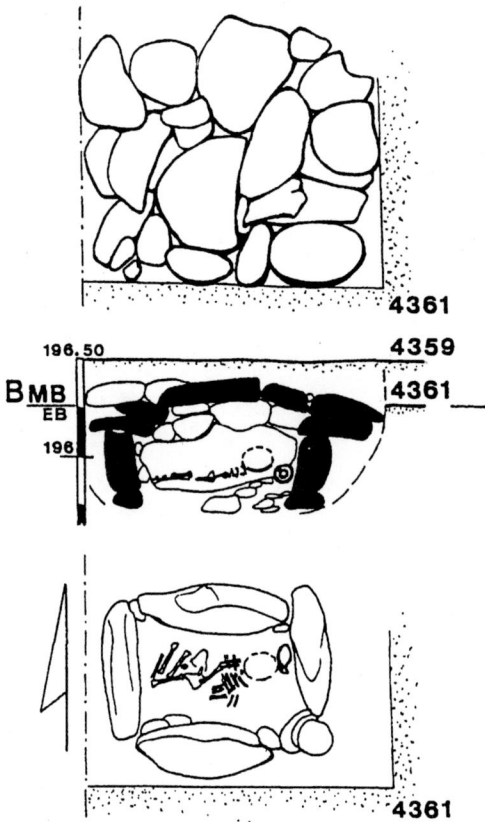

Fig. 15.9: Cist Tomb 4224, top plans and section.

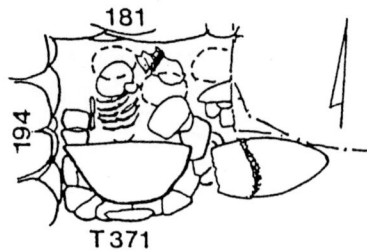

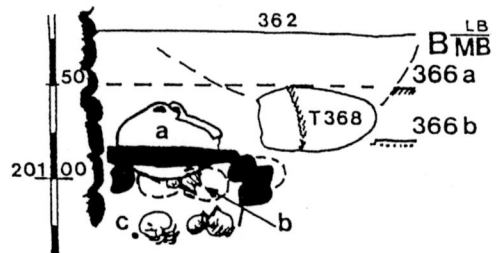

Fig. 15.10: Cist Tomb 371, (two phases, b and c),
surmounted by jar burial, Tomb 371a.

| Tomb[*] | length/width (m) | orientation (direction of mouth) | direction of head | burial mode |
|---|---|---|---|---|
| 902b | 0.74 x 0.62 | ? (?) | ? | fragmentary, surrounding circle of stones |
| 902c | 0.55 x 0.40 | ? (?) | ? | no bones |
| 902d | 0.42 x 0.36 | NW-SE (NW) | - | no bones |
| 4242a | 0.40 x 0.32 | E-W (W) | ? | fragmentary |
| 4356 | 1.38 x 1.28 | upright | - | primary, surrounding circle of stones |
| 1062 | 0.81 x 0.48 | E-W (W) | mouth | primary, flexed, left side? |
| 3050 | 0.42 x 0.37 | N_S(N) | mouth | primary, highly flexed, left side |
| 349 | 0.75 x 0.50 | N-S (?) | ? | fragmentary, two burials (jar and pithos) |
| 371a | 0.55 x 0.40 | E-W (E) | mouth | primary, flexed on right side |
| 367 | 0.59 x 0.34 | N-S (N) | mouth | fragmentary |
| 368 | 0.48 x 0.45 | E-W (E) | mouth | primary, flexed on right side (pithos) |
| 393 | 0.48 x 0.34 | SE-NW (NW) | ? | fragmentary |
| 328a | 0.90 x 0.60 | N-S (S) | mouth | fragmentary, surrounded by a ring of stones |
| 328b | 0.68 x 0.45 | SE-NW (SE) | ? | fragmentary |
| 4648 | 1.28 x 0.78 | NE-SW (NE) | mouth | primary, two burials, flexed, one supine (pithos) |
| 4652 | 0.56 x 0.43 | N-S (S) | mouth? | primary, filled with lentils |
| 8186d | not available | NW-SE (NW) | mouth | primary, jar was semi upright |
| 7161 | not available | N-S (S) | ? | fragmentary |

[*] Jar burials are in store jars unless otherwise specified. Several burials, those with insufficient data available, have not been included in this table.

*Table 15.5. Attributes of jar burials*

## Jar burials (Fig. 15.11)

Jar burials are the most ubiquitous type of interment in the Middle Bronze Age levels of Tel Dan, as they are throughout the Levant. Their primary attributes are summarised in Table 15.5.

Jar burials show several salient characteristics:

1. The orientation of jar burials is mainly, but not always, dictated by the orientation of architecture. This is highlighted by the fact that they are frequently placed next to, and aligned with, walls. Since most of the MB architecture at Tel Dan was found in Areas A and B, and Y, respectively on the tel's southern and eastern flanks, the dominant orientation of jar burials, (and the built tombs as well), is either north-south or east-west. Although photographs or drawings may suggest otherwise, very few jars were intentionally placed *under* walls. Where it seems so, there is frequently an intervening floor level sealing the jar burial beneath the foundations of the wall. In other cases jar burials were inserted from the floor surface obliquely at, or under, the foundations of walls and not just before the wall's construction.

2. The jar's neck and shoulder was usually broken and removed to enable insertion of the corpse. This opening was sometimes covered by a large fragment from another jar.

*Fig. 15.11. Schematic illustration of a jar burial, usually containing the remains of an infant or foetus (drawn by N. Ze'evi).*

3. Where the osteological remains are sufficiently well preserved, burials are observed to be primary.

4. Where the osteological remains are sufficiently well preserved, the cadaver was interred in a flexed or contracted position (to varying degrees at both knees and hips).

5. Where the osteological remains are sufficiently well preserved, the head of the deceased is almost always placed at the jar's opening.

| tomb/ burial | area/ phase | type | no. of burials | sex | age | burial mode | orientation | date/comments |
|---|---|---|---|---|---|---|---|---|
| 23 | A1 | cist | 1 | ? | ? | flexed l. side | N/S | MB I |
| 4244 | B2 | cist | 1 | m | 2-3 yr | flexed, r. side | E/W | MB I |
| 4242a | B3 or 4 | jar | 1 | ? | 5-6 mth | ? | E/W | MB I |
| 4356 | B3 or 4 | jar | 1 | ? | 6-7 mth | not artic. | | MB I |
| 4663 | B8 | chamb. | 0(?) | - | - | - | NE/SW | MB II – cenotaph? |
| 371a | B9-10 | jar | 1 | ? | 6-10 mth | flexed, r. side | E/W | MB III – in corner of walls |
| 371b | B9-10 | over cist | 2: H1 | ? | 2 yr | not artic. | - | MB III – in corner of walls |
| | | | H2 | ? | 5-6 yr | not artic. | | |
| 371c | B9 | cist | 3: H1 | ? | 2-4 yr | not artic. | | MB III – in corner of walls |
| | | | H2 | ? | 4 yr | not artic. | | |
| | | | H3 | m | 2-3 yr | not artic. | | |
| 349 | B9 | pithos jar | 2: H1 H2 | ? ? | inf. inf. | ? not artic. | E/W | MB III – under wall |
| 187a | B10 | cist | 1 | ? | adt. | not artic. | | MB III – frag., next to wall |
| 187b upper | B9-10 | cist/ chamb. | 1: H1 | m | 40+ yr | knees flexed supine | N/S | MB III |
| 187b lower | B10 | " | 7: H1 | m | 50-55 yr | legs flexed | N/S | MB III |
| | | | H2 | m | 18-20 yr | moved | not artic. | MB III |
| | | | H3 | ? | juv. | moved | not artic. | MB III |
| | | | H4 | m | mat. | moved | not artic. | MB III |
| | | | H5 | m? | juv. | moved | not artic. | MB III |
| | | | H6 | ? | ? | moved | not artic. | MB III |
| | | | H7 | ? | ? | moved | not artic. | MB III |
| 367 | B9-10 | jar | 1 | ? | inf. | ? | N/S | MB III – next to wall, frag. |
| 368 | B9-10 | pith | 1 | ? | 5.5-6 yr | flexed, r. side | N/S | MB III – next to wall |
| 393 | B9-10 | jar | 1 | ? | inf. | ? | SE/NW | MB III – next to wall |
| 4648 | B9-10 | pith | 2: H1 | ? | 2-3 yr | flexed | NE/SW | MB III – next to wall |
| | | | H2 | ? | inf. | flexed | NE/SW | MB III |
| 4652 | B9-10 | jar | 1 | ? | 1.5-2 yr | flexed | NE/SW | MB III – filled with lentils, next to wall |

*Table 15.6. The Middle Bronze Age human remains of Tel Dan – data summary*

6. Where osteological remains were sufficiently discernible, the cadaver was usually, but not always, placed on its right side. This may have more to do with a right-handed majority in the population placing the dead infants with their heads next to jar openings, rather than with ideological or social predilections.

7. Several jars, from the MB I and the MB III are either set into a circle of stones or had one built around them. There does not seem to be a practical reason for this and the explanation may have to do with symbolism.

8. Juglets are the most frequently found object accompanying jar burials (see Table 15.7), and probably contained liquids.

9. The human remains are overwhelmingly those of infants under 2 years. There are two exceptions: Burial 368, a pithos containing a 5 1/2-year old child; and Burial 4648, a pithos containing two infants, one probably newborn and one possibly as old as 3 years. Note that the exceptions are both pithoi burials, perhaps an indication of extenuating circumstances, such as mental or physical handicap (not detected in osteological analysis).

## Some general conclusions

1. Tomb orientation is inconsistent; tombs of all types are usually oriented with reference to architecture, i.e., jar burials are usually inserted alongside and parallel to walls, as are built and cist tombs (where the archaeological exposure is sufficient to judge). However, where primary and relatively undisturbed

| tomb/ burial | area/ phase | type | no. of burials | | sex | age | burial mode | orientation | date/comments |
|---|---|---|---|---|---|---|---|---|---|
| 4680 | B9-10 | jar | 1 | | ? | inf. | not artic. | ? | MB III |
| 328a | B10? | jar | 1 | | ? | 2 yr? | | N/S | MB III – next to wall |
| 328b | B10? | jar | 1 | | ? | 2 yr? | | E/W | MB III – next to wall |
| 7161 | B10? | jar | 1 | | ? | inf. | ? | N/S | MB III – under wall |
| 8096 a/b | M b, d | chamb. | 5 | H1 | m | 30-40 yr | not artic. | ? | late MB I-MB III |
| | | | | H2 | f | 30-40 yr | not artic. | ? | MB III |
| | | | | H3 | f? | 18-21 yr | not artic. | ? | late MB I-MB III |
| | | | | H4 | ? | 8-12 yr | not artic. | ? | late MB I-MB III |
| | | | | H5 | ? | <5 yr | not artic. | ? | late MB I-MB III |
| 8185b | Md? | chamb. | 0 | | | | | | late MB I-LB I(?), no bones, reused as silo |
| 8186c | M b | jar | 1 | | ? | inf. | not artic. | | MB III/LB I, under wall |
| 902b | Y1-2 | jar | 1 | | ? | inf. | - | – | MB I, in stone circle |
| 902c | Y1-2 | jar | 0 | | - | - | - | – | MB I, no bones |
| 902d | Y1-2 | krater | 0 | | - | - | - | NW-SE | MB I, no bones |
| 1025 | Y2 | chamb. | 4 | H1 | ? | 19-20 yr | flexed, rt. side | E-W | MB I |
| | | | | H2 | ? | mat. | moved | – | MB1 |
| | | | | H3 | ? | mat. | moved | – | MB1 |
| | | | | H4 | ? | mat. | moved | – | MB1 |
| 1062 | Y5 | jar | 1 | | ? | inf. | flexed, l. side | E-W | MB I |
| 3050 | Y2 | jar | 1 | | ? | inf. | flexed, l. side | E-W | MB I |
| 3126 | Y3 | shaft | 4 | H1 | ? | 25 yr | flexed, r. side | N-S | MB I |
| | | | | H2 | ? | ? | disturbed- | " | MB1 |
| | | | | H3 | ? | ? | disturbed- | " | MB1 |
| | | | | H4 | f? | | not artic. | – | MB1 |
| 3004 | Y11 | cist | 1 | | ? | juv. | ? | .? | MB II?, amorphous, in baulk includes jar |

Note: Tombs and burials are listed by area, each area's burials listed in chronological order (for chronological equivalency of different areas' features, see Table 15.1).

The following abbreviations are used:

| | | | | | | | | H | Homo |
|---|---|---|---|---|---|---|---|---|---|
| adt | adult | artic | articulated | chamb | chamber | frag | fragmentary | | |
| inf | infant | juv | juvenile | l | left | mat | mature (>20 yr) | min | minimum |
| mth | month(s) | r | right | yr | year(s) | | | | |

*Table 15.6. The Middle Bronze Age human remains of Tel Dan – data summary*
(based on Arensberg 1970, Zias 1982, Zorich 1985)

interments can be discerned, the deceased was usually placed with his or her head toward the tomb opening. This is true for all burial types.

2. The early cist tombs (Tombs 23 and 4244) contain single burials. The later cist and constructed tombs (starting with T.1025) contain multiple successive burials. This is best seen in Tombs 1025, 187b and 8096 where the skeletal remains of previous burials were pushed up against the walls to make room for the next, a phenomenon observed at most other sites in the Near East where multiple successive burial took place. The transition from single burial to multiple successive burial can perhaps be seen as an indication of Canaanite society's increasing complexity.

3. Different tomb types are often associated in clusters. Jar burials are frequently found on top of, or next to, chamber or cist tombs. Post-interment offerings are also in evidence. Moreover, the shaft burial (T.3126) is apparently associated with T.1025. In other words, society's interaction with the deceased did not end with burial.

## The geographical and temporal range of Middle Bronze Age tomb and burial types found at Tel Dan

None of the burial types found in the Middle Bronze Age levels at Tel Dan are unique to that site, nor do any categorically represent the earliest occurrence of a type. This section shall briefly outline the geographical and chronological range of each burial or tomb type, in an attempt to show general and readily observable patterns of distribution.[34] These patterns help to place the MB tombs from Tel Dan in their regional and temporal context.

Cist tombs and jar burials appear in the very earliest MB I levels and continue into the terminal MB III and beyond. Built chamber tombs first appear in the mid or late MB I and continue into the LB II at Dan.[35] The shaft burial dates also to the later MB I. However, the first appearance of the latter two types may be earlier as well – our small MB I sample precludes judgment. In brief, all the types seem to coexist over at least a great part of the Middle Bronze Age, and may do so for the period's entirety.

Built chamber tombs do not have true prototypes in Early Bronze or Intermediate Bronze Age Canaan. They first occurred in Mesopotamia in the Early Dynastic period reaching Syria by ED III at the latest, spreading to coastal Syria (i.e. Ugarit), the Egyptian delta (brought there by an Asiatic population originating perhaps in Syria[36]), and Canaan proper, only in the MB I.[37] Tel Dan T.1025 is thus one of the earliest examples of the type. However, built chamber tombs never became common in Canaan, where rock-cut tombs were the standard. Subsequently, sometime in the sixteenth or fifteenth century BC, the form reached Cyprus.[38] Chamber tombs in Mesopotamia (and in the Nile delta) tended to have vaulted roofing as opposed to the slab roofing found in Canaan and Syria. This variance should be seen as reflecting the availability of raw materials; lack of stone required the solution of mud-brick vaulting.

Unlike large chamber tombs, cist tombs do have local predecessors in the previous period (the Intermediate Bronze Age), though not in the Early Bronze Age.[39] However, they are the exception in a period when shaft, cave and 'dolmen' tombs are the rule, as they were in the Early Bronze Age.[40] This may indicate either linear continuity from the IB to the MB I, or a common inspiration and/or source for a technique that reached Canaan at different times. In either case, the concept of the cist tomb is closely related to that of the larger chamber tomb and both have their antecedents in the northern Levant and Mesopotamia of the third millennium BC.[41] This was not merely the transmission of an idea from the north, but the mortuary practice of a people that originated there. This point is expanded on below.

Shaft burial is another widespread phenomenon in the Levant of the third and second millennia BC, though the idea of the shaft does not always seem to have a common source. Some forms of shaft burial were an end in themselves – a sort of deeper pit burial (e.g., at Sukas and Selenkhiye[42]) not associated with other burial forms. Others were probably associated with another, usually chamber, burial located next to them (e.g., at Ur, Tel el-Dab'a and T.3126 at Dan). The former is a phenomenon which may be conceptually related to the typical rock-carved shaft tombs of the Intermediate Bronze Age. The fact that shaft tombs were also a norm of the Early Bronze Age in one form or another precludes the possibility of saying whether any aspect of the type originates outside of Canaan, though the principle has great antiquity in Mesopotamia as well.

The absence of simple, shallow pit (or non-constructed) burials at Dan is an anomaly since the technique was employed at many contemporary urban sites both in Canaan and beyond, e.g., at Hazor,[43] Tell es-Saliheyeh[44] and Alalakh.[45] However, not too much should be made of this dearth since the MB domestic levels uncovered at Dan are restricted.

With the exception of the Pottery Neolithic jar burials,[46] subfloor jar burials do not appear regularly in the Levant until the MB. Much like the chamber and cist burials, the practice of subfloor burial in ceramic vessels can be demonstrated to have first appeared in Mesopotamia in the late fourth or early third millennium BC, becoming quite usual in third- and second-millennium Mesopotamia and Syria,[47] reaching the southern Levant in the early second millennium BC. In the former regions the vessel containing, or more frequently covering, the cadaver was most often a krater or a cooking pot.[48] At certain Mesopotamian sites infants were interred under floors without the use of a ceramic container, e.g., at Chagar Bazar Levels 2-3

---

34 Selected parallels from Canaan, Syria, Mesopotamia and Egypt are listed in the Appendix.
35 E.g., Biran 1994; Gilmour, in this volume.
36 Bietak 1984, 474-475.
37 See parallels in Appendix; and cf. van den Brink 1982, 72.
38 E.g., Pelon 1973.
39 One must also consider the possibility that the megalithic 'dolmens' – found mostly in Jordan (cf. Prag, in this volume), the Golan Heights, the Hula valley and in the hills of Samaria, the Galilee and the Carmel – served as the inspiration or prototype for the cist tomb and perhaps for the chamber tomb as well.
40 Prag 1974, 100-102; Richard 1987, 33.

41 See the parallels in Appendix.
42 Cf. the shaft burial analogues in Appendix.
43 Yadin et al. 1960, 77-85.
44 von der Osten 1956, 40-43, Pls. 20-23.
45 Woolley 1955, 215-222.
46 Cf. Gopher & Greenberg 1987.
47 E.g., Dornemann 1979, 138.
48 Burial in an open vessel is ususual in Canaan, but occurs, e.g., at Hazor (in an oven: Yadin et al. 1960, 77, Pl. XXVIII:9) and perhaps at Tel Dan, T.902d (if it is a burial).

*Table 14.7. Typological Summary of Tomb Contents*

| Period | Stratum | Tombs (in chrono-logical order) | Tomb type | Number of burials | Total no. of burial offerings (1) | B.p | B.h | Bg | B.c | B.g.n | B.g.f | B.f.c | B.c.n | G | CH | CP | K | L | SJ |
|---|---|---|---|---|---|---|---|---|---|---|---|---|---|---|---|---|---|---|---|
| MB I | XII | 23 | cist | 1 | 1 | | | 1 | | | | | | | | | | | |
| | | 4244 | cist | 1 | 2 | 2 | | | | | | | | | | | | | |
| | | 4242a | jb | 1 | 0 | | | | | | | | | | | | | | |
| | | 4356 | jb | 1 | 0 | | | | | | | | | | | | | | |
| | | 3050 | jb | 1 | 0 | | | | | | | | | | | | | | |
| | | 902b | jb | - | 0 | | | | | | | | | | | | | | |
| | | 902c | jb | 1 | 0 | | | | | | | | | | | | | | |
| | | 1025 | chamber | 4? | 35 | 5 | | 10 | 1 | | | | | | | | 1 | 1 | |
| | | 3126 | shaft | 3 | 6 | | | 1 | | | | | | | | | | | |
| MB II | XI | 1062 | jb | 1 | 2 | | | | | | | | | | | | | | |
| | | 8096a (2) | chamber | 3-4 | 6 | | | 1 | 1 | | | | | | | | | | |
| | X | 4663 | chamber | 1? | 22 | 3 | | | | 1 | 2 | | | | 1 | | 1 | 2 | 2 (4) |
| | | 3004 (3) | cist? | 1? | 2 | | | | | | | | | | | | | | |
| MB III | IX | 349 | jb | 2 | 8 | | | | | 1 | 1 | | | 1 | | | | | |
| | | 371c | cist | 3 | 2 | | | | | 1 | | | | | | | | | |
| | | 371b | cist | 1 | 2 | | | | | | | 1 | | | | | | | |
| | | 371a | jb | 2 | 1 | | | | | | | | | | | | | | |
| | | 367 | jb | 1 | 2 | | | | | | | | | | | | | | |
| | | 368 | jb | 1 | 3 | | | | | | | | | | | | | | |
| | | 393 | jb | 1 | 1 | | | | | | | | | | | | | | |
| | | 4648 | jb | 2 | 4 | | | | | | 1 | | | | | | | | |
| | | 4652 | jb | 1 | 1 | | | | | | | | | | | | | | |
| | | 328a | jb | 1 | 4 | | | | | | | | | | | | | | |
| | | 328b | jb | 1 | 0 | | | | | | | | | | | | | | |
| | | 7161 | jb | 1 | 1 | | | | | | | | | | | | | | |
| | | 187b - lower mid | chamber or cist | 7 | 7 | | | | | 3 | | 1 | | | | | | | |
| | | 187b - upper | chamber or cist | 1 | 4 | | | | | | | | 1 | | | | | | |
| | | 187a | cist (6) | 1 | 15 | 4 | | | | 1 | 1 | | | | | | | 1 | |
| | | 8096b (7) | chamber | 1-2 | 33 | 8 | 1 | | | 1 (8) | 3 | 1 | 1 | | 1 | | | 3 | |
| | | 8185b | chamber | - | 1 | | | | | | | | | | | | | | |
| | | 8186c | jb | 1 | 1 | | | | | | | | | | | | | | |
| LB | VIII | 4689b | jb | 1 | 0 | | | | | | | | | | | | | | |
| | | 8096c | jb | - | 1 | | | | | | | | | | | | | | |
| *Totals:* | | | | 49 | 164 (9) | 21 | 1 | 12 | 2 | 5 | 8 | 7 | 2 | 1 | 2 | 0 | 2 | 7 | 2 (10) |

(1) Where multiple pieces comprise a single composite, bone plaques to inlay a box for example, they are calculated as one item.

(2) Several items attributed to T.8096a may be attributable to T.8096b and *vice versa.*

(3) Tomb 3004 was in a balk and its accutrements only partially recovered.

(4) These are of the single-shoulder-handle type which can also be called large jugs.

(5) This is actually a development of the globular necked bowl with the vertical neck.

Table 14.7: *Typological Summary of Tomb Contents (continued)*

| Tombs | J | Jt.d | Jt.g | Jt.o | Jt.p | Jt.c | Cypriot | Stick Pin | Dagger | Projectile point | Other Metal | Ala-baster | Scarab | Cyl. seal | Bone inlay | Beads | Shell | Organic material | Faunal remains |
|---|---|---|---|---|---|---|---|---|---|---|---|---|---|---|---|---|---|---|---|
| 23 | | | | | | | | | | | | | | | | | | | |
| 4244 | | 1 | | | | | | | | | | | | | | 9 | | | |
| 4242a | | | | | | | | | | | | | | | | | 1 | | yes |
| 4356 | | | | | | | | | | | | | | | | | | | yes |
| 3050 | | | | | | | | | | | | | | | | | | | |
| 902b | | | | | | | | | | | | | | | | | | | |
| 902c | 5 | 1 | 3 | 3 | 2 | | | | 1 + pom | | 1 (belt?) | | | | | 1 (glass) | | | yes |
| 1025 | | | 2 | | 2 | 1 | | | | | | | | | | | | | yes |
| 3126 | | | 1 | | | | | | | | | | | | | | | | |
| 1062 | | | | | | | | | | 1 | | | 1 ? | | | 36 (frit) | | | ? |
| 8096a (2) | | | | 1 | 1 | 1 | | | 1 | | | | | | | | | | yes |
| 4663 | 1 | | | 1 | 1 | | 2 | 1 | 1 | | 1 (belt?) | | | 1 | 1 | 1 (bone) | 1 | | yes |
| 3004 (3) | | | | | | 2 | | | | | | | | | | | 4 | | yes |
| 349 | 1 | 1 | 1 | | | | | | | | | | | | | | | | |
| 371c | | | | | 1 | | | | | | | | | | | | | | |
| 371b | | | | | 1 | | | | | | | | | | | | | | yes (tool) |
| 371a | | | 1 | | | | | | | | | | | | 1 | | | | |
| 367 | | | | | | 1 | | | | | | | | | | | | | |
| 368 | | 1 | | | | | | | | | | | | | | | | | |
| 393 | | | | | | 1 | | | | | | | | | | | | | |
| 4648 | | | | | | 1 | | | | | | | | | | 17 (foraminefera) | | lentils | |
| 4652 | | | | | | | | 1 | | | | | | | | | | | |
| 328a | 1 (5) | | | | | 2 | | | | | | | 1 | | | | | | |
| 328b | | | | | | | | | | | | | | | | | | | |
| 7161 | | | | | | | 1 | | | | | | 1 | | | | | | yes |
| 187b- lower mid | | 1 | 2 | | | | | | | | | | | | | | | | |
| 187b- upper | | | | 1 | | | | 1 | | | | | | | | | | | ? |
| 187a | | | 1 | | 1 | 2 | | | | | | | | | | 1 | | | yes |
| 8096b (7) | | 3 | 1 | | | 2 | | 2 | | | | 2 | 2 | | 1-2 | 1 | 1 | | yes |
| 8185b | | | | | | 1 | | | | | | | | | | | | | yes |
| 8186c | | | | | | 1 | | | | | | | | | | | | | |
| 4689b | | | | | | | | | | | | | | | | | | | |
| 8096c | | | | | | | | | | | | | | | | | | | |
| *Totals* | 9 | 8 | 11 | 6 | 9 | 15 | 3 | 5 | 3 | 1 | 3 | 2 | 5 | 1 | 3-4 | 59 (11) | 7 | -- | -- |

(6)  Selected bones only, not a primary burial.
(7)  See note 2.
(8)  Actually a trefoil-mouthed jug with the profile of a necked bowl.

(9)  Including burial jars, 182 vessels total.
(10) Including burial jars, 20 storejars total.
(11) For 6 composite objects--bracelets or necklaces.

dating from the second half of the third to the first half of the second millennium BC.[49]

A significant element of morphological continuity from the third to second millennium BC is embodied by the rock-cut tomb type common throughout the country wherever bedrock is available (though not at Tel Dan). But, as we have seen, most of the different burial techniques practiced at Tel Dan have antecedents in Syria-Mesopotamia.[50] Certainly one must heed Ucko's admonition that burial practices can and do change rapidly without clearly manifest reasons.[51] But burial is an intimate and personal practice that strongly reflects the value system and ideology of individuals and societies. The evidence from the ancient Near East suggests that, in that area at least, it was also the most resilient of cultural expressions, and as such, slow to change. In MB Canaan previous practices *continue*, while newly introduced techniques can be demonstrated to have external origins.[52]

Many other aspects of MB material culture have also been determined to originate in Syria / Mesopotamia: Freestanding earthen embankment fortifications, tripartite city gates, casemate walls, the *Hofhaus*, etc.[53] The question has always been by what mechanism these phenomena were transmitted. Given the supplement of new mortuary practices and the continuity of traditional ones, together with other evidence pointing to large scale cultural transference, we are directed to readopt some aspects of an earlier and once dominant model positing that *people* actually migrated from Syria-Mesopotamia to Canaan.[54] This, of course, is not to advocate a pure Syro-Mesopotamian origin for the Canaanite culture of the Middle Bronze Age. Nor are the crucial roles of trade and independent invention belittled. Our stance does contrast to those that explain MB culture change as directed solely by independent invention or by the transmission of ideas and commodities via trade.[55] What burial practices suggest is that an amalgam of endogenous and exogenous cultural forces was in play.[56]

From a broader perspective, when the archaeological conditions are right, funerary practices can be a powerful tool for understanding processes of information transfer and culture change, a tool that is often neglected.

## Social Implications and Spiritual Meanings

This examination of the Middle Bronze Age burial remains from Tel Dan has been carried out under the assumption that mortuary practices reflect a society's social organisation and cultural values. On the one hand, an attempt has been made to discern societal phenomena such as ranking, social persona, and kinship affiliation, while on the other hand ritual behaviour in its cosmological context was sought out. Ceremonial behaviour, religious beliefs and social systems are clearly interrelated and should not be disassociated. As Huntington and Metcalf have put it, "Close attention to the combined symbolic and sociological context of the corpse yields the most profound explanations regarding the meaning of death and life in almost any society".[57] But in prehistoric contexts (or, rather, protohistoric in the case of Middle-Bronze-Age Canaan), it is difficult to arrive at an understanding of ancient concepts of death wholly on an artifactual basis.[58] For this reason, most recent scholarship tends to lean heavily toward the social orientation – usually with little emphasis on religion.[59] Huntington and Metcalf adopt an integrated approach, but their work deals with contemporary, observable societies.[60]

The shortcomings of the sample outlined in the introduction have obviated the utility of most quantitative methods,[61] as they have for most other burial assemblages in Canaan. And yet some patterns *are* manifest, even in this small assemblage, and require explanation, if only in tentative terms. Moreover, textual sources from related cultural contexts, particularly from second-millennium BC Ugarit and Mari, shed light on mortuary ideology. Thus, some provisional conclusions can be suggested regarding both social organisation and the perception of death amongst the inhabitants of Middle-Bronze-Age Tel Dan.[62]

## Social implications

*Introduction; mortuary practices and social evolution in the Middle Bronze Age*

An increase in social complexity from the IB through the MB III is observable at Dan and throughout Canaan. This process is reflected in the settlement pattern,[63] in

---

49 Mallowan 1936, 15.
50 Cf. also Carter & Parker, in this volume.
51 Ucko 1969.
52 Cf. Steele, in this volume, for a similar phenomenon in early Iron Age Cyprus.
53 E.g., Kaplan 1971.
54 E.g., Kenyon 1966; Albright 1973; Dever 1976.
55 E.g., Gerstenblith 1983; Tubb 1983.
56 Ilan 1994.
57 Huntington & Metcalf 1979, 17.
58 Cf. Jacobsen & Cullen 1981.
59 Cf., e.g., the studies contained in Saxe 1970; Binford 1971; Tainter 1978; Chapman, Kinnes & Randsborg 1981; and for Canaan specifically, Shay 1983; Palumbo 1987.
60 Huntington & Metcalf 1979.
61 Many are detailed by Tainter 1978; and in Chapman, Kinnes & Randsborg 1981.
62 In the following sections the ethnographic record is drawn upon to shore up an idea or to suggest alternative interpretations. For the sake of brevity only selected examples are noted in the appropriate context. This is done with some reservation, keeping in mind Ucko's (1969) warning concerning the multiplicity of possible explanations for mortuary variability in the archaeological record and the problems of sampling error. Since Ucko's contribution, subsequent research has identified a greater degree of commonality in mortuary practices and better founded explanations for variability have been forwarded (e.g., by Binford 1971; Tainter 1978; O'Shea 1984; Morris 1987).
63 Broshi & Gophna 1986.

architecture, in the magnitude of trade contacts, and in ancient literature such as the Execration Texts.[64] Another manifestation of MB social evolution is found in the mortuary remains. At Dan, and apparently at every other MB I site with burial remains, early MB I built (cist) tombs contain single burials, while later MB I and MB II-III built tombs contain multiple successive burials. These changes seem to have accompanied a transition from the pastoralist and small-scale cultivation modes of subsistence of the Intermediate and early Middle Bronze Age, to a dominant mode of settled agriculture, élite-controlled redistributive economies, and urbanism of the MB proper.[65] Thus, burial methods provide a general gauge of cultural and social continuity with the IB, although the lack of secondary burial in the MB contrasts sharply with that practice's frequency in the IB.[66]

### On discerning status and rank in mortuary practices

The four basic burial types – jar burials, cist tombs, chamber tombs and shaft burials, contemporaneous at least from the late MB I on – correspond with the average number of dimensional distinctions in burial calculated by Binford for settled agriculturists in his study of the mortuary practices of different subsistence types.[67] While Binford's conclusions with regard to social persona and ranking in societies of varying complexity have derived support from other scholars' work,[68] subsequent studies have suggested that *status* differences based on age and sex must be considered separately from ascribed or genealogical *ranking* differences which are "not simultaneously ordered on the basis of age and sex".[69] Peebles and Kus' distinction of the *subordinate* (i.e., age and sex) dimension from the *superordinate* dimension (i.e., attributes which crosscut age and sex distinctions and which are determined by class or genealogy), has been useful in the present study. A breakdown of burial practices in relation to demographic data in particular reveals certain status groups based on age and sex.

### Demographic status correlates to tomb types (see Table 15.6)

Most *chamber tomb* interments (N = 17) show a range of age and sex, excluding infants, implying that they are family vaults.[70] The exception is T.187b which contained only males, mostly adult; but this may be an aberrant sample in what is still a family tomb. Conversely, it may represent a differentiation of social personae; several studies have shown that sex can be a determinant of

burial location.[71] In view of what appears to be a dominance of males in the cist tombs (see immediately below), it is worth recalling that T.187b is technically a large cist tomb – it has no side entry.

*Cist tombs* seem to have contained only children or juveniles aged 2 to 12 years (N = 7, or 58% of the total juvenile population identified). The only sexed individuals were male (N = 4). Here we might speculate that these were individuals that had not yet experienced a "rite of passage",[72] such as circumcision, or other initiation ceremony.

With one exception, *jar burials* contained only infants – generally less than 2 years of age but a few possibly as old as 3. These embody perhaps the most obvious evidence for status of the subordinate dimension – at Dan and throughout the Levant. While in some societies infants lack status completely,[73] the patterns observed in jar burials (and especially the accompanying offerings) indicate that infants maintained a social persona of some kind, albeit an ephemeral one.[74]

It can be seen from Table 15.6 that very few skeletons were sexed, 8 out of a sample of 48+ individuals; only 2 female skeletons were identified, both from T.8096. While the sample may be unrepresentative, it is worth noting that in Area B, where most of the burial material was excavated and most of the sexed individuals originated, not one female skeleton was identified. This however, may be an accident of excavation.

From the foregoing discussion it seems that at least three, and probably four, status categories are apparent; infant, juvenile male, adult male, female. The reality is probably more complex.

### Ascribed ranking

Contrary to what one might expect from other indicators of social complexity at Tel Dan and in Middle Bronze Age Canaan, the evidence for class division or ascribed ranking in the mortuary assemblage of Tel Dan is meager.

*Shaft burial* T.3126, associated with chamber T.1025, does show some attribute affinity with 'servant burials' at Ur and Tell ed-Dab°a,[75] but the social implications inherent in a "servant" interpretation, based on so little real evidence, require a cautious approach. Whether it represents an extension of the kinship affiliation suggested for chamber tombs, another status category, or

---

64 E.g., Mazar 1968; Dever 1987. For the archaeological correlates of a ranked society, including burial characteristics, cf. Peebles & Kus 1977.
65 Cf. Dever 1987, 159-160; Ilan 1994.
66 Cf. Prag 1974, 101; Richard 1987, 38; Dever 1987.
67 Binford 1971.
68 E.g., Ucko 1969, 270; Saxe 1970.
69 Peebles & Kus 1977, 431.
70 Cf. the chamber tombs of Ugarit: Salles, in this volume.
71 E.g., Ucko 1969, 270-271; Binford 1971; Randsborg 1975; Huntington & Metcalf 1979, 98-118. We have been unable to identify what the social personae may have been in T.187b; to mention just one possible criterion of social identity, no easily identifiable 'prestige items', such as weapons, were present. The infrequency of metal finds, for example, could be accounted for by plunder in antiquity, or by interpreting all the excavated tombs as representing lower-ranked individuals.
72 Van Gennep 1960.
73 E.g., Ucko 1969, 270-271.
74 Cf. Steele, in this volume.
75 Cf. Appendix.

an imported practice later abandoned, one cannot say; not every case of extra-tomb burial need be considered an indication of status differentiation. Practical circumstances may have prevented a family from opening its tomb. If, for example, two deaths occurred within a short time, and the first corpse had not yet decayed sufficiently to allow opening the tomb, the family may have preferred to inter the remains directly over or next to it.[76] A straightforward kinship explanation seems preferable for the shaft burial.

The position of burial does not seem to have any discernible social significance. Orientation, degree of flexure, and side of inhumation all seem to vary across the sex and age dimensions identified above (and see Table 15.6). The possible exception is the upper burial of T.187b, that of a robust adult male in a supine position with legs flexed to the right. In his analysis of the large population of Intermediate Bronze Age burials at Jericho, Palumbo has suggested that this position characterises the burial of a higher ranking individual,[77] but the evidence and the statistical manipulations are not unequivocal.

There is no reliable indication of wealth differentiation that cross-cuts demographic indices. Wright has suggested that the lack of built tombs in Canaan may testify to a more "egalitarian" society than that of Mesopotamia or, for example, that of Ugarit.[78] However, tomb contents, and those from Tel Dan in particular, give no indication that even the largest built tombs belong to wealthier or higher status individuals than do those of rock-hewn tombs. If the effort-expenditure principle is applicable,[79] a rock-hewn tomb can involve at least as substantial an investment of labour as a built tomb. Indeed, the richest MB tombs known, the MB III tombs of Tell el-Ajjul, are rock-hewn, as are the rich tombs of Jericho and many of those at Megiddo.

In the realm of burial offerings, none of the Tel Dan tombs contain much in the way of prestige items such as metal objects, jewellery and inscribed seals (many of which were probably looted in antiquity). The richest tombs are chamber tombs, which invariably contain the oldest and the greatest number of individuals. Almost all the metalwork (including weapons), and jewellery recovered from funerary contexts came from the chamber tombs. Greater wealth associated with older, more accomplished (and therefore higher ranked) individuals is to be expected, even in an 'egalitarian' society.[80]

Two daggers were found in chamber tombs (1025 and 8096), one of which certainly, and the other probably, contained adult male individuals in consanguine contexts. Both are dated to the earlier MB (MB I and early MB II respectively). These individuals most likely maintained a 'warrior' status of some kind (in the social but not necessarily occupational sense) though not interred in single warrior burials of the classic type.[81]

The burial goods associated with cist tombs are similar in number and type to those of the jar burials – a few ceramic vessels and little else. Looking at infant-containing jar burials, where the sample is larger, little variation in pattern is evident at Dan, or in other contemporary Levantine mortuary contexts. The presence or absence of a juglet or scarab is insufficient evidence for determining the existence of rank. It would seem that the degree of conformity present in infant inhumation at Dan should be interpreted as an indication that the norms of infant burial cut across any differences in rank or wealth that may have existed in Canaanite society.

While the tomb sample from Dan is too small to warrant the drawing of firm conclusions, contemporary tombs at Jericho, more numerous, much richer and less disturbed on the whole, give the impression of a fairly standardised repertoire for grave-offerings, which held good for many families.[82] At Jericho, the richness of a tomb seems to be contingent on the length of time it was in use and the number of individuals interred more than anything else.[83] In the ethnographic record, the frequent lack of correlation between an individual's wealth and the wealth of his or her burial goods demonstrates the risk of making correlative assumptions.[84] Even more to the point is Tainter's observation that in a study of 93 societies, only 5% used grave-goods to symbolise status or wealth differences.[85]

*Kinship-affiliation*

While the variety in burial method indicates the existence of different social statuses or social personae in the Canaanite society of Tel Dan, it is still likely that most or all burials were kin-affiliated, including tombs containing only males or only children, and jar burials placed on or next to built tombs. This hypothesis draws support from the fact that burial was executed under the living surfaces and within the confines of domestic structures or their appendages. The home and the burials it contained can be assumed to have belonged to the same family (cf. the tomb-house unit relationship proposed by Salles for the intramural chamber tombs at Ugarit[86]). A similar model has been proposed for the age-selected distribution of interments in the contemporary burials, of the Larsa period, at Ur, where vaults were constructed for the adults of the family under the chapels or courtyards of many houses, youths buried in coffins outside the tomb

---

76 Cf. Woolley 1976, 33.
77 Palumbo 1987,.
78 Wright 1985, 329.
79 Binford 1971; Tainter 1978, 125.
80 Cf. Peebles & Kus 1977, 431.

81 Philip, in this volume.
82 Kenyon 1960; 1965.
83 Perhaps the only conclusion that can really be drawn from Yasur-Landau's (1993) analysis.
84 E.g., Ucko 1969. The Merina of Madagascar (Bloch 1982, 213-214) provide one of the best examples of this lack of correlation; even commoners build large subterranean tombs that are far grander and richer than their flimsy houses.
85 Tainter's 1978, 121.
86 Salles 1987; and in this volume.

entrances, and infants in jars or bowls under the floors.[87] Much of the ethnographic data show that chamber tombs containing multiple successive burials are kin-oriented.[88]

*Social implications of mortuary practices; summary*

The dimensions of social persona that have been elicited here are sex, age, kin-affiliation and warrior status. No unequivocal evidence has been recognised for ascribed ranking or differential wealth. This picture contrasts to existing indicators of social complexity (such as settlement patterns, craft specialisation, evidence for élite-controlled trade, public architecture, fortifications and differing modes of domestic architecture), at Dan and other sites, which suggest a higher degree of social stratification.[89]

Why do the mortuary data not support hypothetical expectations for the distinguishing of rank and wealth? Three factors may be influencing our perceptions – (a) a small sample limited to a subfloor domestic context; an as yet unidentified extra-mural cemetery, or an undetected burial ground within the tel, may have served higher (or lower) ranking individuals;[90] (b) site formation processes such as poor preservation and plunder; and (c) ideological precepts which act as social leveling mechanisms. A larger-scale study that includes more sites with larger samples is required to clarify the social implications of mortuary practices in the Middle Bronze Age.

# Cosmology

Having demonstrated that certain mortuary practices cross-cut the dimensions of sex and age, and having noted the lack of evidence for ascribed ranking or wealth differentiation in the MB burials at Dan, other explanations must be sought for these practices. The system of religious beliefs is a potentially fruitful area of inquiry, and one that better explains, for example, patterns of burial position and the nature of burial offerings. Not surprisingly, concepts of rebirth, fertility and perhaps an afterlife, are manifest and intertwined in the MB funerary practices at Tel Dan.

*Simulation of womb and birth in mortuary practices*

The idea of return to the womb and rebirth may be illustrated by the following features:

a. Almost all skeletons were contracted to some degree (i.e., bent at the knees and waist) – a posi-

tion that ubiquitously simulates that of the foetus and of sleep in the ethnographic material.[91]

b. In chamber and jar burials, the head of the deceased was most often placed closest to the tomb or jar opening, the position which best facilitates natal delivery and that in which most newborns breach.

c. The configurations of chamber tombs, jar burials and rock-cut tombs (the latter not yet found at Tel Dan), can be interpreted as simulating the female reproductive organs: burial chamber/jar = womb; entry = cervix; corridor, shaft or dromos = birth canal. Ethnographic evidence provides several parallels in this respect,[92] and a similar interpretation has been offered for the tomb configurations of ancient Egypt.[93] Keel has suggested a concept of return-to-the-womb for a particular type of Iron-Age tomb 'headrest'. He introduces evidence from both Scripture (Psalm 139:8-15; Job 1:21) and iconographic material from Mesopotamia as support.[94]

*The fertility function of death*

Augmenting the birth motif is the concept of death's fertility function. The Ugaritic Baal Epic (I AB:II:30-37) depicts the murder of Mot (god of death) by Anath in terms of the grain harvest,[95] while in the Ugaritic poem 'The Birth of the Gods Good and Fair', the death god is described as a grapevine being pruned and bound.[96] The connexion between death and agricultural fertility has long been recognised and was already documented ethnographically by Frazer in *The Golden Bough*.[97] In ancient Near Eastern mythology the death/fertility connexion has been noted by, among others, Astour.[98] In addition, although the mortuary practices of ancient Egypt have not been dealt with here, the chief god of the Egyptian netherworld, Osiris, is a classic case in point; he was also the fertility god *par excellence*.[99]

In the most rudimentary way, death was probably perceived as a debt owed to the earth (and to whatever deity personified the earth and its fertility); bodies were returned to the earth to ensure its fertility.[100] Genesis 3:17-19 should be understood in the same vein:

---

87 Woolley 1976, 33-35.
88 Cf., e.g., the case of the Merina of Madagascar: Bloch 1971; Bloch & Parry 1982.
89 Cf. Dever 1987, 163-165; Ilan 1994.
90 Cf. Yasur-Landau 1993 for such an interpretation for the MB necropolis of Jericho.

91 Examples of this are abundant; cf., e.g., the practices of the Zulu: Ngubane 1976, cited by Block & Parry 1982, 24-25.
92 Cf. once again the Zulu (as n. 95), where the interment ritual comprises the process of being born into another world. The Bara of Madagascar adopt a variation on this theme, including a number of mortuary rituals with overt sexual symbolism, starting with the sexual act and culminating in the birth of the deceased into the world of the ancestors. In this case however, the tomb itself is the next world and the world of the living the womb (Huntington & Metcalf 1979, 115-116.
93 E.g., Romer 1982, 167.
94 Keel 1987.
95 Pritchard 1969, 140.
96 Gordon 1949, 59.
97 Frazer 1890, 351, 357-372.
98 Astour 1967, 228-249; 1980, 230-231.
99 E.g., Frankfort 1948, 28, 103.
100 Here too, numerous examples exist in contemporary ethnographic records to substantiate the ubiquity of the idea

By the sweat of your brow
Shall you get bread to eat
Until you return to the ground -
For from it you were taken.
For soil you are
And to soil you shall return.

The infant jar burial that contained a large quantity of lentils (T.4652) must also be emblematic of the connexion between fertility and death.

*Mortuary practices related to life in the Nether World*

Artifactual correlations to the idea of a Nether World existence in a western Semitic milieu,[101] are only partly forthcoming. The jar burial's connexion to the Nether World is apparently alluded to in several Ugaritic texts.[102] In the Baal Epic (I AB:V:12-13),[103] the entrance to the Nether World is found inside Mt *Knkny*, which must be connected to the Ugaritic, Canaanite (*knkn*), and Akkadian and Aramaic words for store-jar. The use of store-jars in burial is apparently expressed in the Ugaritic Tale of Aqhat (I D:147 or AQHT C), *yqbr nn b[m]dgt bkn[kn]* "he buries him in a dark place(?), in a jar".[104]

Burial offerings invariably accompany a chamber, cist or shaft-pit burial, and usually accompany jar burials. In the multiple burial context of the chamber, cist and shaft tombs, it was frequently difficult to relate particular offerings to a particular skeleton. Where single, primary and undisturbed burials existed, goods were placed next to or on the corpse. The most universal offering, i.e., one that cross-cuts the different burial types, was a juglet placed next to the mouth, a practice typical to other sites as well, such as Hazor, Area C, Strata 3-4;[105] Jericho;[106] Gezer;[107] and Tell es-Salihiyeh.[108] Even after a tomb was closed, perhaps for good, offerings were left above or next to the tomb. As a working hypothesis towards a more precise understanding, it can be suggested that some manifestation of the deceased required sustenance of some kind, possibly during, and definitely after, the burial process.

Burial goods are not always testament to belief in an afterworld,[109] yet when considered with the other evidence, some such belief can be inferred for the Middle-Bronze-Age mortuary practices at Tel Dan. If we assume that the ancient Canaanite inhabitants of Tel Dan conceived of death as a liminal, or transitional, experience in the human life cycle, and of burial as a 'rite of passage',[110] as they almost universally are, even in modern societies, the question is asked: To what phase of the "passage" do the burial goods belong? The choice is between three phases or some combination of them; (a) the pre-interment phase, when the subject is dying or immediately following his or her death; this might comprise a pre-burial funeral feast;[111] (b) the interment phase, at which point the corpse is provisioned for his journey into, or his existence in, the next world; (c) the post-interment phase, when it would be more likely that the spirit of the corpse required provisioning.[112]

In the world of the western Semites, burial offerings were called *kispum* and are widely mentioned in ancient texts.[113] These textual sources suggest at least two possible explanations for *kispum*-offerings, both of which involve the *rpum* (Hebrew *rephaim*) – probably manes or spirits of the underworld.[114] One approach posits that the *kispum* placate the manes of the underworld,[115] while a second implies that the *kispum* sustained venerated ancestors and ensured their goodwill.[116] A combination of the two is highly probable, at least in some places, depending on the relationship of the living to the deceased and the perceived potential of the deceased's spirit for influencing the lives of the living.[117] That the practice was an ongoing one that did not cease with the summation of the interment process is apparent, (a) from the archaeological evidence which features offerings found above or next to tombs (e.g., in the case of Tombs 187a-b, 4663, 1025 and 8096 at Tel Dan), and (b) from the ancient texts.[118]

Finally, it is clear that Canaanite beliefs of this kind also persisted into the later Israelite culture, well into the first millennium BC, where they were to become the object of denigration in the biblical narrative and in Isaiah (57:5-6) in particular.[119]

---

of the corpse's return to the soil as being essential to the fertility of the earth and its inhabitants: The Mambi of Timor (Huntington & Metcalf 1979, 92); the Merina (Bloch 1982, 213-214); the Dobu of Melanesia who 'plant' their dead like yams in the mound in the centre of the village (Bloch & Parry 1982, 28); the Melpa of New Guinea (Strathern 1982, 118); the Cantonese in China (Watson 1982, 173-174). The above examples, and a vast reservoir of data not presented here, show that this is an almost universal concept in pre-industrial societies.

101 And thus, in general terms, it is referred to by most of the authors in Alster 1980. "Underworld" and "afterlife" are equally suitable terms for *kur* (my thanks to the editors for this point).
102 Astour 1980, 229.
103 Pritchard 1969, 139.
104 Ibid., 154.
105 Yadin et al 1960, 82-85.
106 Kenyon 1981, 349.
107 Macalister 1912, 299-300, Figs. 158-159.
108 von der Osten 1956, 40-43, Pls. 20-23.

109 Ucko 1969, 265.
110 E.g., van Gennep 1960.
111 For parallels to this behaviour, cf. the Yoruba of Nigeria (Ucko 1969, 267) and other examples of the "Great Feast" in Hertz 1907. Remains of pre-burial offerings or feasts are usually not preserved in the mortuary context, in fact they are often presented or celebrated away from the tomb itself (e.g., Ucko 1969, 267).
112 For parallels to this behaviour, cf., e.g., the Mambi of Timor: Huntington & Metcalf 1979, 90-91.
113 E.g., Heidel 1946, 150-165; Bottéro 1980, 37-38; Tsukimoto 1980.
114 Although cf. Pitard 1992, 33, and references there cited, on the problem of defining the nature of the *rapi'uma*.
115 E.g., Bayliss 1973.
116 E.g., Astour 1973; Bottéro 1980, 37-38; Skaist 1980.
117 Cf. Skaist 1980.
118 E.g., Thalon 1978, 53- ; Bottéro 1980, 38.
119 Cf., e.g., Keel 1987; Kennedy 1989.

# Conclusion

The patterns that assert themselves in mortuary practices must be addressed systematically, no matter what the size or quality of the data base under consideration. It is essential firstly to confront problems of stratigraphy, typology and chronology in order to lay solid foundations for any further work. But to confine the investigation of ancient burial remains to these goals is to neglect those questions which have greater significance for understanding human behaviour and the evolution of human society. The investigation which proceeds beyond the normative topics of stratigraphy, typology and chronology enters an even wider realm of speculation and false trails. The methods used and the conclusions drawn in this study can perhaps serve as guidelines to be refined or discarded in a more comprehensive and wider sampled analysis of Middle-Bronze-Age funerary practices.

It is probably true that most ancient tombs of the Near East have been plundered, or excavated with inadequate methods. Those of us who deal with the archaeology of death must shun the antiquities trade; it brazenly perpetuates the demand for antiquities supplied by the rampant plunder of tombs. One also hopes that what little remains in the way of mortuary data – including that excavated but never reported – will be excavated, recorded and published with the care and attention befitting its explanatory potential.

*Acknowledgements*
I would like to thank Avraham Biran, director of the Nelson Glueck School of Biblical Archaeology, Hebrew Union College, Jerusalem, and director of the Tel Dan Expedition, and Richard Scheuer, a generous and enthusiastic benefactor, for their support and encouragement.

# Appendix I. Tomb comparanda

## Long rectangular built tombs (cf. 1025, 4663, 187 and possibly 8185):

### Canaan
Kabri: T.498, late MB I or early MB II (Miron 1989, ix-x, 27-30, Figs 9-11).

### Syria/Mesopotamia
Ras Shamra: Tombs 36, 54, 55, 56, and 57, late MB (Ugarit Moyen 3 or Ras Shamra II/3) with a terminal date of approximately 1650/1600 BC (Schaeffer 1938; 1939; 1948; 1949; North 1973; Courtois 1974).

Mari: Three large built tombs under the Ishtar Temple C courtyard, Early Dynastic, (Parrot 1935, 9, Pl. 11:4; 1938:4-8, Figs 2-3, Pl. II; 1956, 10-11, Pl. III).

Tell Hadidi: Hundreds of this type, late third millennium BC (Dornemann 1979:118-122, Figs 7-8, 10).

Til Barsip: The "hypogeum", Early Dynastic III period with a continued placement of offerings into the early second millennium BC, (Thureau-Dangin and Dunand 1936, 96-119, Fig. 28, Pl. 20; Drower and Bottero 1971, 334).

Khafage: Numerous vaulted chamber tombs under the floors of Houses, Levels 8-3, Early Dynastic period, (Delougaz, Hill and Lloyd 1967, 89-123, 136-141, and Table 14.1).

Ur: The Royal Cemetery (sixteen "royal" chamber tombs), Early Dynastic II-III, (Woolley 1934, 232-5: 1954, 59-90); the royal mausoleum, Ur III period, (Woolley 1954, 150-9, Fig. 10, Pl. 19-20; 1976, 34-5); Built tombs under the floors of houses, Larsa period, (Woolley 1976, 33, 35, Fig. 2a-d).

ᶜUsiya: Chamber tomb G.1, first half of the second millennium BC, (Numoto and Yasuyoshi 1987, 172).

Nineveh: Early Dynastic, (e.g. Perkins 1949, 179).

Babylon: (e.g. Reuther 1926, 151).

Chagar Bazar: (Mallowan 1936, 55).

Tell Agrab: (Lloyd 1967, 269).

Tepe Gawra: (Speiser 1935, 140-143).

### Egypt
Tell e-Dab'a: MB (van den Brink 1982).

Tell Maskhuta: MB (van den Brink 1982, 55-65)

## Curvilinear shape, corbelled with "beehive" radial roofing (T.8096):

### Canaan
Megiddo: Tombs 3095, 3175, 4055, MB II-C,(Loud 1948, Figs 33-34, 202-204; Schemata 1908, Pl. VI),

### Syria/Mesopotamia
Ur: Tomb PG 1054 in the Royal Cemetery, Early Dynastic II-III, (Woolley 1934, Fig. 16).

Amrith: The "silo-tombs" IB and MB I, (Dunand, Saliby and Kirichian 1954-55).

### Cyprus
Enkomi: Tomb 1432, Late Cypriote I or II, (Karageorghis 1966, 345; Pelon 1973, 428, Pl. CXXXVIII).

## Built Cist Tombs:

### Canaan:
Beitrawi and Bab edh-Dhra: IB, (Prag 1974, 101).

Tel el Ajjul: IB, (Petrie 1932, 2, Pls. LIII, 1516, 1517).

RafidL: Lebanon, IB, (Mansfeld 1970).

Degania Aleph: IB, (Kochavi 1973).

Aphek: MB I, "Pre-Palace" stage (Kochavi, Beck and Gophna (1979, 132), or Beck's (1985) MB I Phase 1 or 2, (Ory 1936, 101-4, Figs 2-5).

Gezer: MB I, (Macalister 1912, 299-301, Figs 158-9, pls. LX-LXIII).

Megiddo: Tombs 51 and 244 (external cemetery, Guy 1938, pls. 53, 59), Tombs 3075 and 3085 (inside the walls, Loud 1948, 95).

Kabri: T.502, T.503, late MB I or early MB II (Miron 1988, v-vi, 22, Figs 7-8).

### Syria and Mesopotamia
Tel Agrab: the Early Dynastic I tombs (Lloyd 1967, 268-9).

Khafage: Early Dynastic, the smaller unroofed brick tombs (Delougaz, Hill and Lloyd 1967, 89-123).

Til Barsip: Early Dynastic, (Thureau-Dangin and Dunand 1936, Pl. XXXII).

Baghouz: beginning of the second millennium, (du Mesnil du Buisson 1948).

Yabrud, MB I, (Assaf 1967).

Tel Hadidi: Level D, MB, (Dornemann 1979, 132).

Ras Shamra, UM III (Schaeffer 1949, 23, Figs 50-1).

## Shaft Burial:

### Canaan
Jericho: Square HIII, Phase xxii, MB I, (Kenyon 1981, 349).

### Syria/Mesopotamia
Sukas: Tomb IV, MB I-II (Thrane 1978).

Ur: Both the royal tombs and private graves of the Early Dynastic period were placed in shafts (Woolley 1934, 135 ff.; 1955, 54-57).

Selenkiyeh: late ED, circa 2400-2200 BC, (van Loon 1979, 111).

Amrith: (Dunand, Saliby and Kirichian 1954-55).

### Egypt
Tel el-Dab'a: "servant burials" found in front of chamber tombs, (Bietak 1979, 245, 287 and van den Brink 1982, 48).

## Jar Burials:

Since jar burials have been found in almost every MB stratum in Canaan, it would serve little purpose in this framework to inventory even a moderate number of sites. The patterns outlinedd for Tel Dan are all discernible elsewhere. The parallels below are designed to demonstrate, in cursory fashion, the geographical and temporal parameters of the phenomenon outside Canaan.

### Egypt
Tel el-Dab'a: MB I-B, (van den Brink 1982, 19-20, 28-9).

### Mesopotamia (usually krater or bowl burials)
Alalakh: Levels VIII-V, MB II-LB, (Woolley 1955, 202 where they are called "urn burials").

Amrith: MB I, (Dunand, Kirichian and Saliby 1954-1955, 198-9).

Tel Hadidi: Area D, Phase B, MB II, (Dornemann 1979, Fig. 27).

Tell Agrab: ED, (Lloyd 1967, 269).

Ur: Isin-Larsa period, (Woolley 1976, 34).

Tepe Gawra: ED, (Speiser 1935, 140-143).

Beyond the analogous material profiled above, further specific attributes of the Tel Dan jar burials which may be of some significance are paralleled selectively as follows:

Jar burials surrounded by stones: Megiddo T.5062, attributable to Kenyon's (1969) Group B (Loud 1948, Fig. 300); Hazor Area C, T.8 (Yadin et al 1960, 82-85); Gezer, Field VI, Burial 23110 in Stratum 12 (Dever et al. 1986, 15, Pl. 67B).

Use of two vessels, one for interment and the other for the lid (cf. T.4356): Mishrife-Qatna in the coupole de Loth (du Mesnil du Buisson 1930, 153-155).

Adult jar burials are rare. Some exceptions are: Hazor Tombs 8, 19, 23 from Area C (Yadin *et al* 1960, 81).

Multiple burials in one jar like T.4648: Hazor Area C, T.25 and T.26 (Yadin *et al* 1960, 85); Tel el-Dab<sup>c</sup>a (van den Brink 1982, 19-20).

Location of jar burials next to walls and in corners: Hazor and Tel el-Dab'a (see above); Tel Mevorakh Stratum XIII (Stern 1984, 46-47, Fig. 27).)

# 16 Warrior Burials in the Ancient Near-Eastern Bronze Age: the Evidence from Mesopotamia, Western Iran and Syria-Palestine

## Graham Philip

ABSTRACT—*Two clear instances of warrior burials are well-known to scholars and can be readily identified in the archaeological record. The first group occurs in Early Dynastic III Mesopotamia (the mid-third millennium BC), and is exemplified by the Royal Cemetery at Ur. The second, later group, occurs in the Middle Bronze Age of the Levant (roughly the first half of the second millennium BC). The present paper is intended to demonstrate that these two instances are simply the best known parts of a wider pattern. In addition to the well-known Syro-Palestinian burials, new evidence indicates that similar practices can be identified in Mesopotamia and western Iran in the early second millennium. There is now sufficient data to demonstrate continuity of tradition between these early second-millennium Mesopotamian burials, and those of the ED III graves at Ur. An examination of the third-millennium evidence from the Levant follows, in order to ascertain whether a local background can be traced for the tradition in that area also, or whether the evidence suggests its introduction from Mesopotamia.*

## Introduction

### Definition of warrior burials

Warrior burials as defined here are burials interred with artefacts whose design indicates 'weapon' as their primary function. In one sense I am attempting to limit 'weapons' to items which would have been categorized as such by those producing and using them. The term 'weapon' used in this sense does not embrace all tools which could have been used in fighting, chisels or lumps of rock for example. However, it includes weapons decorated with precious materials. These may not have been used in combat, but were weapons in the sense that they looked like the real thing. I suspect that appearance was an important part of the symbolism of ancient implements.

In practice the main grey area is cutting implements, which comprise a heterogeneous range of multi-purpose knives or blades. While such were usable as weapons, they may have had quite different primary functions. Burials equipped with items from this rather heterogeneous range should be distinguished from genuine warrior burials. Within the latter there is an element of overall unity, manifested through repeated combinations of particular artefacts. No single, consistent set of attributes is present in all cases, as there are both regional and temporal variations in the goods interred, not to mention short-term exigencies. However, there are enough superficial resemblances between the various warrior burials to suggest a unity of underlying structure.

### Weapons in burial contexts: recent research

A glance at the published illustrations of metalwork[1] reveals that there exists a complex of typologically similar artefacts, including forms of dagger, spearhead and axe, throughout Western Asia during the later third and much of the second millennia BC. While material from any one area shows greater internal homogeneity than that from distinct regions, the degree of similarity among the material as a whole is striking. Furthermore, the forms in use are such as would be inherently

---

1   E.g., Maxwell-Hyslop 1946; 1949; Deshayes 1960; de Maigret 1976.

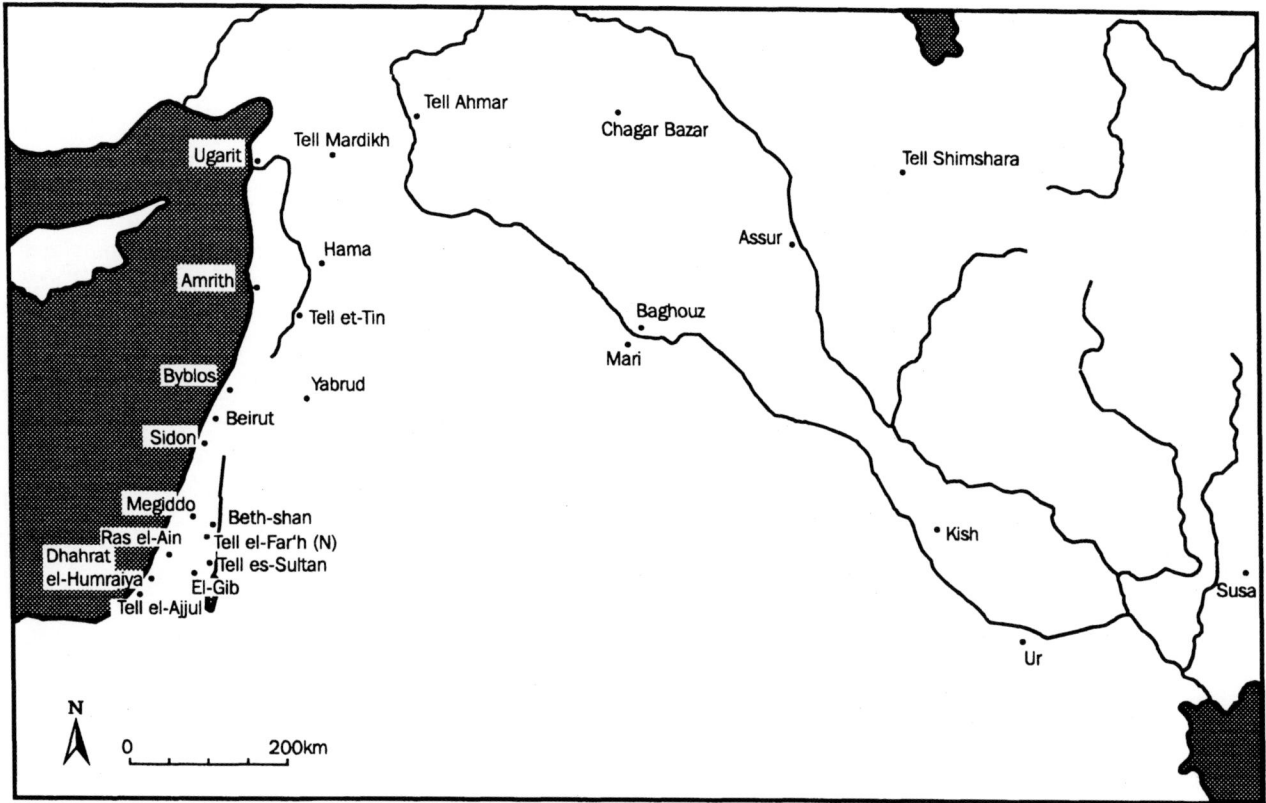

*Fig. 16.1: Some of the sites discussed.*

unlikely to occur simultaneously, in widely separated areas, by chance alone. There is, I believe, an underlying theme traceable with a degree of localised variation, from the Nile valley at least as far as western Iran.

Despite the number of typological studies, little attempt has been made to consider the reasons for the patterns observed. Researchers have noted typological connections between material from different regions, but have not produced an explanatory framework beyond presumed ethnic connections or 'diffusion'. Stewart, for example, writing in the 1940s, noted the occurrence of warrior-equipment in MB II graves at a number of Palestinian sites, and made a connection between this phenomenon and the Hyksos.[2]

The first detailed discussion was that of Oren in his publication of one such burial from Tomb 92 at Beth Shan. Despite the limitations of the evidence then available, Oren clearly perceived warrior burials as a phenomenon, and described their extent in Syria-Palestine during the earlier part of the Middle Bronze Age.[3] His work was followed by Dever, who considered the continuation of this pattern into the later MB periods in the coastal Levant.[4]

A short article by Watkins drew attention to the existence of a similar phenomenon in Mesopotamia during the Early Dynastic III period, i.e. many centuries before the burials discussed by Oren. Working from

Woolley's unpublished notes on the cemetery at Ur, he observed that burials containing weapons overlapped with, but were not identical to, the very rich burials. At Ur we see clearly the employment of standard weapon types in regular combinations, i.e. the patterning which is the keynote of the whole idea of warrior burials.[5]

Pollock, who has also worked on the original records, argued that for high status burials a clear gender distinction can be observed at Ur, with two discrete sets of funerary artefacts.[6] Weapons, along with whetstones and head-bands form part of the 'male' set. Knives and daggers were usually located around the waist, axes in the hand.[7] Pollock bases her assessment on the few skeletons in which sex was identified, and which showed associated sets of grave-goods, supported by evidence from Cemetery A at Kish, where a certain amount of anthropological work was carried out.[8] Pollock's suggestion is supported by textual evidence from Ebla and skeletal data from Tell el-Dab'a.

Moorey suggested that the preponderance of daggers and axes over spears and arrowheads in ED III graves at both Ur and Kish suggested that these represented the personal weapons of an élite, not the equipment of ordinary soldiers.[9] In fact, grave-goods found in the richer graves at these sites resemble the items

---

2    Stewart 1974, 52.
3    Oren 1971.
4    Dever 1975.

5    Watkins 1983.
6    Pollock 1991a, 373.
7    Ibid., 376.
8    Ibid., 375.
9    Moorey 1982, 32.

described in the Grave Inventory of Billala, an important temple official at Kish. This document lists a silver spear, a knife and a copper axe, as well as a 'chariot' and harness donkey (translated by Zarins as a *pair* of animals for hauling a vehicle) among the gifts taken to the grave by this particular individual.[10]

Noting that weapons, jewellery and vessels are present in considerable quantities, while there is little or no grave equipment relating to craft activities, agricultural labour, or textile manufacturing, Pollock suggests that the grave-goods from Ur relate to the individual's ritual or political position.[11] Watkins observed that the many burials with weapons were only "moderately rich".[12] Pollock attributes this to the marking of male status at a lower absolute level than was the case with female burials, for whom mortuary evidence for a similar 'semi-élite' is lacking.[13]

In summary, there is now good evidence to suggest that in ED III Mesopotamia we can detect a connection between the interment of weapons in funerary contexts and matters of status and entitlement. Can this be connected to the Syro-Palestinian phenomenon identified by Oren which dates to the beginning of the second millennium BC? Watkins has pointed out a general similarity in the equipment of west Asiatic warrior burials, which suggests that there may well be a connection of some kind.[14] However, the plausibility of any reconstruction which seeks to unify the two groups of warrior burials is dependent on whether or not a clear connection between them can be demonstrated. These interments in their various regional and chronological manifestations encompass a vast area, and span a period of well over a millennium. The next task is to review the archaeological evidence.

### Identification of warrior burials

The coherence of warrior burials as a group was initially obscured by the fact that many occur in tombs containing multiple successive interments, within which it is difficult to isolate distinct, associated groups of material. Examples include Middle Bronze-Age groups from Ras Shamra[15] and Jericho Tombs 9, D9 and D22.[16] The key contexts for identifying warrior burials as such are single interments. A number of particularly clear examples has been excavated at the Second Intermediate Period site of Tell el-Dab'a in the eastern Nile Delta, e.g., A/II-l/12 Gr 5 (Fig. 16.3).[17]

Having used single burials to identify core sets of associated items, it is possible to discern their occurrence among the larger bodies of material found in multiple-use tombs. While the coastal Levant has been well studied, the significance of this phenomenon elsewhere in western Asia was concealed until recently by the lack of second millennium material with good archaeological context. In the last twenty years or so, excavations in an area extending from north Mesopotamia and western Iran to the Nile Delta, have provided sufficient new evidence to permit a re-assessment of the topic.

## Warrior Burials by Region

It is best to begin with the southern Levant, where there is a useful body of well reported material. Here, early MB IIA burials occur with a distinctive range of items: fenestrated axes, short socketed spearheads, and daggers (several possible types are acceptable). As much of the older evidence from Palestine has already been reviewed by Oren and by Dever, the reader is referred to these publications for fuller references.[18] The present discussion is not intended as an exhaustive catalogue of possible warrior burials, and will concentrate on material published since 1971.

## The Levant in the second millennium BC

### Palestine: MB IIA

In Palestine, several good examples of MB IIA warrior burials are known in the north Jordan valley. At Beth Shan Tomb 92, a re-used multi-chambered EB IV tomb disturbed in Roman times,[19] produced a fenestrated axehead, grooved dagger, spearhead and a small projectile head.[20] All are of early MB IIA types. In a cemetery at Tel Rehov south of Beth Shan,[21] Tomb 2 revealed a single flexed burial inside a chamber which had been blocked with a large stone. The contents included a storage jar probably of early MB IIA type.[22] The weapons comprised a classic set of warrior items: a dagger with central groove and crescent-shaped handle, placed by the pelvis, a fenestrated axe by the head, and two spearheads lying together below the feet of the burial (Fig. 16.2).

Both the Beth Shan and Tel Rehov graves show a grouping of fenestrated axe with a grooved dagger and small spearhead(s). Additional material of this date was recently reported from an early MB IIA cemetery at Gesher, some 13 km south of Lake Tiberias. Here 14 graves were investigated, mostly single, primary burials,

10 Foxvog 1980; cf. Zarins 1986.
11 Pollock 1991b, 180.
12 Watkins 1983, 102.
13 Pollock 1991a, 376.
14 Watkins 1983, 102.
15 Schaeffer 1936, Fig. 17; 1938, Fig. 32.
16 Garstang 1932, 46, Pl. XXXVII; Kenyon 1965, 259, 284, Fig. 111.
17 Bietak 1968, Fig. 3.

18 Oren 1971; Dever 1975.
19 Oren 1973, 12.
20 Ibid., 61-67.
21 Yogev 1985.
22 Ibid., 99.

lying in flexed position with head to east.[23] Offerings include a few pottery vessels,[24] fenestrated axes and small spearheads. Two tombs revealed a fenestrated axe and a spear, and one a single axe. The presence of a notched, narrow-bladed axe in another tomb indicates a late MB IIA date for this particular burial.[25]

Three substantial daggers with crescent-shaped pommels and two ribs flanking a central groove were found in the large Tomb 1100D at Megiddo.[26] Like the fenestrated axes with which they are often found, these occur most often in northern Palestine. While no fenestrated axes were recorded from this tomb, it had been re-used extensively in the LBA, and these daggers are clearly of MB IIA types. Such a large multi-chambered tomb would seem suitable as a setting for warrior burials. Despite certain typological changes including the introduction of notched narrow-bladed axes and daggers with ribbed blades,[27] the essential pattern of axe, dagger and small spearheads continues into the later MB IIA.

## Syria: MB IIA

Groups of similar composition are known from Tomb 1 at Sin el-Fil,[28] the cemeteries at Kfar Jarrah and Lébé'a in southern Lebanon[29] and the '*tombeaux de particuliers*' at Byblos.[30] In none of these however, can clear associations be made between individual artefacts and particular burials. More such material comes from the *Dépôts des Offrandes* at Byblos.[31] Other coastal graves producing similar artefacts include built stone MB IIA tombs from Amrit, south of Tartous.[32]

Further north, similar material occurs at Ras Shamra. However, the contexts from which these weapons come are rather uncertain. Schaeffer ascribed the appearance of new metal types to the arrival at the site, at the beginning of Ugarit *Moyen* I, of the '*Porteurs du torcs*'.[33] Much of the relevant material, fenestrated axes, daggers with triangular blades, rivetted butts and crescent-shaped handles, and the socketed spearheads, is identical to that found in warrior burials throughout Palestine and western Syria during the early second millennium BC. As at many other sites, this phase at Ras Shamra is marked by the presence of single burials with little associated pottery but a noticeable quantity of weapons and other metalwork.[34] I would contend that

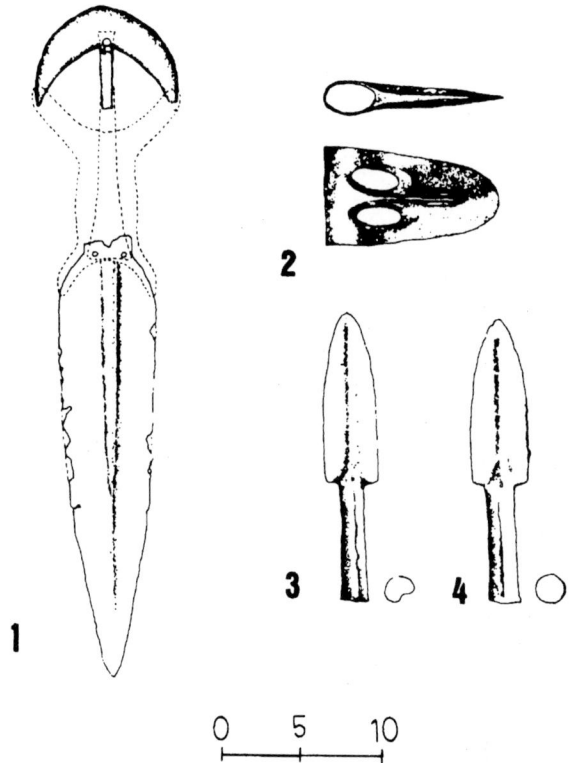

*Fig. 16.2: Set of warrior equipment from Middle-Bronze-IIA Tomb 2 at Tel Rehov. After Yogev 1985, Fig. 4.*

the material ascribed by Schaeffer to the '*Porteurs du torcs*', is simply the local manifestation at Ras Shamra of the phenomenon of warrior burials widespread elsewhere in the Levant at the beginning of the Middle Bronze Age.

## Inland Syria

From inland Syria groups are known from Hama Tombs GI and GIV,[35] in central Syria. Tomb GIV in particular produced one fenestrated axe, a dagger with central groove and two spearheads. Another MB IIA tomb (or tombs), is known from Tell et-Tin in the Lake of Homs. The material includes fenestrated axes, spearheads and at least one dagger with ribbed blade.[36] In both cases, the association of grooved daggers with fenestrated axes and spearheads is clear, although individual groups of material cannot now be isolated. Nearer Damascus, four fenestrated axes and several daggers and spearheads come from MB IIA graves in a cemetery at Yabrud, a multiple interment.[37] Taken together, the evidence suggests that for the MB IIA period, it is possible to identify distinctive items of

23 Garfinkel & Bonfil 1990.
24 Ibid., 106.
25 Cf. Philip 1989, 39.
26 Guy 1938, Pl. 147:2-3; 5-7.
27 Philip 1989, 169.
28 Chehab 1939, 807.
29 Guiges 1937; 1938.
30 Montet 1928, 247.
31 Dunand 1939, 1958; cf. Philip 1988 for a possible interpretation of these deposits.
32 Dunand, Saliby & Kirichian 1955. The writer was able to see this largely unpublished material in Damascus Museum in 1984.
33 Schaeffer 1949, 52-55.
34 Schaeffer 1948, 23-24, Fig. 56, Pl. XIII.

35 Fugmann 1958, Fig. X.
36 Gautier 1895. The material from Tell et-Tin is now in Istanbul Archaeological Museum, where the writer was able to inspect the metalwork in 1985.
37 Assaf 1967.

warrior equipment, in some cases even complete sets, occurring in grave contexts throughout the Levant.

## Palestine and Syria: MB IIB/C

Palestinian warrior burials of MB IIB/C date generally occur without spearheads, and with narrow-bladed axes, and daggers of styles different from their MB IIA precursors.[38] Despite the typological changes the underlying structure, especially the dagger-axe pairing, remains the same, but for the disappearance of the small spearheads. It is worth noting that at Middle Bronze Age Jericho only 10 tombs out of 51 actually contained weapons, less than 20 percent. This includes four axes and around sixteen daggers, distributed between a total number of interments which Kenyon, working from the number of crania, put at 681.[39] It is clear then that weapons were very much a minority item. This is made even more so by that fact that three of the axes, and three daggers, were found, along with the sole instance of a metal belt from the site, in Grave J3, which contained but a single burial.[40] The evidence from Jericho supports the suggestion that the presence of weapons in graves is connected with the marking of status.

Few MB IIB/C burials are known from inland Syria. Those from Ras Shamra on the coast[41] show a number of local peculiarities. All are from tombs used for multiple successive interments, preventing the isolation of individual grave groups. There is clear evidence for the use of socketed axes, but in a style closer to those of Cyprus than to contemporary Palestinian forms.[42] Many of the daggers resemble Middle and Late Cypriot knives, rather than the dagger styles in vogue in the contemporary southern Levant.[43] A final difference is that contrary to the pattern in the southern Levant, spearheads do occur in graves at Ras Shamra, but these are larger than the throwing spears found in MB IIA contexts.[44] The presence of Cypriot pottery in those tombs[45] reinforces the close stylistic ties between coastal Syria and Cyprus during the later Middle Bronze Age.

Despite the underlying structural unity, the typology of north and south Levantine warrior burials differs more in the later Middle Bronze Age than in the early part of the period. This suggests the gradual dissolution of a once unified tradition. If we assume the phenomenon to have a common origin, as the initial widespread homogeneity of MB IIA practices suggests, then it seems reasonable to expect that its introduction

## The Nile delta

In recent years warrior burials similar to those already described have been encountered as far south as the eastern Nile Delta, where they are associated with a spread of Asiatic settlements.[46] An early example of a warrior burial was found in a recently excavated single grave from Tell el-Dab'a (F/I-o/19 Gr 8), which produced a set of weapons very similar to that from Tomb 2 at Tel Rehov; namely, fenestrated axe, grooved dagger, and spearheads, but with the addition of a metal belt.[47] This particular grave is assigned to an early phase (d/2 = H) of the Asiatic settlement at Tell el-Dab'a, and is one of a group of heavily plundered, mudbrick, chambered graves built in an Egyptian manner. The fact that both the tomb architecture and the pottery from this phase at the site are predominantly Egyptian in style[48] makes the characteristically Levantine weapons from this, and the other graves, all the more striking.

Work at Tell el-Dab'a and Tell el-Maskhuta shows that warrior burials were in regular use in the eastern Delta well into MB IIB/C.[49] Besides the typological similarities between the Tell el-Dab'a metalwork and that of the Levant,[50] other, more structural relationships exist. For example, the grave A/II l/12 Gr 5 (Fig. 16.3) assigned to stratum F – that is, the transition from MB IIA to MB IIB/C[51] – contains a single interment, with dagger at the waist and axe at the head. A study of the best preserved burials at Tell el-Dab'a reveals that this was the normal layout,[52] one which resembles that of the weapons found in the Royal Cemetery at Ur.[53] In fact, the same layout is apparent in many well preserved warrior burials found throughout Western Asia.

Also noteworthy is the occurrence of donkey burials in the vicinity of these tombs (Fig. 16.3), and the presence of sheep/goat bones within the graves, indicating meat-offerings. While relatively infrequent in the southern Levant, burials with equids are more common in Mesopotamia.[54] The very fact that these practices are of West Asiatic origin contrasts with a willingness to adopt local Egyptian pottery and grave-construction techniques, and indicates that certain aspects of burial customs were of particular significance to the participants.

38  Philip 1989, 169-170.
39  Kenyon 1965, 569.
40  Kenyon 1960, 313.
41  Summarised in Courtois 1979, 1204-1208.
42  Philip 1991a, 82, Fig. 10.
43  Ibid., 72, Fig. 8.
44  Philip 1989, 170.
45  Courtois 1979, 1204-1208.

46  Bietak 1979.
47  Bietak 1992, Abb. 6.
48  Bietak 1992.
49  Bietak 1979; 1991; Holladay 1982, 44-47.
50  Philip, in press (a).
51  Bietak 1991, Fig. 3, table of overall site phasing.
52  Philip, in press (a).
53  Pollock 1991a, 376.
54  Bietak 1992, 54, nn. 23-25; further discussion below.

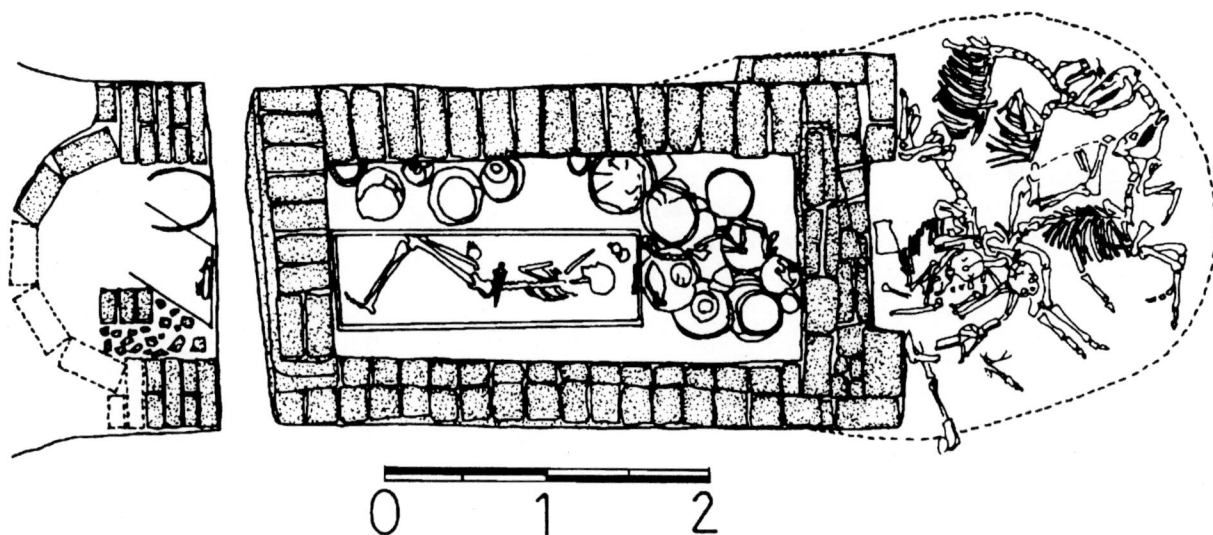

*Fig. 16.3: Tell el-Dab'a, Middle Bronze Age, Grave A/II l/12 No. 5; note multiple donkey burials and position of weapons inside the coffin. After Bietak 1968, Fig. 3.*

In contrast to the Syrian situation, the Delta weapon-types are virtually indistinguishable from those found in Palestine.[55] However, the pattern of alloys used at Jericho and Tell el-Dab'a shows quite clearly that the metalwork from the two sites was the product of two distinct industries.[56] The conclusion is that smiths in both areas were producing metalwork to essentially the same designs, which implies the existence of a stylistic norm, widely accepted throughout the southern Levant.

### Additional paraphernalia

Alongside the weapons themselves, the most striking additional element to warrior burials is metal belts. These consisted of a thin metal sheet sewn onto a leather backing. The holes for stitching are clearly visible around the margins of the metal. Examples from good contexts include those from Jericho Tomb J3,[57] Tell el-Far'ah (N),[58] and four specimens from Tell el-Dab'a.[59] A fragment of a possible example was found in Tomb LVI at Ras Shamra.[60] Metal fragments likely to come from similar belts were found in a MB IIA grave at Tell et-Tin near Homs in Syria.[61] Similar fragments of sheet metal with concentric circle decoration from the *Dépôts* at Byblos[62] should probably be interpreted as belt components. All are of MB IIA or early MB IIB/C date. All Syro-Palestinian contexts from which metal belts have been reported have also produced weapons, including the *Dépôts des Offrandes* at Byblos. The association is

clear. As neither weapons nor belts appear in the majority of graves, this association is unlikely to be a chance one.

Additional examples are known from Cyprus.[63] Although their contexts are generally poor, one was found in association with a narrow-bladed axe of the local Cypriot variety.[64] Although none of the Cypriot examples are from tombs with undisturbed deposits, the occurrence of narrow-bladed axes[65] and metal belts, both in styles resembling those common on the mainland is worthy of note. Both of these items are foreign to local Cypriot metalwork styles, and most likely represent the extension of the mainland idea of 'warrior' burials to the island in the later Middle Bronze Age.[66]

The presence of these belts along with warrior equipment, in Middle-Bronze-Age graves throughout the east Mediterranean littoral and Cyprus, strengthens the argument for a structural unity beneath the superficial typological differences. The warrior burial clearly represents a concept understood and deemed appropriate throughout a wide area, and emphasises the long-range contacts between élites in otherwise quite different regions.

### The end of warrior burials in the Levant

The uniqeness of the phenomenon of the MBA warrior burial is emphasised by its complete absence in the succeeding Late Bronze Age. Although burials with weapons continue to occur in the LBA, these are fewer in number and feature new and different types, mainly

---

55  Philip 1989, 169-170; in press (b).
56  Philip, in press (b).
57  Kenyon 1960, 313 Fig. 117:3.
58  Vaux & Stève 1947, 432, Pl. XX:1.
59  Philip, in press (a).
60  Schaeffer 1938, Fig. 4W.
61  Gautier 1895, 459.
62  Dunand 1954, Nos. 8354-8358, 189-90, Pl. LVII.,

63  Cf. Philip 1991a, 84-85.
64  Overbeck & Swiny 1972, 8, Figs 5-8.
65  Reviewed by Buchholz 1979; Philip 1991a.
66  For further discussion, cf. Philip 1991a.

145

*[handwritten margin note top: Does this difference occur in non-mortuary contexts? It might just be the fashion.]*

long daggers with cast-hilts.[67] The weapons found in LBA graves bear little resemblance to the distinct sets of the earlier period. Axes decline sharply as a component of the grave record. Although occasional examples still occur in the LBA,[68] these are related less to MBA forms than to the shaft-hole axes of north Mesopotamian styles.[69] As with the daggers, the axe-styles of the LBA are of a more 'international' character, with regional stylistic variants being less pronounced than in the MBA.

## The Middle Euphrates valley in the second millennium BC

*[handwritten margin note: But a lot changed from M-LBA. Temples dedicated + palace + separate suggesting new organisation of power - Neuwelite paraphernalia may be a symptom of this.]*

Oren suggested that a similar concept of warrior burials applied in inland Syria.[70] His argument was based on the evidence from the Middle-Bronze-Age cemetery at Baghouz in the Euphrates valley near Mari. Here, a number of single burials in stone-lined cist graves were excavated, some marked by tumuli.[71] Organic grave-goods were exceptionally well preserved in these graves, enabling the excavator to ascertain the spatial arrangement of the grave equipment relative to the deceased (Fig. 16.4:1).

De Mesnil du Buisson excavated around 185 Middle-Bronze-Age graves, and another 47 of this date showing evidence of later re-use. His tabulated data[72] reveals that of these, approximately 25 contained weapons, a little over 10% of the total. The commonest equipment was one or two ceramic vessels; most graves contained little else. The most common weapon in these tombs was a spearhead, followed by fenestrated axes, a strong typological connection with western sites. Wherever positions could be established, an axe was placed by the head (Fig. 16.4:1), as at more westerly sites, and in ED III Mesopotamia, although in several cases the axe could be seen to have rested on the wood and fabric 'bed' on which the deceased had been laid.

Most burials containing axes also contained a spearhead, and wooden grave-furniture, quite rare elsewhere in the cemetery. Furthermore, the bulk of these wealthier graves were concentrated in one area of the cemetery – on a small rise termed *Mamelon II* by the excavator.[73] This pattern provides additional weight to the weapons-status connection. The axe was usually accompanied by a single spearhead, rather than a pair as is more common in the southern Levant (although in one case, Grave Z95, two spearheads were found). Daggers were markedly less frequent than in the coastal Levant. Another local difference is that at Baghouz daggers were generally found in association with the

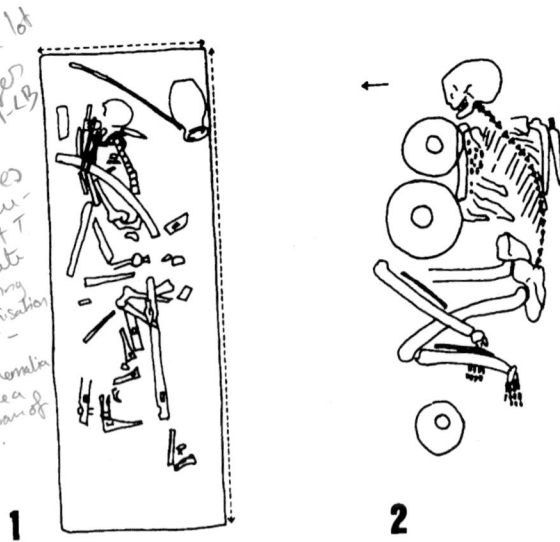

*Fig. 16.4*

*1. Baghouz burial Z121; note fenestrated axe by head of deceased and remains of wooden grave-furniture. After du Mesnil du Buisson 1948, Pl. XLVIII:1.*

*2. Tell Halawa Grave 3, crouched interment with dagger positioned at the back of the deceased; this burial is not untypical of those from the second- millennium BC cemeteries excavated in the Hamrin basin. After excavator's unpublished plan.*

remains of meat-offerings, not by the abdomen of the deceased as was more common at western sites. This suggests that they were playing the role taken by the distinctive curved knives found in many Syro-Palestinian graves.[74] The types of both daggers and spearheads found at Baghouz differ from those of the Levant.[75] Despite these differences, I agree with Oren that Baghouz represents yet another regional variation on the Middle Bronze Age warrior burial theme.[76]

## Mesopotamia

Valuable though Baghouz is, it still leaves us some distance both chronologically and spatially from the Royal Cemetery. However, recent data from northern Iraq permit us to extend the pattern of second-millennium BC warrior burials to Mesopotamia, where the existence of axe-types related to those of the Levant has long been clear.[77] The problem here has always been that apart from occasional isolated finds – from Kish,[78] Assur[79] and Shemshara[80] – most Mesopotamian exam-

---

*[handwritten margin note: are they definitely daggers not knives then? or are they gifts rather than personal items?]*

67  Maxwell-Hyslop 1946, Types 31-32.
68  Cf. Deshayes 1960, 186-191.
69  Philip 1989, 180-181.
70  Oren 1971.
71  Mesnil du Buisson 1948, 31-32.
72  Ibid., 63-93.
73  Ibid., 30.

74  Philip 1989, 141-142.
75  Ibid., 168.
76  Oren 1971, 126.
77  E.g., Maxwell-Hyslop 1949, 115, Type 23.
78  Langdon 1924, Pl. XX.5.
79  Andrae 1922, Pl. 60, below.

ples were museum purchases without site-provenance, let alone archaeological context.

The new material comes from early second-millennium BC cemeteries excavated at several sites in the Diyala valley in north-eastern Iraq. These were investigated during rescue work carried out in advance of the construction of a dam in the Hamrin basin during the late 1970s. Excavations revealed a number of occupation deposits and cemeteries dating to the Isin-Larsa and Old Babylonian periods (c. 2000-1600 BC). Close dating of these tomb-groups is difficult, owing to our more limited knowledge of the ceramics of these periods, and the paucity of published data. However, these burials can be placed securely in the first few centuries of the second millennium BC, broadly contemporary with those from Baghouz and the Levantine sites discussed above.

## The material

The Hamrin metalwork is clearly related to Syro-Palestinian types, but it forms a distinct regional group. The forms of weapon (Figs. 5-6) are rather different from their western counterparts.

Japanese and Italian teams were prominent in the excavation of graves of these periods in the Hamrin. At Tell Songor B, 16 graves were assigned to the Isin-Larsa period.[81] but none contained weapons. However, several of the 21 graves at Tell Songor A were more reminiscent of traditions familiar in the Levant. These rectangular pit-graves contained single crouched interments, several of which were associated with small socketed spear-heads, sometimes in pairs.[82] These were usually positioned by the arms or behind the back of the deceased, as at Baghouz. Note should be taken of the absence of axes and daggers from these graves. Several (including Gr 228 and 71) produced animal bones, no doubt the remains of meat-offerings, another trait observed in the Levant.

Many early second millennium graves were found in the Italian excavations at Tell Yelkhi, which revealed in level V a substantial administrative building of Isin-Larsa date.[83] Most of the richer graves are assigned to this phase and many were found in the domestic areas and in quarters adjacent to the administrative building.[84] These produced various weapons including both fenestrated and socketed axes,[85], daggers and spear-heads, as well as meat-offerings, mainly the long bones of sheep and goats. Some of the graves with weapons may date to late in the third millennium BC,[86] suggesting a local background for the warrior burials of the

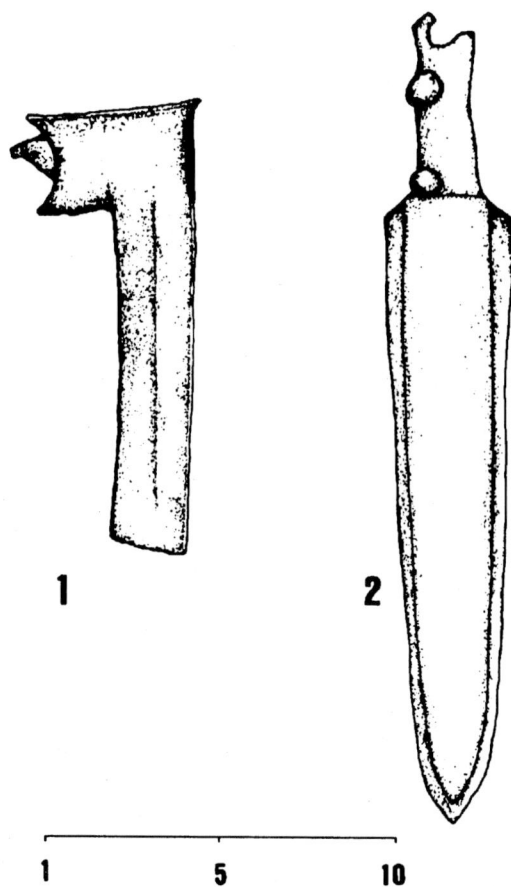

*Fig. 16.5: Axe-dagger set from Tell el-Seib Grave 20.*

Isin-Larsa period. A rich female burial was found to have been dug from the floor of the main room of the level V administrative structure.[87] The lack of weapons from this richly furnished grave further emphasises the male associations of such weaponry.

Graves of the Isin-Larsa period were also found at the small rural sites of Tell Hassan and Tell Abu Husseini, also excavated by Italian teams.[88] Here, weapons were less well represented in grave contexts, as in the Tell Songor cemeteries described above. The contrast between the occurrence of numerous weapons at the important Isin-Larsa period administrative centre of Tell Yelkhi, with their relative paucity at other contemporary sites in the Hamrin, emphasises the connection between arms and status. The concentration of rich graves in the vicinity of the level V administrative building might reasonably be taken as evidence for some connection between high status groups and this structure.

While these sites demonstrate the existence and socio-political setting of warrior burials in Isin-Larsa-period Mesopotamia, too little of the actual data have been published to permit detailed typological comparisons with the Levantine corpus. However, similar

80 Laessøe 1963, Pl. 12B.
81 Yokoyama & Matsumoto 1989.
82 Kamada & Ohtsu 1988, 137-148; see Gr 228, Fig. 3, Bronze 3; Gr 71, Fig. 5:2, Bronzes 1-2; Gr 277, Fig. 8:2, Bronzes 22-23.
83 Bergamini 1985, 49-50.
84 Bergamini 1984, 235-236.
85 Quarantelli 1985, 316, Nos. 122-123.
86 Fiorina 1985, 62-63.
87 Bergamini 1984, 237.
88 Fiorina 1984, Fig. 27; 1985, 63.

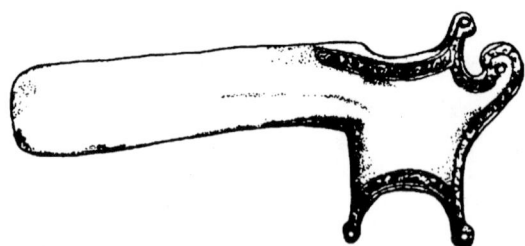

Fig. 16.6: Socketed axe from Chagar Bazar, Level I; this axe is clearly a variation on that from Tell el-Seib depicted in Fig. 16.5. After Mallowan 1937, Pl. XVBb. Actual length 27.0 cm

material from other excavations in the area will allow parallels to be drawn.[89]

Excavations at Tell el-Seib produced a total of 34 early second-millennium BC graves. The burials are generally in crouched position in rectangular pits. As at most sites, metalwork is relatively rare, and many graves contain only a limited range of ceramics. Grave 20, with two burials, produced an axe-dagger set (Fig. 16.5), a silver band, and a toggle-pin, as well as metal vessels.[90] and the remains of a sheep at the north-west side of grave, presumably a meat-offering.[91] The axe and dagger were both located in the vicinity of the abdomen of one of the burials, the former lying as if the handle had been pointing upwards.

Although the axe and dagger types are different from the Levantine examples, this is to be expected. It is the idea of the pairing which is important. The axe is an example of Deshayes' Type C3a.[92] The only example of known provenance in his catalogue is the decorated axe from Chagar Bazar (Fig. 16.6).[93] There are now a number of (unpublished) axes of this type known from sites in the Hamrin, suggesting that it should be seen as a local north Mesopotamian style.

Grave 9 at Tell el-Seib had an equid (donkey ?) burial nearby.[94] This practice is reminiscent of the donkey burials found at Tell el-Dab'a in the Nile Delta. These too are often located just outside graves.[95]

Tell Halawa, located near Tell el-Seib, revealed some 28 Old-Babylonian-period graves[96] The pottery included many thin-walled cylindrical cups, both straight- and concave-sided, some with disc-base. Jars with flaring necks and flaring-sided bowls occur as well. It is interesting that cups and goblets are here such a

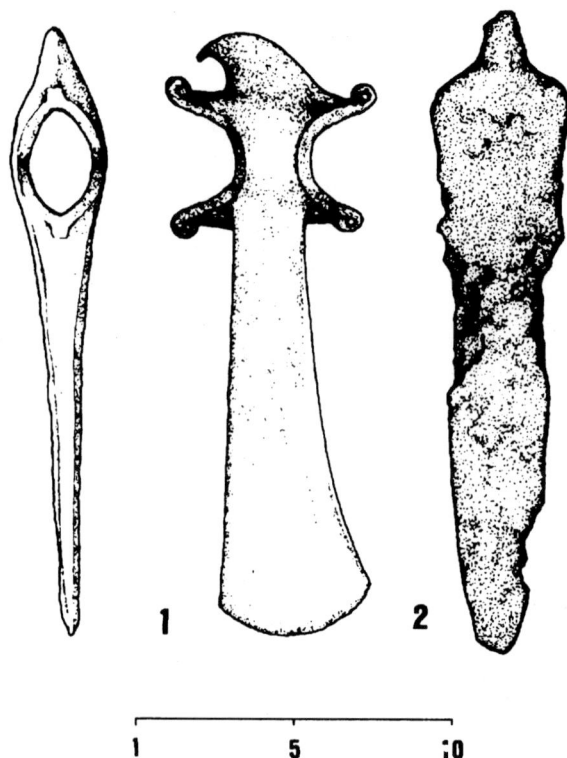

Fig. 16.7: Axe-dagger set from Tell Halawa Grave 5.

feature of the grave repertoire, while the juglets so common in coastal Syria-Palestine are seemingly absent. The metalwork has not been published by grave-group, but a selection is illustrated.[97]

From a draft report in Arabic the following data can be established.[98] Only a minority of graves produced weapons, and of these most contained only a single item, generally a knife or spearhead. The graves were mostly single crouched interments. Grave 3 (Fig. 16.4:2) had a knife/dagger positioned at the back of the deceased. Grave 5 revealed an axe-dagger set (Fig. 16.7), with the axe placed by head. Grave 7, a poorly preserved adult burial, produced a set of axe, a fragmentary knife or dagger, and two spearheads. Two toggle-pins lay behind the head, while a necklace, two copper bracelets or anklets and a dish lying by the legs completed the set of metal artefacts.

Another large cemetery was excavated at Tell Slei-mah, where 85 graves are assigned to levels I and II which span the Isin-Larsa and Old Babylonian periods.[99] As at other Hamrin sites, the grave-goods included metal vessels (beakers and bowls) as well as jewellery and weapons, the latter occurring in a relatively small proportion of the total number of graves. In short, this site conforms to the pattern established by

---

89  This material was excavated by Iraqi archaeologists working in the Hamrin area. Brief preliminary reports have been published on work at these and other Hamrin rescue sites (summaries in Postgate & Watson 1979; Roaf & Postgate 1981)
90  Hannoun 1984, Arabic section, Fig. 21.
91  Ibid., Arabic section, Fig. 19.
92  Deshayes 1960, 179-180.
93  Mallowan 1937, 99, Pls. XVA-B.
94  Hannoun 1984.
95  Cf. above,.
96  Abbu 1984.

---

97  Ibid., Fig. 28.
98  Abbu, unpublished.
99  Rumeidiyeh 1984.

the other early second millennium BC sites in the Hamrin area.

The presence at Chagar Bazar of an axe with typological parallels in the Hamrin (see above) brings us to consider the north of Syria. This axe came from Chagar Bazar Grave 131, which also contained what Mallowan terms a spearhead.[100] However, the photograph suggests that it might actually be a dagger with broken tang,[101] which would indicate the presence of a dagger-axe set in this tomb. The grave also produced two toggle pins, a copper wine-strainer, and one ceramic vessel, a small/medium-sized jar. The limited ceramic element in the tomb echoes the pattern found in Syro-Palestinian burials of the early second millennium BC. At Chagar Bazar only a few of the graves contained weapons. Grave 143, a robbed vaulted grave produced a dagger and a spear. Grave 154, with three burials, also robbed, produced three spears, pottery, beads, and animal bones, probably a meat-offering.[102] Another axe, this one with a ribbed socket, comes from Grave 200, and is also dated to the early second millennium BC.[103] This grave also produced a small spearhead.

### Summary of north Mesopotamia

Several differences between the contents of the graves in the Hamrin and contemporary cemeteries in the Levant are worthy of comment. Single burials are the norm in north Mesopotamia. The frequent re-use of tombs seen in the Levant is less common here. The actual weapon types employed in the two areas differ somewhat and my impression is that there may be rather less emphasis on the dagger as a grave-item in Mesopotamia than in the Levant. The frequency of metal vessels in Mesopotamian graves presumably indicates their greater availability there, than in Palestine, as these are rare in Levantine contexts. Toggle-pins, so common in the Middle-Bronze-Age Levant,[104] also occur in the Hamrin.

It has been suggested that the red-slipped and burnished, carinated bowls and jugs characteristic of MB IIA graves in coastal Syria and Palestine were inspired by the shapes and finish of metal vessels.[105] This idea finds some support in that red-slipped and burnished pottery is absent in Mesopotamia, where copper/bronze vessels, often with carinated profiles, occur in the richer graves, in the Hamrin for example. Tubb has observed that this type of pottery is not found in inland Syria.[106] Unfortunately, the Middle-Bronze-Age graves of this area are little known, but if the Mari texts reflect accurately the prevailing conditions,[107] then

metal vessels were likely to have been quite widely available, perhaps rendering superfluous the production of red-slipped and burnished ceramics in this area, as well as in Mesopotamia. In other words, the familiar red-slipped vessels may have been widely used only where metal vessels were in restricted supply, namely the less economically developed coastal and southern areas of the Levant.

## Warrior burials in Mesopotamia in the third millennium BC

The early second-millennium BC warrior burials in the Hamrin just described have good local predecessors. Tell Madhhur grave 5G revealed a crouched, young adult male burial interred in a large rectangular pit with two equid skeletons.[108] A dagger lay across the waist of the deceased and a socketed adze some 0.25 m from the skull.[109] Again we see the classic pattern of axe by the head and dagger close to the body. Other burial goods included metal beads, pins and silver jewellery as well as copper-base vessels and the remains of food offerings. This grave is dated to the late ED III or early Akkadian period, and is one of four similar burials in varying states of preservation. The earliest of these may be of ED I date.[110] Tell Sabra too has produced an ED III burial containing both a dagger and a socketed adze.[111] Such adzes occur quite often in Mesopotamian graves and are used in the same way as axes. At Tell Razuk a tomb dated to the early Akkadian period housed a burial in one chamber, while the other contained copper tools and weapons along with two equid skeletons lying side-by-side.

The evidence from these three sites shows that there is a strong, local thread of continuity in the Hamrin which will allow us to trace structured warrior burials at least as far back as the later third millennium BC. In fact, as hinted at by the evidence from Tell Madhhur, burials with weapons are known in the Hamrin as early as the ED I period. At ED I Kheit Qasim, for example, copper objects are restricted to the larger tombs, presumably those of the more important personages, who may have had some connection to the elaborate ED I building at nearby Tell Abu Qassem.[112] However, in these early examples the weapon types are less clearly defined and the structuring is less tight, suggesting that the essential form of the warrior burial crystalised somewhere between ED I and ED III when it appears in a developed form in the Royal Cemetery at Ur, that is at some point in the first half of the third millennium BC.

---

100  Mallowan 1937, 120.
101  Mallown 1937, Pl. XIVE.
102  For details of the graves, cf. ibid., 118-124.
103  Mallowan 1947, 85-86, Pl. XLI:1.
104  Henschel-Simon 1938.
105  Amiran 1969, 90.
106  Tubb 1983, 55.
107  Cf., the summary by Dalley 1984.

108  Roaf 1984, 116.
109  Ibid., Fig. 24.4-24.7..
110  Ibid., 116.
111  Tunca 1987, 32, Pl. 33:1-4.
112  Forest 1984, 112-113.

## The end of warrior burials in Mesopotamia

As in the Levant, the tradition does not continue beyond the middle of the second millennium BC. Although little material from second-millennium cemeteries has been published, neither Ur[113] nor Tell Zubeidi in the Hamrin[114] provides any evidence for burials with warrior items of the kind described above. Occasional burials with weapons occur, but these are generally equipped with long daggers with cast-hilts. Examples are known from Nippur,[115] Ur,[116] `Aqar Quf[117] and Tell Zubeidi.[118] These weapons stand at the head of a tradition which continues, with some variation, into the Iron Age.

## The evidence from western Iran

The sketch drawn of developments in Mesopotamia receives support from the evidence from western Iran. The publication of the metalwork from Susa has revealed the sheer quantity of weapons uncovered in the excavations at the site, much of it dating on typological grounds to the third and earlier second millennia BC.[119] Many of these weapons can only be assigned to general chronological periods,[120] as exact contexts are frequently missing. However, the bulk of these are almost certainly from the largely unpublished graves excavated at Susa over many decades.[121]

To make sense of this material, we must begin with those grave-groups which are adequately documented. Carter notes a group consisting of axe, metal belt and a decorated mace-head from Grave 555. This she assigns to her period IVa, the mid-third millennium BC.[122] The material from this group is clearly in the warrior burial tradition, albeit a distinctly Iranian variant. Grave 507 with rich goods including a spearhead and the remains of a meat-offering she assigns to period V (late third and beginning of the second millennia BC).[123] These two graves reveal traits associated with warrior burials elsewhere – weapons, the metal belt and meat-offerings – suggesting that the general phenomenon extends to western Iran.

However, these graves are but two examples. In order to demonstrate clearly the eastward extension of the phenomenon, a larger body of data is required. This exists in outline published form in the numerous graves

excavated during the pre-war seasons at the site, in particular among the 357 graves from the 'Chantier de Donjon' published briefly by de Mecquenem.[124] While this rather cryptic report may not be entirely reliable,[125] it should provide an indication of the nature of the mortuary evidence from Susa.

Of the 357 graves listed, 24 are recorded as containing weapons, about 7%.[126] Most of these occur singly, and include axes, daggers and spears, although a rich group from Grave 89b produced a dagger, an axe, spears and other metal goods.[127] Two graves (16 and 125) produced a pairing of axe and macehead. Rarely found outside Iran, this seems to be a distinctive local set.[128] In one instance, Grave 294, an axe comes from an infant burial,[129] which might argue for a definite association between status and weapons, the interment of the latter being a matter of entitlement rather than related to the deceased's role in the living world. Alternatively, it could be an aberration. Another is from what is alleged to be the burial of an adult female.[130] However, there is little indication of the basis on which the sex of the deceased was determined, other than that the grave contained numerous items of jewellery, a notoriously unreliable indicator. Without full documentation, it is hard to date individual graves exactly, although it is clear that collectively they span a considerable period. A great number are contemporary with Carter's period IV, others including the distinctive coffin burials date to the early second millennium BC.[131]

Tallon dates axe-type B3 from Susa to the Isin-Larsa–Old Babylonian periods.[132] This type of socketed axe features a blade with a very wide cutting edge with concave upper and lower margins which narrow abruptly rendering the blade quite slender at the point where it joins the socket. More than twenty examples are reported from the site.[133] This form is rare at more westerly sites, and represents a local style.

In summary, Susa provides good evidence for warrior burials, clearly related to the standard international pattern but showing certain local peculiarities, just as observed in other regions. Chronologically weapon finds are concentrated in periods IV and V, that is from ED III through to Isin-Larsa/Old Babylonian in Mesopotamian terms. Again this fits with the picture from Mesopotamia. The key feature of Susa, however, is that as far as it can be established from the available data, burials with weapons span the whole of this period

113 Baker, in this volume.
114 Boehmer & Dammer 1985, 35-44.
115 McCown & Haines 1967, 22, Pl. 30:4-5.
116 Woolley & Mallowan 1976, 119, n.1:184.
117 Curtis 1983.
118 Boehmer & Dammer 1985, 63-64, Pl. 149:646-647.
119 Over 70 socketed axes and more than 50 daggers are published by Tallon (1987).
120 Ibid., Catalogue.
121 A coherent publication of the burials from Susa has not yet appeared.
122 Carter 1980, 75-77, Fig. 22. The periodisation used here is that of Carter 1978, 198, Table 1, as used by Tallon 1987, 28-32.
123 Carter 1980, 107-113, Fig. 44.

124 Mecquenem 1943, 76-106.
125 Cf. the remarks of Tallon 1987, 58-59.
126 For illustrations of typical examples see Mecquenem 1943, Fig. 73.
127 Ibid., 89.
128 For discussion of the distinctive maceheads from Susa, cf. Tallon 1987, 128-134, Table 6. These artefacts are not treated in detail in the present paper.
129 Mecquenem 1943, 102.
130 Tallon 1987, 88.
131 Carter & Stolper 1984, 147.
132 Tallon 1987, 83.
133 Ibid., Catalogue Nos. 46-67.

without interruption. Susa provides strong supporting evidence to that cited from the Hamrin for the continuity of a tradition of warrior burials over a period of a millennium or so. In other words, the burials from the Royal Cemetery and those from second millennium BC graves in the Hamrin are parts of a unified phenomenon, which on present evidence has its origins in Mesopotamia in the early third millennium BC.

A similar phenomenon, the placing of quantities of metalwork in graves, can also be seen in Luristan during the later third and early second millennia BC. While most of this material has only been published in preliminary form, summary articles[134] and the illustrations in the interim reports are sufficient to show that burials with weapons, generally of Mesopotamian inspiration, were widespread in the Pusht-i-Kuh area of western Iran. Examples include material from Bani Surmah,[135] Dar Tanha[136] and Kalleh Nisar.[137]

Typologically this material has wide parallels, and compares well with that from Mesopotamia and Susa.[138] However, it should be clearly distinguished from the later 'Luristan' metalwork which dates to the end of the second and the beginning of the first millennia BC. This second group of metalwork is different in many ways from the earlier material and represents a truly local style.[139] Some scholars would go so far as to see a clear break between the earlier material and later 'Luristan' metalwork.[140] The implication is that despite the existence of a late tradition of metalworking in Luristan, the Iranian component of the wider West Asiatic phenomenon, represented by warrior burials at Susa and in the Pusht-i-Kuh, ceases at around the same time as it does in other regions – that is a little before the middle of the second millennium BC.

## The Levant in the third millennium BC

The discussion above should have clarified two points. Firstly that the warrior burials of the Levant are simply a local version of a phenomenon widespread throughout Western Asia. Secondly that this tradition has a long and continuous history in Mesopotamia and neighbouring regions, and that its cessation in Mesopotamia and western Iran, is broadly contemporary with its disappearance from the archaeological record of Syria-Palestine around the end of the Middle Bronze Age.

The next step is to assess whether the Levantine warrior burials have local third-millennium BC precursors, or represent a tradition introduced from outside the region. To do this we must examine the evidence for warrior burials in third millennium BC Syria-Palestine.

### Third millennium BC Syria

The funerary archaeology of third millennium Syria is poorly known. Individual burials with weapons occur, but sets of the kind, easily identifiable in the Middle Bronze Age, are unknown.[141]

The remains of three equids were found in association with burial H-70 at Halawa in north Syria.[142] In Mesopotamia, interments with equids are often understood as those of high status individuals.[143] This early third-millennium BC grave also included a male burial associated with two daggers placed by the chest. The association of the equids and the weapons is clear, and although the ingredients differ from the classic Mesopotamian types, the underlying pattern may well be similar.

The only large quantity of Early Bronze Age weaponry from a single context comes from the *Hypogeum*, a large stone-built grave at Til Barsip on the Euphrates. This structure is later than the burial from Halawa, and should be placed somewhere in the second half of the third millennium BC. Only two adult burials were recorded,[144] although the site was excavated many years ago and important details may have gone unnoticed. Among other things, the chamber produced a large amount of pottery, metal bowls, a wide array of axes, spears and daggers and two rein-rings, suggestive of a vehicle of some kind.[145] Although no equid bones were mentioned in the report, it does state that large quantities of sheep and goat bones were noted, suggesting the presence of meat-offerings.[146] All these points indicate an episode of conspicuous consumption and display. In many ways this tomb echoes elements of the rich Early Dynastic graves of Mesopotamia.

At Mari, some distance down the Euphrates, several big, stone-built tombs, excavated in the 1930s have recently been published in full.[147] Although largely robbed, these are reminiscent of the tomb at Til Barsip, and the surviving material includes jewellery and personal items, weapons including a crescentic axe, metal vessels and various ceramic examples.[148] These tombs date to the late ED I, i.e. the earlier third millennium BC,[149] arguing for a long history of such rich graves in the Euphrates valley, of which the Mari graves and the *Hypogeum* are simply the best known instances.

More evidence for the importance of weapons in third millennium BC Syria comes from recent work on

134 Vanden Berghe 1973.
135 Vanden Berghe 1968, 55-58.
136 Vanden Berghe 1970a, 15-16, Fig. 12.
137 Vanden Berghe 1970b, 69-70, Fig. 72.
138 Moorey 1971, 286; Waele 1982, 36-38.
139 Cf. Moorey 1971, 288-289.
140 Waele 1982, 39.

141 Philip 1989, 164-165.
142 Orthmann 1981, 54-55, Pl. 39.
143 Cf. Zarins 1986.
144 Thureau-Dangin & Dunand 1936, 97, Fig. 28.
145 Cf. ibid., 106-108, Pls. 28-31.
146 Ibid., 97.
147 Jean-Marie 1990.
148 Ibid., 314-316, Pls. IX, XV, XVI.
149 Lebeau 1990, 351.

texts from Tell Mardikh. The frequent mention of weapons, including daggers, spears and axes, often decorated with precious metals is a striking feature of these texts. The items concerned seem to feature as part of a gift-obligation system, linking both internal and external élites to the central palace economy.[150] While Archi has observed the importance of weight in these artefacts, suggesting that it was the amount of precious metal which was of primary concern,[151] the very choice of weapons as one of the appropriate forms of transferring precious materials (as opposed to using ingots, for example) is itself of interest, and argues for an important symbolic role for these artefacts. Archi also notes the existence of a differentiation by sex in the kinds of artefacts given to different individuals, with weapons being a favoured 'gift' for males.[152]

A detailed study of the textual references to weapons at Ebla observes that it is decorated, status items, not military equipment which dominate.[153] These were available in large numbers. In one case there is mention of 540 spears being provided with silver decoration,[154] while other texts clearly relate to weapons fashioned for different gods.[155]

Several forms of dagger feature, frequently with decorated sheaths and handles. Waetzoldt points out that the familiar *gir-Martu* often appears in specific weights and may represent a particular style of dagger.[156] They too are often decorated with precious metal, thus taking the form of prestige items. Axes were treated in the same way.[157] Like elaborate daggers these were not made for the use of ordinary soldiers. The textual evidence from Ebla indicates that weaponry was an accepted way of making gifts to men, and of displaying rank, status and connections. Although few of these precious metal objects have survived, I would suggest that the existence of this symbolic role indicates that weapons played an important part in the ideology of Syria in the third millennium BC, in particular in definitions of high status and 'maleness'.

Given this situation, the appearance of weapons in graves is predictable. While the evidence remains sparse, I suspect that in time Syrian equivalents of the rich cemeteries of ED III Mesopotamia, with a number of warrior burials, will be excavated, and will confirm the existence in both Mesopotamia and parts of Syria, of a common notion regarding the expression of status messages, from an early phase of the third millennium BC.

## First appearance of warrior burials in Palestine

The picture is less clear in the case of Palestine. There are few weapons from EB I-III grave contexts.[158] Despite the existence of walled towns, and good evidence for some sort of social hierarchy during the EB II-III,[159] unequivocal evidence for the expression of status through a warrior idiom is lacking prior to EB IV. The sole published example of an identifiable, rich EB II-III burial, the EB II grave from Kinneret near Khirbet Kerak is completely lacking in weapons.[160] A further difference is provided by the lack of evidence for meat-offerings reported from the numerous EBA burials from sites such as Jericho[161] and Bab edh-Dhra'.[162]

The major increase in the deposition of weapons in graves actually comes in EB IV, a phenomenon once linked to incoming 'Amorites'.[163] However, more recent studies have stressed the degree of ceramic continuity from EB III to EB IV, and interpret the archaeological evidence in terms of changes in settlement patterns and socio-economic organisation rather the arrival of new peoples.[164]

Although there is some regional variation among the weapon types employed in EB IV burials, a standard underlying structure can be identified. They usually feature a narrow-bladed dagger, sometimes accompanied by a hooked-tang spearhead.[165] In many cases these are the sole (surviving) items accompanying the deceased. Sets there are, but the types are very different from those in use in Mesopotamia and Syria. Weapons in Syrian styles are few, and concentrated in north Palestine.[166] EB IV metalwork is generally the product of a local industry, making objects in traditional styles.

The contrast between EB IV individual burials and the multiple successive tombs favoured during the EB II-III is striking.[167] In the latter the isolation of particular individuals is virtually impossible, as is any association between any one burial and particular grave goods. The notion of separating and identifying individuals on burial is more clearly expressed in the EB IV period. More importantly this pattern continues into the succeeding Middle Bronze Age. Although multiple successive burial was the norm at some MBA sites, such as Jericho[168] and el-Gib,[169] this practice may owe to the local availability of large EB IV tombs. Many MBA burials at sites such as Megiddo[170], Ras el-'Ain,[171] Dhahrat el-Humraiya[172] and Tell el-'Ajjul,[173] as well as

150 Archi 1985, 31.
151 Ibid., 30.
152 Ibid., 28-29.
153 Waetzoldt 1990.
154 Ibid., 3.
155 Ibid., 3.
156 Ibid., 17.
157 Ibid., 24.

158 Philip 1989, 164.
159 Palumbo 1990; Esse 1991.
160 Amiran & Haas 1973.
161 Kenyon 1960; 1965.
162 Schaub & Rast 1989.
163 Kenyon 1966, 12-14.
164 Dever 1980; Richard 1980; Palumbo 1990.
165 Philip 1989, 165-166.
166 Ibid., 167.
167 Palumbo 1990, 125.
168 Kenyon 1960; 1965.
169 Pritchard 1963.
170 Loud 1948.
171 Ory 1937.
172 Ory 1948.

the 'warrior' burials at Tel Rehov and Beth Shan described above, are single interments. Single burials with weapons provide a strong thread linking Palestinian Middle Bronze Age burial practices to those of the EB IV period.

Many of the typological differences between the grave-goods of the EB IV and MB IIA periods result from the different technological possibilities open to the craftsmen of the two periods, in particular the greater use of two-piece moulds in the later period, and the different bases on which they may have worked.[174] These should not distract us from an important element of continuity between the two periods, namely single burials with sets of weapons.

Besides a preference for single burials and a marked increase in the use of weapons as grave-goods, the EB IV period also sees the appearance in the southern Levant of the practice of placing meat-offerings in graves.[175]. While this practice continues into local MBA graves, we have already noted that it was a component of Mesopotamian, and probably Syrian, warrior burials of the third millennium BC. Perhaps then, the warrior burials of EB IV Palestine and Jordan are simply a local attempt to emulate practices already well-established to the north, but using locally available metal artefacts. The presence together of weapons and meat-offerings, combined with the clear association of particular items with individual burials, suggests that a common structure may underlie the EB IV burial practices of both the northern and southern Levant, one which contrasts with Palestinian EB II-III practices.

The adoption in the late third millennium BC in the southern Levant of a system of marking status through warrior goods, which had been acknowledged in Syria by the mid-third millennium BC at the latest, provides a possible explanation for the appearance of burials equipped with costly metal goods in a period – the EB IV – which is generally considered to be impoverished, and which lacks major fortified centres. We might consider the possibility that the well-documented settlement shifts,[176] have no relation to the changes in burial practices, other than that they were broadly contemporary.

*Why warrior equpiment at all?*

Possible reasons for the attribution of significance to warrior equipment have been discussed elsewhere.[177] Briefly, they were associated with power and conquest, with the ability to take tribute and lives, i.e. the acquisition of wealth and reputation. The image of the king as conqueror, the warrior-leader as hero, occurs repeatedly in ancient Near Eastern literature, and probably reflects the values of that society. The fact that the concept of weapon-symbolism cuts across a range of ancient ceramic, political and linguistic boundaries, as demonstrated above, argues that it expressed widely held, culturally formed, notions concerning appropriate male high-status behaviour. These views were current throughout a large part of the ancient Near East during much of the third and the early second millennia BC. It is this, the very unity of the phenomenon, which underlies the widespread typological similarities observable in weapon types throughout Western Asia at this time.

## Decline of the Warrior Burial

One of the most striking aspects of warrior burials is that they cease at approximately the same time throughout most of Western Asia. In the southern Levant and Nile Delta, the last classic warrior burials date to the later phases of the Middle Bronze Age (we cannot be more precise than this); a similar date would seem reasonable for burials in Syria.[178] In Mesopotamia, there is no evidence that they continue beyond the end of the Old Babylonian period.[179] For Iran the existence of a possible break between the early second-millennium BC metalwork and the later 'Luristan' bronzework has already been discussed.

The uniqueness of the warrior burial phenomenon is emphasised by its complete absence in the later second millennium BC. The reason for this doubtless lies in the network of complex changes taking place towards the middle of that millennium. However, three main possibilities can be identified.

1. The widespread adoption of the combination of the chariot, the composite bow and scale-armour around the beginning of the LBA[180] had a major impact on the conduct of warfare. It may also have had a concomitant effect on the mode of representing high status, with an associated decline in the deposition of sets of weapons designed for hand-to-hand combat. The growth of a group of highly trained, and high-status chariot troops, the *mari-anna*, may have been an important factor in the decline of the status value of the more traditional weapon-sets. However, Heltzer has pointed out that at LBA Ugarit chariot troops were dependent on royal stores and workshops, and that many *mari-anna* were themselves royal dependents.[181] Changes in the range of grave artefacts may well reflect the greater degree of control by palace organisations of

173 Petrie 1931-34.
174 Philip 1991b, 101.
175 Cf., e.g., the graves from Jericho published by Kenyon 1960; 1965.
176 Palumbo 1990.
177 Philip 1989, 156.

178 Cf. Philip 1989, 217.
179 Cf. Baker in this volume.
180 Moorey 1986.
181 Heltzer 1982, 114.

the new-style élite military equipment such as chariotry and horses. Such costly material may not have been available for use in the graves of individuals.

2.  In the Levant, at least, the LBA has a distinctly cosmopolitan nature.[182] There was a significant increase in long-distance trade in the Late Bronze Age, with more, and more varied, international trade and diplomatic connections, best seen through imported pottery.[183] While there is too little pertinent archaeological data to allow an assessment of the situation in contemporary Mesopotamia, the general ambience of international relations during this time (see below) suggests an increase in long-range political relations. In these circumstances, a greater range of alternative, perhaps imported, prestige-type material would have become available, perhaps contributing to a diminution of the importance of the more traditional weapons in this role.

3.  The decline in warrior equipment may also reflect the changing political landscape during and after the sixteenth century BC. The Late Bronze Age is generally understood as seeing the replacement of the small Middle Bronze Age 'Amorite' kingdoms by larger political units, organised along different lines, the Hittite and Egyptian empires for example, and the kingdom of Mitanni.[184] Foreign powers, governing from relatively distant centres such as Hattusas and Thebes played a greater role in the political life of the region than had hitherto been the case. The appearance of new political units, and the different systems of power relations which would have resulted from this, might well have altered the mode of interchange between élites, causing shifts in the nature of their material expression. Such developments may have contributed to a decline in the importance, and hence the production, distribution and deposition, of 'personal' warrior equipment, artefacts which had only been meaningful in terms of previous sociopolitical structures.

*Acknowledgements*

I wish to express my gratitude to the staff of the Directorate-General of Antiquities and Heritage and other individuals in Iraq, who kindly provided access to material in the Iraq Museum, Baghdad, and at Mosul University, and to various notes and records. Helpful comments on the text were provided by the various participants at the Manchester conference, and by Stephen Bourke, Elizabeth Carter and StJohn Simpson in particular. I also owe a debt to Trevor Watkins, some of whose insights I have hijacked as my own. For the illustrations I am indebted to my wife, Carrie Philip.

---

182  Leonard 1989.
183  Mazar 1990, 261-263; Gonen 1992b, 247-249.

184  Astour 1981; Gonen 1992b, 211-214.

# 17

# Aegean Influence in Late Bronze Age Funerary Practices in the Southern Levant

## Garth Gilmour

ABSTRACT—*The two dominant burial practices in Canaan during the Late Bronze Age were single burials in pits or cists in the coastal plain, and multiple burials in caves and rock-cut tombs in the interior. Several other burial customs are present, four of which have been ascribed to Aegean influence: chamber tombs, stone-built corbelled tombs, larnakes and cremation.*

*Chamber tombs are best represented in the '900' and '500' cemeteries at Tell el-Far'ah (South), though they occur also at Tell el-Ajjul and Beth Shean. Several studies of these tombs have attributed them to either Mycenaean or Cypriote influence. It is here concluded that the 900 cemetery tombs represent a local development of the bilobate tomb tradition of MB IIC, which itself was a concept imported from Cyprus; and the 500 cemetery tombs were cut by the Philistines who drew on their own Aegean as well as Cypriote and the local Canaanite traditions.*

*Stone built corbelled tombs in LB Canaan have been found at Megiddo, Dan and Aphek. It is here concluded that the origin of this tradition lies to the north in Syria, and not in the Aegean.*

*Late Bronze Age larnakes have been found only twice in Canaan, one each in Gezer and at Acco (the 'Persian Garden'). They are typical of burials in Crete in the Middle and Late Minoan periods, and are also found in mainland Greece during LH III. While there seems little doubt about the Aegean origin of the tradition, factors such as the dates and associated finds in each case require caution before ascribing these burials to Aegean groups resident in Canaan.*

*Cremation appears in three different forms, at Jericho, Tell Beit Mirsim, and the Amman Airport building. Some scholars have associated cremations in Syria with the coming of the Sea Peoples, while others have attributed them to the Hittites. However, cremation may be performed for any number of reasons, and these three isolated and different examples suggest that they may be local aberrations; any outside influence is to be ascribed to Anatolia rather than the Aegean.*

## Introduction

Burial practices in Late Bronze Age Canaan followed a consistent pattern of single burials in cists or pits in the coastal plain and multiple burials in caves and rock-cut tombs in the Shephelah and mountainous interior.[1] Nevertheless there were numerous individual exceptions to this pattern, and four of these have been variously ascribed to Aegean influence. These are cut chamber tombs, stone-built corbel vaulted tombs, larnakes and cremation. In each case a detailed study of the practice reveals that the simple invoking of influence from Aegean groups is at best inadequate, and more often unable to explain the practice, and other factors need to be considered.

## Chamber Tombs

### Introduction

At the site of Tell el-Far'ah (South), excavations in the 1920s and '30s exposed a settlement and several surrounding cemeteries. The '900' cemetery, which ranges in date from Late Bronze II into the Iron Age,

---

1    Gonen 1992a.

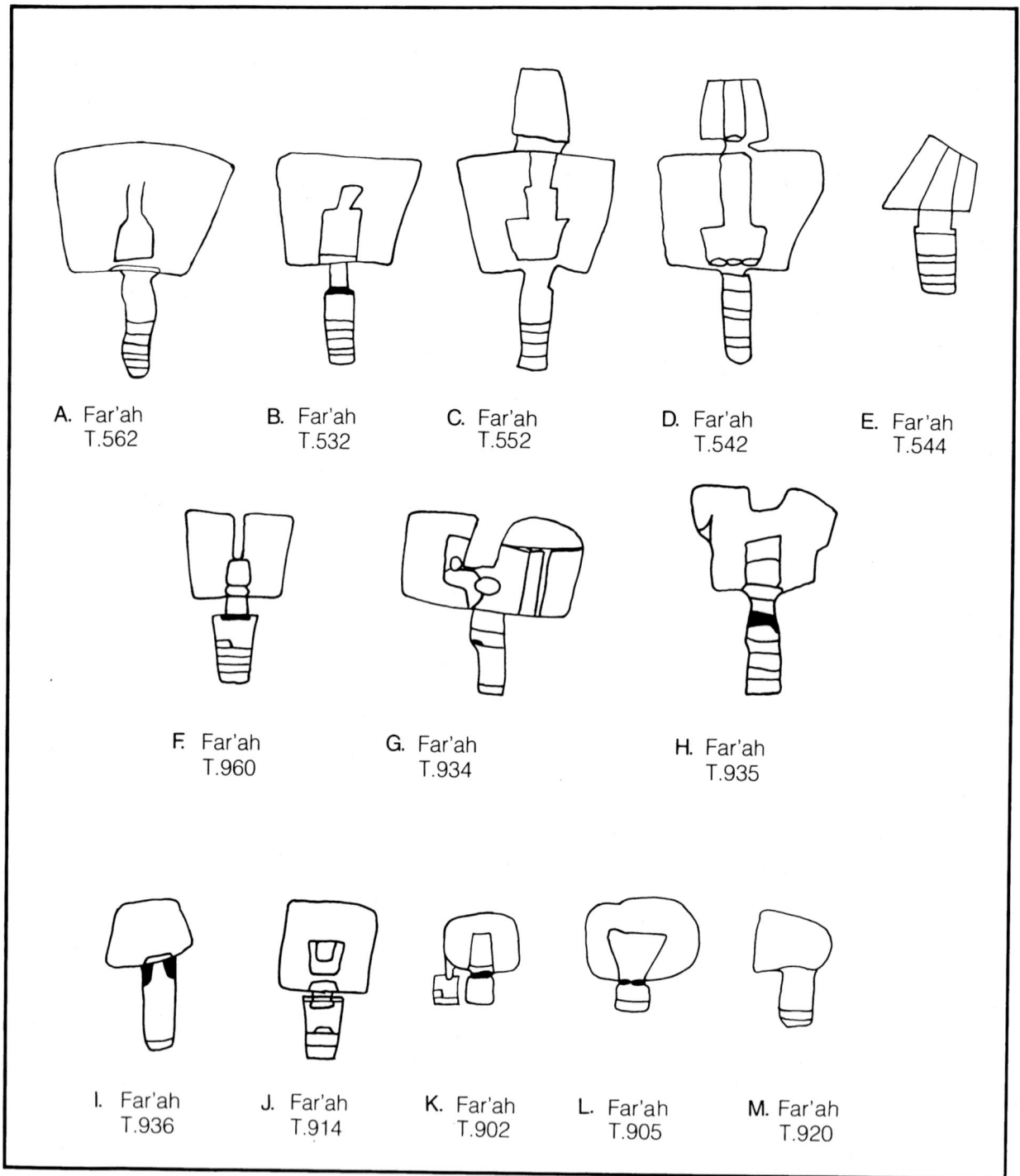

A. Far'ah
T.562

B. Far'ah
T.532

C. Far'ah
T.552

D. Far'ah
T.542

E. Far'ah
T.544

F. Far'ah
T.960

G. Far'ah
T.934

H. Far'ah
T.935

I. Far'ah
T.936

J. Far'ah
T.914

K. Far'ah
T.902

L. Far'ah
T.905

M. Far'ah
T.920

*Fig. 17.1: Chamber tombs from the 500 and 900 cemeteries at Tell el-Far'ah (S). (Scale 1:200).
After BP I, pls XIX, XIII; BP II, pls LIX, LX.*

| Site | No. of chamber tombs | Depression | Benches | Stepped dromos | Step(s) into chamber | Sources |
|------|------|------|------|------|------|------|
| Asine | 8 | 1 (?) | - | 1 | 1 | Frödin & Persson 1938. |
| Dendra | 9 | - | 1 | 2 | 2 | Persson 1931; 1942. |
| Prosymna | 52 | - | 7 | - | 8 | Blegen 1937. |
| Perati | 192 | - | 3 | 1 | 2 | Iakovides 1969. |
| Agora | 21 | - | 1 | 1 | - | Immerwahr 1971. |
| Mycenae | 24 | 1 | 3 | 3 | - | Wace 1932. |

*Table 17.1 Frequency of occurrence of certain features in Mycenaean chamber tombs*

consists of several chamber tombs (Fig. 17.1:F-M) along with many more less elaborate graves.[2] The '500' cemetery comprised two areas, one dating to the 'Hyksos' period and the other to the 'Philistines'.[3] Prominent among the Philistine graves are five large rock-cut chamber tombs, numbers 562, 532, 552, 542 and 544 (Fig. 17.1:A-E), which were attributed by Petrie to the "lords of the Philistines".[4] It is these five tombs, along with some of the chamber tombs in the 900 cemetery, that have been variously attributed to Aegean and Cypriote influence. Both sets of tombs showed signs of being in use for several generations, and each group resembled the other in certain aspects of their architecture, such as roughly square chambers, stepped dromoi, sunken floors, and benches.

Several scholars have contributed to the debate on the origins of these tombs. Waldbaum proposed that the two cemeteries were the product of two different groups of Mycenaean settlers who drew on patterns from Late Helladic Aegean chamber tombs such as dromoi, rectangular shape, the occasional secondary chamber, and benches, in the design of the Tell el Far'ah tombs.[5] She was supported by Oren,[6] but other scholars rejected her argument, preferring to see a Cypriote influence in the tombs. Loffreda and Stiebing both suggested that the tombs reflect a continuation and development of the bilobate tomb tradition imported to Palestine from Cyprus in early MB IIC.[7] T. Dothan follows them with respect to the 900 tombs, interpreting these as a continuation by the local Canaanite population of the MB II bilobate tradition,[8] but supports Waldbaum's attribution of the 500 tombs to "foreign stimuli of Aegean origin".[9] Finally Gonen has proposed that the two sets of tombs were both cut during the reign of Ramesses II, based on Cypriote models. Later the 500

cemetery tombs were cleared of their contents to be used for Philistine burials.[10]

## Analysis

### Mycenaean chamber tombs

Chamber tombs at Mycenae, like those at Tell el-Far'ah, consist of dromoi, stomions and chambers. The dromos is usually long, though in earlier chamber tombs it is short and wide and sometimes has a few rock-cut steps at its entrance (Tombs 515, 516 and 529; Fig. 17.2:D-E).[11] These steps are not a feature of any of the later tombs.

The shape of the chamber in Mycenaean tombs varies from oval to round to rectangular, but usually tends towards a rectangular shape, which occasionally may have one or more smaller chambers leading off the main one. A few of the tombs have benches along one side of the chamber, either built or carved in the rock (Fig. 17.2:D,G); other tombs have grave-pits or cists dug into the floor, while some have none of these features.[12]

While there are clear similarities between the Mycenaean and Tell el-Far'ah tombs, several typical features at Far'ah are infrequent and atypical in the Aegean. These include a central depression, benches, a stepped dromos, and a step into the chamber. Table 17.1 details the frequency of occurrence of each of these features in Mycenaean chamber tombs at six different Aegean sites, and clearly indicates that these features were exceptional in Mycenaean chamber tombs throughout the Aegean.

### Cypriote chamber tombs

Several cemeteries in Cyprus reveal a long tradition, lasting through a large portion of the Bronze Age, of chamber tombs which resemble aspects of those at Tell el-Far'ah (S). These include such features as short, usually stepped dromoi, benches, unitary, bilobal and multilobal chambers, and depressions in the floor (Fig. 17.3).

---

2 Starkey & Harding 1932, 22-27, Pls LIX-LX.
3 The geographical location of Tell el-Far'ah (S) has caused these tombs to be attributed to the Philistines, though the absence of further evidence could mean that another Sea Peoples group is responsible. This paper follows its predecessors in using the label 'Philistine' for the Sea Peoples of Tell el-Far'ah (S).
4 Petrie 1930, Pls. XIX, LXIV.
5 Waldbaum 1966.
6 Oren 1973, 141, 149-150.
7 Loffreda 1968; Stiebing 1970.
8 T. Dothan 1982, 260.
9 Ibid., 263.

10 Gonen 1992a, 24, 128.
11 Wace 1932, 52, 125, Figs. 24, 41; 1949, 14.
12 Wace 1949, 14; Mylonas 1966, 112.

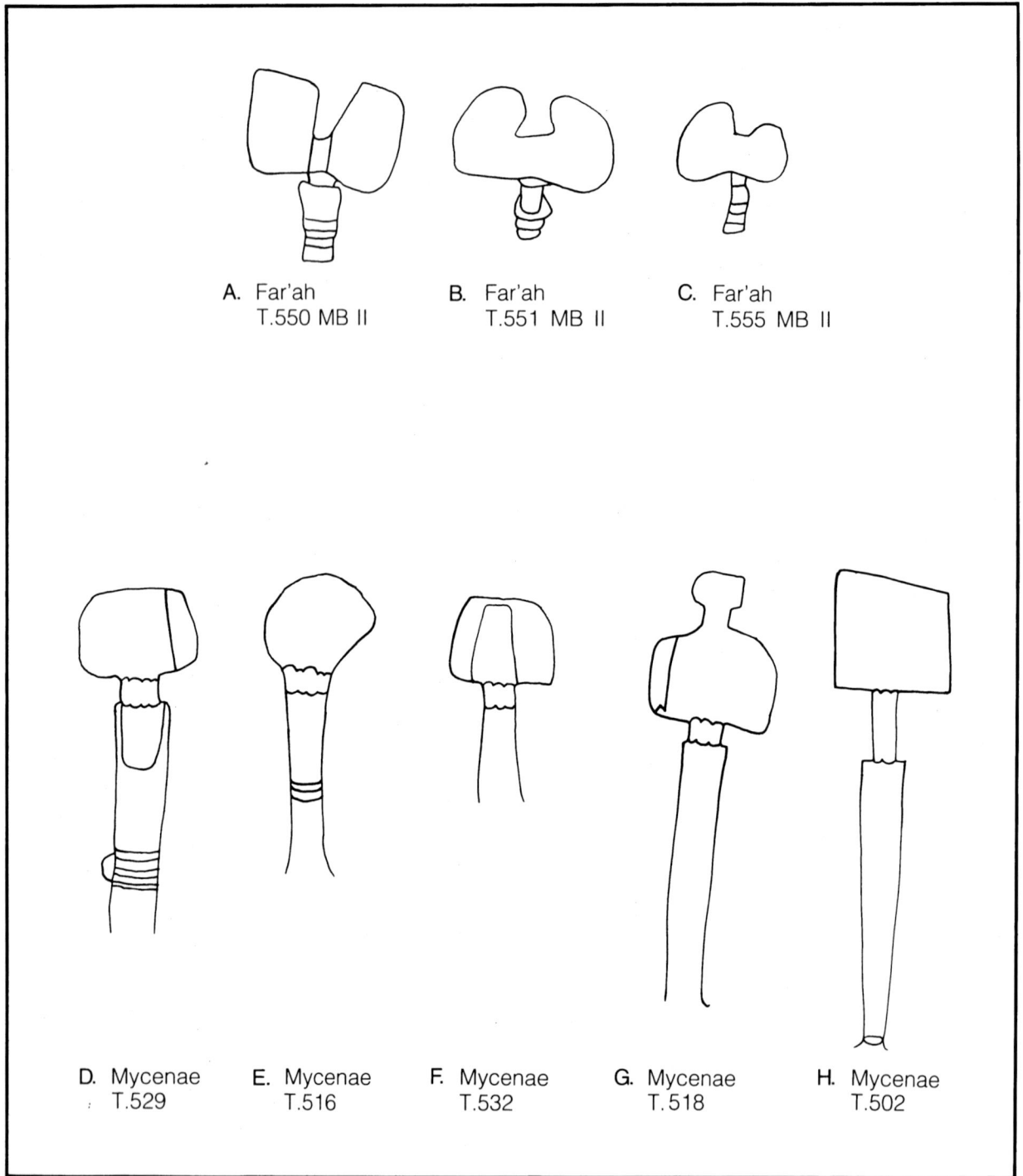

A. Far'ah
T.550 MB II

B. Far'ah
T.551 MB II

C. Far'ah
T.555 MB II

D. Mycenae
T.529

E. Mycenae
T.516

F. Mycenae
T.532

G. Mycenae
T.518

H. Mycenae
T.502

*Fig. 17.2: Chamber tombs at Tell el-Far'ah (S) and Mycenae. (Scale 1:200).*
*After BP I, pl. XVII; Wace 1932, fig 41, 24, 46, 2.*

## The 900-series tombs at Tell el-Far'ah (South)

The 900 tombs were for the most part cut into the outer slopes of the MB II rampart. Dothan has dated this cemetery to the thirteenth and early twelfth centuries BC, with its terminal date being suggested by two scarabs of Ramesses IV from Tombs 934 and 960.[13] Most specifically Tombs 936, 914, 902, 905 and 920 (Fig. 17.1:I-M) each had a sloping stepped dromos, a stomion, and a step down into a large chamber; all except two, Tombs 936 and 920, had central depressions in the chamber surrounded by benches. The other three chamber tombs, Tombs 960, 934 and 935 (Fig. 17.1:F-H), resembled the first group in most respects except that they were larger, and their chambers were divided into two by a section protruding from the rear wall opposite the entrance.

While the scarabs and pottery indicate that the 900 cemetery did continue in use into the early Iron Age, no Philistine pottery has been found there. However, a small amount of Mycenaean "simple style" pottery came from the 900 cemetery, from chamber tombs 905, 936 and 902, as well as from Tomb 939 (pit grave) and Tomb 922 (small circular chamber). Mycenaean imported pottery was not found anywhere else on the site.[14]

There are several points of resemblance between the Cypriote tombs and the 900 chamber tombs at Tell el-Far'ah (S). The short dromos with only a few steps, the step down into the chamber, the side benches and the central depression all feature in both groups, as does the bilobal effect produced by the protruding wall from the back of the chamber. However it is the long development of the chamber tomb in Cyprus that is especially significant in a comparison with Tell el-Far'ah, as the MB cemeteries at this site also contain bilobate chamber tombs quite similar to those in Cyprus.

In comparison to the Cypriote chamber tombs, the Aegean tombs have fewer similarities to the 900 tombs at Tell el-Far'ah. The tradition does not extend as far back in Greece, precluding any possibility that the MB 'Hyksos' chamber tombs at Far'ah are of Aegean inspiration, and undermining the apparent continuity between these tombs and the LB chamber tombs at the site. The dromoi at Mycenae are long and overwhelmingly sloping, while only three – dated to early Late Helladic – have steps. The walls of the Aegean dromoi incline toward the centre as they rise; although the reports of the Far'ah tombs do not mention whether such a feature is present, it seems unlikely that if it existed it would have gone unnoticed or unreported. The stomion at Mycenae seems in the vast majority of cases to be longer than at Far'ah, while the concept of a depression in the centre of the floor is present only in Mycenae Tomb 532.[15]

It seems therefore that the *typical* tomb in Cyprus shows more resemblance to the Far'ah 900 tombs than the *typical* Aegean tomb. The various differences in detail between the Cypriote and Far'ah tombs may be ascribed to the likelihood that the 900 tombs at Far'ah were cut by the local Canaanite residents of Tell el-Far'ah in the Late Bronze Age who were inspired by the Middle Bronze tombs and continued the tradition.

While the exact chronology of the 900 chamber tombs is not discernable due to later interference with their contents, the progression can be seen if they are ordered from north to south as follows: 960, 934, 935, and then 936, 914, 902, 905 and 920. There seems little problem with accepting that a group from Cyprus settled in Palestine in MB IIC, bringing with it the bilobate tomb design already well established on that island. Thus the 900 chamber tombs represent a local development of the bilobate tradition of MB IIC, which in turn was a concept imported from Cyprus. The apparent similarities of these tombs to the chamber tombs at Mycenae are coincidental; the resemblance is in basic appearance only, and not in the finer details.

## The 500-series tombs at Tell el-Far'ah (South)

Each of the 500-series chamber tombs has a similar plan. There is a short sloping stepped dromos leading to a narrow stomion. Through the doorway is a step down into the chamber, which is large and trapezoidal in shape, with generally well-defined corners. In each tomb the floor of the chamber forms a central passage surrounded on the left and right by benches carved into the rock. The skeletal remains were usually, but not exclusively, on these benches. In one tomb, Tomb 562, the passage petered out toward the rear of the chamber as it rose to meet the bench opposite the entrance. In the two earliest tombs, Tombs 542 and 552, the central passage passed through the rear wall into a secondary chamber. In Tomb 542, the passage in the secondary chamber was again flanked by benches on the left and right, but in Tomb 552 there were no benches in the secondary chamber.

Petrie listed the 500-series chamber tombs in the right chronological order, from earliest to latest 542, 552, 532, 562; but his dating was too high. Starkey and others corrected this, and most recently T. Dothan, in a detailed consideration of the pottery and scarabs from these tombs, has concluded the cemetery dates from the mid-twelfth to the first half of the eleventh century BC.[16]

In contrast to the 900 tombs, the five tombs of the "Philistine lords" at Tell el-Far'ah show more uniformity within the group, and bear a closer resemblance to

---

13  T. Dothan 1982, 29[49].
14  Petrie 1930, 6, Pls. XII, XVI; Starkey & Harding 1932, 23-27, Pls. XLIX, LIV; Furumark 1941, 116-118; Waldbaum 1966, 338-339.
15  Wace 1932, 110, Fig. 46.

16  T. Dothan 1982, 29-33.

A. Lapithos
   T.317 EC III

B. Lapithos
   T.320 MC II

C. Paleoskoutella
   T.4 MC III

D. Paleoskoutella
   T.7 MC III

E. A.Jakovos
   T.10 LC I

F. A.Jakovos
   T.8 MC III

G. Enkomi
   T.18 LC II

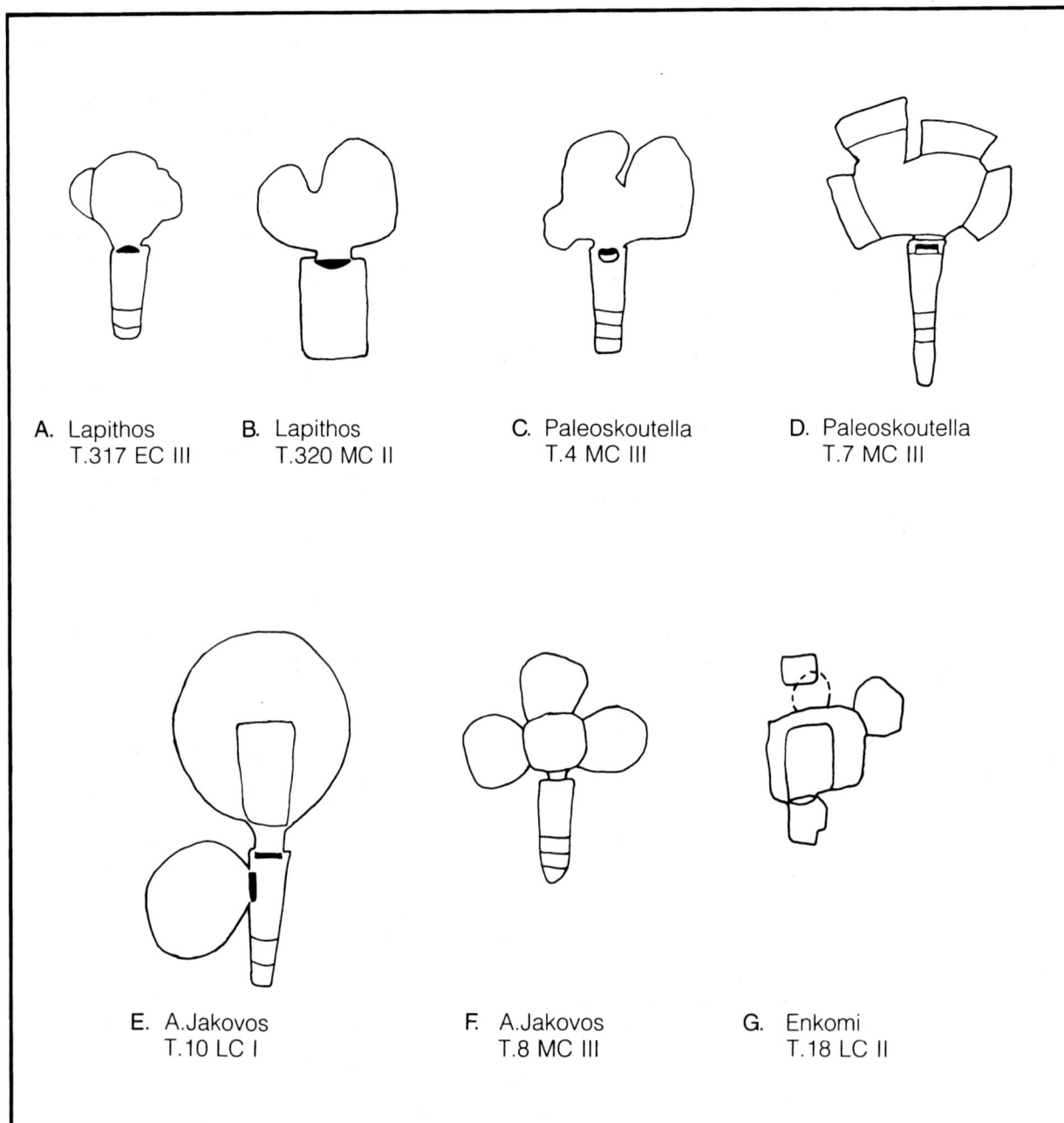

*Fig. 17.3: Cypriote chamber tombs. (Scale 1:200).*
*After Gjerstad, E., Lindros, J., Sjöqvist, E. & Westholm, A., 1934, fig.s 49, 50, 163, 166, 126, 209.*

the Mycenaean chamber tombs. While Stiebing proposed that these tombs represent simply the ongoing development of the 900 chamber tombs, in turn developed from the MB II bilobate tombs,[17] there are several significant differences between the two tomb groups, which require explanation.

The 900 and 500 chamber tombs differ most essentially in size and shape. Except for Tomb 544, the Philistine tombs are considerably larger than the 900 tombs, and their shape too is more standardised than that of the 900 tombs, with the chambers appearing to be almost square or rectangular, with well cut, fairly sharp corners. Other differences are that the central depression is consistently stepped at the sides (except in Tomb 544), and Tombs 542 and 552 have secondary chambers in the rear. It is possible that these differences are due to location, as the 900 tombs were carved into the side of the MB II rampart, while the 500 tombs were carved into the marl, or due to the particular preferences of the group responsible for them. Furthermore, as all the scholars have noted, there are several clear similarities between the two tomb groups. Nevertheless the differences are too striking for an evolutionary interpretation alone.

As noted above, the 500-group shows more resemblance to the Aegean tombs than the 900-group. Nevertheless, the resemblance is still nowhere near as close as it should be if we are talking of a group of Aegeans settling at Far'ah and re-establishing old customs in a new environment. So again this explanation, while pertinent, is inadequate.

Firm evidence has emerged over the last decade or so for Cyprus being the departure point for the move of the Sea Peoples to Canaan after at least a generation on the island.[18] It has been established elsewhere that Mycenaeans were present in small numbers in Cyprus in the second half of the thirteenth century BC, producing Rude Style pottery and Mycenaean-type ivories there.[19] It now seems that this population included Sea Peoples, who were thus in Cyprus long enough to become aware of local funerary practices, as well as tomb architecture. Elements of Cypriote funerary architecture were adopted by the Sea Peoples and, as Stiebing, Loffreda and Gonen have all proposed, were used after their arrival in Philistia, in the 500 cemetery at Tell el-Far'ah (S). Such elements include short stepped dromoi, benches, and perhaps a symmetrical depression in the centre of the chamber.[20]

It has recently been suggested that these tombs reflect Nubian influences both in architecture and in the anthropoid coffins found in Tombs 552 and 562.[21] However, chamber tombs such as those at Buhen, Soleb and Aniba in Nubia show little resemblance in the finer details to the tombs at Far'ah, and as with the Aegean tombs, the similarities should be seen as coincidental. Depressions, benches, stepped dromoi and steps into the chamber are, if anything, less frequent in Nubia than in the Aegean. A second problem with this proposal is that these tombs seem confined to Nubia in this period, and are absent in Lower Egypt and particularly the Delta area. While there is much evidence for influence from Lower Egypt and the Delta in Late Bronze Age Canaan, there is little suggestion of such influence from Nubia.[22]

Thus three influences played a part in the design of the five chamber tombs of the 500 cemetery: The influences of both the Mycenaean chamber tombs and the Cypriote chamber tombs which the Philistines brought with them, and finally, after their arrival at Far'ah itself, that of the chamber tombs of the 900 cemetery, which waere still in use when the 500 tombs were first carved. The newly arrived settlers would thus have had ample opportunity to study the design of these local Canaanite tombs.

## Chamber tombs at Tell el-Ajjul and Beth Shean

### Tell el-Ajjul

In his second season of excavation at Tell el-Ajjul, in 1932, Petrie uncovered a large cemetery to the northeast of the tell, just outside the MB II fosse, which he dated to the XVIII Dynasty. Separate from the cemetery, but clearly associated with it in date, was a chamber tomb, Tomb 1166, cut into the rampart, showing considerable resemblance to the 900-series chamber tombs at Tell el-Far'ah (S) (Fig. 17.4).[23] There was a deep shaft, with a single step leading to a short stomion. Two low steps led into a large trapezoid chamber. In the back left corner was a hollow in the floor surrounded by a wall, and in the back right-hand corner of the chamber a short, high step led to a secondary chamber whose floor was slightly higher than the main one.

The tomb is dated by the pottery to LB IIB, but was cut and in use from perhaps as early as the fourteenth century BC until the reign of Ramesses II. The similarity of the tomb's design and pottery to the 900 tombs at

17 Stiebing 1970, 40.
18 E.g., Karageorghis 1984; Karageorghis & Demas 1984; 1988.
19 Kantor 1956, 250-274; Karageorghis 1965, 231-259; Poursat 1977, 161-165; Anson 1980a, 109-127; 1980b, 1-18; Vermeule & Karageorghis 1982, 59-67; Jones and Catling 1986, 549-553.
20 Cf. Ajios Jakavos Tomb 10 and Enkomi Tomb 18 (fig. 16.3 E, 6). The later introduction of a Mycenaean chamber tomb tradition into Cyprus (e.g., Daniel 1937; Gjerstad 1948, 238-239; Benson 1973, 22-24; Karageorghis 1975, 25; 1983, 3-6) is the result of a much greater influx of a much larger population which settled in Cyprus, and which was thus able to continue former traditions in their new home. Hence this

chamber tomb tradition only appears in LC IIIB and C, after the arrival in Cyprus of the main influx of Aegeans fleeing their homeland.
21 Risser & Harvey 1992.
22 I am grateful to Dr Risser for forwarding me a draft of the unpublished paper presented at the American Institute of Archaeology Annual Meeting in 1992 by herself and Dr Harvey.
23 Petrie 1932, 15, Pls. LII-LIII.

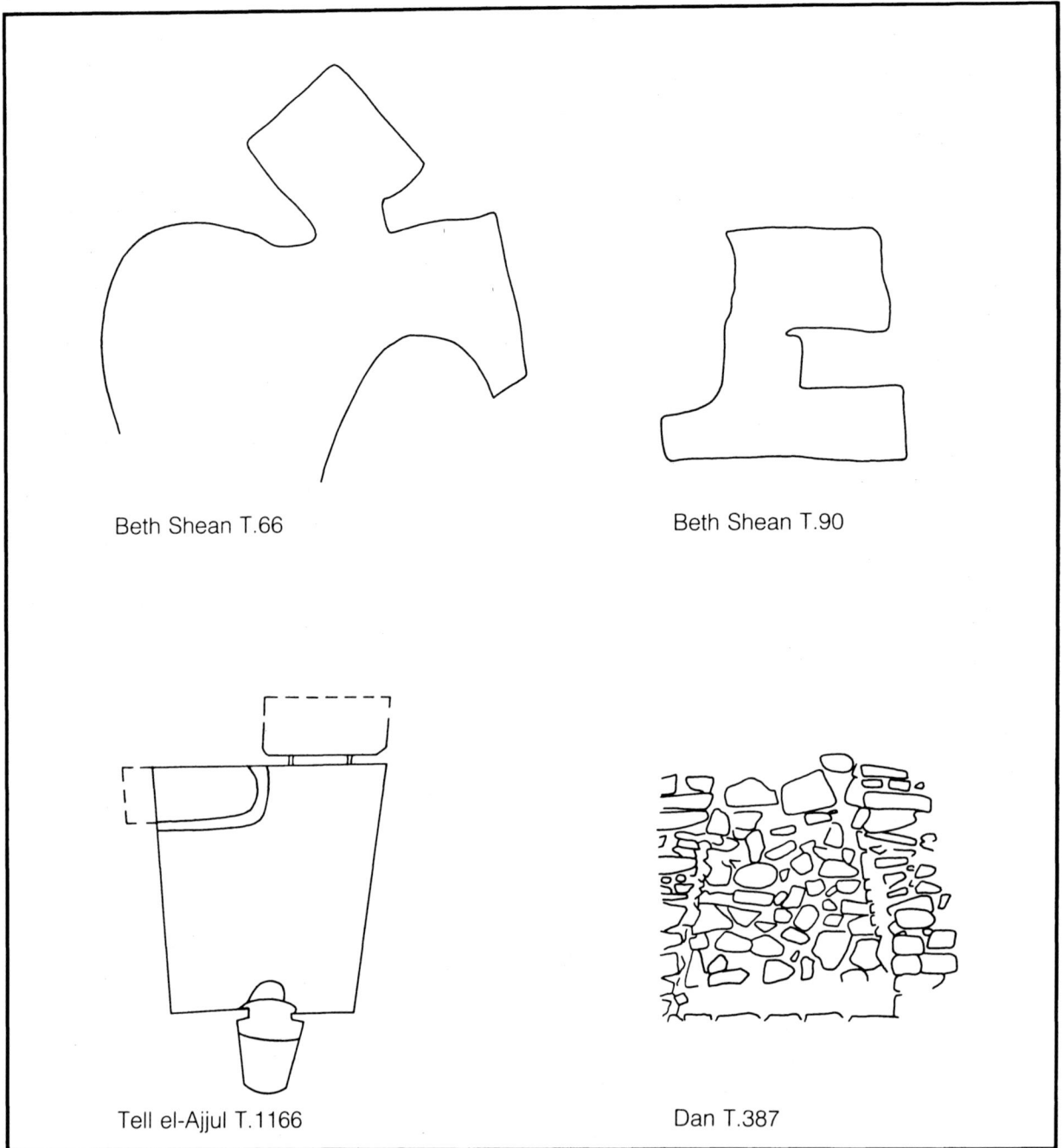

Beth Shean T.66

Beth Shean T.90

Tell el-Ajjul T.1166

Dan T.387

*Fig. 17.4: Chamber tombs from the northern cemetery at Beth Shean and at Tell el-Ajjul. (Scale 1:100). The "Mycenaean" tomb at Dan. (Not to scale). After Oren 1973, figs 9, 12; Ancient Gaza II, pl. LIII.*

Tell el-Far'ah (S), as noted by Gonen,[24] also suggests that the tomb was in use in the late thirteenth and perhaps early twelfth centuries BC.

The tomb's similarities with the Far'ah tombs are not as close as Gonen has suggested. Tomb 1166 has very sharp corners, unlike the Far'ah tombs, and no benches. Furthermore, the smaller chamber is quite different to those in both Far'ah cemeteries. There is no central depression either, only one in the far corner, in all likelihood a secondary alteration to the original design. For these reasons any association with Far'ah, while possible, must be very indirect.

The dromos, which in this case is a shaft, seems to preclude any Aegean connexion to this tomb, as it is quite unlike anything known from the Aegean area. It also seems to bear only a passing resemblance to Cypriote chamber tombs. The pottery too gives no clues as to the origin of the tomb's builders. We can but assume that this tomb, which is unique at Ajjul, was built by people who had perhaps seen other chamber tombs at nearby Tell el-Far'ah (S), and were inspired by them to design such a tomb. As at Tell el-Far'ah, the tomb was built into the MB II rampart, even though this caused it to be situated outside the bounds of its associated cemetery.

*Beth Shean*

Two tombs containing anthropoid coffins in the northern cemetery of Beth Shean, Tombs 66 and 90, display similarities to the chamber tombs of Tell el-Far'ah (S) (Fig. 17.4). Like other tombs in the same cemetery, these originally date from the EB IV (=MB I) period, and were altered and adjusted in the thirteenth century BC to accommodate the coffin burials. They were altered again in the Roman period during quarrying operations in the area. As to their LB II appearance, Oren speculates that Tomb 66 was originally entered from the south, and consisted of one roughly square chamber, with a smaller chamber adjoining at the back. It thus resembles Tombs 542 and 552 at Far'ah. Tomb 90, according to Oren's reconstruction, would have been entered from the west or south-west, and consisted of one possibly rectangular chamber partly divided by a buttress protruding from the centre of the rear wall in to the chamber. This resembles Tombs 934, 935 and 960 at Far'ah.[25]

The pottery and other finds from this group of tombs at Beth Shean suggested a date from the late thirteenth to the early eleventh century BC for these burials. Tomb 66 had Iron Age but no Late Bronze forms, while Tomb 90 had pottery from both periods, indicating it was in use throughout the period.[26]

Although Oren is a supporter of Waldbaum's attribution of the 900 chamber tombs at Tell el-Far'ah to an early Sea Peoples group,[27] and attributes these tombs to the Denyen on the basis of the resemblance of the anthropoid coffins found in them to the images of this group in the Medinet Habu reliefs,[28] Dothan has dated these coffins to the eleventh century BC, long after the tombs were recut in the thirteenth century.[29] Consequently the design of the tomb cannot be ascribed to the Sea Peoples that used the coffins, and it seems wise to accept Dothan's conclusion that "we cannot press the suggestion that the change in funerary architecture is connected with the arrival of the Philistines".[30] Indeed, the state of preservation of the tombs after the Roman quarrying, and especially the absence of an entrance, as well as the evidence that these were reworked EB IV tombs, lead us to an open verdict, not only of the origin of these tombs' design, but also on their original Late Bronze/Early Iron Age appearance.

## Stone-Built Corbelled Tombs

### Introduction

Stone-built corbelled tombs in Late Bronze Canaan have been found at Dan, the so-called "Mycenaean" tomb, dated to the fourteenth and thirteenth centuries BC[31] and at Aphek, dated to the thirteenth century BC.[32] The resemblance of these tombs to the grand tholos tombs at Mycenae has been noted, not only in terms of the similarities in building style and technique, but also – particularly in the case of the Dan tomb – in terms of the large percentage of Mycenaean pottery found.[33] However, it is important to note that stone-built and corbel-vaulted tombs are not unusual in the Near East in the periods leading up to and including the Late Bronze Age. They are found in Mesopotamia, northern Syria and Cyprus, as well as Palestine itself. Therefore any investigation into the origins of these tombs needs to range widely, and take all these factors into account.

The "Mycenaean" tomb, Tomb 387, at Dan was built in the inner slope of the MB II rampart of the city (Fig. 17.4). It is constructed of rough stones, with the floor consisting of flat basalt pavings. The walls slope inwards at an angle of 32°; the roof had collapsed into the tomb, damaging its contents. No entrance to the tomb was found, nor an entrance shaft, though one of the walls was disturbed and the entrance may have been there, or possibly from above.[34]

24  Gonen 1992a, 129-130.
25  Oren 1973, 102-103.
26  Ibid., 129-130.

27  Ibid., 141.
28  Ibid., 138, 140.
29  T. Dothan 1979, 101-102; 1982, 268-276.
30  T. Dothan 1982, 268[20].
31  Biran 1971.
32  Kochavi 1989, 76-78.
33  Gonen 1992a, 27; cf. Schaeffer 1939, 67-69, 99-103.
34  Biran 1974, 34.

The tomb contained approximately 40 burials spread over two generations. Twenty-five percent of the pottery was Mycenaean imported ware, and included one restorable chariot krater. In all there were 21 Mycenaean vessels, four Cypriote and 59 local vessels in the tomb. Other finds included four well-made basalt bowls, cosmetic implements of ivory and bone, gold leaf, and earrings and crescents of silver. There was also a quantity of weapons in the tomb which included swords, spearheads and arrowheads.

The finds date the period of the tomb's use from the mid-fourteenth century to the beginning of the thirteenth century BC. According to Biran, the rich finds and its situation on the edge of the town indicate the importance of the buried people; consequently he suggests this was a tomb of a high-status family, perhaps even that of the governor himself.[35]

The Aphek tomb was discovered on the edge of the tell, outside the limits of the Late Bronze city, and was described as being similar to the Mycenaean tomb at Dan. A Roman floor had cut into and partly destroyed the tomb; the fragmentary remains of the lower sections of the walls suggested it had a corbelled roof. The pottery which accompanied the 8 burials was a typical LB II assemblage of local Canaanite, Mycenaean and Cypriote imported ware dating to the thirteenth century BC, and the other grave-goods included a bronze dagger, a bronze Egyptian-style mirror, a gold earring, scarabs (some dating back to MB II), bracelets and beads. The excavator's opinion was that this too was a tomb belonging to a family of high social status.

## Analysis

Stone-built corbelled tombs are not unusual in the ancient world, and occur throughout the eastern Mediterranean and ancient Near East. They have a long history in the Aegean, where they date from the Neolithic on Crete through to the end of the Bronze Age on the mainland, culminating in the magnificent Mycenaean tholos tombs.[36] In Cyprus, three stone built tombs were found at Enkomi dating from the mid-sixteenth to the thirteenth centuries BC.[37]

In northern Syria and Mesopotamia there is another long record of these tombs. The earliest recorded occurrence is at Goksur in Turkestan, dating to the fifth millennium BC.[38] From the third millennium BC are tombs at Til Barsib (the "hypogeum")[39] and at Tilmen-Hüyük in south-east Turkey.[40] In the first half of the second millennium BC there are several corbel-vaulted

mudbrick tombs from Level I at Chagar Bazar[41] and in the second half of the second millennium BC several different categories of stone-built corbelled tombs occur at Ugarit.[42]

In Palestine itself there is also a stone-built tomb tradition dating to the Middle Bronze Age. Examples are from Aphek, dating to MB IIA,[43] Kabri, where the large stone-built Tomb 498 also dates to MB IIA,[44] Dan, where two such tombs, 1025 and 4663, are dated to MB IIA-B,[45] and at Megiddo, where a series of tombs was excavated by the University of Chicago expedition in strata XII-X, in areas AA and BB, dating to MB IIB,[46] and by Schumacher in his *Mittlereburg* dating to the mid-sixteenth century BC.[47]

Consequently there is no shortage of possible architectural influences on the LB II tombs at Dan and Aphek, and certainly were it not for the proportion of Mycenaean pottery in the Dan tomb there would be little reason to attribute Mycenaean influence in its construction. Biran has noted that during the fourteenth and thirteenth centuries BC Laish had close ties with the cities of the eastern Mediterranean coast, and via them with Cyprus and the Aegean.[48] While the rich pottery assemblage and the large number of young male burials and weapons in the tomb suggest this may have been a group of Mycenaean soldiers who lived at Dan and died there in battle, the construction of the tomb requires a more cautious consideration. Architecturally and chronologically the tomb's closest parallel is with a group of tombs at Ugarit classified as "category 401", of which Tomb 1068 has been described in detail.[49] Indeed, it is more reasonable to seek a parallel to the Dan tomb in the Levant than in the Aegean, and this tomb is very similar in many respects to the Dan tomb.

If the Dan tomb's architecture is thus Syrian, how are the strong Aegean connexions in its contents to be explained? It is possible that the tomb belonged to a wealthy and influential family, who drew on Syrian traditions to build the tombs, and whose wealth is reflected in the pottery and ivory and bone offerings. The large quantity of Mycenaean pottery is a product of the family's status and connexions with the coastal cities. In this respect, the tomb resembles a cave tomb at Sarafend, ancient Sarepta, which also produced a pottery assemblage remarkable for its large proportion of Mycenaean pottery. Here the conclusion too was that the tomb's contents were a product of the strong

35  Biran 1971; 1974.
36  Wace 1949, 16-19; Blegen 1954; Hood 1960; Mylonas 1966, 118-120.
37  Gjerstad et al. 1934, 570-573; Johnstone 1971; Pelon 1973; 1976.
38  Mellaart 1970, 301.
39  Thureau-Dangin & Dunand 1936, 96-97, Fig. 28.
40  Alkim 1969, 289.

41  Mallowan 1936, 14, 55; 1937, 107, 118-121 (Tombs G139, G141, G143, G154), Fig. 8.
42  Salles 1987.
43  Ory 1938.
44  Kempinski 1989, 27-30, III, IX-X, Figs. 6, 9-11.
45  Biran 1980; 1986; cf. also Ilan, in this volume.
46  Loud 1948, 15-16, Figs. 29-34, 379; 87-92, Figs. 202-205, 215-223, 230-235, 398-400.
47  Schumacher 1908, 13-23, Pls. IV-VI; Watzinger 1929, 1-17.
48  Biran 1971.
49  By Salles 1987, 158-173, Figs. 6-14. I am grateful to R. Ben Dov for referring me to Salles' paper and for drawing my attention to the similarities between these two tomb types.

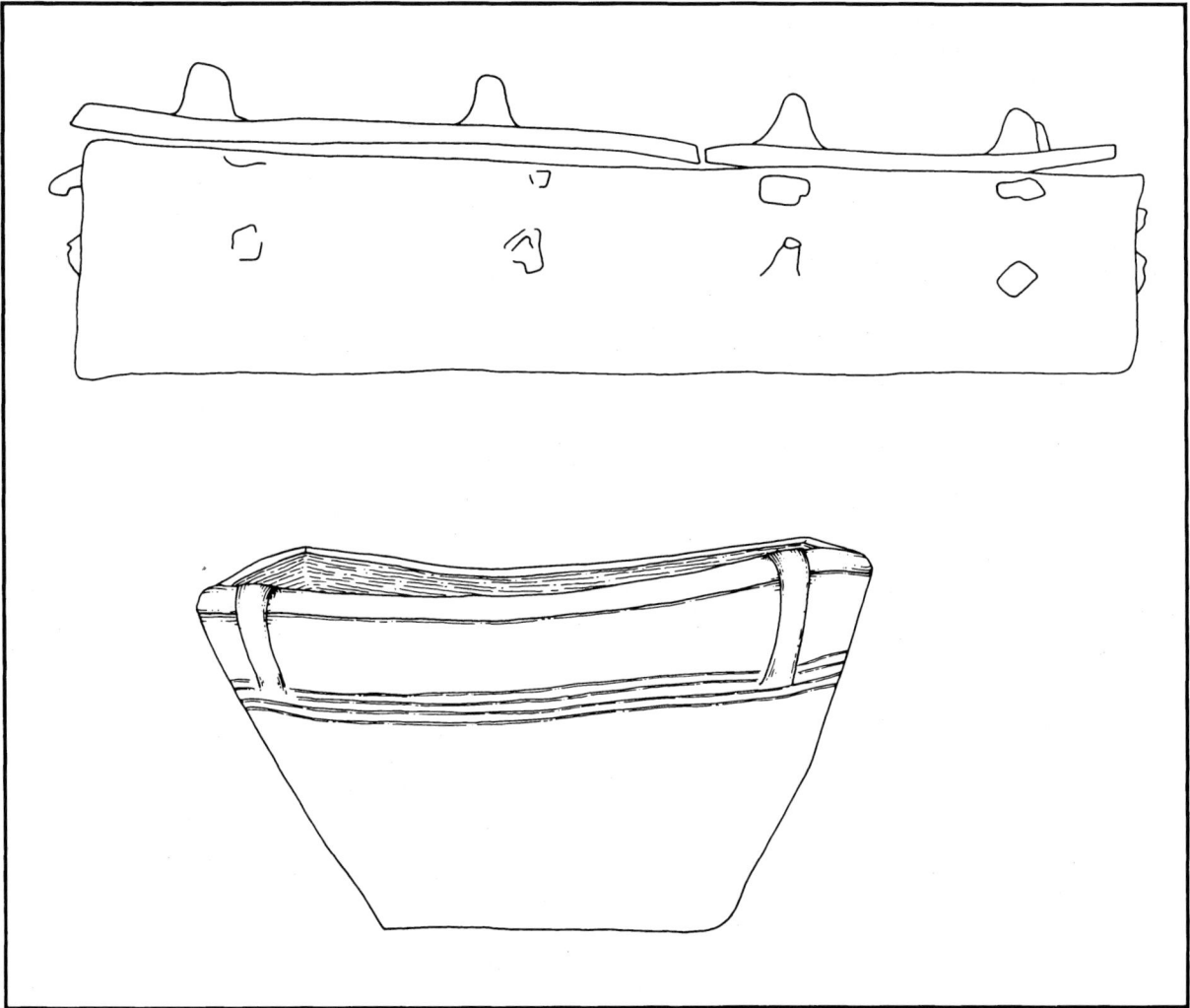

*Fig. 17.5: Larnakes from Gezer (above) and Acco (scale 1:10). After Seger, J.D.,1988 and APG pl.xv.*

commercial ties existing between the Aegean and the Levant in the fourteenth and thirteenth centuries BC, and of the wealth and status of the interred individuals, rather than of any Mycenaean ethnic identity they may have had.[50]

A similar conclusion may be drawn for the Aphek tomb. No plan of the tomb has yet been published, though it appears from the descriptions to be largely similar to the tomb at Dan. The offerings were typical of a LB II tomb, and Kochavi's interpretation of it as the tomb of a wealthy family seems appropriate.[51]

It may therefore be concluded that the appearance of these tombs in Late Bronze Canaan is due wholly or in part to influence from the north, from Syria. Similar tombs had already appeared in Palestine in the Middle Bronze Age, including at both of these sites, probably also due to northern influence, and these traditions may well have been passed on. Thus any proposed Aegean influence in the design or construction of these tombs is to be rejected.

## Larnakes

### Introduction

The larnax, or clay coffin, is typical of burials in Crete from the Middle and Late Minoan periods, though clay vessels containing burials first appear there in the Early Minoan period. The chest-shaped larnax appears in the MM III and LM I periods, replacing the earlier tub or oval shapes. They declined in popularity in LM I, but revived again in LM II and especially LM III, by which time they had spread throughout the island, as testified to by some 500 specimens.[52]

The larnax is rare in the Aegean outside Crete, though not totally unknown. A fragment is reported by Wace from Tomb 502 at Mycenae, dated to LH III. Wace also mentions two further LH III larnakes from tomb contents, one from Tomb 3 at Thebes, the other

---

50  Baramki 1958, 130; 1973, 195; Gonen 1992a, 124.
51  Kochavi 1989, 76-78.

52  Rutkowski 1968.

from Tomb 17 at the Argive Heraion.[53] The most significant Mycenaean manifestation of this method of burial is at Tanagra in Boeotia, dated to the end of LH IIIB/start of LH IIIC, c. 1300 BC.[54] These Mycenaean examples differ from the Cretan larnakes, particularly in their decoration. While the Cretan larnakes are on the whole decorated with marine and plant motifs, the Tanagra specimens have motifs of people in funereal scenes, particularly mourning women with raised hands.

Two larnakes from the Late Bronze Age have been excavated in Israel, at Gezer and at Acco's "Persian Garden" (Fig. 17.5). In the light of the larnax's known provenance, it is hardly surprising that they have been explained as evidence of Minoan groups resident in the land in this period. The Gezer larnax was found among the Lower Phase burials of Tomb I.10A, dated 1450-1380 BC.[55] It is described as "a plain box with multiple handles on the sides and on the lid",[56] and belongs to a type that was common in Crete in MM III but declined in popularity in LM I along with the general decline in larnakes during that period. The renaissance of the larnax in LM II saw a new type, with feet and painted decoration, all but replace the earlier multihandled type. This complicates the dating of the Gezer larnax, for while it is clearly of the earlier, MM III type, it is from a well-defined LB IB context (though this has recently been challenged[57]). Neutron activation analysis has shown that the coffin was manufactured locally. Pottery and other finds in the tomb, itself a transformed cistern, showed Cypriote and Egyptian connexions, and a few finds also indicated links with Syria, perhaps Ugarit. No Minoan or Mycenaean finds came from the cave in any of its four phases. Inside the sarcophagus itself, apart from the human remains, were only two artefacts, a bronze bracelet and a Cypriote Base Ring I tankard. The excavator concluded that the larnax is indicative of a Minoan presence at Gezer in the late fifteenth century BC, perhaps a trading colony but more likely refugees who fled Crete after the early LM IB disasters there.[58]

At the "Persian Garden" site at Acco, five undisturbed graves were excavated in a cemetery consisting of burial pits dug into the ground. The other graves had been disturbed by development works. The larnax was found in tomb C2, which differed from the others in that it incorporated a roughly rectangular cut made in the kurkar stone. Inside this cut were pottery offerings only, while skeletal material, pottery and the overturned larnax were situated some 1.5 m to the east. The excavated tombs were unelaborate, but the offerings, which included local and imported (mostly Mycenaean and Cypriote) pottery, seals, jewellery and weapons, suggest that people of some standing and wealth used them.[59]

In contrast to the Gezer larnax, the one from Acco is bath-tub shaped, and is handmade of coarse, poorly fired clay. It is decorated on three sides with four parallel bands in relief, and has four handles hanging from the rim down to the relief, one in each corner of the two long sides.

The pottery dates the site to the fourteenth century BC. A small amount of Mycenaean pottery came from the other graves, and on the surface was a sherd from a Minoan cup dating to LM IIIA.[60]

While the excavators raise the question of the larnax's origin, and of the possible Aegean influence represented by it, they refrain from drawing any conclusions.

## Discussion

The larnakes from Gezer and Acco would seem at first to provide clear evidence for an Aegean presence in Late Bronze Age Palestine, and Seger has noted the evidence for such an opinion. However, on further examination the theory of Minoan origin is perhaps not as certain as first appears.

It has already been noted that the Gezer larnax is physically closest to a style which was already out of use in Crete by the time it was constructed and used at Gezer. Indeed, while it bears similarities to the MM III larnakes, the Gezer specimen has no precise match in Crete.[61] The bath-tub type larnax from Acco is of a type prevalent in Crete during LM II and III. However, in both date and shape neither larnax can be associated with the Mycenaean larnakes from Tanagra. These were of the chest kind on legs, and are firmly dated to the thirteenth century BC.

Further reservations about any direct Aegean, and especially Minoan, association with these larnakes arise with the examination of the associated finds. As has been noted above, Gezer tomb I.10A is distinguished by the total absence of any Mycenaean and Minoan pottery. Rather, the tomb was particularly rich in Cypriote pottery, and in Israel only Lachish tomb 216 has more Cypriote pottery.[62] At Acco the pottery is more typical of Late Bronze assemblages in Israel. In addition to the local ware, there is a fairly large collection of Cypriote, Aegean (including the one Minoan sherd) and Egyptian material.[63] Thus, in terms of pottery at least, the connexions with Crete are non-existent at Gezer and tenuous at Acco.

53 Wace 1932, 9³, Fig. 4.
54 Spyropoulos 1970; 1972.
55 Seger 1988, 52, 114-115.
56 Ibid., 52.
57 Bourke 1993, 76.
58 Seger 1988, 52, 114, 152.

59 Ben-Arieh & Edelstein 1977, 1, 15.
60 Ben-Arieh & Edelstein 1977, 45-51.
61 Rutkowski 1968; Seger 1988, 114.
62 Seger 1988, 50.
63 Ben-Arieh & Edelstein 1977, 16-19.

Gonen has suggested a possible connexion between the two larnakes on the basis of the metal finds.[64] She points out that among the finds in the Gezer tomb were several bronze arrowheads similar to a group from Acco,[65] but these items are not uncommon in Palestine during this period, and considering the time-gap between the two sites the similarities are probably coincidental.[66]

In addition to the discrepancies in date and associated finds, other lesser factors also serve to blur any proposed Minoan connexion. Among these is the interesting anthropological finding at Gezer that the 88 or more skeletons in Cave I.10A were all members of an extended family group.[67] This being so, the question that needs to be asked is why only one sarcophagus was made, if there were such strong Minoan connexions. It may be significant that 11 of the 12 skeletons in the sarcophagus were of infants and children (the twelfth was an adult woman), yet the total infants and children in the tomb numbered 31, meaning that the majority of them were buried outside the sarcophagus.[68]

Thus, the appearance of the two larnakes in Late Bronze Age Canaan raises more questions than it answers. In the light of these observations, the most that can be said is that while the Aegean, and Crete in particular, remains the only likely origin for the larnax concept as manifested at Gezer and Acco, the association is nevertheless blurred. There is no further evidence at either site for resident Minoan groups; indeed, there is very little evidence at all for Aegean visitors to southern Canaan throughout the Late Bronze Age. Consequently, no more may safely be concluded about these larnakes. The evidence is simply too flimsy, particularly in respect of any Mycenaean connexions, to understand the relationship between these larnakes and their Aegean origins.

---

# Cremation

## Introduction

Cremation burials are not usually associated with the Late Bronze Age in Palestine; they only become common in Iron Age II. However, there are three isolated incidents of Late Bronze Age cremations, at Jericho,[69] Tell Beit Mirsim,[70] and Amman Airport,[71] all dating to LB II.

Further north on the Levantine coast, cremation burials dating to around 1200 BC are reported at Alalakh,[72] Hama,[73] Carchemish,[74] Tell Sukas[75] and other sites. These have been attributed to the influence of the Sea Peoples,[76] an argument which is possibly supported by the excavation of a cremation burial dating to the mid-eleventh century BC at Azor in Philistia.[77] While not common in the Late Bronze Age Aegean, cremation is not unrepresented there, and is found at several sites relating to Mycenae as well as at Troy.

The other area proposed as the origin of this practice is Anatolia, where the Hittites are known to have practised cremation. A series of texts found at Boghazkoy describes the cremation of a king and queen, and cremation cemeteries there and at several other central and southern Anatolian sites suggest the practice was used from an early date for commoners as well.[78]

## Cremation burials in Late Bronze Age Canaan

Garstang's excavations at Jericho uncovered little evidence of occupation during the fourteenth and thirteenth centuries BC. From a necropolis dated by Garstang to around 1200 BC came a pit grave which was isolated from the others, and in the bottom of which were some half-cremated remains, and a scarab of Tutmoses III. The rest of the pit contained incinerated bones as well as offerings, including bracelets of bronze and iron, and Iron Age I pottery. Garstang believed the tomb was evidence of the presence of a garrison of foreign mercenaries, either Hittites or Sea Peoples, established by Ramesses II or III perhaps as early as the fifteenth century BC.[79] Alternatively, Block-Smith has suggested that the fact that the bones were only partially burned may indicate an unintentional tomb fire, or that spontaneous combustion was responsible.[80]

At Tell Beit Mirsim the charred remains of an elderly individual were found relating to the sherds of a large jar, in a fourteenth-century BC context. Albright offers no interpretation of the find.[81]

During preparatory work on the building of the airport at Amman in Jordan, a large square building with massive walls and a nearby platform was uncovered several kilometers from Canaanite Amman. A central room or hall, with a pillar base in the middle, is surrounded by rooms on each side. A wealth of finds, including Aegean pottery, Egyptian stone vessels,

---

64    Gonen 1979, 110.
65    Cf. Seger 1988, Pls.19:10, 27:3-4, with Ben-Arieh & Edelstein 1977, Figs. 18:2, 20-21.
66    Seger 1988, 102-104.
67    Ibid., 131.
68    Ibid., 66, 130.
69    Garstang 1932, 37; 1933, 36.
70    Albright 1938, 75-76.
71    Herr 1983.

72    Woolley 1955, 201-203.
73    Riis 1948, 192-203.
74    Woolley 1952, 225.
75    Riis 1962, 140-141.
76    Culican 1982, 55.
77    M. Dothan 1960; 1961; 1989.
78    Gurney 1990, 137-140.
79    Garstang 1932, 37; 1933, 36.
80    Block-Smith 1992, 38.
81    Albright 1938, 75-76.

scarabs, seals, bronze weapons and gold jewellery, date the structure to the second half of the thirteenth century BC. A very large quantity of burnt human bones of both adults and children was found in and around the structure.[82]

The function of the building found on the Amman Airport site has been a matter of debate ever since its discovery, with opinions ranging from an Iranian-type "fire-temple", to a temple for human sacrifice, to a tribal league centre.[83] Others have rejected a ritual function, preferring to see it as a watchtower or residency.[84] The site was re-excavated in 1976 by Herr, who rejected a domestic function for the building and reinterpreted it as a mortuary where cremations took place. The absence of a cremation tradition among the Canaanites and the lack of settlement evidence in the vicinity led Herr to suggest that the site was used by Hittites or Neo-Hittites who were in the area to defend their strategic interests there against Egypt.[85]

## Discussion

### Cremations in the Aegean in the Late Bronze Age

Although the predominant method of burial in the Aegean during the Mycenaean period was inhumation, a few isolated cremation burials are known. These sites include Traghana in Triphylia (LH II)[86] and Musgebi, Astipalaia and Karpathos in the Dodecanese (LH IIIB).[87] In LH IIIC the practice becomes more common, and cremation burials appear, for example, on the islands of Naxos, Rhodes, Cos[88] and Salamis, at Argos, Athenian Kerameikos,[89] Perati,[90] and at Prosymna.[91]

Thus while cremations were rare in the Greek world during the Mycenaean period, especially before LH IIIC, they gain in popularity in the sub-Mycenaean phase until they become quite widespread in the Proto-Geometric and Geometric periods.

At Troy, outside the Mycenaean sphere of influence, there is more evidence for cremation. A cremation cemetery from level VIh (dated 1325-?1275 BC) was discovered by the British expedition under Blegen.[92] The cemetery was outside the town, and consisted of urns filled with charred human bones and occasionally pottery and animal bones and teeth, which had been closed with a stone or bowl and then buried in pits in the earth. Near the urn cemetery was a structure which may have been a crematory where the dead were incinerated. A place of apparently similar function, though rougher design, was discovered closer to the citadel.[93]

A short distance from Troy itself, at Besik Tepe, a German expedition has more recently uncovered another thirteenth-century BC urn cemetery, again set apart from the settlement, this time only 15 m from the present seashore.[94] Unlike Blegen's cemetery, this one was of wealthy individuals, and the wealthiest grave contained cremation burials. Based on the finds and the cemetery's proximity to the shore, the excavator is of the opinion that the Besik cemetery was of an unidentified merchant community not native to Troy.

### Cremations in north Syria in the Late Bronze Age

Urn burials with cremated human remains were excavated at several sites on the northern Canaanite coast dating to the very end of the Late Bronze Age, around 1200 BC. These sites include Alalakh – where cremation started as early as the sixteenth century BC and increased in use until by the thirteenth century it was "at least as common as burial",[95] Hama,[96] Rasm et-Tanjara and Tell el-Khanzourah,[97] and at Tell Sukas, where the cremations are not recorded as coming from urns, but simply as being found with groups of funerary gifts.[98]

One theory explaining the origin of these north Syrian cremations around 1200 BC is that they were introduced from the Aegean by the Sea Peoples. Thus, Barnett writes in *The Cambridge Ancient History* that the attack by the Sea Peoples on Egypt in the eighth year of Ramesses III was preceded by a series of conquests in north Syria. The introduction of cremation immediately follows these attacks, and Barnett concludes it was therefore an innovation of the Sea Peoples.[99] Support for this view comes from Riis, the excavator of Hama,[100] and from M. Dothan, who ascribes the practice of cremation as it appears in the lone urn burial of this type from Azor, in the eleventh century BC, to the Sea Peoples. However, Dothan suggests that the Sea Peoples may have acquired the practice in northern Syria before settling in southern Canaan.[101]

On the other hand, it is clear that cremation was the exception in Mycenaean Greece, and the likelihood

82  Hennessy 1966; Herr 1983.
83  Wright 1966; Hennessy 1966; Campbell & Wright 1969.
84  Fritz 1971; cf. also Herr 1983, 224.
85  Herr 1983, contra Mazar 1990, 256[21].
86  Mylonas 1966, 112.
87  Mee 1988, 303, and references there cited.
88  Desborough 1975, 663.
89  Kurtz & Boardman 1971, 25-26, 344, and references there cited..
90  Iakovides 1969, 30-36, 40-49, 86-93, 132-144, 159-166, 270-273, 275-284, 422-425; Paidoussis & Sbarounis 1975, 129.
91  Mylonas 1966, 112.
92  Blegen, Caskey & Rawson 1953, 370-391.

93  Ibid., 391-395.
94  Latacz 1986.
95  Woolley 1955, 201-223; 1968, 157.
96  Riis 1948, 4, 28-30, 192-193.
97  Athanassiou 1977, 223[5], 239-240.
98  Riis 1962, 140-141.
99  Barnett 1975, 369-370.
100  Riis 1948, 201-203.
101  M. Dothan 1989.

of any Aegean-based group transporting to foreign lands an exception to tradition, rather than the tradition itself, is very small. Consequently, if Sea Peoples that originated in the Aegean brought with them any particular kind of burial tradition, it would most likely have been some form of inhumation or chamber burials rather than cremation.

Far more likely is that the north Syrian cremations were introduced by newcomers from the northwest. The Hittite texts from Boghazkoy have already been mentioned,[102] and cremation burials at this and other Hittite sites produced cremated remains buried in pairs of jars laid mouth-to-mouth.[103] Further evidence that the Hittites practised cremation comes from a cemetery dating from the first half of the second millennium BC at Osmankayasi. Here the ashes of the dead were placed in small vessels inside jars laid in pairs mouth-to-mouth, which in turn were placed in a burial cave.[104] This use of two jars is characteristic of Hittite burials, and appears in Palestine at Kfar Yehoshua[105] and in large quantities at Tell es-Saidiyeh, where several examples come from the Late Bronze and Early Iron Ages.[106]

Anatolian influence is suggested at Alalakh, where Woolley proposed that immigrants from the north initially trickled in until in the thirteenth century BC they came in large numbers.[107] Pottery and other finds at Rasm-et-Tanjara also suggested Anatolian influence,[108] while for Hama, Riis records that anthropological studies of the human remains from the site suggest that new elements entered this area from the northwest, having crossed the Taurus mountains by 1200 BC.[109]

It is important to note that at north Syrian sites too, cremation is the exception (except, perhaps, at Tanjara, where the cremation cemetery contained the only burials found at the site[110]) and the practice did not become widespread until later in the Iron Age. The end of the Bronze Age in the Aegean and the Near East is known to have been a period of considerable flux, with great migrations of peoples. The collapse of Mycenaean Greece, the movements of the Sea Peoples and the decline of the Hittite empire were all elements in this process. With such a great movement of peoples it is hardly surprising that cremations should appear in both the Aegean and the Near East. Both areas were also important trading centres so that, as at Besik Tepe, foreign merchants may have been resident there, and have been buried in a way that they were accoustomed to.

There is one more alternative that should be considered. The appearance of rare and sporadic cremations, as in Late Bronze Age Canaan, may be an independent local development. Piggott has noted that in the thirteenth century BC in Europe cremation burials began to appear and increase in number until they replaced the barrow inhumations that were the normal method until then. He notes specifically that there was no evidence of newcomers in this change, but rather that it was a method which had been used sporadically in the past and which suddenly gained in popularity.[111] Similarly Snodgrass writes that the move from inhumation to cremation in post-Mycenaean Greece, and in Athens in particular, is probably unrelated to changes in population or religion.[112]

Ethnographic studies have shown quite clearly that burial customs need not always be linked to religious beliefs, that they are not necessarily due to fresh influences from outside, and that any number of factors, both internal and external, may be responsible for such changes.[113] Reasons for cremating individuals rather than burying them by inhumation include death from plague or some other disease, reasons of race, religion, or social standing – either the deceased were social outcasts[114] or were of high social status.[115] A rise in population, economic reasons, or lack of space[116] are all possible reasons for a switch to cremation.

If we return to the three cremation examples from Late Bronze Palestine, it is striking that they are all different. One is an urn burial (Tell Beit Mirsim), one a pit burial (Jericho), and the third is associated with a large building (Amman Airport). Furthermore, cremation had been practised sporadically in Palestine since the late fourth millennium BC.[117] Consequently, while foreign influence may not be ruled out for the LB examples, particularly for the Amman building, it seems at least as possible that other less easily identifiable factors may have been involved. Concerning the north Syrian sites, it seems that while the area was a meeting place of several different non-native groups at this time, any foreign influence in the introduction of cremation appears more likely to have come from Anatolia than from the Aegean.

## Conclusion

Late Bronze Age Canaan had clearly defined funerary traditions of its own. It is therefore perhaps inevita-

102 Cf. above, p.9.
103 Gurney 1980, 168; 1990, 137-140.
104 Bittel et al. 1958, 22-32.
105 Druks 1966.
106 Tubb 1988, 60-61, Fig. 42.
107 Woolley 1955, 202-203; 1968, 157-158.
108 Athanassiou 1977, 241-244.
109 Riis 1948, 202-203.
110 Athanassiou 1977, 240.

111 Piggott 1965, 145.
112 Snodgrass 1971, 144-146.
113 Ucko 1970.
114 E.g., Ur: Woolley 1934, 142-143.
115 E.g., the Boghazkoy text: Gurney 1990, 137-138.
116 E.g., Motya: Whitaker 1921, 229.
117 Bienkowski 1982, 89.

ble that explanations for the exceptions to these customs should have been sought outside the cultural borders of Canaan. The temptation to invoke Mycenaean and other Aegean influences in this regard has proved strong, and not without cause. However, in each of the four categories addressed in this paper it has been shown that arguments for such influence are flawed, and in three of the four cases other explanations are perhaps closer to reality.

Late Bronze Age Canaan's situation meant that it was subject to many and diverse influences, and not only from the Aegean. Egyptians, Cypriotes, Syrians, Mesopotamians and Anatolians all visited Canaan's shores, and all left their mark. Consequently it is hardly surprising that the four cases of exceptional funerary practices discussed here probably reflect four different sources of influence.

*Acknowledgements*
I am grateful to Professor Trude Dothan, Professor Jane Waldbaum and Dr P.R.S. Moorey for advice and encouragement in the preparation of this paper, and to the Director and staff at the W.F. Albright Institute for Archaeological Research in Jerusalem, where I was a research fellow in 1990-91. Financial support came from the University of Cape Town, the Hebrew University of Jerusalem, and the South African Zionist Federation Trust.

# 18 Rituel Mortuaire et Rituel Social à Ras Shamra/Ougarit

## Jean-François Salles

ABSTRACT—*The interpretation of the funerary data from Ras Shamra/Ugarit (ancient excavations by C.F.A. Schaeffer, since 1929, and recent excavation by M. Yon, since 1978) is heavily hampered by the lack of well published material (especially anthropological) – and by a general plundering of the tombs of the city, probably in ancient times. On the other hand, the cuneiform literature from Ugarit is not really profuse about death and funerary rituals. This paper deals with three aspects of what we can try to understand of the conception of death in Ras Shamra. The container of the dead body, i.e. the subterranean built-tomb, provides some paths of interpretation through its architecture and its installations, revealing a few hints of the organization of the society and its beliefs about death. What can be elucidated by the excavation and the texts of the funerary ceremonial at the time of the burial suggests a strong hierarchy, where an elite might have practiced the funerary rituals as an option to strengthen its pre-eminence. Finally, the post-mortem rituals – or cult of ancestors – remain rather confused, without true archaeological basis: their main purpose seems to have brought blessings on the kingdom and its rulers – and on the social body?*

La notion de rituel mortuaire paraît devoir inclure, dans le cas précis de Ras Shamra, trois niveaux d'analyse articulés autour de l'objet-tombe, l'un des problèmes majeurs étant celui de la relation qui s'établit entre les rituels supposés (données socio-religieuses) et l'espace archéologique proprement dit (données matérielles le plus souvent disparues). À chacune des étapes de la mort, en effet, correspondent des comportements sociaux spécifiques se traduisant probablement par des contraintes matérielles qu'on va retrouver – ou que l'archéologue doit tenter de découvrir – dans l'agencement de la tombe: architecture, intégration dans l'espace environnant, aménagements spéciaux, etc., toutes données matérielles structurellement liées à des manifestations sociales. Comme dans l'archéologie des pays bibliques, l'éclairage des textes est indispensable pour saisir ces comportements; mais il faut souligner combien les textes relatifs à la mort sont elliptiques dans la littérature ougaritique, et une adéquation entre les données de l'archéologie et les interprétations des textes est rarement atteinte: les réflexions qui vont suivre relèvent donc plus de l'hypothèse ou de la suggestion que de certitudes, même archéologiques.

Les trois moments du rituel mortuaire – au sens large du terme – sont, successivement:

1. le passage de vie à trépas, l'instant de la mort, celui que les textes mythiques d'Ougarit expriment ainsi: « La vie d'Aqhat s'est échappée comme un vent, son principe vital comme une glaire, comme une fumée de ses narines », Légende de Danel:[1] faut-il rappeler que le terme *npš* qui désigne dans ces textes le principe vital deviendra le *nephès* araméen servant à définir le monument funéraire? Le rituel, ou plutôt les réactions à ce moment, sont plus gestuelles qu'architecturales ou matérielles, donc sans traces archéologiques. Certaines manifestations du deuil sont citées dans les textes: « Il répand sur sa tête l'ordure du deuil, sur son crâne la poussière où il se roule. Il couvre ses reins d'un sac, il se taillade la peau avec une pierre, il tranche sa double tresse au rasoir, il fend par trois fois ses joues et son menton », Baal et la Mort;[2] « Elle couvre ses reins d'un sac, elle se taillade la peau avec une pierre... »,[3] (Cf. le deuil israélite: « Je mettrai le sac sur tous les reins, la calvitie sur toutes les têtes », *Amos*, 8, 10), etc. On ne connaît, bien sûr, presque rien de

---

1 Caquot, Sznycer & Herdner 1974, 440.
2 Ibid., 260-261.
3 Ibid., 254.

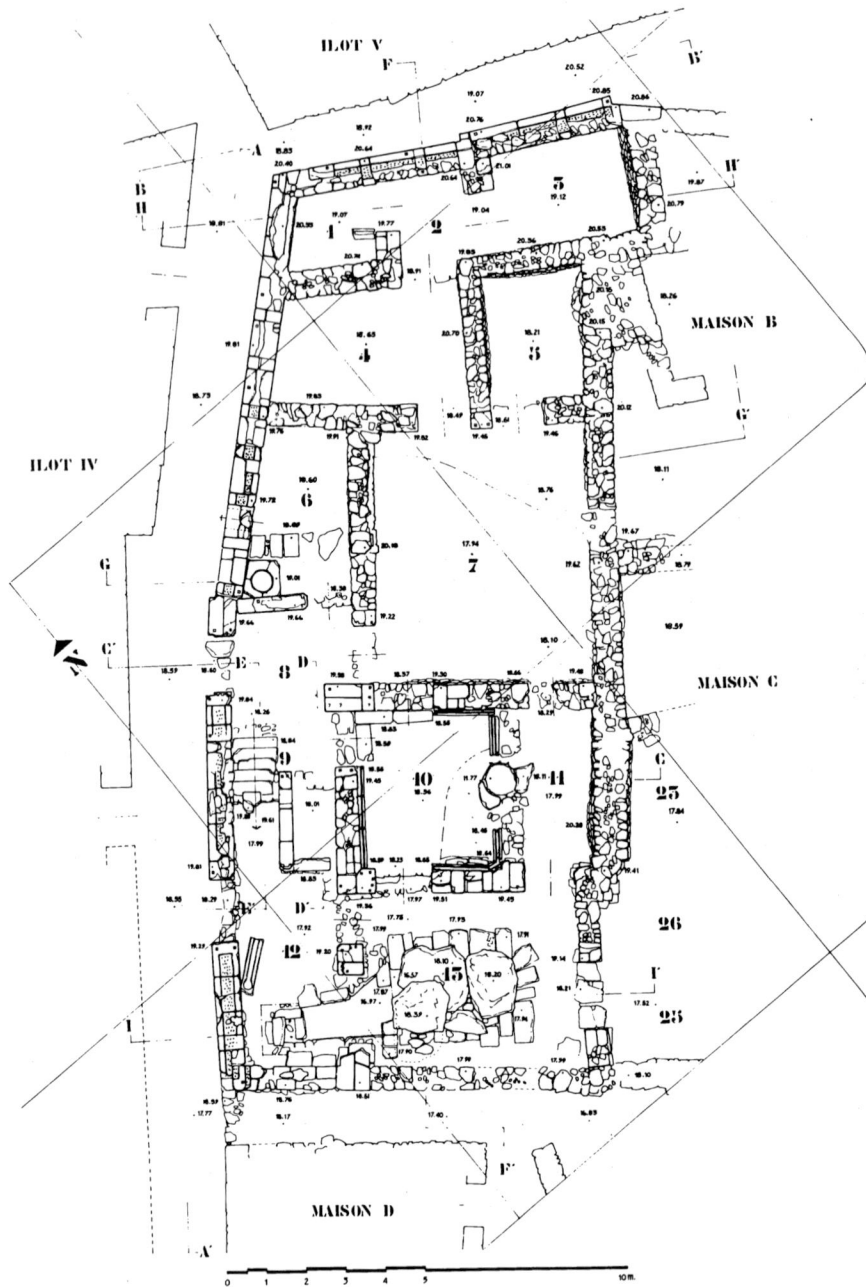

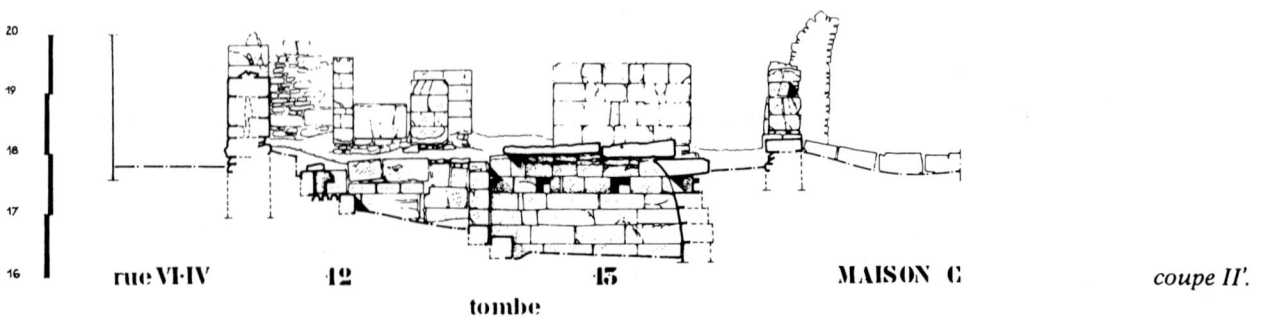

*Fig. 18.1: Plan d'une tombe souterraine de Ras Shamra,*
*à prendre dans Callot 1983.*

ces rituels gestuels instantanés,[4] mais c'est cet événement seul, la mort, qui justifie *l'existence de la tombe*: il y a des morts sans tombe, rarement des tombes sans mort.

2. Puis vient le rite de l'enterrement proprement dit, c'est-à-dire, en termes d'anthropologie contemporaine, le moment où la société se « débarrasse » du cadavre,[5] ou, plus poétiquement en termes ougaritiques, celui où le défunt rejoint le monde des morts, c'est-à-dire la terre (*'arṣ*), en-dessous (*tḥt*). Logiquement, le lieu de l'événement est la tombe, mais *la tombe ouverte*, et les comportements sociaux de cet instant – ainsi que les contraintes matérielles qui leur sont associées – peuvent être désignés comme le « rituel funèbre », par référence au terme de cérémonie funèbre qui caractérise tout enterrement.

3. Plus tard, enfin, le mort enterré est l'objet d'attentions et de soins – plus ou moins réguliers – et les mânes ougaritiques, les *Rephaïm*, sont invoqués pour protéger la famille, le clan, la ville ou le royaume[6] – avec une restriction, cependant: tous les textes sur les *Rephaïm* nous parlent des ancêtres royaux ou des mânes des aristocrates, et on ne sait rien des croyances populaires, sauf à les calquer sur les données bibliques. A ce(s) moment(s)-là, on peut supposer que la *tombe était fermée* (bien que cela reste à démontrer) et, *a priori*, les contraintes matérielles sont alors différentes: ce sont ces comportements qui constituent le « rituel funéraire »

———————

Comme dans tout l'Orient du IIe millénaire av. J.-C., la mort non enterrée est une mort ignominieuse à Ougarit [« Que je regarde s'il y a un lambeau de chair ou un bout d'os pour pleurer et l'enterrer, pour le placer dans la terre, le cimetière divin », Légende de Danel],[7] et le retour à la terre, le « cimetière divin », une nécessité impérieuse. Une caractéristique de Ras Shamra, qui n'est pas unique en Orient, est que les tombes connues sont situées à l'intérieur la ville, en général sous les maisons auxquelles elles sont structurellement associées (Fig. 18.1).[8] L'architecture de ces caveaux souterrains évolue du XVIIIe à la fin du XIIIe s. av. J.-C., et les différents types en ont été présentés à plusieurs re-

prises.[9] Même si de nombreux aménagements changent ou se perfectionnent au cours des siècles, les principes de base de construction et les modes d'utilisation restent les mêmes, et ce qui pourra être dit des grands caveaux de la phase finale de la cité est aussi valable, *mutatis mutandis*, pour les tombes souterraines plus rustiques du Bronze Moyen. Les monuments les plus accomplis, en effet, datent de la dernière période de l'histoire de la ville, fin du XIVe et XIIIe s. av. J.-C.; C.F.A. Schaeffer utilise fréquemment l'expression « tombeaux égéens » pour les désigner, laissant supposer la présence d'une colonie mycénienne à Ougarit qui aurait imposé ses propres coutumes funéraires, mais on a fermement démontré depuis que ces deux traditions étaient totalement indépendantes.[10]

Les tombes construites sous les maisons ne constituent qu'un seul aspect – le mieux connu – des rituels mortuaires dans le royaume d'Ougarit, dont on ignore presque tout. A la fin du IIIe/début du IIe millénaire, des cimetières de sépultures en pleine terre existaient près du temple de Baal, sur l'acropole de Ras Shamra, avant (?) l'apparition des tombeaux construits: mais la chronologie exacte de ces ensembles reste très floue, seuls des rapports sommaires étant disponibles.[11] Pour l'ensemble de la ville, il faudrait pouvoir comparer le nombre total des tombeaux – nombre réel inconnu: l'inventaire des fouilles anciennes n'est pas établi, beaucoup de tombes mentionnées dans les rapports ayant disparu et de nombreuses constructions visibles sur le terrain n'étant mentionnées nulle part; nombre présumé sur la totalité du site, dont moins d'un quart a été fouillé, impossible à établir – avec l'évolution démographique présumée de la population au cours du IIe millénaire, sujet de vifs débats.[12] L'hypothèse généralement admise de caveaux familiaux à inhumations multiples et successives ne suffirait certainement pas à rendre compte de toute la mortalité ougaritaine au IIe millénaire, mais toute étude sérieuse sur ce point se heurte à l'absence de données anthropologiques pour les anciennes fouilles (à l'exception de quelques mentions d'ossements ou de squelettes); les tombes récemment fouillées n'ont livré que des esquilles d'ossements humains. Enfin, absolument rien n'est connu des rites d'inhumation de la population rurale du royaume. Qui, donc, était enterré autrement, et comment, demeurent des questions sans réponse, et c'est un truisme de constater que les rites mortuaires connus à Ras Shamra sont ceux d'une partie seulement d'un société fortement urbanisée.

Il faut d'abord corriger une règle parfois admise trop vite: la présence nécessaire d'un caveau funéraire

———————

4    Gruber 1980.
5    Thomas 1980.
6    Caquot 1981.
7    Caquot, Sznycer & Herdner 1974, 450.
8    Callot 1983; Salles 1987. Cette association est normale et banale, et il faut absolument éviter d'errer dans des interprétations abusives, du type : « A Ras Shamra, les fondations des murs à piliers sont souvent en belles pierres de taille parce que chaque maison avait sa propre tombe souterraine; on sait que les Orientaux, et les Phéniciens en particulier, accordaient beaucoup de soin à la demeure du mort : on ne sera donc pas surpris de ce que l'architecture de la maison souterraine soit plus soignée que celle de la maison des vivants » (Elayi 1980, 172).

9    Schaeffer 1939a; Saadé 1979; Courtois 1979.
10   Servais 1985.
11   Schaeffer 1934.
12   Garr 1987; Yon 1992.

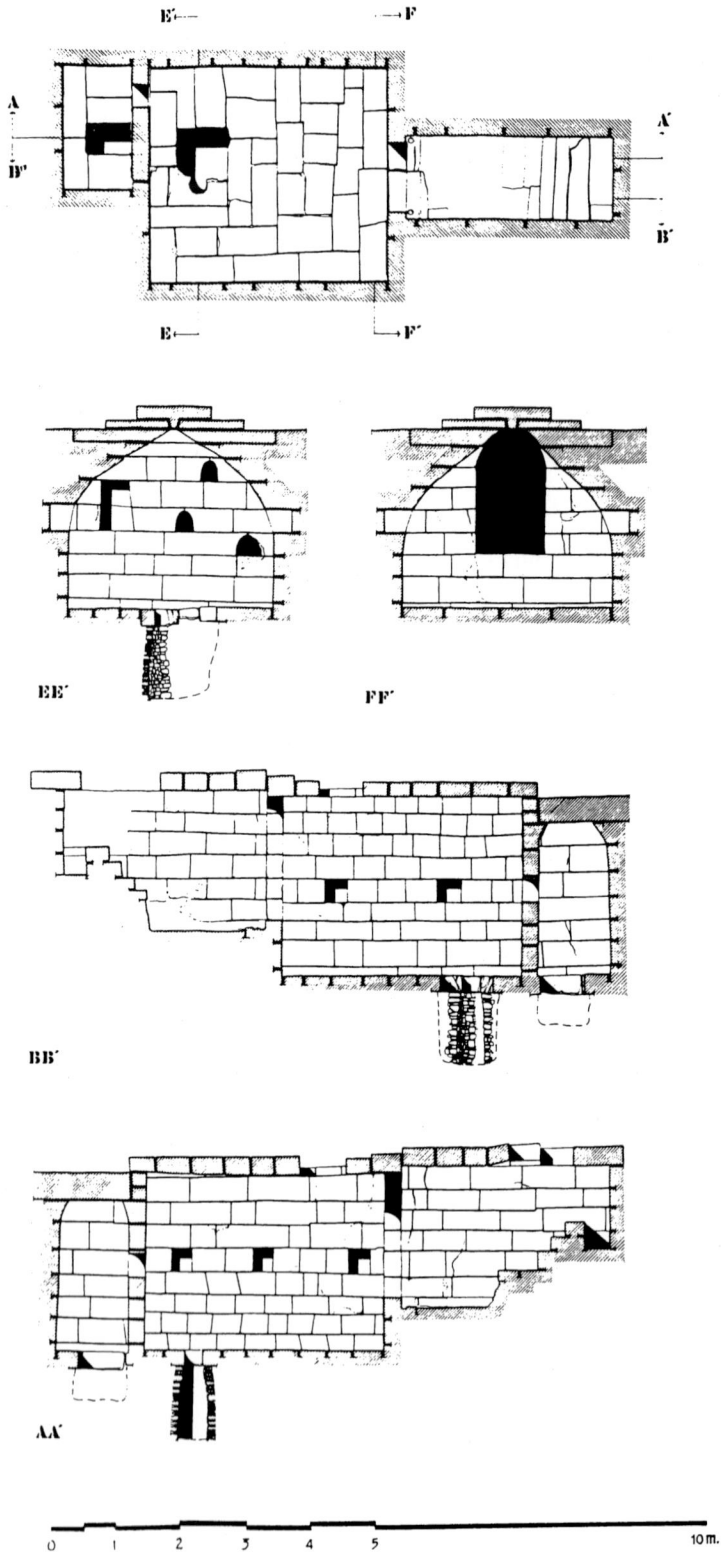

Fig. 18.2: Plan d'un grand caveau.

dans chaque maison.[13] La publication imminente d'un secteur cohérent de l'espace urbain, la tranchée Ville-Sud,[14] démontre que plusieurs maisons ne possédaient pas de tombe construite au sous-sol – et plusieurs autres exemples en existent dans la ville; par contre, un bâtiment dont la fonction demeure inconnue, abritait deux caveaux monumentaux dans son soubassement. Plusieurs hypothèses pourraient justifier cette apparente discordance entre l'existence d'une unité d'habitation familiale caractérisée par l'absence du tombeau des ancêtres. L'une mettrait en avant les fonctions différentes des bâtiments de la ville: il est sûr que les ruines du tell de Ras Shamra correspondent autant à de réelles maisons d'habitation qu'à des boutiques, remises ou hangars, espaces vides, etc., comme le montre bien O. Callot dans son étude;[15] seules les premières seraient dotées d'un caveau funéraire. Mais, dans le secteur tranchée Ville-Sud, l'auteur démontre bien que des unités d'habitation bien reconnaissables étaient dépourvues de tombes: il n'y a pas de règle "une maison = une tombe".

Une autre hypothèse consisterait à tranformer la notion de caveau familial en celle de tombe « clanique », ce que pourrait suggérer un texte sur les devoirs filiaux qui mentionne *le monument du clan* dans les honneurs rendus au père: « [un fils] qui érigera dans le sanctuaire la stèle de son clan ancestral, le monument de son clan... » (Légende de Danel)[16] sur les bétyles.[17] Le nombre de tombeaux dévolus à des groupes sociaux plus larges – des clans regroupant plusieurs familles – serait alors inférieur à celui des unités d'habitation, elles-mêmes peut-être de fonction plus large que seulement familiale: «En définitive, la "maison" ougaritique prise dans le tissu urbain n'est pas une unité architecturale, mais une unité sociologique».[18] Mais l'étude archéologique seule ne peut fournir de réponse exacte en l'absence d'indications anthropologiques, et l'archéologie funéraire reste muette, à Ras Shamra, sur le problème de l'organisation interne de la société.

Les tombes les plus achevées de Ras Shamra témoignent d'une élaboration architecturale tout à fait remarquable, qu'on pourrait qualifier d'aristocratique: c'est le cas des deux tombes des bâtiments désignés comme le Petit Palais,[19] aussi luxueuses que les caveaux de la nécropole royale proprement dite, au cœur de Palais,[20] de la tombe-L [50] de la résidence nord,[21] de la tombe du "Grand Bâtiment" à la limite nord du tell,[22] de la tombe-I [1] du secteur acropole[23] et de plusieurs constructions du quartier dit égéen généralement non publiées. On ne peut qu'imaginer, sur la base des blocs restants, la riche architecture des demeures qui les recouvraient, et ces caveaux funéraires offrent un caractère grandiose qui, s'il était bien le reflet du monde des vivants – ce qui reste à démontrer – , laisserait supposer une supériorité architecturale incontestable par rapport au reste de la ville. Ces innovations en matière de construction ne sont pas seulement chronologiques: les grands caveaux sont datés de la fin du XIVe à la fin du XIIIe s av. J.-C., mais c'est aussi dans cette dernière phase de l'histoire de la ville qu'on trouve des maisons et des tombeaux « moyens », aux techniques architecturales plus banales.[24] Dans tous les exemples de tombes monumentales cités plus haut, les dimensions excèdent les seuls besoins d'une simple inhumation (hauteur sous voûte, surface au sol, *dromoi*, etc.), et si, comme on le suppose dans d'autres sites contemporains,[25] l'investissement matériel, moral et financier supposé pour de telles constructions est significatif d'une position sociale, on se trouve sans conteste dans les couches les plus élevées de la société et dans l'entourage royal. Les variations dans l'élaboration architecturale des tombes seraient ainsi le reflet de la stratification sociale d'Ougarit.

Une telle affirmation doit être fortement nuancée. Comme on l'a dit, la perfection architecturale des tombes monumentales s'accompagne d'un agrandissement fonctionnel. Les dromoi d'accès sont désormais pourvus d'escaliers aisément utilisables, à la différence de nombreux autres passages où la circulation reste très malaisée, même à la période finale de la ville;[26] les toitures permettent une facile station debout, impossible dans les tombes anciennes, mais souvent difficile dans certains caveaux des XIVe-XIII[e] s.; les sols sont dallés, etc. De tels soucis, ainsi que le raffinement de la finition, laissent supposer que ces tombeaux étaient destinés à être vus et admirés par un public élargi, c'est-à-dire par un rassemblement de personnes extérieures à la maisonnée, probable au moment d'un enterrement – mais il ne faut pas exclure d'autres occasions:[27] la

---

13 La difficulté que j'avais soulevée (Salles 1987, 160) du problème de la cession du tombeau lors d'une vente de la maison pourrait trouver un début de réponse à Mari, si on suit l'interprétation du terme *ku-bu-ru* proposée par Durand (1989); mais la proposition de Durand a été récemment rejetée par Scurlock (1993). Sur ces problèmes de cessibilité du tombeau, on évoquera aussi l'exemple de Pétra cité par J. Healey, dans ce volume.
14 Callot 1994
15 Ibid.; voir également l'excellente analyse des spécialisations de l'espace urbain dans Callot et Yon, sous presse.
16 Caquot, Sznycer & Herdner 1974, 421-422.
17 Voir récemment Dietrich *et alii*, 1989.
18 Callot & Yon, sous presse.
19 Non publiées.

20 Non publiés eux aussi, mais voir Schaeffer 1951, 16 et Fig. 8; 1962, 11 et dépliant.
21 Schaeffer 1938, 317 et Pl.XXXV; 1939a, Pl. XV et Fig. 79, 86.
22 Margueron 1983, Fig. 2.
23 Schaeffer 1933, 114-117; 1939a, 87 et Fig. 80.
24 Callot 1983; Callot 1994.
25 Kesnawi 1989b.
26 Margueron 1977, 175.
27 Un texte d'Isaïe (65, 4) décrit des pratiques cultuelles interdites aux Israélites de la période post-exilique : « Ils se tiennent dans des sépulcres, ils passent la nuit dans des grottes, ils mangent de la viande de porc... ». Tout le monde s'accorde pour reconnaître que le premier stique évoque la consultation des morts (nécromancie) comme forme de divination, pratique fréquemment condamnée dans la Bible depuis les rédactions les plus anciennes. Le mode de consultation reste inconnu : rites d'incubation, évocation des morts,

fonction de ces monuments dépasserait ainsi la seule nécessité physique d'y déposer des défunts et revêtirait une dimension sociale difficile à préciser. Si on ajoute qu'aucun matériel ostéologique n'a jamais été mentionné explicitement dans les trouvailles en provenance de ces caveaux, on pourrait être amené à se demander si ces constructions étaient vraiment des tombes destinées à recevoir des cadavres, ou si elles n'étaient pas des sortes de chapelles funéraires, à fonction seulement rituelle, les corps étant disposés ailleurs – mais où, dans ce cas?

L'hypothèse se heurte à deux arguments. Le premier provient de l'une des tombes les plus prestigieuses de Ras Shamra, celle du "Grand Bâtiment" de la bordure nord du tell. On y a en effet retrouvé un sarcophage en pierre,[28] brisé et peut-être jamais utilisé (?), mais qui semble bien avoir été destiné à accueillir un personnage de haut rang, tant la coutume est inhabituelle à Ras Shamra, sauf à envisager l'hypothèse, plausible, de cercueils en bois plus fréquents dont on n'aurait pas retrouvé de traces. On pourrait, bien sûr, suggérer, de manière assez improbable, que ce caveau serait devenu, par le biais du sarcophage, un tombeau de substitution pour un mort tombé « ailleurs » et non ramené dans sa dernière demeure, le sarcophage symbolisant le cadavre absent;[29] le cas serait un *hapax* à Ougarit, et l'argument assez difficile à défendre: quand bien même, on se trouverait bien dans une tombe (sarcophage), et non dans une chapelle. L'autre argument relève de la longue durée: à toutes les époques du IIe millénaire, on constate une telle homogénéité des rituels mortuaires connus à Ras Shamra qu'il paraît difficile d'accepter que, ce qui était auparavant tombe et l'est encore dans plusieurs secteurs de la ville du XIIIe s., soit devenu un espace seulement cultuel dans quelques-unes des résidences des couches les plus élevées de la société.

Une explication plus sociologique peut être avancée, même si elle reste difficile à démontrer. En construisant ces tombes monumentales et somptuaires, l'aristocratie ougaritaine démontrait sa richesse et sa puissance en faisant étalage des investissements financiers qu'elle y consentait; elle cherchait en même temps à s'assurer une meilleure gestion des rituels mortuaires qui, devenus publics ou élargis, permettait un « contrôle » plus étroit des fidèles. Le pouvoir ne s'exprimait plus seulement par la splendeur architecturale, mais aussi par une pratique attentive et communautaire des rites de la mort – et peut-être d'autres

rites de la cité. Si l'hypothèse est juste, les grands caveaux de Ras Shamra pourraient être la manifestation d'une forme d'« intégrisme » de la part de l'aristocratie d'Ougarit, vieille méthode de gouvernement des oligarchies! Ou bien ne s'agit-il, tout simplement, que d'une expression de l'« euphémisme » de la mort, évoqué par J. Healey?[30]

---

Vient le moment de l'enterrement. Le rituel funèbre comprenait peut-être une préparation du corps – sommaire, élaborée?: « On versera sur ma tête quelque chose de blanc, de la cendre sur mon crâne », dit Danel.[31] Une pratique analogue apparaît dans le texte appelé *Le Juste Souffrant*, l. 12: « mes femmes versent (?) de l'huile fine (?) sur mon (corps déjà) prêt (à la tombe) »;[32] mais il s'agit là d'un texte ancien en akkadien, qui ne décrit peut-être pas une coutume ougaritaine. Une pratique similaire paraît avoir existé à Byblos quelques siècles plus tard, d'après une inscription phénicienne du site: « voici que je repose dans ce sarcophage dans la myrrhe et le bdellium »,[33] mais la forte influence égyptienne sur la civilisation giblite empêche qu'on puisse généraliser cette pratique au Levant ancien. Rappelons qu'une interprétation singulière, rejetée par tous les savants, traduit le terme *rp'um* à Ougarit (c-à-d. les *Rephaïm*) par les « embaumeurs ».[34] L'archéologie ne peut fournir aucune indication en l'absence de restes ostéologiques; peut-être faudrait-il scruter les textes économiques pour y trouver trace des ingrédients qui auraient pu servir au traitement du corps des défunts?

J'ai évoqué ailleurs l'accès à la tombe et le transport du cadavre dans son reposoir en-dessous, dans la terre.[35] La tombe, généralement construite en même temps que la maison mais parfois rajoutée dans l'architecture existante[36], possède généralement – il faudrait vérifier tous les cas encore intelligibles pour établir une règle – son accès au caveau souterrain dans une pièce accessible à la fois de la maison et de la rue: la tombe n'est pas isolée dans la partie privée de l'habitat, mais peut être atteinte par des visiteurs venant de l'extérieur qui, ainsi, ne sont pas contraints de pénétrer dans l'espace privatif. Aucune indication en provenance des fouilles anciennes ne permet de discerner une fonction propre pour la pièce de la maison qui abrite l'accès à la tombe: entrepôt, pièce vide, lieu de culte, etc.? Les recherches attentives menées récemment dans le "Centre-Ville" ou dans la tranchée "Ville-Sud" n'ont pas permis non plus de proposer une hypothèse sur le rôle de cette pièce dans l'organisation de la maison:[37] aucun matériel ar-

---

etc.? Faut-il imaginer cette pratique à Ras Shamra, dans des caveaux qui auraient pu accueillir de nombreux participants à la cérémonie? Il est difficile de dessiner l'image « physique » d'une cohabitation passagère entre les cadavres présents dans les caveaux (?) et les vivants invocant leurs ombres, mais toute magie macabre n'est-elle pas inhabituelle? La nécromancie était une pratique courante dans le Proche Orient antique (Finley, 1983-1984; Tropper, 1989). Je remercie Jacques Briend pour son commentaire amical sur le texte d'Isaïe.

28  Margueron 1977; 1983, 19-20
29  par ex. Vernant 1980.

30  J. Healey, dans ce volum.
31  Caquot, Sznycer & Herdner 1974, 432-433.
32  Nougayrol 1968.
33  Teixidor 1986, 479-480.
34  Good 1980.
35  Salles 1987, que je résume ici.
36  Callot 1983; 1985.
37  Salles 1987, 162-163; Callot sous presse.

chéologique particulier ne suggère une fonction qu'on serait en droit de supposer singulière.

L'ouverture de la tombe ne posait pas de difficultés majeures, les dalles de couverture du dromos étant situées juste sous le sol en terre battue ou, parfois, affleurant le sol.[38] Cette présence de lourdes dalles sur l'accès au dromos, souvent renforcée quelques mètres plus loin par une fermeture amovible, dalles ou portes en bois, entre le dromos et la chambre funéraire proprement dite, marquait la limite entre le monde des morts et celui des vivants, et le poids généralement considérable de ces aménagements protégeait les vivants des frayeurs qui pouvaient venir d'en-bas: pestilences, retour des ombres des défunts, etc. Une évolution se manifeste du Bronze Moyen au Bronze Récent et dans le Bronze récent lui-même, qui est l'allongement et l'élargissement des dromoi, permettant un accès plus aisé dans la chambre funéraire: comme on l'a dit plus haut, la descente au tombeau semble occuper une place de plus en plus importante dans le rituel funèbre.

On ignore à peu près tout de la disposition des corps à l'intérieur de la chambre funéraire: déposés à même le sol (généralement en terre battue, dallé dans les grands caveaux), enveloppés dans un linceul, cachés par un cercueil? L'enseignement des tombes du Bronze Moyen de Jéricho ou celui des tombes royales de Byblos, entre autres exemples, pourraient être instructifs sur ce point, mais on ne peut rester que dans le champ des hypothèses en l'absence de rapports anthropologiques à Ras Shamra, et du fait du caractère souvent superficiel des rapports des fouilles anciennes. Plusieurs aménagements visibles à l'intérieur des chambres funéraires restent mal compris. J'ai douté ailleurs que les niches réservées dans les murs aient systématiquement été des emplacements pour des lampes comme fréquemment affirmé dans les rapports anciens:[39] leur fonction exacte demeure cependant énigmatique. Comme J. Margueron, je reste sceptique sur la notion d'ossuaire, peu conforme avec les croyances orientales sur le nécessaire intégrité des morts.[40] Il est vrai qu'il faudrait étudier chaque cas en détail, dans les limites de la documentation disponible. Par ailleurs, le respect des morts n'est pas aussi coercitif qu'on pourrait le supposer puisque, au hasard des ruines de Ras Shamra, on peut voir des constructions qui ont sciemment détruit des tombes plus anciennes. Ce qui était désigné jadis comme des

ossuaires était en général des puits[41] ou des constructions annexes qu'on tentera d'interpréter plus loin, mais il ne semble pas y avoir eu, dans le plan initial de la tombe, un endroit précis dont la fonction était de servir d'ossuaire.

Un autre aménagement paraît avoir échappé à l'attention des chercheurs. Dans les tombes du Palais Royal, mais aussi dans de nombreux autres caveaux de types plus anciens ou plus sommaires, on constate la présence d'une petite ouverture au niveau du sol, vide, intentionnellement aménagée dans la maçonnerie du mur, souvent – mais pas toujours – à la base du mur court face à la porte d'entrée. Ce trou, de taille toujours réduite (il n'est pas accessible à l'homme) ne conduit à rien: il se prolonge par une sorte de tunnel court et étroit qui se perd dans la terre, sans aucun aménagement vers sa fin (dans la tombe 1246 [T.402], ce boyau débouche sur un puits abandonné).[42] Les rapports des fouilles anciennes ne mentionnent aucune trouvaille particulière dans ces recoins, parfois appelés ossuaires, et les fouilles récentes ne sont guère plus explicites. Je serais tenté de donner une signification à ce boyau anodin, celle d'une « porte » ou d'une voie de passage entre le caveau funéraire lui-même, isolé de la terre environnante par sa construction relativement hermétique – pour des raisons évidentes d'hygiène – , et la terre au sens large, domaine des morts par excellence. C'est par cet artifice architectural que le mort pouvait aller et venir entre son lieu de repos permanent, la terre, et le lieu où il était parfois rappelé par le rituel funéraire afin d'accorder ses bénédictions aux vivants. Il faut, en effet, insister sur le fait que, dans la tradition ougaritique, c'est la terre qui est la destination finale des défunts: il n'est pas possible de dire que la *tombe* est la dernière demeure des morts, puisque ceux-ci habitent la *terre*. En ce sens, la chambre funéraire ne constitue plus qu'un lieu de passage du mort promis à la terre, et non son reposoir définitif; elle devient aussi un point de rencontre entre le monde des vivants et celui des morts, celui d'où le défunt pouvait rejoindre sa demeure finale et où il pouvait revenir protéger les vivants.

Si on suit cette hypothèse, on pourrait, peut-être, offrir une explication pour les chambres annexes présentes dans la tombe du "Grand Bâtiment" de la bordure nord du tell, dans une tombe de Ras Ibn Hani, et dans l'une des deux tombes du Petit Palais.[43] Dans ces trois cas, il paraît clair qu'un rituel funèbre ou funéraire devait se dérouler à l'intérieur du caveau, et il se pourrait alors que la chambre annexe ait été un lieu spécialement aménagé pour le retour des *Rephaïm* lorsqu'on les invoquait, emplacement isolé du caveau pour ne pas créer un « mélange » avec les vivants présents. À la même cérémonie auraient participé, côte à côte mais séparés les uns des autres, les vivants en action dans le caveau principal et les *Rephaïm* cachés dans la

---

38  Schaeffer (1938) présente plusieurs tombes dont les systèmes d'accès n'ont pas cette simplicité : épais matelas de terre entre le sol présumé et les dalles de couverture du dromos (0,50 m pour T. XXXVI ou T. LIII, 2,85 m [?] pour T. LIV, 1 m pour T. LVI), dalles de couverture du dromos bloquées sous un seuil de porte (T. XXXVI) ou sous un mur (T. LV), etc. Il s'agit, évidemment, de mauvaises interprétations de la stratigraphie et des évolutions architecturales de la maison (reconstruction des murs, rehaussement de sols, etc.) : tous ces cas « anormaux » devraient faire l'objet de nouvelles études sur le terrain, si cela est encore possible.
39  Salles 1987, 170.
40  Margueron 1983, 14-16; Salles 1987, 172-173.
41  *Infra*
42  Salles 1987, 177.
43  Margueron 1983, 14-17; la tombe du Petit Palais est inédite.

RAS SHAMRA
TOMBE L.

COVPE AB.

PLAN AV NIVEAV GH.

COVPE CD.

PLAN AV NIVEAV LF.

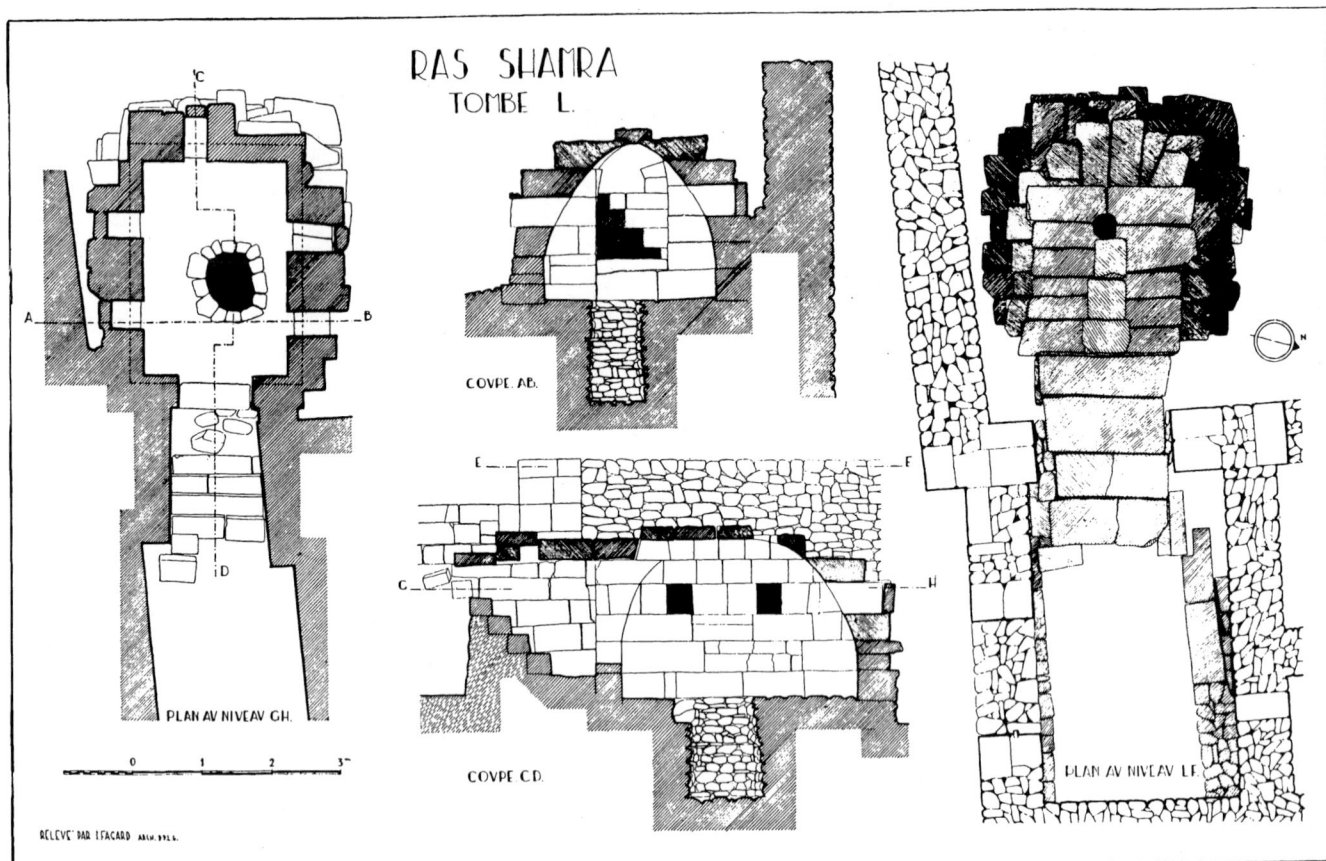

*Fig. 18.3: Tombe L/50, couverture avec trou manquant et autres dessins*

chambre annexe, revenus de la terre et dispensant leurs bénédictions par les petites ouvertures aménagées entre ces deux lieux...

Les tombes qui viennent d'être citées, ainsi que de nombreux autres caveaux du site, possèdent également un puits creusé au centre de la chambre funéraire, aux parois souvent maçonnées sur un mètre de profondeur ou plus; la mention d'un aménagement semblable, plus ou moins élaboré, est fréquente dans les rapports sur les tombes anciennement fouillées de Ras Shamra, mais il est loin d'être démontré qu'il s'agissait d'une règle.[44] En révisant divers témoignages archéologiques anciens, et en analysant avec précision le cas de la tombe du "Grand Bâtiment", J. Margueron a brillamment démontré que ce type d'installation n'était certainement pas un ossuaire, pouvait éventuellement être un lieu de passage vers la terre-domaine des ombres, *supra*, mais était plus sûrement un puits à libation.[45] On reviendra plus loin sur les problèmes archéologiques soulevés par ce rite, mais il faut souligner un paradoxe: les libations en l'honneur des morts sont bien connues dans la littérature mortuaire mésopotamienne, mais il n'y a pas de texte ougaritique analogue[46] et, par exemple, si le rituel

funéraire RS 34.126 fait état d'offrandes au sens le plus large, il n'est question de libations.[47] Pourtant, les vases en albâtre recueillis au fond du puits de la tombe du "Grand Bâtiment" étaient bien destinés à recueillir les offrandes liquides ou autres faites en l'honneur du mort, ne laissant planer aucun doute sur cette fonction particulière du puits; on pourrait en trouver confirmation dans la jarre trouvée au fonds du puits (?) de la tombe-VIII.[48] Dès lors qu'on accepte que les grands caveaux n'étaient pas des chapelles funéraires mais de vrais tombeaux destinés à accueillir des cadavres, *supra*, il devient évident que la cérémonie de libation/offrande était bien un rituel funèbre, au moment où la tombe était ouverte pour l'enterrement: ce rite rassemblait plusieurs participants, et la présence de ces puits à libation démontre *per se* l'existence de cérémonies à l'intérieur de la tombe. Il s'agit, évidemment, d'une cérémonie différente des rituels funéraires évoqués plus loin.

Sans préjuger de la validité de l'exploration archéologique – tous les puits ont-ils été découverts sous les dalles des sols construits ou dans la terre meuble des sols en terre battue? – il semblerait que plusieurs tombes ne possèdent pas ce type d'aménagement, et il faut

---

44    Salles 1987, 172-173.
45    Margueron 1983, 17-19.
46    Pope 1981, 161.

47    Bordreuil et Pardee 1982, 123.
48    Schaeffer 1939a, Fig. 78: 85.

tenter d'expliquer cette disparité. Une explication pourrait être chronologique, les offrandes ou libations constituant un rituel nouveau, spécifique des grands caveaux. On objectera qu'un puits semble présent dans la tombe-LV datée du XVe s.,[49] ou dans la maison B du secteur Centre Ville datée du XIVe s.;[50] de telles démonstrations archéologiques restent fragiles, mais il n'y a aucune raison évidente pour stipuler une nouveauté dans les rituels funèbres.

Un argument paraît plaider en faveur d'une origine relativement ancienne des puits funéraires. Dans la pièce qui abrite la nécropole royale du Palais, dont le caveau le plus ancien est étroitement lié aux fondations du Palais, quelle que soit la date de construction de celui-ci, on trouve un énorme puits, large de 2.10 m de diamètre à l'ouverture et maçonné sur plus de 4 m de profondeur. Il n'existe aucune information publiée sur la fouille de ce puits: quelle est sa réelle profondeur? Qu'a-t-on trouvé dans le remplissage? Et de nouvelles fouilles ne sont pas possibles du fait du danger que fait courir le délabrement de plusieurs constructions supérieures. Une étude préliminaire montre que ce puits pourrait avoir communiqué par un petit boyau avec le caveau le plus ancien (mais n'est-ce pas un résultat de l'érosion ou d'une fouille trop profonde?); il est totalement indépendant de la tombe la plus récente de la nécropole royale. Il occupe une position résolument centrale dans l'ensemble du complexe funéraire, et, bien que n'étant structurellement lié à aucune des trois tombes de la nécropole, il jouait évidemment un rôle de premier plan dans les rituels funèbre et funéraire du Palais Royal.

La taille du puits pourrait permettre d'évoquer le rituel KTU 1.105, qui mentionne les sacrifices de plusieurs dizaines de bêtes en l'honneur du roi mort,[51] sorte d'hécatombe que l'auteur interprète comme un rite funéraire. Toutefois, D. Pardee propose une interprétation sensiblement différente de la même tablette, ne serait-ce qu'en inversant le *recto/verso* du document sur la base d'indices épigraphiques.[52] Il serait bien question de sacrifices en relation avec une fosse – mais sur quelles bases Del Olmo Lete et Pardee fondent-ils leurs affirmations que des sacrifices en rapport avec une fosse seraient particulièrement en rapport avec les morts? – qui auraient lieu en hiver en l'honneur d'un « panthéon » inhabituel, mais qui n'auraient rien de funéraire. Le même puits de la nécropole royale pourrait jouer un rôle central dans le rituel RS 34.126, dont le caractère funéraire ne peut être mis en cause:[53] le texte fait expressément référence à la « descente » du roi – peut-être même du roi assis sur son trône – dans la terre pour y prendre sa place parmi les *Rephaïm*. La vision pourrait être symbolique et purement rituelle, la

« descente » s'accomplissant par n'importe quelle gestuelle que nous ignorons au fur et à mesure que le texte était récité; mais D. Pardee n'exclut pas que la « descente » ait été réellement celle du corps défunt du roi, treuillé jusqu'au fond du puits, c'est-à-dire au cœur même de la terre où il pouvait rejoindre les ancêtres de la dynastie, les *Rephaïm* royaux cités dans la même tablette: « A la suite de tes maîtres descends en terre, descends en terre et plonge dans la poussière... » (l. 20-22).[54] Quoiqu'il en soit de l'interprétation exacte de ce texte, au premier ou au deuxième degré, il paraît certain qu'une étude sérieuse de la nécropole royale et de son puits jetterait une lumière nouvelle sur les coutumes funéraires d'Ougarit.

Une autre explication pourrait être proposée pour justifier l'absence/présence des puits. Ce qui pourrait avoir changé, à défaut des rituels eux-mêmes, c'est le lieu où se déroulait le rituel funèbre, à l'extérieur de la tombe dans les temps anciens et là où aucun puits n'est signalé, à l'intérieur des grands caveaux et des autres tombes où un puits existe. Le perfectionnement progressif dans la maîtrise des techniques architecturales, ainsi que l'enrichissement de la population et des classes aisées qui a permis des constructions de plus en plus luxueuses, auraient conduit à transformer de petites tombes souterraines impraticables où l'on se contentait de déposer les morts tant la circulation y était difficile, en de grands caveaux fonctionnels où il devenait possible de rendre aux morts les honneurs qui leur étaient dûs lors de leur inhumation. Mais s'il s'agit bien d'un simple transfert du lieu du rituel funèbre (tombe ouverte), on est amené à se poser une question complémentaire: où ce rituel se déroulait-il à l'extérieur des tombes plus anciennes et/ou inaccessibles parce que trop exiguës, lorsqu'elles étaient ouvertes pour l'enterrement? Quel était l'espace où se pratiquaient les rites liés à la mort lorsqu'ils ne se déroulaient pas dans la tombe? L'interrogation renvoie ainsi au problème du rituel funéraire, celui du culte rendu aux morts après que la tombe ait été fermée.

———————

Les questions relatives aux rituels funéraires relèvent plus de l'épigraphie et de la littérature ougaritiques que de l'archéologie proprement dite. Les principales données ont été rassemblées par M.H. Pope en 1981,[55] et elles n'ont cessé, depuis, d'être l'objet d'exégèses nombreuses, le plus souvent contradictoires et, parfois, malheureuses.[56] Plusieurs études sur la tablette RS 34.126 (*supra*),[57] éclairent d'un jour nouveau les sacrifices en l'honneur du roi mort – sans qu'il soit possible de décider si la récitation de ce rituel se déroulait devant la tombe ouverte (rituel funèbre) ou fermée (rituel funéraire). Ce n'est pas le lieu de revenir

49  Schaeffer 1938, Fig. 24, 229.
50  Salles 1987, 172-173.
51  Del Olmo Lete 1988.
52  Pardee, à paraître.
53  Dernièrement: Bordreuil et Pardee 1991, 151-163

54  Pardee, à paraître.
55  Pope 1981.
56  Lewis 1989.
57  Bordreuil et Pardee 1991, avec bibliographie antérieure.

ici sur les devoirs filiaux énumérés dans la Légende de Danel,[58] sur la fonction exacte des *Rephaïm*,[59] ou sur le banquet funéraire (?) ou *mrz"*.[60] On relèvera cependant deux problèmes archéologiques en liaison avec ces rituels funéraires.

L'un est celui des aménagements hydrauliques destinés à nourrir les morts depuis l'extérieur de la tombe, question soulevée par C.F.A. Schaeffer en 1939[61] et colportée depuis sans vérification.[62] Un exemple en est fourni par la tombe-L [50] de la résidence nord-ouest (dite *Palais de la Reine-Mère* – sur ce secteur du site),[63] où « les dispositifs pour libations sont nombreux et particulièrement bien conservés ».[64] Aucune autre indication n'est fournie par le fouilleur, et J.-C. Courtois signale seulement l'existence d'un puits à margelle dans la pièce sous laquelle est enterrée la chambre funéraire;[65] aucune relation autre que la proximité ne peut être établie entre la tombe et le puits, et il a été bien établi que les nombreuses installations hydrauliques de la résidence nord n'ont aucun rapport avec la tombe.[66] Quant à la chambre funéraire, sa couverture montre un trou à l'extrémité ouest du caveau (. 18.3), et, à la suite de Sukenik, Lewis affirme que « *through this hole libations would be offered to the deceased* »;[67] faut-il rappeler que cette couverture construite était cachée sous les sols en terre battue, et que si la fouille de 1937 n'a pas préservé l'altitude des sols enlevés, l'étude des seuils avoisinants permet de restituer un matelas de terre épais de 0,40/0,50 m au-dessus de la couverture de la tombe, au moins dans le dernier état du bâtiment? L'hypothèse d'offrandes liquides repose sur l'existence présumée de « tuyaux » de libation, communs dans les rituels mésopotamiens;[68] aucun ustensile de ce type n'a jamais été retrouvé dans les fouilles de Ras Shamra.[69] En fait, ce trou de 0.35 m de diamètre paraît trop étroit pour être un trou de pillage, bien que la possibilité ne puisse pas être totalement écartée; les quatre clefs de voûte qui joignent les corbeaux supérieurs de l'encorbellement mesurent, elles aussi, 0,35 m de largeur: sur les bords du trou, la face supérieure des corbeaux est préparée pour l'encastrement d'une clef de voûte, comme dans de nombreuses autres tombes du site.[70] Il est donc clair que ce trou correspond à une clef de voûte manquante, et il n'y a absolument aucune raison pour affirmer que le

bloc aurait été enlevé dès l'antiquité pour des libations... .[71]

Des pierres circulaires percées existent sur tout le tell de Ras Shamra, parfois à proximité de tombes, mais la plupart de celles qui sont visibles aujourd'hui sont simplement des margelles de puits hors contexte (c'est-à-dire rejetées loin des puits), comme l'étaient sans doute celles qui sont signalées dans les rapports anciens. Il n'empêche que les interprétations les plus abusives ont été proférées à ce propos: « *By the side of each tomb was a pit, the mouth of which was covered with a pierced slab stone to which a stone gutter was connected and liquids poured from above were carried along the gutter into the underground pit* ».[72] à ma connaissance, aucune tombe visible sur le tell à ce jour ne présente la moindre trace de tels aménagements. Des puits sont parfois situés à peu de distance des tombes, mais il s'agit toujours de constructions indépendantes, sans aucune connexion architecturale: en fait, le grand nombre de puits et de puisards répartis sur tout le site est étroitement lié aux problèmes de l'alimentation de la ville en eau, non à celui de ses morts,[73] et ni la photographie ni le plan publiés de la tombe-IV ne justifient l'affirmation selon laquelle le puisard proche était lié à un quelconque rituel funéraire.[74] Il en va de même pour les nombreux fragments de canalisations en pierre retrouvés partout sur le site, souvent en remploi, qui appartiennent à de complexes réseaux d'écoulement,[75] sans aucun rapport avec les tombes. Dans le cas du grand caveau-II,[76] l'unique morceau de rigole recueilli près du dromos paraît appartenir au remplissage ou à un niveau antérieur et ne saurait être assimilé à une structure de libation: les seuils de porte à gauche et au fond de la photo paraissent, à première vue, déterminer un niveau cohérent de sol qui couvrirait les dalles de couverture de la chambre funéraire et du dromos; le morceau de canalisation est situé à environ 0,50 m au-dessous de ce niveau, et aucune libation versée sur le sol d'utilisation de la tombe n'aurait jamais pu atteindre cette canalisation profondément enfouie. Je ne vois aucune raison stratigraphique ou architecturale pour associer les deux rigoles voisines de la tombe-IV au caveau funéraire lui-même et encore moins à un rite de libation:[77] d'après photos et plans (Fig. 18.4), les canalisations ne sont nullement connectées entre elles, l'une aboutissant dans un puisard, l'autre on ne sait où, mais certainement pas

58 Healey 1979.
59 Caquot 1981.
60 Récemment, Pardee 1988, 54-57.
61 Réf. cité, Scheaffer 1939b, 46 sq.
62 Sukenik 1940; Tarragon 1980 – où l'exemple cité par l'auteur, p. 182, pris dans *Syria* 1936, n'a rien de funéraire, *loc. cit.*, p. 113, au lieu de la seule photo p. 110; Lewis 1989, 97-98.
63 Callot 1986.
64 Schaeffer 1938, 317.
65 Courtois 1979b, 114 et Fig. 11, 130.
66 Calvet 1989.
67 Lewis 1989, 98.
68 Pope 1981, 161.
69 Yon 1987, sur les vases à libations d'Ougarit.
70 Par ex., Salles 1987, 186.

71 Il y a même de fortes chances pour que cette clef de voûte ait disparu au cours des fouilles, si mon interprétation des documents cités ci-après est juste. Dans *Syria* 1938, la photo 1 Pl. XXXIII montre la face extérieure du mur du fond de la tombe (côté ouest), et une pierre paraît exister à l'emplacement de ce qui va devenir un « trou », à l'avant de la première clef de voûte visible; sur la photo 2, le bloc a disparu (derrière les pieds du dessinateur), et un trou est visible à l'avant de la même clef de voûte .
72 Sukenik 1940, 60.
73 Calvet et Geyer 1987.
74 Schaeffer 1934, photo 5 Pl. XII, et Fig. 6, 120.
75 Par ex. Calvet 1981.
76 Schaeffer 1934, 112, Fig. 4, 115.
77 Schaeffer 1934, photo 5 Pl. XII, et Fig. 6, 120.

# TOMBE IV

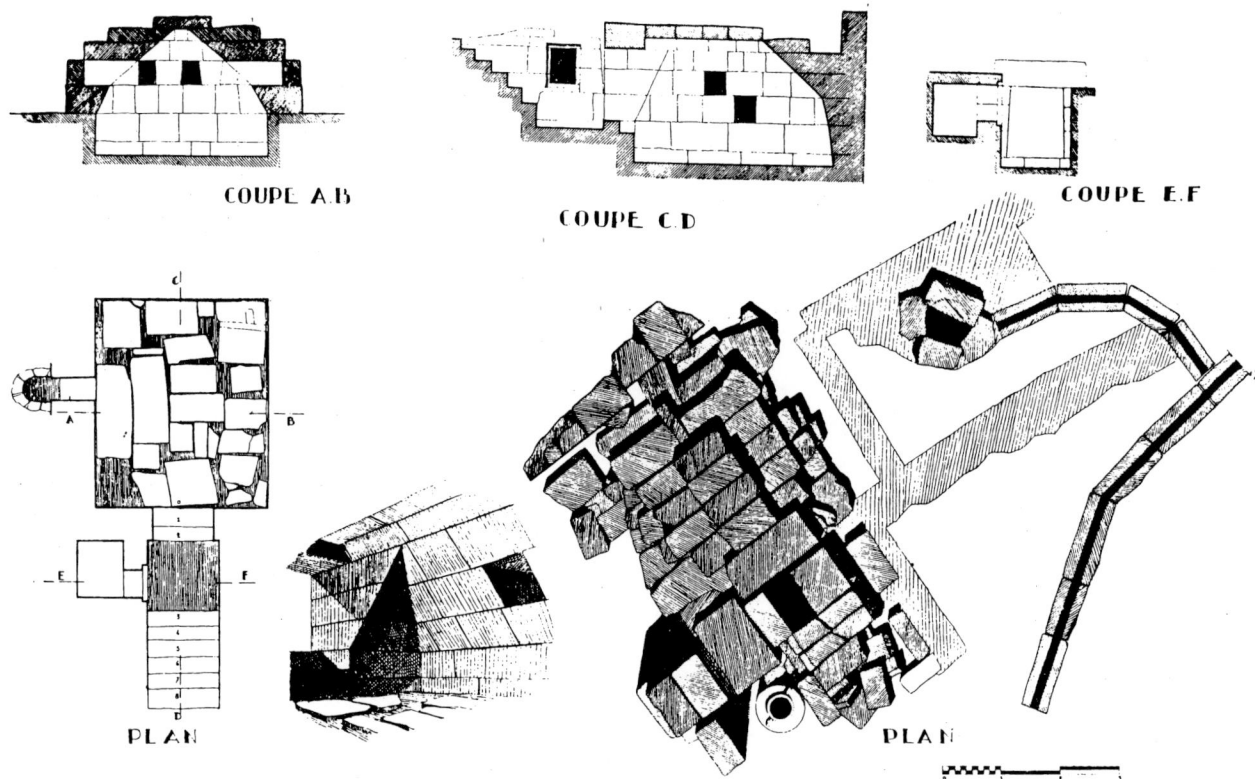

*Fig. 18.4: Tombe IV (rigoles, etc.)*

à l'entrée du dromos comme suggéré par le fouilleur. Il est d'ailleurs paradoxal que tous les commentaires sur les installations pour des libations fassent toujours référence aux rapports de 1934 et aux articles de 1939 et 1940,[78] sans jamais faire état des trouvailles, ou plutôt des non-trouvailles postérieures: plus aucun aménagement de ce type n'est cité dans les rapports de toutes origines publiés depuis les années cinquante.

Reste le cas incertain de la jarre enfouie à l'extérieur du mur sud du dromos de la tombe-IV,[79] mais il semble y avoir là aussi une séquence stratigraphique qui exclut une utilisation simultanée de l'amphore et de la tombe: le niveau du sol recouvrant les dalles de couverture tel qu'il est suggéré par les seuils de porte se situerait très au-dessus de l'ouverture de l'amphore. Que contenait l'amphore? S'agit-il d'une amphore complète ou seulement d'un haut d'amphore, comme pourrait le laisser supposer la photo 1 Pl. XII?[80] L'amphore n'apparaît pas sur les coupes du caveau funéraire, Fig. 18.6, p. 120. Un autre cas douteux est celui de l'amphore retrouvée dans une pièce annexe (?) de la tombe-II:[81] « [...] une grande jarre est prise dans la maçonnerie de l'angle de la cella; son col incliné aboutit à la hauteur d'une « fenêtre » ménagée dans le corps du mur, établissant une communication entre l'intérieur du

caveau et la jarre ».[82] Si cette reconstitution est assurée, on se trouverait alors en présence de libations à l'intérieur de la tombe, comme celles qui ont été mentionnées plus haut dans le cadre du rituel funèbre.

En définitive, il n'esiste aucun élément archéologique qui pourrait soutenir l'hypothèse de libations pratiquées à l'extérieur du tombeau fermé, et, s'il existe bien, comme en Mésopotamie, ce rituel funéraire n'a trouvé, jusqu'à présent, aucun début de preuve dans les données archéologiques disponibles.

Il faut conclure avec un autre problème de rituel, loin d'être unanimement accepté par les spécialistes, et étroitement lié à l'espace archéologique, celui du *mrz"*. On peut d'abord s'interroger sur l'existence d'un lieu réservé à un culte funéraire (tombe fermée) qui aurait inclus, outre les invocations et appels aux mânes des ancêtres, (RS 34 126 pour un rituel royal, donc spécial), un banquet communautaire ou repas commémoratif des morts nécessitant un espace relativement dégagé. Ce lieu pourrait être la salle commune de la maison, mais O. Callot rappelle à plusieurs reprises que la vie quotidienne se tenait à l'étage, c'est-à-dire loin de la tombe; dans la plupart des maisons de type moyen, il paraît exclu d'organiser un banquet dans la pièce qui abrite le caveau souterrain, généralement dépourvue de fenêtres et parfois exiguë. Y aurait-il eu, à cette intention, des lieux plus ouverts à un public élargi, hors de

78    Schaeffer 1934; 1939a; 1940?
79    Références *supra*.
80    Schaeffer 1934.
81    Ibid., Fig. 4, 115.

82    Ibid., 115.

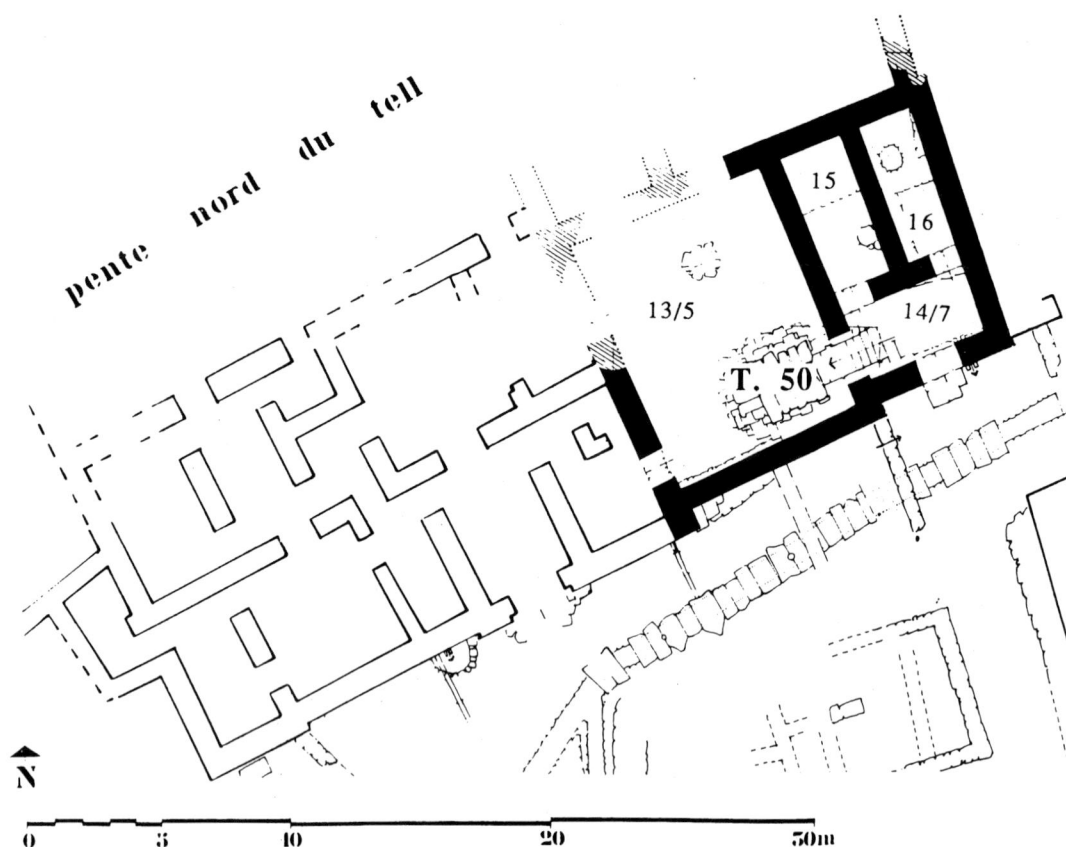

*Fig. 18.5: Plan espace funéraire de la maison de la Reine-Mère.*

l'habitat privé? On pourrait suggérer l'exemple d'un bâtiment de la tranchée "Ville Sud" où deux caveaux funéraires ont été retrouvés dans une construction qui ne peut pas être une maison (elle ne répond en rien aux canons des habitation privées de la ville), et dont la fonction demeure inconnue: mais le cas est trop unique pour être représentatif.[83] Dans d'autres secteurs de la "Ville Sud" et du reste du site, on pourrait évoquer des ensembles funéraires relativement excentrés par rapport à la maison, mais il n'est pas possible d'y individualiser ce qui pourrait être une salle de rassemblement pour le rituel: rien, dans la grande majorité des maisons reconnues à Ras Shamra, ne peut être identifié comme un lieu de rassemblement associé à la tombe, où un groupe de personnes se réunirait pour célébrer le souvenir des défunts enterrés en-dessous.

Le cas est peut-être différent pour la zone des palais, et je serais enclin, sous réserve de discussions à venir avec les spécialistes de l'espace à Ougarit, à identifier deux groupes de restes archéologiques spécialement dévolus au rituel funéraire. L'un serait situé dans la résidence nord-ouest (*Palais de la Reine-Mère*) et peut être étudié à partir des descriptions qu'en donnent Courtois[84] et Callot:[85] cet espace serait constitué par les

pièces "14/Courtois-7/Callot" et "13/Courtois-5/Callot", en y ajoutant probablement les réduits "15" et "16/Courtois" (Fig. 18.5). Cet ensemble, un peu excentré par rapport au reste de la maison – il en constitue toute la partie sud-est – est organisé autour de la grande pièce "13/5", que Courtois interprète comme une cour et Callot comme une salle couverte et qui abrite le caveau souterrain-L [50] ainsi qu'un puits, et de la pièce "14/7", qui ouvre de manière monumentale vers la place située au sud, permettant donc un accès direct depuis l'extérieur. Ce groupe de pièces n'est pas isolé du *Palais de la Reine-Mère* voisin à l'ouest et au nord, et plusieurs ouvertures ou portes assurent la communication entre la maison proprement dite et cette zone. On pourrait trouver là les éléments d'un ensemble centré sur le funéraire: présence de la tombe, bien sûr, abritée dans une pièce accessible de la maison et de l'extérieur; grande salle permettant des rassemblements et, éventuellement, des banquets (pièces annexes "15-16"); existence d'un puits, pour les repas ou pour les besoins des libations... L'hypothèse mériterait d'être examinée de près. Un autre exemple pourrait être celui du lien étroit qui associe la cour-II du *Palais Royal*, la pièce "28" de la nécropole royale et les pièces "38" et "39" situées à l'est de cet ensemble.[86] Il me semble qu'un podium "38" menait vers l'un des accès "39" à la

---

83  Callot 1994.
84  Courtois 1979b, Fig. 11, 130.
85  Callot 1986, Fig 2, 753.

86  Voir dépliant dans Schaeffer 1962 Fig. 6.

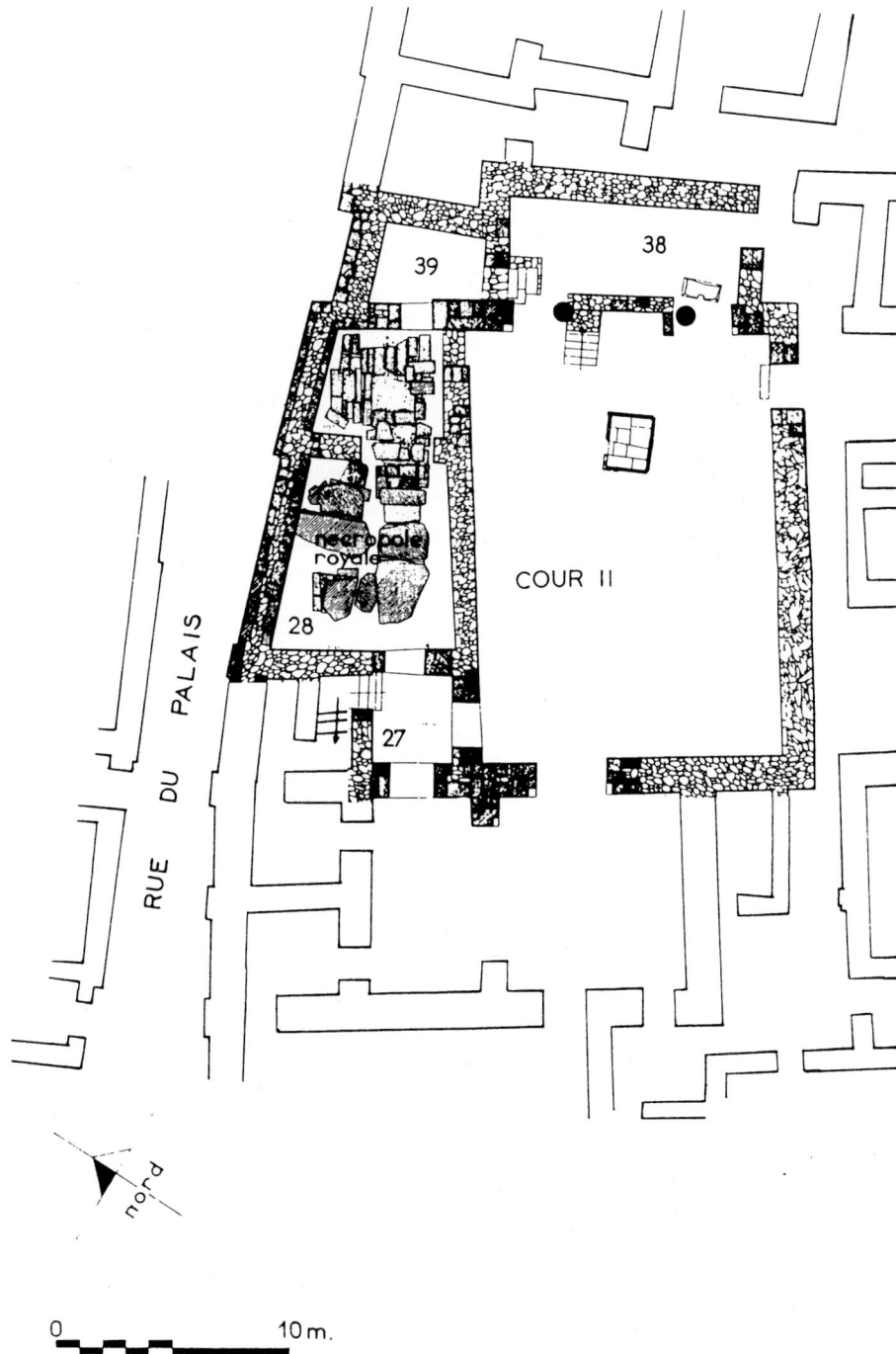

*Fig. 18.6: Plan espace funéraire palais royal.*

nécropole royale, laissant supposer un cérémonial auquel aurait pu assister une assemblée réunie dans la cour-II. Mais il faut attendre l'étude en cours du *Palais Royal* par J. Margueron et O. Callot pour vérifier la validité ou l'inanité de cette hypothèse. Reste qu'il n'est sans doute pas vain de rechercher l'espace archéologique du rituel funéraire à Ras Shamra.

Le volet littéraire de cette quête est la réflexion sur le *mrz"*. On a souvent considéré que le lieu géométrique du rituel funéraire était ce thiase dédié au culte des ancêtres de la famille ou du clan, rassemblé en un lieu cérémoniel autour d'un banquet (cf. la Légende de Danel);[87] sur la base de données bibliques ou extérieures à Ougarit (généralement tardives), M. Pope suggère l'existence de « *Marzeah-houses* » à Ras Shamra,[88] espaces réservés aux thiases funéraires, un peu comme les *triclinia* nabatéens dont J. Healey fait état.[89] L'hypothèse se heurte aux débats sur le *mrzḥ*, que plusieurs commentateurs refusent de considérer comme

---

87 Récemment Llyod 1990.
88 Pope 1981, 176.
89 J. Healey, dans ce volume.

une assemblée proprement funéraire;[90] la manifestation la plus tangible de ces réunions paraît bien être une beuverie, mais le but de l'association semble nous échapper: réunions en l'honneur d'un dieu (plusieurs exemples), évocation éventuelle d'un disparu – les possibilités sont ouvertes et nombreuses. Quant au lieu où se réunissait ce *mrzḥ*, il se pourrait qu'on puisse le reconnaître dans ce qu'on avait coutume d'appeler des « sanctuaires de quartier », tel le *Temple aux Rhytons* dans le "Centre Ville".[91]

---

De trop nombreux problèmes demeurent non résolus pour qu'on puisse prétendre présenter un bilan des croyances et rituels funéraires à Ras Shamra-Ougarit, le principal étant les limites de la documentation disponible – en dépit de l'apparente abondance des données, publiées ou non. Il faudra attendre que des réponses aient été apportées à des questions du type: combien de morts sous les maisons de la ville par rapport au reste de la population inhumée ailleurs? Quels morts particuliers trouve-t-on dans ces tombes, au sein d'une société complexe? Quel sort subissaient les défunts qui n'étaient pas enterrés dans la ville? etc. Pourtant, ce qui se dessine à travers les documents accessibles relatifs à une frange seulement de la population, profondément urbanisée et directement liée au monde du palais, se révèle en quelque sorte paradoxal. Ce qui serait important, ce ne seraient pas les quelques morts enterrés dans les caveaux souterrains de Ras Shamra (et jamais retrouvés lors des fouilles des grandes tombes de la fin de l'histoire de la cité), sorte de prétexte à la présence de la mort et au rite funèbre, mais bien le rite funéraire lui-même, celui des ancêtres rappelés au cours de cérémonies régulières, fondement de la prospérité de la famille, du clan, de la ville et du royaume d'Ougarit, celui de rassemblements figés par des règles strictes autour de l'aristocratie; force de cohésion mais aussi de contrôle, le rituel funéraire devient véritablement rituel social.

Les recherches sur la mort à Ras Shamra/Ougarit s'inscrivent dans le programme que dirige Marguerite Yon sur ce site depuis 1977. Quelques-unes des idées présentées ci-dessous ont été développées en 1989 lors d'une séminaire « Nécropoles » de la Maison de l'Orient de Lyon, Institut d'Archéologie Classique (sous la dir. de R. Étienne). Je tiens à remercier Denis Pardee pour les critiques et commentaires, toujours positifs et enrichissants, qu'il a bien voulu apporter à la première version de ce texte.

---

90 Pardee 1988, 56-57.
91 Yon 1984, 50; Pardee 1988, 56; Bordreuil et Pardee 1990, 67.

# 19  A Case of Symmers' Fibrosis of the Liver during the 18th Dynasty?

## Walter Y. Loebl

ABSTRACT—*The stele of Bak, King Akhenaton's chief sculptor, portrays him with a diffusely swollen abdomen, prominent breasts and swollen ankles. His umbilicus is absent. This is not a depiction of obesity, nor does it resemble the Amarna style. I would propose that Bak shows the classical features of portal hypertension due to chronic hepato-splenic schistosomiasis, which has been endemic in Egypt since antiquity. Unlike liver failure from other causes, the course is usually very slow, without significant debilitation until near the end. Unfortunately, neither remains of Bak's body nor biographical details have been found so far to prove my hypothesis.*

The quartzite stele of the chief sculptor Bak and his wife Taherit (Fig. 19.1) was acquired in London in 1963 by the Egyptian Museum SMPK in Berlin, ninety years after it was first discovered.[1] It is about 64 cm high and the identity of its subject is not in doubt. He was a chief sculptor of King Akhenaton (1352–1336 BC), as had been his father, Men, before him.

Whereas the female figure of Taherit on the stele is of conventional appearance, the portrait of Bak includes some peculiar features. On first inspection, one may actually hesitate to decide which of the pair is the male. Bak has prominent breasts and a diffusely swollen abdomen – better seen on the side views of a plaster cast of the figures, without the surrounding naos (Fig. 19.2). Very unusually for the Amarna period, Bak is also depicted without an umbilicus, and his ankles are clearly swollen.

It might be argued that Bak is portrayed in accordance with the prevailing effeminate artistic style of Amarna. However, that particular style usually includes quite different elongated facial features and a slender neck. Also, the abdomen during the Amarna style is pear-shaped, protuberant mainly in its lower part, and almost invariably a conspicuous umbilicus is present. Neither Bak nor Taherit conform to this Amarna style. Likewise, obesity can also be excluded as the explanation for Bak's unusual appearance. On the contrary – his portrayal includes somewhat hollow cheeks and his arms are slender. No rolls of fat are shown over his chest or abdomen. Nor would simple obesity explain the swollen ankles, or the absence of an umbilicus.

I would propose that the following three assumptions can be made:

a. Bak's portrayal on his stele is a realistic representation of the man:

As detailed above, his features are due neither to the influence of the Amarna Period style, nor to the intention to illustrate prosperous obesity.

b. Bak's appearance is not that of a healthy person:

His abdomen is grossly distended and his ankles are swollen.

c. The stele shows Bak in his customary shape and condition:

Otherwise, if his morbid features had developed rapidly – just when the stele was being made, he would have been portrayed in his former pre-morbid state of health.

Yet despite his unhealthy features, neither Bak's figure nor the stele's inscription indicate any serious physical debilitation or mental impairment at the time. Bak is surrounded by an unremarkable votive formula,[2] which does not suggest any possible infirmity in him.

Among the diagnostic possibilities of gross abdominal swelling, a likely explanation which fits the picture well is chronic liver failure. In that condition, the abdominal distension is due to the enlargement of the spleen and to ascitic fluid – which classically obliterates the umbilicus and can even cause its eversion.[3] Disturbed hormonal metabolism by the liver may lead to enlargement of the male breasts, and the ankle swelling is due to anaemia and reduced serum albumin.

---

1  Krauss 1986, 8.

2  Ibid., 30-38.
3  Papworth 1963, 157.

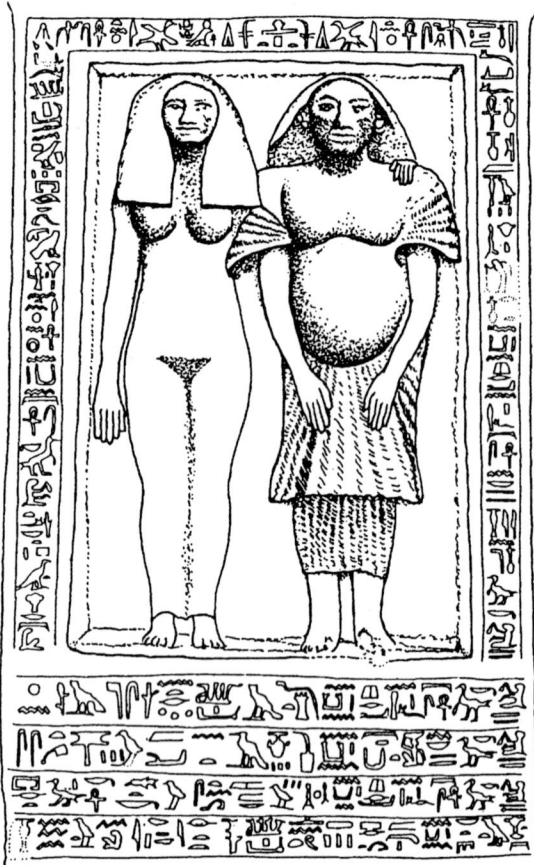

*Fig. 19.1 Bak's Stele – the naos figures and inscription.*

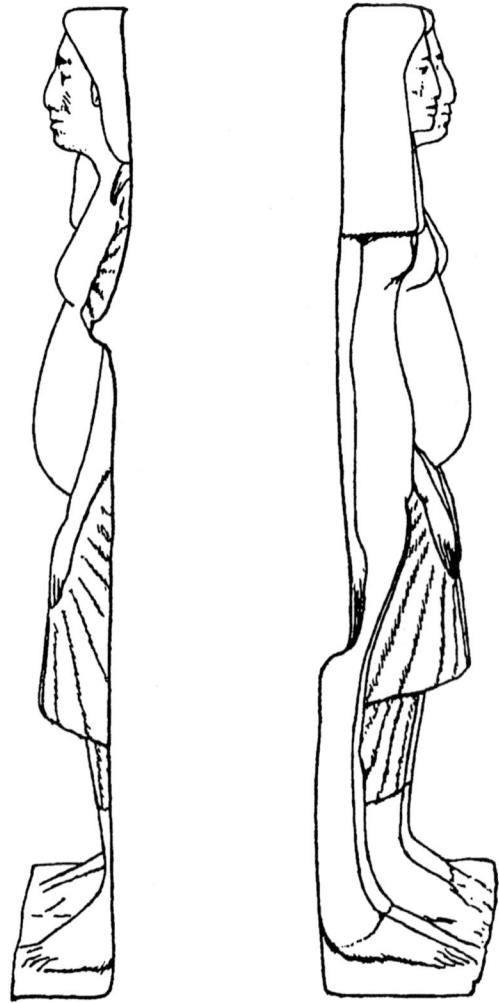

*Fig. 19.2: Side views of a plaster cast of the naos figures.*

Chronic liver disease may result from a large number of causes. The commonest is cirrhosis, often due to alcoholic poisoning. Yet it is unlikely that Bak was an alcoholic – in his high post of a chief sculptor to the king. Furthermore, once cirrhosis had reached the decompensated late stage shown in Bak's relief, it would usually cause rapidly progressive debility followed by death.

These considerations lead me to propose that Bak's chronic liver disease could well have been due to a different disease, namely hepato-splenic schistosomiasis.[4] Also called 'Egyptian Splenomegaly', its course is characteristically much slower than cirrhosis and usually quite benign until near the end. Bak's condition, as seen on the stele and as analysed above, is well advanced but not rapidly progressive; nor does he seem to be physically or mentally impaired.

The life cycle of the schistosomal parasite is astonishing in its complexity.[5] Two of the species are endemic in Egypt, S. haematobium and S. Mansoni; and mixed infection by both species has been found in 60% of one modern series,[6] as well as in some mummies. First described by Bilharz in 1851, the adult worms may live in

the veins of the bowel (S. Mansoni) or the bladder (S. haematobium) for up to 25 years. About 10 to 20 mm long, the male envelopes the longer slender female in a ventral fold along his body. Each pair produces up to 300 eggs daily – tens of thousands over their lifetime.

The eggs contain an embryo miracidium. By its movements, and the secretion of enzymes, the miracidium causes the egg to migrate through the wall of the intestine or the bladder. When the contaminated faeces or urine reach fresh water, the miracidium hatches from the egg and penetrates a specific species of snail host to multiply and evolve into the next two larval stages. Within a few days, infected snails begin to release free-swimming cercariae into the water, at the rate of 1,500 daily for several months.

Upon contact with human skin or the mucous membrane of the mouth or throat, the cercaria penetrates and migrates through the blood stream, ultimately to reach the liver. After 4 to 12 weeks the adult fertile worms migrate to the veins of their target organs and start egg production. In the established disease, it is the migration

4   Mousa et al. 1967.
5   Manson-Bahr & Apted 1982, 693-699.
6   Ibid., 206-224

of these eggs which causes symptoms in the bowel and the bladder respectively. Inflammation, cystitis or diarrhoea predominate, followed by ulceration and bleeding. Other organs can also be involved. Severity depends on the particular species and on how heavily the individual is infected.

Many of the eggs do not find their way into the bowel or bladder but are swept by the bloodstream to other organs, particularly to the liver. That is the principal cause of illness in chronic schistosomiasis. In up to 40% of infected persons (depending on severity), the liver gradually becomes scarred in a characteristic pattern. The fibrosis spares the liver parenchyma and involves mainly the portal spaces, giving the cut surface an appearance resembling sectioned pipe-stems. It was first described by Symmers in 1903.[7] The fibrosis causes a rise in portal venous pressure, resulting in massive enlargement of the spleen and the accumulation of ascitic fluid. The scarring usually progresses very slowly over many years, with liver functions remaining almost unimpaired until very late.[8] Therefore, compared to other types of liver cirrhosis, in Symmers' pipe-stem fibrosis the physical and mental functions are preserved for much longer, and death from hepatic coma is only one third as common.

Schistosomiasis has been prevalent throughout the Middle East since antiquity.[9] It has been found in the mummy of an Egyptian adolescent of the late pre-dynastic period, about 3200 BC.[10] In 1910, Ruffer found the eggs of schistosoma in two mummies of the 20th dynasty.[11] In a series of 23 mummies dating from the third- to the fifth-centuries AD, 65% tested positive to the infection.[12] In the eighteenth century Baron Dominique Larry, Napoleon's Chief Medical Officer to the Expedition to Egypt is reputed to have remarked that the Egyptians were "a nation of menstruating men",[13] obviously referring to the high prevalence of bloody urine due to Bilharzial bladder disease. In modern Egypt, despite knowledge of the cause

and of the risks, a prevalence of almost 100% has been found in 5 to 20 year old subjects in the rural population, dropping to 55% over the age of 50.[14] There is no reason to doubt, that the disease was similarly widespread in the days of King Akhenaton, particularly in the Nile Delta area. Bak's family was presumed to have lived in Helio-polis in lower Egypt[15] – a highly endemic area.

Therefore, if we combine the diagnostic possibility of Bak's chronic liver disease – derived from his appearance on his stele, with the high prevalence of schistosomiasis at the time and the place where Bak lived, the hypothesis achieves a fair degree of probability that the chief sculptor suffered from chronic hepato-splenic schistosomiasis. Final proof will depend on finding Bak's identifiable remains for analysis or the discovery of documents which describe his state of health or recognisable symptoms of disease.

Ruffer and other early investigators had to rely on the microscopic identification of Schistosoma eggs on histological examination of the treated tissues of mummies. In recent years it has become possible to detect the presence of the parasite's antigen in as little as 150 mg of tissue by means of an enzyme-linked immuno-sorbent assay (ELISA).[16] The antigen is a proteoglycan component of the adult worm's gut lining, which it regurgitates into the host's blood and which persists in the body tissues. This sensitive and specific method will facilitate a much wider survey of ancient remains, possibly including cancellous bone, to provide more accurate data on the true prevalence of the disease in antiquity.

*Acknowledgements:*
I am grateful to Dr C.N. Reeves of the Department of Egyptian Antiquities, the British Museum, for his helpful initial advice; and to Mrs M. Büsing of the Egyptian Museum, SMPK Berlin, for photographs of the plaster cast of Bak's stele.

7    Symmers 1903.
8    Mousa et al. 1967.
9    Kinnier Wilson 1967.
10   Deelder 1990.
11   Ruffer 1910.
12   Miller et al. 1992.
13   Theya Molleson personal communication

14   Manson-Bahr & Apted 1982, 209..
15   Krauss 1986, 45.
16   Miller et al. 1992.

# 20 Death in West Semitic Texts:Ugarit and Nabataea

## John F. Healey

ABSTRACT—*There are common themes in ancient Semitic attitudes to death and the dead revealed in various corpora of inscriptions: Ugaritic, Phoenician, Aramaic, Mesopotamian. This paper takes two examples, the Ugaritic texts of LBA Syria and the Nabataean Aramaic texts of Roman period northern Arabia. Four themes are examined: 1. Ideas of life after death and royal ideology; 2. Meals for the dead; 3. Euphemism and death; 4. The violation of tombs and legal aspects thereof.*

## Introduction

There is extensive material on death and the dead in West Semitic texts (the 'traditional' text of the Hebrew Bible and epigraphic material, both literary texts and non-literary documents: Phoenician, Aramaic, etc.). The two particular corpora which I have chosen to discuss are the Ugaritic texts and the Nabataean tomb-inscriptions.[1] The Ugaritic material dates to c. 1300-1200 BC, the end of the Syrian Late Bronze Age, and the Nabataean material dates to the first century AD. There is, therefore, a considerable time-gap between the two corpora, but that gap could be bridged without too much difficulty in a more extensive treatment by reference to other bodies of material from other sources in the first millennium BC (Biblical, Aramaic, Phoenician[2]). I intend to show in this paper that there are common themes which reveal deep-seated aspects of what used in the nineteenth century to be called "Semitic Religion". The term is no longer fashionable, but I hope the reader will be convinced that there is more than coincidence underlying the similarities between Ugarit and Petra in this regard.

I will consider four themes: ideas of life after death and royal ideology; meals for the dead; euphemism and death; the violation of tombs and the consequences thereof.

Before turning to these, note may be made of the fact that in the comparison of the Ugaritic texts with the Nabataean there is a lack of symmetry. From Ugarit we have no tomb inscriptions as such, whereas tomb inscriptions are among our most important sources of information on Nabataean. On the other hand, Ugaritic has a further dimension not found in Nabataean, that of mythological texts and rituals concerned to some extent with death.

Thus the Ugaritic deity or demon Mōtu, who plays a significant part in one of the mythological cycles connected with the storm and fertility god Ba'lu, is essentially a voracious Death god who swallows up enemies. His name, Mōtu, is also the common noun in Ugaritic meaning 'Death'. In some sense he is the personification of Death, one of Ba'al's several enemies. It is not so easy to be sure about what he is supposed to represent in a more precise way, but the most likely explanation of his role is that he represents the death-dealing drought of summer which is annually routed by the coming of Ba'al's fertility-producing rains in the autumn.[3]

---

1   For the Ugaritic literary texts the most accessible work in English is Gibson 1978, which is generally followed here, though many of the most important ritual and administrative texts are not in that volume. Reference to texts in Ugaritic is based on the corpus of Dietrich, Loretz & Sanmart in 1976 (*KTU*). For the Nabataean tomb inscriptions, cf. Healey, 1993a.

2   An excellent survey is provided by Spronk 1986. For the Bible, note Lewis 1989 and, recently, Bloch-Smith 1992.

3   On Mōtu, note Watson 1970. Cf. also Healey 1977, 11-52; in press.

# Life after death and royal ideology

There are several allusions to life after death in the Ugaritic mythological and legendary texts and it is very noticeable that there is an inconsistency in what is said. On the one hand it is clearly established that immortality is something reserved for the gods and denied to men. "Death, the final lot, nothing takes away; nothing takes away death, what comes after. Glaze will be poured upon my head, potash on the top of my pate ... The death of all men I will die; indeed I will surely die" is the hero Aqhatu's response in *KTU* 1.17 vi 35–38 to the goddess Anatu's blandishments in offering him immortality, a theme echoed also in the Mesopotamian Epic of Gilgamesh (in which the barmaid or alewife Siduri tells Gilgamesh he is wasting his time looking for the secret of immortality).[4] On the other hand, when the legendary king Kirtu is about to die, his friends ask what has happened to his immortality: "Shall you die, father, as men?...shall gods die?" (*KTU* 1.16 i 15–22). These texts seem difficult to reconcile, but the answer to the apparent contradiction probably lies in the fact that kings were in a special category of human being. Kirtu's friends in effect ask: "Can *kings* die?" Kings had, it appears, a special relationship with the gods and could expect some sort of immortality.

Ritual texts connected with the cult of the so-called Rephaim (Ugaritic *rāpi'ūma*), especially *KTU* 1.161 combined with 1.20-22, show that the long-dead royal ancestors were invoked to bring blessing upon the living king.[5] There is a king-list (*KTU* 1.113) in which the names of the kings are listed with the word *ilu* ('divine one') before each name. In a list of gods (*KTU* 1.118, etc.[6]) the 'kings' appear alongside other divinities. This does not mean that they were divine in the sense that Ba'al was divine, since the same god-list has included in it such items of cult equipment as the 'divine', i.e. sacred, thurible and metal water-dish.[7]

The special status of dead kings is reflected also in Ebla and Mari texts from earlier in the Bronze Age of Syria. Ebla had a ritual for the lamentations for the dead kings, as well as elaborate royal tombs. Mari had regular offerings 'for the kings'.[8]

Traces of such ideas can be seen also in the Hebrew Bible, notably in royal psalms (e.g., Psalm 16; Isaiah 14:9), but the Hebrew *r$^e$pā'ī m* are basically shades, out of proper contact with God. They are by no means in a blessed state of immortality. The mythological and cultic role of the Rephaim may well have been repressed as a Canaanite idolatry. Only in the late Old Testament age, in the Persian and Greek periods, did notions of blessed immortality for the just emerge in Israel.

Despite the extensive Nabataean materials, especially tomb-inscriptions, there is no clear evidence in writing on what the precise Nabataean attitude to the life of the dead was. That the dead were important is clear enough from the tombs themselves, which are extremely elaborate and must have been very expensive. The reference in Strabo (*Geography* 16.4.26) to the Nabataeans having no regard for the dead and treating them like dung is plainly wrong. It was long ago explained as based on a confusion between one of the Nabataean words for tomb, *kaprā*, and the Greek for 'dung', κόπρος, κοπρία or κοπρών.[9] It is reasonable to presume that the Nabataean upper classes believed that they could buy immortality by investing in tombs cut from the rock, tombs which would be virtually eternal, indeed 'houses of eternity'. More explicit, however, is the Nabataean attitude to dead kings. Apart from having particularly elaborate tombs (at Petra), some at least of the dead kings were regarded as divine, i.e. they achieved ancestral apotheosis. Thus Obodas I, who was buried at 'Avdat in the Negev, was raised to the status of having a cult dedicated to him, probably during the reign of Aretas IV (9 BC – AD 40). Texts refer to "Obodas the god".[10] Personal names like *'Abd'obodat* ("servant of [the god] Obodas") and *'abdḥaretat* ("servant of [the god] Aretas")[11] also suggest the divinisation [divination ?] of kings.

It is a moot question whether this has Semitic roots or came about entirely under Roman or Egyptian-Roman influence. Such ideas certainly existed in the earlier Near East, as we have seen.

# Meals for the dead

A second theme which links Ugarit and Nabataea is that of the feeding of the dead, or more specifically the notion of sharing meals with the dead.

At Ugarit there was, according to C.F.-A. Schaeffer, archaeological evidence of libation arrangements in tombs (which were frequently built under the family house). E.L. Sukenik drew parallels with tombs from Palestine. J.-F. Salles has, however, shown that this evidence is inconclusive. He has also directed attention to special rooms in houses which may have been devoted to the cult of the dead.[12] This kind of special room for the ancestor cult may be what is referred to in *KTU* 1.22 i 24 in a funerary ritual context as *bt 'ikl*, perhaps 'dining-room', though another possibility is that it means 'house of mourning'.[13] But the most striking aspect of the Ugaritic situation is the idea of meals to which the dead, apparently usually the dead kings, were summoned, as in the *rp'um* ritual

---

4   The translation more or less follows that of Healey 1977, 278. For the whole text and an English translation see Gibson 1978, 109. For the Gilgamesh material see Old Babylonian Gilgamesh X iii 3-5: Dalley 1989, 150.

5   On the *rp'um* cf. Healey 1978 and 1989.

6   Cf. Healey 1985 and 1988.

7   Healey 1985, 120.

8   Cf. Healey 1984.

9   Clermont-Ganneau 1895, 146-148.

10   The best known text is *CIS* II 354:1.

11   For personal names, cf. Khraysheh 1986, 129-131.

12   Salles, in this volume.

13   Cf. Akkadian *ikkillu*, *CAD* 7(I/J), 57-59.

(above). This is similar to, though not identical with, the Mesopotamian *kispum* ritual.[14]

In Nabataea it is a well-known feature that there are sometimes *triclinia* associated with tombs – the 'Uneishu tomb and the Urn tomb are, perhaps, the most unambiguous examples. Inscriptions identify various parts of tomb-complexes, notably the inscription of the Turkmaniye tomb inscription of Petra and one of the Madā'in Ṣāliḥ tombs.[15] The best guess is that the *triclinia* were used for commemorative ritual banquets. Such banquets are known from Strabo's description of the Nabataeans (*Geography* 16.4.26), though it is not indicated in Strabo that they had to do with the dead.

In the royal context note should be made of the earlier Aramaic Panamu inscription (*KAI* 214), in which the spirit of the dead king is expected in its afterlife to eat and drink with Hadad. J. C. Greenfield linked this too with the *kispum* ritual.[16]

## Euphemism and the dead

A surprising feature which is part of a widespread phenomenon and which could also be said to link our own attitudes to the the dead with those of the ancient world is the prominence of euphemism.

At Ugarit, in the mythology of the Death god, there is quite frequent mention of epithets of the underworld which are euphemistic. "We two did reach 'Pleasure' the land of pasture, 'Delight' the fields by the shore of the realm of death" (*KTU* 1.5 vi 6-7). *n'my* and *ysmt* are here euphemisms for the underworld. Elsewhere it is called "house of freedom" (*bt ḥptt*: *KTU* 1.4 viii 7).

In the early Near East this is paralleled in Mesopotamian titles of the underworld – "eternal city", "house of eternity" and "pure dwelling",[17] and there are signs of euphemism in the Old Testament: "the house appointed for all the living" (Job 30:23) and, possibly, "house of eternity" (Qo 12:5).

Euphemism is found in a wide variety of late Aramaic tomb inscriptions. Thus in Nabataean,[18] early Syriac[19] and Palmyrene,[20] the tomb may again be called "house of eternity" (*byt 'lm*). Nabataean tomb inscriptions contain such striking euphemisms as "she departed" (*ḥlkt*),[21] "the change of death befell him" (*ḥlp mwt*)[22] and "dwelling" for "tomb" (*'wn*).[23]

## The Violation of Tombs and Law

The violation of tombs was a great fear throughout the Semitic-speaking world and the general material was well reviewed long ago by A. Parrot and more briefly M. Lidzbarski.[24] There is no such material from Ugarit, though there are some remarkable parallels from Lycia.

With regard to the Nabataean material, firstly, it may be noted that most of the inscriptions were prepared by the main person who was to be buried in the tomb, not by relatives. The inscriptions reflect an intense concern with the protection of the tomb from various types of possible violation. In the Nabataean texts, though not generally elsewhere (apart from a few Palmyrene examples), the context is basically legal.

The legal aspect is most evident from the fact that a copy (Nabataean Aramaic *nsḥt '*) of the individual tomb inscription was lodged in a temple registry, as is explicitly stated in the case of one inscription which provides a good example of this material:

> "This is the tomb which Ḥalafu son of Qosnatan made for himself and for Su'aydu, his son, and for their sons and their descendants by hereditary title for ever. And his children (?) may be buried in this tomb: this Su'aydu and Manu'at and Ṣanaku and Ribamat and Umayyat and Salimat, daughters of this Ḥalafu. And none at all of Su'aydu and his brothers, males, and their sons and their descendants has the right to sell this tomb or write a deed of gift or anything else for anyone at all, except if one of them writes for his wife or for his daughters or for a father-in-law or for a son-in-law a document for burial only. And anyone who does other than this will be liable for a fine to Dushara the god of our lord in the sum of five hundred Ḥaretite *sela*s and to our lord the same amount, according to the copy of this deposited in the temple of Qaysha. In the month of Nisan, the fortieth year of Ḥaretat, King of the Nabataeans, lover of his people."[25]

A common feature is the listing of forbidden actions (selling, mortgaging, giving away, etc.). Such clauses are found in burial inscriptions from various sources.[26] Warnings against misuse and disturbance of the tomb, especially in the form of curses, are also a common enough feature,[27] but there are some aspects of the Nabataean texts which are unusual, at least so far as the Semitic sphere is concerned, especially the fact that not

---

14 Cf. esp. Healey 1978; and in relation to the text called "The Genealogy of the Hammurapi Dynasty", cf. Finkelstein 1966. For *kispum* in general cf. *CAD* 8(K), 425-427.

15 *CIS* II 350 and Jaussen & Savignac 1909, 1.

16 Greenfield 1973.

17 Cf. Tallqvist 1934, 15, 16, 36.

18 Negev 1971 50-52:1; Yadin 1962, 243-244.

19 Drijvers 1972, 79.

20 Jean & Hoftijzer 1965, 35.

21 Jaussen & Savignac 1909, 17:4. For recent discussion of this particular text, cf. Healey & Smith 1989. *ḥlkt* may, in fact, be an Arabism rather than a euphemism, since this verb can mean 'to die' in Arabic.

22 Jaussen & Savignac 1909, 9:6.

23 Ibid., 25:1.

24 Parrot 1939.

25 Jaussen & Savignac 1909, 36. The translation is as in Healey, 1993a.

26 Cf., e.g., the text discussed by Beeston 1979.

27 For a survey, cf. Parrot 1939.

only curses but also *fines* are invoked against the wrong-doer.

The recipients of fines are the gods (usually Dushara and associates) and officials (generally the king, once the governor,[28] once the '*pkl*'.[29] Rather difficult to establish is exactly what the fine is supposed to represent. References to the "full price" or "double the price" of the tomb[30] might suggest that the fines, in some cases at least, were meant to represent the price or a multiple of it.

Semitic parallels to the imposition of fines are few,[31] but fines and other features of the texts are found in the Greek and Lycian tomb inscriptions of Lycia (fifth century BC onwards).[32] The similarities between the Nabataean and Lycian formularies are striking, but the various similarities can be explained on the basis of the fact that in both cases, in Lycia and in Nabataea, the inscriptions are legal in character and that there was a widespread common legal ground in the Hellenised, earlier Achaemenid, East.[33] Just as a copy of the Nabataean tomb inscription was lodged in a temple, as is proved by the Nabataean inscription cited earlier, so in the case of the Greek inscriptions a copy (ἀντίγραφον, 'certified copy of an official document') was placed in a public registry.[34] In Nabataean, as we have seen, the term *nsht'* is used for the 'copy'. Nabataean law, incidentally, owes much to the Imperial Aramaic and cuneiform traditions,[35] but cuneiform does not know of tomb inscriptions like the Nabataean ones. Note may be made of royal grants of burial places to eunuchs, in which curses of gods are invoked,[36] but Mesopotamian tomb-curses are otherwise rare.[37]

A final word on the Turkmaniye tomb inscription at Petra.[38] This has been seen as in need of explanation because of the unusual fact that it has no personal name attached to it. M. Gawlikowski suggested there was a ban on putting names on tombs at Petra because of the sanctity of the site.[39] In fact, however, there *are* grave inscriptions at Petra containing personal names (as in a major tomb just outside the Siq[40]) and the absence of the personal name of the owner may be explained in the case of the Turkmaniye tomb by the possibility that it belonged to the temple of the god Dushara. The inscription in fact emphasises, rather unusually, that the tomb is sacred to Dushara and that there are documents deposited elsewhere, presumably in a temple archive, giving further details.

---

28  Jaussen & Savignac 1909, 38.
29  Ibid., 16.
30  Ibid., 1:8; 31:7.
31  Note may be made of a Palmyrene tomb inscription which imposes a fine for misuse of the tomb: Cantineau 1933, 184, discussed by Parrot 1939, 44-45.
32  Cf. Bryce & Zahle 1986, 116-127; Bryce 1981, especially for general burial practices and Lycian inscriptions. For Greek inscriptions, cf. Hirschfeld 1887; Arkwright 1911. The Greek material from Asia Minor is surveyed by Parrot 1939, 103-139. For details of comparison, cf. Keil 1908, esp. 567-572 .
33  Keil 1908, 570-572. Nabataean tombs are discussed in the context of Roman funerary art by Toynbee 1971, 191-199. Balty 1983, 316-324, also discusses Greek and Roman analogies of the Nabataean tombs and especially the legal background of Roman tombs.

34  cf. Parrot 1939, 44-45, 125.
35  Cf. Healey, 1993b.
36  Cf. Postgate 1969, Nos.9-12, and now grave-inscriptions of queens: Fadhil 1990a, 461-470; 1990b, 471-482.
37  Parrot 1939, 9-24.
38  *CIS* II 350.
39  Gawlikowski 1975.
40  Milik 1976.

# 21 Some Concepts of Afterlife in Mesopotamia and Greece

## Charles Penglase

ABSTRACT— *There are a number of parallels between the Classical and Mesopotamian notions of afterlife, but for the most part the concepts of afterlife in the two societies are dissimilar. This paper gives a presentation of the main concepts about afterlife in the mythical literature; a brief overview of the Mesopotamian netherworld in the literature at various periods; consideration of the gods and functions relating to the dead; and of the conditions of the dead. Then follows a discussion of major parallels and contrasts of these three aspects in Greek mythical literature, taking into account the development of Greek ideas of the afterlife down to the end of the Early Archaic period in Greece.*

The afterlife in Mesopotamia and Greece is too large and complex a topic to be examined all at once and must be separated into manageable segments. This comparative discussion is therefore limited to dealing with some aspects of the realm of the dead, and the fate of the dead there in literature of Mesopotamia and early Greece. A number of general similarities, and even specific parallels in the case of some motifs are evident in the beliefs of the two areas. This study is derived from literature, but is highly relevant to the interpretation of archaeological remains.

It is important to be aware that the sources often represent seemingly contradictory pictures of the netherworld and of the fate of the dead. The varying pictures which arise may be due to the different dates of the evidence and a change in beliefs, or to the different findspots and the different cults from which the evidence comes. The dates of the Mesopotamian literary sources on the netherworld range from the Old Sumerian to Neo-Babylonian and Neo-Assyrian times, a period of approximately two thousand years, and the tablets come from all over Mesopotamia. However, despite varying details, the general picture that is gained of the realm of the dead is that of a gloomy and sometimes hostile place inhabited by lowerworld gods, demons and the dead, a place which the Mesopotamian peoples often had due cause to fear. This is echoed to some extent in Greek texts of the eighth and seventh centuries BC.

In Mesopotamia the place of the dead is situated under the surface of the earth, the netherworld. It is the realm of Ereshkigal and Nergal, the queen and (consort) king of the netherworld. Other divine figures inhabit the netherworld, prominent among which are the Anunna gods, a group of seven judges in the netherworld, as seen in the Sumerian work *Inana's Descent to the Netherworld* (line 163). In later times Anunnakku seems to have been a collective name for the underworld gods.[1] Besides the main gods and lesser gods (some texts mention six hundred) there are various monsters, demons and, of course, the dead.[2]

The netherworld has several names some of which are descriptive.[3] The most common is ki (Sumerian) or *erṣetum* (Akkadian), meaning 'earth'. This is frequently compounded with adjectives such as dagal, Akkadian *rapsu*, 'wide'. Another name, Arallu (Sumerian Arali), is of uncertain derivation. Urugal, meaning 'great city', refers to the conception of the netherworld as a city filled with the dead; another term which may also refer to the city nature of the netherworld is Kutû, which is the name of an actual city. The god of this city was Nergal, the netherworld god himself, so the term may have originally been symbolic. Ki-gal 'great earth' is another Sumerian term for the netherworld; it is part of

---

1   Falkenstein 1965, 127-140; Kienast 1965, 141-158; Tsukimoto 1985, 10; Edzard 1990, 37.
2   Lambert 1980, 59.
3   Tallqvist 1934; Meier 1943: 213-214; Tsukimoto 1980, 7; Groneberg 1990, 258-259.

the netherworld queen's name, Ereshkigal, 'queen of the great earth, or netherworld'. An important term is kur-nu-gi₄-a, or in Akkadian *erṣet la-târi*, meaning the 'Land of No Return', which describes a significant aspect of the netherworld. Another term is edin, Akkadian *ṣeru*, 'desert', 'steppe'. There are other possible designations, a few of which are ambiguous.

One important but ambiguous term is kur, the Sumerian word for 'mountain', or 'foreign land', sometimes with a hostile connotation of 'enemy land', but this word is also used to designate the netherworld.[4] The use of this word may either be a result of the conception of kur as 'land' or possibly it may have some connexion with the way in which the netherworld is sometimes approached, via the mountains at the edge of the world. Indeed the netherworld can be approached from various directions. Although Ereshkigal's realm is below the earth, it can be approached from a horizontal direction. One entrance is commonly located in the far west where the sun, Sumerian Utu, Akkadian Shamash, descends each night to the netherworld. The place is called ka.gal ᵈUtu.šu.a, Akkadian *abul ereb ᵈ šamši*, 'place of lying down of the sun', and other similar names.[5] According to one view the gidim, Akkadian *etemmu*, the spirit of the dead, is sent like the demons to the netherworld across the earth in a horizontal fashion, crossing a desert, a mountain and finally the Hubur river, beyond which is the netherworld.[6] At the River Hubur there seems to be a boatman named Humuṭ-tabal, meaning 'take away quickly', who ferries the *etemmu* across the frontier of the Land of No Return.[7] However, any tomb or grave in which the dead were laid was understood to be an entrance to the netherworld.[8] The way in which they were supposed to reach Ereshkigal's realm is not clear in this situation, but it may be straight down, since the netherworld is conceived as beginning a short distance below the surface of the earth. As seen in the case of the god Dumuzi, the lowerworld may also be entered via the kur, a mountain or mountains in the east, where the sun rises from the netherworld every morning.[9] The River Hubur can also be located in the mountainous land at the place where the sun rises.

The netherworld is generally presented as a dark, gloomy, dusty, unattractive place, at least as it is portrayed in the Neo-Assyrian *Ishtar's Descent to the Netherworld* (lines 4-11), the Akkadian version of the Old Babylonian Sumerian myth, *Inana's Descent to the Netherworld*.[10] However, one text suggests a belief that the sun travels through the netherworld during the night of the world above.[11] This text indicates that the moon god Nanna-Suen also visited the netherworld once every month on his 'day of lying down', and, with Utu, carried out some kind of judgement of the dead.

The spirit of the dead, the gidim/*etemmu* is an insubstantial ghost.[12] In *Ishtar's Descent to the Netherworld* it is seen to be winged (line 10), and in some texts is bird-like.[13] For the mortal dead the netherworld is the Land of No Return. The reason for this description is transparent as the dead never come to life again. However, if the spirit is not cared for by the living, neither receiving offerings, nor hearing its name uttered, it can return to the world above and haunt the living. The spirit must then be despatched to the netherworld by exorcistic rituals.[14] There is also the evocation of spirits of the dead. For instance, in the literary work *Gilgamesh, Enkidu and the Netherworld* (lines 240-243), the hero Gilgamesh makes a hole in the earth and with the help of the sun-god Utu the spirit of his friend Enkidu rises via this connecting shaft to speak to him.[15]

There is no reincarnation or return to life in the world above. However, death appears to some extent to be a continuation in the netherworld of the life which the person had lived in the world of the living. Life in the underworld is in fact a pale and often unpleasant imitation of life on earth.[16] After the death of the body, the spirit travels to the netherworld across the earth and River Hubur, or to the mountains in the east, and enters through the gates. Burial and the correct rites are required for the *etemmu* to be allowed to enter the netherworld. Otherwise it is forced to wander around on the earth, generally acting inimically towards the living, causing especially what are recognised as psychological illnesses. These spirits must be dispatched to the netherworld by incantations.[17]

On entrance to the netherworld the *etemmu* of the recently dead seem to undergo some kind of judgement (*The Death of Ur-Nammu*, lines 128-143). Depending on the texts, the judges are the Anunna-gods, or Gilgamesh, or Utu and Nanna as seen in the Pushkin elegy published by Kramer.[18] The exact nature of the judgement is uncertain, but it seems that the newcomer is allocated his place in the netherworld. The allocation of the dead's place in the netherworld seems to be made on the basis of his or her position and achievements while alive, but there does not seem to be any moral judgement.[19]

4   Limet 1978, 1-12; Steiner 1982, 633-663.
5   Stola 1972, 267; Bottéro 1980, 34; 1982; 376.
6   Bottéro 1983, 191.
7   Heidel 1949, 171-172; Stola 1972, 267; Behrens 1978, 192-194; Cooper 1980, 179-180, 183-184, 187-188.
8   Heidel 1949, 171; Tsukimoto 1985, 6, 8.
9   Sladek 1974, 62, n.4; Lambert 1985, 202.
10  Stola 1972, 268-270.
11  Kramer 1960, 62-63; Stola 1972, 271; Heimpel 1986, 127-128,, 149-150.
12  Tsukimoto 1985, 10; Groneberg 1990, 251.
13  Deller, in press.
14  Stola 1972, 268; Bottéro 1980, 41; 1983, 177-179.
15  Tropper 1986, 19-20.
16  Kramer 1960: 66; 1967, 104-122; Bottéro 1982, 375-376.
17  Ebeling 1931, 122-123; Heidel 1949, 155; Bottéro 1983, 153-154, 191-192.
18  Kramer 1960.
19  Ibid., 62-3, 67¹⁶; Stola 1972, 268; Bottéro 1983, 200; Tsukimoto 1985, 14-19; Bauer 1989, 21-27.

In summary, life after death is continued in the netherworld and appears in many texts to be a curse more than a blessing. There is, however, one text, the Pushkin elegy, which suggests that there may at one time have been less pessimistic beliefs held at least by some. In this text a man intercedes on behalf of his dead father with Nanna, Shamash, and other gods for a favourable destiny in the netherworld, with sympathy and with pure fresh water to drink.[20] Finally, a rather obscure line at the end of *Ishtar's Descent to the Netherworld* (lines 136-138) presents the idea that the dead rise with Dumuzi as he rises from the netherworld.[21] However, just what this rise is, the state of the dead in it, where the dead rise from, where they go to, and for what purpose, remain unclear.

Some general features of the Mesopotamian beliefs directly parallel features of the early Greek concepts, and there are some specific parallels of motif. The area of this comparison is restricted to the early Greek times and the relevent works of literature are the Homeric epics *The Iliad* and *The Odyssey*, which were written down between approximately 750 and 700 BC, Hesiod's *Theogony*, written down perhaps a little later, and the *Homeric Hymn to Demeter*, of about 650 to 600 BC.[22] These works were of course compositions based on the formulaic tradition. This material reveals customs and beliefs of early historical Greece, but it may also present ideas of Greece in the preceding Dark Age, as it is called, a period which spanned approximately the two hundred years from 1100 to 900 BC after the fall of the Bronze-Age Mycenaean civilisation in Greece. Bronze-Age traditions may also be preserved in this material.

As in Mesopotamia the world of the dead is situated in the subterranean region, the netherworld, and is similarly ruled by a divine king and queen, of which pair the queen is likewise more prominent in myth. There are also similar ambiguities of approach to the netherworld. In fact, in *The Iliad* (3.276 and 19.258) and *The Odyssey* (Books 10 and 12) the references to the actual location or method of approach to it are somewhat conflicting as the poet seems to be indifferent to the actual location of the realm of the dead. This indifference is also shared by Hesiod in *Theogony* (lines 622, 746), because sometimes the netherworld is below and at other times at the edge of the earth.[23] Nevertheless, in *The Iliad* it is always below the earth, while in *Homeric Hymn to Demeter*, Hades is also clearly directly below the earth since the netherworld king, also named Hades, carries off the young goddess Persephone down through a chasm in the earth; but it is interesting to note that the field in which Persephone is playing when she is abducted lies at the edge of the earth near the streams of River Ocean, which encircles the earth. Similarly, when Persephone returns from the netherworld at the end of the work, she returns over the earth to Eleusis as though from the edge of the earth (lines 1-37, 375-385). In these literary works, it is probably the entrance which is located at the edge of the earth, while the netherworld is below.

The idea in *The Odyssey*, that one must cross the River Ocean at the edge of the earth to enter Hades, is similar to the crossing of the River Hubur in Mesopotamia. There is also the boatman who carries the souls across the river into Hades, Humuṭ-tabal in Mesopotamia, Charon in Greece. With Charon the river is called the Acheron and this is sometimes seen to be beneath the earth.

In the Homeric epics the deceased must similarly receive the proper funerary rites before the spirit may cross to Hades, otherwise it is not allowed into Hades and wanders over the earth (*Iliad* 23.71; *Odyssey* 11.72).[24] However, in the epics this occurs after cremation, not just by burial as in Mesopotamia. Nevertheless, funerary customs varied in different periods and in the archaeological evidence it is clear that burial was also at times the custom.[25] As in Mesopotamia, the dead often received provision at burial, perhaps also for the journey to the netherworld as it was in Mesopotamia. There seems also to have been in Greece a cult of the dead where offerings were made to the shades in the netherworld. Evidence for this may be seen in the bottomless and other vessels which were placed over the graves.[26] This seems, however, to indicate merely funerary offerings and perhaps evocational offerings rather than the continual supply of offerings seen with the Mesopotamian peoples.

In Mesopotamia the spirit of the dead has wings as does the Greek spirit, the *psyche*, and, as in Mesopotamia, it is at times comparable with birds.[27] Souls with wings are often shown on Greek pottery. In the Homeric epics the conception is also evident that the dead remain as they were at the point of death. For instance, in *The Odyssey* (11.36-41), Odysseus sees soldiers who have been killed, still in their uniforms with bleeding wounds visible. This parallels to some extent the description of the dead in Tablet XII of the *Epic of Gilgamesh*. However, unlike in Mesopotamia, the souls can never return to haunt the living (*Iliad* 23.75).[28]

Moral judgement of the dead seems to be absent in the early Greek conception of the netherworld, just as it was absent in Mesopotamian belief. The passages which indicate punishment in *The Odyssey*, besides being considered additions of later times when there was a belief in moral judgement,[29] are not evidence for moral judgement among the dead, but are rather clearly

---

20 Kramer 1960, 62-63, lines 87-112.
21 Tsukimoto 1985, 11-14.
22 West 1966, 40-41, esp. 46; Richardson 1974, 5-6, 11-12.
23 West 1966, 339.

24 Mylonas 1948, 61-62; Sourvinou-Inwood 1983, 36.
25 Mylonas 1948, 60, 68-69, 74, 79; Andronicus 1968, 37-39.
26 Ibid., 57, 91-102, 106-107.
27 Mühll 1939, 10.
28 Mylonas 1948, 62, 70; Sourvinou-Inwood 1983, 36.
29 Büchner 1937, 104.

special cases of revenge that Zeus takes on specific mythical figures (*Odyssey* 11.568-627).[30]

In the Homeric epics, the same gloomy view is held of the netherworld and life after death as seen in Mesopotamia. As the spirit of the hero Achilles says to Odysseus, it is better to be a poor serf on earth among the living than to be the king of the dead in the netherworld (*Odyssey* 11.487-491). There is no evidence in these Greek works of the paradise offered for instance to the Orphics, whether this paradise is in the sky, beneath the earth or on the Isles of the Blessed. The *Homeric Hymn to Demeter*, on the other hand, ends with a promise of a favourable destiny for those initiated in the Eleusinian mysteries (lines 480-482), but it does not disclose exactly what the nature of this destiny is or where it is located.

The parallels of the boatman, the river at the edge of the netherworld, and even the winged, bird-like souls, are specific. Other parallels are more general. There are, however, also many differences, and above all differences in detail even in the parallels which can be seen. Nevertheless, if one compares the Greek concepts in these works with the Egyptian beliefs of the afterlife, beliefs which even in general terms are almost entirely different,[31] one is struck by the similarity in many basic features between the netherworlds and concepts of afterlife in Mesopotamia and early Greece. If there is some connexion between the beliefs of these two areas, as a similar framework and some specific parallels may suggest, it must have been a very ancient connexion, since the parallels are of the more general and basic kind while the details are usually quite different.

---

30   Stola 1972, 260, 268.

31   Scandone Matthiae 1987, 11-47.

# 22 A Typology of Dilmun Burial Mounds

## *Abdulaziz Soweileh*

ABSTRACT—*This paper examines the evidence of mortuary practices from recently excavated 'Dilmun' cemeteries at Hamad Town, Buri, Al-Hajjar and Saar, and attempts to establish a typology for the development of burial cemeteries on Bronze-Age Bahrain.*

The burial mounds of the State of Bahrain provide one of the world's most notable archaeological sites. Since the eighteenth century these mounds have challenged archaeologists and collectors alike in their attempts to unearth and analyse their contents. The large number of mounds prompted some researchers to conclude that they were burial sites for civilizations from outside Bahrain and that the main island was a cemetery for the whole region.[1] Some researchers interpreted the evidence from cuneiform documents to suggest that Dilmun (Bahrain) was a sacred Holy Land, hence the reason for its use as a burial site.[2]

The total number of mounds is most recently estimated at some 172,000[3] and they are located mainly in the centre and northern part of the main island, covering an area of 20 square miles. They constitute the largest readily visible (i.e., showing above ground) archaeological burial site in the world and some can apparently be dated as far back as the second half of the third millennium B.C. They are constructed by hand from stone, gravel and sand. Occasionally larger stones were mixed with the sand, usually in the centre of the main burial chamber.

## Early excavations

In 1879 Captain Durand and his soldiers excavated a 45 foot high mound and came to the conclusion that the mounds were Phoenician in origin.[4] In 1889 Theodore Bent and his wife visited Bahrain and after excavating

another large mound expressed their agreement with Durand's theory.[5] Colonel Prideaux also came to the same conclusion in 1906.[6]

It was in 1925 that Ernest MacKay, following excavation work at Kish, visited Bahrain and carried out the excavation of 50 mounds. As a result of his work, he went on to develop the theory that Bahrain was a burial site for a larger civilization.[7] However, from 1940-44, P.B. Cornwall carried out a programme of excavation and research which led him to contradict the theories of MacKay and Durand and propose that the burial mounds were for the indigenous population.[8] His conclusions were confirmed by a Danish archaeological team in 1953 which unearthed the first Dilmun settlement at Qala'at al-Bahrain (Bahrain Fort).[9]

Since 1970 teams of Bahraini, Arabic and other foreign archaeologists have conducted more-or-less continuous 'rescue' excavations aimed at discovering the secrets of Bahrain's mounds. As a result of this work, I would suggest that there are, in fact, four distinct types of mound, each showing differences in their architecture, design and contents.

## 1. Early type (?2500–2300 BC)

These mounds are small in size and, viewed from a distance, resemble a pile of medium and large stones. In the centre lies a burial chamber constructed from the same type of stone but of a larger size. These are piled on

---

1 MacKay 1929; Lamberg-Karlovsky 1982; During Caspers 1984. Against this view, Bibby 1969, 18; 1986 (or 1985); Frohlich 1983; and Lowe 1986, 81-82.
2 Cf especially Burrows 1921. Alster 1983, 52-59 contradicts this interpretation of the cuneiform sources.
3 Larsen 1983, 45. For varying estimates, cf. Lamberg-Karlovsky 1986, 156 (or 1985, 15).
4 Durand 1879, partly reproduced as 1880.

5 Bent 1890; Bent & Bent 1900.
6 Prideaux 1912.
7 MacKay 1929.
8 Cornwall 1943; 1944; 1946; 1948.
9 Qala'at al Bahrain: Glob 1954a; 1955. For burial mounds excavated by the Danes, cf. Glob 1954b. See also on the Danish expedition, Bibby 1969.

top of one another in such a way that rows of stones overlap inwards to roof the chamber. Occasionally the chamber is covered with a large flat capstone, but generally speaking the first method was used. The chamber is surrounded by a ring wall made from larger stones and it may contain smaller chambers for the burial of infants, some of whom were found to have died between the ages of 1 month and 7 years.

This Early type of mound is found scattered along the edges of valleys and in open spaces, indicating that it was the prototype for the larger burial mounds which came later. The contents of this type of mound were most commonly Umm an-Nar pottery, which is red in colour and decorated in a black ribbon design or with black triangles in the upper part of the pot; shell amulets (perhaps seals); 'Dilmun' seals; bronze spears; and necklaces made of semi-precious stones. On the basis of the finds, these mounds may possibly be dated to c. 2500-2300 BC. Local archaeologists believe this to have been the time of the beginning the civilisation of 'Dilmun'.

## 2. Intermediate type (?2300–2000 BC)

These are fewer in number and located mainly in the area which is now Hamad Town.[10] The Intermediate mounds are larger with a flat top. Some of the stones of both the main and subsidiary chambers are often visible in the side of the mound, a feature which distinguishes them from other types. They are usually 1–1.5 metres in height, but occasionally reach 2 metres and the diameter ranges from 6 to 12 metres. The burial chamber itself usually faces east-west, measures 3 or more metres in length and 1 metre in height, and is built on a clay floor overlying bedrock. The grave is wider at the base, approximately 1 metre gradually narrowing to approximately 0.5 m. It is usually covered by 4-8 (small to medium) calcite stones. This type of burial chamber may be surrounded by a ring wall, and sometimes has support walls radiating out from the central chamber to the ring wall. These support walls sit above a deposit of in-filled sand. Another similarity to the Early type is the occasional addition of subsidiary chambers extending from the ring wall and usually situated on the south-east and north-east sides.

Contents of the Intermediate type include pottery, Dilmun seals, amulet shells and bronze weapons. There are also tools used to make Dilmun seals such as needles with animal and bird bone handles; bronze sewing needles; and bronze cups. The finds seem to date this building period to between c. 2300 and 2000 BC.

## 3. Late type (?2000–1400 BC)

This type of mound takes the shape of a dome and most are single burials, while a few are family mounds with more than one main chamber and subsidiary chambers for infants. As with the earlier types most of the burial chamber and the circular wall are covered by sand or a calcite gravel. A cross section shows that the cavity between central chamber and wall is filled with sand in such a way that the sand is piled higher towards the chamber than around the central wall, thus creating the form of a cone.

The evidence suggests that this type of chamber was built before the death of the occupant. After the burial the chamber was then covered and the last layer of fill added to create the cone-shaped appearance. It appears that if the main chamber was used to bury an adult member of the family then no smaller chambers were added. However, if any children in the family died before the adult, then the mound would contain chambers added to the main burial chamber. Any additional chambers usually contain skeletons of children under the age of 12 years.

The Late type of grave is normally cut into bedrock. However, in some cases the grave and side walls are built above ground. Most graves have alcoves in the south-east and north-east corners, while a few have an alcove in each corner. Ovoid jars similar to those found by the Danish expedition Group in City II at Bahrain Fort, apparently dating to 2000–1400 BC,[11] were found in many graves of the this type.

The main burial chamber of this type of mound is rectangular with a smoothly dressed face of stones on the inside (externally roughly hewn). It is usually covered by three large cap-stones and is wider at the base than at the top. The western wall of the chamber was not bonded and offered an easy entry into the tomb through which many grave-thieves and 'amateur archaeologists' obtained access to the contents. The family mound has more than one main grave and each of these contains a main burial chamber with additional smaller ones attached to the ring-wall. There is usually a small alcove in the side wall of the chamber. The lapse of time between the construction of the main and additional side chambers can easily be determined when, as was sometimes the case, part of the ring-wall was demolished in order to add another chamber.

Generally speaking, the position of the body in the three early types of mound is the same. The dead were placed in a 'foetal' position usually lying on the right side, but occasionally on the left. The knees were drawn up to the chest and hands crossed with palms outstretched as if the person were praying. My interpretation of the use of the 'foetal' position is that it reflects a society's belief that death also entails a 're-birth' into the afterlife. Similarly, pottery vessels and food offerings often found in the alcove may suggest a belief in the afterlife, representing

---

10    Unpublished, cf. summary by Lowe 1986.

11    Cf Bibby 1969, 130.

perhaps the food and drink required by the occupant after death.[12] Other contents of the Late type of burial mound include the usual collection of pottery, Dilmun seals, shell seals, bronze utensils and weapons such as spears, short swords and daggers. In addition there were necklaces made from semi-precious stones such as carnelian, indicating that there was an early trade connexion between Dilmun, Baluchistan and Yemen. The finding of soap stone utensils again suggests connections between Bahrain and Baluchistan, Elam and Oman. Unique to the Late type mounds are locally made palm leaf baskets coated with bitumen.

# 4 Tylos period type (c.300 BC–AD 200)[13]

These mounds are large and conical or flat-topped. Unlike Dilmun-period burials, they do not have ring walls. These graves are normally built of small stones and covered with sand. Some graves were built on a specially prepared surface. Additional graves were later dug into the fill of the earlier ones. Jar burials were also used for children; the jars used for infant burials were household storage jars. In some cases, a simple pit was cut for an infant burial and a large sherd or stone used to cover the burial.

In each mound there may be many single burial chambers, arranged in a concentric ring around the centre of the mound. Originally each of these single burial chambers formed its own small mound, but over time became amalgamated into one larger mound. Internal evidence of the finds suggests some of these amalgamated mounds were in use for up to a century.

The chambers of the Tylos period mounds were built from calcite stones joined together with mortar. Occasionally the inner surface was coated with gypsum mixed with ashes. The chambers are rather long and contain only a single skeleton. In some cases, the bones from more than one skeleton were found, all mixed up and pushed to one end of the grave suggesting that the chamber was partly emptied and reused. In a few cases a group of skeletons was found together in one chamber, each properly buried. This suggests that the group died at the same time. The chambers are covered either by slabs of 'sea-stone' or calcite stones joined together with mortar. In some cases, glazed bowls and charcoal were found resting upside-down above the cap-stones, perhaps used in burial ceremonies of some sort.

As for the contents of the chambers themselves, these typically include plates and small glass containers in green, blue or gold, similar to specimens found elsewhere in the region of the Gulf States, Iraq and Syria. They date to the Hellenistic period, c.300 BC to 200 AD. Wherever a female or a child was buried, their gold and jewellery were interred with them.

This type of burial structure was used until the early Islamic period; approximately the seventh to eighth centuries AD. Some Islamic burial chambers have been found interspersed between the layers of large Tylos mounds and in fact some modern villages have located their graveyards in the middle of these mounds.

# Concluding remarks

1. Burial fields in Bahrain are located on non-productive land, i.e. on limestone outcrops where bedrock is only 20-30 cm below the surface. For this reason, there seems to have been a preference for building tombs above bedrock rather than to cut them into the bedrock, below ground, which would have been a difficult and time-consuming endeavour. Alternatively, religious belief may have dictated a preference for burial above rather than below ground. Since some of the burial mounds were prepared before the death of any member of the family, it may be that they needed to be identified above ground by the family to make them easy to locate when a burial was to take place. The different layers of pottery sherds found around the perimeter walls and the chamber indicate frequent visits by relatives of the deceased. Perhaps the design was made in such a way so as to make the mounds easily identifiable for visiting purposes.

2. Each family had its own burial ground which was marked and identified by a round fence or wall, isolating it from neighbouring burial grounds. Once the burial process was completed, the chambers were covered by sand and small stones, as a result of which a mound was made, marking the burial site.

3. Building a mound on top of a burial chamber was part of a ceremonial ritual, particularly between the period 2300-2000 BC, when no chambers were cut into the bedrock.

In conclusion, simple burial mound construction from around 2800 BC had evolved by the third century BC into the practice of building elaborate burial mounds, a practice and development which may be explained to some degree by the points here made.

*Acknowledgements*
The excavations of the moundfields at Hamad Town and elsewhere are financed by the State of Bahrain Ministry of Information and organized by the Directorate of Archaeology and Museums. I should like to thank Dr Robert Killick of the London-Bahrain Archaeological Expedition for facilitating my attendance at the Manchester conference, and the British Council in Manama, Bahrain, for the grant of financial support for the visit.

---

12  Cf., for Mesopotamia, Postgate 1980; Bolt & Green, in press.
13  'Tylos' or 'Tyros' was apparently the Hellenised form of Dilmun/Tilmun.

# 23  Differential Burial Practices in Cyprus at the Beginning of the Iron Age

## *Louise Steel*

ABSTRACT—*In this paper I discuss patterns in the funerary record of Cyprus in the eleventh-tenth centuries BC. I examine the evidence for differential treatment of individuals on the basis of age, sex and social position. (1) Child remains. Initial results are promising. Newly born and premature babies are excluded from burial in formal cemetery areas, and instead are located in settlement contexts, generally close to the city walls. More excavations however, are needed within Early Iron-Age settlements to determine whether it is exclusively this age group which is denied access to formal burial areas. Older children are admitted to 'adult' cemeteries, though they may be buried in pit/cist graves, rather than in chamber tombs. They tend to be inhumed, though the practice of cremation is not reserved exclusively for adults. The range of grave-goods deposited with child burials has also produced interesting results. Problems arise, though, due to poor recovery and insufficient analyses of the skeletal remains. The ages of the children who are represented in the formal cemeteries are unknown, and so differential treatment according to age is not apparent. (2) Sex differentiation. The results are less promising, as the vast majority of the skeletons have not been sexed. What evidence is available indicates that there is no serious differentiation in a) the treatment/preparation of the corpse, b) the type of burial facility and c) the range of grave furniture. There are certain artefacts that may be restricted to a particular sex though this is only a tentative suggestion. (3) Ranking may be identified by wealth of grave-goods, the occurrence of 'symbols of office' and the size and type of burial facility. Whilst the contents of most tomb-groups are largely compatible, certain tombs do stand out because of the range and quality of their funerary furniture. It is suggested that these are indicative of ranking.*

## Introduction

Funerary remains are frequently the only source of information for the archaeologist. This is a common problem for many periods of Cypriot prehistory, including the eleventh century BC. The study of funerary material is of intrinsic interest, however, as it represents a group of associated remains that were intentionally deposited at one time, rather than the chance survival of finds from a settlement context. It is important to remember, however, that the archaeologist only has reference to the material residue of a funeral, rather than the ritual in its entirety. Ideally, interpretations of these remains should be based on literary sources, or other, non-verbal records, such as Greek LG vase paintings. Unfortunately we do not have such records for the EIA of Cyprus, and so are entirely dependent on the material remains from tombs. In this paper I shall discuss patterns which are discernible in the funerary record of Cyprus at the transition from the

Bronze to the Iron Age. I shall discuss the evidence for the differential treatment of individuals on the basis of age and sex, and examine the evidence for ranking.

There were a number of important changes in funerary ritual in Cyprus in the eleventh century BC.[1] These may in part be attributed to the appearance of a new ethnic element and in part to a change in social organisation at the beginning of the Iron Age. Throughout the Late Bronze Age Cypriot burial practices consisted of multiple inhumations in small chamber tombs within the perimeter of the settlement. Though a new tomb-type (the shaft grave, which housed between one and three burials) was introduced for some of the burying group in the twelfth century BC, traditional burial practices continued unabated throughout the island, for the rest of the population.

In the eleventh century BC new funerary practices were introduced to Cyprus, contemporary with a major

---

1  Steel 1993, 165-169.

change in the island's settlement pattern and material culture.[2] (1) Formal areas, used exclusively for burial, were established outside the settlement area. (2) A new, intrusive tomb type was introduced, presumably from the Aegean. This comprises a rock-cut chamber (circular, square or trapezoidal in shape) approached by a passage dromos, up to 8.3 m long. (3) The chamber tomb was used to house a small number of burials, usually only one or two, but on occasion up to five burials. This contrasts with the large, 'family' vaults of the LC period, which were in use over several generations, and may indicate a shift in emphasis in social organisation, away from large, corporate, 'kinship' groups to a smaller social unit. (4) Whilst inhumation continued to be the typical rite, cremation occurs sporadically for the first time.[3]

## Child burials

The study of the child burials has produced interesting results,[4] though it is hampered by uneven recovery of child remains, due to their fragile nature and the limited study of human remains. Frequently the identification of a child burial is dependent on the absence of skeletal remains, and it is probable that many child burials have gone undetected. Child burials fall into two main categories. The first group consists of a small number of intramural burials, but the main category comprises those child burials admitted to the formal, extramural cemeteries.

1. Infant (or foetal) remains have been uncovered at both Salamis and Kition-*Bamboula*, within the city walls, in association with PWP and WP I pottery, and at Salamis they continue into the tenth, ninth and eighth centuries BC.[5] They were deposited in re-used Canaanite Jars placed in small pits, in no fixed orientation. These burials have been found in association with domestic structures and along the city walls. The infants were provided with no grave-gifts other than the vessel in which they were buried, which should be viewed merely as a receptacle for the body, rather than equipment for the afterlife.

   More excavations are needed within the EIA settlements to establish whether it was this age-group alone that was denied burial within the formal cemeteries. These abbreviated funerary rites would cause minimum disruption to community life, thus indicating that the infant had not yet been admitted formally into the community.[6] Some infants/children were admitted to the formal burial

areas. As their ages are unknown, it is unclear at what age children were accepted into society, though on present evidence it appears that only new-born and pre-term infants were excluded from burial within the formal burying grounds.

2. Child burials in the extramural cemeteries would either be deposited in a pit or cist grave,[7] or in a chamber tomb.[8] The infant/child burial in Lapithos-*Kastros* Tomb 420 was not admitted into the burial chamber itself, but was deposited in the dromos niche, together with a couple of pots. A similar deposit in the dromos niche of Episkopi-*Kaloriziki* Tomb 33, in which no skeletal remains were found, might also be interpreted as an infant or child inhumation. The other child burials were deposited within the burial chamber, which in some cases had been constructed especially for the child burial.[9] Inhumation was the usual rite, but there is one recorded incident of cremation.[10]

   The child burials had a modest provision for the afterlife. The usual grave furniture consisted of a range of ceramic vessels. Though these were not deposited in the quantities typical of adult burials, they comprised a similar range of vessels. The emphasis was on bowls, plates and storage vessels. Sometimes miniature vessels were buried with the children[11] and the amphoriskoi and amphoroid craters might be miniatures of the large storage vessels and mixing craters that furnished adult burials. Most of the children were buried wearing simple bronze jewellery and dress accessories, such as bracelets, pins and fibulae, and in Episkopi-*Kaloriziki* Tomb 25 and Kouklia-*Skales* Tombs 48A and 68 the children also wore gold earrings. Other, utilitarian, grave-goods are more restricted. These include a stone spindle-whorl on an ivory distaff in Amathus Tomb 22, a stone scraper and an ivory distaff and spindle-whorl in Episkopi-*Kaloriziki* Tomb 25 and a bronze needle in the dromos niche of Episkopi-*Kaloriziki* Tomb 33. The burial in Episkopi-*Kaloriziki* Tomb 25 was also furnished with a pair of stone pestles and a mortar, presumably toiletry articles for the preparation of cosmetics.

Some grave-goods were exclusive to child burials.[12] Of these the most important is the feeding bottle, or side-spouted jug with basket handle. Its occurrence in Episkopi-*Bamboula* Tomb 33 and Kouklia-*Skales* Tombs

2 Ibid., 165-166, 221.
3 Episkopi-*Bamboula* Tomb 30, Episkopi-*Kaloriziki* Tombs 19, 39 and 40, and Kouklia-*Skales* Tombs 83, 89, Pyre A.
4 Steel 1993, 173-177.
5 Calvet 1980, 115-118; Yon & Caubet 1985, 29.
6 Cf. Binford 1972, 233.

7 Episkopi-*Bamboula* Tomb 30, Episkopi-*Kaloriziki* Tomb 22, Kouklia-*Skales* Tombs 48A, 68.
8 Amathus Tomb 22, Episkopi-*Kaloriziki* Tombs 25, 33, 36E, Gastria-*Alaas* Tomb 17, Kouklia-*Skales* Tomb 92, Lapithos-*Kastros* Tombs 406, 420, Lapithos-*Prostemenos* Tomb 74.
9 Amathus Tomb 22, Episkopi-*Kaloriziki* Tombs 25, 36 East and Kouklia-*Skales* Tomb 92.
10 Episkopi-*Bamboula* Tomb 30.
11 These include a kalathos (Episkopi-*Kaloriziki* Tomb 36 East/11), a hydria (Kouklia-*Skales* Tomb 48A/15) and a tripod (Kouklia-*Skales* Tomb 92/10).
12 Steel 1993, 175.

45, 67 and 91 suggests that these tomb groups housed child burials that had not been detected by the excavator. The duck askoi in CG I contexts might also be intended specifically for child burials, as toys, though in the LC IIIB period these, and other slow-pouring vessels, were commonly deposited with adult burials. Other possible toys include quadruped askoi and a wheeled terracotta horse.[13] Other items of funerary furniture were rarely, if ever, deposited with child burials. Military equipment was never deposited with a child, nor were the majority of status symbols (discussed below), though the simplest gold jewellery, bronze bowls, a faience plaque and a steatite stamp seal are found with children. Near Eastern imports were usually restricted to adult burials.

## Sex differentiation

The evidence for differential treatment of burials on the basis of their sex is more ambiguous.[14] The vast majority of the skeletons have not been sexed anthropologically, though a number have been sexed according to their associated grave-gifts. The data therefore, are biased at the start by a number of *a priori* assumptions, for example that only males were buried with military equipment and that a spindle-whorl denotes a female burial. It is certain, though, that the type of burial facility, treatment of the corpse and the range of pottery deposited with the burial did not vary according to the sex of the individual. Adults of either sex were buried in chamber tombs of both the indigenous LC type and the new 'Mycenaean' type. There are no examples of adults buried in pit or cist graves. The vast majority of burials were inhumations, but a few examples of cremation are known at Kouklia and Episkopi, for both sexes.

It is suggested that the sex of the deceased will be recognised in funerary contexts by their funerary furniture. This should be apparent in differences in dress and the types of tools and other artefacts buried with the dead, reflecting a male/female division of labour and perhaps social position.[15] Though it must be stressed that the data are somewhat inadequate, the following results seem to emerge.

Both sexes wore clothing which was fastened by fibulae, and there is no difference in the type of fibulae used by either sex. Pins, however, are apparently restricted to female burials, as is simple jewellery, such as rings and earrings. More elaborate gold jewellery, however, may have been worn by either sex. For the most part the skeletons associated with these finds have not been sexed,[16] but reference to representational art,

such as terracottas, ivories and sculpture, indicate that gold head-dresses and pendants were female artefacts,[17] whilst men would wear diadems and clothing adorned with gold rosettes.[18]

A male/female division of labour is more difficult to establish! As far as can be established, spindle-whorls were found exclusively with female burials, and are a standard piece of funerary equipment, implying that spinning was an important, and exclusively female, occupation. Toiletry articles, such as pestles for the preparation of cosmetics, tweezers and an ivory comb, might also be restricted to female burials. Knives were deposited with both sexes, but only with male burials were they associated with whetstones. Though it is usually assumed that military equipment would be restricted to male burials, the female from Lapithos-*Plakes* Tomb 602 was equipped with a bronze spear. Moreover, the only excavated burial from Episkopi-*Kaloriziki* Tomb 40 was that of a female, even though the tomb was equipped with one of the most elaborate displays of military paraphernalia. It should be added however, that this tomb had suffered badly from looting and so evidence of a second, male burial might have been lost.

Though extremely limited, there is some evidence for differential treatment of the sexes in Cypriot burial customs. This picture would be enhanced by a more rigorous study of skeletal remains, which might also reveal other examples of differentiation at present undetected.

## Ranking and social position

An attempt to identify social stratification within the LC IIIB-CG IB burial group is more successful. I have attempted to establish not only if there was a stratified society in Cyprus, but also the degree to which ranking cross-cut age and sex distinctions. The criteria used are (1) the type and size of burial facility, (2) the wealth of the grave-goods and (3) the occurrence of 'symbols of office'.[19]

1. The construction, size and elaborateness of the burial facility is an important means of establishing rank within a group of burials.[20] In Cyprus, at the transition from the Bronze to Iron Age, the obvious distinction is between the individuals buried in the new type of rock-cut chamber tomb, and those who were excluded from such tombs. The latter were buried in pit or cist graves or in indigenous LC

13  Kouklia-*Skales* Tomb 45/82: Karageorghis 1983, Pl. XII.
14  Steel 1993, 177-180.
15  Binford 1972, 233.
16  Only two skeletons associated with elaborate jewellery have been sexed, and both are female: Lapithos-*Kastros* Tomb 417, wearing a gold head-dress, and Lapithos-*Kastros* Tomb 420, wearing a necklace with circular gold pendant.
17  Karageorghis 1983, Pl. CXII; Maxwell-Hyslop 1971, Pls. 106-107; Ohnefalsch-Richter 1893, Pls. L:1, 4, 5, LI:7, LII:16, LVI, CCX:1-4, 7.
18  Myres 1914, Nos. 1045, 1047, 1251-1252, 1254.
19  Steel 1993, 180-201.
20  Tainter 1975, 2; 1978, 125- .

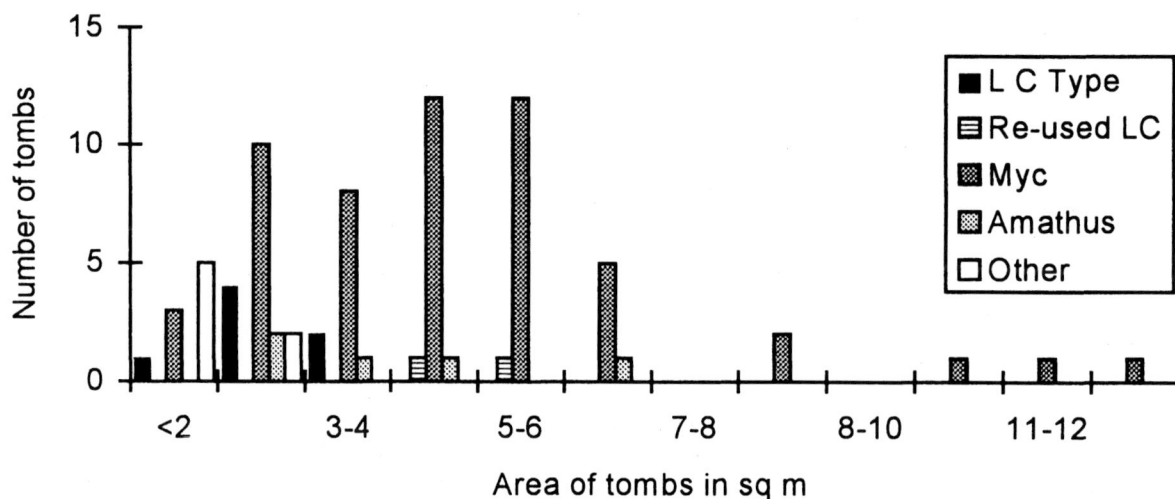

*Fig. 23.1: Area of LCIIIB and CGI tomb groups.*

type chamber tombs. Pit and cist graves required the minimum expenditure of effort to construct and were reserved specifically for child burials. Presumably these children were of little social consequence, and merited only the simplest form of funerary ritual. The area of the tomb chamber suggests that there is a real social distinction between the incumbents of the new type of chamber tomb and those buried in the traditional LC type chamber tomb.[20] The latter group is amongst the smaller of the CG I tombs, and has an area of between 2 m² and 3 m², whereas the area of the majority of the Mycenaean type chamber tombs falls between 2 m² and 6 m², and a small group falls between 6.5 m² and 12.54 m² (Fig. 23.1). It is evident that greater energy was expended in cutting the new type of chamber tomb, particularly considering the effort involved in excavating the long corridor dromos. Of particular interest are the largest tombs, which form only a small percentage of the CG I tomb groups, and might well belong to members of an economic or political élite. An unusual group of tombs, found only at Amathus, are not amongst the largest of the CG I tombs. Their method of construction, however, which involved lining the chamber shaft with large, dressed limestone blocks, is indicative of a certain input of labour not seen in other contemporary tombs.

2. Differences in the range and quality of the funerary furniture might also be indicative of social stratification. The typical grave-offering is pottery, and even the poorest burial would be provided with a small ceramic deposit. Around 28% of the tomb-groups contained only ceramic grave-gifts. Some burials, however, were provided with a surprisingly large array of pottery, which may reflect the wealth of the incumbents or their families (that they could acquire and deposit a large number of vessels on a single occasion), and/or the importance of the incumbents themselves (that they merited a large funerary ritual to which all the participants would bring some sort of ceramic funerary offering).

The accumulation of large quantities of imported pottery may also have been used to display the high social status of the deceased, or their relatives. These were presumably imported for their contents rather than the intrinsic worth of the vessel. Phoenician imports are found in around 39% of the tombs, and the vast majority (61%) come from Kouklia-*Skales*. The Paphos region in particular, therefore, appeared to benefit from commercial activity with the Levant, and it appears that eastern imports were quite widely enjoyed there. Elsewhere, the imports were restricted to only a small minority of the tomb groups and were probably indicative of wealth and high status.

The second most commonly represented class of artefact comprises jewellery and dress ornaments. Simple bronze jewellery and dress accessories are so widely distributed as not to be indicative of rank. Gold jewellery, however, was restricted to only a quarter of the tomb groups, and was only very occasionally used for pins and fibulae. These adornments are characterised by the very sparing use of gold.[21] It is apparent, therefore, that this was a rare, valuable commodity and that the small proportion of the population who had access to it probably belonged to a social or economic élite.

---

20   Steel 1993, 181-182.

21   Goring 1983, 422.

Another "reliable index of wealth is an accumulation of bronze vessels".[23] Less than a quarter of the tomb groups contained at least one bronze vessel. The most commonly represented is the shallow hemispherical bowl, found in 22% of the tomb groups. In Cyprus as a whole they were restricted to only the wealthiest tombs, and should be considered a luxury item. At Kouklia-*Skales*, however, they were relatively abundant. This cemetery also produced the largest quantities of Levantine imports and gold jewellery. It would appear, therefore, that at the beginning of the Iron Age the inhabitants of the Paphos region had greater access and ability to acquire luxury goods than their counterparts in the rest of the island. Other, larger, more elaborate vessels, which were restricted to only 6% of the tomb groups, may be interpreted as a status symbol. Four tombs in particular stand out, because of the large number of bronze vessels deposited at one time.[24] These should be considered in the light of the general paucity of metal artefacts in contemporary tomb-groups, and probably should be interpreted as an elaborate display of wealth and status. It is interesting to note that three of these tombs are amongst the largest recorded for this period.[25]

3.  I also have identified a number of artefacts which were restricted to only a small percentage of the LCIIIB-CGIB/II burials, and might be interpreted as symbols of authority. They include distinctive elements of costume, ritual paraphernalia and military equipment.[26]

Certain items of gold jewellery were restricted to about 10% of the tomb-groups.[27] These might be interpreted as elements of dress reserved for members of an élite group, and used to convey their position in society. This category includes a series of rectangular gold mountings, which were worn as a head-dress, necklaces with a gold circular pendant, inlaid gold signet rings, gold rosettes and silver bracelets. The use of gold or silver for pins and fibulae was also restricted, and might be interpreted as an distinctive feature of costume belonging to the élite group.

Ritual paraphernalia are more difficult to identify.[28] During the CA period a series of bronze sceptres, and one of agate, might have functioned as 'royal' insignia, yet these are not found in the earliest Iron-Age tomb-groups, either because they were not in use, or because they were too valuable to be deposited as part of the funerary ritual. The only example of this class of artefact which can be placed with certainty at the beginning of the Iron Age is a ceremonial bronze crook from a looted tomb in the *Kastros* cemetery at Lapithos. The oft-cited cloisonné sceptre from Kourion is difficult to reconcile with an eleventh century BC date and should be treated with great caution.[29] The small number of scarabs and seals might also be interpreted as insignia of the élite group.

Military equipment is restricted to around 22% of the tombs.[30] Over half of the weapons (54%) are from the cemetery of Kouklia-*Skales*, in which 7 of the 18 CG I tombs were furnished with military equipment. Usually the weapons comprised only a single bronze spearhead, but on occasion there was more elaborate military display, such as armour (shields and corselets), swords, pairs of spears and a single dagger. Obeloi, which were later to be associated with Greek and Cypriot warrior burials, are found with a small percentage of these tombs.

## Conclusions

It is expected that certain elements of social differentiation would be given formal recognition in mortuary ritual, such as age, sex and rank or social position. It has been shown that the age of the deceased is an important factor governing funerary treatment. Only when an individual had reached a certain age, and was fully accepted into society, was he or she allowed burial within the formal cemetery. Even then the child might be excluded from burial in the 'family' chamber, either being buried in a pit grave or in a dromos niche. Whether this treatment was due to the age or social position of the child cannot as yet be ascertained from the available information. There is less evidence that the sex of the deceased was an important dimension in the choice of funerary ritual.

There is, however, plenty of evidence for disparity of wealth in Cyprus at the very beginning of the Iron Age. This was recognised in the funerary ritual by the type and size of the burial facility, the range and quantity of funerary furniture and the presence of certain 'status symbols' reserved for only a small percentage of the burial population. On the whole, these correlate closely.

It is apparent that ranking cut across age and sex boundaries. Whilst objects indicative of wealth (such as imports, gold jewellery and simple bronze vessels) might be deposited with children, the most impressive status symbols are always associated with adult burials, thereby indicating that children were not admitted to the highest stratum of society. Adult burials might be accorded high status regardless of their sex, although the

---

23  Coldstream 1989, 328.
24  Episkopi-*Kaloriziki* Tombs 39, 40 and Kouklia-*Skales* Tombs 49 and 58.
25  Episkopi-*Kaloriziki* 40 and Koulia-*Skales* 49 and 58.
26  Brown 1981, 29-30; Coldstream 1989, 325-334; Steel 1993, 193-201.
27  Steel 1993, 193-195.
28  Ibid., 196-197.
29  MacFadden 1954, 131, 141, Pl. 18, Fig. 2; cf. Goring 1992.
30  Steel 1993, 197-200.

fine objects deposited with some females might, in fact, reflect the wealth and position of their families. Indeed, a richly adorned female might even be regarded as a status symbol for her male relatives.

In conclusion, there is evidence that there was a degree of social stratification in Cyprus at the transition from the Bronze to the Iron Age. The élite were buried in the same type of tomb as much of the rest of the populace, though these involved greater expenditure of effort. They were also buried with a similar range of funerary furniture, though this increased in quality, variety and quantity with the increased social position of the deceased. At the top end of the social scale there was a small group who had greater wealth and access to the products of craft specialists. This group used funerary ritual, elaborate dress and ritual paraphernalia to establish and maintain their position.

# 24 Urartian Funerary Customs

## Charles Burney

ABSTRACT—*Urartian funerary practices are hard to distinguish, partly owing to a lack of written sources. Hurrian elements might reasonably be sought; and there are arguments for aspects attributable to Indo-European, and perhaps specifically Iranian, influences, as well as survivals in pre-Christian Armenia.*

*Stelae, sometimes associated with tombs, are among features which can be related to a cult of the earth and underworld, as can the insertion of cremations in crevices in the rock. There could perhaps have been a role also for human sacrifice, though evidence is meagre.*

*The rock tombs of Urartu represent a tradition beginning only with the establishment of the Vannic kingdom and the introduction of iron tools. The inspiration for their design is uncertain, but there is evidence for burnt and liquid offerings.*

*While it seems that cremation was popular with many of the inhabitants of Urartu, with rock tombs reserved for the governing class, inhumation in a variety of stone-built graves continued from pre-Urartian times, providing evidence for centuries hitherto devoid of archaeological data on villages or towns, let alone fortresses. Whether or not any external influence on the design of some graves is discernible is another matter.*

It is indeed difficult to distinguish any single distinctively Urartian tradition in funerary practices.[1] This need not, however, cause undue amazement, seeing that a diversity of funerary customs is found widely in the ancient Near East. The later the period, it seems, the greater the diversity, although there are exceptions to this rule.

For any profound understanding of funerary customs two categories of evidence are required: a range of grave-goods associated with burials from different social strata; and textual sources on the rituals and beliefs related to these burials. Outside Egypt and certain periods in Mesopotamia such evidence is sadly incomplete. Textual evidence – far more reliable than that of physical anthropology – is essential for any attempt to set the archaeological material in an ethnic context.

Alas, whereas (for example) we have funerary texts to elucidate aspects of Hittite religion – at least that of the royal dynasty – in the second millennium BC in central Anatolia,[2] no such inscriptions survive from the kingdom of Urartu or from its contemporary neighbours. What would one give for a text related to the graves of Hasanlu![3] It would be reasonable to expect Hurrian elements to be prominent in any Urartian funerary text, since the relationship of the Urartian language to Hurrian is by now well attested: it is a question either of direct descent or, more generally accepted nowadays, of derivation from a common Proto-Hurrian progenitor (*Ursprache*) in the old homeland (*Urheimat*) of eastern Anatolia with Transcaucasia and the Urmia basin of north-western Iran.[4]

The presence also of an Indo-European element, more specifically Iranian, seems highly probable, though there are no adequate comparative data from Achaemenid Iran, whose diversity of burial practices and religious traditions has perplexed Iranologists and provoked endless controversies on such problems as the role of Zoroastrianism.[5] The general archaeological picture from Urartu might appear to indicate connec-

---

1 Barnett 1963.
2 Gurney 1977, 59-63; Bittel 1958; 1975.
3 Dyson & Voigt 1989.
4 Diakonoff & Starostin 1986; Wilhelm 1989, pp.3-4; Kamp & Yoffee 1980; Burney 1989.
5 Dandamaev & Lukonin 1989, 320-347, on the religion of the ancient Iranians; Frye 1962, 27-34; Zaehner 1961, 339-348 (bibliography).

tions with, or influence on, Iran, notably in the tradition of rock-cut tombs. Yet, with the exception of the tomb at Doğubayazit, any definite parallel is hard to discern.[6] Iran under the Achaemenid kings displayed an even greater variety of burial customs than obtained (it seems) in Urartu. In Iran the body might be preserved in wax, perhaps thus circumventing the Zoroastrian prohibition of defiling the earth; or the body might be exposed to the elements and the vultures, a tradition first manifest at Çatal Hüyük in the seventh millennium BC;[7] or it might be cremated. Classical sources record the attachment of the magi to exposure of the dead.[8]

Where, then, was there any Iranian element in Urartian cult or funerary customs? In the former, it seems, the presence of the goddess Bagbartu, as consort of Haldi and thus second in command in the local pantheon in the principality of Musasir, indicates an Iranian presence. The political and religious role of Musasir in the crucial formative phase of Urartian history, the later ninth century BC, makes this Iranian influence more significant than it would otherwise have been, even though the references to Bagbartu come a century later, with the eighth campaign of Sargon II (714 BC).[9] Haldi himself seems distinctively associated with Musasir and Urartu, acting as the clearest link between the two, while the city-state held a delicate position between Urartu and Assyria.[10] Haldi was recognised as one of the leading deities of the Near East in a tablet of the eighth to seventh century BC listing the gods and goddesses of Assyria and its surrounding regions. The use of the term Hald to describe the Pontic highlands south of Trebizond may or may not have some connection with the god Haldi.[11]

Iranian elements specific to Urartian funerary customs are scarcely discernible, although one aspect of these is perhaps to be seen in one of the major Urartian citadel sites, Altintepe in the stony plain of Erzincan, near the north-western limit of the kingdom. This is particularly significant, in that the rock-cut tombs at Van Kale and elsewhere have survived entirely stripped of their contents, including human remains. For relevant evidence one must turn to the comparable tombs excavated at Altintepe, not cut out of bedrock but built of masonry and terraced into the steep hillside. Here is a courtyard, an integral part of the funerary complex, with three fine stone stelae of beautifully dressed basalt, smooth-faced yet entirely devoid of any inscription or relief carving.[12] There are of course many examples of inscribed stelae in Urartu, among them the

two set into round-topped rock-cut niches at the foot of the north slope of Van Kale, the so-called Anneli Kiz, in fact the shrine of Sarduri II (764-735 BC).[13] But this was probably associated not with his funeral ceremonies – even if his is the uninscribed rock tomb immediately across from this shrine in the south cliff of the citadel rock of Van – but with celebrations of his accession, arguably the high water-mark of Urartian power. Earlier stelae at Hasanlu are to be associated not with funerary cult but with a major temple, Burned Building II.[14] Following the initial expansion of Urartian control into north-western Iran and the erection of a bilingual stele at Kel-i-shin, in the mountains on the modern Iran-Iraq frontier, the same king, Ishpuini, had a major record of his religious reforms inscribed in a rock-cut niche close to Van citadel; the Mehr Kapisi inscription takes the form of a list of standardised offerings of bulls and sheep to Haldi, Tesheba, Shivini and a host of lesser divinities.[15]

The rock-cut niche is agreed to represent a feature of relevance to the state cult, most probably the temple doorway, as likewise at Yeşilaliç (formerly Pagan), well to the east of Van, close to the modern frontier with Iran.[16] Significantly there are slots cut into the rock platform immediately beside the Yeşilaliç inscription; clearly these were for stelae. While the analogy with the temple doorway seems perfectly acceptable, an alternative explanation is that such niches, inscribed or not, were intended as places of offerings to the gods and goddesses of Urartu. They may have had a funerary role, for similarly recessed doorways occur in tombs, such as that at Kayalidere, where the entrance was carefully sealed with dressed blocks, the lowest of which remained in situ. Against the face of this block, as shown by traces of fire, a food offering would have been cooked, before the rock-cut dromos was filled with roughly laid stones.[17]

Association of stelae with the earth and specifically with the bedrock seems to imply that a major significance was attached to chthonic deities and cults in Urartian religion. That this was not restricted to the royal house and nobility is surely demonstrated by the habit of inserting cremation burials into crevices in the rock, evident at Iğdir beneath Mount Ararat[18] and at Altintepe.[19] The design of rock tombs to include deep shafts for the burials may bear a similar interpretation, relevant both to the tomb of Argishti I at Van and to the Kayalidere tomb, the latter having two bottle-shaped shafts originally sealed with a stone plug. Both these tombs yield evidence of some sort of funerary ceremonies – in the tomb of Argishti I are shallow insets in the rock floor, doubtless emplacements for altars or offering

6   Forbes 1983, 103-105; Zimansky 1985, 25; Kleiss & Hauptmann 1976, 19 (site 115 in Turkey).
7   Mellaart 1964; 1967, 82-84, Fig. 44, etc.
8   Dandamaev & Lukonin 1989, 337, quoting Strabo, *Geography* 15.3.20.
9   Luckenbill 1927, I, paras. 173, 176.
10  Zimansky 1985, 10420.
11  Burney 1993.
12  Özgüç 1969, 28-33, 73-74, Pls. XXVI-XXVII.

13  Melikishvili 1960, No. 155.
14  Dyson & Voigt 1989, 107-127.
15  Melikishvili 1960, No. 27; Salvini, in press.
16  Sevin & Belli 1977; Tarhan & Sevin 1975.
17  Burney 1966, esp. 101-108.
18  Barnett 1963.
19  Özgüç 1969, 72.

tables; at Kayalidere fragments of dressed basalt give hints of altars or other features set in the chambers above. Whether the room (6) with small depressions cut into its rock floor had these filled with liquid offerings or as insets for round-bottomed offering vessels makes no difference to the indication of funerary offerings in the Kayalidere tomb. The porous nature of the rock makes the second suggestion the likelier.[20] These offerings can hardly have been made much after the final burial, seeing that the tomb was so carefully walled up; but this tomb probably served successive generations, perhaps of district governors, among whom would surely have been the builder of the temple in the upper citadel above the cliff into which was cut the tomb, in spite of the many natural fissures in the rock.[21]

The lack of textual sources to illuminate funerary customs and attitudes to death in Urartu has already been deplored. Some kind of belief in a life after death is surely implied by the two small ventilation shafts cut through the rock on either side of the doorway into the first anteroom of the Kayalidere tomb. What other explanation makes sense?

The most dramatic but often least well documented aspect of funerary practices in the ancient Near East is human sacrifice, best known in the so-called Royal Cemetery of Ur.[22] It is well known that there is no Sumerian text directly clarifying the thinking behind this holocaust. The suggestion of semi-voluntary suicide occurs in relation to servants and slaves in pre-Christian times in Armenia, when the deceased was a king or high-ranking noble;[23] but there is no documentation to indicate beyond speculation that this tradition was inherited from Urartu, even if the Indo-European newcomers from the west, according to the meagre historical sources, had intermingled with survivors of the older population. Human sacrifice seems to occur from time to time in widely separated contexts, suggesting perhaps that there was no widespread taboo on ethical grounds. Amestris, wife of Xerxes, enjoyed a long life, and in old age is reputed to have ordered fourteen aristocratic youths to be buried alive, evidently as a sacrificial offering to a chthonic god in thanksgiving.[24] Thus human sacrifice was not invariably in a funerary context. The one Urartian example appears to be at Toprakkale, the royal citadel close to Van Kale (Tushpa), founded by Rusa II and occupied until the destruction of the kingdom (c. 590 BC) by the Medes. Here the presence of human and animal bones in the same area close to the temple could indicate deliberate slaughter as part of ritual ceremonies of offerings to Haldi and other members of the pantheon.[25] But the evidence is unclear, and could relate instead to the final

onslaught on this royal fortress. Animal bones from butchered offerings were numerous at Bastam, another of Rusa II's foundations.[26] Earlier examples of human sacrifice are the skeletons of young women holding lion-headed pins found both at Hasanlu and at the Urartian palace at Giriktepe, near Aznavurtepe (Patnos), most probably therefore of Menua's reign.[27]

The presence of a series of rock tombs of impressive scale marks Van Kale, the citadel securely identified (with the city at its foot) as Tushpa, as the chief seat of government in the kingdom of Urartu,[28] at least until the attack by Tiglath-Pileser III in the campaign dated by the *limmu* list to 735 BC.[29] Rock tombs do indeed appear as one of the innovations associated with the Vannic state, marked as a perquisite of royalty and of some others such as district governors. Funerary customs, in Urartu as elsewhere, are of necessity to be seen in the context of the available technology and resources. Nearer to this gathering here in Manchester, the celebrated prehistoric tombs of Orkney, such as Maes Howe on Mainland, demonstrate a standard of design and finish unthinkable in those regions not blessed with the appropriate geology, in that case a type of sandstone occurring ubiquitously in strata which break easily into thin slabs ready for use by builder of tomb and house alike.[30] No such gift was available in the Urartian lands: round Lake Van the predominant formations are crystalline limestone, at Van Kale and elsewhere including Çavuştepe, and basalt. The invention of iron tools, notably chisels whose marks survive on Van Kale and other fortresses, made it possible for the first time to carve out rock tombs.[31] The sources of iron, however, are not entirely clear in their dating.[32]

What significance is attributable to the design of the Van tombs is arguable: the obvious explanation is imitation of houses. An alternative would be that they derive from elaborate tents or marquees. In spite of later tradition, they never served as marriage chambers! Much importance seems to have been attached to the access to these tombs, often by a broad rock-cut stairway. The shape of the ceiling varied from flat to that of a barrel vault, suggesting that there was no fixed, traditional design.

Derivation of Urartian tombs from Assyria is a theory supported by reference to stone-lined and -roofed graves found both to the south of Lake Van and particularly at Evditepe, near Ernis on the north-east shore of the lake, and attributed to a pre-Urartian phase.[33] Assyrian interest in the iron sources in the mountains of

20  Forbes 1983, 108; Burney 1966, 101-108.
21  Burney 1966, 68-75.
22  Moorey 1977; Pollock 1985; Forest 1983; Bayliss 1973.
23  Burney & Lang 1971, 222; Strabo, *Geography* 11.4.7.
24  Dandamaev & Lukonin 1989, 338, quoting Herodotus VII:14.
25  Lehmann-Haupt 1931, 453; Barnett 1950; 1954; Lynch 1901, 64, the victims being described as prisoners of war.

26  Krauss 1975.
27  Balkan 1964; Burney & Lang 1971, 141.
28  Zimansky 1985, 78-80; Loon 1966, 70-71.
29  Luckenbill 1927, I, paras. 785, 813; II, p. 436 (*limmu* list).
30  Renfrew 1985, esp. 94-107.
31  Kleiss 1976; Kleiss & Calmeyer 1979, 84, Fig. 96; cf. Curtis *et al.* 1979.
32  Belli 1986; 1987.
33  Evditepe: Erzen 1964, 570-572; Mellink 1964, 158; 1965, 359-60. Note by Kirsopp Lake (1938) on "stone boxes of considerable size formed of megaliths", cited by Sevin 1987, 48.

the Van region and its surroundings,[34] as well as the well-known documentation of Assyrian military intrusions, are cited in support of an Assyrian inspiration, dating back to the Middle Assyrian period, for the design of Urartian tombs.[35] While there may be parallels with graves of comparable status, these too are largely pre-Urartian, including some burials excavated in 1992 at Karagündüz, near Lake Erçek east of Van.[36] Significant as providing evidence for the archaeologically otherwise obscure, indeed virtually unknown, period immediately preceding the rise of the Vannic kingdom in the ninth century BC, these graves can hardly be related to the imposing rock tombs of Van Kale or their provincial counterparts, with which they have nothing in common. Perhaps some answers may eventually emerge from the excavations in progress at Horom, in the northwest of the former Armenian SSR.[37]

Alas, these scattered hints provide no clue to what was thought, said or sung at Urartian funerals. They must indeed have had much in common with the customary practices of their contemporaries elsewhere in the Near East. One day the looked-for text will tell all.

---

34  Maxwell-Hyslop 1974; Pigott 1989.
35  Sevin 1987. The case is forcefully argued, but remains debatable.
36  Personal communication 1992, James Stedman.
37  Badaljan *et al.*, 1992; Badaljan *et al.* 1993.

# 25 Neo-Babylonian Burials Revisited

## Heather Baker

ABSTRACT—*This paper aims to synthesise the evidence for burial practices from post-Kassite Babylonia down to the end of the Achaemenid period. The various aspects of mortuary data – burial typology, treatment of the dead, stratigraphic and other evidence for dating, chronological and geographical variability, grave goods etc. – will be taken into account in the analysis.*

## Introduction

The only study of Neo-Babylonian burials to date remains an article by Eva Strommenger published thirty years ago.[1] Her work was based on stratigraphic sequences from the private houses in the Merkes area of Babylon, as published by Reuther.[2] It concentrated on the typological development of the burials excavated there.

My aim in carrying out the present study was, firstly, to assemble all of the published evidence relating to Neo-Babylonian burial practices in an attempt to provide an updated synthesis incorporating, in particular, burials which have come to light in the time since Strommenger's article was published. Recent work has enabled a revised dating to be proposed for certain burial types. Secondly, my intention was to broaden the scope of the enquiry to include aspects of burial practices other than the strictly typological, on the grounds that this is essential for comparing Neo-Babylonian mortuary practices with those from other periods and other areas.

The study is based on data collected from around one thousand graves. This large number masks the inevitable difficulties of variable excavation techniques, observation, recording and publication which afflict any study based on published archaeological reports. It includes almost 400 graves from Ur, for example, for which details of find-spots and stratigra-

phy are mostly lacking, and the pottery typology difficult to use.[3] Constraints are imposed also by the preliminary nature of some of the reports; for example, entire grave groups are rarely illustrated. These comments are by no means intended to diminish the contributions made by former excavators, which remain of enduring importance, but rather to illustrate the conditions under which the study was carried out. It goes without saying that statistical evaluations are difficult to perform on data of such uneven quality, and are better suited to data which have been collected from the start with such a purpose in mind. However, it is clear that the large amount of evidence contained within earlier excavation reports cannot be overlooked, and an attempt has been made systematically to extract information relating to typological features, physical attributes including age and sex, treatment of the dead, stratigraphy and location of the graves, and the presence of pottery and other grave goods, wherever such details were available.

Our treatment will consist of two parts. In the first section we will review the typological sequence. Secondly, we will consider the treatment of the dead and other aspects of burial practices; to date no such synthesis exists for this period. It should be remarked that, although 'Neo-Babylonian' is the nominal scope of this paper, we shall be considering burials ranging from the late Kassite through to the Achaemenid period, since, as will be seen below, recent advances

---

1   Strommenger 1964
2   Reuther 1926.

3   Curtis 1983 p. 92.

have affected our understanding of the dating of burials at both ends of this chronological span.

The principal sites on which this work is based are Babylon, Isin, Kish, Nippur, Sippar, Tell ed-Dēr, Tell el-Laḥm, Ur and Uruk. Although a large number of burials from various of these sites have been published in the thirty years since Strommenger's article, the Babylon sequence remains central to any study of these burials. It provides the only stratigraphic sequence in which all of the different burial types discussed here have been found, and includes one or two which have not been encountered elsewhere. Moreover, as Strommenger observed, the graves can often be related to the plans and sections, so that with care it is possible to locate many of them in three dimensions.[4] The relative sequence at Babylon therefore continues to provide a good point of reference

Neo-Babylonian graves have also been found in large numbers at Uruk. Our treatment of the Uruk graves is inevitably provisional, pending the availability of their final publication, announced for 1994. In the meantime information has been obtained from brief summaries contained in volumes of the Uruk preliminary reports (*UVB*); from the publication of excavations in areas J-K/23 and H/24-25,[5] and from summary information concerning graves cited as find-spots for pottery, beads and other finds.[6]

Nippur has been similarly productive of graves, particularly the TA Sounding.[7] The post-Kassite stratigraphy of this and other soundings has recently been thoroughly revised in a study which has far-reaching implications both for Nippur and for other Babylonian sites with levels of the later second to early first millennia BC[8] The resultant pottery typology distinguishes between forms of Kassite, post-Kassite and early Neo-Babylonian date, and includes a couple of types attributed to the Achaemenid period. In addition to this, recently published pottery from well-dated levels at various northern Babylonian sites means that we can begin to distinguish more easily between graves of Neo-Babylonian and those of Achaemenid date.[9] Work on the metal items from Babylonian graves has also helped to clarify some chronological problems.[10] It remains difficult to relate the historical labels 'Neo-Assyrian', 'Neo-Babylonian' and 'Achaemenid' to the grave sequence with any precision, but progress has clearly been made; the debt which this study owes to these developments will be evident in the pages which follow.

## Typology

### Type 1: The double-pot burial

The earliest occurring burial type to be considered here is the double-pot grave, which was in use in various regions of the Near-East during the second millennium BC.[11] At Ur Woolley identified a transitional form deriving from Early Kassite brick burial vaults, which comprised a pair of jars set apart with a stretch of brick vaulting covering the gap between them.[12]

It seems clear that the double-pot burial, treated by Strommenger as a single type spanning a period c. 1000-700 BC at Babylon,[13] can be divided into two chronologically distinct types. The first consists of two large, wide-mouthed ring-based jars placed rim to rim, and the second comprises one large ring-based jar together with a bowl, often with a protruding stem base, which was generally perforated. For convenience these will be referred to as types A and B respectively. This distinction was first noted by Reuther;[14] those of type A were called by him '*Doppeltopfgräber*', and Type B '*Topfgräber mit irdenen Deckeln*'. The distinction has also been observed at Uruk, where burials of our type B are the more numerous of the two varieties.[15] It is not always possible to determine from excavation reports which form of double-pot burial is in question, and the desirability of publishing illustrations of the burial jars themselves, as well as of the ceramic grave goods, should be evident. The chronological implications of the distinction between these two forms will now be discussed.

### Type 1A

Burials of type A have been found at Babylon, Isin, Tell ed-Dēr, Ur and Uruk. Reuther considered this type to be characteristic of the Late Kassite period.[16] At Babylon such burials were generally the deepest of all the types considered in this study. According to the excavation sections they were almost invariably not found within the architecture labelled as "JK" (*jungkassitische*), but above it, occurring in a level between the Kassite building level and the "MBA"

4   Strommenger 1964, 159. However, it should be noted that the graves are not numbered on the plans or sections, so that the combined evidence of square, grave type, depth and description must be used to identify individual burials with those in Reuther's catalogue. Also, the sections are somewhat composite, in that graves not located on a section-line may be projected onto the section drawing, thereby occasionally implying a misleading stratigraphic relationship.
5   Boehmer 1987.
6   Strommenger 1967, Boehmer 1984, Limper 1988 and Salje 1992.
7   McCown & Haines 1967 pp. 117-144.
8   Armstrong 1989.
9   E.g. Gasche *et al.* 1989 a. 39-42 (Ḥabl aṣ-Ṣahr); Gasche *et al.* 1989 b, 25-34 (Abū Qubūr).
10  Braun-Holzinger 1988.

11  Strommenger 1971, 583.
12  Woolley 1965, 85-86, Fig. 5.
13  Strommenger 1964, Fig. 1.
14  Reuther 1926, 185 ff.
15  Boehmer 1987, 14; See also 37, n. 81.
16  Reuther 1926 , 185.

(*mittelbabylonische-assyrische*) architecture, and sometimes cutting the former.[17] There was apparently a gap in occupation between the ruins of the LK housing and the later MBA buildings, during which the area was used as a burial ground,[18] and to judge from the evidence of the sections it is this, the latest Kassite phase, to which the majority of double-pot graves of Type A belong. According to Reuther's account, one example, grave 42 in square 25p, lay between layers containing tablets of the First Dynasty of Babylon and those of Enlil-nādin-šumī, Melišipak and Marduk-apla-iddin.[19] Other early double-pot graves were found at the same depth as tablets of Kudur-Enlil, Kadašman-Turgu and Kurigalzu, suggesting a date around the later thirteenth century BC or later.

Evidence from other sites supports the dating of these earlier double-pot burials to the Late Kassite period, and into the early post-Kassite period. Several graves of our Type A were found at Isin, some of which have been attributed by the excavators to the Neo-Babylonian period,[20] but which should in fact be assigned to the late second millennium BC[21] They came predominantly from the Level 2 building in the *Nordabschnitt* II area, dated by the excavators to the Isin II period on the evidence of tablets found there.[22]

The Isin double-pot graves contained pottery similar to forms from Tell Imlihiye and Tell Zubeidi in the Hamrin, including the frit situlae found in graves 34 and 91 (a type also found in double-pot grave 49 at Babylon). Close parallels can also be found with late Middle-Babylonian pottery from Tell ed-Dēr, Chantier E, Ensemble O, which has produced globular jars comparable to those from Isin graves 53, 57 and 58.[23] A number of double-pot graves from Isin (for example nos. 27, 34 and 49) also contained a type of round-based aryballos of post-Kassite date.[24] In fact, all of the graves at Isin assigned to the Neo-Babylonian period, with the exception of two which contained no grave goods, have produced pottery which is certainly pre-Neo-Babylonian, and which has good parallels in the Late-Kassite-early post-Kassite period. In addition to the evidence of the pottery, it must surely be significant that, of the relatively numerous double-pot burials, there are none that can be seen to cut the walls of the Level 2 building,[25] in contrast to the later bathtub coffins and jar burials, which not infrequently do so; it seems likely that the

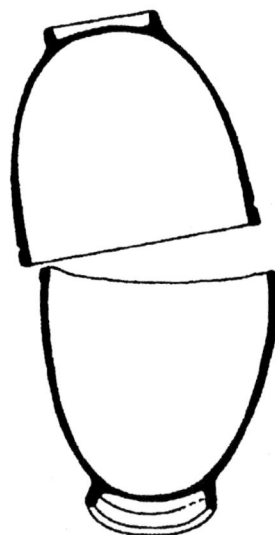

*Fig. 25.1  Type 1a. Double pot. Uruk W.21260 (after Boehmer 1984, 193, Fig. 1)*

building was still in use, or at least standing, when these burials were deposited there.

At Tell ed-Dēr a grave of Type A was found in sub-phase Ia0 in Chantier E3. This burial, no. 368,[26] contained a tall goblet which is typical of Ensemble O at Tell ed-Dēr,[27] representing a phase which has been tentatively linked to the restoration of the Eulmaš by Šagarakti-Šuriaš (1245-1233 BC).[28] Another burial of this period (earth grave 337A) contained a faience situla.[29]

A number of double-pot burials have been uncovered from various locations at Ur, including the EM and AH sites; these graves have all been attributed a Kassite date.[30]

Finally, some graves of Type A from area J-K/23 at Uruk have been dated to the Late Kassite period;[31] this type was considerably less common at Uruk than the later form of double-pot grave. Other examples from Uruk, graves W.21260, 13463 and 13464, have been dated by Boehmer to the eleventh and tenth centuries BC on the basis of cylinder seal styles and the presence of bronze '*Tropfenbecher*'.[32] A number of other double-pot graves also contained this vessel type.[33] The graves with this type of bronze beaker and/or cylinder seal style appear to have been concentrated in the area of squares N-O/16.

We may conclude from the above that, as Reuther observed, graves consisting of two large jars were current in the Late Kassite period. They contin-

17  Ibid., Taf. 3-5.
18  Ibid., 21.
19  Ibid., 185.
20  Hrouda *et al.* 1981, 40-48. 'Neo-Babylonian': double-pot graves 43a, 45, 49, 53, 56, 57, 58, 59, 67; 'Later than Old Babylonian': 77; 'Isin II': 90, 92; 'Later than Isin II': 92a.
21  Boehmer 1985 p. 11; Armstrong 1989 pp. 89-90.
22  Hrouda *et al.* 1981, 34.
23  Gasche 1991, 44 Pls. 7-10.
24  Hrouda *et al.* 1977 Taf. 28, vessels IB 407& IB 600d; Hrouda *et al.* 1981 Taf. 34 vessels IB 789 c-d; cf. Armstrong 1989, 314 Fig. 67.2 type 13.
25  Hrouda *et al.* 1981, plan 5.

26  Gasche 1991, 25, Fig. 7, Pl. 5:1-2.
27  Ibid. Pls. 11.1-2.
28  Ibid., 30.
29  Ibid., 1991, 24, n. 59 & Fig. 4.
30  Woolley 1965., 89-90, "Analysis of Kassite Graves", nos. KG 44-54, 56.
31  Boehmer 1987, 14, nos. 3, 4, 8, 14-16.
32  Boehmer 1984 , 191 ff.
33  Braun-Holzinger 1988, 125, Pl. 92.

ued to be used into the early post-Kassite period, but no example is demonstrably later than the late second or beginning of the first millennium BC.

## Type 1B

Double-pot burials of type B are recorded from Babylon, Isin, Nippur, Tell el-Laḥm, Ur and Uruk. At Babylon they begin to occur just above the level at which type A is found, and are probably to be dated to the earlier centuries of the first millennium BC;[34] Strommenger placed their terminus at c. 700 BC[35]

At Isin two burials of this type have been found.[36] One, grave 86, was found in the corner of a room in the *Nordabschnitt* NII building, while the other, 87, was buried in open(?) land.[37] The latter grave contained 11 round-based aryballoi of the type discussed above in connection with the Type A burials at Isin, and also a frit situla as found at Tell Imlihiye.[38] Since these two burials clearly shared the same context and ceramic repertoire as the more numerous examples of Type A at Isin, they must also date to the late Second Millennium; it seems likely that the transition between the two forms of double-pot grave is represented here.

The TA sounding at Nippur produced a number of these burials, which have been attributed by Armstrong to the Early Neo-Babylonian period.[39] One of these, 1B 235, contained a glazed bottle of his Type 33 decorated with Glaze Pattern A.[40] It should be noted that, while TA 1B 215 is said to consist of a perforated bowl plus jar,[41] full details of the other graves are not available.

Excavations on the main mound at Tell el-Laḥm unearthed 6 Type B burials, 5 of which came from sounding 6 (graves 3-7) and one from sounding 3 (grave 2).[42] All were relatively close to the surface, at the level of (and probably intrusive into) the latest extant architectural phase, the Late Kassite.

Fourteen of the double-pot burials found at Ur were assigned by Woolley to the Neo-Babylonian period.[43] He described them collectively in the following terms:

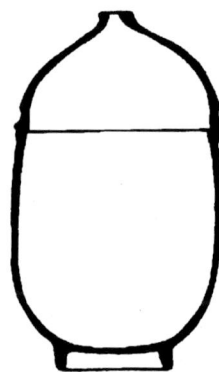

*Fig. 25.2 Type 1b. Double pot. Babylon grave 52 (after Reuther 1926, Pl. 60).*

Two large clay vessels, either wide-mouthed jars or bell-shaped bowls, were laid on the ground mouth to mouth; the body was placed in them, the head in one pot, the legs in the other, and the rims of the pots were brought together and often fastened one to the other with bitumen or cement.[44]

It is not entirely clear which type of double-pot grave is in question here. In Woolley's catalogue grave NB 34 is described as a "large urn with bowl cover", which identifies it with Type B, while some are described as "two large urns" (graves NB 36-37, 39-41), and others were disturbed. A number of graves were said to contain items of iron,[45] which would place them somewhat later than the graves of Type A discussed above.

Some of these double-pot graves assigned to the Neo-Babylonian period came either from the XNCF area, or from the YC site, both of which produced Late Kassite housing levels.[46] It is possible that the graves in XNCF and YC actually belonged with the (post-Kurigalzu) houses in whose rooms they were found (often at some depth below surface), and that these houses continued in use later than Woolley recognised. In any case, given the presence of iron in some of them, it seems likely that these graves date to the earlier first millennium. They may be earlier than the denuded Neo-Babylonian and Persian levels covering these areas, and they probably belong with our Type B, though without further details as to their form we risk imposing a distinction not observed by their excavator.

At Uruk most of the double-pot burials belonged to Type B.[47] By far the majority of these graves have been found in the area of Neo- and Late-Babylonian private housing to the west and south-west of Eanna, and they have been said by the excavators to comprise

34 Reuther 1926, 52-71.
35 Strommenger 1964, 158 Fig. 1.
36 Hrouda *et al.* 1981, 46-47 nos. 86- 87.
37 Ibid., Plan 5.
38 Ibid., Taf. 35; cf. Boehmer & Dämmer 1985, 11; for examples of situlae from Babylon, Ur and isin cf. ibid, 13, Abb. 6; for situlae from Tell Imlihiye cf. ibid, Taf. 27.
39 Armstrong 1989, 158, Table 17, graves TA IB 215, 218-19, 235-36, 255.
40 Mc Cown &Haines 1967, Pl. 101: 10; Armstrong 1989, 69, Figs. 75. 1-2, 81.
41 McCown & Haines 1967, 133.
42 Safar 1949, 161-162.
43 See Woolley 1962, 61-62 for catalogue of "Double-pot burials assigned in the field notes, on external evidence, to the Neo-Babylonian period", nos. NB 28-41.

44 Woolley 1962, 53.
45 Ibid., nos. 28, 29, 32, 36, 41.
46 Woolley 1965, 75-7.
47 Boehmer 1987, 14.

the characteristic form of burial at Uruk until the slipper coffins of the Parthian period,[48] although it is likely that they went out of use some centuries earlier. These double-pot graves share pottery types in common with the early Neo-Babylonian assemblage defined at Nippur,[49] and so far as I can tell there is an absence of types which can reasonably be identified as 'Achaemenid'. This would accord with the dated archival tablets found in this area, which span the period c. 700-488 BC.[50]

In summary, the earliest examples of this type appear to date to the early post-Kassite period at Isin, though the form is generally characteristic of the earlier 1st millennium BC. At Uruk they survive a little later than at other sites (except for Ur?), and probably went out of use around the 6th century BC.

## Type 2: The 'Bathtub' Coffin

As Strommenger observed, burials of the 'bathtub' type spread into Babylonia from Assyria in the Neo-Assyrian period.[51] They have been linked with the first appearance of fibulae in Babylonia.[52] Examples have been found at Babylon, Isin, Kish, Nippur, Sippar, Tell el-Lahm, Ur, Uruk, and as far south as Qala'at al-Bahrain. In spite of their shape, they were, in fact, purpose-built coffins.[53]

There is a definite sequence of development to be observed in the form of the bathtub coffins. This was made clear by Reuther, who divided those from Babylon into an earlier and a later group.[54] Basically, the earliest examples, which predated the foundation of the Neo-Babylonian houses, were higher in relation to their length than the later ones. A third group of coffins developed from the bathtub type, being even longer and lower, with a pronounced rim and a rounded end which was wider than the straight end; they tended to be inverted over the body.[55] These eventually evolved into a type which was long enough to accommodate a body fully outstretched.[56] Other features of the ceramic bathtub coffins, such as the impressed bands with which they were typically decorated, remained constant.

Fig. 25.4 illustrates the development between these three groups of bathtub-type coffins in terms of the relationship between height and length. It shows

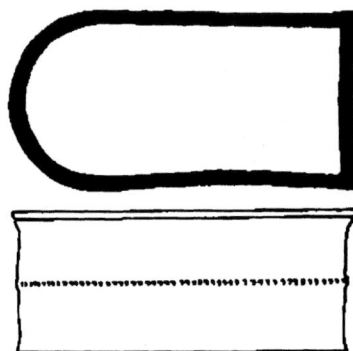

*Fig. 25.3 Type 2. Bathtub coffin. Babylon grave 115 (after Reuther 1926, Pl. 67).*

only the examples from Babylon, as measurements are usually lacking for those from other sites (but see below concerning the Sippar examples). We have also plotted, for the sake of comparison, the four examples of bronze coffins for which measurements are available. from Ur (2 examples), Sinjirli and Dailaman-Amlash.[57] In terms of date these belong with our earliest group, but they are clearly not directly comparable in terms of their size-range.

In the context of his study of the bronze bathtub coffins, Curtis has discussed the dating of coffins equipped with handles.[58] In addition to the example he cites from Babylon (grave 153), a couple of terra-cotta bathtub coffins with handles have been found more recently at Isin, one of which was dated to the Late-Babylonian period by the excavators, that is, somewhat later than the previously known examples, said to be of the eighth-to-seventh century BC.[59]

Bathtub coffins were quite often equipped with a lid of palm-wood planks, as for example Babylon graves 112-114;[60] Nippur TA 1B 201, 227, WB 10;[61] Tell-al-Lahm G 16,[62] and Uruk W. 12313.[63] At Babylon both coffin and lid were sometimes spread with bitumen and/or covered with palm matting, the whole then secured with twisted reeds or palm-fibre ropes, for example graves 119 and 143.[64] Lids of baked brick have also been found in Babylon graves 116 and 154,[65] as has one of unbaked brick in Nippur grave TA 1B 183,[66] and a ceramic lid in Nippur TA 1B 268.[67] In one Nippur grave, TA 1B 204, a second, inverted bathtub coffin was used as a lid.[68]

48 Lenzen *et al.* 1964, 21.
49 Armstrong 1989, types 15-43.
50 Kessler 1991, 3.
51 Strommenger 1964, 171.
52 Braun-Holzinger 1988, 125.
53 Curtis 1983, 87.
54 Reuther 1926, 218-232 nos. 112-140 (earlier), nos. 141-150 (later).
55 Ibid., 234-245, *"Stülpgräberi"* nos. 160-189; dated by Strommenger (1964, 158, Fig. 1) to the second half of the first millennium BC.
56 Strommenger dates these to the Hellenistic/Parthian period. Ibid., Fig 1.

57 References in Curtis 1983, 85.
58 Ibid., 86.
59 Hrouda [*et al.*] 1981, 40, graves 44 &44a.
60 Reuther 1926, 218-219.
61 McCown & Haines 1967, 132, 143; Gibson *et al.* 1978, 70-71.
62 Safar 1949, 162.
63 UVB 5 p. 24.]
64 Reuther 1926,. 220-221, 230.
65 Ibid. 220, 233-234.
66 McCown & Haines 1967, 131.
67 McCown & Haines 1967, 137.
68 McCown & Haines 1967, 132.

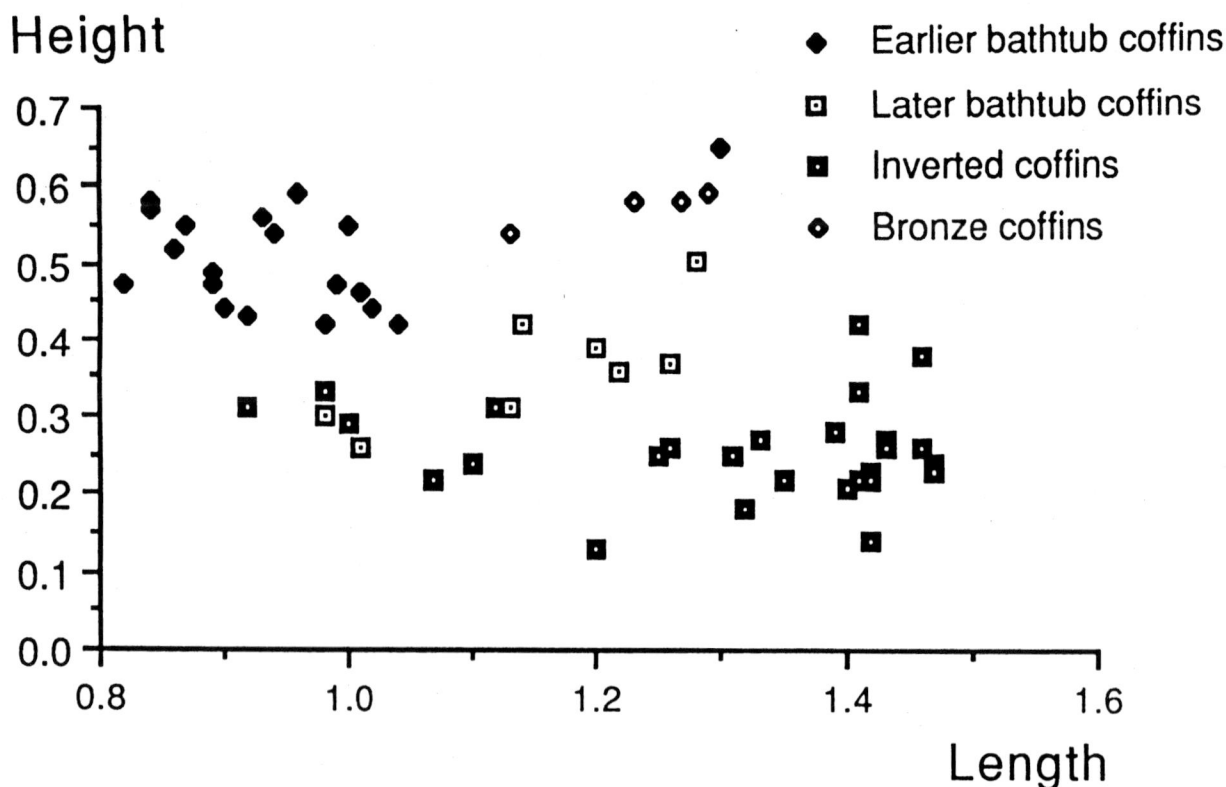

*Fig. 25.4 'Bathtub' coffin groups according to size (from Babylon, except for bronze coffins).*

The earliest bathtub coffins at Babylon have been attributed to the eighth century BC,[69] and according to Reuther's sections they were sometimes found in the same horizon as double-pot graves of Type B, jar burials and oval coffins.[70]

In addition to the two bathtub coffins with handles mentioned above, a further two plain bathtubs were found in the same area at Isin.[71] One of these, grave 75, contained an Achaemenid bottle,[72] a jar, a dish, and some items of jewellery, including a pair of bronze earrings consisting of hoops with 'grape-clusters' attached.[73]

At Kish baked clay coffins with one rounded end and one straight end have been found on the surface of Mound W. They have been dated by Moorey to the fifth century BC or later.[74] A number of these were inverted over the body, as in the third group at Babylon mentioned above. One such grave, no. 6 from the third season, contained a pair of bracelets with serpent's-head terminals which are very similar to

examples from the 'Résidence Achéménide' at Abū Qubūr.[75]

A number of bathtub coffins have been found at Nippur. Most of them came from the TA area, and according to Armstrong's revised stratigraphy for this sounding, the earliest burials of this type are to be dated to the third quarter of the seventh century BC.[76] Other bathtub coffins are shown to have contained pottery of approximately Achaemenid date.[77]

Three bathtub coffins have been found at Sippar, graves T. 138, 144 and 145.[78] The two complete examples, T. 138 and T. 144, were long, with straight, parallel sides; they measured 1.16 x 0.48 and 1.18 x 0.52 m respectively, and thus fall within the size-range of the later coffins of this type from Babylon (see Fig. 25.4). The pottery from these tombs indicates a date in the Achaemenid period,[79] including a tall jar from T.145 which is similar to Armstrong's Type 44.[80]

At Ur most of the published burials were of this type, and were dated by the excavator to the

69   Strommenger 1964, 171 & Fig. 8.
70   E.g., Reuther 1926 Taf. 3 House III in square 26 o 1.
71   Hrouda *et al.* 1981, 45-46 graves 75-76.
72   Ibid., Pl. 35 (pottery and other grave contents); cf. also Armstrong 1989, 144 n.71.
73   Cf. Braun-Holzinger 1988, 122.
74   Moorey 1978, 51. Microfiche 1 C08-D06 "Catalogue of the grave groups on Mound W".

75   Ibid., Microfiche 1 C09 (illustration); cf. Pons 1993, 6, Pl. 2: 1-2.
76   Armstrong 1989, 146.; graves 1B 183, 209, 227, 268, 269.
77   Ibid., 141-45, 151-153; graves 1B 168, 173, 178-181, 206.
78   De Meyer 1980, 55.
79   Ibid., 66.
80   Ibid., 70, Pl. 5:5, 15:10, jar S2016.

Achaemenid period.[81] They were, however, less numerous than the graves assigned by Woolley to the Neo-Babylonian period, which, more often disturbed in antiquity and less-well preserved, are under-represented in the final publication. However, the dating of the bathtub coffins to the Persian period has been questioned, and it is likely that some of them belong to the preceding period.[82]

The few bathtub coffins from Uruk have been discussed by Boehmer and others.[83] One in Eanna cut an NB wall; others have been found in P13, J-K/23 and in H/24-5, where they were intrusive into Kassite architecture. They are very rare in the area around Eanna, presumably because they were in use at Uruk after the abandonment of the housing-area there.

One bathtub coffin from Bahrain has been dated by the excavators to the eighth-seventh centuries BC, that is, as early as the earliest examples from Babylon.[84]

To summarise, bathtub coffins were introduced into Babylonia in the late Neo-Assyrian period. They continued in use in the Achaemenid period, though by this time they had undergone a change in shape, becoming longer and lower; this transition probably took place in the later years of Neo-Babylonian rule. As the Achaemenid period advanced, coffins of even longer and lower dimensions were regularly inverted over the bodies.

## Type 3: Jar-Burials

This form of burial has been found at Babylon, Kish, Isin, Nippur, Tell el-Laḥm, Ur and Uruk. The vessel used was typically a large, wide-mouthed jar with a ring base, for example Kish grave G 15,[85] Nippur WB3,[86] and Ur NB 44.[87] The jars could be laid on the ground on their side, or stood vertically in the grave shaft. They were sometimes equipped with a wooden lid, for example Babylon graves 74, 76, 78-82; the burial jar from grave 81 had traces of bitumen at the neck with impressions of rope, presumably in order to secure a lid. Grave 85 at Babylon had a lid of spirally-woven palm-fibre rope spread with bitumen.

At Babylon jar-burials were first found in levels containing earlier bathtub coffins, which would place them in the late Neo-Assyrian period and later; they also overlapped with the use of later double-pot burials and oval coffins.[88] They were often located below the level of Reuther's Neo-Babylonian houses; grave 82, for example, was overlain by a wall of

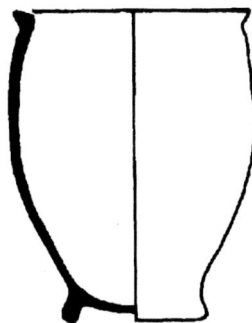

*Fig. 25.5 Type 3. Jar. Nippur grave WB6 (after Gibson et al. 1978, Fig. 52.2b)*

House 2. Grave 83 is said to have been found together with two early bathtub burials (nos. 133-134) in a house whose abandonment pre-dated the reconstruction of the temple of Ishtar by Nabonidus. Three jar burials, 74-76, were found together in the same room of House VII.

Two jar-burials were found at Isin (nos. 38 and 112), both of which contained a jar form similar to an Achaemenid type found at Nippur.[89]

Two jar-burials were among the graves on Mound W at Kish; they were found at 2.5 m below the surface.[90] One was a child burial with no grave goods, the other contained a single jar.

An unusual example from Nippur, jar burial WB 5, had a narrowed neck and was decorated on the shoulder and neck with wavy lines; it had an internal seating to accommodate a flat lid with a handle on top.[91] A jar with similar wavy-line decoration was found in a double-pot grave at Uruk, where it was dated 'nb/sb' (*neubabylonisch/spätbabylonisch*); the Uruk example had a comparable rim form, together with handles and a tripod footed base.[92] Within the cut around WB 5 a large number of clay tablets were packed; these are said to date to the mid to late eighth century BC.[93] In the TA sounding at Nippur over twenty jar burials were among the graves dated by Armstrong to the early first millennium BC.[94] One of them, 1B 220, contained an Assyrian bowl.[95] A number of these graves have been shown to pre-date the resettlement of TA in the latter half of the eighth century BC.[96]

---

81 Woolley 1962, 67-87 "Analysis of the Persian Graves".
82 Braun-Holzinger 1988, 123-124.
83 Boehmer 1987, 68-69.
84 Glob 1956, 172-173.
85 Matsumoto 1991, Fig. 17: 1.
86 Gibson *et al.* 1978, Fig. 55.
87 Woolley 1962, Pl. 59, type 238.
88 Reuther 1926, 199-202.

89 Hrouda *et al.* 1977 Pl. 28 IB 627; 1987, Pl. 31:6 IB 1430; cf. Armstrong 1989 325, Fig. 80, Type 44 (found in jar burial TA 1B 177).
90 Moorey 1978, Microfiche 1 D01.
91 Gibson *et al.* 1978, 72-73, Figs. 52: 1a-c, 53: 1-2.
92 Strommenger 1967, 27, Pl. 29: 2.
93 Armstrong 1989, 181.
94 Ibid., 158, Table 17.
95 Ibid., 147.
96 Graves 1B 256, 257, 263, 266 , 284.

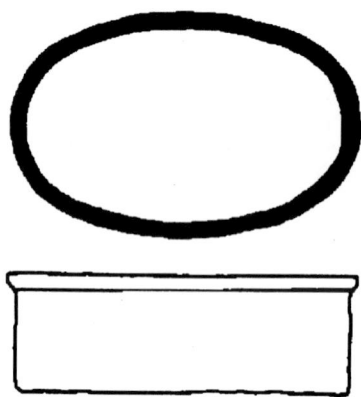

*Fig. 25.6  Type 4. Oval Coffin. Babylon grave 100*
*(after Reuther 1926, Pl. 62)*

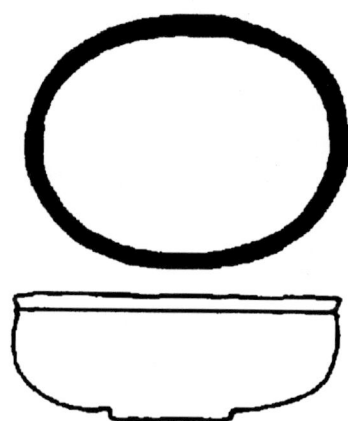

*Fig. 25.7  Type 5. Bowl. Babylon grave 102*
*(after Reuther 1926, Pl. 63).*

Some of the jar burials at Ur were located against Nebuchadnezzar's *temenos* wall;[97] the fill against another such jar contained tablets of Nabopolassar.[98]

Jar burials were found at Uruk together with double-pot burials of Type B in the area of 'nb/sb' housing to the SW of Eanna. The same considerations apply to their dating as have been stated above for the double-pot burials there.

The earliest dateable examples of jar burial therefore belong to before the late eighth century BC. Jar burials continued in use into the Achaemenid period, but they were considerably less common than during Neo-Assyrian/Neo-Babylonian times.

## Type 4: Oval coffins

Oval coffins have been encountered at Babylon, Kish, Nippur, Tell el-Laḥm and Ur. In around one third of the 61 examples known to me, the body was that of a baby or child, suggesting that it was a preferred method of burial for juveniles; this was the case in all but one of the oval coffins at Babylon.

At Babylon these coffins were generally found in levels associated with bathtubs of the earliest group (graves 94-95), with double-pot graves of Type B (92), and with jar burials (94).[99] Graves 100 and 101 were associated with a later bathtub coffin, grave 143; together with a bowl burial (102), this group post-dated the foundation of NB House 4.

The exact stratigraphic context of the oval coffins at Kish is unknown, but they were found on Mound W at the same depth as coffins of the later bathtub types, including inverted ones (see above).[100]

In the TA sounding at Nippur four oval coffins were found in House B, in a level designated as Achaemenid.[101]

Two examples from Tell el-Laḥm were found in sounding 7, one of which rested on the upper floor,[102] as did a cylinder of Nabonidus in a different room (Room 8) of the same building range;[103] the coffins are probably to be dated to the Achaemenid period.

Finally, at Ur over 30 oval coffins have been found at various sites including the AH house site, the NH building, and "on the line of the town wall".[104]

## Type 5: Bowl-burials

Bowl-burials have been encountered at Babylon,[105] Kish,[106] Nippur[107] and Ur.[108] Some of the bowls, including all of those from Babylon, were oval in form. These differed from the preceding type in that they had a base like a bowl, with curving rather than straight sides. Again, infants were over-represented, having been found in at least two-thirds of the bowl-burials studied. At Kish the graves dug into Mound W were located at a depth of up to 3m below surface. The Nippur examples, from loci 46 and 76, belong to the early seventh century BC. and later. Bowl-burials from Ur came mainly from the AH house site.

97  Woolley 1962, 62, graves NB 42-44.
98  Ibid., 58, grave NB 2.
99  Reuther 1926, 206-208 graves 92-101.
100  Moorey 1978, Microfiche 1, pp. C11, third season graves G3, 8, 13, 23, 26, 79.

101  Armstrong 1989, Fig. 57 'TA II*'; cf. Fig. 38 for the location of burials TA 1B 132-133 & 138-139.
102  Safar 1949, 159 no. 14.
103  Ibid., 159.
104  Woolley 1962, 60, 74-87.
105  Reuther 1926, 208-212, graves 102-111.
106  Moorey 1978, Microfiche 1, C11-D05, third-season graves 10, 20, 28, 29, 35, 38, 39, 43-45, 60, 72, 86.
107  McCown & Haines 1967, 132-133 TA 1B 205, 210. Cf. Armstrong 1989, 299 Fig. 54. (revised level 'TA IV*').
108  Woolley 1962, 64-, NB 73, 88; P 191, 195, 243, 246, 282.

## Type 6: Bathtub-bowls

This type, Reuther's '*Hockertöpf*', appears to be a coffin-form transitional between the usual burial-bowls and the bathtub coffins. It has a bowl base and curving sides terminating in a rim which, in plan, has one straight and one rounded end, like the bathtub coffins. The form has only been found at Babylon, where both examples came from House XVI, considered by Reuther to pre-date the rebuilding of the temple of Ishtar by Nabonidus.[109] One of the bodies was of an immature individual, and the other was an infant.

## Type 7: Earth graves

Graves consisting of simple pits are, by their nature, difficult to date unless equipped with diagnostic grave goods. At Sippar three earth graves (T. 139, 142 and 143) were well-stratified in relation to the three bathtub coffin burials discussed above.[110] Both T. 142 and 143 were located above bathtub coffins T. 144 and 145, while the latest earth grave in this sequence, T. 139, was disturbed by bathtub T. 138. In both T. 142 and T. 143 a lateral chamber was separated from the main pit by baked bricks, some of which were stamped with an inscription of Nebuchadnezzar II.

The same two earth graves each contained a bowl inverted over the mouth of a jar; in the case of T. 142 the bowl was of fine ware, and in T. 143 it was of eggshell-ware.[111] A fine-ware bowl was found together with a jar in the third (disturbed) earth-grave, T. 139.[112] The fine-ware bowls from tombs 139 and 142 (and a similar one from bathtub coffin T. 138) have been compared to examples from Achaemenid levels at sites in Iran.[113] These bowls are also somewhat similar to an example from the so-called '*Résidence Achéménide*' at nearby Abū Qubūr, which dates to the later Achaemenid period.[114] T. 142 also contained a fragment of a bronze bangle with serpent's-head terminal for which the excavators cite Achaemenid parallels, and which may be also compared to an example from Abū Qubūr.[115]

To digress slightly, the practice of inverting eggshell-ware bowls over jars has long been observed in graves from Achaemenid and Seleucid Babylonia, and Fleming has suggested that eggshell pottery may have functioned as a funerary ware.[116] He cites Peters as providing the single known exact find-spot for an eggshell-ware vessel; the example from Sippar T. 143

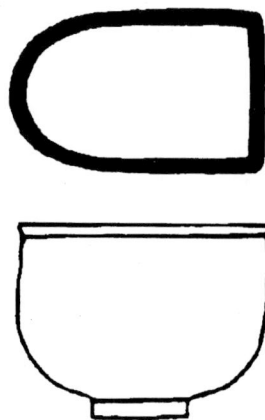

*Fig. 25.8 Type 6. Bathtub bowl. Babylon grave 152 (after Reuther 1926, Pl. 78).*

can be added to this, as can a ribbed eggshell ware bowl inverted over a jar in Isin earth- grave 107,[117] and a bowl in a similar position in Nippur earth grave TA IB 164.[118] Eggshell-ware was also found in another Isin earth grave, 106, together with a large jar and an Achaemenid bottle.[119] These examples appear to strengthen the association of eggshell-ware with funerary contexts.

A number of earth graves with lateral chambers have been found more recently at Tell ed-Dēr, and have been attributed by the excavators to the late Achaemenid and/or Seleucid periods.[120] As with some of our examples above, the cavity in some cases had been sealed with baked bricks, some of which bore inscriptions of Nebuchadnezzar II (for example graves T. 213, 252). Other graves consisted of a simple pit covered over with baked bricks, including stamped ones, which were set at an angle to form a roof (for example tombs 346 and 362). It is likely that the inhabitants of Sippar and Tell ed-Dēr pillaged the bricks for use in their tombs from the nearby wall of Nebuchadnezzar II, Ḥabl aṣ-Ṣahr.

Graves consisting of pits with side chambers have also been found at Nippur in the WB sounding, where they were dated to Level G ('Late N. Ass/NB (?)').[121] However, one of these, WB7, contained a bottle of Armstrong's Achaemenid type 45.[122] It also produced a jar similar to one found in an oval coffin (grave 14) at Tell al-Laḥm, which was said to lie just above the latest floor of room 11 in Sounding 7;[123] elsewhere in this building range a cylinder of Nabonidus was

---

109  Reuther 1926, 232 graves 151-152.
110  De Meyer 1980, 56-61.
111  Ibid., Pl. 12:14 (bowl S2000) & Pl.10: 5 (bowl S2006).
112  Ibid., Pl. 12: 12 (bowl S1989).
113  Ibid., Pl. 12.
114  Gasche *et al.* 1989b, Pl. 8:11.
115  De Meyer 1980 Pl. 6:.3; cf. Pons 1993, 6, Pl. 2:1-2.
116  Fleming 1989, 167.
117  Hrouda *et al.* 1987 16, Pls. 31: 2 (jar IB 1358), 31:5 (bowl IB 1357).
118  McCown & Haines 1967, 129, Pl. 103, type 66.
119  Hrouda *et al.* 1987, 15, Taf. 31.1 (jar IB 1353), 31.3 (bottle IB 1354; cf. Armstrong 1989 Type 45) & 31.4 (eggshell-ware bowl IB 1352).
120  Gasche 1991 pp. 32-33.
121  Gibson *et al.* 1978, 70 ff. graves WB 1, 4, 7.
122  Ibid., Fig. 77: 6.
123  Safar 1949, 163, Pl. 3: 2.

found on the latest floor. The Nippur graves of this form may therefore be later than was originally suspected.

Although simple pit graves may have been used at all periods as an alternative to burial in containers, it appears that earth-graves with lateral chambers came into use during the course of the Achaemenid period and continued in use into the Seleucid period.

## Burial Practices

## Location

It was Strommenger's contention that the burials at Babylon (as in the ancient Near East in general) were intramural,[124] and in order to demonstrate this she correctly questioned the assumptions on which Reuther's arguments to the contrary were based. However, it is not necessary to propose one single choice of burial location to the exclusion of others. It is clearly possible that more than one mode was in use at the same time; Barrelet has suggested five alternative types of burial location, both extra- and intramural.[125] Cultural, religious and practical considerations may all to varying degrees have played a part in the choice of location. The use of cemeteries in urban areas must relate in some way to the availability of open ground. It may be that the distribution of burials at times reflected the changing fortunes of urban society, for example, when burial grounds spread over previously inhabited areas or disused public monuments. The spatial distribution of burials is therefore of interest not only to students of burial practices, but to anyone interested in the changing uses of urban space.

Firstly, a few comments about methodology are needed. In order to be able to demonstrate intramural burial, it is evidently necessary to be able to show that a grave was dug at a time when the room or building in question was still in use. However, the evidence upon which such a judgement relies is often absent. The tops of grave-cuts can be difficult to detect, and were frequently truncated in antiquity, so that unless adequately detailed sections and descriptions are available, we are forced to rely upon other, circumstantial evidence, such as alignment with walls etc. In the case of Babylon, it is sometimes easier to prove that a grave was *not* intramural (for example, because it is said to lie beneath a wall of the house above it) than to prove that it *was*, since grave-cuts are rarely indicated on the published sections. Burials found at the surface of a site pose another problem, in that

they are often said to belong with houses which have entirely eroded away. The assumption of intramural burial therefore introduces circularity into the argument, and the question of whether the graves belong instead to cemeteries is not always addressed.

Reuther claimed that the Merkes area was used as a burial ground in the late Kassite period, after the buildings there had fallen into disuse. The same may be true of the period immediately following his MBA level, at least for parts of Merkes. Judging from the sections and other published information, there are a number of graves at or above the level of the MBA architecture which cannot have been dug down from the NB houses above, either because they are too far down, or because such a possibility is contradicted by Reuther's description.

It has been suggested for Uruk that cemeteries must have been used, since intramural burial could not have accounted for all the graves that would have been required.[126] If we apply this reasoning to the Merkes area, a similar conclusion follows. Allowing a minimum span of 800 years for the burials studied here (that is, c. 1200-400 BC.), ranging from the early double-pot graves to the inverted coffins, then the number of burials in Reuther's catalogue (some 147 in all) would imply that one individual from the Merkes quarter was being buried approximately every 5 years and 5 months. Admittedly, there are a smaller number of graves which Reuther noted without including them in his catalogue, but these are insufficient to overturn the conclusion that the number of burials in this area could not have matched the likely number of inhabitants and their rate of dying.

The double-pot graves at Isin may belong with the building in which they were found, while the level from which the later graves in that area were dug is not preserved. The graves in the TA sounding at Nippur are thought to have been mostly intramural.[127] Bathtub coffins and earth graves in the sounding by the city wall at Sippar were related to occupation levels. At Uruk a cemetery was said to have spread densely over the Eanna enclosure wall of Sargon II.[128] A cemetery has also been identified in the H/24-25 area at Uruk, where bathtub coffins were intrusive into Late Kassite architecture.[129] In the absence of information on context nothing can be deduced about the modes of burial location used at Kish and Ur.

From the above we may conclude that both intramural burial and inhumation in cemeteries were practised. The case of intramural burial raises the question of whether or not there was any variability in the spatial distribution of burials within houses, for

124 Strommenger 1964, 157.
125 Barrelet 1980, 7.

126 Lenzen & Nissen 1974, 24-25.
127 Armstrong 1989, 156.
128 Nöldeke *et al.* 1932, 25-26.
129 Boehmer 1987, 68.

example, were certain rooms preferred for this purpose? In view of the methodological constraints outlined above, we can only observe that occasionally concentrations of burials do seem to occur. At Nippur a small room at the corner of TA house C, leading off the reception room, has been identified as a burial room.[130] A group of burials was also found in a small room to the east of the courtyard of House 4 at Babylon (graves 100, 101, 102, 143; respectively two oval coffins, an oval bowl and a bathtub coffin).

## The Treatment of the dead

Individual burial was the norm. Inhumation was almost invariably crouched, since with the exception of pit graves, the grave forms discussed here did not allow fully outstretched disposal. Graves containing more than one occupant were very rare, and usually consisted of an adult and neonate or small child; for example Isin, grave 38 and Babylon grave 52. Cremation was also extremely rare; at Babylon three examples were placed in bathtub coffins, both of the earlier group (153-155), and two in jars with sherd lids (156-157).

It was not uncommon for the dead to be wrapped in cloth. At least thirty graves contained remnants or impressions of textiles. It is notable that, where these were observed in any quantity, or in a recognisable form, the graves in question were predominantly double-pot graves, and the remainder were jar burials. It is unlikely that this fact is of any chronological significance, but rather that the presence of a more or less closed grave 'capsule' protected the fabric remains, so that they tended to be much better preserved. Shrouds were recorded by the excavators in a number of cases; for example, Babylon grave 63; Nippur TA 1B 236; Ur NB 34, 36, 39 & 41; Uruk W. 10997 (all double-pot graves); and Ur NB 21 & 23 (jar-burials). A sash of twisted textile was found in Nippur TA 1B 255 (double-pot grave), and a number of graves contained textile remnants on or near the skull, as in Isin grave 27; Nippur TA 1B 218; Babylon 63 (all double-pot graves); and Nippur TA 1B 223 (jar burial; the cloth was associated with a fibula). Leather fragments at the feet were recorded in the case of Nippur grave TA 1B 219.

## Grave offerings (foodstuffs)

In a number of graves evidence for offerings of foodstuffs was found. Heaps of date stones were reported from Babylon graves 63 (in the bend of the knee; double-pot grave Type B) and 113 (along the right side of the body; bathtub coffin). In grave 129

(bathtub coffin) date stones were heaped up by the feet, near to some bones of a small ruminant. Grave 86 (a ceramic box) contained a heap of well-preserved dates, together with three pomegranates next to a pot, and some figs by the hip.

Animal bones were placed in graves 48, 69, 112 and 151 at Babylon. Several graves from the TA sounding at Nippur contained animal bones (TA 1B 168, 178, 206, 227 and 269; all bathtub coffins), and one produced fish bones (1B 246; jar burial). In T. 143 at Sippar, an earth grave with side-chamber, some bones of a juvenile sheep or goat were covered by a plate and placed on the hands of the dead.

Several graves at Babylon had numerous carbonised date stones mixed in with the fill. In most of these there was evidence for burning at the top of the grave-cut, sometimes in the form of a hearth which seemed to the excavator to have been used on more than one occasion (e.g., grave 58, Type B double-pot grave; 106, oval bowl). The ash of these hearths sometimes contained date stones, as in grave 106 (with wood carbon and burnt bone fragments) and grave 52 (Type B double-pot grave; the hearth was contained in a brick-edged trough). Above the grave-cut of 109 (oval bowl) the excavator identified a thick ashy layer with many burnt bone fragments and date stones, but no sign of a hearth. The cut of grave 87 (ceramic box), whose fill also contained many carbonised date stones, was sealed by a thick deposit of pure clay, which was cut at one side by a fire pit. The fill of a bathtub grave at Uruk also contained much organic material, including barley, date stones and sheep bones (grave 1 in area J23/100).

The presence of carbonised date stones and other organic material in these grave fills could point merely to the use of refuse as backfill, but combined with the evidence for fires, is suggestive of some activity associated with or following upon the act of burial.

## Grave-goods and social differentiation

Approximately 15% of the graves studied here contained no grave-goods at all. Most grave assemblages consisted of a small number of pots and/or items of personal adornment or utensils. Twenty-three graves containing cylinder seals were noted, of which 6 contained more than one seal. A further 45 contained stamp seals, of which 12 graves produced more than one. Thirty-six graves contained metal vessels, including 11 graves with more than one. Only a small proportion of grave occupants, amounting to about 140 individuals, have had their gender positively or tentatively identified. Of these, women were more likely to be buried with ornaments of gold, silver and bronze than men; around 50% of female graves contained beads compared with less than 5% of

---

130 Armstrong 1989, 167, 281, fig. 36.

male ones. Men, on the other hand, were slightly more likely to be buried with metal vessels, or with iron.

The grave types themselves are a possible indicator of social differentiation, though the reasons why one form of burial was chosen in preference to another at a time when several types were in use are likely to remain obscure. As we have seen, Braun-Holzinger observed that fibulae were associated with those buried in bathtub coffins. Among the Merkes graves it is noteworthy that, of those containing gold and/or silver, over half were bathtub coffins but none were jar burials. A couple of types, the oval coffin and the bowl, were the preferred recipients for child burials. One of these, grave 109 (oval bowl), was very richly furnished, including jewellery of gold and semi-precious stones, a carved ivory head, and glass vessels.

There are few other indicators of differentiation among the graves studied. The burials from Merkes appear to be consistently richer in their accompanying goods than burials from other sites, both in terms of the range and quantity of material; this must reflect the size and quality of the prestigious houses in this part of the capital city. At Nippur, an increase in the wealth of the inhabitants was observed between the revised Levels V-IV and III-II on the basis of the grave-goods found with burials there.[131]

## Conclusions

At the beginning of our period disposal of the dead was dominated by a single grave type, the double-pot grave. The second quarter of the first millennium BC saw a greater diversity in the range of burial forms used. By the later Achaemenid period this diversity has declined and the predominant form of disposal was in ceramic coffins, often inverted, or in earth graves. We have been able to provide confirmation of typological distinctions first made by Reuther at Babylon for certain burial forms, namely the double-pot graves and bathtub coffins, and to elucidate their chronological implications in the light of recent work. It has also been shown that the use of the earth grave with lateral side chamber is distinctive of the Achaemenid period and later. The use of both cemeteries and intramural burial at this period is indicated; it is hoped that study of the spatial distribution of burials within housing areas will be facilitated by better contextual information in the future. Finally, the evidence for burial practices, including the provision of foodstuffs and textiles as well as the more commonly preserved and reported items, has been outlined.

*Acknowledgements*
This study was conducted with the generous assistance of the G.A. Wainwright Near Eastern Archaeological Fund. The revision of the paper following the conference benefited from comments and contributions by participants too numerous to enumerate individually; responsibility for errors and omissions is mine alone.

---

[131]Armstrong 1989, 172.

# 26

# The Tombs of Lycia Evidence for Social Stratification?

## Antony G. Keen

ABSTRACT—*The tombs of Lycia fall into four broad categories: Pillar tombs, heroön-type tombs, sarcophagi, and rock-cut house-tombs. They have attracted scholarly attention ever since Lycia was 'rediscovered' by Westerners in the early nineteenth century, but particularly since the Second World War. Jan Zahle has argued that different categories reflect a fairly clear hierarchy in Lycian society. This paper examines that contention, and looks at the evidence available to determine whether a Lycian's social class determined which type of tomb they were buried in. The answer arrived at also provides some lessons for the study of funerary monuments in general.*

Lycia lies in south-western Turkey. In ancient times it was the home of a flourishing and original culture, which reached its height in the so-called 'epichoric' period (roughly 550-300 BC). The tombs from this period have attracted scholarly attention ever since Lycia was 'rediscovered' by Westerners in the early nineteenth century, but particularly since the Second World War, through the work of French, German, Austrian, Danish and British archaeologists and art-historians. The earliest tombs, belonging to the class known as pillar tombs, date to c. 540 BC, whilst house-tombs and sarcophagi seem to have appeared first in the mid-fifth century BC.[1] Though the period of these tombs coincides with Lycia's time as a province of the Achaemenid Persian empire, it can be safely said that these tombs largely represent a local phenomenon, only superficially touched by Iranian influences, which mainly impinged upon the iconography used in the late fifth and early fourth centuries BC.[2]

In what is the most thorough modern treatment of the tombs, Jan Zahle lists approximately known 1,085 examples, and divides them into four broad types: Monumental or heroön-type tombs (6 known); pillar tombs (35); 'gothic' sarcophagi (60); and rock-cut house-tombs (about 950).[3] On the basis of these categories he

has argued that there may in the tombs be found a reflection of a fairly clearly defined stratification in Lycian society;[4] the heroön tombs belonged to the families of the highest social standing, and the house-tombs to those lower down the scale.

There are, however, fundamental problems with trying to reconstruct social history out of the Lycian tombs. The Classical archaeologist A.M. Snodgrass has argued persuasively that archaeological data are of a quite different sort to the data required by historians, and hence do not always fit historical models;[5] this is undoubtedly the case with Lycia. Sometimes the historical material does match the archaeological; for instance, the archaeological richness of the city of Xanthos fits well with the conclusion from historical sources that it was the most important city in the region.[6] On the other hand, the city of Limyra possesses something in the region of 500 tombs, five times as many as any other city in Lycia (indeed, almost as many as all the other cities of Lycia put together), which might lead one to argue that it was a very important city; yet historical evidence would suggest that it was only so for a period of thirty to forty years in the early fourth century BC.[7] The city with the next highest number of

---

1   Zahle 1983, 198.
2   On which cf. Shahbazi 1975; Borchhardt 1990, 47.
3   Zahle 1983; esp. pp. 142-143 for the figures, made approximate by uncertainty about the exact number of house-tombs

4   Ibid., 39-63, 163-164.
5   Snodgrass 1987, 36-66.
6   Zahle 1980, 40-42.
7   Keen 1992a, 207-227.

to be found at the site of Limyra (approx. 485 known in 1983; more continue to be found).

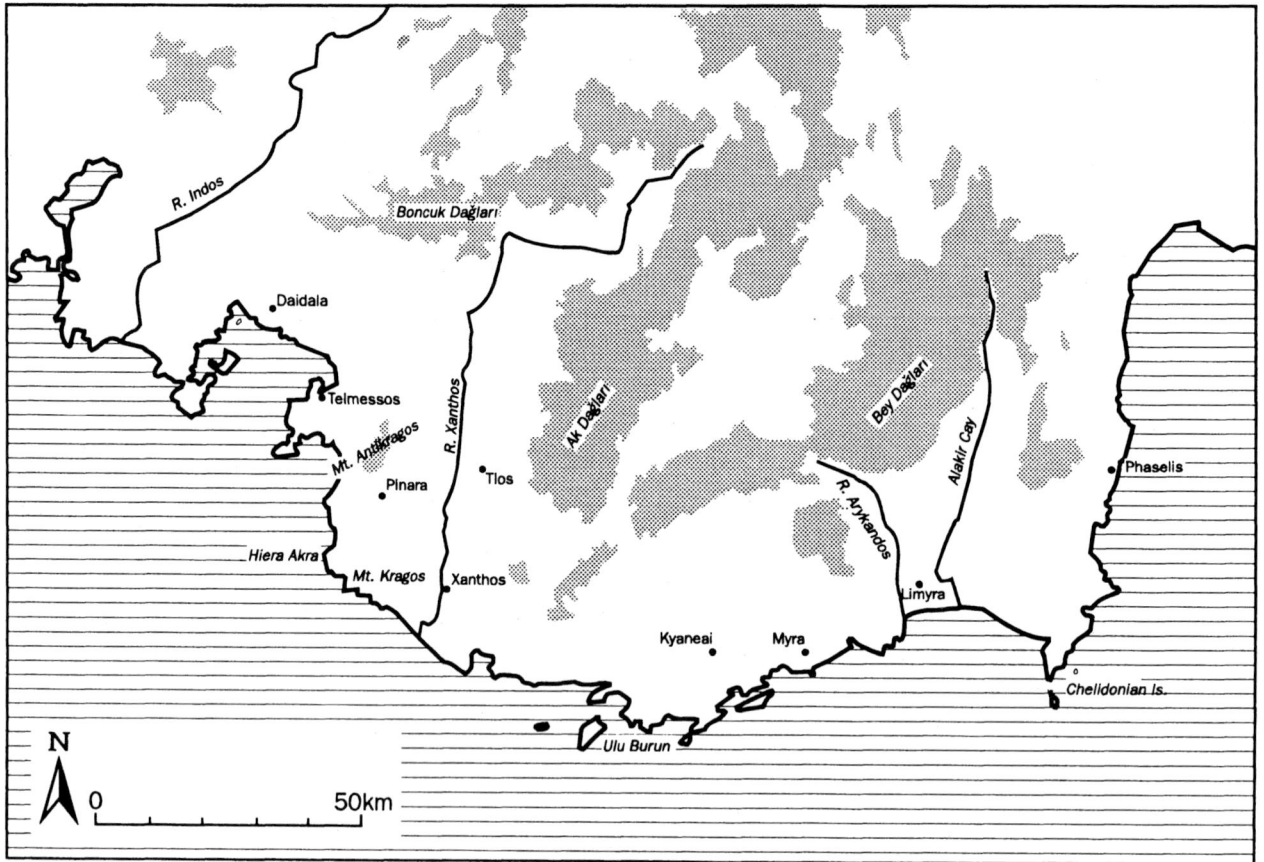

*Fig. 26.1: Lycia (land over 1500m shaded)*

tombs, Myra (which has 99), does not even merit a mention before Hellenistic times (by Artemidoros, writing in the second century BC, quoted in Strabo 14.3.7).

Most of the tombs of Lycia were emptied of their contents long before Westerners 'rediscovered' them. In the early nineteenth century, Captain Beaufort found a sarcophagus with its single occupant still inside, but lacking any grave-goods;[8] Phaselis, however, was a Greek colony, culturally distinct from the rest of Lycia in the epichoric period,[9] and it is therefore most unlikely that the sarcophagus concerned was pre-Hellenistic. Sir Charles Fellows in 1840 found bones in a tomb in Pinara,[10] but this tomb carried an inscription solely in Greek, and seems again to be post-Classical. Epichoric period house-tombs with their burials intact have recently been unearthed at Limyra,[11] but there has been little indication in publication of significant grave-goods. In any case, even if there were, the lack of undisturbed sarcophagi and pillars mean that the comparative material needed to deduce social stratification simply is not present.

It must further be remembered that all the recorded tombs of Lycia represent only a minority of the entire population of the country in the epichoric period; for the vast majority of the population, there is no trace of their burial-practices,[12] unless their tombs are represented by the pigeon-hole tombs that honeycomb the acropolis of Pinara (the only city in Lycia, however, with such tombs).[13] If there is a defined hierarchy within the tomb-owners then these are élites within an élite. T. R. Bryce notes that where family connections can be traced, sarcophagus-owners seem to have come from families with an already established tradition of tomb-ownership.[14] (A problem here is the high number of tombs at Limyra compared to those at other sites[15] – perhaps Limyra had an abnormally large catchment area?)

No serious objection can be raised to the four basic categories Zahle uses; it has long been recognised that the four tomb types are distinct. Nor does it seem unlikely that some sort of social divide is represented by the division between pillar tombs and sarcophagi. It has long been believed that the pillar tombs were tombs of

---

8  Beaufort 1818, 62.
9  Bean 1979, 121; Bryce 1986, 38[47], 205.
10 Fellows 1841, 143-144.
11 Cf. Großschmidt 1991 for an anthropological analysis of the skeletal remains.

12 Zahle 1983, 29.
13 Cf. Wurster & Wörrle 1978, 87, who suggest that they may be the oldest tombs in Lycia.
14 Bryce 1991, 84.
15 On the necropoleis at Limyra, cf. Schulz 1990.

the ruling dynasts of Lycia,[16] who in Xanthos probably styled themselves 'kings'.[17] The only pillar tomb whose owner can positively be identified, the 'Inscribed Pillar' of Xanthos,[18] is attributed to the coin-issuer Kheriga;[19] a number of sarcophagi are inscribed with the name of the owner (e.g., the sarcophagi of Pajawa[20] and Merehi[21] at Xanthos), but none of these can be equated with names known from the coinage record.

However, the right to have oneself buried in a pillar tomb seems to have been a sign of political rank, rather than necessarily a sign of a rigid caste-system. It seems most likely that the pillars were tombs for individuals, rather than family tombs, simply on the grounds of the limited size of the burial chamber (it should be noted that no tombs from Lycia have yielded any evidence for the practice of cremation); therefore the other members of a pillar-owner's family must have been buried elsewhere. And whilst the hereditary principle seems to have been important in determining who were dynasts, there does not seem to have been an exclusive dynastic class.

The division between the owners of pillar tombs and those of heroön tombs, as Zahle would have it between rulers and "super-rulers",[22] seems far less clear-cut. The six monumental tombs known fall into two broad chronological groups; two are of the mid-fifth century BC, and the remainder belong to the period 390-360 BC, a period when the use of the pillar as a method of burial began to wane (there is a late fourth-century BC pillar from Hoiran,[23] but this is in many respects atypical, and seems more likely to be an imitation of Greek funerary stelae). The two fifth-century BC heroön tombs seem curiously out of place, and it has been argued elsewhere that at least one of them, the so-called 'Building G' on the fifth-century acropolis at Xanthos, is not in fact the tomb of a historical personage at all, but a hero-cult centre;[24] the other, a building at Apollonia,[25] may well have had a similar function. The later heroön tombs were probably a development of the pillar tombs. The earliest, the 'Nereid Monument' attributed to the Xanthian ruler Erbbina,[26] was probably erected as a symbol of Erbbina's heroic qualities at a time when his control over Lycia

seems to have been weakening,[27] and the remaining three such tombs were claims by rulers in other cities to similar heroic qualities; in other words, a direct challenge to Erbbina's authority.

To turn to the division between sarcophagi and house-tombs, it is certainly true that house-tombs tremendously outnumber sarcophagi, by a factor of more than fifteen to one; but does this mean that sarcophagi automatically belonged to people from a higher social stratum than house-tombs? In favour of the argument, it can be said that the house-tomb virtually disappeared in the Hellenistic age, and the sarcophagus became the universal method of burial; it might perhaps be argued that the increased popularity of the sarcophagus was due to a more egalitarian atmosphere removing social barriers to such burials (or perhaps it represents an increasing Carian influence on Lycia).

For the epichoric period, however, it must be mentioned that the actual division between sarcophagi and house-tombs can become a little blurred at times. Consider, for instance, a tomb near the agora at Xanthos.[28] The façade of this monument is typical of the rock-cut house-tomb, yet it is free-standing like a sarcophagus. On the other hand, there are rock-cut tombs whose façades deliberately imitate sarcophagi; examples of these are to be found at Kyaneai,[29] Myra[30] and Pinara.[31] These are probably the tombs of people who would have liked to have been buried in proper sarcophagus tombs, but for one reason or another were unable to be so; but if the division between social strata was well-defined, might not such aspirations have been frowned upon as the actions of people who did not know their place?

Some house-tombs even went as far as imitating the façades of heroön tombs; the most spectacular of these is the Tomb of Amyntas at Telmessos,[32] but there are other examples from Telmessos,[33] and also from Daidala,[34] Tlos[35] and Kyaneai (the so-called 'Ionic Tomb').[36] This may well, however, be something of a blind alley. Daidala and Telmessos are in the Lycio-Carian border region, which had certain cultural differences from the rest of Lycia; coinage in this area is sometimes inscribed with Lycian names in Carian rather than Lycian, suggesting that the population might have been bilingual.[37] Furthermore, the style of letters in the Greek inscription on the tomb of Amyntas identifies it as belonging to the fourth century BC,[38] and the name, common in Macedon but not it seems, often found

16  Zahle 1980, 38; 1983, 32-33, 64-65, 107-111.
17  Keen 1992a, 31, 139-140.
18  Demargne 1958, 79-102, Pls. 25-44; 1974, 113; Bean 1978, 57-58, 177-179, Pl. 15; Deltour-Levie 1982, 163-167; Meiggs & Lewis (eds) 1988, 282-283.
19  Identification by Bousquet 1975, 139-141, argued against by Childs 1979. Identifications for all the pillar tombs at Xanthos are suggested by Keen 1992b.
20  Demargne 1974, 61-87, Pls. XXX, 28, 30, 32-45:1; Idil 1985, 82-83, Pls. 87-88.
21  Demargne 1974, 88-96, Pls. XXI, XXXII, 46-53; Idil 1985, 81-82, Pls. 85:2-85:4, 86.
22  Zahle 1983, 107-111.
23  Deltour-Levie 1982, 41-49.
24  Keen 1992b, 54-56; 1995.
25  Kjeldsen & Zahle 1976.
26  Demargne 1975, 150; 1976, 81⁴; 1979, 99-100¹⁶; Childs & Demargne 1989, 401; Demargne 1990, 69; Keen 1992b, 59.

27  Bryce 1986, 109-111; Keen 1992a, 186-190.
28  Demargne 1974, 21-24, Pls. II-V:1-2.
29  Bean 1978, 111, Pl. 58.
30  Zahle 1983, Pl. 7.
31  Bean 1978, 77, Pl. 34.
32  Ibid., 40, Pl. 2.
33  Ibid., Pl. 3.
34  Ibid., 35, Pl. 1.
35  Önen 1990, 13, Pl. 12.
36  Bean 1978, 111, Pl. 59; Zahle 1983, 19, 20, 114, Pl. 8.
37  Masson 1974, 124-130.
38  Bean 1978, 40.

elsewhere before Alexander's conquests, suggests that the tomb is post-333 BC, supported by the fact that its inscription is in Greek alone; all pre-Hellenistic Greek inscriptions in Lycia are found on bilinguals. It would not be altogether surprising if the other examples also turned out to be very late fourth-century BC (particularly as the Ionic Tomb from Kyaneai also carries an inscription in Greek only). If that is so – since the Macedonian conquest and subsequent influx of new settlers would have wrought significant social changes – these tombs are little help in determining the social structures in place before 333 BC.

Decoration of tombs must also be considered. Many sarcophagi were adorned with relief sculpture; most house-tombs were not. But this is not a universal rule. A few house-tombs, such as the 'Painted Tomb' at Myra,[39] were decorated to a very high standard, whilst a number of sarcophagi were unadorned (as indeed were some pillars, e.g., the 'Acropolis Pillar' at Xanthos[40]). Three sarcophagi at Pinara, for instance, carry no relief sculpture,[41] yet a house-tomb there, the so-called 'Royal Tomb', does.[42] Were the inhabitants of the undecorated sarcophagi people at the bottom of one social stratum, with the right to sarcophagus burial, but no money to adorn their tombs, and those in the decorated house-tombs people at the top of another, with money but no right to a sarcophagus?

It is known from their inscriptions that many Lycian house-tombs were tombs for families.[43] There are only seven occasions when such inscriptions are found on sarcophagi;[44] three of them also carry Greek inscriptions,[45] which may or may not be significant. Since, however, there are no more than a dozen or so sarcophagi that have inscriptions in any case, the sample is statistically too small to draw any worthwhile conclusions, and no epichoric period sarcophagus has ever been found with its occupants.

The inscriptions do, however, provide a very important clue. Bryce has studied the names recorded in the Lycian inscriptions with a view to seeing whether family associations can be detected to support Zahle's argument.[46] His reconstruction of family units in Lycia rests on the assumption that the same name in different inscriptions relates, if not to the same individual, at least to individuals of the same family group, an assumption he admits is "unprovable";[47] but it seems possible , and the fact that this seems to point to family

units with connexions with two or more cities is quite compatible with inferences of upper-class mobility within Lycia that may be drawn from the coinage record.[48] For the purposes of this paper, however, the important point is that some of these family units cut across the divide between sarcophagi and house-tombs. Bryce himself concludes that there "may well have been important exceptions to J. Zahle's proposition";[49] it is perhaps acceptable to go further and suggest that if Bryce's conclusions hold any weight, then there was no rigid social barrier between sarcophagus ownership and house-tomb ownership.

It cannot be argued that the ownership of a sarcophagus tomb (or indeed of a pillar or heroön) was not a symbol of social status; but it was perhaps a status symbol conceivably achievable by those lower down the social scale, rather like a Rolls-Royce or a large house in Surrey is today. It seems likely that pillar and heroön tombs were a mark not of social class but of personal distinction,[50] and this may well also be the case with sarcophagi, particularly if it is correct that they were usually single burials. Therefore, instead of a four-tier social hierarchy amongst the tomb-owners, there was only a general class of house-tomb-owners, out of whom certain individuals of particular distinction, either by social or political rank or quite possibly simply by wealth (although the three are not easily separable given the level of evidence), proclaimed that distinction by choosing to be buried (or exercising their right, in the case of dynasts buried in pillar tombs) in different types of tomb.

How these different status symbols evolved is a very interesting question, but not one that is easy to answer. The evolution of heroön tombs is fairly easily deduced, from the genuine heroa of the mid-fifth century BC, influenced by both Greek architecture from the west and oriental tombs such as that of Cyrus the Great at Pasargadae.

Where the pillars and sarcophagi came from is far less clear. A link has been suggested between pillar tombs and the modern beehives of north Lycia,[51] but this must be a case of the tombs (which may have been of wood before stone tombs became common) influencing the shape of the beehives (if indeed there is any connexion at all).

The prime lesson to be drawn from the study of Lycian tombs for the study of funerary monuments in general is one of caution. The distinct categories of Lycian tombs initially attract one into the belief that some conclusions about social structures can be drawn from it. As has been seen, such conclusions are probably unwarranted. It is particularly salutary that one of the most important pieces of evidence against the hypothe-

39   Ibid., 123-124, Pls. 72-76.
40   Demargne 1958, 113-116, Pls. 49-51; Bean 1978, 60, Pl. 18. Deltour-Levie 1982, 168-170.
41   Idil 1985, 61-62.
42   Bean 1978, 76-77.
43   E.g. *TAM* I 3.3; 4.3; 6.2 & 5-6; 7.3; 56.2 & 6; 61.1; 84.2; 88.2; 101.2; 102.1-2; 107.*a*.1; 108.2-3; 139.2-3; Neumann 1979, No. 322.
44   *TAM* I 11.1-2; 23.7-8; 29.2 (post-333 BC); 36.5-6; 117.3-4 & 7-8; 143. 2-3.
45   *TAM* I 23, 117, 143.
46   Bryce 1991.
47   Ibid., 83.

48   Keen 1992a, 30.
49   Bryce 1991, 84.
50   Ibid.
51   Dinstl 1990; see Mellink 1969 on general links between Lycian tombs and modern wooden buildings.

sis of a divide between sarcophagi and house tombs comes from epigraphic evidence; were the Lycians a prehistoric people, that evidence would be missing, and it would have been much easier to draw what are probably incorrect inferences. Hence the case-study of the Lycian tombs draws out important considerations for all archaeologists dealing with funerary monuments.

# 27 Gold Face-Masks in the Ancient Near East

## John Curtis

ABSTRACT—*The practice of covering the faces of corpses with gold face-masks, mostly in the first few centuries AD, is described, and extant masks of this type are listed. A previously unpublished mask from Jerusalem given to the British Museum as part of the A.W. Franks Bequest, is introduced, and compared with two masks from Nineveh which were published in 1976. The opportunity is taken now to review new evidence, and also to include evidence that was overlooked at that time. Lastly we shall attempt to place these gold face-masks in a wider context, and trace the origin and spread of the tradition.*

In 1976 I published an article in *The British Museum Yearbook* describing some tombs at Nineveh of Romano-Parthian date in which two gold face-masks had been found.[1] At that time I attempted to collect together gold face-masks from the ancient Near East and surrounding areas, and to review what was known about them. Since then, another gold face-mask, from Jerusalem, has been acquired by the Department of Western Asiatic Antiquities at the British Museum, and in publishing it now (Fig. 27.1) the opportunity is taken to include some more recent evidence about gold face-masks as well as including some information that was overlooked in the former article.

The new face-mask is made of thin gold-foil and is roughly circular in shape, measuring 14 x 12 cm with a weight of 13g. On it are crudely moulded details of eyes, eyebrows, nose and mouth. The eyes have large, circular pupils. On either side of the mask there are two pairs of holes to bind it to the head. This mask was originally part of the collection formed by Sir Augustus Wollaston Franks (1826-1897) and bequeathed by him to the British Museum".[2] No further information is available about the mask, save that the provenance "Jerusalem" is written on it, presumably indicating that it was originally found or purchased in that city. This Jerusalem mask is of thinner gold than the two examples from Nineveh, is slightly smaller and of rather different shape, but it clearly belongs to the same tradition.

The two masks from Nineveh (Figs 27.2 and 27.3) are angular in shape, tapering towards the bottom, and each is pierced in the four corners to tie it to the head of the corpse. On each, outlines of eyes, nose and mouth are crudely indicated. The tombs were discovered apparently somewhere near the centre of the Kouyunjik mound at Nineveh between January and July 1852. By this time Layard had returned to Britain and the excavations were under the overall control of Colonel H.C. Rawlinson, the British Consul-General at Baghdad and the East India Company's Political Agent in Turkish Arabia. But Rawlinson was based in Baghdad, and day-to-day supervision of the excavations was undertaken by Christian Rassam, the British Vice-Consul at Mosul and the eldest brother of Hormuzd Rassam. Contemporary accounts of the discovery were given by Matilda Rassam, the wife of Christian, in letters to Layard and by Rawlinson in reports to Sir Henry Ellis, the Principal Librarian of the British Museum. It seems that about a dozen tombs were discovered. Each was roughly built from slabs of stone forming the sides and the top. Most of them had been looted, probably in antiquity, but at least three seem to have escaped the attention of the tomb-robbers. The richest tomb was discovered in January 1852. It contained the smaller of the two face-masks (Fig. 27.3); a sheet gold mouth-piece; a sheet gold eye-cover in the shape of a pair of spectacles; a pair of elaborate gold earrings inlaid with garnets and with pendants set with garnets and turquoise; a pair of earrings with gold wire bindings and filigree decoration; two gold finger-rings, one set with a garnet engraved with the figure of a nude boy; a gold *aureus* of Tiberius; two glass bottles; a necklace of small gold beads; some glass beads; and a

---

1 Curtis 1976.
2 It is item no. 17 in a list of material in the Franks Bequest, and was registered in the Department of British and Medieval Antiquities with the number O(ld) A(cquisition) 1429. It was transferred to the Department of Western Asiatic Antiquities in 1983, and now has the number WA139535/1983-6-7, 1.

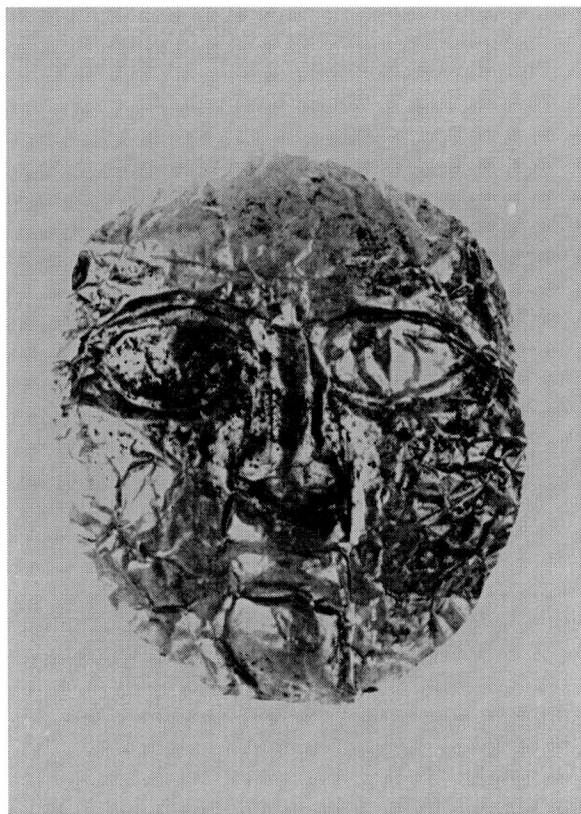

*Fig. 27.1: Gold mask from Jerusalem, BM 139535.*
*Photograph courtesy Trustees of the British Museum.*

*Fig. 27.2: Gold mask from Nineveh, BM 123894.*
*Photograph courtesy Trustees of the British Museum.*

cylinder with a cuneiform inscription that was obviously an antiquity when it was buried. There were also a number of small gold plaques for sewing to clothing. Altogether from the tombs there were nearly 200 plaques, mostly small circular discs with embossed centres, either with loop fasteners at the back or pierced with small holes at the sides. Mrs Rassam thought this first tomb was "apparently of a female", which in view of the accompanying earrings may well be correct. What is less certain is how many bodies there were in this tomb. The finding of eye and mouth coverings *in addition to* the mask might be an indication of two corpses, but it is also possible the mask was placed on top of the other coverings. The evidence of the earrings is equivocal, as often two pairs are worn by one person. The tomb with the second face-mask (Fig. 27.2) was less rich, containing only "a few gold buttons" with the mask. This grave was assumed by Matilda Rassam – probably not for any good reason – to have been that of a man. In other tombs were found "buttons (i.e. clothing plaques) and strips of gold leaf which seem to have been bound round the handles of knives or daggers". There were also sixteen gold leaves and four gold-leaf impressions of a coin of Trajan, probably all part of a funeral wreath. How should these tombs be dated? The coin of Tiberius was minted in the period AD 16-21, while the coin of Trajan from which the gold leaf impressions were produced can be dated to *c*. AD 115. Parallels for

the earrings with triple pendants and garnets and turquoise, including representations on a funerary bust from Palmyra, suggest a date in the second-third century AD.[3] Such a date would also be quite acceptable for the gold ring with engraved garnet and for the *unguentarium* now in the British Museum and assumed to come from the tombs. Therefore, if it is assumed that the tombs are of various dates, with the burial-ground having been in use for several generations, bracket dates of first-third century AD must be proposed. If, on the other hand, the tombs are contemporary, or nearly so, they cannot be earlier than AD 115.

The best-known, and also the earliest gold masks, are the famous examples from the shaft graves at Mycenae, dating from a period shortly after 1600 BC.[4] These masks, of sheet gold, show men with handlebar moustaches and tightly closed eyes. The eyebrows are indicated by hatching. The wide, rounded shape of the masks includes ears. On either side of the masks there are small holes for fixing them to the head of the corpse.[5]

---

3    Curtis 1976, 54.
4    Schliemann 1878, Figs. 331-332, 473-474; Evans 1929, Figs. 2-3; Stubbings 1973, 629-633, 822.
5    In a lecture at the annual conference of the British Association for Near Eastern Archaeology in Liverpool on 15 December 1992, Dr Christopher Mee suggested that the Mycenaean masks were made by Minoan craftsmen, on the

Surprisingly, these Mycenaean examples seem to be an isolated phenomenon. There is a long gap between them and the gold face-masks from tombs at Trebenishte near Ohrid in the former Yugoslav Republic of Macedonia.[6] These masks are dated to the sixth-fifth centuries BC.[7] They are roughly triangular in outline and each has a wide border, in one case decorated with a cable pattern and in the other with linear designs. Ears are not shown.

Probably belonging to the same cultural horizon and of similar date is a gold mask in the Walters Art Gallery, Baltimore, that is believed to come from a tomb at Chalkidike in Northern Greece.[8] The grave is thought to be of a warrior who was equipped with a helmet of Illyrian/Thracian type; it is dated to the last quarter of the sixth century B.C. This mask is unlike those from Mycenae in that here the ears are not shown and the piece to cover the nose was made separately, perhaps because the mask split when it was being pressed into shape. The gold masks from the nearby site of Sindos, however, are made from single sheets of gold.[9] They sometimes occurred together with bronze helmets. We should also consider here a gold mask now in the Ashmolean Museum Oxford that was allegedly obtained in Boeotia in Central Greece. It was once in the possession of Sir Arthur Evans who bought it at *Sotheby's* in 1927.[10] It shows a bearded man with a thick head of hair. Unlike the other masks it is rectangular and there is evidence that it was fixed to something by tacks at the four corners. This - and the fact that it is only two-thirds life size – prompted Evans to suggest that it was not placed on the face of the corpse but was fixed to the coffin.[11] This seems very plausible.

The next occurrence of gold face-masks is on the north coast of the Black Sea, an area that was heavily colonised by Greeks. There are two examples. The first is a mask found at Olbia by Count Alexis Ouvaroff in 1842.[12] It is a fairly crude representation. It is now in the Hermitage Museum in St. Petersburg where it is dated to the fourth century B.C., but this might well be too early. The date is uncertain.[13] More securely dated is the famous mask from Glinishche near Kerch (Chersonesus).[14] This comes from a grave that is commonly known as the Tomb of the Queen with the Gold Mask. It is dated by coins to the first half of the

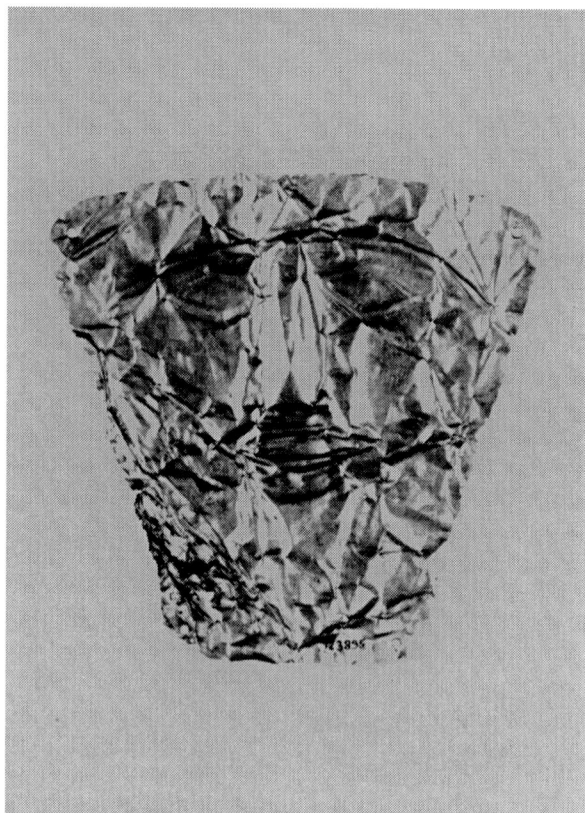

*Fig. 27.3: Gold mask from Nineveh, BM 123895. Photograph courtesy Trustees of the British Museum.*

third century B.C.[15] The grave-goods from this tomb are quite comparable to those from Nineveh with (in addition to the mask) a number of garnets mounted in bezels and several hundred small stamped gold plaques. The mask is more realistic than the examples from Nineveh, and is perhaps an accurate representation of the queen's face.

From the area of Sidon there is allegedly quite a large number of gold masks, but none of them has a secure archaeological provenance and dating is therefore a matter of speculation. Perhaps exceptional is a mask in the Museum für Kunst und Gewerbe in Hamburg which can allegedly be dated by associated material in the Hamburg Museum, including coins, to the second-third century AD.[16] By contrast, a mask attributed to Sidon, acquired by the Louvre in 1902,[17] has been dated by Gubel to the third quarter of the first millennium B.C.[18] and a very similar mask in the Louvre, formerly in the de Clercq collection,[19] is ascribed by Moscati to the fifth-fourth century B.C.[20] These datings are presumably on the basis that these masks should be linked with the Phoenician anthropoid sarcophagi from

---

grounds that there was little or no tradition of goldworking in Mycenae at this time.

6    Popovic 1956, Pls. I-II; 1974, Pls. 1-2.
7    Popovic 1974, 11-12.
8    Canby 1979, No. 235; Ogden 1982, Pl. 5.
9    Vokotopoulou 1985, Nos. 115, 239, 282, 322, 451. I am indebted to Dr N.V. Sekunda for this reference.
10   Evans 1929, Fig. 4. I am indebted to Dr Michael Vickers of the Ashmolean Museum who provided me with information about this mask.
11   Ibid., 10.
12   Ouvaroff 1855, Pl. XIV/l; *Historische Schätze* 1966, No. 248.
13   Minns 1913, 390.
14   Phillips 1965, Pl. 84; Rostovtzeff 1922, 174-175, 177.

15   The queen is identified as Rhescuporis III, *Hermitage* 1990, 32.
16   Hoffmann and von Claer 1968, No. 131.
17   AO 3988; Parrot 1970, Pl. on p. 46.
18   Grubel 1986, No. 242.
19   AO 25065 *bis*.
20   Moscati 1988, 593, No. 55.

Sidon, but there is no evidence for this. More realistically, perhaps, the first of the Louvre masks is dated to the "période romaine" in *Sauvegarde de Tyr*.[21] Also said to be from Sidon is a gold mask formerly in the Hermitage Museum and sold at *Sotheby's* in 1931.[22] It is dated to the sixth or fifth century B.C., but it was allegedly found with a gold wreath, which would presumably make it later. Yet another gold mask ascribed to Sidon was in the former von Nelidow collection.[23] Again it was dated to the sixth-fifth centuries B.C., but no reasons are given for this dating. It has a flattened border around the edge, and the face is quite naturalistic. Two gold masks that recently passed through the London salerooms[24] were said by the owner to come from Sidon, and I am informed that a number of gold masks from Byblos and Sidon are in a private collection in Beirut.[25] A mask in the Louvre, acquired in 1872, is said to be from nearby Tartus.[26]

Like some of the examples from Sidon, a face-mask from Homs (Emesa) in Syria is quite naturalistically modelled.[27] It is dated by Seyrig to the 1st century AD.

Further east, in Mesopotamia, there are a number of examples of gold masks apart from the two examples from Nineveh. There is, for example, a gold mask from Nippur, now known only from a photograph and therefore of uncertain size.[28] Very probably, however, it is the mask found by Peters in a blue-glazed slipper-shaped coffin. He refers to "a large leaf of gold for covering the face".[29] Inside the coffin were also found "123 button-like gold objects made for sewing on stuff of some description. They were distributed all over the body, and had evidently been sewed on the garment worn". This is reminiscent of the tomb at Nineveh, as are "two large elaborate gold earrings with bell pendants, in the centre of which were once pearls". There was also "a fillet of gold leaf for the head". Another gold face-mask whose whereabouts is now unknown was found in a tomb at Halebiye on the Upper Euphrates by Captain H.B. Lynch of the Euphrates Expedition.[30] It is said by Chesney to have been exhibited at India House. Layard believed it to have been preserved in the museum of the East India Company.[31]

*Fig. 27.4: Gold mask in Musées Royaux d'Art et d'Histoire, Brussels. Photograph courtesy A.C.L., Brussels.*

The practice of covering the faces of corpses with gold masks may have been more widespread in Mesopotamia than is generally believed, perhaps because the gold was of very thin foil and easily destroyed. For example, Rassam says that at Babylon he found "some skeletons with thin gold-leaf covering the faces, and others with bands of the same gold-leaf placed across the foreheads".[32] At Warka according to Loftus, "thin gold leaf sometimes appears to have covered the face like a veil".[33] At Babylon, Koldewey tells us that "the face (of the corpse) was often wrapped in pieces of thin gold-leaf".[34]

In addition to the above examples, there are various unprovenanced gold masks in museums and private collections, and this paper makes no pretence at listing all of them.[35] A particularly interesting specimen is exhibited in the Hellenistic World gallery in the Musées Royaux d'Art et d'Histoire in Brussels (Fig. 27.4). It is more naturalistic than the Nineveh and Jerusalem examples, and shows a small, chubby face with eyes

21  AO 3988.*Sauvegarde de Tyr*, No. 140.
22  Sotheby's Catalogue 9th November 1931, lot No. 147.
23  Pollak 1903, 19, Pl. 7, No. 40. This is now exhibited in the Antiken Museen in Berlin together with another example.
24  They were twice offered for sale by Bonhams and were listed in their catalogues for 5th July 1994 (lot Nos 210-211) and 6th December 1994 (lot Nos 114-115), on both occasions with illustrations.
25  The Pharahon collection. I am indebted to Dr Jean-François Salles for this information.
26  MNB 1315; Sargon 1969, Pl. on p. 56. For information about material in the Louvre I am very grateful to Mme Agnès Spycket.
27  Seyrig 1952, Pl. XXVI; Chad 1972, p. 53.
28  Legrain 1928, 211-212, Fig. 18.
29  Peters 1898, II, 227.
30  Chesney 1850, 418; Hoffmann 1878.
31  Layard 1853, 592-594, note.

32  Rassam 1897, 350.
33  Loftus 1857, 211.
34  Koldewey 1914, 218.
35  For example, a gold mask was in the *Sotheby's* New York sale on 8 June 1994 (lot No. 259 with illustration in catalogue), and another was brought into the British Museum for an opinion in 1968 by a Madame Khonsari.

closed and wavy hair.[36] Then there were seven masks in the former de Clercq collection.[37] Two of them were given to the Louvre in 1968 by Count H. de Boisgelin, and bear the numbers AO 25065 and AO 25065 *bis*.[38]

Lastly, we might mention a curious gold mask that was found in the Shamshi Cemetery in Kirgiziya in Central Asia.[39] It measures 20.4 x 15.3 cm and is dated to the fourth-fifth century AD. The eyes are inlaid with red stones, and the surface of the gold is decorated with lines of white paste, perhaps in imitation of tattoos. It clearly seems to belong to a different tradition to the other masks discussed here. There is also a mask from another cemetery in Kirgiziya but this example is miniature and therefore beyond the scope of our present investigation.[40]

The custom of covering all or part of a dead person's face has a long history in the ancient world. It is generally thought that the intention was to preserve, or at any rate to conceal the decay of, those organs which would be most needed in the afterlife. As only a completely physical existence beyond the grave was envisaged, it was essential that the deceased would be able to see, eat, breathe and speak. Gold was extensively used as the covering material because of its incorruptible property. In addition, covering the face of the dead person would have made it more presentable at the funeral ceremony and less painful to look upon. The use of gold leaf to cover the eyes and mouth of the corpse is common in the ancient Near East, and is attested from at least *c.* 2000 BC onwards. It was particularly widespread, however, in the Hellenistic and Romano-Parthian periods, both in the Near East and in Egypt

where pieces of gold foil are often found in mummy wrappings. It is from these later periods that we have the distinctive gold "spectacles" to cover the eyes.[41] Clearly the gold mouth and eye coverings and the gold masks served the same purpose, and to some extent they belong to the same tradition, but the gold masks are far less common and not so widely distributed.

What, then, can be deduced about the date and distribution of the gold-masks? In 1976, I concluded that the gold face masks in the ancient Near East were probably inspired by the Phoenician anthropoid sarcophagi of the fifth-third centuries B.C., which derive from Egyptian mummy cases.[42] The apparent concentration of masks in the Sidon area tends to support this idea, and I see little reason to change that view now, in spite of the fact that most of the Near Eastern masks seem to date from the early centuries AD, including those that are allegedly from Sidon. There is a dearth of examples securely dated to the Hellenistic period, at least in the Near East proper, that would bridge the gap between the Phoenician sarcophagi and the Romano-Parthian period, but the closely related practice of covering the eyes and mouth of the corpse with strips of gold was certainly prevalent during that time. Also, we do of course have masks of Hellenistic date from the north coast of the Black Sea. The only difficulty with accepting a Phoenicio-Egyptian influence for the gold masks is that it does not explain the Mycenae masks or the later examples from Thrace and Macedonia. In some ways it is tempting to see a continuing Greek tradition from Mycenae right through to Kerch, but this cannot be supported. We are forced to conclude, therefore, that these masks are isolated phenomena that are not connected to the gold masks of the Hellenistic and Romano-Parthian periods.

This is not the only problem with these gold masks. It is clear from the most superficial examination they are very different. Some are very stylised, and cannot possibly be meant to represent the features of the deceased, whereas others are apparently quite naturalistic. Whether these are actually death-masks, or whether they are simply funerary portraits, is unknown. Amongst other differences, sometimes the eyes are open and sometimes they are closed. In short, there is considerable variety in these masks, and it is possible that further detailed study would lead to interesting conclusions. It also needs to be seen how the gold masks relate to masks in other materials such as plaster. Another interesting line of enquiry could focus on whether the masks had any particular social significance. Obviously they must derive from the graves of wealthy people, but whether they are an indication of hierarchy is unknown. Much still remains to be done, therefore, and the need for a comprehensive study remains as great now as it

---

36 Information about this mask and permission to publish it was very kindly given by Dr Jean-Charles Balty. The inventory number is A411, and it measures 17 cm x 12 cm. It came to the Musées Royaux from the Hagemans Collection in 1861. There is no information about provenance, but in Hagemans 1863, 374, No. 120, it is described as "masque étrusque en or repoussé ... Cette pièce ... rappelle l'usage des Etrusques de mettre des plaques semblables sur le visage des morts de qualité".

37 de Ridder 1911, 16-18, Nos. 17-23.

38 Mentioned in Devambez 1968, 328, and illustrated in Coche de la Ferté 1956, 37. Another mask formerly in the de Clercq collection was sold at Sotheby's on 7th November 1977, Lot No. 68.

39 Kanimetov 1983, No. 141. This publication was kindly brought to my attention by Dr St. John Simpson.

40 Ibid., No. 109. As well as miniature masks, we have taken no account here of masks in materials other than gold or of masks that were not for funerary purposes such as theatre-masks. For a brief but interesting discussion of death-masks in general with emphasis on plaster masks in the Roman period, see Berg, Rolle & Seemann 1981, 154-156 ("Das Gesicht im Tode: Masken und Abgüsse"). Life-size masks in plaster and clay, definitely death-masks, are also known from tumuli of the first-third century AD in the region of the Abakar River, a tributary of the Yenisey, in the Altai Mountains (Kyzlasov 1960, 147-151, Fig. 56). See also Jettmar 1967, 81. I am indebted to Mr M. Kruszynski for this information. As pointed out by Jettmar some of these masks show Mongolian features, and it is interesting that from Mongolia itself, dating from the time of the Liao Dynasty (AD 907-1125), these are life-size funerary masks of gold, silver and gilded bronze (Kessler 1994, 9, Fig. 10).

41 In Curtis 1976, 59, with notes, I collected together some examples of gold mouth and eye coverings from the ancient Near East, but there are many more.

42 Curtis 1976, 57.

was in the last century. Writing more than a hundred years ago the eminent politician and classical scholar W.E. Gladstone expressed the hope, in his preface to Schliemann's *Mycenae*, that the discovery of the Mycenae masks would "lead to a full collection of the evidence of this rare and curious practice", i.e. using masks of gold for the dead. His subsequent comments on masks are extremely illuminating and have stood the test of time extremely well. He records that there is no evidence for this custom in Greece, and refers to the discovery of masks in the Crimea, Campania, Mesopotamia and Phoenicia. He points to the considerable Phoenician influence in Hellenistic culture, and concludes that the "use of the metallic mask may have been a Phonenician adaptation from the Egyptian custom of painting the likeness of the dead on the mummy case".[43] In other words, our own conclusions differ little from those of Gladstone, and his basic hypothesis still stands up to scrutiny. Nevertheless, there is still scope for a careful study of these masks which might yet lead to a fresh appraisal.[44]

---

43  Gladstone, in Schliemann 1878, xxxv-xxxvi.
44  In Mack 1994 there is inportant information about masks in Egypt and in Greece and Rome. Also, the Department of Egyption Antiquities at the British Museum is organising a conference on 13th-14th July 1995 on 'Portraits and Masks: Burial Customs in Roman Egypt', at which interesting reviews for the evidence will surely be presented.

# 28 Cannabis Sativa (Hashish) as an Effective Medication in Antiquity: the Anthropological Evidence

## Joe Zias

ABSTRACT—*While the use of cannabis as a drug in the ancient Near East was widely known from literary sources as early as the sixteenth century BC, it is rarely found in archaeological contexts. Of considerable medical importance was its use by many ancient cultures to reduce haemorrhage and pain in childbirth. Nineteenth-century European physicians reported that not only was hashish widely used but was therapeutically effective in reducing pain and increasing uterine contractions during the birthing process.*

*Recent excavations carried out by the Israel Antiquities Authority west of Jerusalem uncovered a fourth-century AD burial complex which contained the remains of 40 individuals. One individual, a young woman of 14 was discovered with a full term foetus in the pelvic area. The anterior-posterior distance of the pelvic outlet was c. 70 mm, less than that usually necessary for a normal vaginal delivery. Lying on the abdominal cavity of the woman was a solidified mass of carbonised material weighing 6.97 g. Subsequent chemical analysis of the material using gas chromatography showed the presence of THC, the active ingredient in Cannabis sativa. The finding of this substance in association with the foetal/maternal death would seem to indicate that its use was intended to increase uterine contractions in the mother and prevent haemorrhaging which would have been considerable given the cephalopelovic disproportion of the maternal pelvis.*

*Seven glass vessels found in the locus were tested using a forensic aerosol spray to determine if the drug was burned in one of the vessels as inhalation therapy. One of the vessels provided positive forensic evidence that the substance was originally burned in the glass vessel.*

Literary evidence for the medicinal use of cannabis first appears in the Egyptian Ebers Papyrus of the sixteenth-century BC.[1] Nine centuries later, the plant is again mentioned in ancient Assyrian texts as being used in rituals, as an intoxicant, and as a medicinal agent, specifically for difficult childbirth. While in Greek and Roman sources it appears only as a minor drug (unrelated to obstetrics),[2] Herodotus was aware of the use of cannabis as an intoxicant in Scythian funerary customs and possibly in everyday life.[3] Cannabis seeds have been found in Scythian tombs.[4] However, direct physical evidence of cannabis use in the ancient Middle East until recently had not been discovered.

Excavations carried out by the Israel Antiquities Authority west of Jerusalem have uncovered a fourth-century AD burial chamber which contained the remains of 40 individuals. One young woman, 14 years of age, was found lying on her back in a fully extended position with the skeletal remains of a full-term (40-week) foetus in the pelvic area. The finding of a full-term foetus would seem to indicate that the woman was in the last stages of pregnancy, or in the birthing process, at time of death. Three bronze coins found in the family burial tomb, dating from AD 315-392, indicate that the tomb was in general use during the fourth century AD.

In the abdominal area of the skeleton 6.97 gm of a grey carbonized material was recovered and sent for scientific analysis to three independent laboratories. The initial non-destructive microscopic analysis, undertaken by the Israel Police Division of Identification and Forensic Science revealed the possible presence of Cannabis sativa while an additional sample, examined under the light microscope by the Hebrew University Department of Botany, showed the apparent presence of reed (phragmites) and minute quantities of

---

1    Mechoulam 1986, 1-19. Cf. below, n. 6.
2    Gunther 1934, 390.
3    Brunner 1973, 344-355.
4    Artamanov 1965, 106.

carbonised fruit or seed. The sample was then submitted to the Hebrew University, Department of Pharmacology for further study.

## Chemical analysis

The sample examined by Professor R. Mechoulam at the Hebrew University Pharmacy School was a grey powder on a hardened, stone-like matrix of dark earth. The grey powder (1 g) was separated, covered with ether (75 ml) and stirred for 48 hours. The ether was decanted and a second portion of ether (75 ml) was added to the powder and stirred for further 72 hours. The ether solutions were combined and evaporated to dryness. A yellow oil (10 mg) was obtained. On thin layer chromatography (TLC) (15% ether in petroleum ether, silica gel plates) mainly one spot was observed, with an Rf value 0.72, identical with that of Δ6-THC.

In order to prevent the possibility of contamination from Δ6-THC present in the laboratory, the glassware and instruments used in the isolation of the THC were thoroughly cleaned and a blank experiment was done giving completely negative results. Repetition of the extraction gave Δ6-THC again.

Gas chromatography (GC) was performed on a Varian gas chromatograph, model 3700, under the following conditions; injector-2700°C: detector-2600°C; capillary column fused silica, DB 17, film thickness 0.25 μm, column dimensions x 0.245 mm at 2600°C. One main peak was observed (retention time 11.06 min). The proton nuclear magnetic resonance (NMR) spectrum recorded on a Varian VXR-300 S instrument at 300 MHz contained the main peaks of Δ6-THC (δ in CDCl3), 0.89 (w-CH3), 1.10, 1.38, 1.70 (CH3 groups), 3.20 (C-2 protons), 5.42 (C-6 proton), 6.10, 6.25 (aromatic protons). On mass spectrometry (MS) the typical peaks of Δ6-THC at 314 (molecular peak), 299, 271, 258, 231 (base peak), 193 were recorded. The GC, NMR and MS were identical with those obtained in parallel from authentic Δ6-THC. The above data indicate therefore the presence of Δ6-THC.

Δ6-THC is a minor, highly stable constituent of cannabis and its presence presumably indicates conversion of the major components, Δ1-THC and cannabidiol into Δ-THC, a process well known to occur on acid catalysis, apparently during the burning process.[5]

## Discussion

Scattered literary references indicate that hashish enjoyed continual widespread usage over a period of 4,000 years for a wide variety of medical reasons.[6]

In the mid-nineteenth century Christison remarked that cannabis had the "remarkable power of increasing the force of uterine contractions, concomitant with a significant reduction of labour pain."[7] Finding this[8] herapeutically effective medicinal plant on the abdominal area of a young woman who died during her last stages of pregnancy would seem to indicate that the drug Cannabis sativa enjoyed widespread usage in the eastern Mediterranean during the fourth century AD. While phragmites (the common reed) does not possess any chemical properties which are known to be medically effective, its inclusion in the medication may be in the form of sympathetic value, as it is mentioned many times in the Bible;[9] or simply as a contaminant, as reeds were frequently used as containers in transport.

Several glass vessels found near the body were tested by forensic scientists using spray reagents to determine if the cannabis had originally been placed in such a vessel for inhalation. One of the glass vessels tested positive to the reagent; therefore, it would appear that the cannabis was originally burned in this vessel and given to the young woman as an inhalant.

A reconstruction of the female pelvis showed that the anterior-posterior internal dimensions (Conjugata vera), which are of critical importance in the normal birth process, were approximately 70-75 mm. According to obstetricians, it is unlikely, though not impossible, that a normal vaginal delivery can ever be affected when the anterior-posterior diameter of the pelvis is less than 90 mm.[10] Therefore, the immature pelvic structure in which a full-term foetus was required to pass through an underdeveloped birth canal, led to a medical condition termed cephalopelvic disproportion.[11] The probable cause of death in such circumstances, where the cephalopelvic disproportion is great, is due to rupturing of the cervix and eventual hemorrhaging.

## Conclusion

From the context of the find it appears that the medication was given as an inhalant to increase uterine contractions and sedate the young mother. In antiquity this procedure would normally have been carried out by a midwife as physicians in the third and fourth centuries AD were, by law, prohibited from attending women in labour.[12] While this therapeutic attempt to increase uterine activity by inhaling smoke from hashish may have been medically effective in minor degrees of cephalopelvic disproportion, the immature pelvic morphology of the young mother led to the eventual

5    Mechoulam 1973, 1-99.
6    Worf Estes 1989, 91. While the Ebers Papyrus is the first literary reference to the use of Cannabis sativa, recent publication tells us that the sixteenth-century BC document may be a copy of an Eleventh Dynasty text (2040-1991 BC).
7    Christison 1851, 26-45.
8    Zias et. al. 1993, 215.
9    Faliks 1971, 18.
10   Hibbard 1988, 410.
11   Ibid., 413.
12   Myles 1981, 711.

death of both the mother and foetus during the birthing process.

234

*Acknowledgements*
Special thanks to Professor R. Mechoulam and Dr E. Werker of the Hebrew University and Dr R. Levy of the Israel Police Department of Forensic Science for examining the specimen. Thanks are also due to the British Council for their generosity in allowing me a travel grant to attend the conference and to Dr M. Stark of the Misgav Ladach Hospital, Jerusalem, for his valuable advice. Mr E. Shor of Erez Forensic Technology Ltd provided the forensic drug testing kit.

# 29 Deathly Links between China and Islam? Relief-Moulded Lead-Glazed Pottery

## Madeleine Sarley

ABSTRACT—*This paper attempts to address the nature of the relationship between Early Islamic relief-moulded lead-glazed wares (seventh to ninth/tenth centuries AD) and the Pre-Han through to the Liao dynasty of China (c. second century BC to twelfth century AD) use of the relief-moulded lead-glazed wares, especially as funerary offerings or 'mingqi'. I hope that by this work, in the early stages of my research, it will be possible to air some of the questions and puzzles that I have encountered.*

## Introduction

Chinese relief-moulded lead-glazed wares have long been of interest to scholars and the antiquities market alike, due to their imposing craftsmanship, appealing expression and, in some T'ang examples, their size. In contrast, Islamic relief-moulded lead-glazed wares, whilst arousing curiosity and having a rarity value rather than a perceived artistic value, have eceived relatively little attention in the past.

Lane, in his important article "Glazed relief ware of the ninth century A.D.", produced the first detailed study of the majority of Early Islamic wares in museum collections.[1] This remains the basis of study in this area. In this work, Lane recognised the possible oriental as well as occidental influences. As Philon summarises it:

"The three influences to be traced through most of the ceramics under discussion are the Classical heritage of the Graeco-Romans, the Persian taste bequeathed by the Sassanian kings, and finally the those richly prized imports from China brought to the Islamic land by Arab sea merchants."[2]

The Early Islamic ware is found on excavations from Fustat in Egypt in the west to Sind in Pakistan in the east, and between the 25th and 33rd latitudes. The greatest quantities found in excavation, at present, were at Fustat in Egypt, Samarra in Iraq and Susa in Iran.

There have also been the odd finds in Jordan, and on the Iranian plateau. My own research at present suggests that this type of pottery is conspicuous by its almost complete absence from Syria.

This study is based on primary research of the Islamic ware from Egypt, Jordan, Syria, Susa and Samarra, where available, and a rudimentary knowledge of Chinese ceramics, gleaned from secondary sources.

## General techniques and shapes of manufacture

Lead-glaze is a very simple technique and can be applied in the form of a galena, or dry dust, although, when applied in this raw state, it is very poisonous. As it can take metal oxides well, it can come in a variety of colours, including amber, brown, aubergine, as well as in the main green. Lead-glaze has a low firing temperature, thus facilitating manufacture in unsophisticated workshops and kilns. The fabric of Islamic types, particularly the eastern examples, is of fine, light-buff to white clays with almost no inclusions. Whether the clay is levigated by man or by nature (i.e. in the form of riverine clays), cannot be addressed here. From the western Islamic types we see that the fabric is of a pink or salmon through to dark rose and has fine to medium silica inclusions. The pre-Han Chinese wares were of a pink or red fabric but by the T'ang this had changed to a pale buff or white. Also by the T'ang period, glaze application had developed a blue variant, possibly due to the importation from Persia of 'glass-cakes'.

---

1 Lane 1939.
2 Philon 1980, 2.

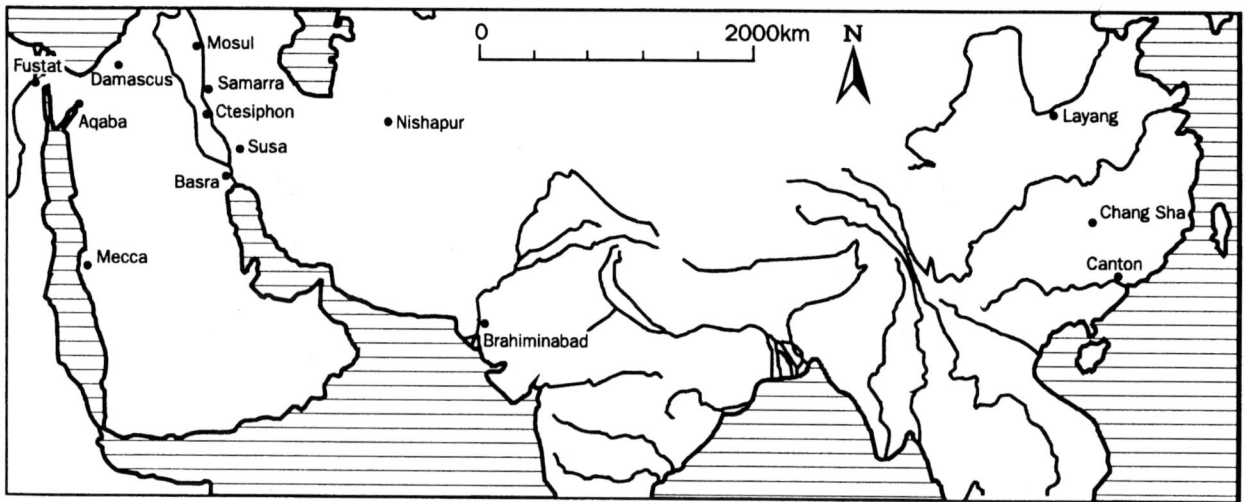

*Fig. 29.1: Chinese and Islamic sites mentioned in the text.*

The moulded decoration of Islamic ceramics was restricted to those shapes which afforded a good space for decoration; i.e., in the west, lamps, in the east, bottles and jugs; and in all areas open bowls and plates. In fact they can be seen to be executed in the parallel metalwork forms that also showed scope for decoration.[3] It is unknown whether the moulds into which the prepared clay was pushed were of wood, plaster (as some of the Classical lamps had been), or of ceramic, like the later Mamluk lead-glazed reliefware.

The mortuary pottery of Han China had an extensive range of forms, some of which were lead-glazed earthenwares. The Chinese names for lead-glaze, *liu-li* and *po-li*, both also mean "glass". Many of the contemporary bronze and lacquer styles were imitated, both by using moulds and by hand. By the sixth century AD the northern wares are produced from finely carved moulds, depicting lively scenes. There are a number of examples left to us of seemingly western-influenced pilgrim flasks and bottles. In the T'ang period this ware continued to be predominantly for *mingqi*, and consisted of both figures and objects. The larger figures of camels, horses and people were made in several moulds and luted together afterwards. By the eighth century AD polychrome glazes had become the dominant form of decoration.

## Dating of the Islamic types

"The annunciatory role played by the Chinese imports was emphasised by Sarre, Koechlin, and later by Arthur Lane. In his *Early Islamic Pottery* of 1947, Lane summarised his views that the white-glazed Islamic pottery evolved in imitation of Chinese porcelain and that Islamic wares decorated with dabs, spots, splashes or incised decoration, imitated similarly decorated Chinese vessels. This im-pressive development of Islamic pottery was attributed by Lane to the 9th century. While it is probable that the Chinese white ware and porcelain inspired a new path for the Islamic potter, Lane's assertion that Islamic splash wares imitate Chinese prototypes must to day be seen as open to doubt."[4]

As Philon continues to discuss, the originally-thought short occupation of Samarra can no longer be used as such an accurate ceramic dating tool. It is now generally accepted that Samarra was occupied from AD 836-883 by the Abbasid court and well into the tenth century, by a general population, although the seat of power had been regained by Baghdad.

The export of T'ang lead-glazed wares can be seen through the excavated sherds from ninth- and tenth-century AD Islamic sites, including Samarra and Ctesiphon in Iraq, Nishapur in Iran, Fustat in Egypt, and sites in India and on the east coast of Africa.[5]

## Dating of the Chinese types

In China in the later Chou period (770-256 BC) it had become the custom to place *mingqi* in the grave to represent the people and things that the dead person had loved in life. The first known lead-glazed relief ceramics are mould-made lidded jars and pots from the third century BC; the fabric is earthenware, soft and red with a brown/green glaze. It was with the succession of the first emperor of the Han Dynasty, Liu-Pang, in 206 BC, that the great imperial period began. The Han Dynasty was temporarily split by strife during AD 9-23, establishing a new and stronger capital at Lo-yang in Honan. The Dynasty lasted there until AD 221. Lead-glazed ware reappears in tombs in China in the sixth

---

3   Cf. Vickers, Impey & Allan 1980, Pl. 63.

4   Philon 1980, 2.
5   Cf. Valenstein 1975, 76.

century AD. This was a time that saw dynamic trade links with Western Asia, as well as foreign traders setting up in import /export businesses in the major trading centres. It is believed that it was from these and envoy contacts that foreign ways and tastes became fashionable.

It was under the T'ang Dynasty, especially in the seventh century AD, that China became unified and expanded to its western boarders with Persia, Khorezm and Sogdia. The solidity that this produced was in no small part facilitated by spending on infrastructure, such as routes of communication and repairs to the Great Wall. The taste for foreign imports and fashions continued, as noted by Medley,

The evidence is most clearly seen in the splendours of the lead-glazed pottery intended for the customarily elaborate furnishings of the tomb.[6]

It is important to remember that it was not until comparatively recently that the Chinese identified the lead-glazed wares within their archaeological record.[7] Also until quite recently the chronologies of T'ang ceramics as a whole presented real difficulties, mainly due to the lack of archaeological work carried out on T'ang-dynasty sites.[8]

## Lead-glazed relief pottery during the Han Dynasty, 206 BC–AD 221.

Han pottery continued the tradition of being heavily influenced by contemporaneous metalwork, with the added difference of a taste in naturalistic decoration.

"Visions of immortality meet with scenes of daily life in the tombs of the Han Dynasty. The number of excavated tombs of this period is large, and the tombs illustrate important changes in burial practices."[9]

According to Rawson, the end of the Han "China was relatively isolated from the outside world. Little in the way of innovation can be directly attributed to outside influence".[10]

On the other hand, Valenstein argues that during the Han Dynasty "China sent its precious silk to the Western world and received in return a wealth of ideas and products, from lands as far away as the Roman Empire".[11]

A development in the Western Han had produced a technique for the low-fired glazes. The quality was not high, but as the results were for symbolic use, it was, after all, their attractiveness that counted. Early examples are

from a tomb dated 141-87 BC, in Shanxi Province, near Xian, Li Zhiya.[12]

## The Six Dynasties period, AD 220–580.

This refers to the period of disunity after the fall of the Han, c. AD 220, when China experienced three and a half centuries of division. In general it was, however, a period of surprisingly substantial technological and cultural growth.

Having fallen in favour during the earlier part of the 6 Dynasties, it was during the fifth century AD that the green and brown glazes became popular again. Tombs, including that of Sima Jinlon (d. AD 489) in Datony Shanxi Province, Northern Wei, produced a large number of lead-glazed *mingqi*. Excavations in various provinces, including Hebei, Henan, Shanxi and Shandong have revealed lead-glazed *mingqi* figures and jars belonging to the later Northern Dynasties. Some of these objects have decoration, including the use of splashes of contrasting glaze colours, or tricolour, decoration.[13]

## Sui period, AD 581–618.

During this short period, China was reunited with a new strong, centralised government. The ancient capitals were rebuilt, the important canals improved and the Great Wall was constructed. Both China's political and military influence extended in many directions. The Sui empire collapsed due to over-ambitious building projects.

There are a few Sui ceramics with lead-glaze, but they were not moulded in relief.[14] However, the ceramic wares of this bustling period "continued the evolution of Chinese pottery ... [and] heralded the coming of the T'ang Dynasty".[15]

## T'ang lead-glazed relief pottery, AD 618-906.

This was a period during which China flourished and its culture surpassed the previous dynasties. It was a prosperous, well developed, civilisation which, especially in the early part, craved for the new and unusual. There was a renewed internationalism, as China traded widely and took from all artistic influences with which it came into contact, merging these new styles with the indigenous taste, to produce a highbred pottery style.

---

6   Medley 1989, 77.
7   Cf. Valenstein 1975, 54.
8   Cf. Medley 1981.
9   Rawson 1980, 199.
10  Ibid., 212.
11  Valenstein 1975, 41.

12  Cf. ibid., 47-48.
13  Ibid., 49.
14  Cf. ibid., 59, for discussion.
15  Ibid.

Valenstein notes that although the lead-glazed relief ware was produced in profusion, few kilns have been identified through excavation as having produced it.[16]

In the last quarter of the seventh century AD, some elaborate green-glazed vessels were made, the sides of which are decorated with applied relief. There are also some examples of small moulded cups of unusual shape, such as the rhyton in the British Museum collection. The rhyton shows the survival of late classical artistic elements in the art of the western side of Asia. Medley deduces that T'ang glazes were made of fritted lead. The raw lead was melted down with the other components, including clay, to a glassy state, which shattered if placed in water. The next stage would have been to crush-down the mixture into a fine powder. This could then have been mixed with water to form a liquid-glaze which could easily be used to coat the pot in a variety of ways. Medley believes that that this advance was developed to enhance the brightness of the glaze, but it would also have greatly reduced the health hazards of the raw lead. As evidence to support her theory, Medley points to the appearance of cobalt blue in China, introduced from Persia in the form of blue glass-cakes or *liuli*".[17]

A recognisable symbol to the west of the T'ang dynasty are the large tomb figures of the seventh and eighth centuries AD, moulded and lead-glazed. It is not directly through technology of manufacture that a link is found between the Chinese and Islamic lands, but it is in the characterisation of these highly individual pieces. The high proportion of western Asiatics represented among these models has been traced through facial attributes and especially through their mode of dress.[18] In AD 651, as Mahler states, "the Chinese first came into contact with the Arabs when an embassy reached China from the fourth Caliph Othman".[19] Mahler continues her study using both Chinese and Arab sources to understand the relationship, at a political level, between the two empires, which took the form of envoys exchanging gifts, as well as some trade-links. She refers to the fact that these envoys were sent by both the Umayyad and Abbasid caliphs; she then makes reference to the defeated An Lu-shan rebellion and the successful part in it that Arab and other western Asians played (AD 756-766). She concludes by dispelling the "popular belief" that there was a large number of settled Arabs in mainland China, whilst confirming their presence in south China as merchants, travellers, diplomats, and sailors, at least in and around Canton.[20]

The An Lu-shan rebellion (AD 756) and the resultant Tibetan invasion (AD 763) caused permanent economic damage. From this time large tomb figures disappear, although the smaller moulded objects continued in production for grave-goods until at least the end of the eighth century. Paul-David considers this type of ware to be for domestic use,[21] although there are finds of bowls and small dishes from the Yung-tiai tomb. Again these forms can be seen to have derived from both local and foreign trends. One of the popular Chinese shapes is a globe-shaped pot, some examples having lug handles and others with three lion feet, or both. There are many examples of moulded open bowls, in flower-inspired shapes with petalled, wide lips. Some bowls of this type were uncovered by Herzfeld at Samarra and are now in Berlin. Philon refers to a host of T'ang wares excavated at Samarra, Susa, Siraf and at Fustat.[22] A base of an open bowl from Fustat, now in the Victoria & Albert Museum, London,[23] which Lane and Philon see as being of Chinese inspiration,[24] is of a four-lobed shape with relief decoration showing one fish leaping above another. On personal inspection, the sherd looked like a Chinese import. In an unpublished note, Oliver Watson states that the piece is not of a usual Islamic type, and refers to Rose Kerr, asserting that the piece is, indeed, Chinese.[25]

Medley makes mention of the western inspired ewers decorated in lead-glaze and made from two half-moulds, the pieces being stuck together with the joint running vertically, and the handles being added afterwards. There are also two-handled amphora types, which can be seen to echo the Hellenistic pottery of the cities of Central Asia. The decorative techniques for these small vessels include the use of splash-glazing (a very simple device), together with the general lead-glazing of the moulded relief wares. Together with a white-slip, a wax resist type effect was possible, and blank areas of dots or florets were produced.

## Southern wares

During the T'ang Dynasty, the kiln sites in the south of China were widely spread; Ch'ang-sha in Hunan Province is the best known. Both earthenwares and stonewares were produced. Medley notes that excavated examples at Siraf off of the Iranian coast in the Gulf, are similar to, and perhaps from, the Ch'ang-sha kiln.[26]

## Yueh ware

This ware, with its distinctive thin olive-green glaze over a grey stoneware, is seen in large quantities in the sherd collections of Fustat and Samarra, but is not moulded.

16  Ibid., 63.
17  Medley 1981, 25.
18  Cf. Mahler 1959.
19  Ibid., 98.
20  Ibid., 99-100.
21  As cited by Medly 1981, 25.
22  Philon 1980.
23  V & A accession no. 866:1902.
24  Lane 1939; Philon 1980, .
25  V & A ceramics department registry entry for 24/4/1986.
26  Medley 1981, 96.

# Liao wares, AD 907-1125.

The Khitan tribes of Manchuria took the dynastic name Liao when they first united AD 907. Under the dynasty, fine moulded wares, decorated in delicate polychrome lead-glazes continued to be made; the ceramic knowledge was due to contact with late T'ang China in the north-eastern region. The shapes show flower-inspiration while the themes of moulded decoration are naturalistic and exhibit stylised flora and fish.

# Conclusion

How this long and complex history of the Chinese mortuary lead-glazed relief moulded wares interweaves with the varied, but small, production-history of the Islamic types is hard to trace. Philon states that

"The Muslim potter looked to China for the improvement of shape, glaze, and the body of his vessel; whilst he sought inspiration and in fact borrowed directly from, the decorative vocabulary ... of late Classical and Persian culture. At any one time, one of these two influences will be seen to predominate. ... While it is probably true that Chinese white ware and porcelain inspired a new path for the Islamic potter, Lane's assertion that Islamic splashed wares imitate Chinese prototypes must today be seen as open to doubt."[27]

Work by Rawson, Tite and Hughes on exported T'ang lead-glazed wares of the highly fired white fabric type (Chinese *sancai*) is of interest here. *Sancai* wares excavated at Fustat, Samarra, and Mantai in Sri Lanka, were in the first instance tested by scanning electron microscope and later by X-ray fluorescence. It was shown that the sherds fell in to two separate groups, for, as Rawson records

Only a small minority of the 'sancai' fragments in the British Museum's collections resemble in any way closely the main 'sancai' tradition. Many of the sherds are not Chinese at all but local products.[28]

The Chinese examples have a clear, white fabric and the Islamic examples a light, buff fabric. Rawson adds that the findings could imply specially designed exports from China to take advantage of west Asian tastes.[29] Her overall date for the export of these pieces is to the late T'ang (i.e. ninth century AD) or as late as the Liao period (i.e. tenth century AD).

Are we any nearer to any concrete connections between the traditions of the lead-glazed relief moulded wares of Early Islam and China? We have seen that there was direct envoy and trade contact in both directions, and that each seems to have copied and adapted the other's technology and artistry. So much for form, decoration and distribution; what about function? The Chinese pieces have, on the whole, been seen to have been used in the tombs as *mingqi*, a fitting task for objects covered in such a deadly poisonous glaze. In contrast, at present there is no evidence to suggest that the Islamic types were used for any particular non-domestic function.

*Acknowledgements*
I would like to express my gratitude to the following people and organisations for their help, support and encouragement during my study. The World of Islam Festival Trust; The Palestine Exploration Fund; The British Institute for Archaeology and Ancient History at Amman; British Institute of Persian Studies; The American University, Cairo; The Egyptian, Jordanian and Syrian Antiquities Services, their directors and staff; The Louvre Museum and its curators; The Berlin Islamic Museums and curators. Dr R.D. King, School of Oriental and African Studies (London); Dr C.J. Lenzen, Jordan; Mr A. Lupton, Cambridge; Mr R. Pinder-Wilson, London; Mr L.H. Pontin, London; Ms A. Porter, Aleppo; Ms V. Porter, British Museum; Dr M. Rogers, School of Oriental and African Studies (London); Dr G. Scanlon, American University at Cairo; Dr O. Watson of London's Victoria and Albert Museum.

---

27    Philon 1980, 2.

28    Rawson, Tite & Hughes 1988, 43.
29    Ibid., 5.

# 30 Death and Burial in the Late Islamic Near East: Some Insights from Archaeology and Ethnography

## St John Simpson

ABSTRACT—*There are well-known inherent interpretational problems in the comparison of data collected by social anthropologists and archaeologists. A number of attempts have been made to link these disciplines as part of a so-called ethnoarchaeological approach to the ancient Near East. However, little attention has yet focused on equivalent mortuary data from this region despite increasing comparative analyses based on case studies from Africa, Europe, the Far East and New World. Such a study does suggest new means of cautiously interpreting aspects of the archaeology of death in the ancient Near East.*

*This paper will address some of the problems by means of reference to written and excavated evidence for recent graves and mortuary customs in Iran, Iraq, Jordan, Palestine and Syria. Possible explanations will be proposed for the location, orientation and internal zoning of cemeteries belonging to both sedentary and nomadic communities; possible reasons will be suggested for variation in the preferred type of grave construction. The possible roles of certain associated objects as deliberate or accidental grave goods will be explored and avenues outlines for renewed research.*

The study of burials and burial-practices can throw considerable light on populations past or present and their beliefs, superstitions and cultural attributes.[1] In some cases, within the Near East, reconstruction of ancient societies is certainly enhanced through the integration of excavated data with contemporaneous written sources relating to death and burial.[2] In other cases, the written sources are absent or remain comparatively silent and greater reliance is placed on the interpretation of excavated evidence.[3] Cautious use of ethnographic data as comparative material is instructive.[4] However, although a number of ethnoarchaeological studies have been undertaken in the Near East, relatively little attention has focused on death and burial.[5] Indeed, most available ethnographic accounts

for this region at best usually only provide incidental information on the subject.[6]

In recent years, there has been growing awareness among Near Eastern archaeologists that careful study of Islamic burials can provide useful additional information on past societies within the Near East.[7] Attention has particularly focused on burials of the late and post-mediaeval periods (henceforth: Late Islamic). Late Islamic burials have been excavated at a large number of sites in Iraq,[8] Israel/Palestine,[9] Jordan[10] and Syria,[11]

---

1  Brown (ed.) 1971; Chapman, Kinnes & Randsborg (eds.) 1981; Pader 1982.
2  Alster (ed.) 1980; Barrelet 1980.
3  Fiedel 1979; Forest 1983.
4  Ucko 1969; Binford 1971; O'Shea 1984.
5  Solecki 1979; Watson 1979; Yoffee 1979; Kramer 1982; Seeden 1985.

6  Granqvist (1965) is a notable exception.
7  Toombs 1985; Eakins 1993; Lancaster & Lancaster 1993.
8  Published and unpublished data from salvage excavations in Iraq include, within the Hamrin Dam basin, Tepe al-Atiqeh (Gibson (ed.) 1981, 15); T. Gubba (Odani & Ii 1981, 152); T. Madhhur (Roaf et al. 1984, 113); T. Razuk (Gibson (ed.) 1981, 81-82); T. Songor (Kamada & Ohtsu 1988; Matsumoto & Yokoyama 1989; Yokoyama & Matsumoto 1990) and T. Yelkhi (Invernizzi 1980, 30-31; cf. Fiorina 1985b, 74) plus T. Abu Dhahir (Simpson in preparation), T. Khirbet Salih (Wilhelm 1993), Seh Qubba (Ball & Gill in press) and possibly T. Karrana 3 (Wilhelm & Zaccagnini 1991, 12-13; Stein 1993) in the Saddam Dam Salvage Project.
9  Caesarea (Toombs 1978, 228-229, 1985, 18; Chase 1992; Holum et al. 1988, 224-225; T. Dan (Spauer 1992, 57-59); T.

with further cases known from Bahrain,[12] Egypt,[13] Turkey[14] and India.[15] All of these are non-urban cemeteries which may be compared directly with ethnographic or eighteenth-nineteenth century European travellers' observations of rural and bedouin Muslim communities in the Near East. Although excavated Late Islamic graves are often casually referred to as 'bedouin' burials, many probably represent village cemeteries.[16] The following comments represent an attempt to integrate these major archaeological and ethnographic sources of evidence for death and burial in the Late Islamic Near East.

## Treatment of the body

Procedures for the proper treatment of the dead are prescribed in the Islamic law manuals although the Qur'an itself says nothing about funerals.[17] The body should be buried before sunset or early the following day, before which time all the necessary preparations must have been made. The body is firstly stretched out in the house, courtyard or morgue with the face and soles of the feet towards Mecca.[18] It must then be washed, except in the case of martyrs for whom the blood is their hallmark of martyrdom. Washing with water and soap or lotus leaves, followed by sprinkling with camphor and dried leaves, is carried out either by the spouse or by persons of the same sex as the deceased;[19] the use of camphor may be a continuation of a

Sasanian mortuary practice.[20] The body is sometimes hennaed and perfumed, the head shaved (in the case of men) or hair plaited (for women), beard trimmed, nails pared and – if necessary – body circumcised.[21] A striking throwback to earlier customs is illustrated by a further description of the painting and gilding of the faces of dead young virgins at the Muslim village of Artas, south of Bethlehem.[22] Bedouin undertake similar, but simpler, preparations at or close to the place of burial. Rectangular paved areas found close to bedouin graves at T. el-Hesi and in north-east Jordan were probably used during this stage of preparations.[23]

The burning of a light close to the corpse is generally disapproved of although there are local exceptions.[24] Prayers are recited over the body; watch is kept over the corpse and, in Egypt, the blood of an animal sacrifice is scattered over the spot where the person died in order to facilitate departure of the soul or ghost and to expiate minor sins.[25] The body is then wrapped in shrouds, generally white in colour, which should be left open at the head so as to allow the soul to escape freely. A green outer shroud is used by Muslims and Copts alike in Egypt;[26] other grave clothes are described from Egypt and Palestine.[27] Variation in the type of cloth used as shrouds reflects the relative wealth of the deceased[28] but valuable shrouds were deliberately torn in order to reduce the risk of later pilfering.[29] Traces of cloth noted in bedouin graves at T. el-Hesi, El-Lejjun and T. esh-Shari'a presumably represent the remains of such shrouds.[30] It is notable that burials without shrouds were compared by villagers at Artas with the graves of gipsies.[31] Coffins are rarely used by Muslims although these are not strictly forbidden.[32] Christian and Druze communities do use coffins,[33] and Butcher describes an incident in Egypt where the discovery of coffins in an

---

Dor, Site K-60 (Guz-Silberstein & Raveh 1990, 51); T. Gezer (Macalister 1912, I, 312, 315, Fig. 166; Dever, Lance & Wright 1970, 1); T. el-Hesi (Fargo & O'Connell 1978, 169-170, 172-173; Eakins 1980, 1993; Toombs 1985); T. Jemmeh and area (Petrie 1928, 25, Pl. LXVII, 4-8; Schaefer 1989, 59); Jerusalem/Bethany (Saller 1957, 327); T. Jezreel (Ussishkin & Woodhead *et al.* 1991/92, 29/31, 42); T. Mevorakh (Stern *et al.* 1978, 4-9, Figs. 1, 23, Pls. 6, 21, 41, 46; Toombs 1985, 17-18); T. Qiri (Avissar 1987); T. esh-Shari'a (Oren 1976, 11-13); T. Sheikh 'Ahmed el-'Areyny (Yeivin 1961, 3-4, Pls. 1-2; Toombs 1985, 16); T. Yoqne'am (cited by Avissar 1987, 7); T. Zeror (Ohata (ed.) 1966, 2-3, 31, Pl. X; Ohata (ed.) 1967, 6, 9-19, Pls. XII-XIII; Toombs 1985).

10  T. Deir 'Alla (Van der Kooij & Ibrahim (eds) 1989, 90, 110); T. Iktanu (Prag 1989, 42); el-Lejjun (De Vries 1987, 341-46; Groot 1987, 497; Parker 1988, 142, 146); Mt. Nebo (Saller 1941, I, 314); Pella (Hennessy *et al.* 1983, 359, Bourke 1992, 221, 223-224, Browne 1992); Umm Qais (Mershen 1990, 1991a, 1991b).

11  T. Chagar Bazar (Mallowan 1936, 6, Fig. 29); T. Mohammed Diyab (Bachelot *et al.* 1990, 13, 26: Fig. 4); T. al-Raqai (Curvers 1987); T. Tuneinir (Fuller & Fuller 1989/90).

12  Qal'at al-Bahrain (Kervran 1982, 75-76, Pl. VI).

13  Bahia oasis (Fakhry 1950, II, 110, Pls. LXVII-LXVIII).

14  Alisar hüyük (Schmidt 1933, 118-120; von der Osten 1937, 193, 195); Girnavaz (Erkanal 1988, 142-143).

15  Rang Mahal (Halbert 1959). The range of evidence for Muslim burial practices from Africa, South Asia and the Far East lies beyond the scope of this paper however (cf. Burton-Page 1986).

16  Cf. Gibson (ed.) 1981, 15, 23.

17  Roberts 1982, 127-128

18  Hansen 1967, 54-55; Algar 1990, 563.

19  White 1845, III, 329-330; Lane 1890, 475; Al-Khaysi 1986, 175.

20  A'lam 1990, 743-744.

21  White 1845, III, 329-330; Conder 1889a, 127; Musil 1908, III, 423-424; Granqvist 1965, 62-67.

22  Granqvist 1965, 63; cf. Curtis, in this volume.

23  Eakins 1993, 13, Pl. 20; Lancaster & Lancaster 1993, 152-153, 155.

24  Algar 1990, 563; also Drower 1937, 181.

25  Lane 1890, 485; Blackman 1968, 110-111. Blackman's (1968: 110) reference to the slaughtering of a camel near the grave of a wealthy Egyptian individual recalls the discovery of camel skeletons in or close to relatively rich Parthian graves in Arabia (Potts 1990, II, 278-279; cf. also Lane 1890, 488; 1987, 261; Wilson 1906, 159; Granqvist 1965, 253; Sweet 1974, 215). The belief amongst Egyptian fellahin today that a man's shadow is a separate entity that accompanies a person throughout his life and into the grave clearly descends from Pharaonic times (Blackman 1968, 113).

26  Blackman 1968, 110, 123.

27  Butcher n.d., 52; Granqvist 1965, 58-63, 138.

28  Lane 1890, 475-476; 1987, 259; cf. Drower 1941, 185; Algar 1990, 563.

29  Lane 1890, 484.

30  Oren 1976, 12; Fargo & O'Connell 1978, 169; Toombs 1985, 105-106, 112; De Vries 1987, 346; cf. also Halbert 1959, 185. Fragments of cloth survived in only two of the excavated graves in Field VI at T. el-Hesi: both were of linen.

31  Granqvist 1965, 58.

32  Exceptions are described by White (1845, III, 335).

33  E.g. Conder 1889a, 125.

old disputed cemetery determined that the ground had belonged to Christians rather than Muslims.[34]

The corpse is then placed on a ladder or bier with low sides, covered with a shawl or rug (variations in which signify the sex or status of the deceased) and carried to the freshly dug grave by male relatives, sometimes accompanied by boy singers, professional wailers, musicians, paupers and female relatives.[35] It is sometimes considered unlucky to precede the bier as this is the position of the angels of death. Similarly, as the angels proceed on foot, it is often considered improper to ride to a Muslim funeral. In contrast to Christian practice, these funeral processions travel rapidly because, on the one hand, the righteous should be allowed to reach heaven as rapidly as possible, whereas in the case of sinners the cortège should reduce as much as possible the length of contact with the corpse.[36] However, it is believed that the speed of the funeral procession is also affected by the wishes and goodness of the deceased.[37] There are no restrictions on other religious minorities attending the funeral, but some consider it inappropriate to stand beside the open grave as this is considered a Jewish custom.[38]

## Grave construction

This usually varies according to the materials available or the local type of subsoil but there may be other factors at work; the T. Abu Dhahir excavations suggest chronological change possibly related to different socio-ethnic groups[39] and the T. el-Hesi data suggest somewhat greater care being paid to the construction of graves for women.[40] The most important feature common to many regions is the belief that women should be buried deeper (i.e. at c. 1.5 m) than men (c. 1-1.3 m), i.e. shoulder and breast height respectively, the aim being to cover the respective sexual characteristics.[41] Infants may be interred in more shallow graves however: those excavated at T. Songor B ranged from 0.20–0.80 m depth.[42] Burials of all ages were excavated at T. el-Hesi, ranging in depth from c. 0.20–1.50 m, again the shallowest generally belonging

to infants or secondary burials and the deepest to an exceptionally tall adult.[43] Further differences apparently occur depending on whether the deceased was bedouin, semi-sedentary or fully sedentary.[44]

Common types of Late Islamic grave vary from stone[45] or mudbrick-lined cist[46] (the latter suggestive of a mudbrick village in the vicinity and perhaps even the season as fresh bricks can only be made during the dry season) to simple shaft graves[47] or shafts with undercut side-chambers blocked with re-used mudbricks, stones, fired bricks, slag or even bushes.[48] The latter obviously leave no archaeological traces.[49] The size of the side-chamber should be sufficient to allow the deceased to sit upright during its interrogation by the angels.[50] The bases of the graves should be pure earth.[51] Multiple graves are permissible in times of war or epidemic but care should be taken to ensure that the first interment is that of the most pious.[52] Graves at Artas were unusual in that the villagers here also used caves as tombs: there was careful avoidance of those caves that contained undecomposed bodies but old burials were simply swept to one side before the new interment was placed.[53] Granqvist noted the sealing of tomb-entrances with stone slabs which were then plastered over in order to reduce the chance of disturbance by men or animals; channels were also dug around the tomb for drainage.[54]

34    Butcher n.d., 51.
35    Lane 1890, 476-481; 1987, 260-261; Jaussen 1927, 335; Granqvist 1965, 92-95, 158-161; Sweet 1974, 214.
36    White 1845, III, 334; Roberts 1982, 128.
37    Blackman 1968, 113; Atiya 1987, 58.
38    Roberts 1982, 128.
39    Simpson, in preparation.
40    Toombs 1985, 71-72.
41    Musil 1928, 670; Drower 1941, 185; Dickson 1949, 212; Watson 1979, 215. This factor would be interesting to compare with graves of other periods where both the anthropological data and the tops of the grave-cuts are recorded: unfortunately, the latter are usually eroded away or are unrecognised in excavation. Some of the Islamic graves at T. Zeror (north mound) were 1.5 m deep but the sex of the occupants are not mentioned (Ohata (ed.) 1966, 3).
42    Matsumoto & Yokoyama 1989, 295; Yokoyama & Matsumoto 1990, 189, 195.

43    Fargo & O'Connell 1978, 169; Toombs 1985, 36-37; Eakins 1993, 9-10, 12, 15, 18.
44    Musil 1928, 670-671; Fiorina 1985b, 74; Toombs 1985, 43; Hobs 1989, 65-66.
45    Balawat (Curtis, Collon & Green 1993, 31, 33: Fig. 30.a-b); Caesarea, area KK (Chase 1992; Toombs 1978, 229); T. el-Hesi, Grave Types II-IV (Toombs 1985, 38-39, 63; Eakins 1993, 9, 15); T. Iktanu (Prag 1989, 42); T. Mevorakh (Stern et al. 1978, 4, Fig. 23, Pl. 6: 1-3): (adults and children); T. Mohammed Diyab (Bachelot et al., 1990, 13, 26: Fig. 4); T. Qiri (Avissar 1987, 7); T. Sh. 'Ahmed el-'Areyny (Yeivin 1961, Pl. 1); Umm Qais (Mershen 1990; 1991a, 137); T. Yoqne'am (cf. Avissar 1987, 7); T. Zeror, north mound, including re-used grinding stones (Ohata (ed.) 1966, 2-3, Pl. X; Ohata (ed.), 1967, 9-10, Pls. XII-XIII).
46    T. Songor A, Grave 111: a single infant, out of a total of some 235 Islamic graves excavated at this site (Kamada & Ohtsu 1988, 151, Pl. 44B).
47    Caesarea, area KK (Chase 1992); T. el-Hesi, Grave Types I-II (Toombs 1985, 37-38, 63; Eakins 1993, 9, 15); T. Mevorakh (Stern et al. 1978, 4); Pella (Hennessy et al. 1983, 359; Bourke 1992, 221); T. Songor A (Kamada & Ohtsu 1988, 150-151); T. Zeror, north mound (Ohata (ed.) 1966, 3).
48    Alishar hüyük (Schmidt 1933, 119); T. el-Hesi, Type I (Toombs 1985, 37, Pocket Inserts 1-2); T. Karrana 3 (Stein 1993, 206); T. Madhhur (Roaf et al. 1984, 113); T. Songor A (Kamada & Ohtsu 1988, 151, Pl. 44A); T. Yelkhi (Invernizzi 1980, 30). Cf. also Dickson 1949, 210.
49    The type with undercut side-chambers was probably rather common in antiquity but as burials were often only recognised when the excavator made direct contact with the bones or grave-goods many published attributions of 'shaft' graves are somewhat suspect (cf. Toombs 1985, 37).
50    Lane 1890, 484; Blackman 1968, 115.
51    Algar 1990, 564.
52    Bell 1911, 99; Al-Khaysi 1986, 178.
53    A ninth-tenth century Early Islamic instance of the same practice was found at Siraf (Ball, pers comm.).
54    Granqvist 1965, 56, 85, 104.

In parts of Egypt, family vaults are constructed above ground.[55]

Other unusual excavated burials include simple interments placed beneath a cairn of stones.[56] Thomson[57] mentions that robbers' tombs were marked by such cairns, that were added to and cursed by passers-by. Cairn burials are more common in Afghanistan and India.[58] Finally, at T. Mevorakh and T. el-Hesi, miscarried foetuses and young babies were buried in so-called 'Gaza-ware' pots.[59] Incidentally, these provide a clue as to the late date (probably early eighteenth century AD or later) of these graves.[60] Other Islamic jar-burials have been reported from T. Zeror, north mound (?),[61] Beersheba & T. Sera'[62] and other Palestinian sites.[63]

## Cemetery location

Owing to religious prohibitions on intramural burial, Islamic graves tend to cluster in distinct cemeteries beyond the settlement. The distance maintained between the living and the dead varies from a track-width at T. Abu Dhahir[64] to almost a kilometre at Aliabad and Godin Tepe[65] or more at Hasanabad[66] and T. Yelkhi.[67] Cemeteries are often found on dry raised ground (i.e. agriculturally poor or useless areas), particularly on nearby deserted tells,[68] or rocky outcrops.[69] In cases where an old cemetery becomes full, a new spot is chosen.[70]

In some cases there is shared use by different villages of one mound as a place of burial, the nearest side of the mound corresponding to the village.[71] Whereas archaeologists would probably refer to such cases as single cemeteries, the villagers in question see distinct areas as being representative of different communities. Instances of longer-distance transport of the dead are provided by the extensive Shi'ite cemeteries at Kerbela, Najaf, Meshed, Qom and (in the Safavid period) Ardabil, whence the deceased used to be wrapped in shrouds or reeds, supported on wooden boards and carried on horse, mule or camel-back.[72] In the case of Coptic funerals where the burial takes place at a monastery, the coffin of the deceased is usually carried on camel-back.[73] Significantly, improvements in transport may contribute towards an increase in long-distance transport of the dead.[74]

In urban cases, where cemeteries become full and/or pressure on space precludes expansion of the cemeteries, two solutions are possible. The first is reburial in crypts (as in the case of Christian communities in Mosul); the second is the creation of separate cemeteries outside the walls (Muslim Mosul). The latter tend to become the focus of certain other activities considered hazardous or 'antisocial', such as pottery production or car-repair garages[75] Incidentally, Chase also cites the case of Bosnian Muslim cemeteries being located close to threshing floors.[76] Finally, Barth describes a preference by some nomads for burial either in a village cemetery or close to a perennial water supply;[77] less concern seems to have been shown by other bedouin tribes, who simply buried the corpse near the tent.[78] The size of bedouin cemeteries varies from a few dozen to several hundred.[79] All cemeteries are usually avoided at night when they are considered to be haunted by *jinns*.[80]

55  Blackman 1968, 116; Lane 1987, 262.
56  T. Mevorakh, Tomb 40 (Stern *et al.* 1978, 4): adult.
57  Thomson 1911, 488.
58  Halbert 1959, 187-188; Ball, pers comm.
59  Stern *et al.* 1978, 4-5, 9, Fig. 1, Pls. 6: 4-5, 21; Toombs 1985, 39-40, 107, Pls. 26-27, 84; Eakins 1993, 9, 11-12, 18, Pls. 13-19, 28-29.
60  Amino acid epimerisation analysis of stratified landsnail shells from a site in the Negev suggests a date of *c.* 1700 for two associated sherds of 'Gaza-ware' (Rosen & Goodfriend 1993).
61  Ohata (ed.) 1967, Pl. XIIIA
62  Stern *et al.* 1978, 8.
63  Canaan 1927, 8; Ohata (ed.), 1970, 74 commented on the prevalence of infants/children among Late Bronze Age-Iron Age-Seleucid jar-burials at T. Zeror Cemetery.
64  Simpson, in preparation.
65  Kramer 1982, 76.
66  Watson 1979, 15.
67  Fiorina 1985b, 74.
68  E.g. T. Abu Dhahir: Simpson, in preparation; T. al-Hawa: Ball, Tucker & Wilkinson 1989, 20-21; T. Mevorakh: Stern *et al.* 1978, 4.
69  Middle Euphrates: Bell 1911, 84. The same is found in other periods (Simpson, 1992).
70  T. Abu Dhahir: Simpson, in preparation; Aiuni/T. Yelkhi: Fiorina 1985b, 74; T. Songor/T. Gubba/T. Baradan: Matsumoto & Yokoyama 1989, 297; Umm Qais: Mershen 1991a, 136-137, 140-141; cf. also El-Lejjun: De Vries 1987, 346.
71  Balawat: Rassam 1897, 201-207 & John Curtis, personal communication, December 1993; T. Yelkhi: Fiorina 1985b, 74. The mound of Balawat was shared by at least seven different nearby villages (Balawat, Kabarli, Badana Alia, Badana

Sufla, Karashaw, Tiwajna and Zara Khatun); T. Yelkhi was shared by villagers from Aiuni (or Uyun) al-Kheshalat and elsewhere. This situation was also suggested at T. Deir 'Alla.
72  Loftus 1857, 54-56, 65-66; Bird 1988, I, 35-36; Breasted 1922, 14, ORINST 6799; cf. Marcanti 1977, Fiche E5; Browne 1970, 78; Algar 1990, 564. These have inspired some archaeologists to interpret Bronze Age cemeteries on Bahrain (Mackay 1929; Lamberg-Karlovsky 1984/85) and Parthian graves at Warka (Loftus 1857, 66; cf. also Ward 1886, 21) as being evidence for similar long-distance transport of the dead. In both these cases, however, the discovery and excavation of nearby contemporaneous settlements suggests instead that they simply served local populations (Frohlich 1983).
73  Blackman 1968, 124.
74  Adams 1989, 195.
75  Mosul has both; cf. also Burder 1847, 419-420. Pottery production may be reflected in the archaeological record with the coincidence of Early Dynastic graves and kilns at T. Ingharra, Kish (Matson 1974, 346).
76  Chase 1992, 179.
77  Barth 1980, 142. Cf. also Haiman 1992, 49; Lancaster & Lancaster 1993, 162-163.
78  Musil 1928, 418; Dickson 1949, 207.
79  E.g. Haiman 1986, 127; Dagan 1992, 101. De Vries (1987, 345) estimated that there may be over a thousand bedouin burials at El-Lejjun; over a hundred individuals have already been excavated.
80  Dickson 1949, 208.

## Cemetery organisation

Graves within a cemetery are normally regularly spaced.[81] The combination of this with regular alignments theoretically contributes to a more efficient use of space. However, most cemeteries tend to be rather organic in their growth, developing first laterally then vertically as pressure of space precludes further spread and finally shifting away altogether to a new location. This sequence was partly demonstrated by the Stratum II Islamic cemetery at T. el-Hesi.[82] At T. Toqaan, there was clustering of graves according to family (rather than social) status and graves of close kin were located as close together as possible.[83] However, as death does not respect family ties, in practice the development of family plots is complicated by the natural outward growth of the cemetery.[84] Blackman, Granqvist and Lane each describe segregation of corpses according to sex where the burials are placed in shared vaults or caves.[85] In the Hamrin basin of Iraq, the mound of T. Madhhur is said to have been used only for women and children.[86]

Separated areas or distinct cemeteries for children and infants are frequent.[87] At Hasanabad, the two cemeteries were 140 metres apart.[88] The reason given was that babies were too young to know sin and therefore should be kept separate.[89] However, there are also exceptions.[90] Granqvist records the occasional burial of children in the same graves as adults if they died at the same time, the reason being that the children help protect the associated adults.[91] Fakhry has noted that in the Bahia oasis (Egypt) newborn babies may be buried anywhere, including the house, and without a grave-marker, but children over three days of age have to be interred individually within a cemetery, unless they died shortly after a parent when they may be interred in the parent's grave.[92] Excavated instances of this have been demonstrated from T. el-Hesi, including one case of a pair of young infants possibly despatched immediately after birth because of the difficulty of simultaneously

rearing two children.[93] A further discovery at this site was that greater care was paid to the grave-construction and laying out of the body of children who died at about three years of age, suggesting a possible change in their family status at this age.[94]

Finally, there are numerous cases of graves clustering around the tombs of shaikhs and other important figures, who are themselves interred close to a mosque or shrine.[95] In most cases, it seems as if it is the presence of the shrine that dictates the growth of a cemetery, the main reasons apparently being that proximity to a holy person will help protect the grave from disturbance and increase the amount of blessing in the afterlife.[96] A similar reason evidently lies behind the storage of grain, heavy agricultural equipment or other possessions near a tomb or shrine.[97]

## Interment & orientation

Islamic burials are normally primary inhumations, hence normally fully articulated when excavated. Both articulated and disarticulated burials have been excavated at T. el-Hesi and El-Lejjun. The latter were presumed to belong to "bedouin nomads who brought their deceased from temporary burials in the winter pasture to be reburied here".[98] However, a strong case was put forward by the excavators of T. el-Hesi that most, if not all, of the secondary burials represented the remains of individuals accidentally disturbed during later grave-digging.[99] Cremation is strictly forbidden to Muslims and it is said that a corpse is as capable of suffering pain as a live person.[100]

The orifices of the body usually are closed in order to hinder evil influences; however, the ears are left open so that the deceased may reply correctly upon subsequent questioning by visiting angels.[101] Curiously, the jaw may be tightly bound in order to prevent the lower portion from accidentally opening;[102] any cords around the shroud are loosened.[103] In some cases the shrouds themselves are removed, carefully folded and placed in the grave beneath the body.[104] These observations suggest that the T. el-Hesi excavator's interpretation of

---

81 At Aliabad they were approximately a metre apart. (Kramer 1982, 78).
82 Fargo & O'Connell 1978, 169; Toombs 1985, 22-29; Eakins 1993.
83 Sweet 1974, 214-215; cf. also Granqvist 1965, 57. This is difficult to demonstrate archaeologically although attempted at T. el-Hesi (Toombs 1985, 22-29, 46-47).
84 Kramer 1982, 78.
85 Blackman 1968, 116; Granqvist 1965; Lane 1890, 484.
86 Roaf et al. 1984, 113.
87 E.g. T. Abu Dhahir: Simpson, in preparation; Aliabad: Kramer 1982, 76; Bethlehem: Granqvist 1965, 58; T. Iktanu: Prag 1989, 42; T. Songor B: Matsumoto & Yokoyama 1989; Yokoyama & Matsumoto 1990; cf. also Canaan 1927, 8.
88 Watson 1979, 15, 214-215.
89 Watson 1979, 215. Although the reasons are unknown, similar segregation is found at a number of ancient Near Eastern sites, for instance Samarran T. es-Sawwan (Campbell, this volume), 'Ubaid T. Abada (Jasim 1985, I, 33-36) and Bronze Age Saar (Ibrahim 1982, 25, Fig. 32, Pl. 40).
90 Cf. Toombs 1985; Eakins 1993.
91 Granqvist 1965, 83.
92 Fakhry 1950, II, 121.

93 Toombs 1985, 23-24, 26; Eakins 1993, 11, 17, Pls. 4-11.
94 Toombs 1985, 41, 69-71.
95 Yeivin 1961, 3; Barth 1980, 142; Toombs 1985, 30-32; Haiman 1986, 127; Schaefer 1989, 59; Mershen 1991a, 136, 140-141; Eakins 1993, 13; Ball & Gill, in press.
96 Canaan 1927, 7-9.
97 Lewis 1971, 50; Adams & Nissen 1972, 237: Site 449; Mershen 1991a, 136; Prag, this volume; cf. also Lancaster & Lancaster 1993, 154.
98 De Vries 1987, 345.
99 Toombs 1985, 22, 44-47; Eakins 1993, 9-11, 15-17, Pl. 3.
100 Roberts 1982, 129.
101 Granqvist 1965, 82-84; Roberts 1982, 128. For coins in graves see n. 124-127, 142-143. On the other hand, Musil (1928, 670) states that Rwala bedouin do not close the eyes or nostrils.
102 Al-Hamadhání 1973, 85.
103 Blackman 1968, 115.
104 Butcher n.d., 53, 57.

pins found in two graves as means of securing such shrouds[105] is incorrect. It is interesting to note here that red staining, thought to derive from skin coloration, was found on the bones of three womens' skeletons at T. el-Hesi.[106] The body is laid in the grave facing Mecca and usually with the head to the west; specific grave orientation of course varies throughout the Islamic world.[107] At T. Abu Dhahir, slight shifts in orientation during different sub-phases were noted although the reasons for these are unknown. A minority of burials excavated at T. el-Hesi were plainly orientated away from Mecca; the excavators suggested this may have been either because of a wish to face Jerusalem, Islam's third holiest city[108] or perhaps even through genuine uncertainty on the part of one or more individuals as to the true direction of Mecca.[109]

Minor variations occur in the laying out of the body but it is unclear whether this was truly random or whether it reflects minor variations in chronological and social groupings. Some 235 Islamic graves were excavated at T. Songor A, in the Hamrin basin of Iraq: the bodies were either placed on their back or on their side, with legs extended but arms either flexed or straight by the sides.[110] At T. el-Hesi, the majority of the excavated burials were either extended on their back or placed on their right side; a minority were placed in other positions, including that of a young woman who had been decapitated, possibly as a punishment for suspected adultery; at least one other individual may have been buried alive.[111] At T. Zeror (north mound), the excavators found that bodies were placed with the head either to the west or the east;[112] crucially, however, all the bodies faced south, i.e. towards Mecca. In many cases, the body was placed on one side,[113] in others, the bodies were placed on their back with the right arm extended by the side but the left arm bent and the left hand placed over the pelvis or (less commonly) the chest.[114] At

Artas, the right hand was placed beneath the head; if necessary, the body or head was propped up on bricks or stones to ensure that they remained correctly orientated.[115]

At T. Deir 'Alla, the bodies are said to have been covered with sherds and mudbricks.[116] This may reflect concern in protecting the corpses from being disinterred, particularly by dogs; for this reason, villagers in western Iran placed large stones over the bodies.[117] Alternatively, it may reflect an aversion to letting the earth touch the dead body.[118] Finally, each of the mourners throws dust or three handfuls of earth into the grave before the backfilling begins.[119]

## Grave-goods

Late Islamic graves containing objects are surprisingly frequent in excavations, despite Islamic prohibitions on grave-goods.[120] Excavated categories of finds comprise coins; European tokens; items of jewellery,[121] including beads, bells, pendants, finger-rings, earrings, hair-rings, toe-rings, bracelets, anklets and headdresses (sometimes utilising perforated coins or unperforated metal discs); pins; combs; mirrors; knife blades; glass bottles; ceramics and natural coloured stones arranged around the head of the corpse.[122] The range and relative frequency of these objects can be judged from the accompanying Appendix.

The funerary significance of many of these grave-objects is uncertain. The occasional discovery of unperforated coins in Islamic graves recalls classical and Partho-Sasanian practices and would seem to be at complete variance with Islamic belief.[123] However, Empson records that Yezidis in northern Iraq occasionally placed gold coins with the deceased as a means

---

105 Toombs 1985, 104.
106 Cf. Musil 1908, III, 424. Their unusual physical characteristics and clustering suggested that they may represent "women from a different tribal group, characterized by longer crania, [who] entered the community which used the cemetery by marriage, and that these women adorned their skin with ochre in a manner not practised by the other women of the community" (Toombs 1985, 90). This discovery recalls similar cases of ochre-stained burials from earlier periods in the Near East.
107 The Yezidis of northern Iraq are said to be interred with their faces to the east (Drower 1941, 36-37, 185). Lane (1890, 474) hints at further variation as some Muslims orientated the top of the head rather than the face towards Mecca at the time of death. I am grateful to Dr A.A. Soweleh for kindly pointing out other exceptions (Manchester, December 1993).
108 Toombs 1985, 79.
109 Eakins 1993, 25, 32, 35. Toombs (1985, 78) also observes that minor variation in orientation of the head could easily occur if the shroud was not fully removed during the final stages.
110 Kamada & Ohtsu 1988, 151.
111 Fargo & O'Connell 1978, 169; Toombs 1985, 66-90, 112-113; Eakins 1993, 21-35.
112 Ohata (ed.) 1966, 2-3; 1967, 9-10, Pl. X.
113 E.g. T. Zeror, north mound: Ibid., 3, Pl. X.
114 Caesarea: Chase 1992; T. el-Hesi: Toombs 1985, 71, 82-86, Eakins 1993, 26-27, 33, 35; El-Lejjun: De Vries 1987, 345,

Parker 1988, 142, 146: Fig. 14; T. Zeror, north mound: Ohata (ed.) 1967, 9-10, Pl. XII. Toombs (1985, 76-77) concluded that reasons of modesty may have dictated this practice whereby genitalia and breasts were covered.
115 Granqvist 1965, 79; Toombs 1978, 229; 1985, 41-42, Pl. 28; Lane 1987, 262; Holum *et al.* 1988, 224; Eakins 1993, 9, 11, 15; cf. also Musil 1928, 670; Dickson 1949, 214.
116 Van der Kooij & Ibrahim (eds) 1989, 90.
117 Watson 1979, 214-215; Kramer 1982, 78.
118 Wilson 1906, 157; Jaussen 1927, 336; Empson 1928, 63; Dickson 1949, 214. Curiously, traces of single wooden boards were found placed over Islamic burials excavated at Qal'at al-Bahrain (Kervran 1982, 75; and personal observation).
119 Roberts 1982, 128.
120 Found in *c.* 40 % of graves at T. el-Hesi Field I (Toombs 1985, 42-43).
121 Unspecified "jewellery" is reported from Islamic graves excavated at T. Dor, Site K-60 (Guz-Silberstein & Raveh 1990, 51) and T. Jezreel, Area B (Ussishkin & Woodhead *et al.* 1991/92, 29/31); "imitation jewellery and cornelian" was found with burials at the Qal'at al-Bahrain (Kervran 1982, 75, Pl. VIB) and "necklaces" were reported from graves excavated at T. esh-Shari'a in the Negev (Oren 1976, 11, 13).
122 Miscellanious objects/fragments of uncertain function, some possibly representing accidental inclusions in the fill, are also reported from T. el-Hesi (Toombs 1985, 108-109).
123 Simpson 1992. The lack of perforations suggest that they were not simply re-used as items of jewellery.

of rewarding the examining angels who questioned the deceased in the grave during the first night of burial;[124] and in the Bahia oasis of the Egyptian Western Desert, Fakhry mentions that people still occasionally placed a coin in the mouth of the old-aged in order to prevent other deaths in the family.[125] An Iranian adaptation of this practice is described by Sykes, who refers to the placing in the mouth of an etched carnelian carrying the names of the twelve imams.[126]

According to Butcher, Copts as well as Muslims may be buried with items of jewellery.[127] Some objects may be gender-specific: Invernizzi observed that bracelets and beads were found associated particularly with young girls' burials at T. Yelkhi,[128] and Ohata stated that grave-goods were associated with womens' burials at T. Zeror.[129] Grave-goods of any sort were less common in male graves at T. el-Hesi although exceptions included burials with metal rings and bracelets.[130] Significantly, at this site, the discovery of bracelets too large to have been worn by the children with whom they were found suggests that at least some of the jewellery may have belonged to mourners rather than the deceased.[131]

There is a certain amount of known ethnographic detail linking items of dress with local Near Eastern superstitions. Certain materials were preferred as a means of protection for the wearer. These include the wearing of a blue glass or stone bead in order to reflect the 'Evil Eye' back onto itself, or cowries (known among the Qashqa'i as *Bibin Tarak* "Eye-Crackers") designed to break the 'Evil Eye'. Dark green stone beads were considered by some to prevent post-natal diseases and protect against any ill effects of menstruation. Similarly, serpentine was regarded as being effective against insect bites, goldstone against poison, certain yellow glass beads against jaundice, tortoise-shell and alum against illness; and red agate, carnelian or amber were regarded as a means of healing, preventing ear/throat inflammation, abortion, internal bleeding and other dangers, and promoting love and fertility. Brown/black and white banded agate or glass ('butter and honey') beads were worn as a means of increasing marital affection; a smooth opaque white bead to promote lactation;

turquoise to ensure prosperity; coral was associated with kindness and good fortune; and cloves were worn at weddings.[132] Among these materials, blue glass beads and bracelets, cowries, and agate, carnelian and coral beads are found within Islamic (as well as earlier) graves; cloves are unlikely to survive into the archaeological record (and in any case are less likely to have formed part of the death assemblage).

It is worth noting that frequently the colour or shape of a bead is regarded as more important than the raw material itself – hence the substitution of, for example, red glass or, more recently, red plastic for carnelian or agate beads. In addition, the specific forms of certain beads and types of jewellery were significant; circular or triangular shapes were considered powerful magic and bells and reflective surfaces were also regarded as effective means of protection against evil influences.[133] Triangular pendants, bells and mirrors all occur in Late Islamic graves. Cowries at T. el-Hesi were interpreted as fertility charms and bracelets with snake-head terminals regarded as possible insurance against snake bites.[134] It is interesting, however, that many of the more elaborate ethnographically attested styles of metal jewellery – let alone gold or silverwork – do not appear in Islamic graves; instead, cheaper versions made of glass or plastic are more abundant within the mortuary context, as are crude beads of bone, shell or mother-of-pearl.[135] A possible explanation of deliberate manufacture for the afterlife is inappropriate here and an explanation should be sought within the social and economic context. A detailed comparative study of regional urban, village and bedouin jewellery styles, associated beliefs and the excavated mortuary evidence would be very useful.[136] In the meantime, the available evidence strongly suggests that costly jewellery was retained in circulation whereas items with amuletic significance were preferred grave-goods.

The available ethnographic accounts are usually silent on the topic of grave-goods, possibly because many of their authors did not witness closely the burial ceremonies.[137] Exceptions are Granqvist and Musil who mention the burial of a strike-a-light in a village grave at Artas, a set of coffee utensils in another, a comb and a piece of soap in the graves of virgins, a needle and thread or kohl with women and a water-filled pitcher beside the head of bedouin.[138] It is interesting to note

---

124 Empson 1928, 63.
125 Fakhry 1950, II, 122. Alternatives were to bury an onion in the grave or to lay a nail in the earth over the head of the deceased (ibid.). The Mandaeans have a similar belief: in order to prevent the deceased from returning and taking close relatives with him, perhaps an allusion to the spread of infectious disease within a family, stones are placed on the mouth and shroud (Drower 1937, 185-186). The closing of the orifices of the deceased has a lengthy tradition (cf. Curtis this volume).
126 Sykes 1902, 167. A yet further variation is illustrated by the apparent discovery of single plain carnelian beads in the mouths of early Seleucid burials excavated at Saar on Bahrain (Herling 1994).
127 Butcher, 52.
128 Invernizzi 1980, 30.
129 Ohata (ed.) 1966, 3.
130 Fargo & O'Connell 1978, 169; Toombs 1985, 92-93, 104-105.
131 Toombs 1985, 92-93, 101, 103.

132 Allgrove et al. 1976, 45; Weir 1989, 193-202; Mershen 1991a, 139-140, 1991b; cf. also Budge 1930, 306-330.
133 Allgrove et al. 1976, 45.
134 Toombs 1985, 105; Eakins 1993, 60-61.
135 This is despite the fact that metal bracelets and both gold and silver jewellery were manufactured in villages as well as the urban centres (e.g. cf. Buckingham 1825, 140).
136 Cf. Buckingham 1827, 292, 382; Lane 1890, 519-532; Spauer 1992, 57. Attempted by Jero (n.d.) for Late Assyrian graves excavated at Assur.
137 Cf. e.g. Sweet 1974, 215.
138 Granqvist 1965, 62-63, 84; Musil 1908, III, 424. On historic period lithics, cf. Miller 1984. Coffee appeared throughout the Near East in the sixteenth century (Hattox 1991) following an initial period of religious disapproval similar to that

that at least some of these items (coffee sets, mirrors, combs) are occasionally left as offerings on top of the graves or are depicted on Late Islamic gravestones.[139]

The presence or absence of objects are clearly unreliable means of distinguishing 'pre-Islamic' from 'Islamic' graves. Indeed, firmly identifiable Early Islamic graves are surprisingly rare. From the point of view of the archaeologist, this material culture therefore is potentially most useful in dating graves within the Islamic period: as these graves provide relatively closed groups, they may be considered representative of minor categories of Ottoman and later material culture.[140] The occasional discovery of earlier coins re-used as elements of jewellery[141] suggests that extreme caution should be used before attempting to date graves on the basis of associated coins.[142] However, some success has been had through comparison of imported glass 'trade beads' found, for instance, in Late Islamic graves at Caesarea with dated assemblages from North America.[143]

Finally, although technically not grave-goods, mention should be made of the Iraqi Shi'ite practice of placing small inscribed clay "prayer-stones" in the graves of pilgrims who had made the journey to Kerbela (whence they were made).[144] The Yezidis of northern Iraq have a similar custom.[145] Conder also mentions the inclusion in certain Palestinian Shi'ite graves of character commendations written on palm-leaves or the writing of prayers on the shroud.[146] These practices recall the occasional occurrence of scroll amulets in graves of earlier periods.[147]

## Grave-markers

Muslim law disapproves of inscribed or ornamented graves. It is therefore ironic that many of the most splendid monuments of Islam comprise tombs.[148] A primary purpose of grave-markers is to prevent people from accidentally treading on or otherwise disturbing the dead;[149] Qur'anic quotations are rarely used, however, lest the inscriptions become accidentally defiled in this way. The extent and type of grave-marker varies considerably from site to site. Ethnographic accounts from Egypt,[150] Palestine,[151] Jordan,[152] Iraq,[153] Kuwait[154] and India[155] attest the use of temporary palm-frond, reed, brick, pottery or sand mound markers. In Baluchistan, there is even deliberate selection of third millennium carved stone objects as markers for recent graves or shrines.[156] Similarly, in eastern Jordan, old Safaitic inscriptions seem to have been re-used as bedouin grave-markers.[157] The placing of palm-fronds, aloes, myrtle and sometimes sweet basil above graves in Egypt, Iraq, Syria and Turkey are believed to bestow a blessing on the dead;[158] likewise, flowers are grown over Druze, Iranian and Turkish graves[159] and scarlet flowers are placed over Yezidi headstones on feast days.[160] According to Lewis, cypresses were planted in Ottoman cemeteries because "the aromatic resinous scent which they gave off was considered an antidote to the graveyard smells, and because of the implications of immortality in their evergreen leaves".[161] The scale and importance of these beliefs in late Ottoman Syria is illustrated by Buckingham's description of mule caravan trade in myrtle.[162]

Significantly, most of these types of markers tend to erode rapidly and are unlikely to leave recognisable traces in the archaeological record.[163] Use of these may explain, however, the occasional accidental discovery of entire cemeteries of unmarked graves (T. el-Hesi;[164] T. Mevorakh;[165] T. Songor A;[166] T. Tuneinir;[167] T. Yelkhi).[168] At T. Abu Dhahir, Aliabad and

---

accorded smoking a century later (Simpson 1990). Thereafter, coffee-making apparatus achieved a symbolism reminiscent of Near Eastern 'wine-sets' of the first millennium BC (Sherratt, in press; cf. also Yassine (ed.) 1988, 273).

139 Cf. belowGrave-markers.

140 Mershen 1991a, 1991b; Spauer 1992.

141 E.g. at T. Razuk: Gibson (ed.) 1981, 82, Pl. 104.

142 Mershen 1991a, 138-139; Ilisch 1993. A medieval (Crusader) date was suggested by the excavators for some of the late graves at T. Mevorakh (Stern et al. 1978, 5, 20, Pl. 46: 15). This was based on the discovery of a perforated twelfth century silver coin in one grave. This clearly represents re-use of an old coin as an item of jewellery: a highly worn bronze coin of Trajan was found in another late grave at the site (Stern et al. 1978, 9, 20, Pl. 46: 10). See also n. 101, 124-127.

143 Cited by Mershen, 1991a. It should be possible to identify products of the Hebron glasshouses in some of these Late Islamic graves (cf. Arkell 1937; Spauer 1992).

144 Niebuhr 1780, II, 222-223; cf. Hansen 1967, 30-31.

145 Empson 1928, 61-62.

146 Conder 1889a, 127.

147 Simpson 1992.

148 Ball, pers comm..

149 Cf. Dickson 1949, 208.

150 Blackman 1968.

151 Jaussen 1927, 336; Dagan 1992, 94.

152 Buckingham 1825, 122-123.

153 Loftus 1857, 59; Bell 1911, 80; Roux 1960, 28; Postgate 1980a, 101.

154 Dickson 1949, 210.

155 Halbert 1959, 187-188.

156 Dales 1977.

157 Lancaster & Lancaster 1993, 154, 157.

158 Thomson 1911, 84; Blackman 1968, 115-117, 259, 260; Lane 1987, 263.

159 Burder 1847, 408-409, 416-417; Conder 1889, 125; Barth 1980, 143; Llewellyn 1986, 59.

160 Drower 1941, 105.

161 Lewis 1971, 106; cf. also Drower 1937, 183, 190.

162 Buckingham 1825, 400-401.

163 The use of temporary grave-markers in antiquity can be inferred by common orientation and a lack of intersecting grave-cuts. However, at T. Songor A, many of the grave-cuts did intersect, supporting the excavators' comment that no postholes from such markers could be traced (Kamada & Ohtsu 1988, 137, 150).

164 Toombs 1985; Eakins 1993.

165 Stern et al. 1978, 4.

166 Kamada & Ohtsu 1988, 150.

167 Fuller & Fuller 1989/90, 333.

168 Invernizzi 1980, 30. Earlier this century, Mandaean cemeteries rarely included grave-markers although "some wealthier Mandaeans, copying their [Muslim] neighbours, have begun to erect brick tombs with the name of the buried person on the slab." In earlier times, according to local belief, the dead were excarnated (Drower 1937, 184).

Hasanabad, many of the childrens' graves were unmarked.[169]

Unworked stones are frequently used as gravemarkers, for instance in Iran,[170] northern Iraq,[171] Jordan,[172] Palestine and the Negev.[173] More unusual types of marker are found in Central Asia: at Kounia-Urgench (Turkmenistan), the ladders used as biers in the funeral-procession were then left upright above the grave, whereas at Kaminskoye (Kyrgyzia) aluminium yurt frames placed over the graves were used to imitate the former homes of the deceased.[174]

Where present, tombstones may indicate the name, family or tribe and profession of the deceased. This is particularly well-defined in the case of Ottoman tombs in Istanbul and other Turkish cities.[175] Conversely, according to Kramer,[176] villagers at Aliabad were usually unable to identify grave occupants "unless the deceased were close kin, the death was very recent, or the grave has an inscription". At Artas, different shapes of stone were used to correspond to different sexes;[177] in Egypt, sex was distinguished by different numbers of sticks or projections at the top of the tomb[178] and in western Iran the addition of a third stone over the centre of the grave marked the womens' graves.[179] Elsewhere, womens' graves are denoted by garments or plaits of hair placed over the top[180] although Drower[181] implies that plaits simply mark a sign of mourning by widows. Upright gravestones may also be attributed another function as St Clair[182] was informed that on occasion they represented the angels of death. Individuals who died in battle may have weapons depicted on the tombstone, as in the case of tombs observed immediately outside Mosul in 1758[183] and more recent graves in Iraq.[184]

Yassine has briefly described bedouin cut tombstones found in Jordan and decorated with "some of the symbols of bedouin hospitality, such as the coffee grinder, and the coffee pot and cups".[185] These may reflect a bedouin belief reported by Granqvist that "coffee utensils mourn on the death of a sheikh. They are hung up and turned upside down."[186] Significantly, a number of bedouin graves in eastern Jordan possess a "short distance from the foot of the grave ... a circle of stones, often built up against a large standing stone, with a variable number of upright stones within it and, perhaps, a pile of small spherical stones nearby." These "represent a coffee hearth(s), the stones within it being coffee pots and the smaller ones being camel-dung fuel".[187] Further elaborate adult gravestones are occasionally found in western Iran and south-east Turkey: examples include the depiction of a prayer stone, prayer beads, ewer and bowl (=washing set) or a semi-circular comb for a man and scissors, a mirror or a double-sided comb for a woman. Others depict scenes with armed horsemen, ibex, gazelles or weaving, with the front and back sides of the stele corresponding to 'life' and 'death'.[188] In some Yezidi cases, the scene may symbolise the manner of death of the individual interred beneath.[189]

## Post-funerary ceremonies

Dyeing of the face and hands, tearing of garments, scratching of cheeks, wailing and occasionally the playing of musical instruments (drums or flutes) at the grave by female relatives of the deceased are customary amongst Muslims (and minority groups[190]) although forbidden by the Prophet and disapproved of by the orthodox.[191] Necklaces and bracelets may be broken and discarded.[192] Suggestions that this sometimes occurred at the grave-side are provided by the discovery of glass bracelet fragments near Late Islamic graves at T. Abu Dhahir,[193] T. Iktanu,[194] T. Razuk[195] and T. Songor A.[196] The period of mourning is characterised also by the wearing of dull-coloured or old clothing, and a temporary stop in manufacture of bright textiles or basketry.[197] Quotations from the Qur'an are recited over the grave and incense is burnt at Yezidi funerals.[198]

Throughout the Near East, there is a strong Late Islamic tradition of undertaking ritual meals at the grave-side. In Egypt, specially-baked loaves are brought regularly to the grave where they are often donated in the name of the deceased to assembled paupers.[199] Bread, figs, dried fruit, water, clothes and even cash offerings were also made at the grave-side in Egypt, Palestine, Syria and Iraq as an act of charity on behalf of

169 Personal observation; Kramer 1982, 76; Watson 1979, 215.
170 Kramer 1982, 76-77.
171 Drower 1941, 36-37.
172 Yassine (ed.) 1988, 273.
173 Schaefer 1989, 59; Dagan 1992, 101.
174 Personal observations, 1991. The conical roofs of Seljuk and later tomb-towers may be influenced by tent designs
175 White 1845, III, 347-358.
176 Kramer 1982, 78.
177 Granqvist 1965, 86.
178 Fakhry 1950, II, 121; cf. also Musil 1928, 670; Mershen 1991a, 137.
179 Kramer 1982, 76.
180 Granqvist 1965, 106-107; Roberts 1982, 128.
181 Drower 1941, 36-37.
182 St Clair 1887, 236.
183 Ives 1773, 323.
184 Personal observations, 1985-1987.
185 Yassine (ed.) 1988, 273; cf. Prag, this volume.
186 Granqvist 1965, 105-106.

187 Lancaster & Lancaster 1993, 152-155.
188 Watson 1979, 215; Mortensen & Mortensen 1989, 932-934, 950-951, Pls. II-III; Vanden Berghe & Tourovets 1992, 20-35, Pls. 13-18; personal observation, Mardin 1986.
189 Drower 1941, 36-37.
190 Cf. Drower 1937, 180-181.
191 Fakhry 1950, II, 122; Granqvist 1965, 53-54, 142-143; Blackman 1968, 109-114, 122-125.
192 Al-Hamadhání 1973, 85; Dickson 1949, 209-210.
193 Simpson, in preparation.
194 Prag 1989, 42.
195 Gibson (ed.) 1981, 81, Pl. 55: 24-26.
196 Kamada & Ohtsu 1988, 159, 170: Fig. 17.
197 Granqvist 1965, 108.
198 Drower 1941, 98.
199 Butcher n.d., 59-60; Lane 1890, 485; Blackman 1968, 115, 118-120, 259, 261.

the soul of the deceased;[200] special care was taken in some cases to take the favourite food of the deceased.[201] Early nineteenth century "bedouin" graves in the Amman area were covered in "numerous propitiatory offerings and tokens in memory of the tenants of the graves";[202] Musil confirms that specially baked bread offerings and water libations were offered at bedouin graves,[203] a practice that continues today.[204] Drower details the carefully prescribed ingredients of and customs at Mandaean ritual meals in the marshes of southern Iraq.[205] Baldensperger[206] mentions that other Palestinian gravestones had scooped-out tops in order to collect rainwater as a drink for the departed souls.[207] The same reason presumably lies behind the Egyptian practice of placing a full water-jar at the head of the grave[208] and may explain the discovery of six water juglets (*abariq*) above the capstones of an excavated man's grave at T. el-Hesi.[209]

Thereafter, the cemeteries become places of solitude and grazing, hence perhaps the discoveries of Late Ottoman smokers' pipes at T. Abu Dhahir,[210] T. el-Hesi,[211] T. Madhhur[212] and T. Razuk.[213]

# Conclusions

The diversity in excavated rural Late Islamic graves reflects variation in the age, sex and social status of the deceased. Anthropological verification is required if these factors are to be tested as alternatives to the prevalent archaeological tendency to extrapolate social hierarchy from mortuary evidence. Detailed anthropological studies of excavated Late Islamic populations are still at an early stage[214] but their potential importance has been highlighted with reference to data from the Negev and Hamrin basin.[215] The relationship between different contemporaneous ethnic and religious groups

is unclear from archaeology yet similarity between Muslim and Coptic mortuary ceremonies has been demonstrated from Egypt[216] and Betts has alluded to "marked tribal differences in burial customs" in the Eastern Desert of Jordan.[217] The ethnographic record for the Near East points to relatively rapid changes in fashion and wide variation of detail within even relatively small geographical areas: the implications of these variables for appreciating variability in associated material culture and death-assemblages should not be under-estimated. There are hints also of regional continuity in burial-practices from pre-Islamic times, particularly concerning treatment of the body and the placement of grave-goods (albeit within an altered theological context). For instance, in Egypt funeral ceremonies are "performed largely for the benefit of the departed, to ensure them happiness in the life beyond".[218] Throughout the Late Islamic Near East there are strong suggestions that local superstitions, popular beliefs and orthodox religion all play important roles in death and funerary ceremonies. Where present, many grave-goods seem to have been selected for their perceived apotropaic properties rather than material value: major disparities with the corresponding above-ground ethnographic record demonstrate the potential unreliability of economic reconstructions based solely on mortuary data. Finally, there are strong suggestions of simple practicality in terms of grave construction and cemetery organisation. On the basis of these observations, it is not surprising that considerable intra- and inter-site variation also occurs in the Ancient Near East. Indeed, cemeteries from different periods may have more in common than do different sites within a single period.[219] Comparative studies of the mortuary evidence from different periods would be useful in future.[220]

---

200  Conder 1889a, 126; Wilson 1906,159; Canaan 1927,188-193; Empson 1928, 63; Drower 1941, 98; Fakhry 1950, II, 121; Granqvist 1965, 90, 98-100, 157; Sweet 1974, 215.
201  Fakhry 1950; II, 122.
202  Buckingham 1825,122-123.
203  Musil 1928, 671-672.
204  Lancaster & Lancaster 1993, 153-154.
205  Drower 1937, 186-188, 204-224.
206  Baldensperger 1893, 217.
207  Cf. also White 1845; III, 347; Lewis 1971, 105.
208  Fakhry 1950; II, 121.
209  Toombs 1985, 106-107. The roots of these practices can be traced back to at least the third millennium in Mesopotamia, whereby libations were offered with the intention of preventing the dead from returning to haunt the living (Thompson 1903: I, xxvii-xxxi; Healey, this volume). Ultimately related to ancestor cults, the latter can be detected in the Near East as early as the aceramic neolithic (Bienert 1991).
210  Matney forthcoming.
211  Bliss, cited by Toombs 1985, 18.
212  Roaf *et al.* 1984, 113-114, 159-160, Fig. 24, 2-3.
213  Gibson (ed.) 1981, 81, Pl. 104: 4.
214  Eakins 1980, 1993; Ishida & Wada 1981; Kervran 1982, 76; Wada 1982; Curvers 1987; Bourke 1992, 221; Browne 1992.
215  Toombs 1985, 90; Matsumoto & Yokoyama 1989, 297; Eakins 1993, 47-55.

216  Blackman 1968, 109-128.
217  Betts 1989, 86.
218  Blackman 1968, 120.
219  Reece 1982.
220  Cf. Nadel, this volume.

## Appendix: Artifact categories from excavated Late Islamic graves in the Near East

### Coins

Balawat (Curtis, Collon & Green 1993, 30), T. Dor, Site K-60 (Guz-Silberstein & Raveh 1990, 51), T. el-Hesi (Toombs 1985, 95, 100-101, 116, Pls. 68b, 69a-b, 70), El-Lejjun (Betlyon 1985, 32-33, 1987: 683-684; De Vries 1987, 344-346), T. Karrana, Burial 16 (Wilhelm & Zaccagnini 1991, 12-13; Ilisch 1993), T. Mevorakh (Stern et al. 1978, 4-5, 9, 20, Pl. 46: 15), Mt. Nebo (Saller 1941, 285), Qal'at al-Bahrain (Kervran 1982, 75), Rang Mahal, Grave 1 (Halbert 1959, 185, Pl. 86: 41), Umm Qais (Mershen 1991a, 137-138), T. Yoqne'am (Avissar 1987, 7).

N.B. Some examples at T. el-Hesi and El-Lejjun were hammered flat, hence the legends were illegible.

### Tokens

T. Chagar Bazar, Trench A (Mallowan 1936, 6; Christie Mallowan 1983, 136-137; 17th century, Hans Krauwinkel of Nuremburg).

### Beads

Silver: T. el-Hesi (Toombs 1985, 99, Pl. 65a).

Copper alloy: T. el-Hesi (Toombs 1985, 97, 99, Pls. 62a: 4, 63a).

Glass: T. el-Hesi (Fargo & O'Connell 1978, 173; Toombs 1985, 94-100 & Pls.), El-Lejjun (De Vries 1987, 344), T. Mevorakh, Tomb 28 (Stern et al. 1978, 5, 9, 103, Pl. 41: 4, 6), Mt. Nebo (Saller 1941, I, 314), T. Qiri, Tombs 5-7 (Avissar 1987, 8, 48-49: Figs. 6: 14-15, 17, 21-22), T. al-Raqai (Curvers 1987, 7, 29: Fig. 17: 89), T. Razuk, Burial 5 (Gibson (ed.) 1981, 82, Pl. 104: 8), T. Songor A, Graves 46-47, 55, 154, 251 (Kamada & Ohtsu 1988, 160-161, 171: Fig. 18), Umm Qais (Mershen 1990, 332), T. Yelkhi (Invernizzi 1980, 30), T. Yoqne'am (Avissar 1987, 8).

Venetian glass (?): T. Qiri, Tomb 5 (Avissar 1987, 8, 48-49: Fig. 6: 18).

Composition: T. el-Hesi (?) (Toombs 1985, 94, 96-99), T. Qiri, Tomb 5 (Avissar 1987, 8, 48-49: Fig. 6: 16), T. Songor A, Graves 46, 278 (Kamada & Ohtsu 1988, 151, 160, 171: Fig. 18).

Plastic: El-Lejjun (De Vries 1987, 344, 346).

Blue plastic: T. Razuk, Burial 4 (Gibson (ed.) 1981, 82, Pl. 104: 5).

Amber: T. Iktanu (Prag 1989, 42; cf. also Prag 1991, 55), T. Mevorakh, Tomb 17 (Stern et al. 1978, 5, 9, 103, Pl. 41: 2), T. Qiri (Avissar 1987, 8, 48-49: Fig. 6: 19), Umm Qais (Mershen 1990, 332). N.B. Mershen (1991a, 139) suggests a possible source for amber on the river Zarqa in Jordan.

Bone: T. el-Hesi (Toombs 1985, 95-96, 98 & Pls.), T. Razuk, Burial 4 (Gibson (ed.) 1981, 82, Pl. 104: 5), Umm Qais (Mershen 1991a, 139).

Shell: T. el-Hesi (Toombs 1985, 98, 100, Pls. 67a: 8-9, 67b: 3, 5, 8, 10), El-Lejjun (De Vries 1987, 344), T. Qiri, Tomb 5 (Avissar 1987, 8, 48-49: Fig. 6:19), T. Razuk, Burials 2, 4 (Gibson (ed.) 1981, 81-82, Pls. 55: 8-15, 104: 5), T. Songor A, Graves 55, 154, 278 (Kamada & Ohtsu 1988, 151, 160-61, 170: Fig. 18), Umm Qais (Mershen 1991a, 139).

Coral: T. Songor A, Grave 278 (Kamada & Ohtsu 1988, 151).

Wood: T. Songor A, Graves 46, 55 (Kamada & Ohtsu 1988, 160-161, 171: Fig. 18).

Carnelian/agate: T. el-Hesi (Fargo & O'Connell 1978, 173; Toombs 1985, 93, 95, 97, 99-100 & Pls.), T. Mevorakh, Tombs 13, 17, 30, 35 (Stern et al. 1978, 5, 9, 103, Pl. 41: 5, 7-12), T. Songor A, Graves 46, 47, 55, 278 (Kamada & Ohtsu 1988, 151, 160-161, 171: Fig. 18), Umm Qais (Mershen 1991a, 139).

Crystal: T. Songor A, Grave 278 (Kamada & Ohtsu 1988, 151).

Soapstone: T. Mevorakh, Tomb 17 (Stern et al. 1978, 5, 9, 103, Pl. 41: 1, 3).

Black stone: T. Zeror, north mound (Ohata (ed.) 1967, 9-10, Pl. XII).

Red stone: T. Razuk, Burial 4 (Gibson (ed.) 1981, 82, Pl. 104: 5).

White stone: T. Razuk, Burial 4 (Gibson (ed.) 1981, 82, Pl. 104: 5).

Unspecified stone: T. Razuk, Burial 2 (Gibson (ed.) 1981, 81-82, Pl. 55: 8-15), T. Songor A, Grave 46 (Kamada & Ohtsu 1988, 160, 171: Fig. 18), Umm Qais (Mershen 1990, 332, 1991a: 139).

Unspecified: El-Bawiti (Fakhry 1950, II, 110, Pl. LXVII), T. el-Hesi (Toombs 1985, 18), T. Jezreel, Area B (Ussishkin & Woodhead et al. 1991/92, 29/31), Mt. Nebo (Saller 1941, I, 314), T. Sh. 'Ahmed el-'Areyny (Yeivin 1961, Pl. 2), Umm Qais (Mershen 1990, 332), T. Yoqne'am (Avissar 1987, 7), T. Zeror, north mound (Ohata (ed.) 1966, 3).

N.B. Some of these beads may derive from bracelets (see below).

### Bells

Silver: T. Mevorakh, Tomb 17 (Stern et al. 1978, 5, 9, 103, Pl. 41: 15).

Copper alloy: T. Gubba (Ii 1989, 224, Pl. 49, No. 210), T. el-Hesi (Toombs 1985, 101, Pl. 69c-d, with traces of cloth), El-Lejjun (De Vries 1987, 344), T. Mevorakh, Tomb 29 (Stern et al. 1978, 5, 9, 103, Pl. 41: 13-14), T. Songor A, Grave 100 (Kamada & Ohtsu 1988, 158, 170: Fig. 17, Pl. 52A).

Unspecified: T. Sh. 'Ahmed el-'Areyny (Yeivin 1961, Pl. 2: 21).

### Pendants

Silver: T. Mevorakh, Tomb 4 (Stern et al. 1978, 5, 9, 103, Pl. 41: 18).

Copper alloy: T. Mevorakh, Tombs 31, 33 (Stern et al. 1978, 5, 9, 103, Pl. 41: 16-17).

Glass: T. el-Hesi (Toombs 1985, 100).

Composition: Balawat (Curtis, Collon & Green 1993, 30).

Shell: mother-of-pearl: T. el-Hesi (Toombs 1985, 100, Pls. 59a: 43, 62c: 1, 66a: 23, 68c).

Green stone: T. Qiri (Avissar 1987, 7-8, 48-49: Fig. 6: 20).

Travertine: T. el-Hesi (Toombs 1985, 98, 100, Pl. 67a: 4).

Unspecified: T. Yoqne'am (Avissar 1987, 7).

### Finger-Rings

Copper alloy: T. el-Hesi (Toombs 1985, 101-102, Pl. 71b, silver-plated), El-Lejjun (De Vries 1987, 344), Pella (?) (Hennessy et al. 1983, 359), T. al-Raqai (Curvers 1987, 8), T. esh-Shari'a (Oren 1976, 12), T. Songor A, Grave 154 (Kamada & Ohtsu 1988, 158, 170: Fig. 17, Pl. 52A).

With stone insets: T. el-Hesi (Fargo & O'Connell 1978, 173; Toombs 1985, 101-102), Umm Qais (Mershen 1991a, 137, 139), T. Zeror, north mound (Ohata (ed.) 1966, 3).

With glass insets: El-Bawiti (Fakhry 1950, II, 110, Pl. LXVIII), T. el-Hesi (Toombs 1985, 101-102).

Iron: T. el-Hesi (Toombs 1985, 101, Pls. 71a, 72c).

Bone: T. el-Hesi (Toombs 1985, 101, Pl. 71c: 1-2).

Unspecified: T. Sh. 'Ahmed el-'Areyny (Yeivin 1961, Pl. 2), Umm Qais (Mershen 1991a, 137, 139).

### Earrings

Copper alloy: El-Bawiti (Fakhry 1950, II, 110), T. Deir Alla (Van der Kooij & Ibrahim (eds) 1989, 90, 110, two with traces of textile), T. Gubba (Ii 1989, 224, Pl. 49, No. 211, with traces of cotton), T. el-Hesi (Toombs 1985, 97, 102, Pl. 62d, with glass drops and traces of cloth), Pella (?) (Hennessy et al. 1983, 359), T. Songor A, Grave 47 (Kamada & Ohtsu 1988, 170, Fig. 17, Pl. 52A, each with a pair of drops).

Unspecified: T. Sh. 'Ahmed el-'Areyny (Yeivin 1961, Pl. 2), Umm Qais (Mershen 1991a, 137).

### Hair-Rings

Copper alloy: El-Bawiti (Fakhry 1950, II, 110, Pl. LXVIII).

Twisted glass: T. Deir Alla (Van der Kooij & Ibrahim (eds) 1989, 90, 110).

### Toe-Rings

Copper alloy & iron: T. el-Hesi (Toombs 1985, 102 & Pls.).

### Bracelets

Copper alloy: El-Bawiti (Fakhry 1950, II, 110, Pl. LXVIII), T. Deir Alla (Van der Kooij & Ibrahim (eds) 1989, 110), T. el-Hesi (Fargo & O'Connell 1978, 173; Toombs 1985, 103-104 & Pls, some with snake-head terminals and traces of cloth), El-Lejjun (De Vries 1987, 344), T. Mevorakh, Tomb 17 (Stern *et al.* 1978, 5, 9, 103, Pl. 41: 20), T. esh-Shari'a (Oren 1976, 12, one with traces of cloth), T. Songor A, Grave 278 (Kamada & Ohtsu 1988, 151, Pl. 44A: on both arms), Umm Qais (Mershen 1991a, 139), T. Yoqne'am (Avissar 1987, 7), T. Zeror, north mound (Ohata (ed.) 1966, 3).

Iron: Caesarea, area KK (Chase 1992), T. Deir Alla (Van der Kooij & Ibrahim (eds) 1989, 110), Gezer, Cave 30 (?) (Macalister 1912, I, 312), T. el-Hesi (Toombs 1985, 104, Pl. 81a-c), El-Lejjun (De Vries 1987, 344), T. Mevorakh, Tombs 5, 17, 31 (Stern *et al.* 1978, 5, 9, 103, Pl. 41: 19), T. Songor A, Graves 264, 278 (Kamada & Ohtsu 1988, 151, Pl. 44A: on left arm), Umm Qais (Mershen 1991a, 139), T. Zeror, north mound (Ohata (ed.) 1966, 3).

Unspecified metal: Umm Qais (Mershen 1990, 332).

Blue glass: T. el-Hesi (Toombs 1985, 102-103 & Pls.), T. Mevorakh, Tombs 2, 25, 31 (Stern *et al.* 1978, 5, 9, 103, Pl. 41: 21-22), T. al-Raqai (Curvers 1987, 7, 29: Fig. 17: 90).

Amber glass: T. el-Hesi (Toombs 1985, 102-103, Pl. 76a: 4).

Coloured twisted or trailed glass: T. Dan, area B (Spauer 1992, 57-59), Gezer, Cave 30 (Macalister 1912, I, 312, 315, Fig. 166), T. el-Hesi (Toombs 1985, 103 & Pls.), T. Jemmeh (Petrie 1928, 25, Pl. LVXVII: 4-8), Jerusalem: Bethany (Saller 1957, 327), Mt. Nebo (Saller 1941, I, 314), T. Sh. 'Ahmed el-'Areyny (Yeivin 1961, Pl. 2).

Unspecified glass: T. Gubba, Graves 295-303, 352-353 (Ii 1989, 221, 234: Fig. 23, Pl. 44), T. el-Hesi (Toombs 1985, 18), El-Lejjun (De Vries 1987, 344), Qal'at al-Bahrain (Kervran 1982, 75, Pl. VIB), T. esh-Shari'a (Oren 1976, 12), Umm Qais (Mershen 1990, 332, 1991a: 137, 139), T. Yelkhi (Invernizzi 1980, 30).

Plastic: T. Razuk, Burial 4 (Gibson (ed.) 1981, 82, Pl. 104: 7).

Leather studded with metal: T. el-Hesi (Toombs 1985, 104).

Leather studded with glass: Umm Qais (Mershen 1990, 332, 1991a: 137, 139).

Unspecified: T. Sh. 'Ahmed el-'Areyny (Yeivin 1961, Pls. 1-2).

N.B. Bracelets formed of glass, composition, shell and silver beads were found with Burial 3 at T. Razuk (Gibson (ed.) 1981,

82). Further bead-bracelets were excavated in Graves 154 & 251 at T. Songor A (Kamada & Ohtsu 1988, 161, 171: Fig. 18).

### Anklets

Copper alloy: T. Deir Alla (Van der Kooij & Ibrahim (eds) 1989, 90, 110).

Iron: T. Deir Alla (Van der Kooij & Ibrahim (eds) 1989, 90, 110).

### Head-dresses

T. el-Hesi (Toombs 1985, 105-106, Pl. 80a), El-Lejjun (Betlyon 1985, 32-33; De Vries 1987, 344), Umm Qais (Mershen 1990, 332, 1991a: 139).

### Pins

Copper alloy: T. el-Hesi (Toombs 1985, 104, Pl. 64b).

### Combs

Wooden: El-Lejjun (De Vries 1987, 344), Rang Mahal (Halbert 1959, 185).

### Mirrors

Bronze: T. Songor A, Grave 278, circular mirror found close behind the cranium of an adult (Kamada & Ohtsu 1988, 151, 158, Pls. 44A, 53).

Glass: T. Mevorakh, Tomb 17 (Stern *et al.* 1978, 5-7, Pl. 41: 23-25). Traces of silvering survived on the backs suggesting that they were originally mounted on a perishable (perhaps cloth) backing.

N.B. Mirror fragments are also reported from bedouin graves at El-Lejjun (De Vries 1987, 344).

### Knife Blades

Iron: El-Lejjun (De Vries 1987, 344).

### Glassware

T. el-Hesi (?) (Toombs 1985, 108), El-Lejjun (De Vries 1987, 344; Parker 1988, 142, 146: Fig. 14), T. Sh. 'Ahmed el-'Areyny (Yeivin 1961, 4, Pl. 2: 1-8).

### Ceramics

T. Dor, Site K-60 (Guz-Silberstein & Raveh 1990, 51), T. el-Hesi (Toombs 1985, 106-108, Pls. 82-83, 85, 88b).

### Natural Coloured Stones

T. Khirbet Salih, Burials 2-3 (Wilhelm 1993, 261).

# BIBLIOGRAPHY

A'lam, H.,
1990    'q.v. Camphor', *Encylopedia Iranica* IV, 743-47.

Abbu, N.A.,
1984    'Excavations at Tell Halawa', *Sumer* 40, 122-129.
n.d.    Tell Halawa, 1979 [in Arabic].

Adams, R.McC.,
1989    [Point arising], Discussion of Frank Hole's paper, in Henrickson, E.F. & Thuesen, I., (eds), *Upon this Foundation – The 'Ubaid reconsidered* (Copenhagen: The Carsten Niebuhr Institute of Ancient Near Eastern Studies), 194-195.

Adams, R.McC. & Nissen, H.J.,
1972    The Uruk Countryside: The Natural Setting of Urban Societies (Chicago/London: University of Chicago).

Akkermans, P.A. *et al.*,
1983    'Bouqras revisited; preliminary report on a project in eastern Syria', *Proceedings of the Prehistoric Society* 49, 335-372.

Akkermans, P.M.M.G.,
1989    'Halaf mortuary practices: a survey', in Haex, O.M.C., Curvers, H.H. and Akkermans, P.M.M.G. (eds), *To the Euphrates and Beyond: Archaeological Studies in Honour of Maurits N. van Loon* (Rotterdam: A.A. Balkema), 75-88.

Al-Adami, K.A.,
1968    'Excavations at Tell es-Sawwan (second season)', *Sumer* 24, 57-94.

Al-Soof, B.A.,
1971    'Tell es-Sawwan, fifth season's excavations', *Sumer* 27, 3-7.

Al-Hamadhání, Badí' al-Zamán
1973    *The Maqámát*, tr. Prendergast, W.J. (London: Curzon Press).

Al-Khaysi, M.I.
1986    Morals and Manners in Islam: A Guide to Islamic Adab (Leicester: Islamic Foundation).

Al-Khraysheh, F.,
1986    *Die Personennamen in der nabatäischen Inschriften des Corpus Inscriptionum Semiticarum* (Marburg: Philips-Universität).

Albright, W.F.,
1938    *The Excavations of Tell Beit Mirsim, vol. 2: The Bronze Age*, Annual of the American Schools of Oriental Research, 17 (New Haven: ASOR).
1973    'The historical framework of Palestinian archaeology between 2100 and 1600 BC (EB IV, MB I, MB IIA-B)', *BASOR* 209, 12-18.

Alden, M.J.,
1981    Bronze Age Population Fluctuations in the Argolid from the Evidence of Mycenaean Tombs, SIMA Pocket Book 15 (Göteborg).

Aldred, C.,
1965    Egypt to the End of the Old Kingdom (London: Thames & Hudson).

Alessio, M., L. Allegri, C. Azzi, F. Bella, G. Calderoni, S. Improta & V. Petrone.,
1983    '14C dating of Arslantepe', in Frangipane, M. & Palmeri, A. 1983 (eds), *Perspectives on protourbanization in eastern Anatolia: Arslantepe (Malatya). An interim report on the 1975-1983 campaigns*, Origini 12 (Rome: Università degli studi 'la sapienza'), 575-580.

Algar, H.,
1990    'q.v. Burial. iv. in Islam', *Encyclopedia Iranica* IV, 563-65.

Algaze, G.,
1986    *Mesopotamian Expansion and its Consequences; Informal Empire in the Late Fourth Millennium BC*, Ph.D. thesis (Chicago: University of Chicago).
in press 'Excavations at Titris Höyük; a Small mid-late third millennium urban center in southeastern Anatolia, 1992', *Kazi Sonuçlari Toplentisi*.

Algaze, G. (ed.),
1990    *Town and Country in Southeastern Anatolia*, Oriental Institute Publications 110 (Chicago: Oriental Institute of the University of Chicago).

Algaze, G., Misir, A. & Wilkinson, T.,
1992    'sanliurfa Museum/University of California excavations and surveys at Titris Höyük, 1991: A preliminary report', *Anatolica* 18, 33-60.

Alkim, U.B. & Alkim, H.,
1966    'Excavations at Gedikli (Karahüyük) – first preliminary report', *Türk Tarih Kurumu Belleten* 30, no. 117, 27-57.

Alkim, U.B.,
1962    'Tilmen Höyük Çalişmalari (1958-1960)', *Türk Tarih Kurumu Belleten* 26, 447-499.
1968    *Anatolia I,* Archaeologia Mundi (Geneva: Nagel).
1969    'The Amanus region in Turkey; new light on the historical geography and archaeology', *Archaeology* 22(4), 280-289.

Allgrove, J.,
1976    *The Qashqa'i of Iran* (Manchester: Whitworth Art Gallery).

Alpagut, B.,
1986    'The human skeletal remains from Kurban Höyük (Urfa Province)', *Anatolica* 13, 149-174.

Alster, B.,
1983    'Dilmun, Bahrain, and the alleged paradise in Sumerian myth and literature', in Potts, D.T. (ed.), *Dilmun; New Studies in the Archaeology and Early History of Bahrain* (Berliner Beiträge zum Vorderen Orient 2 (Berlin: Dietrich Reimer Verlag), 39-74.

Alster, B. (ed.),
1980 Death in Mesopotamia; Papers Read at the XXVIe Rencontre Assyriologique Internationale, Mesopotamia 8 (Copenhagen: Akademisk Förlag).

Amiran, R.,
1969 *Ancient Pottery of the Holy Land* (Jerusalem: Massada Press).

Amiran, R. & Haas, N.,
1973 'An Early Bronze Age II tomb at Beth-Yerah (Kinneret)', *Eretz-Israel* 11, 176-193 [in Hebrew].

Andrae, W.,
1922 *Die Archäischen Ischtar-Tempel in Assur*, Wissenschaftliche Veröffentlichungen der Deutschen Orient-Gesellschaft 39 (Leipzig: J.C. Hindrichs'sche Buchhandlung).

Andronicus, M.,
1968 *Totencult*. Archaeologia Homerica 3 (Göttingen: Kapitel W, Vandenhoeck & Ruprecht).

Angel, J.L.,
1944 'Greek teeth; ancient and modern', *Human Biology* 16, 283-297.
1953 'The human remains from Khirokitia', in Dikaios, P.K., *Khirokitia*, Monograph of the Department of Antiquities of the Government of Cyprus 1 (London: Oxford University Press), 416-430.
1961 'Neolithic crania from Sotira', in P. Dikaios, *Sotira* (Philadelphia), 223-229; 250-252,
1972 'Late Bronze Age Cypriotes From Bamboula: The Skeletal Remains' in J.L. Benson, *Bamboula at Kourion, The Necropolis and the Finds* (Pennsylvania).

Angel, L. & Bisel, S.C.,
1986 'Health and stress in Early Bronze Age Anatolia', in Canby, J.V., Porada, E., Ridgway, B.S.& Stech, T. (eds), *Ancient Anatolia; Aspects of Change and Cultural Development. Essays In Honor of Machteld J. Mellink* (Wisconsin Studies in Classics; Wisconsin: University of Wisconsin Press), 12-30.

Anson, D.,
1980a 'Composition and provenance of Rude Style and related wares', *Report of the Department of Antiquities of Cyrprus* 1980, 109-127.
1980b 'The Rude Style in Late Cypriote IIC-III pottery; an analytical typology', *Opuscula Atheniensia* 13, 1-8.

Archi, A.,
1982 'About the organization of the Eblite State', *Studi Eblaiti* 5, 201-220.
1985 'Circulation d'objets en métal precieux de poids standardise à Ebla', in Durand, J.-M. & Kupper, J.-R. (eds), *Miscellanea Babylonica; Melanges à Maurice Birot* (Paris:Editions Récherche), 25-34.

Archi, A., Pecorella, P.E. & Salvini, M.,
1971 *Gaziantep e la sua Regione; uno Studio Storico e Topografico degli Insediamenti Preclassici,* Incunabula Graeca 48 (Rome: Edizioni dell'Ateneo).

Arensburg, B.,
1970a 'The Human Remains from 'Ein el-Jarba', *BASOR* 197, 49-52.
1977 'New Upper Palaeolithic human remains from Israel', *Eretz-Israel* 13, 208-215.

Arensburg, B. & Bar-Yosef, O.,
1973 'Human remains from Ein Gev I, Jordan Valley, Israel', *Paléorient* 1(2), 201-206.

Arensburg, B. & Hershkovitz, I.,
1988 'Nahal Hemar Cave, Neolithic human remains', *'Atiqot* 18, 50-58.
1989 'Artificial skull 'treatment' in the PPNB period; Nahal Hemar', in I. Hershkovitz (ed.), *People and Culture in Change,* BAR International Series 508 (Oxford: BAR), 115-131.

Arensburg, B. & Nathan, H.,
1980 'A Mousterian third cervical vertebra from Hayonim Cave, Israel', *Journal of Human Evolution* 9, 193-195.

Arensburg, B., Bar-Yosef, O., Belfer-Cohen, A. & Rak, Y.,
1990 'Mousterian and Aurignacian human remains from Hayonim Cave, Israel', *Paléorient* 16(1), 107-109.

Arensburg, B., Belfer-Cohen, A. & Schepartz, L.A.,
n.d. 'Cultural continuities in the Levant from the Epipaleolithic through the Neolithic', in Pap, I. (ed.), Cultural and behavioral continuities in the Levant: Proceedings of the third symposium on Upper Paleolithic and Neolithic populations of Europe and the Mediterranean Basin, Budapest September 3-8, 1990.

Arensburg, B., Smith, P. & Yakar, R.,
1978 'The human remains from Abou Gosh', in Lechevallier, M. (ed.), *Abou Gosh et Beisamoun* (Paris: Association Paléorient), 95-105.

Arkell, A.J.,
1937 'Hebron beads in Darfur', *Sudan Notes & Records* 20, 300-305.

Arkwright, W.,
1911 'Penalties in Lycian epitaphs of Hellenistic and Roman times', *Journal of Hellenic Studies* 31, 269-275.

Armitage, P.L. & Clutton-Brock, J.,
1980 *An Investigation of the Mummified Cats held by the British Museum (Natural History),* Museum Applied Science Centre for Archaeology Journal, Mummification Supplement 1(6) (Philadelphia: University of Pennsylvania).

Armstrong, J.A.,
1989 The Archaeology of Nippur from the Decline of the Kassite Kingdom until the Rise of the Neo-Babylonian Empire, PhD. thesis (Chicago: University of Chicago).

Artamanov, M.I.,
1965 'Frozen tombs of the Sythians', *Scientific American* 212(5), 101-109.

Ashe, G.,
1971 *Man, Myth and Magic*, Vol. 84, 2353-.

Ashton, L.,
1934 'China and Egypt', Transactions of the Oriental Ceramic Society 1933-1934.

Assaf, A.A.,
1967 'Der Freidhof von Yabrud', *Les Annales Archéologiques Arabes Syriennes* 17, 55-68.

Astour, M.C.,
1967 *Hellenosemitica*, 2nd ed. (Leiden: E.J. Brill).
1980 'The nether world and its denizens at Ugarit', in B. Alster (ed.), 227-238.
1981 'Ugarit and the great powers', in Young, G.D. (ed.), *Ugarit in Retrospect; Fifty Years of Ugarit and Ugaritic* (Winona Lake: Eisenbrauns), 3-30.

Athanassiou, H.,
1977 Rasm et-Tanjara; a Recently Discovered Syrian Tell in the Ghab, part 1: Inventory of the Chance Finds, PhD thesis (University of Missouri-Columbia).

Atiya, N.,
1987 Khul-Khaal. Five Egyptian Women tell their Stories (Cairo: American University in Cairo).

Avissar, M.,
1987 'The Medieval to Persian Periods: architecture, stratigraphy and finds', in Ben-Tor, A., Portugali, Y., Avissar, M., Baruch, U. & Hunt, M. 1987, *Tell Qiri. A Village in the Jezreel Valley. Report of the Archaeological Excavations 1975-1977*, 7-26, Qedem 24 (Jerusalem: Institute of Archaeology).

Avner, U.,
1989 'Eilat – burial cairns', *Hadashot Archaologiyot* 94, 64-65. [in Hebrew].
1991 'Eilat', American Journal of Archaeology 95, 496-497.

Axmacher, B. & Hjortsjö, C-H.,
1958 Examen anthropologique des crânes constituant le matériel préhistorique mis à jour à la suite de fouilles effectuées par les archéologues français à Iskender, Chypre, *Lund Universitets Årsskrift*, N.F. Avd.2, Bd. 54 Nr.4 (Lund: Lund Universitets).
1959 Examen anthropologique des crânes constituant le matériel protohistyorique exhumé à Bamboula Kourion, Chypre, *Lund Universitets Årsskrift*, N.F. Avd.2, Bd. 55 Nr.2 (Lund: Lund Universitets).

Bachelot, L. *et al.*,
1990 *Tell Mohammed Diyab. Campagnes 1987 et 1988*, Supplément à N.A.B.U 1 (Paris: Société pour l'Etude du Proche-Orient Ancien).

Badaljan, R., Edens, C., Kohl, P. & Armen, T.,
1992 'Archaeological investigations at Horom in the Shirak plain of north-western Armenia, 1990', *Iran* 30, 31-48.

Badaljan, R.S. *et al.*,
1993 'Preliminary report on the 1992 excavations at Horom, Armenia', *Iran* 31, 1-24.

Baker, S.,
1879 Cyprus as I Saw it in 1879 (London).

Baldensperger, P.J.,
1893 'Peasant Folklore of Palestine', *Palestine Exploration Fund Quarterly Statement* 1893 (July), 203-219.

Balkan, K.,
1964 [Report on Giriktepe], *Ataturk Konferanslari* 1, 239.

Ball, W. & Gill, S.,
in press 'Excavations at Seh Qubba', in Ball, W. (ed.), Ancient Settlements in the Zummar Region. Excavations carried out in the Saddam Dam Salvage Project by the British Archaeological Expedition to Iraq, vol. 1, British School of Archaeology in Iraq Reports (London: Aris & Phillips).

Ball, W., Tucker, D. & Wilkinson, T.J.,
1989 'The Tell al-Hawa Project: Archaeological Investigations in the North Jazira 1986-87', *Iraq* 51, 1-66.

Balty, J.C.,
1983 'Architecture et société à Pétra et Hégra', in *Architecture et Société; Actes du Colloque du Rome 1980* (Rome), 303-324.

Bar Adon, P.,
1980 *The Cave of the Treasure* (Jerusalem: Israel Exploration Society).

Bar-Yosef, O.,
1973 'Nahal Ein Gev I, preliminary report', *Mitekufat Haeven* 11, 1-7.
1978 'Man – an outline of the prehistory of the Kinneret area "C"', in Serruya, C. (ed.), *Monographiae Biologicae* 32 (The Hague), 447-464.
1983 'The Natufian of the southern Levant', in Smith, P.E.L. & Mortensen, P. (eds), *The Hilly Flanks and Beyond* (Chicago: Chicago University Press), 11-42.

Bar-Yosef, O. & Alon, D. (eds),
1988 *Nahal Hemar Cave*, 'Atiqot 18; English Series.

Bar-Yosef, O. & Belfer-Cohen, A.,
1988 'The Early Upper Palaeolithic in Levantine caves', in Hoffecker, J.F. & Wolf, C.A. (eds), *The Early Upper Palaeolithic, Evidence from Europe and the Near East*, BAR International Series 437 (Oxford: BAR), 23-41.
1989 'The origins of sedentism and farming communities in the Levant', *Journal of World Prehistory* 3(4), 447-498.

Bar-Yosef, O., Laville, H., Meignen, L., Tillier, A-M., Vandermeersch, B., Arensburg, B., Belfer-Cohen, A., Goldberg, P., Rak, Y. & Tchernov, E.,
1988 'La sepulture neandertalienne de Kebara (unite XII)', in O. Bar-Yosef (ed.), *L'Homme de Neandertal*, vol. 5, La Pensee (Liege: ERAUL), 17-24.

Bar-Yosef, O. & Valla, F.R. (eds),
1991 *The Natufian Culture in the Levant*, International Monographs in Prehistory 1 (Michigan: Ann Arbor).

Bar-Yosef, O., Vandermeersch, B., Arensburg, B., Belfer-Cohen, A., Goldberg, P., Laville, H., Meignen, L., Rak, Y., Speth, J.D., Tchernov, E., Tillier, A-M. & Weiner, S.,
1992 'The excavations in Kebara Cave, Mt Carmel', *Current Anthropology* 33(5), 497-534, 543-550.

Bar-Yosef, O., Vandermeersch B., Arensburg, B., Goldberg, P., Laville, H., Meignen, L., Rak, Y., Tchernov, E. & Tillier, A.-M.,
1986 'New data on the origin of modern man in the Levant', *Current Anthropology* 27(1), 63-64.

Baramki, D.C.,
1958 'A Late Bronze Age Tomb at Sarafend, Ancient Sarepta', *Berytus* 12 (2), 129-142.
1973 'The impact of the Mycenaeans on ancient Phoenecia', in *Acts of the International Archaeological Symposium 'The Mycenaeans in the Eastern Mediterranean (1972)* (Nicosia: Department of Antiquities), 192-197.

Bard, K.A.,
1989 'The Evolution of Social Complexity in Predynastic Egypt: An Analysis of the Naqada Cemeteries', *Journal of Mediteranean Archaeology* 2/2, 223-248.

Barnett, R.D.,
1950 'The excavations of the British Museum at Toprakkale near Van', *Iraq* 12, 1-43.
1954 'The excavations of the British Museum at Toprak Kale, near Van – addenda', *Iraq* 16, 3-22.
1963 'The Urartian cemetery at Igdyr', *Anatolian Studies* 13, 153-198.
1975 'The Sea Peoples', *CAH* 3rd ed. (Cambridge: Cambridge University Press), vol. 2(2), 359-378.

Barrelet, M.-Th.,
1980 "Les pratiques funéraires de l'Iraq ancien et l'archéologie, état de la question et essai de prospective", *Akkadica* 16, 2-27.

Barrett, J.C.,
1987 'The Glastonbury Lake Village; models and source', *Archaeological Journal* 144, 409-423.
1988 'The living, the dead and the ancestors; Neolithic and early Bronze Age mortuary practices', in Barrett, J.C. & Kinnes, I.A. (eds) 1988, *The Archaeology of Context in the Neolithic and Bronze Age; Recent Trends* (Sheffield: John R. Collis), 30-41.

1991 'Review of B.G. Trigger, A History of Archaeological Thought and H. Kragh, An Introduction to the Historiography of Science', Proceedings of the Prehistoric Society 57(2), 211-212.

Barrett, J.C., Bradley, R. & Green, M.,
1991 Landscape, Monuments and Society; the Prehistory of Cranborne Chase (Cambridge: Cambridge University Press).

Barth, F.,
1980 Nomads of South Persia: The Basseri Tribe of the Khamseh Confederacy (Oslo: Universitetsförlag).

Bauer, J.,
1989 'Der "schlimme Tod" in Mesopotamien', in Behrens, H., Loding, D. & Roth, M.T. (eds), *Dumu-e₂-dub-ba-a; Studies in Honor of Ake W. Sjöberg* (Philadelphia: The University Museum, Samuel Noah Kramer Fund), 21-27.

Baxevani, P.A.,
1994 The Evolution of Social Complexity in the Early Bronze Age East Mediterranean: A Cross-Cultural Analysis of Tomb Groups from the Southern Levant, Cyprus and Crete, Ph.D. Thesis (Edinburgh: University of Edinburgh).

Bayliss, M.,
1973 'The cult of dead kin in Assyria and Babylonia', *Iraq* 35, 115-125.

Bean, G.E.,
1978 *Lycian Turkey; an Archaeological Guide* (London: Ernest Benn).
1979 Turkey's Southern Shore; an Archaeological Guide, 2nd ed. (London: Ernest Benn).

Beaufort, F.,
1818 Karamania, or a Brief Description of the South Coast of Asia Minor and the Remains of Antiquity, 2nd ed. (London: R. Hunter).

Beck, P.,
1985 'The Middle Bronze Age IIA pottery from Aphek, 1972-1984; first summary', *Tel Aviv* 12, 181-203.

Beeley, J.G. & Lunt, D.A.,
1980 'The nature of the biochemical changes in softened dentine from archaeological sites', *Journal of Archaeological Science* 7, 371-377.

Beeston, A.F.L.,
1979 'Nemara and Faw', Bulletin of the School of Oriental and African Studies 42, 1-6.

Behm-Blancke, M. R. *et al.*,
1984 'Hassek Höyük; vorläufiger Bericht über die Ausgrabungen in den Jahren 1981-1983', *Istanbuler Mitteilungen* 34, 31-150.

Behrens, H.,
1978 *Enlil und Ninlil; ein Sumerischer Mythos aus Nippur*, Studia Pohl: Series Maior 8 (Rome: Biblical Institute Press).

Belfer-Cohen, A.,
1988a   *The Natufian Settlement at Hayonim Cave; a Hunter-Gatherer Band on the Threshold of Agriculture*, PhD thesis (Jerusalem: Hebrew University).
1988b   'The Natufian graveyard in Hayonim Cave', *Paléorient* 14(2), 297-308.
1989    'The Natufian issue; a suggestion', in Bar-Yosef, O. &. Vandermeersch, B. (eds), *Investigations in South Levantine Prehistory*, BAR International Series 497 (Oxford: BAR), 297-307.
1991a   'The Natufian in the Levant', *Annual Review of Anthropology* 20, 167-186.
1991b   'Art items from layer B, Hayonim Cave; a case study of art in a Natufian context', in Bar-Yosef & Valla (eds) 1991, 569-588.

Belfer-Cohen, A. & Hovers, E.,
1992    'In the eye of the beholder; Mousterian and Natufian burials in the Levant', *Current Anthropology* 33(4), 463-471.

Belfer-Cohen, A., Arensburg., B., Bar-Yosef, O. & Gopher, A.,
1990    'Human remains from Netiv Hagdud – a PPNA site in the Jordan Valley', *Mitekufat Haeven* 23, 79-85.

Belfer-Cohen, A., Schepartz, L.A. & Arensburg, B.,
1991    'New biological data for the Natufian populations in Israel', in Bar-Yosef , O. & Valla, F. R. (eds) 1991, 411-424.
in press Cultural behavioral continuities in the Levant, in Pap I. (ed.), Upper Palaeolithic, Mesolithic and Neolithic Populations of Europe and the Mediterranean Basin (Budapest).

Bell, G.,
1911    *Amurath to Amurath* (London: John Murray).

Belli, O.,
1986    'Untersuchungen zur Eisenmetallurgie in Hubuskia', *Anadolu Arastirmalari* 10, 271-299.
1987    'Demir Çagda dogu Anadolu bolgesinde demir metalurjisi / Ironworking in eastern Anatolia in the Iron Age', in Çilingiroglu, A. & French, D.H. (eds), *Anatolian Iron Ages; Proceedings of the First Anatolian Iron Ages Symposium*, Oxbow Monographs 13 (Oxford: Oxbow), 89-107.

Ben-Arieh, S. & Edelstein, G.,
1977    'Tombs Near the Persian Garden', *'Atiqot* 12 (English ser.), 1-86.

Ben-Tor, A.,
1992b   'The Early Bronze Age', in Ben-Tor (ed.) 1992a, 81-125.

Ben-Tor, A., (ed.),
1992a   *The Archaeology of Ancient Israel* (New Haven: Yale University Press).

Bennett, K.A.,
1965    'The etiology and genetics of wormian bones', *American Journal of Physical Anthropology* 23, 255-260.

Benson, J.L.,
1972    *Bamboula at Kourion; the Necropolis and Finds* (Philadelphia: University of Pennsylvania Press).
1973    *The Necropolis of Kaloriziki*, Studies in Mediterranean Archaeology 36 (Göteborg: Paul Åströms Förlag).

Bent, J.T.,
1890    'The Bahrain islands in the Persian Gulf', *Proceedings of the Royal Geographical* Society 12, 1-18.

Bent, J.T. & Bent, Mrs,
1900    *Southern Arabia* (London: Smith, Elder & Co).

Bentley, G.,
1987    Kinship and Social Structure at Early Bronze Age IA Bab edh Dhra', Jordan: A Bioarchaeological Analysis of the Mortuary and Dental Data, Ph.D thesis, (Chicago: University of Chicago).

Berg, S., Rolle, R. & Seemann, H.,
1981    Der Archäologie und der Tod. Archäologie und Gerichtsmedizin (Munich & Lucerne: C.J. Bucher).

Bergamini, G.,
1984    'The excavations in Tell Yelkhi', *Sumer* 40, 224-244.
1985    'Tell Yelkhi', in Quarantelli, E. (ed.) 1985, 41-56.

Bergman, C.A. & Stringer, C.B.,
1989    'Fifty years after; Egbert, an early Upper Palaeolithic juvenile from Ksar Akil, Lebanon', *Paléorient* 15(2), 99-111.

Betlyon, J.W.,
1985    'Coins from the 1982 Excavations at Lejjun and Qasr Bshir', in Rast, W.E. (ed.), *Preliminary Reports of ASOR-Sponsored Excavations 1981-83* (Baltimore: ASOR), 25-34.
1987    'Coins, Commerce, and Politics: Coins from the *"Limes Arabicus"* Project, 1976-1985', in Parker, S.T. (ed.), *The Roman Frontier in Central Jordan. Interim Report on the Limes Arabicus Project, 1980-1985*, II, BAR International Series 340 (Oxford: BAR), 655-689.

Betts, A.,
1989    'The Edinburgh University/B.I.A.A.H. expedition to Qasr Burqu'/Ruweishid', *Palestine Exploration Quarterly* 121 (January-June), 85-86.

Betz, H.D. (ed.),
1986    The Greek Magical Papyri in Translation, including the Demotic Spells, vol. 1: Texts (Chicago: University of Chicago Press).

Bibby, T.G.,
1969    *Looking for Dilmun* (Harmondsworth: Penguin).
1985    '"The Land of Dilmun in holy..."', *Dilmun* 12 (1984-85), 3-4.
1986    '"The land of Dilmun in holy..."', in Sh.H.A Al Khalifa & M. Rice (eds), *Bahrain Trough the Ages; the Archaeology* (London: KPI), 192-194.

Bienert, H.-D.,
1991 'Skull cult in the prehistoric Near East', *Journal of Prehistoric Religion* 5, 9-23.

Bienkowski, P.A.,
1982 'Some remarks on the practice of cremation in the Levant', *Levant* 14, 80-89.
1989 'The division of the MB IIB-C in Palestine', *Levant* 21, 169-176.

Bietak, M.,
1968 'Vorläufiger Bericht über die erst und zweite Kampagne der Österreichisches Ausgrabungen auf Tell el-Dab'a in Ostdelta Ägypten, 1966, 1967', *Mitteilungen des Deutschen Archäologischen Institüt Abteilungen Kairo* 23, 79-114.
1979 'Avaris and Piramesse: archaeological exploration in the Eastern Nile Delta', *Proceedings of the British Academy* 65, 225-290.
1984 'Problems of Middle Bronze Age chronology; new evidence from Egypt', *American Journal of Archaeology* 88, 471-485.
1991 'Egypt and Canaan during the Middle Bronze Age', *BASOR* 281, 27-72.
1992 'Der Friedhof in einem Palastgarten aus der Zeit des späten mittleren Reiches und andere Forschunsergebnisse aus dem ostlichen Nildelta (Tell el-Dab'a 1984-1987)', *Ägypten und Levänte* 2, 47-75.

Bikai, P.M.,
1983 'Appendix II; the imports from the East', in V. Karageorghis (ed.) 1983, 396-406.
1987a *The Phoenician pottery of Cyprus* (Nicosia: The Leventis Foundation).
1987b 'Trade networks in the Early Iron Age; the Phoenicians at Palaepaphos', in Rupp, D. (ed.) 1987, *Western Cyprus – Connections; an Archaeological Symposium*, Studies in Mediterranean Archaeology 77 (Göteborg: Paul Åströms Förlag), 125-128.

Binford, L.R.,
1971 'Mortuary practices: their study and potential', in Brown, J.A. (ed.) 1971, 6-29

Binford, S.,
1966 'Me'arat Shovakh (Mughaert esh-Shubabaiq)', *Israel Exploration Journal* 16, 18-32.
1968 'A structural comparison of disposal of the dead in the Mousterian and the Upper Palaeolithic', *Southwestern Journal of Anthropology* 24, 139-154.

Biran, A.,
1971 'Laish-Dan – secrets of a Canaanite city and an Israelite city', *Qadmoniot* 4/1(13), 2-11 [in Hebrew].
1974 'Tel Dan', *Biblical Archaeologist* 37, 26-51.
1980 'Tel Dan five years later', *Biblical Archaeologist* 43, 168-182.
1981 'The discovery of the Middle Bronze Age gate at Dan', *Biblical Archaeologist* 44, 139-144.
1986 'The dancer from Dan, the empty tomb and the altar room', *Israel Exploration Journal* 36, 168-187.
1994 *Biblical Dan* (Jerusalem: Israel Exploration Society/Hebrew Union College – Jewish Institute of Religion).

Bird, I.L.,
1988 *Journeys in Persia and Kurdistan*, reprint (London: Virago).

Bittel, K., Herre, W., Otten, H., Röhrs, M. & Schaeuble, J.,
1958 Boǧazköy-Hattusa, vol. 2: Die hethitischer Grabfunde von Osmankavasi (Berlin: Gebr. Mann).

Bittel, K., Boessneck, J., Damm, B., Güterbock, H.G., Hauptmann, H., Naumann, R. & Schirmer, W.,
1975 Boǧazköy-Hattusa, vol. 9: Das hethitische Felsheiligtum Yazilikaya (Berlin: Gebr. Mann).

Bittel, K., Otten, H., Röhrs, M. & Schaeuble, J.,
1958 Die hethitischen Grabfunde von Osmankayasi (Berlin: Gebr. Mann).

Blackman, W.S.,
1968 The Fellahin of Upper Egypt. Their Religious, Social and Industrial Life with Special Reference to Survivals from Ancient Times (London: Frank Cass).

Blegen, C.W.,
1937 *Prosymna. The Helladic Settlement Preceding the Argive Heraeum* (Cambridge: Cambridge University Press).
1954 'An early tholos tomb in western Messenia', *Hesperia* 23, 158-162.

Blegen, C.W., Caskey, J.L. & Rawson, M.,
1953 *Troy, vol. 3: The Sixth Settlement* (Princeton: Princeton University Press).

Bloch, M.,
1971 *Placing the Dead; Tombs, Ancestral Villages and Kinship Organization in Madagascar.* (London & New York: Seminar Press).
1982 'Death, women and power', in Bloch, M. and Parry, J. (eds) 1982, 211-230.

Bloch, M. & Parry, J. (eds),
1982 *Death and the Regeneration of Life* (Cambridge: Cambridge University Press).

Bloch-Smith, E.,
1992 Judahite Burial Practices and Beliefs about the Dead (Sheffield: Sheffield Academic Press).

Boddington, A., A.N. Garland & R.C. Janaway,
1987 Death, Decay and Reconstruction: Approaches to Archaeology and Forensic Science (Manchester).

Boehmer, R.M.,
1983 'Dolche vom Tell Subedi (Hamrin)', *Baghdader Mitteilungen* 14, 101-108.
1984 'Uruk: Funde im Zusammenhang mit Tierknochen', *Baghdader Mitteilungen* 15, 191-196.
1987 Uruk, Kampagne 38. 1985 Grabungen in J-K/23 und H/24-25, Ausgrabungen in Uruk-Warka,

Endberichte Band 1 (Mainz-am-Rhein:Phillip von Zabern).

Boehmer, R.M. & Dammer, H-W.,
1985 *Tell Imlihye, Tell Zubeidi, Tell Abbas*, Baghdader Forschungen 7 (Mainz am Rhein: Phillip von Zabern).

Bolt, D. & Green, A.,
in press 'The burial of the dead', in Weiss, H. (ed.), *The Origins of North Mesopotamian Civilization; Ninevite 5 Chronology, Economy, Society* (New Haven: Yale University Press).

Bonechi, M.,
1991 'Onomastica dei testi di Ebla; nomi propri come fossili-guida?', *Studi Epigrafici e Liguistici sul Vicino Oriente Antico* 8, 59-79.

Bonhams
1994 *Bonhams Catalogue* 5th July 1994 (London: Bonhams).

Borchhardt, J.,
1990 'Kunst in Lykien', in Jacobek, R. & Dinstl, A. (eds) 1990, 45-49.

Bordreuil, P. & Pardee, D.,
1982 'Le rituel funéraire ougaritique RS 34.126', *Syria* 54, 121-128.
1990 'Le papyrus du marzea''', *Semitica* 34, *Hommages à Maurice Sznycer,* 49-69.
1991 'Les textes ougaritiques', in P. Bordreuil (ed.), *Une bibliothèque au Sud de la Ville,* Ras Shamra Ougarit VII (Paris: Éditions Recherche sur les Civilisations), 139-180.

Bottéro, J.,
1980 'La mythologie de la mort en Mesopotamie ancienne', in Alster, B. (ed.) 1980, 25-52.
1982 'Les inscriptions cunéiformes funéraires', in Gnoli, Gh. & Vernant, J.-P. (eds), *La Mort; les Morts dans les Sociétés Anciennes,* Éditions de la Maison des Sciences de l'Homme (Cambridge & Paris: Cambridge University Press), 373-406.
1983 'Les mort et l'au-dela; dans les rituels en accadien contre l'action des "revenants"', *Zeitschrift für Assyriologie* 73(2), 153-202.

Bourke, S.J.
1992 'First preliminary report on the excavation and study of human remains', in McNicoll, A.W., Edwards, P.C., Hanbury-Tenison, J.B., Potts, T.F., Smith, R.H., Walmsley, A & Watson, P. (eds), *Pella in Jordan 2. The Second interim report of the Joint University of Sydney and College of Wooster excavations at Pella 1982-1985,* Mediterranean Archaeology Supplement 2 (Sydney: University of Sydney), 215-26.
1993 'Review article: the field I caves at Gezer', *Palestine Exploration Quarterly* 125, 75-77.

Bousquet, J.,
1975 'Arbinas, fils de Gergis, dynaste de Xanthos', *Comptes Rendus de l'Académie des Inscriptions,* 138-148.

Bowman, S.G.E. & Ambers, J.C.,
1989 'Radiocarbon dates for Tell Brak, 1987', *Iraq* 51, 213-215.

Boyd, B.,
1992 'The transformation of knowledge; late Epipalaeolithic (Natufian) mortuary practices at Hayonim, western Galilee', *Archaeological Review from Cambridge* 11(1), 19-38.

Brabant, H.,
1969 'Observations sur les dents des populations megalithiques d'Europe occidentale', *Bulletin du Groupement International pour la Recherche Scientifique en Stomatologie* 12, 429-460.
1971 'Etude des dents trouvees dans les cimetieres neolithiques de Barmaz I, Barmaz II et Chamblandes (Valais et Vaud, Suisse)', *Archives Suisses d'Anthropologie generale* 34, 1-34.

Bradley, R.,
1990 *The Passage of Arms* (Cambridge: Cambridge University Press).

Braidwood, R.J. & Braidwood, L.,
1960 *Excavations in the Plain of Antioch, vol. 1: The Earlier Assemblages, Phases A-J,* Oriental Institute Publications 61 (Chicago: University of Chicago Press).

Braun-Holzinger, E.A.,
1988 'Bronze Objects from Babylonia', in Curtis, J. (ed.) 1988, 119-134.

Breasted, J.H.,
1922 'The Oriental Institute of The University of Chicago. A beginning and a problem', *Oriental Institute Communications* 1.

Breniquet, C.,
1987 'Nouvelle Hypothèse sur la Disparition de la Culture de Halaf', 231-242, in Huot, J.-L. (ed.), *Préhistoire de la Mesopotamie,* (Paris: CNRS).
1990 *La Disparition de la Culture de Halaf ou les Origines de la Culture d'Obeid dans le Nord de la Mesopotamie,* PhD thesis (Paris).
1991 'Tell es-Sawwan: réalitès et problèmes', *Iraq* 53, 75-90.

Bright, L.,
1994 'A Possible Case for the Practice of Abandonment during the Late Cypriot and Cypro-Geometric Periods', in C. Morris (ed) *Klados: Essays in Honour of Professor J.N. Coldstream,* BICS 63, 35-.

Brook, A.H.,
1984 'A unifying aetiological explanation for anomalies of human tooth number and size', *Archs Oral Biol.* 29, 373-378.

Broome, E.C.,
1940 'Dolmens of Palestine and Transjordania', *Journal of Biblical Literature* 59, 479-497.

Broshi, M. & Gophna, R.,
1986 'Middle Bronze Age II Palestine; its settlement and population', *BASOR* 261, 73-90.

Brothwell, D.R.,
1963b   The Macroscopic Dental Pathology of some
        Earlier Human Populations. in Brothwell (ed.)
        1963a, 271-288.
1972    *Digging Up Bones.* 2nd ed. (London: British
        Museum – Natural History).

Brothwell, D.R., (ed.),
1963a   *Dental Anthropology* (Oxford: Pergamon).

Brown, J.A.,
1981    'The search for rank in prehistoric burials', in
        Chapman, R., Kinnes, I. and Randsborg, K. (eds)
        1981, 25-38.

Brown, J.A. (ed.),
1971    *Approaches to the Social Dimensions of mortuary
        practices,* Memoir 25 (Washington DC: Society
        for American Archaeology).

Brown, P.,
1981    'Artificial cranial deformation: a component in
        the variation in Pleistocene Australian
        Aboriginal crania', *Archaeoogy Oceania* 16, 156-
        167.

Browne, C.D.,
1992    'Palaeopathological survey of the human remains
        from Pella', in McNicoll, A.W., Edwards, P.C.,
        Hanbury-Tenison, J.B., Potts, T.F., Smith, R.H.,
        Walmsley, A & Watson, P. (eds), *Pella in Jordan
        2. The Second interim report of the Joint University
        of Sydney and College of Wooster excavations at
        Pella 1982-1985,* Mediterranean Archaeology
        Supplement 25 (Sydney: University of Sydney),
        215-26.

Browne, E.G.,
1970    A Year amongst the Persians. Impressions as to
        the Life, Character, & Thought of the People of
        Persia Received during Twelve Months
        Residence in that Country in the Years 1887-
        1888, reprint (London: Adam & Charles Black).

Brunner, T.F.,
1973    'Marijuana in ancient Rome and Greece? The
        literary evidence', *Bulletin of the History of
        Medicine* 47, 344-355.

Brunton, G. & Caton Thompson, G.,
1928    *The Badarian Civilisation* (London: British School
        of Archaeology in Egypt).

Bryce, T.R.,
1981    'Disciplinary agents in the sepulchral
        inscriptions of Lycia', *Anatolian Studies* 31, 81-93.
1986    *The Lycians; a Study of Lycian History and
        Civilisation to the Conquest of Alexander the Great,
        vol. 1: The Lycians in Literary and Epigraphic
        Sources* (Copenhagen: Museum Tusculanum).
1991    ' Tombs and the social hierarchy in ancient
        Lycia', *Altorientalische Forschungen* 18, 73-85.

Buchholz, H.G.,
1979    'Bronzen Schaftrohäxte aus Tamassos und
        Umgebung', in *Studies presented to Porphyrios
        Dikaios* (Nicosia: Lions Club), 76-88.

Büchner, W.,
1937    'Probleme der homerischen Nekyia', *Hermes* 72,
        104-122.

Buckingham, J.S.,
1825    *Travels among the Arab Tribes* (London: Longman
        & Co)
1827    Travels in Mesopotamia. Including a journey
        from Aleppo, across the Euphrates to Orfah, (the
        Ur of the Chaldees,) through the plains of the
        Turcomans, to Diarbekr, in Asia Minor; from
        there to Mardin, on the borders of the great
        desert, and by the Tigris to Mousul and Bagdad:
        with researches on the ruins of Babylon,
        Nineveh, Arbela, Ctesiphon, and Seleucia
        (London: Henry Colburn

Budge, E.A.W.,
1930    *Amulets and Superstitions* (London: Oxford
        University Press).

Bunimovitz, S.,
1992    'The Middle Bronze Age fortifications in
        Palestine as a social phenomenon', *Tel Aviv* 19,
        221-234.

Burder, S.,
1847    *Oriental customs,.* fourth edition (London:
        Longman)

Burney, C.A.,
1966    'A first season of excavations at the Urartian
        citadel of Kayalidere', *Anatolian Studies* 16, 55-
        111.
1989    'Hurrians and Proto-indo-europeans; the ethnic
        context of the early Trans-Caucasian culture', in
        Emre, K., Hrouda, B., Mellink, M. & Özgüç, N.
        (eds), *Anatolia and the Ancient Near East. Studies
        in Honor of Tashin Özgüç* (Ankara: Türk Kurumu
        Basimevi), 45-51.
1990    'The Indo-european impact on the Hurrian
        world', in Markey, T.L. & Greppin, J. (eds), *When
        Worlds Collide,* 45-49.
1993    'The god Haldi and the Urartian state', in
        Mellink, M.J., Porada, E. & Özgüç, T. (eds),
        *Aspects of Art and Iconography; Anatolia and its
        Neighbours – Studies in Honor of Nimet Özgüç*
        (Ankara: Türk Tarik Kurumu Basimevi), 107-
        110.

Burney, C.A. & Lang, D.M.,
1971    The Peoples of the Hills; Ancient Ararat and
        Caucasus (London: Weidenfeld and Nicholson).

Burrows, E.,
1928    *Tilmun, Bahrain, Paradise* (Rome: Sumptibus
        Pontificii Instuti Biblici).

Burton-Page, J.,
1986    'Muslim graves of the "Lesser Tradition": Gilgit,
        Punial, Swat, Yusufzai', *Journal of the Royal
        Asiatic Society* 1986(2), 249-54.

Butcher, E.L.,
n.d.    *Things Seen in Egypt* (London: Seeley, Service &
        Co).

Buxton, L.H.D,
1920    'The anthropology of Cyprus', Journal of the
        Royal Anthropological Institute of Great Britain
        and Ireland 1, 183-235.

Byrd, B.,
1989    'The Natufian; settlement variability and
        economic adaptations in the Levant at the end of
        the Pleistocene', *Journal of World Prehistory* 3(2),
        159-198.
1992    in Gebauer & Price (eds) 1992.

Callot, O.,
1983    *Une Maison à Ougarit, Étude d'Architecture
        Domestique*, Ras Shamra Ougarit I (Paris: Édition
        Recherche sur les Civilisations).
1985    'Rôle et méthodes des "constructeurs de
        maisons" à Ras Shamra-Ougarit', in *Le Dessin
        d'Architecture dans les Sociétés Antiques* (Colloque
        Strasbourg 1984), Travaux du CRPOGA 8
        (Strasbourg), 19-28.
1986    'La région nord du Palais Royal d'Ougarit',
        *Comptes Rendus de l'Académie des Inscriptions et
        Belles Lettres*, 735-755.
1994    *La Tranchée "Ville Sud"*, Ras Shamra Ougarit X
        (Paris: Édition Recherche sur les Civilisations ).

Callot, O. & Yon, M.,
n.d.    'L'habitat à Ougarit à la fin du Bronze Récent',
        Colloque *La Maison Syrienne* (Damas: IFAPO).

Calvet, Y.,
1980    'Sur certaines rites funéraires à Salamine de
        Chypre', in *Salamine de Chypre: Histoire et
        Archéologie* (Paris: C.N.R.S.), 115-121.
1981    'Installations hydrauliques d'Ougarit', in Métral,
        J. et Sanlaville, P. (eds), *L'Homme et l'Eau en
        Méditerranée et au Proche Orient* I (Lyon: La
        Maison de l'Orient), 33-48.
1989    'La maîtrise de l'eau à Ougarit', Comptes Rendus
        de l'Académie des Inscriptions et Belles Lettres,
        308-326.

Calvet, Y. & Geyer, B.,
1987    'L'eau dans l'habitat', *RSO* III, in M. Yon (ed.),
        *Le Centre de la Ville. 38ᵉ-44ᵉ campagnes (1978-
        1984)* (Paris: Éditions Recherche sur les
        Civilisations), 129-156.

Campbell, E.F. & Wright, G.E.,
1969    'Tribal league shrines in Amman and Shechem',
        *Biblical Archaeologist* 32, 104-16.

Campbell, S.,
1992    Culture, Chronology and Change in the Late
        Neolithic of North Mesopotamia, Ph.D. thesis
        (Edinburgh: University of Edinburgh).

Canaan, T.,
1927    *Mohammedan Saints and Sanctuaries in Palestine*,
        Oriental Religion Series 5 (London: Luzac).

Canby, J. V.,
1979    *Jewelery: Ancient to Modern* (New York: The
        Viking Press/ The Walters Art Gallery).

Cantineau, J.,
1933    'Tadmorea', *Syria* 14, 169-202.

Caquot, A.,
1981    'Rephaïm', in *Supplément au Dictionnaire de la
        Bible*, fasc. 55, col. 344-357.

Caquot, A., Sznycer, M. & Herdner, A.,
1974    Textes Ougaritiques, I. Mythes et Légendes
        (Paris: Les Éditions du Cerf ).

Carmi, I. & Segal, D.,
1992    'Rehovot radiocarbon measurements IV',
        *Radiocarbon* 34(1), 115-132.

Carr, H.G.,
1960    'Some dental characteristics of the Middle
        Minoans', *Man* 60, 119.

Carter, E.,
1978    'Suse "Ville Royale', *Paléorient* 4, 197-211.
1980    'Excavations in the Ville Royale I at Susa; the
        third millennium BC occupation', *Délégation
        Archéologique Français en Iran* 11, 11-134.

Carter, E. & Stolper, M.W.,
1984    *Elam Surveys of Political History and Archaeology*,
        University of California Press Near Eastern
        Studies 25 (Berkeley: University of California
        Press).

Castellin, G.,
1957    'Urnammu: three religious texts', *Zeiscrift fur
        Assyriologie* 52, 1-57.

Castillos, J.J.,
1983    'A study of the spatial distribution of large and
        richly endowed tombs in Egyptian Predynastic
        and Early Dynastic cemeteries', in Kolos, D.M.
        (ed.), Society for the Study of Egyptian
        Antiquities 2 (Toronto).

Cassimatis, H.,
1973    *Les Rites Funeraires à Chypre*, Report of the
        Department of Antiquities of Cyprus, 118-.

Cate, P.,
1990    'Ancient Anatolia', *The Encyclopaedia Britannica*,
        vol. 1 (Chicago: Encyclopaedia Britannica) , 900-
        906.

Chad, C.,
1972    *Les Dynastes d'Emèse* (Beirut:Dar el-Machzeq).

Chapman, R. & Randsborg, K.,
1981    'Approaches to the archaeology of death', in
        Chapman, R., Kinnes, I. & Randsborg, K. (eds)
        1981, 1-24.

Chapman, R., Kinnes, I. & Randsborg, K., (eds),
1981    *The Archaeology of Death* (Cambridge: Cambridge
        University Press).

Charles, R.P.,
1967    'Étude des Restes Humains de la Tombe 31', in
        V. Karageorghis, *Excavations in the Necropolis of
        Salamis I, Text and Plates*, Appendix VI (Nicosia),
        147-.

Chase, J.W.,
1992 'Mortuary analysis of the recent burials in area KK: preliminary report, 1990', in Vann, R.L. (ed.), *Caesarea Papers. Straton's Tower, Herod's Harbour, and Roman and Byzantine Caesarea,* Supplementary Series No. 5, Journal of Roman Archaeology (Ann Arbor: Journal of Roman Archaeology), 177-180.

Chehab, M.,
1939 'Tombe phénicienne de Sin el-Fil', in *Mélanges Syriens offert à R. Dussaud,* vol. 2, (Paris: Paul Geuthner) 803-810.

Chesney, F.R.,
1850 The Expedition for the Survey of the Rivers Euphrates and Tigris, carried on by order of the British Government, In the Years 1835, 1836, and 1837; preceded by geographical and historical notices of the regions situated between the rivers Nile and Indus, vol. 1 (London: Longman, Brown, Green & Longmans).

Cheverud, J.M., Kohn, A.P.L., Konigsberg, L.W. & Leigh, S.R.,
1992 'Effects on fronto-occipital artificial cranial vault modifications on the cranial base and face', *American Journal of Physical Anthropology* 88, 323-345.

Childe, V.G.,
1956 *Piecing Together the Past* (London: Routledge & Kegan Paul).
1957 *The Dawn of European Civilization* (London: Routledge & Kegan Paul).

Childs, W.A.P.,
1979 'The authorship of the Inscribed Pillar of Xanthos', *Anatolian Studies* 29, 97-102.

Childs, W.A.P., and Demargne, P.,
1989 Fouilles de Xanthos, vol. 8: Le Décor Sculpté du Monument des Néréides (Paris: Institut Francais d'Archéologie d'Istanbul).

Christie Mallowan, A.,
1983 *Come, Tell Me How You Live* (London: Bodley Head).

Clarke, D.L.,
1979 'The Beaker Network; social and economic models; the theoretical aspects (or the games that archaeologists play)', in Hammond *et al.* (eds) 1979, 333-362.

Clermont-Ganneau, C.,
1895 *Études d'Archéologie Orientale I* (Paris: Bibliothéque de l'école des hautes études)

Cobham, C.D.,
1908 Excerpta Cypria, Materials for a history of Cyprus (Cambridge).

Coche de la Ferté, E.,
1956 'Luxe de l'Orient romain', *L'Oeil* 15 (March), 34-38.

Coldstream, J.N.,
1989 'Status symbols in Cyprus in the eleventh century BC', in Peltenberg, E.J. (ed.), *Early Society in Cyprus* (Edinburgh: Edinburgh University Press), 325-335.

Cole, D.,
1984 *Shechem, vol. 1: The Middle Bronze Age IIB Pottery* (Philadelphia: American Schools of Oriental Research).

Collon, D.,
1987 *First Impressions; Cylinder Seals in the Ancient Near East* (London & Chicago: British Museum Press & University of Chicago Press).

Collon, D., Otte, C. & Otte, M.,
1975 'Les sépultures de la couche III (A2 et A3)', in D. Collon, C. & M. Otte & A. Zaqzouq (eds), *Sondages au flanc sude du Tell de Qal'at El-Mu,* Fouilles d'Apamée de Syrie – miscellanea 11 (Brussels: Centre Belge de Recherches Archéologiques à Apamée de Syrie), 107-158.

Conder, C.R.,
1889a 'Report on Answers to the "Questions"', *Palestine Exploration Fund Quarterly Statement* (July), 120-33.
1889b The Survey of Eastern Palestine, vol. 1: The Adwan Country. (London: Palestine Exploration Fund).

Coon, C.S.,
1949 'The Eridu crania preliminary report', *Sumer* 5, 103-106.

Cooper, J.S.,
1980 [Review-article of Behrens 1978], *Journal of Cuneiform Studies* 32(3), 175-188.

Cornwall, P.B.,
1943 'The tumuli of Bahrain', *Asia and the Americas* 43(April), 230-234.
1944 *Dilmun; the History of Bahrain Island before Cyrus,* PhD thesis (Harvard University).
1946 'On the location of Dilmun', *BASOR* 103(October), 3-11.
1948 'In search of Arabia's past', *National Geographic* April 1948, 493-522.

Cornwall, I.B.,
1981 'The Pre-Pottery Neolithic burials', in Kenyon, K.M., *Excavations at Jericho, vol. 3: The Architecture and Stratigraphy of the Tell* (London: British School of Archaeology in Jerusalem), 395-404.

Courtois, J-C.,
1974 'Ugarit grid, stratigraphy, and find localizations; a reassessment', *Zeitschrift des Deutschen Palästina-Vereins* 90, 102-105.
1979a 'Ras Shamra; archéologie', in *Dictionnaire de la Bible:* supplément 52 (Paris:), 1126-1295.
1979b L'architecture domestique à Ugarit au Bronze Récent', *Ugarit-Forschungen* 11, 105-134.
1979c 'Ras Shamra', in Letouzey & Ané (eds), *Supplément au Dictionnaire de la Bible,* fasc. 52-53,

col. 1126-1295 (col. 1200-1202 pour les tombes, avec la bibliographie antérieure).

Covello-Paran, K.,
In press Tombs at Kibbutz HaGoshrim, *'Atiqot* [English Series].

Creutz, U.,
1977 'Zur Architektur des menschlichen Schädelaches im Bereich der Pars bregmatica suturae sagittalis', *Gegenbaurs morph. Jahrb.* 123, 666-688, 787-814.

Culican, W.,
1982 'The repertoire of Phoenician pottery', in Niemeyer, G.(ed.), *Phönizer am Westen* (Mainz am Rhein: Philipp von Zabern), 45-82.

Curtis, J.E.,
1976 'Parthian gold from Nineveh', *The British Museum Yearbook* 1, 47-66.
1983a 'Late Assyrian Bronze Coffins', *Anatolian Studies* 33, 85-95.
1983b 'Some axe-heads from Chagar Bazar and Nimrud', *Iraq* 45, 73-81.
1988 Bronzeworking Centres of Western Asia c. 1000-539 BC (London: Kegan Paul International).

Curtis, J., Collon, D. & Green, A.,
1993 'British Museum excavations at Nimrud and Balawat in 1989', *Iraq* 55, 1-37.

Curtis, J.E.,
1979 'Neo-Assyrian ironworking technology', *Proceedings of the American Philosophical Society* 123, 369-390.

Curvers, H.,
1987 'The Middle Habour Salvage Operation: Excavation at Tell al-Raqai, 1986', *Akkadica* 55(November/December), 1-29.
1988 'The period VI pottery', in van Loon, M. (ed.), *Hammam et Turkman I* (Istanbul: Nederlands Historisch-Archeologisch Instituut), 351-395.
1989 'The beginning of the third millennium in Syria', in Haex, O.M.C., Curvers, H.H. & Akkermans, P.M.M.G. (eds), *To the Euphrates and Beyond: Archaeological Studies in Honour of Maurits N. van Loon* (Rotterdam: A.A.Balkema ), 173-193.

Dagan, Y.,
1992 Archaeological Survey of Israel. Map of Lakhish (98) (Jerusalem: Israel Antiquities Authority).

Dajani, R.W.,
1968 'Excavations in dolmens', Annual of the Department of Antiquities of Jordan 12/13, 56-64.

Dales, G.F.,
1977 'Hissar IIIC Stone Objects in Afghan Sistan', in Levine, L.D. & Cuyler Young, T. Jnr. (eds), *Mountains and Lowlands: Essays in the Archaeology of Greater Mesopotamia*, Bibliotheca Mesopotamica 7 (Malibu: Undena Publications), 17-27.

Dalley, S.,
1984 *Mari and Karana: Two Old Babylonian Cities* (London: Longman).
1989 *Myths from Mesopotamia*, paperback ed. 1991, The World's Classics (Oxford: Oxford University Press).

Dandamaev, M.A. & Lukonin, V.G.,
1989 *The Culture and Social Institutions of Ancient Iran*, tr. Kohl, P.L. & Didson, D.J. (Cambridge: Cambridge University Press).

Daniel, J.F.,
1937 'Two Late Cypriot III tombs from Kourion', *American Journal of Archaeology* 41, 56-85.

Dascoulis, G.,
1956 'Die Kariesfrequenz in Griechenland von der Vorgeschichte bis zur Neuzeit', *Deutsche Zahnärztliche Zeitschrift* 11, 1470.

David, A.R.,
1982 The Ancient Egyptians; their Religious Beliefs and Practices (Manchester: Manchester University Press).

Davies, G.I.,
1986 Meggido, Cities of the Biblical World, (Cambridge: Lurtelworth).

Davidson, T.E.,
1977, Regional Variation within the Halaf Ceramic Tradition, Ph.D. Thesis, (University of Edinburgh).

Davidson, T.E. & Watkins, T.,
1981 'Two seasons of excavations at Tell Aqab in the Jezirah, north east Syria', *Iraq* 43, 1-18.

Davies, N. de G.,
1925 *The Tomb of the Two Sculptors at Thebes* (New York: Metropolitan Museum of Art).
1927 *Two Ramesside Tombs at Thebes* (New York: Metropolitan Museum of Art).

Davies, N.M.,
1936 *Ancient Egyptian paintings, vol. 1* (Chicago: The University of Chicago Press).

Davis, S.J.M. & Valla, F.R.,
1978 'Evidence for the domestication of the dog 12,000 years ago in the Natufian of Israel', *Nature* 276, 608-610.

de Contenson, H.,
1966 'Seconde campagne a Tell Ramad 1965. Raport preliminaire', *Ugaritica* 4, 477-519.
1967 'Troisieme campagne a Tell Ramad 1966. Raport preliminaire', *Les Annales Archeologiques Arabes Syriennes* 17, 17-24.
1972 'Tell Aswad. Fouilles de 1971', *Les Annales Archeologiques Arabes Syriennes* 23, 85-103.
1992 'Les coutumes funeraires dans le Neolithique syrien', *Bulletin de la Societe Prehistorique Français* 89(6), 184-191.

de Mesnil du Buisson, R.,
1930   'Compte rendu de la quatrieme campagne de fouilles a Mishrife-Qatna', *Syria* 11, 146-163.
1948   *Baghouz, l'Ancienne Corsoté; le Tell Archaique et la Necropole de l'Age du Bronze* (Leiden: E.J. Brill.)

de Maigret, A.,
1976   *Le lance nell'Asia Anteriore nell'eta dell Bronzo* (Rome: Universita di Roma Istituto di Studi del Vicino Oriente).

de Mecquenem, R.,
1943   'Fouilles de Suse 1933-1939', *Mémoires de la Mission Archéologique en Iran* 29(Paris: Presses Universitaires de France), 3-161.

de Meyer, L. (ed.),
1980   Tell ed-Der III. Souding at Abu Habbah (Sippar) (Leuven: Peeters).

de Ridder, A.,
1911   Collection de Clercq, vol. VII: Les Bijoux et les Pierres Gravées (Paris: Ernest Leroux).

de Saulcy, L.F.,
1865   Voyage en Terre-Sainte, vol. 1 (Paris).

de Vaux, R.,
1966   'Palestine during the Neolithic and Chalcolithic periods', *CAH* 3rd ed. (Cambridge: Cambridge University Press), vol. 1(1), 498-520.
1976   'El-Far'a, Tell North', in Avi-Yonah, M. (ed.), *Encyclopedia of Archaeological Excavations in the Holy Land* (London: Oxford University Press), 395-404.

de Vaux, R. & Steve, A.M.,
1947   'La première campagne de fouilles à Tell el-Far'ah, près Naplouse', *Révue Biblique* 54, 394-433.

de Vries, B.,
1987   'The Fortifications of El-Lejjun', in Parker, S.T. (ed.), *The Roman Frontier in Central Jordan. Interim Report on the Limes Arabicus Project, 1980-1985,* BAR International Series 340 (Oxford: BAR), 311-351.

de Waele, E.,
1982   *Bronzes du Luristan et d'Amlash,* Publications de l'histoire de l'art et d'archéologie de l'Université Catholique de Louvain 34 (Louvain-la-Neuve: Université Catholique de Louvain).

Deelder, A.M., Miller, R.L., De Jonge, N. & Krijger, F.W.,
1990   'Detection of schistosome antigen in mummies', *The Lancet* 335, 724.

Deller, K.,
in press 'Bird-text', Paper delivered at the XXXIXᵉ *Rencontre Assyriologique Internationale*, Heidelberg, 1992.

Del Olmo Lete, G.,
1988   'Un ritual funerario de Ugarit (KTU 1.105)', *Aula Orientalis* 6(2), 189-194.

Delougaz, P., Hill, H. & Lloyd, S.,
1967   *Private Houses and Graves in the Diyala Region,* Oriental Institute Publications 88 (Chicago: University of Chicago).

Deltour-Levie, C.,
1982   *Les Piliers Funéraires de Lycie,* Publications d'Institute de l'Art et d'Archéologie de l'Université de Louvain 31 (Louvain-la-Neuve: Institut Supérieur d'Archéologie et d'Histoire de l'Art).

Demargne, P.,
1958   *Fouilles de Xanthos, vol. 1: Les Piliers Funéraires* (Paris: Institut Français d'Archéologie d'Istanbul).
1974   *Fouilles de Xanthos, vol. 5: Tombes-Maisons, Tombes Rupestres et Sarcophages* (Paris: Institut Français d'Archéologie d'Istanbul).
1975   'Observations on Bousquet 1975', *Comptes rendus de l'Académie des Inscriptions,* 148-150.
1976   'L'iconographie dynastique au Monument des Néréides de Xanthos', in Chamoux, F. (ed.), *Recueil Plassart; Études sur l'Antiquité Grecque Offertes à André Plassart par ses Collèges de la Sorbonne* (Paris: Société d'Édition 'Les Belles-Lettres'), 81-95.
1979   'Athéna; les dynastes lyciens et les héros grecs', in *Florilegium Anatolicum; Mélanges Offerts à Emmanuel Laroche* (Paris: Éditions E. de Boccard), 97-101.
1990   'Das Nereiden-Monument von Xanthos', in Jacobek, R. & Dinstl, A. (eds) 1990, 65-69.

Demirjian, A. & Goldstein, H.,
1976   'New systems for dental maturity based on seven and four teeth', *Annals of Human Biology* 3, 411-421.

Demirjian, A., Goldstein, H. & Tanner, J.M.,
1973   'A new system of dental age assessment', *Human Biology* 45, 211-227.

Desborough, V.R. d'A.,
1975   'The end of Mycenaean civilization and the Dark Age; the archaeological background', *CAH* 3rd ed. (Cambridge: Cambridge University Press), vol. 2(2), 658-677.

Deshayes, J.,
1960   Les Outils de Bronze de l'Indus au Danube (IVᵉ au IIᵉ millénaire) (Paris: Paul Geuthner).

Devambez, P.,
1968   'Antiquités grecques et romaines', *La Revue du Louvre et des Musées de France* 18, 321-328.

Dever, W.G.,
1975   'Middle Bronze IIa cemeteries at 'Ain es-Samiyeh and Sinjil', *BASOR* 217, 23-36.
1976   'The beginning of the Middle Bronze Age in Syria-Palestine', in Cross, F.M., Lemke, W.E. & Miller, P.D. (eds), *Magnalia Dei; the mighty acts of God; essays on the Bible and archaeology in memory of G. Ernest Wright* (Garden City, New York: Doubleday), 3-38.

1980 'New vistas on the EB IV ("MB I") horizon in Syria-Palestine', *BASOR* 237, 35-64.

1987 'Middle Bronze Age; the zenith of the urban Canaanite era', *Biblical Archaeologist* 50, 148-177.

1992 'Pastoralism and the end of the Urban Early Bronze Age in Palestine', in Bar-Yosef, O. and Khazanov, A. (eds), *Pastoralism in the Levant*, Monographs in World Archaeology 10 (Madison, Wisconsin: Prehistory Press).

Dever, W.G., Lance, H.D. & Wright, G.E.,
1970 *Gezer I: Preliminary Report of the 1964-66 Seasons* (Jerusalem: Hebrew Union College Biblical and Archaeological School).

Dever, W.G., Lance, R.G., Cole, D.P., Gitin, S., Holladay, J.S., Seger, J.D., Walker, A.M. & Wright, R.B.,
1986 Gezer, vol. 4: Report of the 1969-71 Seasons in Field VI, the 'Acropolis' (Jerusalem: Hebrew Union College).

Diakonoff, I.M. & Starostin, S.A.,
1986 *Hurro-Urartian as an Eastern Caucasian Language*, Münchener Studien zur Sprachwissenschaft, neue Folge, Beiheft 12 (Munich: R. Kitzinger).

Dickson, H.R.P.,
1949 The Arab of the Desert. A Glimpse into Badawin Life in Kuwait and Sau'di Arabia (London: George Allen & Unwin).

Dietrich, M., Loretz, O. & Mayer/Münster, W.,
1989 'Sikkanum "Betyle"', *Ugarit-Forshungen* 21, 133-139.

Dietrich, M., Loretz, O. & Samart, J.,
1976 *Die keilalphabetischen Texte aus Ugarit* (Neukirchen/Vluyn: Neukichener Verlag).

Dikaios, P.,
1938 'Vounous-Bellapais in Cyprus, 1931-2', *Archaeologia* 88, 1-.

Dingwall, E.J.,
1931 *Artificial Cranial Deformation* (London: Bale, Sons and Danielsson Ltd).

Dinstl, A.,
1990 'Bienenhaus in der Tuerkei', in Jacobek, R. & Dinstl, A. (eds), 205.

Dixon, D.M.,
1972 'Masticatories in ancient Egypt', *Journal of Human Evolution* 1, 433-449.

Domurad, M.,
1989 'Whence the First Cypriots?', in E. Peltenburg (ed) 1989, 66-

Donjon, C.,
1975 La Transcaucasie aux Époques Chalcolithique, Bronze Ancien et Bronze Moyen, Mémoire de Maîtrise (Paris: Université de Paris I).

Dornemann, R.H.,
1979 'Tell Hadidi; a millennium of Bronze Age city occupation', in Freedman, D.N. (ed.), *Archaeological Reports from the Tabqa Dam Project* – *Euphrates Valley, Syria*, Annual of the American Schools of Oriental Research 44 (Cambridge MA: ASOR), 113-150.

1988 'Tell Hadidi; one Bronze Age site among many in the Tabqa Dam salvage area', *BASOR* 270, 13-42.

1990 'The Beginning of the Bronze Age in Syria in Light of Recent Excavations', in Matthiae, P., van Loon, M. & Weiss, H. (eds.), *Resurrecting the Past. A Joint Tribute to Adnan Bounni* (Istanbul: Nederlands Historisch-Archaeologisch Instituut te Istanbul), 85-100.

Dothan, M.,
1959a 'Excavations at Meser, 1957', *Israel Exploration Journal* 9, 13-29.

1959b 'Excavations at Horvat Beter (Beersheva)', *'Atiqot* 2, 1-42.

1960 'Azor', *Israel Exploration Journal* 10, 259-260.

1961 'Excavations at Azor, 1960', *Israel Exploration Journal* 11, 171-175.

1989 'A cremation burial at Azor – a Danite city', *Eretz-Israel* 20, 164-174 [in Hebrew] 200 [English summary].

Dothan, T.,
1979 *Excavations at the Cemetery of Deir El-Balah*, Qedem 10 (Jerusalem: Hebrew University).

1982 *The Philistines and their Material Culture* (Jerusalem: Israel Exploration Society).

Downs, D.,
1984 'The human skeletal remains', in Roaf, M. (ed.), 'Tell Madhur: A summary report on the excavations', *Sumer* 43, 127.

Drijvers, H.J.W.,
1972 Old-Syriac (Edessean) Inscriptions (Leiden: Brill).

Drower, E.S.,
1937 *The Mandaeans of Iraq and Iran. Their Cults, Customs, Magic, Legends, and Folklore* (Oxford: Clarendon Press).

1941 Peacock Angel. Being some Account of Votaries of a Secret Cult and their Sanctuaries (London: John Murray).

Drower, M. & Bottero, J.,
1971 'Syria before 2200 B.C.', *CAH* 3rd ed. (Cambridge: Cambridge University Press), vol. 1(2), 315-362.

Druks, A.,
1966 'A "Hittite" burial near Kfar Yehoshua', *Bulletin of the Israel Exploration Society* 30(3/4), 213-220 [in Hebrew].

Dunand, M.,
1939 *Fouilles de Byblos, vol 1: 1926-1932* (Paris: Paul Geuthner).

1958 *Fouilles de Byblos, vol. 2: 1933-1938* (Paris: Paul Geuthner ).

1973 Fouilles de Byblos, vol. 5: l'Architecture, les Tombes, le Material Domestique, des Origines Neolithiques à l'Avenement Urbain (Paris: Adrien Maisonneuve).

Dunand, M., Saliby, N. & Khirichian, A.,
1955    'Les fouilles d'Amrith en 1954; rapport préliminaire', *Les Annales Archéologiques Arabes Syriennes* 4/5, 189-204.

Durand, E.L.,
1879    *The Antiquities of Bahrein* (Calcutta: Foreign Department Press), report 4806-E No. 164.
1880    'Extracts from report on the islands and antiquities of Bahrein', *Journal of the Royal Asiatic Society* 12, 189-201 .

Durand, J.-M.,
1989    'Tombes familiales et culte des Ancêtres à Emar', *Nouvelles Assyrologiques Brèves et Utilitaires* 1989/4, 85-88.

During Caspers, E.C.L.,
1984    'Dilmun; international burial ground', *Journal of the Economic and Social History of the Orient* 27, 1-32.

Dyson, R.H. & Voigt, M.M. (eds),
1989    'East of Assyria; the highland settlement of Hasanlu', *Expedition* 31 (Philadelphia: University Museum).

Eakins, J.K.,
1980    'Human Osteology & Archaeology', *Biblical Archaeologist* 43(2), 89-96.
1993    *Tell el-Hesi: The Muslim Cemetery in Field V and VI/IX (Stratum II)*, The Joint Archaeological Expedition to Tell el-Hesi, vol. 5 (Winona Lake, Indiana: Eisenbrauns).

Ebeling, E.,
1931    *Tod und Leben nach den Vorstellungen der Babylonier* (Berlin: Walter de Gruyter).

Edwards, P.C.,
1991    'Wadi Hammeh 27; an early Natufian site in Pella, Jordan', in Bar-Yosef, O. & Valla, F.R. (eds) 1991, 123-148.

Edwards, P.C., Bourke, S.J., Colledge, S.M., Head, J. & Macumber, P.G.,
1988    'Late Pleistocene prehistory in Wadi al Hameh, Jordan Valley', in Garrard, A.N. and Gebel, H.G. (eds.) 1988, 525-565.

Edzard, D.O., (ed.),
1990    *[Igigu-,], Anunna und. A. Nach sumerischen Quellen*, *Reallexikon der Assyriologie und Voerderasiatische Archäologie* (Berlin & New York: Walter de Gruyter) 5, 37-40.

Egami, N.,
1959    *Telul eth Thalathat, the Excavation of Tell II 1956-57, vol. 1* (Tokyo: The Institute for Oriental Culture, The University of Tokyo).

Ehrich, R.W. (ed.),
1992    *Chronologies in Old World Archaeology* (Chicago: University of Chicago Press).

Eisenberg, E.,
1986    'Tel Teo', *Excavations and Surveys in Israel* 5, 107-109.

1987a   'Excavations at Tell Teo', *Israel Exploration Journal* 37, 173-175.

Elayi, J.,
1980    'Remarques sur un type de mur phénicien', *Rivista di Studi Fenici* 8(2), 165-180.

Eldar, I. & Baumgarten, Y.,
1985    'Neve Noy; a Chalcolithic site of the Beersheba culture', *Biblical Archaeologist* 48, 134-139.

El-Wailly, F. & Abu al-Soof, B.,
1965    'The Excavations at Tell es-Sawwan; first preliminary report (1964)', *Sumer* 21, 17-31.

Empson, R.H.W.,
1928    The Cult of the Peacock Angel. A Short Account of the Yezidi Tribes of Kurdistan (London: H.F. & G. Witherby).

Epstein, C.,
1974    'Middle Bronze Age tombs at Kfar Szold and Ginosar', *'Atiqot* 7, 13-39 [in Hebrew].
1984    'A Pottery Neolithic site near Tel Qatif', *Israel Exploration Journal* 34, 209-219.
1985    'Dolmens excavated in the Golan, *'Atiqot* (English series) 17, 20-58.

Erkanal, H.,
1988    'Girnavaz', Mitteilungen der Deutschen Orient-Gesellschaft zu Berlin 120, 139-52.

Erdélyi, J.,
1930    'Schädelveränderungen bei gesteigertem Hirndruck', *Fortschr. Geb. Röntgenstr.* 52, 153-179

Erzen, A.,
1964    'Toprakkale, Çavaştepe ve Ünsel (Ernis) kazıari, *Turk Tarih Kurumu Belleten* 28: 568-573.

Esse, D, L.,
1991    *Subsistence, Trade and Social Change in Early Bronze Age Palestine*, Studies in Ancient Oriental Civilization 50 (Chicago: Oriental Institute Publications).

Evans, A.,
1929    The Shaft Graves and Bee-Hive Tombs of Mycenae and their Interpretation (London: Macmillan & Co.).

Ewing, J.F.,
1947    'Preliminary note on the excavation at the Palaeolithic site of Ksar 'Akil, Republic of Lebanon', *Antiquity* 21, 186-196.

Fadhil, A.,
1990a   'Die in Nimrud/Kalhu aufgefundene Grebinschrift der Jabâ', *Baghdader Mitteilungen* 21, 461-70.
1990b   'Die Grabinschrift der Mulissu-Mukannisat-Ninua aus Nimrud/Kalhu und andere in ihrem Grab gefundere Schriftträger', *Baghdader Mitteilungen* 21, 471-82, Taf. 39-45.

Fakhry, A.,
1950    *The Egyptian Deserts. Bahria Oasis, vol. 2* (Cairo: Service des Antiquités de l'Egypte).

Falkenstein, A.,
1965 'Die Anunna in der sumerischen Überlieferung', in Güterbock, H.G. & Jacobsen, T. (eds), 127-140.

Fargo, V.M. & O'Connell, K.G.,
1978 'Five Seasons of Excavation at Tell el-Hesi (1970-1977)', *Biblical Archaeologist* 41(4), 165-182.

Faris, J.C.,
1983 'From form to content in the structural study of aesthetic systems', in Washburn, D.K. (ed.), *Structure and Cognition in Art* (Cambridge: Cambridge University Press), 90-112.

Faliks, J.,
1971 'Reed', *Encyclopedia Judaica* 14, 18.

Fellows, C.,
1841 *An Account of Discoveries in Lycia, being a Journal kept during a Second Excursion in Asia Minor* (London: John Murray).

Ferembach, D.,
1959 'Note sur un crane brachycephale et deux mandibules du Mesolithique d'Israel', *Israel Exploration Journal* 9, 65-73.
1969 'Étude anthropologique des ossements humains neolithiques de Tell Ramad (Syrie)', *Les Annales Archeologique Arabes Syriennes* 19, 49-70.
1970 'Étude anthropologique des ossements humains neolithiques de Tell Ramad (Syrie)', *L'Anthropologie* 74(3/4), 247-254.

Ferembach, D. & Lechevallier, M.,
1973 'Découverte de cranes surmodeles dans une habitation du VII ème millenaire, è Beisamoun, Israel', *Paléorient* 1(2), 223-230.

Ferembach, D., Schwidetzky, I. & Stloukal, X.,
1980 'Recommendations for age and sex diagnoses of skeletons', *Journal of Human Evolution* 9, 517-549.

Fiedel, S.J.,
1979 *Intra- and Inter-Cultural Variability in Mesolithic and Neolithic Mortuary Practices in the Near East*, Ph.D. thesis (University of Pennsylvania, microfiche 1981 Ann Arbor: University Microfilms International).

Filer, J.M.,
1989 *Cats in Ancient Egypt; an Archaeozoological Study*, BA thesis (London: University College).

Finkel, I.L.,
1984 'Necromancy in ancient Mesopotamia', *Archiv für Orientforschung* 29/30, 1-7.

Finkelstein, I.,
1991 'The central hill country in the Intermediate Bronze Age', *Israel Exploration Journal* 41, 19-45.
1992 'Middle Bronze Age "fortifications"; a reflection of social organization and political formation', *Tel Aviv* 19, 201-220.

Finkelstein, J.J.,
1966 'The genealogy of the Hammurapi dynasty', *Journal of Cuneiform Studies* 20, 95-118.

Fiorina, P.,
1984 'Excavations at Tell Hassan; preliminary report', *Sumer* 40, 277-289.
1985a 'Funeral Customs', in E. Quarantelli (ed.) 1985, 62-63.
1985b 'Ethnoarchaeology', in Quarantelli, E. (ed.) 1985, 72-74.

Fischer, P.M.,
1986 *Prehistoric Cypriot Skulls*, SIMA LXXV (Göteborg).

Flannery, K.V.,
1972 'The cultural evolution of civilisations', *Annual Review of Ecology and Systematics* 3, 399-426.

Fleming, D.,
1989 'Eggshell Ware Pottery in Achaemenid Mesopotamia', *Iraq* 51, 165-185.

Forbes, T.,
1983 *Urartian Architecture*, BAR International Series 170 (Oxford: BAR).

Forest, J-D.,
1983 *Les Pratiques Funéraires en Mésopotamie du 5e Millénaire au Début du 3e, Étude de Cas*. Editions Recherche sur les civilisations Mémoire 19 (Paris: CNRS).
1984 'Kheit Qasim; an ED I cemetery', *Sumer* 40, 107-114.

Foxvog, D.A.,
1980 'Funerary furnishings in an early Sumerian text from Adab', in Alster, B. (ed.) 1980, 67-75.

Frangipane, M. & Palmieri, A. (eds),
1983a *Perspectives on Protourbanization in Eastern Anatolia. Arslantepe (Malatya). An Interim Report on 1975-1983 Campaigns*, Origini 12/2 (Rome: Università degli Studi 'La Sapienza').

Frangipane, M. & Palmieri, A. (eds),
1983b 'A protourban center of the Late Uruk period', in Frangipane, M. & Palmieri, A. (eds) 1983a, 287-454.
1983c 'Cultural developments at Arslantepe at the beginning of the third millennium', in Frangipane & Palmieri (eds) 1983a, 523-574.

Frankfort, H.,
1948 *Ancient Egyptian Religion; an Interpretation* (New York: Harper).

Frazer, J.G.,
1890 *The Golden Bough; a Study in Magic and Religion*, 1963 ed. (New York: Macmillan).

Fritz, V.,
1971 'Erwägungen zu dem spätbronzezeitlichen Quadratbau bei Amman', *Zeitschrift des Deutschen Palästina-Vereins* 87, 140-152.

Frödin, O. & Persson, A.W.,
1938 *Asine; results of the Swedish excavations, 1922-1930* (Stockholm: Generalstabens Litografiska Anstalts Förlag i Distribution).

Frohlich, B.,
1983    'The Bahrain Burial Mounds', *Dilmun* 11, 4-9.

Frye, R.N.,
1962    *The heritage of Persia* (London: Weidenfeld & Nicolson).

Fugmann, E.,
1958    *Hama; Fouilles et Recherches, 1931-1938, vol. II 1: L'Architecture des Périodes Pre-Hellénistiques* (Copenhagen: Nationalmuseets Skrifter).

Fukai, S. & Matsutani, T.,
1981,   Telul eth-Thalathat. The Excavations of Tell II, vol. 4 (Tokyo: Institute of Oriental Culture).

Fuller, M.J. & Fuller, N.B.,
1989/90 'Tall Tuneinir 1986 and 1987', *Archiv für Orientforschung* 36/37, 332-335.

Fürst, C.M.,
1933    Zur Kenntnis der Anthropologie der prähistorischen Bevölkerung der Insel Cypern, Lunds Universitets Årsskrift, Bd.29, Nr 6. (Lund: Lunds Universitets).

Furumark, A.,
1941    *The Chronology of Mycenaean Pottery* (Stockholm: Kungl Vitterhets Historic och Antikvitets Akademien).

Galili, E.,
1987    'A late Pre-Pottery Neolithic B site on the sea floor at Atlit', *Mitekufat Haeven* 20, 50*-71*.

Galili, E., Hershkowitz, I., Gopher, A., Weinstein-Evron, M., Lernau, O., Kislev M. & Horwitz, L.,
1993    'Atlit-Yam; a prehistoric site on the sea floor off the Israeli coast', *Journal of Field Archaeology* 20, 133-157.

Galili, E., Weinstein-Evron, M., Hershkovitz, I., Gopher, A., Kislev, M., Lernau, O. & Kolska-Horwitz, L.,
1993    'Atlit-Yam; a prehistoric site on the sea floor off the Israeli coast', *Journal of Field Archaeology* 20, 133-157.

Gamkrelidze, T.V.,
1990    'On the problem of an Asiatic original homeland of the Proto-Indo-Europeans', in Markey, T.L. & Greppin, J. (eds) 1990, 5-14.

Gardiner, A.H.,
1938    'The Mansion of Life and the Master of the King's Largesse', *Journal of Egyptian Archaeology* 24 (London: Egypt Exploration Society), 83-91.

Gardner, E.A. Hogarth, D.G, James, M.R, Elsey Smith, R.,
1888    'Excavations in Cyprus, 1887-8', *Journal of Hellenic Studies* 9, 147-271.

Garfinkel, Y. & Bonfil, R.,
1990    'Graves and burial Customs of the MB IIA period in Gesher', *Eretz-Israel* 21, 132-147 [in Hebrew].

Garr, W.R.,
1987    'Population in Ancient Ugarit', *BASOR* 266, 31-44.

Garrard, A., Betts, A., Byrd, B. & Hunt, C.,
1987    'Prehistoric environment and settlement in the Azraq Basin; an interim report on the 1985 excavation season', *Levant* 19, 5-25.

Garrard, A., Betts, A., Byrd, B., Colledge, S. & Hunt, C.,
1988    'Summary of palaeoenvironmental and prehistoric investigations in the Azraq basin', in Garrard, A.N. & Gebel, H.G. (eds), 311-337.

Garrard, A.N. & Gebel, H.G. (eds),
1988    *The Prehistory of Jordan.* BAR International Series 396 (Oxford: BAR).

Garrod, D.A.E.,
1932    'A new Mesolithic industry; the Natufian of Palestine', *Journal of the Royal Anthropological Institute* 62, 257-269.
1937    'Notes on some decorated skeletons from the Mesolithic of Palestine', *Annual Report of the British School at Athens* 37, 123-127.
1942    'Excavations at the Cave of Shukbah, Palestine, 1928', *Proceedings of the Prehistoric Society* 8, 1-20.
1957    'Notes sur le Paleolithique Superieur du Moyen-Orient', *Bulletin de la Societe Prehistorique Francaise* 55, 439-445.

Garrod, D.A.E. & Bate, D.M.A.,
1937    *The Stone Age of Mount Carmel* (Oxford: Clarendon Press).

Garstang, J.,
1932    'Jericho: city and necropolis', *(Liverpool) Annals of Archaeology and Anthropology* 19, 3-22, 35-54.
1933    'Jericho: city and necropolis', *(Liverpool) Annals of Archaeology and Anthropology* 20, 3-42.

Gasche, H. (ed.),
1989a   'Habl as-Sahr 1986, nouvelles fouilles. L'ouvrage défensif de Nabuchodonosor II au nord de Sippar', *Northern Akkad Project Reports* 2, 23-70.
1989b   'Abu Qubur 1987-1988, Chantier F. La Résidence Achéménide', *Northern Akkad Project Reports* 4, 3-43.
1991    'Tell Ed-Der 1985-1987. Les Vestiges Meso-Babyloniens', *Northern Akkad Project Reports* 6, 9-94.

Gautier, J.E.,
1895    'Notes sur les fouilles entrepris dans le haute Vallée de l'Oronte', *Comptes rendues des séances de l'Academié des Inscriptions et Belles-lettres,* 4eme ser. 23, 441-464.

Gawlikowski, M.,
1975    'Les tombeaux anonymes', *Berytus* 24, 35-41.

Gebauer, A.B. & Price, T.D. (eds),
1992    *Transitions to Agriculture in Prehistory* (Madison: Prehistory Press).

Gebel, H.G.,
1988 'Late Epipalaeolithic – Aceramic Neolithic sites in the Petra area', in Garrard, A.N. & Gebel, H.G. (eds), 67-100.

Gebel, H.G., Muheisen, M.S., Nissen, H.J., Qadi, N. & Starck, J.M.,
1988 'Preliminary report on the first season of excavations at the late aceramic Neolithic site of Basta', in Garrard, A.N. & Gebel, H.G. (eds), 101-134.

Geraads, D. & Tchernov, E.,
1983 'Femurs humains du Pleistocene Moyen de Gesher Benot Ya'akov (Israel)', *L'Anthropologie* 87(1), 138-141.

Gerstenblith, P.,
1983 *The Levant at the Beginning of the Middle Bronze Age*, Americal Schools of Oriental Research dissertation series 5 (Indiana: Eisenbrauns).

Gibson, J.C.L.,
1978 *Canaanite Myths and Legends* (Edinburgh: T & T Clark Ltd).

Gibson, McG. (ed.),
1981 *Uch Tepe I. Tell Razuk, Tell Ahmed Al-Mughir, Tell Ajamat*, Hamrin Report 10 (Chicago/Copenhagen: Universities of Chicago/Copenhagen).

Gibson, McG. *et al.*,
1978 *Excavations at Nippur, Twelfth Season*, Oriental Institute Publications 23 (Chicago: Oriental Institute).

Gilead, I.,
1983 'Upper Palaeolithic occurrences in Sinai and the transition to the Epi-Palaeolithic in the southern Levant', *Paléorient* 9(1), 39-53.
1988 'The Chalcolithic period in the Levant', *Journal of World Prehistory* 2(4), 397-443.
1989 [Review of Perrot, J., Ladiray, D. & Solivères-Masséi, O. 1988], *Mitekufat Haeven* 22, 132*-138*.
1990 'The Neolithic-Chalcolithic transition and the Qatifian of the northern Negev and Sinai', *Levant* 22, 47-63.
1994 'Dead and burial customs in Israel during the Palaeolithic', in Zinger, I. (ed.), *Graves and Burial Customs in Israel in Ancient Times*, (Jerusalem: Yad Yizhak Ben-Zvi and the Israel Exploration Society), 9-30.

Gimbutas, M.,
1985 'Primary and secondary homelands of the Indo-Europeans: Comments on the Gamkrelidze-Ivanov articles', *Journal of Indo-European Studies* 13(1-2), 185-202.

Gisis, I. & Bar-Yosef, O.,
1974 'New excavations in Zuttiyeh Cave, Wadi Amud, Israel', *Paléorient* 2(1), 175-180.

Gjerstad, E.,
1926 *Studies on Prehistoric Cyprus* (Uppsala).

1948 *The Swedish Cyprus Expedition, vol. 4/2: The Cypro-Geometric, Cypro-Archaic and Cypro-Classical Periods* (Stockholm: The Swedish Cyprus Expedition).

Gjerstad, E., Lindros, J., Sjöqvist, E. & Westholm, A.,
1934 *The Swedish Cyprus Expedition; Finds and Results of the Excavations in Cyprus 1927-1931, vol. 1* (Stockholm: The Swedish Cyprus Expedition).
1935 *The Swedish Cyprus Expedition; Finds and Results of the Excavations in Cyprus 1927-1931, vol. 2* (Stockholm: The Swedish Cyprus Expedition).

Glob, P.V.,
1954a 'Bahrains oldtidshovedstad / the ancient capital of Bahrain', *Kuml* 1954, 164-169.
1954b 'Bahrain. Oen med de hundredtusinde Gravhoje / Bahrain – island of the hundred thousand burial-mounds', *Kuml* 1954, 92-105.
1955 ' Udgravninger på Bahrain. Dansk Arkæologisk Bahrain – Ekspeditions 2. udgravingskanpagne / The Danish Archaeological Bahrain – Expedition's Second Excavation', *Kuml* 1955, 178-193.
1956 'Et nybabylonisk gravfund fra Bahrains oldtidshovedstad / A Neo-Babylonian burial from Bahrain's prehistoric capital', *Kuml* 1956, 164-174.

Goldman, H.,
1956 *Excavations at Gözlü Kule, Tarsus*, Vols I & II (Princeton: Princeton Universtity Press).

Gonen, R.,
1979 *Burial in Canaan of the Late Bronze Age as a Basis for the Study of Population and Settlements*, [in Hebrew, with English summary], PhD thesis (Jerusalem: Hebrew University).
1992a *Burial Patterns and Cultural Diversity in Late Bronze Age Canaan*. American Schools of Oriental Research dissertation series 7 (Winona Lake: Eisenbrauns).
1992b 'The Late Bronze Age', in Ben-Tor, A. (ed.) 1992a, 211-257.
1992c 'Structural tombs in the second millennium B.C.', in Katzenstein, H., Nezer, E., Kempinski, A. & Reich, R. (eds), *The Architecture of Ancient Israel from the Prehistoric to the Persian Periods* (Jerusalem: Israel Exploration Society), 151-160.

Good, R.M.,
1980 'Supplementary remarks on the Ugaritic funerary text RS 34.126', *BASOR* 239, 41-42.

Gopher, A.,
1985 *Flint Industries of the Neolithic Period in Israel*, PhD thesis (Jerusalem: Hebrew University).
1989 'Horvat Galil and Nahal Betzet I; two Neolithic sites in the Upper Galilee', *Mitekufat Haeven* 22, 82-92.

Gopher, A. & Gophna, R.,
1993 'Cultures of the eighth and seventh millennia B.P. in the southern Levant; a review for the 1990s', *Journal of World Prehistory* 7(3), 297-353.

Gopher, A. & Greenberg, R.,
1987 'Pottery Neolithic levels at Tel Dan', *Mitekufat Haeven* 20, 91*-113*.

Gopher, A. & Orrelle, E.,
1991 'Preliminary report on excavations of Nahal Zehora II- seasons 1990-1991', *Mitekufat Haeven* 23, 169-172.

Gopher, A., Sadeh, S. & Goren, Y.,
1992 'The Neolithic Pottery of Nahal Betzet I', *Israel Exploration Journal* 42(1/2), 4-16.

Gopher, A., Tsuk, T., Shalev, S. & Gophna, R.,
1990 'Earliest gold artefacts in the Levant', *Current Anthropology* 31(4), 436-443.

Gophna, R.,
1992 'The Intermediate Bronze Age', in Ben-Tor, A. (ed.) 1992a, 126-158.

Gophna, R. & Lifschitz, S.,
1980 'A Chalcolithic burial cave at Palmachim', *'Atiqot* 14, 1-8.

Gordon, C.H.,
1949 *Ugaritic Literature* (Rome: Pontificum Institutum Biblicum).

Goren, Y.,
1990 'The "Qatifian culture" in southern Israel and Transjordan; additional aspects for its definition', *Mitekufat Haeven* 23, 100-112.

Goren, Y. & Fabian, P.,
1993 'Nahal Kisufim', *Hadashot Archeologiot* 99, 81-82 [in Hebrew].

Goring, E.,
1983 'Appendix VI. Techniques of the Palaepahos-Skales jewellery', V. Karageorghis (ed.) 1983, 418-422.
1988 *A Mischievous Pastime, Digging in Cyprus in the Nineteenth Century*, (Edinburgh: National Museums of Scotland).
1989 'Death in Everyday Life', in E. Peltenburg (ed) 1989.
In press 'The Kourion Sceptre; some facts and factoids', *Klados; Essays in Honour of Professor J.N. Coldstream.*

Goring-Morris, A.N.,
1991 'A PPNB settlement at Kfar Hahoresh in Lower Galilee; a preliminary report of the 1991 season', *Mitekufat Haeven*, 24, 77-101.

Gottlieb, K.,
1978 'Artificial cranial deformation and the increased complexity of the lambdoidal suture', *American Journal of Physical Anthropology* 48, 213-214.

Granqvist, H.,
1965 *Muslim Death and Burial. Arab Customs and Traditions Studied in a Village in Jordan*, Commentationes Humanorum Litterarum t. XXXV:1 (Helsinki: Societas Scientiarum Fennica).

Green, P. (tr.),
1974 *Juvenal, The Sixteen Satires* (London: Penguin).

Greenfield, J.C.,
1973 'Un rite religieux araméen et ses parallèles', *Revue Biblique* 80, 46-52.

Gregory, C.,
1982 *Gifts and Commodities* (London: Academic Press).

Griffith, F. Ll. (ed.),
1900 *Beni Hasan, vol. 4: Zoological and other Details* (London: Egypt Exploration Fund.

Grilletto, R.,
1973 'Caries and dental attrition in the early Egyptians as seen in the Turin Collection', Brothwell, D.R. & Chiarelli, B.A. (eds), *Population Biology of the Ancient Egyptians*, 289-295.

Groneberg, B.,
1990 'Zu den mesopotamischen Unterweltvorstellungen; das Jenseits als Fortsetzung den Diesseits', *Altorientalische Forschungen* 17, 244-261.

Groot, J.C.,
1987 'The Small Finds', in Parker, S.T. (ed.), *The Roman Frontier in Central Jordan. Interim Report on the Limes Arabicus Project, 1980-1985*, volume II, BAR International Series 340, (Oxford: BAR), 497-521.

Großschmidt, K,
1991 'Die menschlichen Skelettreste von Limyra. Anthropologische und paläopathologische Untersuchungen, XIII', *Kazi sonuçlari toplantisi* 2, 215-216.

Grube, E.,
1976 *Islamic Pottery of the Eighth to Fifteenth Century in the Keir Collection* (London: Faber).

Gruber, M.,
1980 Aspects of Non-Verbal Communication in the Ancient Near East (Rome: Studia Pohl).

Grupe, G.,
1982 'Zur Variabilität der Diploestructuren ethnisch deformierter Schädel', *Zeitschrift.Morph.Anthrop.* 73,157-173.
1984 'On diploic structures and their variability in artificially deformed skulls', *Journal of Human Evolution* 13, 307-309.

Gubel, E. (ed.),
1986 Les Phéniciens et le Monde de Méditerraneen (Brussels: Générale de Banque).

Guiges, P.E.,
1937/38 'Lébé'a, Kafer-Garra, Qrayé; nécropoles de la région Sidonienne', *Bulletin du Musée de Beyrouth* 1, 35-76; 2, 27-72.

Gunther, R.T. (ed.),
1934 *Dioscorides, The Greek Herbal* (Oxford: Oxford University Press).

Gurney, O.R.,
1977   *Some Aspects of Hittite Religion,* Schweich lectures of the British Academy 1976 (Oxford: Oxford University Press).
1980   *The Hittites,* 3rd ed. (Harmondsworth: Penguin).
1990   *The Hittites,* 4th ed. (Harmondsworth: Penguin).

Güterbock, H.G., & Jacobsen, T. (eds),
1965   *Studies in Honor of Benno Landsberger on his Seventy-Fifth Birthday* (Chicago: University of Chicago Press).

Guy, P.L.O.,
1938   *Megiddo Tombs,* Oriental Institute Publications 33 (Chicago: University of Chicago Press).

Guz-Silberstein, B. & Raveh, K.,
1990   'Tel Dor. Maritime Archaeology – 1987/1988', *Excavations and Surveys in Israel 1988/89* 7/8, 50-51.

Haas, N.,
1973   'The human fossil remains', in Anati, E., Avnimelech, M., Haas N. & Meyerhof E. (eds), *Hazorea I* (Brescia Edizioni del Centro Camuno di Studi Preistorici), 44-48.
1974   'Les restes squelettiques decouverts a Tel-Ely (Sheikh-Aly)', *Mitekufat Haeven* 12, 36-46.

Haas, N. & Nathan, H.,
1973   'An attempt at a social interpretation of the Chalocolithic burials in the Nahal Mishmar caves', in Aharoni, Y. (ed.), *Excavations and Studies in the Honour of Professor Shmuel Yeivin* (Tel Aviv: Institute of Archaeology), 143-153.

Hagemans, G.,
1863   Un Cabinet d'Amateur; Notices Archéologiques (Liège & Leipzig: Charles Gnusé)

Haiman, M.,
1986   *Archaeological survey of Israel. Map of Har Hamran – Southwest (198) 10-00* (Jerusalem: Israel Antiquities Authority).
1992   'Har Loz (Northeast) Map, Survey', *Excavations and Surveys in Israel 1991* 10, 48-49.

Halbert, L.,
1959   'The Mohammedan graves', in Rydh, H., Arbman, H., Eriksson, K.G. (eds.), *Rang Mahal. The Swedish Archaeological Expedition to India 1952-1954.* Acta Archaeologica Lundiensia (Lund: Lunds Universitats Historiska Museum), 185-188.

Hamburg, M.,
1979   *Basic Statistics: a Modern Approach,* 2nd ed. (New York: Harcount Brace Jovanovich).

Hammond, N. *et al.* (eds),
1979   *Analytical Archaeologist; the Collected Papers of D.L. Clarke* (London: Academic Press).

Hanbury-Tenison, J.W.,
1986   *The Late Chalcolithic to Early Bronze I Transition in Palestine and Transjordan,* BAR International Series 311 (Oxford: BAR).

Hanoun, N.,
1984   'Excavations at Tulul Baradan, Al-Seib and Haddad', *Sumer* 40, 70-72 [English section], 65-70 [Arabic section].

Hansen, H.H.,
1967   *Investigations in a Shi'a Village in Bahrain,* Ethnographical Series Vol. XII (Copenhagen: National Museum of Denmark).

Harrold, F.,
1980   'A comparative analysis of Eurasian Palaeolithic burials', *World Archaeology* 12(2), 195-211.

Hartweg, R.,
1945   'Remarques sur la denture et statistiques sur la carie en France aux epoques prehistoriques et protohistoriques', *Bulletin et Mémoires de la Societé d'Anthropologie de Paris* 6, 71-113.

Hasluck, M.,
1947   'Head-deformation in the near east', *Man* 47, 130-131.

Hassan, F. & Robinson, S.W.,
1987   'High precision radiocarbon chronometry of ancient Egypt, and comparisons with Nubia, Palestine and Mesopotamia', *Antiquity* 61, 119-135.

Hattox, R.S.,
1991   Coffee and Coffeehouses. The Origins of a Social Beverage in the Medieval Near East, reprint (Seattle/London: University of Washington).

Hauptmann, H.,
1982a   'Lidar', *American Journal of Archaeology* 86(4), 562-563.
1982b   'Lidar Höyük', *Türk Arkeoloji Dergisi* 26(1), 93-110.
1982c   'Lidar Höyük', *Anatolian Studies* 32, 17-18.
1983   'Lidar', *American Journal of Archaeology* 87(4), 433.
1988   'Lidar', *American Journal of Archaeology* 92(1), 110-111.
1993   'Vier Jahrtausended Siedlungsgeschichte am mittleren Euphrat', *Archäologie in Deutschland* 1[Jan.-Mar. 1993], 10-15.

Healey, J.-F.,
1977   *Death, Underworld and Afterlife in the Ugaritic texts,* PhD thesis, (London University).
1978   'Mlkm/rp'm and the Kispam', *Ugarit-Forschungen* 10, 89-91.
1979   'The *pietas* of an ideal son in Ugarit', *Ugarit-Forschungen* 11, 353-356.
1984   'The immortality of the king: Ugarit and the Psalms', *Orientalia* (New Series) 53, 245-254.
1985   'The Akkadian 'Pantheon' list from Ugarit', *Studi epigrafici e linguistici* 2, 115-125.
1988   'The Ugaritic 'Pantheon': further notes', *Studi epigrafici e linguistici* 5, 105-112.
1989   'The last of the Rephaim', in Cathcart, K.J. & Healey, J.F. (eds), *Back to the Sources; Biblical and Near Eastern Studies in Honour of Dermot Ryan* (Dublin: Glendale Press), 33-44.

1993a    *The Nabataean Tomb Inscriptions of Mada'in Salih* (Oxford: Oxford University Press).

1993b    'Sources for the study of Nabataean law', *New Arabian Studies* 1, 203-214.

1994    'Mōtu', in van der Toorn, K. (ed.), *Dictionary of Deities and Demons in the Old Testament* (Leiden: E.J. Brill).

Healey, J.F. & Smith, G.R.,
1989    'Jaussen-Savignac 17 – The Earliest Dated Arabic Document (A.D. 267)', *Atlal* 12, 77-84.

Hedges, R.E.M., Housley, R.A., Bronk, C.R. & van Klinken, G.J.,
1992    'Radiocarbon dates from the Oxford AMS system; archaeometry datelist 14', *Archaeometry* 34(1), 141-159.

Heidel, A.,
1949    *The Gilgamesh Epic and Old Testament Parallels* (Chicago: University of Chicago Press).

Heimpel, W.,
1986    'The sun at night and the doors of heaven in Babylonian texts', *Journal of Cuneiform Studies* 38, 27-151.

Helms, S.W.,
1987    'Jawa, Tell Um Hammad and the EB I/Late Chalcolithic landscape', *Levant* 19, 49-81.

Heltzer, M.,
1982    *The Internal Organisation of the Kingdom of Ugarit* (Wiesbaden: Dr. Ludwig Reichert).

Helwing, B.,
1991    *Die frühbronzezeitliche Keramik aus den Gräberfeldern von Titriş, Türkei*, Magisterarbeit, (Heidelberg: Ruprecht-Karls-Universität).

Hennessy, J.B.,
1966    'Excavation of a Bronze Age temple at Amman', *Palestine Exploration Quarterly* 98, 155-162.

1969    'Preliminary report on a first season of excavations at Teleilat Ghassul', *Levant* 1, 1-24.

Hennessy, J.B., McNicoll, A.W., Hanbury-Tennison, J.W., Watson, P.M., Randle, L. & Walmsley, A.G.,
1983    'Preliminary Report on the Fourth Season of Excavations At Pella, 1982', *Annual of the Department of Antiquities of Jordan* 27, 325-361.

Henry, D.O.,
1985    'Preagricultural sedentism; the Natufian example', in Price, T.D. & Brown, J.A. (eds), *Prehistoric Hunter-Gatherers; the Emergence of Cultural Complexity* (New York: Academic Press), 365-384.

1989    *From Foraging to Agriculture* (Philadelphia: University of Pennsylvania Press).

Henschel-Simon, E.,
1938    'The "toggle-pins" in the Palestine Archaeological Museum', *Quarterly of the Department of Antiquities of Palestine* 6, 169-209.

Herr, L.G.,
1983    'The Amman airport structure and the geopolitics of ancient Transjordan', *Biblical Archaeologist* 46(4), 223-229.

Herling, A.,
1994    'Excavation of a Tylos Period Cemetery at Sar (Bahrain)', Paper presented at the Seminar for Arabian Studies, Oxford, 22 July 1994.

Hermitage,
1990    The Hermitage; Selected Treasures from a Great Museum (Leningrad: Stere Hermitage Museum).

Herscher, E.,
1981    Southern Cyprus: the Disappearing Early Bronze Age and the Evidence from Phaneromeni, Studies in Cypriot Archaeology Monograph XVIII.

Hershkovitz, I. (ed.),
1989    *People and culture in change.* BAR International Series, 508. (Oxford: BAR).

Hershkovitz, I. & Galili, E.,
1990    '8,000 years-old human remains on the sea floor near Atlit, Israel', *Journal of Human Evolution* 5(4), 319-358.

Hershkovitz, I. & Gopher, A.,
1988    'Human burials from Horvat Galil; a Pre-Pottery Neolithic site in the Upper Galilee, Israel', *Paléorient* 14(1), 119-125.

1990    'Paleodemography, burial customs, and food-producing economy at the beginning of the Holocene; a perspective from the southern Levant', *Mitekufat Haeven* 23, 9-47.

Hershkovitz, I., Galili, E. & Ring, B.,
1991    'Des squelettes humains 8,000 ans sous la mer; indications sur la vie sociale et economique des habitants de la cote sud du Levant a la periode neolithique preceramique', *L'Anthropologie* 95(2/3), 639-650.

Hershkovitz, I., Garfinkel, Y. & Arensburg, B.,
1986    'Neolithic skeletal remains at Yiftahel area C (Israel)', *Paléorient* 12(1), 73-81.

Hershkovitz, I., Edelson, G., Spiers, M., Arensburg, B. & Nadel, D.,
1993    'Ohalo II man – unusual findings in the anterior rib cage and shoulder girdle of a 19,000 year-old specimen', *International Journal of Osteoarchaeology* 3, 177-188.

Hertz, R.,
1907    *Death and the Right Hand*, 1960 ed., tr. by R. & C. Needham (London: Cohen & West).

Hibbard, F.M.,
1988    *Principles of Obstetrics 410.* (London: Butterworth).

Higgs, A. & Noy, T.,
1971    'Rakefet Cafe – 1971', *Hadashot Archeologiyot* 40, 6-7 [in Hebrew].

Hijara, I.,
1978    'Three new graves at Arpachiyah', *World Archaeology* 10, 125-128.
1980    'Arpachiyah 1976', *Iraq* 42, 131-154.

Hillson, S.,
1986    *Teeth* (Cambridge: Cambridge University Press).

Hirschfield, G.,
1887    'Über die griechischen Grabinschriften, welche Geldshafen anordner', *Königsberger Studien* 1, 83-144.

Historische Schätze,
1966    *Historische Schätze aus der Sowjetunion*, exhibition at Kunsthaus Zurich 17 December 1966 – 26 February 1967.

Hjortsjö, C-H.,
1947    'To the knowledge of prehistoric craniology of Cyprus', Särtryck Ur Kungl. Human. Vetenskapssamfundets: Lund, Årsberättelse 1946-47.

Hodder, I.,
1980    'Social structure and cemeteries; a critical appraisal', in Rahtz, P., Dickinson, T. & Watts, L. (eds), *Anglo-Saxon Cemeteries 1979*, BAR British Series 82, (Oxford: BAR), 161-169.
1989    'Writing archaeology', *Antiquity* 63, 268-274.

Hoffmann, G.,
1878    'Über eine am Euphrat gefundene Mumie mit goldener Gesichtsmaske', *Archäologische Zeitung* 35, 25-27.

Hoffmann, H. & von Claer, V.,
1968    Museum für Kunst und Gewerbe Hamburg: Antiker Gold- und Silberschmuck, (Mainz am Rhein: Philipp von Zabern).

Hole, F., Flannery, K.V. & Neely, J.A.,
1969    *Prehistory and Human Ecology of the Deh Luran Plain*, Memoirs of the Museum of Anthropology, University of Michigan 1, (Ann Arbor: University of Michigan), 248-253.

Holladay, J.S.,
1982    *Tell el-Maskhuta. Preliminary report on the Wadi Tumilat project 1978-79 part 3; Cities of the Delta*, American Center in Egypt Reports 6 (Malibu: ACE).

Holland, T.A.,
1975    'Preliminary report on excavations at Tell es-Sweyhat, Syria, 1975', *Levant* 9, 36-65.

Holum, K.G., Hohfelder, R.L., Bull, R.J. & Raban, A.,
1988    *King Herod's Dream. Caesarea on the Sea* (New York/London: W.W. Norton & Co).

Hood, M.S.F.,
1960    'Tholos tombs of the Aegean', *Antiquity* 34, 166-176.

Hornblower, G.,
1930    'Funerary designs on Predynastic jars', *Journal of Egyptian Archaeology* 16, 10-18.

Howells, W.W.,
1978    'Was the skull of the Moriori artificially deformed', *Arch.Phys.Anthrop. Oceania* 13,198-203.

Hrouda, B. (ed.),
1977    *Isin-Išān Bahrîyāt II. Die Ergebnisse der Ausgrabungen 1973-1974*, Bayerische Akademie Der Wissenschaften Philosophisch-Historische Klasse Abhandlungen, Neue Folge, Heft. 79 (Munich: Bayerischen Akademie der Wissenschaften).

Hrouda, B. et al.,
1981    *Isin-Išān Bahrîyāt II. Die Ergebnisse der Ausgrabungen 1975-1978*, Bayerische Akademie Der Wissenschaften Philosophisch-Historische Klasse Abhandlungen, Neue Folge, Heft. 87 (Munich: Bayerischen Akademie der Wissenschaften).

Hrouda, B. et al.,
1987    *Isin-Išān Bahrîyāt II. Die Ergebnisse der Ausgrabungen 1983-1984*, Bayerische Akademie Der Wissenschaften Philosophisch-Historische Klasse Abhandlungen, Neue Folge, Heft. 94 (Munich: Bayerischen Akademie der Wissenschaften).

Humphreys, S.C. & King, H.,
1981    *Mortality and Immortality; the Anthropology and Archaeology of Death* (New York & London: Academic Press).

Huntington, R. & Metcalf, P.,
1987    *Celebrations of Death; the Anthropology of Mortuary Ritual* (Cambridge: Cambridge University Press).

Huot, J.,
1982    *Les Céramiques Monochromes lissées en Anatolie à l'poque du Bronze Ancien*, 2 Vols, Bibliotheque Archéologique et Historique 111 (Paris: Paul Geuthner).

Iakovides, S.,
1969    *Perati; the necropolis, vol. 1: The Tombs and the Finds*, [in Greek], Library of the Archaeological Service in Athens 67 (Athens).

Ibrahim, M.,
1982    Excavations of the Arab Expedition at Sar el-Jisr, Bahrain (Manama: Ministry of Information, Bahrain).

Idil, V.,
1985    'Likya Lahitleri', *Türk Tarih Kurumu Yayinlari* ser. 6, 24. (Ankara: Türk Tarih Kurumu Basimevi).

Ilan, D.,
1994    'The dawn of internationalism; the Middle Bronze Age', in Levy, T. (ed.) 1994, *The Archaeology of Society in the Holy Land* (Leicester).
in press 'The Middle Bronze Age tombs', in Biran, A., Ilan, D. & Greenberg, R. (eds), *Tel Dan, vol. 1: History of Excavations, the Pottery Neolithic, the Early Bronze Age Levels and the Middle Bronze Age*

*Tombs*, Annual of the Nelson Gluek School of Biblical Archaeaology (Jerusalem: Keter).

Ilisch, L.,
1993    'The *dirham* from Burial 16', in Wilhelm, G. & Zaccagnini, C., *Tell Karrana 3, Tell Jikan, Tell Khirbet Salih*, Baghdader Forschungen Bd. 15 (Mainz am Rhein: Philipp von Zabern), 221-222.

Immerwahr, S.A.,
1971    *The Athenian Agora; vol. 13: The Neolithic and Bronze Ages,* (Princeton: American School of Classical Studies in Athens).

Ingold, T.,
1992    'Foraging for data, camping with theories; hunter-gatherers and nomadic pastoralists in archaeology and anthropology', *Antiquity* 66, 790-803.

Invernizzi, A.,
1980    'Excavations in the Yelkhi Area', *Mesopotamia* 15, 19-49.

Irby, C.L. & Mangles, J.,
1823    *Travels in Egypt and Nubia, Syria and Asia Minor, during the years 1817 and 1818* (London: 'Printed for private distribution').

Ishida, H. & Wada, Y.,
1981    'Human remains from Hamrin. Preliminary report of excavations at Gubba and Songor', *Al-Rafidan* 2, 206-15.

Ives, E.,
1773    A Voyage from England to India, in the Year MDCCLIV (London: Edward & Charles Dilly).

Jacobek, R. & Dinstl, A. (eds),
1990    *Götter, Heroen, Herrscher in Lykien* (Vienna: Anton Schroll).

Jacobsen, T.W. & Cullen, T.,
1981    'A consideration of mortuary practices in Neolithic Greece; burials from Franchthi Cave', in Humphreys, S.C. & King, H. (eds) 1981, 79-101.

Jasim, S.A.,
1985    The Ubaid Period in Iraq. Recent Excavations in the Hamrin Region, BAR International Series 267 (Oxford: BAR).

Jaussen, J.-A.,
1927    Coutumes Palestiniennes I. Naplouse et son District (Paris: Paul Geuthner).

Jaussen, A. & Savignac, R.,
1909    *Mission Archéologique en Arabie, vol.* I (Paris: Leroux/Geuthner).

Jean, C.F. & Hoftijzer, J.,
1965    *Dictionaire des Inscriptions Sémitiques et de l'Ouest* (Leiden: Brill).

Jean-Marie, M.,
1990    'Les tombeaux en pierres de Mari', *Mari Annales de Recherche Interdisciplinaires* 6, 303-336.

Jero, A.M.,
n.d.    'The tombs discovered at Ashur in the second season (1979)', *Sumer* 42, 110-113, 44-50 [Arabic section].

Jettmar, K.,
1967    *Art of the Steppes.* (London: Methuen).

Joffe, A.H.,
1991    'Early Bronze Age I and the Evolution of Social Complexity in the Southern Levant', *Journal of Mediteranean Archaeology* 4/1, 3-59.

Johanson, G.,
1971    'Age determinations from human teeth', *Odontologisk Revy* 22 supplement, 27-39.

Johnstone, W.,
1971    *A Late Bronze Age tholos tomb at Enkomi*, in Schaeffer, C. (ed.), *Alasia, vol. 1* (Paris: Mission Archéologique d'Alasia), 51-122.

Jones, R.E. & Catling, H.,
1986    'Cyprus, the Aegean and the Near East, 1500-1050 BC', in Jones, R.E. (ed.), *Greek and Cypriot Pottery; a Review of Scientific Studies,* Fitch Laboratory Occasional Papers 1 (Athens : British School at Athens), 523-625.

Joussaume, R.,
1988    *Dolmens for the Dead; Megalith Building throughout the World* (London: Batsford).

Kafafi, Z., Rollefson, G. & Simmons, A.,
1990    'The 1989 season at 'Ain Ghazal; preliminary report', *Annual of the Department of Antiquities of Jordan* 34, 11-25.

Kalinka, E.,
1920    *Tituli Asiae Minoris, vol. 2: Tituli Lyciae linguis Graeca et latina conscripti, fasc. 1-2* (Vienna: Alfred Hoelder).
1944    Tituli Asiae Minoris, vol. 2: Tituli Lyciae linguis Graeca et latina conscripti, fasc. 3 (Vienna: Alfred Hoelder).

Kamada, H. & Ohtsu, T.,
1988    'Report on the excavations at Songor A; Isin-Larsa, Sassanian and Islamic graves', *Al-Rafidan* 9, 135-172.

Kamp, K. & Yoffee, N.,
1980    'Ethnicity in ancient Western Asia during the early second millennium B.C.; archaeological assessments and ethnoarchaeological prospectives', *BASOR* 237, 85-104.

Kampschulte, I. & Orthmann, W.,
1984    *Gräber des 3. Jahrtausends im syrischen Euphrattal, vol. 1: Augrabungen bei Tawi 1975 und 1978,* Saarbrücker Beiträge zur Altertumskunde 38 (Bonn: Rudolf Habelt GmbH).

Kanimetov, A., *et al.* (eds.),
1983    *Pamyatniki Kulturi i Iskusstva Kirgizii*, catalogue of an exhibition, (Leningrad).

Kantor, H.,
1956 'Syro-Palestinian ivories', *Journal of Near Eastern Studies* 15, 153-174.

Kaplan, Y.,
1959 *The archaeology and history of Tel Aviv – Jaffa* (Ramat-Gan: Massada Press).
1963 'Excavations at Benei Beraq, 1951', *Israel Exploration Journal* 13(4), 300-312.
1969 *Ain el-Jerbah, Chalcolithic remains in the Esdraelon Valley* (Tel Aviv-Jaffa: Publications of the Museum of Antiquities) [in Hebrew].
1970 'Tel Aviv', in Mazar, B. *et al.* (eds), *Encyclopaedia of Archaeological Excavations in the Holy Land*, vol. 2 (London: Oxford University Press), 563-564 [in Hebrew].
1971 'Mesopotamian elements in the Middle Bronze II culture of Palestine', *Journal of Near Eastern Studies* 30, 293-307.

Karageorghis, V.,
1965 *Nouveaux Documents pour l'Étude du Bronze Récent à Chypre* (Paris: E. de Boccard).
1966 'Chronique de fouilles de Chypre en 1965; fouilles de Enkomi', *Bulletin de Correspondance Héllénique* 90, 343-345.
1967 'An early XIth century BC tomb from Palaepaphos', *Report of the Department of Antiquities of Cyprus*, 1-24.
1974 *Excavations at Kition, vol. 1: The Tombs* (Nicosia: Zavallis Press).
1975 *Alaas; a Protogeometric Necropolis in Cyprus* (Nicosia: Department of Antiquities).
1977 'More Material from the Protogeometric necropolis of "Alaas"', *Report of the Department of Antiquities of Cyprus*, 141-9.
1983 *Ausgrabungen in Alt-Paphos auf Cypern, vol. 3: Paleopaphos-Skales; an Iron Age Cemetery in Cyprus* (Konstanz: Universitätsverlag).
1984 'New light on Late Bronze Age Cyprus', in Karageorghis, V. & Muhly, J.D. (eds), *Cyprus at the Close of the Late Bronze Age* (Nicosia: Leventis Foundation), 19-22.
1987 *The Archaeology of Cyprus, The Ninety Years After Myres*, The Thirteenth J.L. Myres Memorial Lecture (London).

Karageorghis, V. & Demas, M.,
1984 *Pyla-Kokkinokremos* (Nicosia: Department of Antiquities).
1988 *Maa-Paleokastro; Excavations 1979-1986* (Nicosia: Department of Antiquities).

Karageorghis, V. & Iacovou, M.,
1982 'Cypro-Geometric material from Palaepaphos', *Report of the Department of Antiquities of Cyprus*, 123-137.
1990 'Amathus T.521; a Cypro-Geometric I group', *Report of the Department of Antiquities of Cyprus*, 75-100.

Kaufman, D.,
1989 'Observations on the Geometric Kebaran; a view from Neve David', in Bar-Yosef, O. & Vandermeersch, B. (eds), *Investigations in South Levantine Prehistory*, BAR International Series 497 (Oxford: BAR), 275-286.

Kaufman, D. & Ronen, A.,
1987 'Le sepulture kebarienne geometrique de Neve-David, Haifa, Israel', *L'Anthropologie* 91, 335-342.

Keel, O.,
1987 'Peculiar tomb headrests may depict return to the womb', *Biblical Archaeology Review* 13, 50-53.

Keen, A.G.,
1992a *A Political History of Lycia and its Relations with Foreign Powers During the 'Dynastic' Period, 545-362 BC*, PhD thesis. (Manchester: University of Manchester).
1992b 'The dynastic tombs of Xanthos; who was buried where?', *Anatolian Studies* 42, 53-63.
1995 'The identification of a hero-cult centre in Lycia', in M.P.J. Dillon (ed.), *Religion in the Ancient World* (Amsterdam: Hakkert), 223-237.

Keil, B.,
1908 'Über kleinasictische Grabinschriften', *Hermes* 43, 522-577.

Kelly-Buccellati, M.,
1978 'The Early Bronze Age pottery; descriptive and comparative analysis', in van Loon, M.N. (ed.), *Korucutepe; Final Report on the Excavations of the Universities of Chicago, California (Los Angeles) and Amsterdam in the Keban Reservoir, Eastern Anatolia, 1968-1970*, Vol. 2, Studies in Ancient Civilization (Amsterdam, New York & Oxford: North-Holland Publishing Company), 67-88.

Kempinski, A.,
1983 'Syrien und Palastina (Kanaan) in der letzten Phase der Mittelbronze II-B-Zeit (1650-1570 v. Chr.)', *AAT* 4. (Wiesbaden)
1992 'Dan and Kabri; a note on the planning of two cities', *Eretz-Israel* 23, 76-81 [in Hebrew, with English summary].

Kempinski, A. (ed.),
1988 *Excavations at Kabri; preliminary report of 1987 season* (Tel Aviv: Tel Aviv University) [in Hebrew, with English summary ].
1989 *Excavations at Kabri; preliminary report of the 1988 season* (Tel Aviv: Tel Aviv University) [in Hebrew, with English summary].

Kendall, D.G.,
1963 'A statistical approach to Flinders Petrie's sequence dating', *Bulletin of the International Statistical Institute* 40, 657-680.

Kennedy, C.A.,
1989 'Isaiah 57, 5-6; tombs in rocks', *BASOR* 275, 47-52.

Kenyon, K.M.,
1956 'Tombs of the Intermediate Early Bronze-Middle Bronze Age at tell el-Ajjul', *Annual of the Department of Antiquities of Jordan* 3, 41-55.

1960    *Excavations at Jericho, vol. 1: The Tombs Excavated in 1952-54* (London: British School of Archaeology in Jerusalem).

1965    *Excavations at Jericho, vol. 2: The Tombs Excavated in 1955-58* (London: British School of Archaeology in Jerusalem).

1966    *Amorites and Canaanites.* The Schweich Lectures of the British Academy. (London: Oxford University Press).

1969    'The Middle and Late Bronze Age Strata at Megiddo', *Levant* 1, 25-60.

1970    *Archaeology in the Holy Land*, 3rd ed. (New York: Praeger).

1979    *Archaeology in the Holy Land*, 4th ed. (London: Ernest Benn Ltd).

1981    *Excavations at Jericho, vol. 3: The Architecture and Stratigraphy of the Tell* (London: British School of Archaeology in Jerusalem).

Kervran, M.,
1982    'Preliminary report on the excavation of Qal'at al-Bahrain', in Kervran, M., Negre, A. & Pirazzoli t'Sertstevens, M., *Fouilles a Qal'at al-Bahrain. Iere partie (1977-1979)* (Manama: Ministry of Information, Directorate of Archaeology & Museums), 59-84.

Kesnawi, P.S.,
1988    'Dimensions of a social hierarchy on Late Bronze Age Cyprus: An analysis of the mortuary data from Enkomi', *American Journal of Archaeology* 92, 245.

1989a   *Mortuary Ritual and Social Hierarchy in Bronze Age Cyprus*, Ph.D Thesis (University of Michigan, Ann Arbor: University Microfilms).

1989b   'Dimensions of social hierarchy in Late Bronze Age Cyprus. An analysis of the mortuary data from Enkomi', *Journal of Mediterranean Archaeology* 2(1), 49-86.

Kessler, A.T.,
1994    'Beyond the Great Wall of China: archaeological treasures from Inner Mongolia', *Minerva* 5(3), 6-11.

Kessler, K.,
1991    *Uruk. Urkunden aus Privathäusern. Die Wohnhäuser westlich des Eanna-Tempelbereichs. I*, AUWE 8 (Mainz-am-Rhein:Philipp von Zabern).

Kienast, B.,
1965    'Igigu- und Anunnakku-; nach den akkadischen Quellen', in Güterbock, H.G. & Jacobsen, T. (eds), 141-158.

1990    'Igigu-, Anunnakku- und. B. Nach akk. Quellen', in *Reallexikon der Assyriologie und vorderasiatischen Archäologie* 5 (Berlin & New York: Walter de Gruyter), 40-44.

Kinnier Wilson, J.V.,
1967    'Organic diseases in ancient Mesopotamia', in Brothwell, D. & Sandison, A.T. (eds), *Diseases in Antiquity*, (Springfield, Illinois: Thomas), 194 – 196.

Kirkbride, D.,
1966    'Five seasons at the Pre-Pottery Neolithic village of Beidha in Jordan', *Palestine Exploration Quarterly* 98, 8-72.

1967    'Beidha 1965; an interim report', *Palestine Exploration Quarterly* 99, 5-13.

Kislev, M.E., Nadel, D. & Carmi, I.,
1992    'Epipalaeolithic (19,000 B.P.) cereal and fruit diet at Ohalo II, Sea of Galilee, Israel', *Review of Palaeobotany and Palyntology* 73(1-4), 161-166.

Kiszely, I.,
1978    'The origins of artificial deformatiom in Eurasia',. in BAR International Series 50 (Oxford: BAR), 1-76.

Kjeldsen, K. & Zahle, J.,
1976    'A dynastic tomb in central Lycia; new evidence for the study of Lycian architecture and history in the Classical period', *Acta Archaeologica* 47, 29-46.

Kleiss, W.,
1976    'Urartäische Architektur', in Kellner, H.-J. (ed.), *Urartu; ein Wiederentdeckter Rivale Assyriens*, Katalog der Ausstellung (Munich: Mann), 28-44.

Kleiss, W. & Calmeyer, P.,
1979    *Bastam, vol. 1: Ausgrabungen in der urartäischen Anlagen 1972-1975*, Tehraner Forschungen 4 (Berlin).

Kleiss, W. & Hauptmann, H.,
1976    *Topographische Karte von Urartu*, Archäologische Mitteilungen aus Iran, Erganzungsband 3 (Berlin).

Kochavi, M.,
1973    'A built shaft-tomb of the Middle Bronze Age I at Degania A', *Qadmoniot* 6, 50-53 [in Hebrew].

1989    *Aphek-Antipatris; Five Thousand Years of history*, [in Hebrew] (Tel Aviv: Hakibbutz Hameuchad).

Kochavi, M., Beck, P. & Gophna, R.,
1979    'Aphek-Antipatris, Tel Poleg, Tel Zeror and Tel Burga; four fortified sites of the Middle Bronze Age IIA in the Sharon Plain', *Zeitschrift des Deutschen Palastina-Vereins* 95, 121-165.

Koeppel, R., Senes, H., Murphy, W. & Mahan, G.S.,
1940    *Teleilat Ghassul II* (Rome: Institut Biblique Pontifical).

Koldewey, R.,
1914    *The Excavations at Babylon*, tr. Johns, AS (London: Macmillan & Co. Ltd).

Kramer, C.,
1982    *Village Ethnoarchaeology. Rural Iran in Archaeological Perspective* (New York: Academic Press).

Kramer, S.N.,
1944    'The Death of Gilgamesh', *BASOR* 94, 2-12.

1960    'Death and nether world according to the Sumerian literary texts', *Iraq* 22, 59-68.

1967 'The death of Ur-nammu and his descent to the netherworld', *Journal of Cuneiform Studies* 21, 104-122.

Krauss, R.,
1975 *Tierknochenfunde aus Bastam in Nordwest-Azerbaidjan / Iran; Fundmaterial der Grabung 1970 und 1972* (Munich)
1986 'Der Oberbildhauer Bak und sein Denkstein in Berlin' Jahrbuch der Berliner Museen 28, 5 – 46.

Kühne, H.,
1976 *Die Keramik vom Tell Chuēra und ihre Beziehungen zu Funden aus Syrien-Palaestina, der Türkei und dem Iraq*, Max Freiherr von Oppenheim-Stiftung, Vorderasiatische Forschungen der Max Freiherr von Oppenheim-Stiftung 1 (Berlin: Gebr. Mann).

Kuijt, I., Mabry, J. & Palombo, G.,
1991 'Early Neolithic use of upland areas of Wadi el-Yabis; preliminary evidence from the excavations of 'Iraq ed-Dubb, Jordan', *Paléorient* 17(1), 99-108.

Kunter, M.,
1981 'Anthropologische Befunde; Kampagnen 1977 und 1978', in Orthmann, W. (ed.) 1981, 67-83.

Kunter, M. & Wahl, J.,
1981 'Anthropologische Befunde; Kampagne 1979', in Orthmann, W. (ed.) 1981, 89-101.

Kurth, G.,
1958 'Zur Stellung der neolithischen Menschenreste von Khirokitia aus Cypern', *Homo* 9, 20-31.

Kurth, G. & Rohrer-Ertl, O.,
1981 'On the anthropology of the Mesolithic to Chalcolithic human remains from the Tell es-Sultan in Jericho, Jordan', in Kenyon, K. 1981, 407-499.

Kurtz, D. & Boardman, J.,
1971 *Greek Burial Customs* (London: Thames & Hudson).

Laessøe, J.,
1963 *People of Ancient Assyria; their Inscriptions and Correspondence* (London: Routledge & Kegan Paul).

Lamberg-Karlovsky, C.C.,
1982 'Dilmun; gateway to immortality', *Journal of Near Eastern Studies* 41, 45-50.
1985 'Death in Dilmun', *Dilmun* 12 (1984/85), 15-24.
1986 'Death in Dilmun', in Sh.H.A Al Khalifa & M. Rice (eds), *Bahrain Trough the Ages; the Archaeology* (London: KPI), 156-165.

Lambert, P.J.,
1979 'Early neolithic cranial deformation at Ganj Dareh Tepe, Iran', *Canadian Review of Physical Anthropology* 1, 51-54.

Lambert, W.G.,
1980 'The theology of death', in Alster, B. (ed.), 53-66.
1985 'The pair Lahmu-Lahamu in cosmology', *Orientalia* (New Series) 54, 189-202.

Lancaster, W. & Lancaster, F.,
1993 'Graves and funerary monuments of the Ahl al-Gabal, Jordan', *Arabian archaeology epigraphy* 4(3), 151-69.

Lane, A,
1939 'Glazed relief ware of the ninth century A.D.', *Ars Islamica* 6(1) (Michigan: University of Michigan Press), 56-65.

Lane, E.W.,
1890 *An Account of the Manners and Customs of the Modern Egyptians. Written in Egypt during the Years 1833-1835*, reprint (London: Ward, Lock & Co.).
1987 Arabian Society in the Middle Ages. Studies from The Thousand and One Nights, reprint (London: Curzon Press Ltd.).

Langdon, S.,
1924 *Excavations at Kish, vol. 1: 1923-1924* (Paris: Paul Geuthner).

Larnach, S.L.,
1974 'Frontal recession and artificial deformation', *Archaeology and Physical Anthropology in Oceania* 9, 214-216.

Larsen, C.,
1983 *Life and Land Use on Bahrain Islands* (Chicago: University of Chicago Press).

Latacz, J.,
1986 'News from Troy', *Berytus* 34, 97-127.

Layard, A.H.,
1853 Discoveries in the Ruins of Nineveh and Babylon; with travels in Armenia, Kurdistan and the desert: being the result of a second expedition undertaken for the trustees of the British Museum (London: John Murray).

Le Brun, A.
1989 'Le traitement des morts et les représentations des vivants à Khirokitia', in E. Pelenburg (ed) 1989, 77-.

Le Mort, F.,
1989 'PPNA burials from Hatula (Israel)', in Hershkovitz, I. (ed.), *People and Cultures in Change*, BAR International Series 508 (Oxford: BAR), 133-140.

Lebeau, M.,
1990 'La céramique du tombeau 300 de Mari (temple d'Ishtar)', *Mari Annales Recherches Interdisciplinaires* 6, 349-383.

Lechevallier, M.,
1978 (ed.), *Abou Gosh et Beisamoun. Deux Gisements de VIIe Millenaire avant l'Ere Chretienne en Israel* (Paris: Centre de Recherches Préhistoriques français de Jérusalem, Mémoires et travaux No. 2).

Lechevallier, M. & Ronen, A.,
1985 Le Site Natoufien-Khiamien de Hatoula, près de Latroun, Israel, Les cahiers de C.R.F.J no.1 (Jerusalem: C.R.F.J).

Leek, F.F.,
1966    'Observations on dental pathology seen in ancient Egyptian skulls', *Journal of Egyptian Archaeology* 52, 596.
1972    'Teeth and bread in ancient Egypt', *Journal of Egyptian Archaeology* 58, 126-132.

Legrain, L.,
1928    'Small sculptures from Babylonian tombs', *The Museum Journal* (of the Museum of the University of Pennsylvania) XIX, 195-212.

Lehmann-Haupt, C.F.,
1931    *Armenien einst und jetzt, vol. 2/2* (Berlin).

Lenzen, H. J.,
1968    XXIV. vorläufiger Bericht über die von dem Deutschen Archäologischen Institut und der Deutschen Orient-Gesellschaft aus Mitteln der Deutschen Forschungsgemeinschaft unternommenen Ausgrabungen in Uruk-Warka. Winter 1965/66 (Berlin: Gebr. Mann Verlag).

Lenzen, H.J. & Nissen, H.J.,
1974    XXV. vorläufiger Bericht über die von dem Deutschen Archäologischen Institut und der Deutschen Orient-Gesellschaft aus Mitteln der Deutschen Forschungsgemeinschaft unternommenen Ausgrabungen in Uruk-Warka. Winter 1966/67 (Berlin,Gebr. Mann Verlag).

Lenzen, H.J. et al.,
1964    XX. vorläufiger Bericht über die von dem Deutschen Archäologischen Institut und der Deutschen Orient-Gesellschaft aus Mitteln der Deutschen Forschungsgemeinschaft unternommenen Ausgrabungen in Uruk-Warka. Winter 1961/62 (Berlin,Gebr. Mann Verlag).

Leonard, A.L.,
1989    'The Late Bronze Age', *Biblical Archaeologist* 52, 4-39.

Levy, T.E.,
1986    'The Chalcolithic period', *Biblical Archaeologist* 49, 82-108.

Levy, T.E. (ed.),
1987    *Shiqmim I; studies concerning Chalcolithic Societies in the Northern Negev Desert, Israel (1982-1984)*, BAR International Series 356 (Oxford: BAR).

Levy, T.E. & Alon, D.,
1982    'The Chalcolithic mortuary site near Mezad Aluf, northern Negev Desert; a preliminary study', *BASOR* 248, 37-59.
1985    'Shiqmim; a Chalcolithic village and mortuary center in the northern Negev', *Paléorient* 11(1), 71-83.
1991    'Gilat – 1990', *Hadashot Archeologiyot* 97, 83-84 [in Hebrew].

Levy, T.E., Alon, D., Grigson, C., Holl, A., Goldberg, P., Rowan, Y. & Smith, P.,
1991    'Subterranean Negev settlement', *National Geographic Research and Exploration* 7(4), 394-413.

Lewis, R.,
1971    *Everyday Life in Ottoman Turkey* (London/New York: Batsford/Putnam's Sons).

Lewis, T.J.,
1989    *Cults of the Dead in the Ancient Israel and Ugarit*, Harvard Semitic Museum Monographs 39 (Atlanta: Scholars Press).

Lieberman, D.E.,
1993    'The rise and fall of seasonal mobility among hunter-gatherers; the case of the southern Levant', *Current Anthropology* 34, 599-631.

Limet, H.,
1978    'Étude sémantique de *ma-da, kur, kalam*', *Revue d'Assyriologie* 72, 1-12.

Limper, C.,
1988    *Uruk. Perlen, Ketten, Anhänger. Grabungen 1912-1985*, AUWE 2 (Mainz-am -Rhein:Philipp von Zabern).

Llewellyn, B.,
1986    'The Catalogue of Oil Paintings, Watercolours, Drawings, Prints and Books', in Cochrane, B., LLewellyn, B. & Searight, S., *Romantic Lebanon. The European View 1700-1900* (London: The British Lebanese Association).

Lloyd, J.B.,
1990    'The Banquet Theme in Ugaritic Narrative', *Ugarit-Forschungen* 22, 169-194.

Lloyd, S.,
1967    'Tell Agrab', in Delougaz, P, Hill, H. & Lloyd, S. (eds), *Private Houses and Graves in the Diyala Region*, Oriental Institute publications 88 (Chicago: University of Chicago Press), 267-273.

Lloyd, S. & Safar, F.,
1945    'Tell Hassuna – Excavations by the Iraq Government Directorate General of Antiquities in 1943-4', *Journal of Near Eastern Studies* 4, 255-289.

Loffreda, S.,
1968    'Typological sequence of Iron Age rock cut tombs in Palestine', *Liber Annus* 18, 244-287.

Loftus, W.K.,
1857    Travels and researches in Chaldaea and Susiana; with an account of excavations at Warka, the "Erech" of Nimrod, and Shush, "Shushan the palace" of Esther, in 1849-52 (London: James Nisbet & Co).

Loud, G.,
1948    *Megiddo, vol. 2: Seasons of 1935-39*, Oriental Institute Publications 62 (Chicago: University of Chicago Press).

Lowe,
1986    'Bronze Age burial mounds on Bahrain', *Iraq* 48, 73-84.

Luckenbill, D.D.,
1926    *Ancient Records of Assyrian and Babylonia*. 2 vols (Chicago: University of Chicago Press).

Lunt, D.A.,
1974 'The prevalence of dental caries in the permanent dentition of Scottish prehistoric and mediaeval populations', *Archives of Oral Biology* 19, 431-437.
1985 'Discussion of the human dentitions', in Peltenburg, E.J. (ed.), *Excavations at Lemba Lakkous, 1976-1983* (Göteborg: Paul Åströms Förlag), 245-249.
1986 'Mediaeval dentitions from St. Andrews', in Cruwys, E. & Foley, R.A. (eds), *Teeth and Anthropology*. BAR International Series 291. (Oxford: BAR), 215-224.

Lüth, F.,
1989 'Tell Halawa B', in Orthmann, W. (ed.) 1989, 85-109.

Lynch, H.F.B.,
1901 *Armenia; Travels and Studies, vol. 2,* 1965 reprint (Beirut : Khayats).

Macalister, R.A.S.,
1912 The Excavation of Gezer 1902-1905 and 1907-1909 (London: John Murray).

Mack, J. (ed.),
1994 *Masks: The Art of Expression* (London: British Museum Press).

Mackay, E.,
1929 'The islands of Bahrein', in MacKay, E., Harding, L. & Petrie, F., *Bahrein and Hamamieh,* British School of Archaeology in Egypt 47[1925] (London: BSAE).

Mahler, J.,
1959 *The Westerners among the Figurines of the T'ang Dynasty of China,* Serie Orientale 20 (Rome).

Maier, F.G. & V. Karageorghis
1984 Paphos History and Archaeology (Nicosia).

Malek, J.,
1993 *The Cat in Ancient Egypt* (London: British Museum Press).

Mallon, A.,
1929 'Notes sur quelques sites du Ghôr oriental', *Biblica* 10, 94-99; 214-232.

Mallon, A., Koeppel, R., & Neuville, R.,
1934 *Teleilat Ghassul I, 1929-32* (Rome: Pontifical Biblical Institute) 4.

Mallowan, M.E.L.,
1936 'The excavations at Tall Chagar Bazar, and an archaeological survey of the Habur region, 1934-5', *Iraq,* 3, 1-86.
1937 'The excavations at Tall Chagar Bazar and an archaeological survey of the Habur region; second campaign, 1936', *Iraq* 4, 91-178.
1947 'Excavations at Brak and Chagar Bazar', *Iraq* 9, 1-259.
1969 'Rediscovered skulls from Arpachiyah', *Iraq* 31, 49-58.

Mallowan, M.E.L. & Rose, J.C.,
1935 'Excavations at Tell Arpachiyah, 1933', *Iraq* 2, 1-178.

Mansfeld, G.,
1970 'Ein bronzezeitliches Steinkammergrab bei Rafid im Wadi at-Taym', in Hachmann, R. (ed.), *Bericht uber die Ergegnisse der Ausgrabungen in Kamid el-Loz (Libanon) in den Jahren 1966 und 1967* (Bonn: Rudolf Habelt), 117-128.

Manson-Bahr, P.E.C. & Apted, F.I.C.,
1982 *Manson's Tropical Diseases,* 18th ed. (London: Balliere Tindall).

Marcanti, P.,
1977 The 1919/20 Breasted Expedition to the Near East. A Photographic Study (Chicago/London: University of Chicago).

Maréchal, C.,
1991 'Elements de parure de la fin du Natoufien; Mallaha niveau I, Jayroud 1, Jayroud 3, Jayroud 9, Abu Hureyra et Mureybet IA', in Bar-Yosef, O. & Valla, F.R. (eds) 1991, 589-612.

Margueron, J.,
1977 'Ras Shamra 1975 et 1976. Rapport préliminaire sur les campagnes d'automne', *Syria* 59, 151-188.
1980 *Le Moyen Euphrate, Zone de Contacts et d'Échanges* (Leiden: Brill)
1983 'Quelques réflexions sur certaines pratiques funéraires d'Ugarit', *Akkadica* 32, 5-31.

Markey, T.L. & Greppin, J. (eds),
1990 *When Worlds Collide,* Rockefeller Foundation's Conference Center, Bellagio, Lake Como, Italy, (Ann Arbor: Karoma).

Marro, C.,
1993 'Introduction à la céramique du haut-Euphrate au Bronze Ancien', *Anatolia Antiqua* 2, 43-69.

Masson, O.,
1974 'Notes d'épigraphie carienne', *Kadmos* 13, 124-132.

Matney, T.,
forthcoming 'Ottoman clay tobacco pipes from the Zummar region, Iraq', in Ball, W. (ed.), *Ancient Settlements in the Zummar Region. Excavations Carried out in the Saddam Dam Salvage Project by the British Archaeological Expedition to Iraq,* vol 3, British School of Archaeology in Iraq Reports (London: Aris & Phillips).

Matson, F.R.,
1974 'The Archaeological Present: Near Eastern Village Potters at Work (summary)', *American Journal of Archaeology* 78, 345-347.

Matsumoto, K,
1991 'Preliminary Report on the Excavations at Kish/Hursagkalama, 1988-1989', *Al-Rāfidān* 12, 261-297.

Matsumoto, K. & Yokyama, S.,
1989 'Report on the Excavations at Tell Songor B. The graves', *Al-Rāfidān* 10, 245-298.

Matthers, J.,
1981b 'EBIV', in Matthers (ed) 1981a, 327-348.

Matthers, J. (ed.),
1981a *The River Qoueiq, Northern Syria, and its Catchment; Studies arising from the Tell Rifa'at Survey 1977-1979*, BAR International Series 98 (Oxford: BAR).

Matthews, R. & Wilkinson, T.J.,
1991 'Excavations in Iraq, 1989-90', *Iraq* 53, 169-182.

Matthiae, P.,
1980 'Two princely tombs at Tell Mardik-Ebla', *Archaeology* 33/2, 8-17.
1988 'On the economic foundations of the early Syrian culture of Ebla', in Waetzoldt, H. & Hauptmann, H. (eds) 1988, 75-80.
1989 *Ebla; un Impero Ritrovato*, 2nd ed. (Turin: Giulio Einaudi).

Maxwell-Hyslop, K.R.,
1946 'Daggers and swords of Western Asia', *Iraq* 8, 1-65.
1949 'Western Asiatic shaft-hole axes', *Iraq* 11, 90-129.
1971 *Western Asiatic Jewellery ca. 3000-612 BC* (London: Methuen).
1974 'Assyrian sources of iron', *Iraq* 36, 139-154.

Maytie, A.,
1972 'Le systeme maxillo-dentaire du Neolithique a l'age du Bronze en France; notes et statistiques', *Bulletin du Groupement International pour la Recherche Scientifique en Stomatologie* 15, 323-349.

Mazar, A.,
1990 *Archaeology of the Land of the Bible 10000-586 BCE.* (New York: Doubleday).

Mazar, B.,
1968 'The Middle Bronze Age in Palestine', *Israel Exploration Journal* 18, 65-97.

Mazzoni, S.,
1985a 'Elements of ceramic cultures of early Syrian Ebla in comparison with Syro-Palestinian EB IV', *BASOR* 257, 1-18.
1985b 'Frontières céramiques et le haut Euphrate au Bronze Ancien IV', *Mari 4 Annales Recherches Interdisciplinaires*, 561-577.
1988 'Economic features of the pottery equipment of Palace in G', in Waetzoldt, H. & Hauptman, H. (eds)1988, 81-105.

McCown, D.E. & Haines, R.C.,
1967 *Nippur I. Temple of Enlil, Scribal Quarter, and Soundings*, Oriental Institute Publications 78 (Chicago: Oriental Institute).

McCown, T.D.,
1937 'Mugharet es-Skhul; description and excavations', in Garrod, D.A. & Bate, D. (eds), *The Stone Age of Mount Carmel* (Oxford: Clarendon Press), 91-107.

1939 *The Natufian crania from Mount Carmel, Palestine and their Inter-Relationships*, PhD thesis (Berkeley: University of California).

McCown, T.D. & Keith, A.,
1939 *The Stone Age of Mount Carmel*, Vol. II (Oxford: Clarendon Press).

McFadden, G.H.,
1954 'A Late Cypriote III tomb from Kourion-Kaloriziki no. 40', *American Journal of Archaeology* 58, 131-142.

McGuire, R.H.,
1983 'Breaking Down Cultural Complexity: Inequality and Heterogeneity', in Schiffer, M.B. (ed.), *Advances in Archaeological Method and Theory* 6 (London and New York: Academic Press), 91-142.

McNeill, R.W. & Newton, G.N.,
1965 'Cranial base morphology in association with intentional cranial vault deformation' *American Journal of Physical Anthropology* 23, 241-256.

Mechoulam, R.,
1973 in Mechoulam, R. (ed.), *Marijuana; Chemistry, Pharmacology, Metabolism and Clinical Effects* (New York: Academic Press), 1-99.
1986 in Mechoulam, R. (ed.), *Cannabinoids as Therapeutic Agents* (Boca Raton, Fl.: CRC Press), 1-19.

Medley, M.,
1981 *T'ang Pottery and Porcelain* (London: Faber).
1989 *The Chinese Potter; a Practical History of Chinese Ceramics* (Oxford: Phaidon).

Mee, C.,
1988 'A Mycenaean thalassocracy in the eastern Aegean?', in French, E.B. & Wardle, K.A.(eds), *Problems in Greek Prehistory* (Bristol: Bristol Classics Press), 301-305.

Meier, G.,
1943 [Review of Tallqvist, K., *Sumerisch-Akkadische Namen der Totenwelt* (Studia orientalia, 4) (Helsingfors: Akademiska Bokhandeln & Leipzig: O. Harrassowitz; 1934)], *Orientalistische Literaturzeitung* 46, 213-214.

Meiggs, R., and Lewis, D.M. (eds),
1988 A Selection of Greek Historical Inscriptions to the End of the Fifth Century BC, 2nd ed. (Oxford: Clarendon Press).

Meijer, D.J.W.,
1980 'The Excavations at Tell Selenkahiye', in Margueron, J.Cl. (ed.), *Le Moyen Euphrate; Zone de Contacts et d'Échanges*, Travaux du Centre de Recherche sur le Proche-Orient et la Grèce Antiques 5, (Leiden: E.J. Brill), 117-126.

Meiklejohn, C., Agelarakis, A., Akkermans, P.A., Smith, P.E.L. & Solecki, R.,
1992 'Artificial cranial deformation in the Proto-neolithic Near East and its possible origin: evidence from four sites', *Paléorient* 18, 83-97.

Melikishvili, G.A.,
1960    *Urätskie klinoobraznve nadpisis* [Urartian cuneiform inscriptions; in Russian] (Moscow).

Mellaart, J.,
1964    'Excavations at Çatal Hüyük 1963; third preliminary report', *Anatolian Studies* 14, 39-119.
1967    *Çatal Hüyük* (London: Thames & Hudson).
1970    'The earliest settlements in Western Asia from the ninth to the end of the fifth millennium BC. *CAH* 3rd ed. (Cambridge: Cambridge University Press), vol. 1(1): 248-326.
1975    *The Neolithic of the Near East* (London: Thames & Hudson).

Mellink, M.,
1964    'Archaeology in Asia Minor ', *American Journal of Archaeology* 68, 149-166.
1967    'Excavations at Karataş-Semayük in Lycia 1966', *American Journal of Archaeology* 71, 251-267.
1969    'The Early Bronze-Age in southwest Anatolia; a start in Lycia', *Archaeology* 22, 290-299.
1972    'Archaeology in Asia Minor', *American Journal of Archaeology* 76, 165-188.
1989    'Anatolia and the foreign relations of Tarsus in the Early Bronze Age', in Emre, K., Hrouda, B., Mellink, M. & Özgüç, N. (eds), *Anatolia and the Ancient Near East; Studies in Honor of Tahsin Özgüç* (Ankara: Türk Tarih Kurumu Basimi), 319-331.
1992    'Anatolian chronology', in Ehrich, R.W. (ed.) 1992, *Chronologies in Old World Archaeology* (Chicago: University of Chicago Press), Vol. 1, 171-184, Vol. 2, 207-220.

Merpert, N.I. & Munchaev, R.M.,
1987    'The earliest levels at Yarim Tepe I and Yarim Tepe II in northern Iraq', *Iraq* 49, 1-37.
1993    'Burial practices of the Halaf Culture', in Yoffee, N. & Clark, J.J. (eds), *Early Stages in the Evolution of Mesopotamian Civilisation: Soviet Excavations in Northern Iraq* (Tucson & London: University of Arizona Press), 207-224.

Merpert, N.I., Munchaev, R.M. & Bader, N.D.,
1978    'Soviet investigations in the Sinjar Plain', *Sumer* 34, 27-70.

Mershen, B.,
1990    'The Islamic cemetery of Abu an-Naml', *Annual of the Department of Antiquities of Jordan* 34, 331-332.
1991a   'The Islamic cemetery of Abu en-Naml', in Kerner, S. (ed.), *The Near East in Antiquity. German Contributions to the Archaeology of Jordan, Palestine, Syria, Lebanon & Egypt. Vol. 2* (Amman: Goethe-Institut), 135-141.
1991b   'Folk Jewellery in Jordan', in Bienkowski, P. (ed.), *Treasures from an Ancient Land: the Art of Jordan* (Stroud: Alan Sutton), 162-174.

Metcalf, P. & Huntington, R.,
1991    Celebrations of Death: The Anthropology of Mortuary Ritual, 2nd ed. (Cambridge: Cambridge University Press.)

Metzger, H.,
1963    *Fouilles de Xanthos, vol. 2: L'Acropole Lycienne* (Paris: Institut Français d'Archéologie d'Istanbul).

Meyer, J.,
1989    'Die Grabungen im Planquadrat Q', in Orthmann, W. (ed.) 1989, 11-18.

Michalowski, P.,
1985    'Third millennium contacts: observations on the relationship between Mari and Ebla', *Journal of the American Oriental Society* 105, 293-302.

Mienis, H.K.,
1987    'Molluscs from the excavation of Mallaha (Eynan)', in Bouchard , J. (ed.), *La Faune du Gisement Natoufien de Mallaha (Eynan), Israel*, Memoires et travaux du Centre Recherche Francais de Jerusalem 6 (Paris: Association Paléorient), 157-178.

Milano, L.,
1991    'Mozan 2; the epigraphic finds of the sixth season', *Syro-Mesopotamian Studies* 5(1), 1-34.

Miles, A.E.W.,
1963    'The dentition in the assessment of individual age in skeletal material', in Brothwell, D. (ed.) 1963a, 191-209.

Milik, J.T.,
1976    'Une inscription bilingue nabatéenne et grecque à Pétra', *Annual of the Department of Antiquities of Jordan* 21, 143-147.

Miller, R.,
1984    'Flaked Stone Industries of Arabia and the Gulf from Late Iron Age to early Islamic Times', in Boucharlat, R. & Salles, J-F. (eds), *Arabie Orientale, Mésopotamie et Iran méridional de l'Age du Fer au début de la Période Islamique*, Mémoire 37, (Paris: Editions Recherche sur les Civilisations), 145-150.

Miller, R.L., Armelagos, G.J., Ikram, S, De Jonge, N., Krijger, F.W. & Deelder, A.M.,
1992    'Paleoepidemiology of schistosoma infection in mummies', *British Medical Journal* 304, 555-556.

Minns, E.H.,
1913    *Scythians and Greeks* (Cambridge: Caambridge University Press).

Miron, E.,
1988    'Area C2; stratigraphy, architecture and the ceramic assemblage', in Kempinski, A. (ed.) 1988, 15-29.
1989    'Area C2', in Kempinski, A. (ed.) 1989, 24-30.

Montet, P.,
1928    *Byblos et l'Égypte* (Paris: Paul Geuthner).

Moore, A.M.T.,
1978    *The Neolithic of the Levant*, PhD thesis, (Oxford University).

Moorey, P.R.S.,
1971    Catalogue of ancient Persian Bronzes in the Ashmolean Museum (Oxford: Clarendon Press).
1977    'What do we know about the people buried in the Royal Cemetery? Expedition 20, 24-40'.
1978    Kish Excavations 1923-1933. With a Microfiche Catalogue of the Objects in Oxford Excavated by the Oxford-Field Museum, Chicago, Expedition to Kish in Iraq, 1923-1933 (Oxford:Clarendon Press).
1982    'The archaeological evidence for metallurgy and related technologies in Mesopotamia c. 5500-2100 BC', Iraq 44, 13-38.
1986    'The emergence of the light horse-drawn chariot in the Near East c. 2000-1500 BC', World Archaeology 18, 196-215.

Moorrees, C.F.A., Fanning, E.A. & Hunt, E.E.,
1963    'Age variation of formation stages for ten permanent teeth', Journal of Dental Research 42, 1490-1502.

Morris, I.,
1987    Burial and Ancient Society (Cambridge: Cambridge University Press)
1992    Death-ritual and Social Structure in Classical Antiquity (Cambridge: Cambridge University Press).

Mortensen, I.D. & Mortensen, P.,
1989    'On the Origin of Nomadism in Northern Luristan', in de Meyer, L. & Haerinck, E. (eds.), Archaeologica Iranica et Orientalis. Miscellanea in honorem Louis Vanden Berghe II (Gent: Peeters), 929-51.

Moscati, S. (ed.),
1988    The Phoenicians, catalogue of an exhibition (Milan: Fabbri Bompiani).

Mousa, A.H., Ata, A.A., El Rooby, A., El Garem, A., Abdel Wahab, M.F. & El Raziky, E.,
1967    'Clinico pathological aspects of hepatosplenic bilharziasis', in Mostofi, F.K. (ed.), Bilharziasis (Berlin: Springer-Verlag), 15-30.

Muhesien, M.,
1988    'The Epipalaeolithic phases of Kharane IV', in Garrard, A.N. & Gebel, H.G. (eds) 1988, 353-367.

Müller, U.,
1970    'Kritische Bemerkungen zu den straten XIII-X im Megiddo', Zeitschrift des Deutschen Palästina-Vereins 86, 50-86.

Munchaev, R.M. & Merpert, N.I.,
1981    Раннеземледельческие Поселения Северной Месопотаии, (Earliest Agricultural Settlements of Northern Mesopotamia) (Moscow: Nauka).

Munro, J.A.R. & Tubbs, H.A.,
1890    'Excavations in Cyprus, 1889. Polis tes Chrysochou, Limniti', Journal of Hellenic Studies 2, 1-99.

Murray, A.S, Smith, A.H, & Walters, H.B.,
1900    Excavations in Cyprus (London).

Murray, M.A.,
1973    The Splendour that was Egypt (London :Book Club Associates).

Musgrave, J. & Evans, S.,
1978    'By Strangers Honored', XI International Congress of Classical Archaeology, University College, London September 1978.

Musil, A.,
1908    Arabia Petraea, Three volumes (Wien: Alfred Hölder).
1928    The Manners and Customs of the Rwala Bedouins, Oriental Explorations & Studies No. 6 (New York: American Geographical Society).

Myles, M.F.,
1981    Textbook for Midwives 711, 9th ed. (London: Livingstone).

Mylonas, G.E.,
1948    'Homeric and Mycenaean burial customs', American Journal of Archaeology 52, 56-81.
1966    Mycenae and the Mycenaean Age (Princeton: Princeton University Press).

Myres, J.H.,
1910    'A tomb of the Early Iron Age from Kition in Cyprus, containing bronze examples of the "sigynna" or Cypriot javelin', (Liverpool) Annals of Archaeology and Anthropology 3, 107-117.
1914    Handbook of the Cesnola Collection from Cyprus (New York: Metropolitan Museum of Art).

Nadel, D.,
1990    'Ohalo II – a preliminary report', Mitekufat Haeven 23, 48-59.
1991    'Ohalo II – the third season (1991)', Mitekufat Haeven 24, 158-163.
1992    Bones and Spirits; Prehistoric Burial Customs in Israel. Catalogue of Exhibition, [in English & Hebrew] (Haifa: Stekelis Museum of Prehistory).
1994    'Levantine Upper Palaeolithic burial customs; Ohalo II as a case study', Paléorient, 20(1), 1130122.

Nadel, D. & Hershkovitz, I.,
1991    'New subsistence data and human remains from the earliest Levantine Epipalaeolithic', Current Anthropology 32(5), 631-635.

Nadel, D., Danin, A., Werker, E., Schick, T., Kislev, M.E. & Stewart, K.,
1994    '19, 000 years-old twisted fibers from Ohalo II', Current Anthropology 35(4), 451-458.

Nadel, D., Carmi, I., & Segal, D.,
In press 'Radiocarbon dating of Ohalo II: archaeological and methodological implications', Journal of Archaeaological Science.

Negev, A.,
1971    'A Nabatean epitaph from Trans-Jordan', Israel Exploration Journal 21, 50-52.

Neumann, G.,
1979    *Neufunde lykischer Inschriften seit 1901*, Ergänzungsbände zu den Tituli asiae minoris 7 (Vienna: Verlag der Oesterreichischen Akademie der Wissenschaften).

Neuville, R.,
1930    'La nécropole megalithique d'el-Adeimeh (Transjordanie)', *Biblica* 11, 249-265.
1934    'Le prehistoire du Palestine', *Revue Biblique* 43, 237-259.
1951    *Le Paleolithique et Mesolithique du desert de Judee.* Archives de l'Institut de Paleontologie Humaine, 24. (Paris: Masson).

Newberry, P.,
1893    'Tomb No. 15' in *Beni Hasan*, vol. 2 (London: Egypt Exploration Fund).

Ngubane, H.,
1976    'Some notions of "purity" and "impurity" among the Zulu', *Africa* 46, 274-283.

Nicolaou, K.,
1965    'Γεωμετικοι ταφοι Κυθραιασ', *Report of the Department of Antiquities of Cyprus*, 30-73.
1976    *The Historical Topography of Kition*, Studies in Mediterranean Archaeology 43 (Göteborg: Paul Åströms Förlag).

Niebuhr, C.,
1776/80 *Voyage en Arabie & en d'autres Pays Circonvoisins*, 2 vols (Amsterdam/Utrecht: S.J. Baaldé/Barthelemy Wild).

Niklasson, K.,
1983    'Tomb 23. A shaft grave of the Late Cypriote III period', *Studies in Mediterranean Archaeology* 45:8 (Göteborg), 169-187

Nissen, H.J., Muheisen, M. & Gebel, H.G.,
1987    'Report on the first two seasons of excavations at Basta (1986-7)'. *Annual of the Department of Antiquities of Jordan* 31, 79-119.
1991    'Report on the excavations at Basta 1988', *Annual of the Department of Antiquities of Jordan* 35, 13-40.

Noldeke, A. *et al.*
1932    Vierter vorläfiger Bericht über die von der Notgemeinschaft der Deutschen Wissenschaft in Uruk unternommenen Ausgrabungen (Berlin).

North, R.,
1973    'Ugarit grid, strata and find locations', *Zeitschrift des Deutschen Palastina-Vereins* 89, 113-160.

Nougayrol, J.,
1968    '(Juste) Souffrant (RS 25.460)', in Nougayrol, J., Laroche, E., Virolleaud, Ch. & Schaeffer, C.F.A., *Ugaritica V* (Paris: Paul Geuthner), 265-273.

Noy, T.,
1980    'Hagoshrim', *Hadashot Archeologiyot* 74/75, 3-4 [in Hebrew].
1989    'Some aspects of Natufian mortuary behaviour at Nahal Oren', in Hershkovitz, I. (ed.), *People and Cultures in Change*, BAR International Series 508 (Oxford: BAR), 53-57.

Noy, T., Legge, A.J. & Higgs, E.S.,
1973    'Recent excavations at Nahal Oren, Israel', *Proceedings of the Prehistoric Society* 39, 75-99.

Numoto, H. & Yasuyoshi, O.,
1987    'Iraq; Rettungsaktivaten: 'Usiya', *Archiv für Orientforschung* 34, 166-175.

O'Connor, D.,
1986    'New Kingdom and Third Intermediate period, 1552-664 BC', in Trigger, B, Kemp, B., O'Connor, D. & Lloyd, A., *Ancient Egypt; a Social History* (Cambridge: Cambridge University Press).

O'Shea, J. M.,
1984    Mortuary Variability: An Archaeological Investigation (New York/London: Academic Press).

Oakley, K.P.,
1964    *Frameworks for Dating Fossil Man* (London).
1972    Man the Toolmaker (London).

Oates, J.,
1978    'Religion and ritual in sixth-millenium B.C. Mesopotamia', *World Archaeology* 10, 117-124.

Ochanine, L.,
1925    'L'ancienneté millénaire de la dolichocéphalie des Turcomans', *Journal Russe d'Anthropologie* 14,69-70.

Odani, N. & Ii, H.,
1981    'Tell Gubba. Preliminary report of excavations at Gubba and Songor', *Al-Rafidan* 2, 141-163.

Oenen, U.,
1990    Lycia: Western section of the southern coast of Turkey, 2nd ed. (Istanbul: NET).

Ogden, J.,
1982    *Jewellery of the Ancient World* (London: Trefoil Books).

Ohata, K. (ed.),
1966    *Tel Zeror I. Preliminary Report of the Excavation First Season 1964* (Tokyo: Society for Near Eastern Studies).
1967    *Tel ZerorII. Preliminary Report of the Excavation Second Season 1965* (Tokyo: Society for Near Eastern Studies).
1970    Tel Zeror III. Preliminary Report of the Excavation Third Season 1966 (Tokyo: Society for Near Eastern Studies).

Ohnefalsch-Richter, M.,
1893    *Kypros, die Bibel und Homer* (London: Asher).

Okley, J.,
1979    'An anthropological contribution to the history and archaeology of an ethnic group', in Burnham, B.C. & Kingsbury, J. (eds), *Space, Hierarchy and Society*, BAR International Series 59 (Oxford: BAR), 81-92.

Oldfather, C.H. (tr.),
1933    *Diodorus Siculus* vol. 1: Books I and II, 1-34 (Cambridge, Massachusetts: Harvard University Press).

Olivier, G.A.,
1801    Travels in the Ottoman Empire, Egypt, & Persia (London: Longman).

Olszewski, D.,
1991    'Social complexity in the Natufian? Assessing the relationship of ideas and data', in Clark, G.A. (ed.), *Perspectives on the Past; Theoretical Biases in Mediterranean Hunter-Gatherer Research* (Philadelphia: University of Pennsylvania Press), 322-340.

Önen, Ü.,
1990    *Lycia; Western Section of the Southern Coast of Turkey*, 2nd ed. (Istanbul: NET).

Oren, E.D.,
1971    'A Middle Bronze Age I warrior tomb at Beth Shan', *Zeitschrift des Deutschen Palästina-Vereins* 87, 109-139.
1973    *The northern cemetery of Beth Shan* (Leiden: E.J. Brill).
1976    *Explorations in the Negev and Sinai* (Beersheba: Ben Gurion University of the Negev).

Orthmann, W.,
1963    *Die Keramik der Frühen Bronzezeit aus Inneranatolien*, Istanbuler Forschungen Band 24 (Berlin: Gebr. Mann).
1980    'Burial customs of the 3rd millennium B.C. in the Euphrates Valley', in Margueron, J.-Cl. (ed.), *Le Moyen Euphrate: Zone de Contacts et d'Échanges*, Travaux du Centre de Recherche sur le Proche-Orient et la Grèce Antiques 5 (Leiden: E.J. Brill), 97-105.
1982    'Ausgrabungen in Halawa 1978', *Les Annales Archéologiques Arabes Syriennes* 32, 143-176.
1986    'The origin of Tell Chuera', in Weiss , H. (ed.), *The Origins of Cities in Dry-Farming Syria and Mesopotamia in the Third Millennium BC* (Guilford, Conn.: Four Quarters Publishing Co.), 61-70.
1989    *Halawa 1980 bis 1986; Vorläufiger Bericht über die 4.-9. Grabungskampagne*, Saarbrücker Beiträge zur Altertumskunde 52 (Bonn: Dr Rudolf Habelt.)

Orthmann, W. (ed.),
1981    , *Halawa 1977 bis 1979; Vorläufiger Bericht über die 1. bis 3. Grabungskampagne*, Saarbrücker Beiträge zur Altertumskunde 31 (Bonn: Rudolf Habelt.)

Orthmann, W., Klein, H. & Lüth, F.,
1986    *Tell Chuēra in Nordost-Syrien 1982-1983*, Schriften Der Max Freiherrvon Oppenheim-Stiftung (Berlin: Verlag Gebr.Mann)

Orton, C.R. & Hodson, F.R.,
1981    'Rank and class; interpreting the evidence from prehistoric cemeteries', in Humphreys, S.C. & King, H. (eds), *Mortality and Immortality: The Anthropology and Archaeology of Death* (London: Academic Press), 103-116.

Ory, J.,
1936    'Excavations at Ras el 'Ain', *Quarterly of the Department of Antiquities of Palestine* 5, 111-112.
1938    'Excavations at Ras el 'Ain II', *Quarterly of the Department of Antiquities of Palestine* 6, 99-120.
1946    'A Chalcolithic necropolis at Benei Beraq', *Quarterly of the Department of Antiquities of Palestine* 12, 43-57.
1948    'A Bronze Age cemetery at Dhahrat el-Humraiya', *Quarterly of the Department of Antiquities of Palestine* 13, 75-89.

Ossenberg, N.S.,
1970    'The influence of artificial cranial deformation on discontinuous morphological traits', *Americam Journal of Physical Anthropology* 33, 357-372.

Otten, C.
1948    'Note on the cemetery of Eridu', *Sumer* 4, 125-127.

Ouvaroff, A.,
1855    Recherches sur les Antiquités de la Russie Méridionale et des côtes de la Mer Noire (Paris: Imperial Archaeological Commission).

Overbeck, J.C. & Swiny, S.,
1972    *Two Cypriot Bronze Age sites at Kafkallia (Dhali)*, Studies in Mediterranean Archaeology 33 (Göteborg: Paul Åströms Förlag).

Özbek, M.,
1974    'Étude de la déformation crânienne artificielle chez les chalcolithiques de Byblos (Liban)', *Bulletin et Mémoires de la Société d'Anthropologie de Paris* 1, 455-481.

Özgen, E.,
1987    'Gaziantep-Kilis bölgesi höyük yüzey araştirmalari: Oylum Höyük', *Araştirma Sonuçlari Toplant ii*4, 239-248.
1988    'Oylum Höyük – 1987', *Kazi Sonuçlari Toplant ii* (1), 95-102.
1989-1990    'Oylum Höyük', *Anatolica* 16, 21-29.
1993    'An Early Bronze Age Burial at Oylum Höyük near Kilis', in Mellink, M.J., Porada, E. & Özgüç, T.(eds), *Aspects of Art and Iconography; Anatolia and its Neighbours – Studies in Honor of Nimet Özgüç* (Ankara: Türk Tarik Kurumu Basimevi), 467-472.

Özgen, E., Carter, A., Parker, A. & Ziadeh.,
n.d.    'A preliminary report on the excavations at Oylum Höyük, 1989-1990'.

Özgen, E. & Carter, E.,
1991    'Oylum Höyük, 1989', *Kazi Sonuçlar Toplant ii*12, 259- 268.

Özgüç, T.,
1948    *Die Bestatungsbräuche im vorgeschichtlichen Anatolien*, Wissenschafliche Reihe 5 (Ankara: Ankara Üniversitesi yayinlari).
1963    'Early Anatolian archaeology in the light of recent research', *Anadolu* 7, 1-21.

1969     *Altintepe, vol. 2,* Turk Tarih Kurumu yayalarindan 5. seri, 25 (Ankara: Turk Tarih Kurumu).

1978     *Excavations at Maşat Höyük and Investigations in its Vicinity* (Ankara: Türk Tarih Kurumu).

1986     'New observations on the relationship of Kültepe with southeast Anatolia and north Syria during the third millennium B.C.', in Canby, J.V., Porada, E. , Ridgway, B.S. & Stech, T. (eds), *Ancient Anatolia, Aspects of Change and Cultural Development. Essays in Honor of Machteld J. Mellink.* Wisconsin studies in classics, Madison (Wisconsin: University of Wisconsin Press), 31-47.

1988     ınandiktepe, an Important Cult Center mitte Old Hittite Period (Ankara: Türk Tarih Kurumu Basim Evi, V/43).

Pader, E.J.,
1982     Symbolism, Social Relations and the Interpretation of Mortuary Remains, BAR International Series 130 (Oxford: BAR).

Paidoussis, M. & Sbarounis, Ch.N.,
1975     'A study of cremated bones from the cemetery of Perati (LH IIIC)', *Opuscula Atheniensa* 11, 129-159.

Paley, S.M. & Porath, Y.,
1979     'The regional project in 'Emeq Hefer, 1979', *Israel Exploration Journal* 29, 236-239.

Palumbo, G.,
1987     '"Egalitarian" or "stratified" society? Some notes on mortuary practices and social structure at Jericho in EB IV', *BASOR* 267, 43-59.

1990     *The Early Bronze Age IV in the southern Levant; Settlement Patterns, Economy and Material Culture of a 'Dark Age'.* (Rome: Herder).

Palumbo, G., Mabry, J. & Kuijt, I.,
1990     'Survey in the Wadi el-Yabis', *Syria* 67, 479-481.

Papworth, M.H.,
1963     *A Primer of Medicine,* 2nd ed. (London: Butterworths).

Pardee, D.,
1988     *Les Textes Para-mythologiques de la 24ᵉ Campagne (1961),* Ras Shamra Ougarit IV (Paris: Édition Recherche sur les Civilisations).

in prep. *Les Textes Rituels,* Ras Shamra Ougarit, Édition Recherche sur les Civilisations. (Paris: ADPF).

Pariselle, C.,
1985     'Le cimitière d'Eridu: essai d'interpretation', *Akkadica* 44, 1-13.

Parker, A.,
in preparation     *Indo-europeans in Early Anatolia,* PhD thesis (Los Angeles: University of California).

Parker, A. & Berger, R.,
in press 'Radiocarbon dating at Oylum Höyük Turkey', *Radiocarbon.*

Parker, S.T.,
1988     'Preliminary Report on the 1985 Season of the *Limes Arabicus* Project', in Rast, W.E. (ed.), *Preliminary Reports of ASOR-Sponsored Excavations 1982-1985* (Baltimore: John Hopkins University Press), 131-61.

Parker Pearson, M.,
1992     Review in *Antiquity* 66, 566-568.

Parrot, A.,
1935     'Les fouilles de Mari', *Syria* 16, 1-28.
1938     'Mari et Chagar Bazar', *Syria* 19, 308-310.
1939     *Maledictions et violations de tombes* (Paris: Geuthner).
1956     *Mission archeologique de Mari, vol. 1: Le temple d'Ishtar* (Paris: Paul Geuthner).
1970     Les merveilles du Louvre (Paris: Hachette).

Pearson, G. W. *et al.,*
1986     'High precision 14-C measurements of Irish oaks to show the natural 14-C variation from AD 1840 to 5210 BC', in Stuiver, M. & Kra, R. (eds), *Radiocarbon* 28, 911-934.

Peebles, C.M. & Kus, S.M.,
1977     'Some archaeological correlates of ranked societies', *American Antiquity* 42, 421-448.

Pelon, O.,
1973     'Les "tholoi" d'Enkomi', in *Acts of the international archaeological symposium 'The Mycenaeans in the eastern Mediterranean (1972)'* (Nicosia: Department of Antiquities of Cyprus), 245-253.

1976     *Tholoi, tumuli et cercles funeraires.* (Athens: École Françaisé d'Athènes).

1985     *Excavations at Lemba Lakkous, 1976-1983,* Lemba Archaeological Project Vol. 1, Studies in Mediterranean Archaeology 70(1) (Göteborg: Paul Åströms Förlag).

1991     'Kissonerga-Mosphilia: A major Chalcolithic site in Cyprus', *BASOR* 282(3), 17-36.

Peltenburg, E. (ed.),
1989     *Early Society in Cyprus* (Edinburgh: University of Edinburgh Press).

Perkins, A.,
1949     *The Comparative Archaeology of Early Mesopotamia* (Chicago: University of Chicago Press).

Perrot, J.,
1955     'The excavations at Tell Abu Matar, near Beersheba', *Israel Exploration Journal* 5(3), 167-189.

1960     'Excavations at 'Eynan ('Ein Mallaha); preliminary report on the 1959 season', *Israel Exploration Journal* 10(1), 14-22.

1961     'Une tombe à ossuaires de IVe millenaire à Azor près de Tel Aviv', *'Atiqot* 3, 1-83.

1966     'Le gisement natoufien de Mallaha (Eynan), Israel', *L'Anthropologie* 70(5/6), 437-483.

1967     *La Palestine prehistorique* Bible et Terre Saint 93.

1968     'La prehistoire palestinienne', in *Dictionnaire de la Bible;* supplement 8, 286-446.

1984 'Structures d'habitat, mode de vie et environment. Les villages souterrains des pasteurs de Beersheva, dans le sud d'Israel, au IVe millenaire avant l'ere chretienne', *Paléorient* 10(1), 75-96.

1993 'Eynan', in Stern, E. (ed.), *The New Encyclopedia of Archaeological Excavations in the Holy Land* (Jerusalem: The Israel Exploration Society), vol. 2, 389-393.

Perrot, J. & Ladiray, D.,
1980 *Tombes à Ossuaires de la Region Cotiere Palestinienne au IVe millenaire avant l'Ere Chretienne* (Paris: Association Paléorient).

Perrot, J., Ladiray, D. & Soliveres-Massei, O.,
1988 *Les hommes de Mallaha (Eynan), Israel, vol. 1: Les Sepultures,* Memoires et travaux du Centre de Recherche Francais de Jerusalem 7 (Paris: Association Paléorient).

Persson, A.W.,
1931 *Royal tombs at Dendra near Midea* (Lund: Gleerup).

1942 *New tombs at Dendra near Midea* (Lund: Gleerup).

Peters, J.P.,
1898 Nippur, or Explorations and Adventures on the Euphrates, the narrative of the University of Pennsylvania expedition to Babylon in the years 1888-1890 (New York: G.P. Putnam's Sons).

Petersen, A.,
1989 'Early Ottoman forts on the Darb al-Haj', *Levant* 21, 97-117.

Petrie, W.M.F. & Quibell, J.E.,
1896 *Naqada and Ballas 1895* (London: Bernard Quaritch).

Petrie, W.M.F.,
1900 *The Royal Tombs of the First Dynasty 1900,* Part 1 (London: Egypt Exploration Fund).

1920 *Prehistoric Egypt* (London: British School of Archaeology in Egypt & Bernard Quaritch).

1928 *Gerar* (London: British School of Archaeology in Egypt).

1930 *Beth Pelet, vol. 1: Tell Farah* (London: British School of Archaeology in Egypt & Bernard Quaritch).

1931 *Ancient Gaza, vol. 1: Tell el Ajjul* (London: Bulletin of the British School of Archaeology in Egypt & Bernard Quaritch).

1932 *Ancient Gaza, vol. 2: Tell el Ajjul* (London: Bulletin of the British School of Archaeology in Egypt & Bernard Quaritch).

1933 *Ancient Gaza, vol. 3: Tell el Ajjul* (London: Bulletin of the British School of Archaeology in Egypt & Bernard Quaritch).

1934 *Ancient Gaza, vol. 4: Tell el Ajjul* (London: Bulletin of the British School of Archaeology in Egypt & Bernard Quaritch).

Pettinato, G.,
1991 *Ebla; a New Look at History* (Baltimore: Johns Hopkins University Press).

Philip, G.,
1988 'Hoards of the Early and Middle Bronze Ages in the Levant', *World Archaeology* 20(2), 190-208.

1989 *Metal Weapons of the Early and Middle Bronze Ages in Syria-Palestine,* 2 vols, BAR International Series 526 (Oxford: BAR).

1991a 'Cypriot bronzework in the Levantine world; conservatism, innovation and social change', *Journal of Mediterranean Archaeology* 4(1), 59-108.

1991b 'Tin, Arsenic Lead; alloying practices in Syria-Palestine around 2000 B.C.', *Levant* 23, 93-104.

in press (a) 'Tell el-Dab'a metalwork; patterns and purpose', in Davies, W.V., *Egypt, the Aegean and the Levant.* (London: British Museum Press).

in press (b) 'The same but different; a comparison of Middle Bronze Age metalwork from Jericho and Tell el-Dab'a', *Studies in the History and Archaeology of Jordan* 5 (Amman: Department of Antiquities of Jordan).

Philipps, E.D.,
1965 The Royal Hordes: Nomad Peoples of the Steppes (London: Thames & Hudson).

Philon, H.,
1980 Benaki Museum Athens. *Early Islamic Ceramics; Nineth to Late Twelfth Centuries,* Benaki Museum, Athens (Saudi Arabia: Islamic Art Publications).

Pichon, J.,
1983 'Parures natoufiennes en os de Perdrix', *Paléorient* 9(1), 91-98.

1991 'Les oiseaux au Natoufien, avifaune et sedentarite', in Bar-Yosef, O. & Valla, F.R. (eds) 1991, 371-380.

Pieridou, A.,
1964 'A Cypro-Geometric cemetery at 'Vathyrkakas'-Karavas', *Report of the Department of Antiquities of Cyprus,* 114-129.

1965 'An early Cypro-Geometric tomb at Lapethos', *Report of the Department of Antiquities of Cyprus,* 74-111.

1966 'A tomb-group from Lapithos-'Ayia Anastasia'', *Report of the Department of Antiquities of Cyprus,* 1-12.

1972 Ταφοσ υπ' AP.503 εκ λαπνθου, "Αγια Αναστασια'", *Report of the Department of Antiquities of Cyprus,* 237-250.

Piggott, S.,
1965 *Ancient Europe from the Beginnings of Agriculture to Classical Antiquity* (Edinburgh: Edinburgh University Press).

1969 'Conclusion', in Ucko, P.J. & Dimbelby, G. (eds), *The Domestication and Exploitation of Plants and Animals* (London: Gerald Duckworth), 555-560.

Pigott, V.C.,
1989 'The emergence of iron use at Hasanlu', in Dyson, R.H. & Voigt, M.M. (eds) 1989, 67-79.

Pitard, W.T.,
1992 'A new edition of the *"rapi'uma"* texts: KTU 1,20-22', *BASOR* 285, 33-77.

Pollak, L.,
1903    Klassisch-Antike Goldschmiedearbeiten im Besitze Sr Excellenz A J von Nelidow (Leipzig: Karl W. Hiersemann).

Pollock, S.,
1985    'Chronology of the Royal Cemetery at Ur', *Iraq* 47, 129-158.
1991a   'Women in a man's world; images of Sumerian women', in Gero, J.M. & Conkey, M.W. (eds), *Engendering Archaeology* (Oxford: Basil Blackwell), 366-387.
1991b   'Of priestesses, priests and poor relations; the dead in the Royal Cemetery at Ur', *Cambridge Journal of Archaeology* 1, 171-189.

Pons, N.,
1983    'Abu Qūbūr. Les objets en métal d'époque achéménide tardive', *Northern Akkad Project Reports* 8, 3-17.

Pope, M.H.,
1981    'The cult of the Dead at Ugarit', in Young, G.D. (ed.), *Ugarit in Retrospect* (Winona Lake: Eisenbrauns), 159-179.

Popovic, L.,
1956    *Katalog nalaza iz nekropole kod Trebenita*, (Belgrade: Narodni Muzej).
1974    *Greek-Illyrian Treasures from Yugoslavia*. Catalogue of exhibition at Sheffield City Museum, (Sheffield: Sheffield City Museums).

Porath, Y.,
1985    'Ma'abarot, burial caves', in Porat, Y., Dar, S. & Epelbaum, S. (eds), *Qadmoniot Emeq Hefer* (Hakibutz Hameuhad Press), 185-191.

Postgate, J.N.,
1969    *Neo-Assyrian Royal Grants and Decrees* (Rome: Pontifical Biblical Institute).
1980a   'Palm-trees, Reeds and Rushes in Iraq Ancient and Modern', in Barrelet, M-Th. (ed.), *L'Archéologie de l'Iraq du Début de l'Époque Néolithique a 333 avant notre ere. Perspectives et Limites de l'Interpretation Anthropologique des Documents,* Colloques internationaux no. 580 (Paris: CNRS), 99-111.
1980b   'Early Dynastic burial customs at Abu Salabikh', *Sumer* 36, 65-82.

Postgate, J.N. & Moon, J.A.,
1982    'Excavations at Abu Salabikh', *Iraq* 44, 103-136.

Postgate, J.N. & Watson, P. (eds),
1979    'Excavations in Iraq 1977-1978', *Iraq* 41, 141-181.

Potts, D.T.,
1990    *The Arabian Gulf in Antiquity,* Two vols (Oxford: Clarendon Press).

Poursat, J.-C.,
1977    *Les Ivoires Mycéniens* (Athens: École Française d'Athènes).

Prag, J.,
1988    quoted in 'Revealed: the long-lost face of King Midas', *Sunday Times* 9th October 1988.

Prag, K.,
1959    'The 1959 Deep Sounding at Harran in Turkey', *Levant* 2, 63-94.
1971    *A Study of the Intermediate Early Bronze-Middle Bronze Age in Transjordan, Syria and Lebanon,* D.Phil. thesis (Oxford University).
1974    'The Intermediate Early Bronze-Middle Bronze Age: an interpretation of the evidence from Transjordan, Syria and Lebanon', *Levant* 6, 69-116.
1984    'Ancient and Modern Pastoral Migration in the Levant', *Levant* 17, 81-88.
1986    'Byblos and Egypt in the fourth millennium BC', *Levant* 18, 59-74.
1989    'Preliminary Report on the Excavations at Tell Iktanu, Jordan, 1987', *Levant* 21, 33-45.
1990    'Preliminary report on the excavations at Tell Iktanu, Jordan, 1989', *Annual of the Department of Antiquities of Jordan* 34, 119-130.
1991a   'A walk in the Wadi Hesban', *Palestine Exploration Quarterly* 123, 48-61.
1991b   'Preliminary Report on the Excavations at Tell Iktanu and Hammam, Jordan, 1990', *Levant* 23, 55-66.
1992    'Bronze Age settlement patterns in the south Jordan valley; archaeology, environment and ethnology', *Studies in the History and Archaeology of Jordan* 4 (Amman: Department of Antiquities & Maison de l'Orient Méditerranéen), 155-160.

Prausnitz, N.W.,
1962    'Khirbet Sheikh Ali', *Revue Biblique* 65, 414.
1970    *From Hunter to Farmer and Trader* (Jerusalem: Sivan Press).

Prideaux, F.B.,
1912    'The sepulchral tumuli of Bahrain', *Archaeological survey of India Annual Report* 1908-9(Calcutta), 60-78.

Pritchard, J.B.,
1963    *The Bronze Age Cemetery at Gibeon,* University of Philadelphia Museum monographs (Philadelphia: University Museum).
1969    *Ancient Near Eastern Texts Relating to the Old Testament,* 3rd ed., with supplement (Princeton: Princeton University Press).

Puech, P.F.,
1977    *Les Caries Dentaires d'une Population du Neolithique en Basse Provence,* Le Chirurgien-Dentiste de France 47(353), 51-55.

Quarantelli, E. (ed.),
1985    *Land between Two Rivers.* Twenty years of Italian Archaeology in the Middle East. The Treasures of Mesopotamia (Turin: Il Quadrante Edizioni).

Rajkowski, W.,
1946    'A Visit to Southern Kurdistan', *Geographical Journal* 107(3/4), 128-134.

Rak, Y., Kimbel, W.H & Hovers, E.,
1994    'A Neandertal infant from Amud Cave, Israel', *Journal of Human Evolution* 26, 313-324.

Rassam, H.,
1897    *Asshur and the Land of Nimrod* (New York: Eaton & Mains/Cincinnati: Curts & Jennings).

Rast, W.,
1980    'Palestine in the 3rd millennium: Evidence for interconnections', *Scripta Mediterranea I*, 5-20.

Rawson, J., Tite, M, & Hughes, M,
1989    'The export of Tang "sancai" wares; some recent research', *Transactions of the Oriental Ceramic Society* 1988-89, London.

Redman, C.L.,
1978    The Rise of Civilization from Early Farmers to Urban Society in the Ancient Near East (San Francisco: W.H. Freeman & Co.).

Reece, R.,
1982    'Bones, bodies and dis-ease', *Oxford Journal of Archaeology* 1(3), 347-58.

Renfrew, C.,
1976    'Megaliths, territories and populations', in de Laet, S.J. (ed.), *Acculturation and Continuity in Atlantic Europe*, IV Atlantic colloquium, Ghent, 1975 (Brugge: De Tempel).
1990    'Some preliminary issues', in Markey, T.L. & Greppin, J. (eds.) 1990, 15-24.

Renfrew, C. (ed.),
1985    [1990] *The Prehistory of Orkney BC 4000 – 1000 AD*.

Reuther, O.,
1926    *Die Innenstadt von Babylon*, Merkes Veroffentlichnungen der Deuthschen Orient-Gesellschaft 47 (Leipzig: J.C. Hinrichs).

Richard, S.L.,
1980    'Towards a consensus of opinion on the end of the Early Bronze Age in Palestine-Transjordan', *BASOR* 237, 5-34.
1987    'The Early Bronze Age; the rise and collapse of urbanism', *Biblical Archaeologist* 50(March), 22-43.

Richardson, N.J.,
1974    *The Homeric Hymn to Demeter* (Oxford: Clarendon Press).

Riis, P.J.,
1948    *Hama, Fouilles et Recherches 1931-193, vol. II/3: Les Cimetières à Crémation* (Copenhagen: Gyldendalske Boghandel, Nordisk Forlag).
1962    'L'activité de la Mission Archéologique Danoise sur la Côte Phénicienne en 1960', *Les Annales Archéologiques de Syrie* 11/12, 133-144.

Riley, J.,
1981    'Petrological examination of Bronze Age IV fabrics', in Matthers, J. (ed.) 1981a, 349-360.

Risser, M.K, & Harvey, S.P.,
1992    'A re-examination of chamber tombs at Tell el-Far'ah (South) [abstract]', *American Journal of Archaeology* 96, 344.

Roaf, M. (ed.),
1984    'Tell Madhhur: A Summary Report on the Excavations', *Sumer* 43, 108-167.

Roaf, M.D. & Postgate, J.N.,
1981    'Excavations in Iraq, 1979-1980', *Iraq* 43, 167-198.

Roberts, D.S.,
1982    *Islam. A Westerner's Guide* (Feltham, Middlesex: Hamlyn).

Rochetti, L.,
1976    'Tombe Geometriche presso Aghia Irini in località Kharangas', *Studi Ciprioti e Rapporti di Scavo* 2, 131-163.

Rohrer-Ertl, O., Frey, K-W. & Neweely, H.,
1988    'Preliminary note on the Early Neolithic human remains from Basta and Sabra 1', in Garrard, A.N. &. Gebel, H.G. (eds) 1988, 135-136.

Rollefson, G.O.,
1983    'Ritual and ceremony at 'Ain Ghazal (Jordan)', *Paléorient* 9(2), 29-38.
1986    'Neolithic 'Ain Ghazal (Jordan); ritual and ceremony, II', *Paléorient* 12(1), 45-51.

Rollefson, G.O. & Simmons, A.H.,
1986    'The Neolithic village of 'Ain Ghazal, Jordan; preliminary report on the 1984 season', *Bulletin of the American Schools of Oriental Research Supplement* 24, 145-164.
1988a   'The Neolithic village of 'Ain Ghazal, Jordan; preliminary report on the 1985 season', *Bulletin of the American Schools of Oriental Research Supplement* 25, 93-106.
1988b   'The Neolithic settlement at 'Ain Ghazal', in Garrard, A.N. & Gebel, H.G. (eds) 1988, 393-421.

Romer, J.,
1982    *Romer's Egypt* (London: Michael Joseph Ltd).

Ronen, A.,
1976    'The Skhul burials; an archaeological review', IXe Congres UISPP, Nice. *Colloque* 12, 27-40.

Roodenberg, J.J.,
1979-1980    'Premiers résultats des recherches archéologiques à Hayaz Höyük', *Anatolica* 7, 3-19.

Rosen, S.A. & Goodfriend, G.A.,
1993    'An early date for Gaza ware from the northern Negev', *Palestine Exploration Quarterly* 125(2), 143-148.

Rostovtzeff, M.,
1922    Iranians and Greeks in South Russia (Oxford: Clarendon Press).

Roux, G.,
1960    'Recently Discovered Ancient Sites in the Hammar Lake District (Southern Iraq)', *Sumer* 16, 20-31.

Ruffer, A.A.,
1920    'Study of abnormalities and pathology of ancient Egyptian teeth', *American Journal of Physical Anthropology* 3, 335-382.

Ruffer, M.A.,
1910    'Note on the Presence of "Bilharzia haematobia" in Egyptian mummies of the twentieth dynasty (1250 – 1000 B.C.)', *British Medical Journal* 1, 16.

Rumeidiyeh, S.S.,
1984    'Excavations at Tell Sleima', *Sumer* 40, 43-54 [Arabic sec.].

Rupp, D.W.,
1989    'High status in the Iron Age', in E. Peltenburg (ed) 1989.

Rutkowski, B.,
1968    'The origin of the Minoan coffin', *Annual of the British School at Athens* 63, 218-227.

Saadé, G.,
1979    *Ougarit, Métropole Cananéenne* (Beirut: Imprimerie Catholique).

Safar, F.,
1949    'Soundings at Tell al-Lahm', *Sumer* (2), 154-164, Pls.I-VII.

Sagona, A.G.,
1984    *The Caucasian Early Bronze Age*, BAR International Series 214 (Oxford: BAR).

Salje, B.,
1992    'Keramik der neubabylonischen Zeit aus den Grabungen in Uruk-Warka', *Baghdader Mitteilungen* 23, 371-464, Taf. 72-100.

Saller, S.J.,
1941    *The Memorial of Moses on Mount Nebo*, Publications of the Studium Biblicum Franciscanum, No. 1 (Jerusalem: Franciscan Press).
1957    *Excavations at Bethany (1949-1953)*, Publications of the Studium Biblicum Franciscanum, No. 12 (Jerusalem: Franciscan Press).

Salles, J-F.,
1987    'Deux nouvelles tombes de Ras Shamra', in Yon, M. (ed.), *Ras-Shamra-Ougarit, vol 3: Le Centre de la ville, 38e-44e Campagnes (1978-1984)* (Paris: Édition Recherche sur les Civilisations), 157-195.

Salman, I.,
1971    'Foreword', *Sumer* 27, a-k.

Sargnon, O.,
1969    'Prestige de l'or chez les Anciens', *Archaeologia* 31, 52-59.

Sauvegarde de Tyr,
1980    *Sauvegarde de Tyr* (Paris: UNESCO).

Saxe, A.A.,
1970    *Social Dimensions of Mortuary Practices*, PhD thesis (Ann Arbor: University of Michigan).

Scandone Matthiae, G.,
1987    'L'aldila nell'antico egitti', in Xella, P. (ed.), *Archeologia dell'inferno* (Verona: Essedu Edizione), 11-47.

Scanlon, G.,
1986    'Moulded early lead-glazed wares from Fustat; imported or indigenous?', in Green, A.H. (ed.), *In Quest of an Islamic Humanism; Arabic and Islamic Studies in Memory of Mohammad al-Nowayhi* (Cairo: AUC Press), 65-96.
1991    'Early lead-glazed wares in Egypt; an imported wrinkle', in Seikaly, S. (ed), *Quest for Understanding; Arabic and Islamic Studies in Memory of Malcolm H. Kerr* (Beirut: AUB Press), 253-262.

Schaefer, J.,
1989    'Archaeological Remains from the Medieval Islamic Occupation of the Northwest Negev Desert', *BASOR* 274 (May), 33-60.

Schaeffer, C.F.A.,
1933    'Les fouilles de Minet el-Beida et de Ras Shamra. Quatrième campagne (printemps 1932)', *Syria* 14, 94-127.
1934    'Les fouilles de Ras Shamra. Cinquième campagne (printemps 1933)', *Syria* 15, 105-131.
1936    'Les fouilles de Ras Shamra-Ugarit, septième campagne (printemps 1935)', *Syria* 17, 105-149.
1938    'Les fouilles de Ras Shamra-Ugarit, neuvième campagne (printemps 1937)', *Syria* 19, 193-255.
1939a   'Ras Shamra-Ugarit et le monde égéen', in Schaeffer, C.F.A., *Ugaritica* I, Bibliotheque Archéologique et Histoirie (Paris: Paul Geuthner), 53-106.
1939b   *The Cuneiform Texts of Ras Shamra*, Sweich Lectures (London: British Academy).
1939c   *Ugaritica, vol. 1: Etudes relatives aux découvertes de Ras Shamra*, Premiere serie, Mission de Ras Shamra 3 (Paris: Paul Geuthner).
1948    *Stratigraphie Comparée et Chronologie de l'Asie Occidentale (IIIe et IIe millénaires)* (London: Oxford University Press).
1949    *Ugaritica, vol 2: Nouvelles Études Relatives aux découvertes de Ras Shamra*, Mission de Ras Shamra 5 (Paris: Paul Geuthner).
1951    'Reprise des recherches archéologiques à Ras Shamra-Ugarit. Sondages de 1948 et 1949, campagne de 1950', *Syria* 28, 1-21.
1962    'Fouilles et découvertes des XVIIIe et XIXe campagnes, 1954-1955', in Schaeffer, C.F.A., *Ugaritica IV* (Paris:Paul Geuthner), 1-150.

Schaub, R.T. & Rast, W.E.,
1989    *Reports of the Expedition to the Dead Sea Plain, Jordan, vol. 1: Bab edh-Dhra'; Excavations in the Cemetery directed by Paul W. Lapp (1965-67)* (Winona Lake: American Schools of Oriental Research).

Schliemann, H.,
1878    Mycenae:a Narrative of Researches at Mycenae and Tiryns (London: John Murray).

Schmidt, E.F.,
1933    *The Alishar Hüyük seasons of 1928 and 1929. Part II*, Oriental Institute Publications 20, Researches in Anatolia 5 (Chicago: University of Chicago).

Schour, I. & Massler, M.,
1941    'The development of the human dentition', *Journal of the American Dental Association* 28, 1153-1160.

Schroeder, B.,
1991    'Natufian in the central Beqaa Valley, Lebanon', in Bar-Yosef, O. & Valla, F.R. (eds) 1991, 43-80.

Schulte-Campbell, C.,
1983    'The human remains from Palaepaphos-Skales', Apppendix XII in V. Karageorghis, *Alt-Paphos 3* (Konstanz), 439-.

Schulz, K.J.,
1990    'Bauten für den Tod; die Nekropolen von Limyra', in Jacobek, R. & Dinstl, A. (eds) 1990, 59-64.

Schumacher, G.,
1908    *Tell el-Mutesellim, vol 1: Fundbericht.* (Leipzig: R. Haupt).

Schwartz, G.,
1987    [Review of Kampschulte, I. & Orthmann, W. *Gräber des 3. Jahrtausends im syrischen Euphratal, vol 1: Ausgrabungen bei Tawi 1975 und 1978* Saarbrücher Beiträger zur Altertumskunder 38 (Bonn: Rudolf Habelt Gmblt)], *Bibliotheca Orientalis* 44, 240-243.

Schwartz, G. & Weiss, H.,
1992    'Syria, ca. 10,000-2000 B.C.', in Ehrich, R.W. (ed.), *Chronologies in Old World archaeology* (Chicago: University of Chicago) Vol. I, 185-202, Vol. II, 221-243.

Schwartz, J.H.,
1974    'The Human remains from Kition and Hala Sultan Tekké: A Cultural Interpretation', in V. Karageorghis, *Excavations at Kition I: The Tombs:* (Text), Appendix IV (Nicosia), 151-.

Scurlock, J.,
1993    'Once more ku-bu-ru', Nouvelles Assyriologiques Brèves et Utilitaires 8, 15-18.

Seeden, H.,
1985    'Aspects of prehistory in the present world: observations gathered in Syrian villages from 1980 to 1985', *World Archaeology* 17(2), 289-303.
1992    'Archäologische Neuigkeiten: Evidence for Child Cemeteries and Burial Customs from Tyre and Nustell (abstract)', *XXXIXe Rencontre Assyriologique Internationale Résumés (Assyrien im Wandel der Zeiten)* (Heidelberg: Institut für Ur- und Fruhgeschichte und Verderasratische Archäologie), 64.

Seeher, J.,
1993    'Tod und Bestattung in der Vorgeschichte', *Arkeoloji ve Sanat* 15, 2-8.

Seger, J.D.,
1988    *Gezer, vol 5: The Field I Caves* (Jerusalem: Hebrew Union College).

Selincourt, A. de., (tr.),
1988    *Herodotus. The Histories* (reprint) (Harmondworth: Penguin).

Şenyürek, M.S. & Tunakan, S.,
1951    'The skeletons from Şeyh Höyük', *Belleten* 15, 431-445.

Servais, J.,
1985    'Architectures funéraires mycénienne et ougaritique: un parallèle à éviter', in Homès-Fredericq, D. (ed), *Studia Phoenicia, III. Phoenicia and its Neighbours* (Leuven: Peeters), 59-67.

Sevin, V.,
1987    'Urartu oda-mezar mimarisin kokeni üzerine bazi gozlemler / Some insights into the origin of Urartian chamber tombs', Cilingiröglu, A. (ed.), *Anatolian Iron Ages* (Izmir: Üniversitesi Edebiyat Fakültesi) 35-55.

Sevin, V. & Belli, O.,
1977    'Yegsilalic Urartu kutsal alani ve kalesi / Urartian sacred area and fortress at Yegisilaliç', *Anadolu Arastirmalari* 4(5), 367-393.

Seyrig, H.,
1952    'Antiquités de la nécropole d'Émèse', *Syria* 29: 204-250.

Shahbazi, A.S.,
1975    *The Irano-Lycian Monuments; the Principal Antiquities of Xanthos and its Region as Evidence for Iranian Aspects of Achaemenid Lycia*, Institute of Achaemenid Research Publications 2 (Tehran: IAR).

Shay, T.,
1983    'Burial customs at Jericho in the Intermediate Bronze Age', *Tel Aviv* 10, 26-37.

Sherratt, A.,
1989    [review of Joussaume 1985], *Historical and Archaeological Review* 4, 59.
1990    'The genesis of megaliths; monumentality, ethnicity and social complexity in Neolithic north-west Europe', *World Archaeology* 22(2), 147-167.
In press *Instruments of Conversion? The Role of Megaliths in the Mesolithic/Neolithic Transition in North-West Europe.* Paper presented to the International Conference *Comparative Studies of Megaliths,* Reiss-Museum, Mannheim, 1993.
in press 'Alcohol and its alternatives: symbol and substance in early Old World cultures', in Goodman, J. & Lovejoy, P., (eds), *Peculiar Substances: Essays in the History and Anthropology of Addictive Substances* (London: Routledge).

Simmons, A.H., Kafafi, Z., Rollefson, G.O. & Moyer, K.,
1989    'Test excavations at Wadi Shu'eib, a major Neolithic settlement in central Jordan', *Annual of the Department of Antiquities of Jordan* 33, 27-42.

Simpson, St J.,
1990 'Ottoman clay pipes from Jerusalem and the Levant: a critical review of the published evidence', *Society for Clay Pipe Research Newsletter* 28, 6-16.
1992 'Sasanian burials: an archaeological viewpoint', Unpublished paper given at *The Archaeology of Death in the Ancient Near East*, Manchester.
in prep. 'Excavations at Tell Abu Dhahir', in Ball, W. (ed.), Ancient Settlements in the Zummar Region. Excavations Carried out in the Saddam Dam Salvage Project by the British Archaeological Expedition to Iraq, Vol. 2, British School of Archaeology in Iraq Reports (London: Aris & Phillips).

Skiast, A.,
1980 'The ancestor cult and succession in Mesopotamia', in Alster, B.(ed.) 1980, 123-128.

Sladek, W.,
1974 *Inanna's Descent to the Netherworld*, PhD thesis (Ann Arbor: University Microfilms).

Smirnov, Y.A.,
1989a 'Intentional human burial; Middle Palaeolithic (Last Glaciation) beginnings', *Journal of World Prehistory* 3, 199-233.
1989b 'On the evidence for Neandertal burial', *Current Anthropology* 30, 323-324.

Smith, B.H.,
1991 'Standards of human tooth formation and dental age assessment', in Kelley, M.A. & Larsen, C.S. (eds) 1991, *Advances in Dental Anthropology* (New York: Wiley-Liss), 143-168.

Smith, P. & Arensburg, B.,
1977 'A Mousterian skeleton from Kebara Cave', *Eretz-Israel* 13, 164-176.

Smith, P. & Tillier, A.-M.,
1989 'Additional infant remains from the Mousterian strata, Kebara Cave (Israel)', in Bar-Yosef, O. & Vandermeersch, B. (eds), *Investigations in South Levantine Prehistory*, BAR International Series 497 (Oxford: BAR), 323-335.

Snodgrass, A.M.,
1971 *The Dark Age of Greece* (Edinburgh: Edinburgh University Press).
1987 *An Archaeology of Greece; the Present State and Future Scope of a Discipline*, Sather Classical Lectures 53 (Berkeley: University of California Press ).

Solecki, R.S.,
1979 'Contemporary Kurdish winter-time inhabitants of Shanidar Cave, Iraq', *World Archaeology* 10(3), 318-330.

Soliveres, O.,
1977 'Restes humains natoufiens du Jebel Saiide (Epipalaeolithique du Liban)', *Paléorient* 3, 293-294.

Soliveres-Massei, O.,
1988 'Etude anthropologique', in Perrot, J., Ladiray, D. & Soliveres-Massei, O., 1988, 107-237.

Sotheby's
1931 = *Sotheby's Catalogue* 9th November 1931 (London: Sotheby's).
1977 = *Sotheby's Catalogue* 7th November 1977 (London: Sotheby's).
1994 = *Sotheby's Catalogue* 8th June 1994 (New York: Sotheby's).

Soto-Heim, P.,
1986 'Déformation cranienne artificielle dans l'Iran ancien', *Bulletin et Mémoires de la Société d'Anthropologie de Paris* 3, 105-116.

Sourvinou-Inwood, C.,
1983 'A trauma in flux; death in the 8th century and after', in R. Hägg, R. (ed.), *The Greek Renaissance of the Eighth Century B.C.; Tradition and Innovation* (Stockholm: Paul Astroms Förlag), 33-48.

Spauer, M.,
1992 'The Islamic Glass Bracelets of Palestine: Preliminary Findings', *Journal of Glass Studies* 34, 44-62.

Spronk, K.,
1986 *Beatific Afterlife in Ancient Israel and the Ancient Near East*, Alter Orient und Altes Testament 219 (Neukircher-Vluyn: Neukirchener Verlag).

Spyropoulos, T.G.,
1970 'Excavations in the Mycenaean cemetery of Tanagra in Boeotia', *Athens Annals of Archaeology* 3, 184-197 [in Greek, with English summary].
1972 'Terracotta sarcophagi', *Archaeology* 25, 207-209.

Starkey, J.L. & Harding, L.,
1932 *Beth Pelet Cemetery*, in *Beth-Pelet*, vol. 2 (Warminster: British School of Archaeology in Egypt & Bernard Quaritch), 22-33.

St Clair, G.,
1887 'Boat-shaped graves of Syria', *Palestine Exploration Fund Quarterly Statement* (October), 236-38.

Steel, L.,
1993 *Burial Customs in Cyprus at the Transition from the Bronze Age to the Iron Age*, PhD thesis (London: University College).

Steele, C.S.,
1990 *Living with the Dead; House Burial at Abu Salabikh, Iraq*, PhD thesis (Ann Arbor: State University of New York at Binghamton).

Stein, D.,
1993 'Burials', in Wilhelm, G. & Zaccagnini, C. (eds.), *Tell Karrana 3, Tell Jikan, Tell Khirbet Salih*, Baghdader Forschungen, Bd. 15 (Mainz am Rhein: Philipp von Zabern), 203-206.

Steiner, G.,
1982   'Der Gegensatz "Eigenes Land"; "Ausland, Fremdland, Feindland" in den Vorstellungen des alten Orients', in Nissen, H.-J. & Renger, J. (eds), *Mesopotamien und seine Nachbarn; Politische und Kulturelle Wechselbeziehungen im alten Vorderasien vom 4. bis 1. Jahrtausend v. Chr.* 25e Rencontre Assyriologique Internationale [Berlin, 1978], Berliner Beiträge zum vorderen Orient 1 (Berlin: Dietrich Reimer) 633-663.

Stekelis, M.,
1935   *Les monuments mégalithiques de Palestine*, Archives de l'Institute de Paléontologie Humaine, Mémoire 15 (Paris: Masson et cie, Editeurs).
1961   *La Nécropolis Megalítica di Ala-Safat, Transjordania* (Barcelona).
1972   *The Yarmukian Culture of the Neolithic Period*, English ed. (Jerusalem: Magnes Press).

Stekelis, M. & Yizraeli, T.,
1963   'Excavations at Nahal Oren', *Israel Exploration Journal* 13, 1-12.

Stern, E.,
1978   Excavations at Tel Mevorakh (1973-1976). Part One: from the Iron Age to the Roman Period, Qedem 9 (Jerusalem: Institute of Archaeology, Hebrew University).

Steuernagel, C.,
1924   'Der Adschlun', *Zeitschrift des Deutschen Palästina-Vereins* 47, 191-240.
1925   'Der Adschlun', *Zeitschrift des Deutschen Palästina-Vereins* 48, 1-144, 201-392.

Stewart, J.R.,
1974   *Tell el-'Ajjul; the Middle Bronze Age Remains*, Studies in Mediterranean Archaeology 38 (Göteborg: Paul Åströms Förlag).

Stewart, T.D.
1941   'The circular type of cranial deformity in the United States', *American Journal of Physiacl Anthropology* 28, 343-351.

Stiebing, W.H.,
1970   'Another look at the origins of the Philistine tombs at Tell el-Far'ah (S)', *American Journal Archaeology* 74, 139-143.

Stola, R.,
1972   'Zu den Jenseitsvorstellungen im alten Mesopotamien', *Kairos* 14(4), 258-272.

Stordeur, D.,
1988   *Outils et Armes en Os du Gisement Natoufien de Mallaha (Eynan), Israel*, Memoires et Travaux du Centre de Recherche Francais de Jerusalem 6 (Paris: Association Paléorient).

Strathern, A.,
1982   'Witchcraft, greed, cannibalism and death; some related themes from the New Guinea highlands', in Bloch, M & Parry, J. (eds) 1982, 111-133.

Strommenger, E.,
1957-71 'Grab', *Reallexicon der Assyriologie und Vorderasiatischen Archäologie III* (New York: de Gruyter), 581-593
1964   'Grabformen in Babylon', *Baghdader Mitteilungen* 3, 157-173.
1967   Gefässe aus Uruk von der neubabylonischen Zeit bis zu den Sasaniden, ADFU 7 (Berlin:Gebr. Mann Verlag)

Stubbings, F.H.,
1973   'The rise of Mycenaean civilization', *CAH* 3rd ed. (Cambridge: Cambridge University Press), vol. 2(1), 627-658.

Stuiver, M. & Becker, B.,
1993   'High precision decadal calibration of the radiocarbon timescale, A.S. 1950-6000 BC', *Radiocarbon* 35, 35-66.

Stuiver, M & Reimer, P.J.,
1993   'Extended $^{14}$C data base and revised calibration 3.0.3 $^{14}$C age calibration program', *Radiocarbon* 35, 215-230.

Sukenik, E.L.,
1937   'A Chalcolithic necropolis at Hederah', *The Journal of the Palestine Oriental Society* 17, 15-30.
1940   'Arrangements for the Cult of the Dead in Ugarit and Samaria', in *Mémorial Lagrange (Cinquantenaire de l'École Biblique et Archéologique Française de Jérusalem)* (Paris: Gabalda), 59-65.

Suleiman, A.,
1984   'Excavations at Ansari-Aleppo for the seasons 1973-1980; Early and Middle Bronze Ages', *Akkadica* 40, 1-16.

Suleiman, A. & Gritsenko, A.,
1987   'Landmarks of the ancient city of Ansari (Yamhad)', *Syria* 64, 231-243.

Sürenhagen, D.,
1973   'Friedhöfe in Habuba Kabira-Süd', in Heinrich, E. et al., *Habuba Kabira 1971-1972. Mitteilungen der Deutsche Orient-Gesellschaft* 105 (Berlin: DOG) 33-38.

Sussman, V. & Ben-Arieh, S.,
1963   'A grave field in Giv'atayim', *'Atiqot* 5, 27-39.

Suzuki, H. & Takay, F.,
1970   *The Amud Man and his Cave site* (Tokyo: Academic Press of Japan).

Swauger, J.L.,
1965   '1962 study of three dolmen sites in Jordan', *Annual of the Department of Antiquities of Jordan* 10, 3-36.

Sweet, L.E.,
1974   *Tell Toqaan: a Syrian Village*, Anthropological Papers, No. 14 (Ann Arbor: University of Michigan).

Swiny, S.,
1981   'Bronze Age Settlement Patterns in South-West Cyprus', *Levant* 13, 51-87.

Sykes, P.M.,
1902 'A fourth journey in Persia, 1897-1901', *Geographical Journal* 19, 121-173.

Symmers, W.St.C.,
1903 'Note on a new form of liver cirrhosis due to the presence of the ova of B. haematobia', *Journal of Pathalogical Bacteriology* 4, 237 – 239.

Tadmor, M.,
1990 'A group of figurines and small objects from the Chalcolithic period', *Eretz-Israel* 21, 249-258.

Tainter, J.A.,
1975 'Social inference and mortuary practices; an experiment in numerical classification', *World Archaeology* 7, 1-15.
1978 'Mortuary practices and the study of prehistoric social systems', in Schiffer, M.B., (ed.), *Advances in archaeological method and theory, vol. 1* (New York, Chicago & London: Academic Press), 105-141.

Tallon, F.,
1987 *Métallurgie susienne I et II; de la fondation de Suse au XVIIIe siècle avant J.-C.,* Notes et documents de musées de France 15 (Paris: Editions de la Reunion des Musées Nationaux).

Tallqvist, K,
1934 'Sumerisch-akkadische Namen der Totenwelt', *Studia Orientalia* 4, 1-47.

Tarhan, M.T. & Sevin, V.,
1975 'The relation between Urartian temple gates and monumental rock niches', *Türk Tarih Kurumu Belleten* 39, 401-412.

Tarragon, J.-M. ,
1980 *Le Culte à Ougarit,* Cahiers de la Revue Biblique 19 (Paris).

Tchernov, E.,
1991 'Biological evidence for human sedentism in Southwest Asia during the Natufian', in Bar-Yosef, O. & Valla, F.R. (eds) 1991, 315-340.

Teixidor, J.,
1986 Bulletin d'Épigraphie Sémitique (1964-1980), BAH 127 (Paris: Paul Geuthner).

Thalon, P.,
1978 'Les offrandes funeraires a Mari', *Annuaire de l'Institut de Philologie et d'Histoire Orientales et Slaves* 22.

Thissen, L.C.,
1985 'Pottery from Hayaz Höyük', *Anatolica* 12, 75-130.
1989 'An Early Bronze III pottery region between the Middle Euphrates and Habur: new evidence from Tell Hammam et-Turkman', in Haex, O.M.C., Curvers, H.H. and Akkermans, P.M.M.G. (eds), *To the Euphrates and Beyond: Archaeological Studies in Honour of Maurits N. van Loon* (Rotterdam: A.A.Balkema,), 195-211.

Thomas, L.V.,
1980 Le Cadavre. De la Biologie à l'Anthropologie (Paris: Éditions Complexe).

Thompson, R.C.,
1903 The Devils and Evil Spirits of Babylonia, being Babylonian and Assyrian Incantations against the Demons, Ghouls, Vampires, Hobgoblins, Ghosts, and Kindred Spirits, which Attack Mankind (London: Luzac & Co).

Thomson, W.M.,
1911 The Land and the Book or, Biblical Illustrations drawn from the Manners and Customs, the Scenes and Scenery of the Holy Land (London: Thomas Nelson & Sons).

Thornton, F.,
1990 *Oral Pathology Comparison of Discrete Ancient Nile Valley and Concurrent Populations,* M.Phil thesis (Bradford University).

Thrane, H.,
1978 *Sukas, vol. 4: A Middle Bronze Age collective grave on Tell Sukas,* Publications of the Carlsberg Expedition to Phoenicia 5 (Copenhagen: Munksgaard).

Thureau-Dangin, F. & Dunand, M.,
1936 *Til Barsib;* 2 vols, Bibliothèque archéologique et historique 23 (Paris: Paul Geuthner).

Tillier, A.-M.,
1989 'Les enfants proto-Cro-Magnons de Qafzeh (Israel) mise au point', in Bar-Yosef, O. & Vandermeersch, B. (eds) 1989, *Investigations in South Levantine Prehistory.* BAR International Series 497 (Oxford: BAR), 343-350.
1990 'Une controverse depasee; l'existence de pratiques funeraires au Paleolithique moyen', *Les Nouvelles de l'Archeologie* 40, 22-24.

Tillier, A.-M. & Tixier, J.,
1991 'Une molaire d'enfant aurignacien a Ksar 'Akil (Liban)', *Paléorient* 17(1), 89-93.

Tobias, P.V.,
1966 A member of the genus Homo from 'Ubeidiya: Jerusalem, *The Israel Academy of Science and Humanities.*

Tobler, A.L.,
1950, *Excavations at Tepe Gawra. Vol. 2* (Philadelphia: University of Pennsylvania Press).

Toombs, L.E.,
1978 'The Stratigraphy of Caesarea Maritima', in Moorey, R. & Parr, P. (eds), *Archaeology in the Levant. Essays for Kathleen Kenyon* (Warminster: Aris & Phillips), 223-232.
1985 Tell el-Hesi: Modern military trenching and Muslim cemetery in Field I, Strata I-II, The Joint Archaeological Expedition to Tell el-Hesi, Vol. 2 (Waterloo, Ontario: Wilfrid Laurier University).

Toynbee, J.C.M.,
1971 *Death and Burial in the Roman World* (London: Thames & Hudson) .

Trinkaus, E.,
1987   'The Upper Pleistocene human molar from Me'arat Shovakh (Mugharet esh-Shubbabiq), Israel', *Paléorient* 13(1), 95-100.

Tropper, J.,
1986   '"Beschwörung" des Enkidu?', *Die Welt des Orients* 17, 19-24.
1989   *Nekromantie: Totenbefragung im AltenOrient und im Alten Testament*, Alter Orient und Altes Testament 223 (Neukirchen-Vluyn: Neukirchener Verlag).

Tsukimoto, A.,
1980   'Aspekte von *Kipsu(m)* als Totenbeigabe', in B. Alster (ed.) 1980, 129-138.
1985   *Untersuchungen zur Totenpflege (kispum) im alten Mesopotamien*, Alter Orient und Altes Testament 216 (Neukirchen-Vluyn: Neukirchener Verlag).

Tubb, J.N.,
1983   'The MB IIA period in Palestine; its relationship with Syria and its origin', *Levant* 15, 49-62.
1988   'Tell es-Sa'idiyeh; preliminary report on the first three seasons of renewed excavations', *Levant* 20, 23-88.

Tunca, O.,
1987   *Tell Sabra*. Akkadica supplementum 5 (Leuven: Peeters).

Turville-Petre, F.,
1932   'Excavations in the Mugharet el-Kebarah', *Journal of the Royal Anthropological Institute* 62, 271-276.

Ubelaker, D.H.,
1989   *Human Skeletal Remains*, 2nd ed. (Washington DC: Taraxacum).

Ucko, P.J.,
1969   'Ethnography and archaeological interpretation of funerary remains', *World Archaeology* 1(2), 262-80.

Ussishkin, D. & Woodhead, J.,
1991/92 'Excavations at Tel Jezreel 1990-1991: preliminary report', reprint from *Tel Aviv* 18(1991), 72-92 & 19(1992), 3-70.

Valenstein, .S.G.,
1975   *A Handbook of Chinese Ceramics* (New York: Metropolitan Museum of Art).

Valla, F.R.,
1981   'Les établissements natoufiens dans le nord d'Israel', in Cauvin, J. & Sanlaville, P. (eds), *Préhistoire du Levant*, Colloques Internationaux du CNRS 598 (Paris: Editions du CNRS), 409-419.
1987   'Chronologie absolue et chronologie relative dans le Natoufien', in Aurenche, O., Evin, J. & Hours, F. (eds), *Chronologies in the Near East: Relative and Absolute Chronologies 16,000-4,000 BP*, BAR International Series 379 (Oxford: BAR), 267-294.
1988   'Aspects du sol l'abri 131 de Mallaha (Eynan)', *Paléorient* 14(2), 283-296.

1991   'Les natoufiens de Mallaha et l'espace', in Bar-Yosef, O. & Valla, F.R. (eds) 1991, 111-122.
1994   'Natufian seasonality; a guess', in Bar-Yosef, O. & Rocek, T. (eds), *Identifying Seasonality in Archaeological Sites; Old and New World Perspectives*

Valla, F.R. & Lechevallier, M.,
1989   'Notes à propos de quelques foyers natoufiens de Mallaha (Eynan, Israel)', in Olive, M. & Taborin, Y. (eds), *Nature et Fonction des Foyers Préhistoriques* (Nemours: Editions APRAIF), 293-302.

Valla, F.R., Le Mort, F. & Plisson, H.,
1991   'Les fouilles en cours sur la Terrasse d'Hayonim', in Bar-Yosef, O. & Valla, F.R. (eds) 1991, 93-110.

Vallois, H.V.,
1936   'Les ossements natoufiens d'Erq el-Ahmar (Palestine)', *L'Anthropologie* 46, 529-539.
1957   'Le squellet de foetus humain fossile d'Antelias (Liban)', *Quaternaria* 4, 1-11.

Vallois, H.V. & Movius, H.L.,
1952   *Catalogue des Hommes Fossiles*, XIX Congres International de Geologie, Alger.

Van den Brink, E.,
1982   *Tombs and Burial Customs at Tell el-Dab'a*, Beitrage zur Agyptologie 4 (Vienna).

Van der Kooij, G. & Ibrahim, M.M. (eds.),
1989   *Picking up the Threads. A Continuing Review of Excavations at Deir Alla, Jordan* (Leiden: University of Leiden, Archaeological Centre).

Van Gennep, A.,
1960   *The Rites of Passage*, tr. Vizedom, M.B. & Caffee, G.L., original edition 1909 (Chicago: University of Chicago Press).

Van Loon, M.N.,
1966   *Urartian Art; its Distinctive Traits in the Light of New Excavations* (Istanbul: Nederland-Archaeologisch Instituut te Istanbul) .
1968   'First results of the 1967 excavations at Tell Selenkahiye', *Les Annales Archéologiques Arabes Syriennes* 18, 21-32.
1973   'First results of the 1972 excavations at Tell Selenkahiye', *Les Annales Archéologiques Arabes Syriennes* 23, 145-158.
1979   '1974 and 1975 preliminary results of the excavations at Selenkiyeh near Meskene, Syria', in Freedman, D.N. (ed.), *Archaeological Reports from the Tabqa Dam Project – Euphrates Valley, Syria*, Annual of the American Schools of Oriental Research 44 (Cambridge, MA: ASOR), 97-112.

Vanden Berghe, L.,
1968   'La necropole de Bani Surmah', *Archéologia* 24, 53-63.
1970a  'Luristan prospections archéologique dans la région de Badr', *Archéologia* 36, 10-21.
1970b  'La necropole de Kalleh Nisar', *Archéologia* 32, 64-73.

294

1973 'Le Luristan de l'age du bronze; prospections archéologique dans le Pusht-i-Kuh Central', *Archéologia* 63, 24-36.

Vanden Berghe, L. & Tourovets, A.,
1992 'Prospections archéologiques dans le district de Shirwan-Chardawal (Pusht-i Kuh, Luristan)', *Iranica Antiqua* 27, 1-73.

Vandermeersch, B.,
1969 'Les nouveaux skelettes mousterienes decouverts a Qafzeh (Israel) et leur signification', *Compte rendus de l'Academie des Sciences* 268, 2562-2565.
1970 'Une sepulture mousterienne avec offrandes decouverte dans la grotte de Qafzeh', *Compte rendus de l'Academie des Sciences* 270(D), 298-301.
1981 *Les Hommes Fossiles de Qafzeh (Israel)* (Paris: Editions CNRS).

Verhaaren, B.,
1989 *Architecture and* Archaeological *Analysis between the Early and Middle Bronze Ages at Kurban Höyük, Turkey*. PhD thesis (University of Chicago).

Vermeule, E.D.T. & Karageorghis, V.,
1982 *Mycenaean Pictorial Vase Painting* (Cambridge, MA & London: Harvard University Press).

Vernant, J.-P.,
1965 'Figuration de l'invisible et catégorie psychologique du double: le *colossos*', in Vernant, J.-P. (ed.), *Mythe et Pensée chez les Grecs*, (Paris: Maspéro), 65-78.
1982 'Introduction' in Gnoli, G. and Vernant, J.P. (eds.) *La Mort, les Morts dans les Sociétés Anciennes* (Cambridge: Cambridge University Press), 5-15.

Vickers, M., Impey, O. & Allan, J.,
1986 *From Silver to Ceramic; the Potter's Debt to Metalwork in the Graeco-Roman, Oriental and Islamic Worlds* (Oxford: Ashmoleon).

Vinitzky, L.,
1992 'The date of the dolmens in the Golan and the Galilee; a reassessment', *Tel Aviv* 19(1), 100-112.

Vita-Finzi, C.,
1964 'Observations on the Late Quaternary of Jordan', *Palestine Exploration Quarterly* 96, 19-31.

Vokotopoulou, J.,
1985 *Sindos: Katalogos tis ekthesis* (Thessaloniki: Archaeological Museum).

Von der Mühll, P.,
1939 'Zur Erfindung in der Nekyia der Odyssey', *Philologus* 93[1938-39], 3-11.

Von der Osten, H.H.,
1937 *The Alishar Hüyük Seasons of 1930-32. Part 3*, Oriental Institute Publications 30, Researches in Anatolia 9 (Chicago: University of Chicago).
1937 *The Alishar Hüyük; seasons of 1930-32*, Oriental Institute Publications 28/29 (Chicago: University of Chicago Press).
1956 *Svenska Syrien Expeditionen 1952-1953, vol. 1: Die Grabung von Tell es-Salihiyeh. Skrifter utgivna av Svenska Instituet, 1* (Lund: CWK Cleerup).

Wace, A.J.B.,
1932 'Chamber tombs at Mycenae', *Archaeologia* 82.
1949 *Mycenae; an Archaeological History and Guide* (Princeton: Princeton University Press).

Wada, Y.,
1982 'Anthropological Studies on the Skulls of the Islamic Period, Unearthed in the Hamrin Basin, Iraq', [in Japanese], *Anthropological Report* 43, 1-32.

Waetzoldt, H.,
1990 'Zur Bewaffnung des Heeres von Ebla', *Oriens Antiquus* 29, 1-38.

Waetzoldt, H. & Hauptmann, H. (eds),
1988 *Wirtschaft und Gesellschaft von Ebla*, Heidelberger Studien zum alten Orient 2 (Heidlberg: Heidelberger Orientverlag).

Waldbaum, J.C.,
1966 'Philistine tombs at Tel Fara and their Aegean prototypes', *American Journal of Archaeology* 70, 331-340.

Ward, W.H.,
1886 *Report on the Wolfe expedition to Babylonia 1884-85* (Boston, MA: Archaeological Institute of America).

Warren, C.,
1870 'Expedition to East of Jordan', *Palestine Exploration Fund Quarterly Statement* for 1870, 284-305.

Watkins, T.F.,
1983 'Sumerian weapons, warfare and warriors', *Sumer* 39, 100-102.

Watkins, T. and Campbell, S.,
1987 'The chronology of the Halaf culture', in Aurenche, O., Evin, J. & Hours, F. (eds), *Chronologies in the Near East: Relative and Absolute Chronologies 16,000-4,000 BP*, BAR International Series 379 (Oxford: BAR), 427-464.

Watson, J.L.,
1982 'Of flesh and bones; the management of death pollution in Cantonese society', in Bloch, M. & Parry, J. (eds) 1982, 155-186.

Watson, P.J.,
1979 Archaeological Ethnography in Western Iran (Tucson: University of Arizona).

Watson, P.L.,
1970 *Mot, the God of Death, at Ugarit and in the Old Testament*, PhD thesis (New Haven: Yale University).

Wattenmaker, P.,
1990 *The Social Context of Specialized Production; Reorganization of Household Craft and Food Economies in an Early Near Eastern State*, PhD thesis (Ann Arbor: University of Michigan).

Watzinger, C.,
1929 *Tell el Mutesellim, vol. 2: Die Funde* (Leipzig).

Webley, D.,
1969a 'A note on the dolmen field at Tell el-Adeimeh and Teleilat Ghassul', *Palestine Exploration Quarterly* 101, 42-43.
1969b 'A note on the pedology of Teleilat Ghassul', *Levant* 1, 21-33.

Weir, S.,
1989 *Palestinian Costume* (London: British Museum Press).

Weiss, H.,
1983 'Excavations at Tell Leilan and the origins of north Mesopotamian cities in the third millennium B.C.', *Paléorient* 9, 39-52.
1990 'Tell Leilan 1989; new data for mid-third millennium urbanization and state formation', *Mitteilungen der Deutschen Orient-Gesellschaft 20 Berlin* 122, 193-218.

West, M.L. (tr.),
1966 *Hesiod, Theogony* (Oxford: Oxford University Press).

Whitaker, J.I.S.,
1921 *Motya; a Phoenecian Colony in Sicily* (London: G. Bell and Sons).

White, C.,
1845 *Three years in Constantinople; or, Domestic Manners of the Turks in 1844* (London: Henry Colburn).

Wienstein-Evron, M.,
1991 'New radiocarbon dates from the Early Natufian of el-Wad Cave, Mt. Carmel, Israel', *Paléorient* 17, 95-98.

Wienstein-Evron, M. & Belfer-Cohen, A.,
1993 'Natufian Figurines from the New Excavations of the el-Wad Cave, Mt. Carmel, Israel', *Rock Art Research* 10(2), 102-106.

Wilhelm, G.,
1989 *The Hurrians* (Warminster: Ares and Phillips).
1993 'Excavations at Tell Khirbet Salih', in Wilhelm, G. & Zaccagnini, C. (eds.), *Tell Karrana 3, Tell Jikan, Tell Khirbet Salih*, Baghdader Forschungen Bd. 15 (Mainz am Rhein: Philipp von Zabern), 261-262.

Wilhelm, G. & Zaccagnini, C.,
1991 'Excavations at Tell Karrana 3 (1985 and 1986)', *Mesopotamia* 26, 5-14.

Wilson, C.T.,
1906 *Peasant Life in the Holy Land* (London: John Murray).

Woolley, C.L.,
1914 'Hittite burial customs', *(Liverpool) Annals of Archaeology and Anthropology* 6(3), 87-98.
1934 *Ur Excavations, vol. 2: The Royal Cemetery*. 2 vols (London & Philadelphia: The British Museum & the Museum of the University of Pennsylvania).
1952 'The excavations in the inner town', in C.L. Woolley & R.D. Barnett, *Carchemish, vol. 3: The Excavations in the Inner Town and the Hittite*

*Inscriptions* (London: The British Museum), 157-258.
1954 *Excavations at Ur* (London & New York: Barnes and Noble).
1955 *Alalakh; an Account of Excavations at Tell Atchana in the Hatay, 1937-1949* (Oxford: Oxford University Press).
1962 *The Neo-Babylonian and Persian Periods*, Ur Excavations 9 (London: British Museum & the University Museum Pennsylvania).
1965 *The Kassite Period and the Period of the Assyrian Kings*, Ur Excavations 8 (London: British Museum and the University Museum Pennsylvania).
1968 *A Forgotten Kindgdom*. (New York: W.W. Norton).
1970 *Ur of the Chaldees*, revised P.R.S. Moorey (London: The Herbert Press).

Woolley, C.L. & Mallowan, M.E.L.,
1976 *Ur Excavations, vol. 7: The Old Babylonian Period* (London/Philadelphia: British Museum & University Museum of Pennsylvania).

Woolley, C.L. & Moorey, P.R.S.,
1982 *Ur 'of the Chaldees'* (London: The Herbert Press).

Whorf Estes, J.,
1989 *The Medical Skills of Ancient Egyp.* ( Science History Publications USA).

Wright, G.A.,
1978 'Social differentiation in the early Natufian', in Redman, C.L., Berman, M.J., Curtin, E.V., Langhorne, W.T, Versaggi, N.H. & Wanser, J.C. (eds), *Social Archaeology; beyond Subsistence and Dating* (New York: Academic Press), 201-223.

Wright, G.R.H.,
1966 'The Bronze Age temple at Amman', *Zeitschrift für die altestamentliche Wissenschaft* 78, 351-357.
1985 *Ancient Building in South Syria and Palestine*. 2 vols. (Leiden: E.J. Brill).

Wurster, W.W. & Wörrle, M.,
1978 'Die Stadt Pinara', *Archäologischer Anzeiger*, 74-101.

Yadin, Y.,
1962 'Expedition D – the Cave of Letters', *Israel Exploration Journal* 12, 227-257.

Yadin, Y., Aharoni, Y., Amiran, R., Dothan, T., Dunayevsky, M. & Perrot, J.,
1960 *Hazor* II. An account of the second season of excavations, 1956 (Jerusalem: Hebrew University Press).

Yakar, J.,
1985 *The Later Prehistory of Anatolia*, BAR International Series 268 (Oxford: BAR).

Yakar, J. & Gürsan-Salzmann, A.,
1979 'Archaeological survey in the Malatya and Sivas provinces', *Tel Aviv* 6, 34-44.

Yasin, W.,
1970 'Excavation at Tell es-Sawwan 1969: Report on the sixth season of excavations', *Sumer* 26, 39-42.

Yassine, K. (ed.),
1988    *Archaeology of Jordan: Essays and Reports* (Amman: Department of Archaeology, University of Jordan).

Yasur-Landau, A.,
1993    'Socio-political and demographic aspects of the Middle Bronze Age cemetery at Jericho', *Tel Aviv* 19, 235-246.

Yeivin, E. & Olami, Y.,
1979    'Nizzanim – a Neolithic site in Nahal Evtah; excavations of 1968-1970', *Tel Aviv* 6, 99-135.

Yeivin, S.,
1961    First Preliminary Report on the Excavations at Tel "Gat" (Tell Sheykh 'Ahmed el-'Areyny). Seasons 1956-1958 (Jerusalem: Department of Antiquities).

Yener, K.A., Özbal, H., Kaptan, E., Necip, A. & Goodway, M.,
1989    'Kestel; an Early Bronze Age source of tin ore in the Taurus mountains, Turkey', *Science* 244 [April 1989], 200-203.

Yoffee, N.,
1979    'Decline and Rise of Mesopotamian Civilisation: An Ethnoarchaeological Perspective', *American Antiquity* 44, 5-35.

Yogev, O.,
1985    'A Middle Bronze Age cemetery South of Tell Rehov', *'Atiqot* 17, 90-114.

Yokoyama, S. & Matsumoto, K.,
1989    'Report on the excavations at Tell Songor B', *Al-Rafidan* 10, 245-298.
1990    'The graves at Tell Songor B', *Al-Rafidan* 11, 189-199.

Yon, M.,
1971    *La tombe T.I du XIe s. av. J.-C. Salamine de Chypre, 2* (Paris) .
1984    'Sanctuaires d'Ougarit', in G. Roux (ed.), *Temples et Sanctuaires* (Lyon: Collection Travaux de la Maison de l'Orient 7), 37-50.
1987    'Les rhytons du sanctuaire', in Yon, M. (ed.), *Le Centre de la Ville*, Ras Shamra Ougarit III (Paris: Édition Recherche sur les Civilisations), 343-350.
1992    'Ugarit: The Urban Habitat. The Present State of the Archaeological Picture', *BASOR*, 286, 19-34

Yon, M. & Caubet, A.,
1985    *Le sondage L-N 13 (Bronze Récent et Géometrique I). Kition Bamboula*, 3 (Paris: Editions Recherches sur les Civilisations).

Zaehner, R.C.,
1961    *The Dawn and Twilight of Zorozstrianism* (London: Weidenfeld & Nicolson).

Zahle, J.,
1980    'Lycian tombs and Lycian cities', in Metzger, H. (ed.), *Actes du Colloque sur la Lycie Antique*, Bibliothèque de l'Institut Français d'Etudes Anatoliennes d'Istanbul 27 (Paris: Institut Francais d'Archéologie d'Istanbul), 37-49.
1983    *Arkæologiske Studier i Lykiske Klippegrave og Deros Relieffer fra ca. 550-300 f.Kr.; Sociale og Religiøse Aspeketer* (Copenhagen: Museum Tusculanum).

Zarins, J.,
1986    'Equids associated with human burials in third millennium B.C. Mesopotamia', in Meadow, R.H. & Uerpmann , H.-P. (eds), *Equids in the Ancient World*, Beihefte zum Tubinger Atlas des vorderen Orients, Reihe A Nr. 19/1 (Wiesbaden: Reichert).

Zias, J.,
1982    *Tel Dan, 1982 season; preliminary anthropological report* Unpublished ms.

Zias, J., Stark, H., Seligman, J., Levy, R., Werker, E., Breuer, A. & Mechoulam, R.,
1993    'Early use of medical cannabis', *Nature* 363[May 1993], 215.

Zimansky, P.E.,
1985    *Ecology and Empire; the Structure of the Urartian State*, Studies in Ancient Oriental Civilization 41 (Chicago: University of Chicago Press).

Zohar, M.,
1989    'Rogem Hiri; a megalithic monument in the Golan', *Israel Exploration Journal* 39, 18-31.

Zorich, D.,
1985    *Report on the Excavation of Skeletal Material from Area B1, 1985*. Unpublished ms..